The Child in His Family

VULNERABLE CHILDREN

VOLUME 4

YEARBOOK OF THE INTERNATIONAL ASSOCIATION
FOR CHILD PSYCHIATRY AND ALLIED PROFESSIONS

EDITOR-IN-CHIEF—E. JAMES ANTHONY, M.D. (U.S.A.)

CO-EDITORS—CYRILLE KOUPERNIK, M.D. (FRANCE)

COLETTE CHILAND, M.D., Ph.D. (FRANCE)

Volume 1 **The Child in His Family**

E. James Anthony and Cyrille Koupernik, Editors

Volume 2 **The Child in His Family:**
The Impact of Disease and Death

E. James Anthony and Cyrille Koupernik, Editors

Volume 3 **The Child in His Family:**
Children at Psychiatric Risk

E. James Anthony and Cyrille Koupernik, Editors

Volume 4 **The Child in His Family:**
Vulnerable Children

E. James Anthony, Cyrille Koupernik, and
Colette Chiland, Editors

Volume 5 **The Child in His Family:**
Children and Their Parents in a Changing World

E. James Anthony and Colette Chiland, Editors

The Child in His Family

VULNERABLE CHILDREN

VOLUME 4

Edited by

E. JAMES ANTHONY, M.D.
St. Louis, Missouri, U.S.A.

and

CYRILLE KOUPERNIK, M.D.
Paris, France

COLETTE CHILAND, M.D., Ph.D.
Paris, France

Foreword by

ANNA FREUD, LL.D., Sc.D.
London, England

Epilogue by

MARGARET MAHLER, M.D., Sc.D.
New York, New York, U.S.A.

CALIFORNIA SCHOOL OF PROFESSIONAL PSYCHOLOGY LOS ANGELES

A WILEY-INTERSCIENCE PUBLICATION

JOHN WILEY & SONS, New York · Chichester · Brisbane · Toronto

Library of Congress Catalogue Card Number: 78-120701

ISBN 0-471-04433-4

Printed in the United States of America

10 9 8 7 6 5 4 3 2 1

To a great pioneer in our field, *THERESE BENEDEK,* whose thoughts enriched the lives of all of us around her and lit up the psychodynamic climate of our times

Contributors

Bruno J. Anthony (M.A., M.Ph.), Doctoral Candidate, Columbia University, New York, New York, U.S.A.

E. James Anthony (M.D.), Blanche F. Ittleson Professor of Child Psychiatry, and Director, Division of Child Psychiatry, Washington University School of Medicine, St. Louis, Missouri, U.S.A.

Lea Baider (Ph.D.), Child Development Project, Western Psychiatric Institute, Pittsburgh, Pennsylvania, U.S.A.

Larry Bass (Ph.D.), Department of Psychiatry, The Jewish Hospital, St. Louis, Missouri, U.S.A.

Frank I. Bishop (M.D.), Department of Psychiatry, Royal Children's Hospital, Parkville, Victoria, Australia

Michael Bohman (M.D., Ph.D.), Umea Universitet, Barn- och ungdomspsykiatriska kliniken, Umeå, Sweden

Ellen Boorse (M.A.), Irving Schwartz Institute for Children and Youth, Philadelphia Psychiatric Center, Philadelphia, Pennsylvania, U.S.A.

Waln K. Brown (Ph.D.), The National Center for Juvenile Justice, Pittsburgh, Pennsylvania, U.S.A.

Gudrun Brun (M.D.), Department of Child Psychiatry, Bispebjerg Hospital, Copenhagen, Denmark

Justin D. Call (M.D.), Professor and Chief of Child and Adolescent Psychiatry Division, Department of Psychiatry and Human Behavior, California College of Medicine, University of California Irvine Medical Center, Orange, California, U.S.A.

Loretta Cass (Ph.D.), Department of Psychology, Washington University, St. Louis, Missouri, U.S.A.

Michael J. Chandler (Ph.D.), Department of Psychology, University of British Columbia, Vancouver, British Columbia, Canada

M. Chazan, Reader in Education, University College of Swansea, South Wales, Great Britain

Colette Chiland (M.D., Ph.D.), Professeur de Psychologie Clinique à L'Université René Descarte de Paris (Sorbonne), Paris, France

A. D. B. Clarke (Ph.D.), Professor of Psychology, University of Hull, Hull, England

Ann M. Clarke (Ph.D.), Department of Psychology, University of Hull, Hull, England

Alan H. Cohen (B.S.), University of Vermont, Burlington, Vermont, U.S.A.

Beatrice Cooper (M.S.W.), Reiss-Davis Child Study Center, Los Angeles, California, U.S.A.

Henry P. Coppolillo (M.D.), University of Colorado Medical Center, Denver, Colorado, U.S.A.

Anthony J. Costello, Clinical Scientific Officer, Medical Research Council, London School of Economics, London, England

M. Coval (M.A.), Vancouver, British Columbia, Canada

Rudolf Ekstein (Ph.D.), Clinical Professor of Medical Psychology, University of California, U.C.L.A., Los Angeles, California, U.S.A.

L. Erlenmeyer-Kimling (Ph.D.), Principal Research Scientist, Department of Mental Hygiene, New York State Psychiatric Institute, New York, New York, U.S.A.

Selma Fraiberg (M.D.), Child Development Project, Ann Arbor, Michigan, U.S.A.

Lois Franklin (Ph.D.), Research Instructor, Clinical Medical Psychology, Edison Child Development Research Center, Washington University School of Medicine, St. Louis, Missouri, U.S.A.

Anna Freud (LL.D., Sc.D. Hon.), Director, Hampstead Child-Therapy Course and Clinic, London, England

Yvon Gauthier (M.D.), Professor and Chairman, Department of Psychiatry, St. Justine Hospital, Montreal, Canada

Michael J. Goldstein (Ph.D.), Professor of Psychology, University of California at Los Angeles, Los Angeles, California, U.S.A.

M. Joyce Grant (M.S.W.), Royal Children's Hospital, Parkville, Victoria, Australia

A. Jack Hafner (Ph.D.), Professor of Psychology, and Consultant, Hazelden Rehabilitation Center, University of Minnesota, Minneapolis, Minnesota, U.S.A.

Joel H. Hetler (Ph.D.), University of Minnesota, Minneapolis, Minnesota, U.S.A.

Hans R. Huessy (M.D.), University of Vermont Medical Alumni Building, Burlington, Vermont, U.S.A.

Wallace Ironside (Ph.D.), Department of Psychological Medicine, Monash University, Melbourne, Australia

Susanne S. Jakobi (M.S.W., A.C.S.W.), Irving Schwartz Institute for Children and Youth, Philadelphia Psychiatric Center, Philadelphia, Pennsylvania, U.S.A.

E. Keinänen (Ph.D.), Aurora Hospital, Helsinki, Finland

Cyrille Koupernik (M.D.), Membre Associé, Collige de Médecine de Hôpitaux de Paris, Paris, France

Robert Krell (M.D.), Associate Professor, Division of Child Psychiatry, Health Sciences Center Hospital, University of British Columbia, Vancouver, Canada

Harriet S. Lander (M.S.), Research Assistant, Edison Child Development Research Center, Washington University School of Medicine, St. Louis, Missouri, U.S.A.

Diane E. Liebert (Ph.D.), State University of New York, Stony Brook, New York, U.S.A.

Margaret Mahler (M.D., Sc.D.), Director, Masters Children's Center; Clinical Professor of Psychiatry, Albert Einstein College of Medicine; and Senior Consultant, Child and Adolescent Service, Roosevelt Hospital; New York, New York, U.S.A.

Katri Malmivaara (M.D.), Child Psychiatrist, Aurora Hospital, Helsinki, Finland

Joseph Marcus (M.D.), Department of Psychiatry, University of Chicago, Chicago, Illinois, U.S.A.

Paul E. McQuaid (D.P.M.), Department of Child Psychiatry, Mater M. Hospital, Dublin, Ireland

Miriam S. Moss (M.A.), Northwest Community Mental Health Center, Northwest Philadelphia, Pennsylvania, U.S.A.

Sidney Z. Moss (M.S.W., A.C.S.W.), Northwest Community Mental Health Center, Philadelphia Pennsylvania, U.S.A.

Humberto Nagera (M.D.), Children's Psychiatric Hospital, Ann Arbor, Michigan, U.S.A.

John M. Neale (Ph.D.), State University of New York, Stony Brook, New York, U.S.A.

Clare Claiborne Park (Litt. D.), Williams College, Williamstown, Massachusetts, U.S.A.

Wentworth Quast (Ph.D.), Professor of Psychology, University of Minnesota, Minneapolis, Minnesota, U.S.A.

Carlos J. Robles (M.D.), In private practice, Buenos Aires, Argentina

Eva Rosenfeld (Ph.D.), Department of Education, Municipality of Jerusalem, Israel

M. Rouyer (M.D.), Hopital des Enfants Malades, Paris, France.

Marja Saarelma (M.D.), Aurora Hospital, Helsinki, Finland

Arnold J. Sameroff (Ph.D.), Department of Psychology, University of Rochester, Rochester, New York, U.S.A.

Jean Livermore Sanville (M.S.S.), Clinical Social Worker, Los Angeles, California, U.S.A.

Leila Seitamo (Ph.D.), Chief Psychologist, Department of Pediatrics, University of Oulu, Oulu, Finland

Michael J. Shea (Ph.D.), Assistant Professor, Division of Health Care Psychology, Department of Psychiatry, University of Minnesota Medical School, Minneapolis, Minnesota, U.S.A.

Sören Sigvardsson (B.A.), University of Umeå, Umeå, Sweden

Albert J. Solnit (M.D.), Professor, Departments of Pediatrics and Psychiatry, and Director, Child Study Center, Yale University School of Medicine, New Haven, Connecticut, U.S.A.

Pierre Straus (M.D.), Hopital Des Enfants Malades, Paris, France

Susan Threlfall (M.A.), University College of Swansea, Wales, Great Britain

Peggy L. Vaughan (M.S.S., A.C.S.W.), Pre-School Unit Staff, Irving Schwartz Institute for Children and Youth, Philadelphia, Pennsylvania, U.S.A.

Elisabeth M. Wann (M.D.), Royal Children's Hospital, Parkville, Victoria, Australia

Betty H. Watts (Ph.D.), Reader in Education, University of Queensland, Brisbane, Australia

Sheldon Weintraub (Ph.D.), Psychology Department, State University of New York, Stony Brook, New York, U.S.A.

Elenaor S. Wertheim (Ph.D.), Department of Paediatrics, Monash University, Queen Victoria Memorial Hospital, Melbourne, Victoria, Australia

Martin Wolins (Ph.D.), School of Social Welfare, University of California, Berkeley, California, U.S.A.

Julien Worland (Ph.D.), Department of Child Psychiatry, Washington University, St. Louis, Missouri, U.S.A.

Lyman C. Wynne (M.D., Ph.D.), Strong Memorial Hospital, Rochester, New York, U.S.A.

Foreword

I THANK YOU VERY WARMLY FOR THE CORDIAL INVITATION TO JOIN
with you in presenting a picture to the clinical world at large a
profile of *the vulnerable child,* since the subject you have chosen for
discussion is one of greatest interest to me.

Like most of the people from the many disciplines represented
in this volume, I have been dealing with a wide range of
vulnerable children all my life, counting among them the socially,
racially, and financially disadvantaged, the physically and
mentally handicapped, the rejected and unloved, the
overprotected, the oversensitive, the overconscientious, the slow
developers, the precocious and others that are well known and are
mentioned in the various sections of this book. Like many other
workers in the field, I too have felt bewildered by the seemingly
unending series of factors that expose a child to danger.

I remained bewildered until I arrived at the conviction that
vulnerability cannot be explained in terms of the qualities
characterizing a child but has to be understood in more general
and impersonal terms. I now assume that any child's forward
movement along developmental lines toward maturity depends
on a number of favorable external influences to interact with
favorable innate givens and favorable internal structural
advances. This means that all children born with normal
potentialities also need sufficient bodily care, membership in an
intact and welcoming family, affection and support on a
continuing basis, ongoing stimulation of their intellectual
capacities, and opportunity for identification with parents who are
themselves healthy members of a community. Not all our
children, by any means, enjoy this combination of internal and
environmental advantage. Nevertheless, it is a fact that whenever

one or more of these conditions are not fulfilled, the result is unfortunate. It reveals itself to us as arrests, deviations, distortions, complications of psychological growth, and failures to reach the aims prescribed by the first social groups that the child must enter and become a part of, whether family, school, or community.

What is vulnerable, therefore, is less the child than the process of development itself, and to see it as such marks, I believe, an advance in our understanding of what vulnerability entails. My expectation is that many of the articles collated in this book will join me in taking this particular line toward a grasp of the hazards that have at all times beset the healthy growth of every child generation.

ANNA FREUD, LL.D., SC.D.

Director, Hampstead
Child-Therapy Course and
Clinic, London, England

Preface

The making of a book, like the making of a baby, runs the gamut of feeling from ecstasy to despair, with the specter of miscarriage always in the offing to haunt the expectant parents. Editorially, the final act of parturition has always seemed to be the most exacting, the most painful, the most prolonged. The moment of delivery never seems to come, even though our publishers have repeatedly demonstrated their skills at bibliomidwifing. In the book world, there is no such thing as natural childbirth—instruments are always needed to extract some contributions held up in the third trimester and sometimes, alas, even earlier! We do not speak of the afterbirth—the bits and pieces, footnotes and corrections, and additions and subtractions that continue to come down the birth canal even after the volume has gone to press and is merely awaiting a splendid jacket in which to make its first appearance in the world. On the whole, it is a lot easier to make a baby and were it not for the intrusion of Father Time, we might well have stayed with that!

Needless to say, there would have been no bibliobirth at all were it not for the indispensable labors of Martha Kniepkamp and Sally Clayburgh who watched over every phase from conception onward, who reworked carelessly delivered manuscripts and in their several ways helped to render the making of this book more of a joy and less of a pain.

E. JAMES ANTHONY, M.D.

St. Louis, Missouri
May, 1978

Contents

The Child in His Family

VULNERABLE CHILDREN

VOLUME 4

CONCEPTS OF VULNERABILITY

A New Scientific Region to Explore*

E. James Anthony, M.D. (U.S.A.)

It must be 10 years since I first became what we have now come to call a "risk researcher," although at the time I had no idea at all that this was what I was. Like Molière's bourgeois gentlemen, I began to talk the language of risk research without being aware that I had entered a new scientific region that was developing its own vocabulary, its own resarch approach, and its own population of subjects, otherwise known as "children at risk" who were on their way to becoming patients of various types. The objective of the risk researcher, unlike that of the usual clinical investigator, was to explore the growth and development of these children prior to the outcome of disorder so as to discover in what way and to what degree their lives were shaped by the risks they encountered, the vulnerabilities and immunities they carried into situations, and the defenses, competences, and coping skills that they forged for themselves in the service of psychological survival. Compounding these various exposures, attributes, and mechanisms, a few succumbed altogether, about half suffered to greater or lesser degrees, and a few came through mysteriously unscathed.

Why do we as clinicians and clinical investigators need to become more risk-conscious and why should we, as a profession,

* The Presidential Address to the VIIIth International Congress of Child Psychiatry and Allied Professions in Philadelphia, 1974.

3

direct our limited resources of personnel and funds toward this end? The answers to these questions are on the way to becoming clinical aphorisms and axioms: "earlier better than later," "before better than after," and "prevention better than cure." When I presented it to our executive 4 years ago when I first became president of the International Association of Child Psychiatry and Allied Professions, my colleagues recognized it as novel and challenging but wondered whether it offered as much to the clinician, as to the public health official. In defense, I pointed to my own reorientation as a "risk clinician" whose perspective had been enlarged to include the intergenerational component and whose clinical skills had been enhanced in dealing with a new kind of case. I felt that the alternative proposal of Childhood Sexuality as a separate study was undoubtedly interesting but, if I could say so without misunderstanding, not nearly as invigorating or innovating. Besides, it was almost 65 years to the day that little Hans had first had his sexual problems aired, and he was clearly due for an honorable retirement. When two major funding bodies, The Grant Foundation and The Commonwealth Fund,[1] expressed their interest in the topic of risk and its many vicissitudes, little Hans was sadly put back on the shelf for a future congress, and for the subsequent 4 years (and hopefully, for many years to come) the "vulnerable child" became the center of our professional interests and lives.

The Three Dolls of Jacques May

I have told the story of the three dolls of Jacques May so often to illustrate the subject of risk and vulnerability that I have almost begun to believe in their actual existence. They were featured in the last brochure put out by the Congress Administration and have become the symbols of the Congress itself.

[1] The International Association of Child Psychiatry and Allied Professions and the International Study Group are deeply indebted to these two foundations for their support, along with the National Institute of Mental Health under the leadership of Dr. Bertram Brown. The Grant Foundation, in particular, has helped the International Association to not only survive, but to flourish.

Children, as Piaget has so clearly demonstrated to us, are by nature preabstract and prepropositional in their thinking, and child clinicians have come to recognize this and have learned to communicate concretely often through the medium of dolls. The Jacques May dolls, you will recall, are made of glass, plastic, and steel and exposed to the equal blow of a hammer. This results in a complete breakdown in the first doll, permanent scarring in the second, and apparent invulnerability in the third. Later I very concretely wrapped the dolls in a protective coating to symbolize the concept of prevention. There seemed to be, however, no place in the model for the mechanisms of defense and coping since the dolls are inherently unable to develop reactive capacities in response to experience. One could not speak, even imaginatively, of competent dolls.

Four years ago, the three dolls served the purpose of illustrating new notions of structure and function regarding the human child, but as time went on and knowledge accrued they were shown to be a deficient and oversimplified model of the human condition. It became necessary to complicate our concepts if we wished them to serve a useful purpose in our work. As I realized this, I was reminded of a passage in the writings of Kierkegaard [1] that brought the lesson home very compellingly. He was sitting one Sunday afternoon in the Frederiksberg Garden in Copenhagen, smoking a cigar and meditating on the somewhat dismal fact that although he was quite unknown, many men of his age had made names for themselves through the ingenuous expedient of simplifying complex issues. It suddenly occurred to him that he might carve a niche in posterity for himself by doing just the opposite, that is, by complicating rather than simplifying matters. He would do this not simply to be contrary but to demonstrate that life, the circumstances of life, and the problems associated with life, could only be simplified at the risk of losing their essence. As a clinician, this resonated at all levels of my own experience since cases frequently turned out to be far more complicated than they appeared on a first assessment and the wider one's frame of reference grew, the more multivariate the picture became.

The Three Children

The three dolls soon gave place to three flesh-and-blood children as new knowledge about risk and vulnerability flowed in from all parts of the world as part of the activities of the International Study Group. The children, unlike the dolls, had undergone development in a variety of different environments, had been buffeted by a range of traumatic events, had reacted with feelings, thoughts, and fantasies to everything that happened to them, and had built their own conception of the world on the basis of their different experiences. There were differences, therefore, in both hammers and constitutions, in risks and in vulnerabilities, and in offensiveness as well as defensiveness. One had to take into account the genetic expectancies, constitutional differences, reproductive hazards, physical illnesses, environmental traumata, and developmental crises in relation to the psychological assets of the individual as epitomized in his competence to handle the many problems presented to him in the process of living.

Let us then turn from the glass, plastic, and steel dolls to the case histories provided by three children where the outcomes were similar but the path to those outcomes highly complicated. The first case broke down completely, the second was left with residual deficits, and the third appeared to thrive on the many difficulties and disasters to which she had been exposed.

CASE 1

The first case is a short and sorry one. Dora had two schizophrenic parents who had met each other in a mental hospital and developed an affinity that flourished within the walls of the institution but rapidly deteriorated when they were both discharged. They then set up a miniinstitution in an apartment where they remained together chaotically crazy. Dora was exposed from birth to almost every indignity and hurt conceivable in the human lexicon of sadism. She was neglected, battered, seduced, alternately over- and under-stimulated, and at times even tortured, as when she was dragged screaming across a room by her hair. The grossness and constancy of the attacks were such that when she was first observed she presented as an undifferentiated zombie who only occasionally performed like a child but more often seemed less than human. In her case a high genetic expectancy was coupled with a child-rearing environment that could only be described as anarchic and shocking. Young organisms sometimes give the impression of immense plasticity and adaptability, but this can be strained to breaking point sooner in the more predisposed. Dora underwent a rapid primitivization in the second year of life when her mother once again became chaotically psychotic and has remained institutionalized since then, resembling in many respects a burnt-out schizophrenic. In Freud's terms, she underwent "too searching a destiny."

CASE 2

John was an 8-year-old suburban child of well-to-do parents who brought him up with loving care. He and his father were especially close and proud of each other. Whatever rivalry they had was seemingly dissolved in the mutual affection. When John was 5 his father died in a street accident. John had no overt reaction to this but was described at the time as looking "lost." He drew nearer to his mother, but the relationship with her was more ambivalent. When I saw him 4 years later he was curiously quiet and unforthcoming during the interview. I asked him to tell me about himself and he replied guardedly, "There is nothing to tell. I am just me. I go to school and then I go home." I said that he did not make his life sound very interesting, and he quickly answered, "It's boring." When asked whether he had any friends, the response was equally terse, "No friends. I only like my mother and she is mean to me and then I don't like her." I wondered whether there was anybody around him who might enjoy hearing how he was doing at school, but his reply remained negative, "I am no good at school. I am no good at anything." Although not depressed in the classical sense, his inner core of depression was evident in his apathy, anhedonism, boredom, and poor self-concept. When I asked him about his "three wishes," he said immediately, "I don't want to wish. That's a baby's game." I pressed a little further. Did he not want sometimes to be young again? He looked startled, then thoughtful, and then said quietly, "I'd like it to be the time when my dad was still living but that's impossible. It's no use wishing for things you can't ever have." There were no tears; it was a simple statement of fact.

CASE 3

Mary was the child of a "poor white" family, living in a two-roomed dilapidated and dirty apartment in the inner city. She had been the seventh of nine children, prematurely born with a congenital dislocation of the hip that was so inadequately treated at the city hospital that she developed a permanent limp. She was hospitalized several times in the first 2 years of life for "chest trouble" from which she almost died. Between 2 and 5 years of age she was placed in a home with three of her siblings because the family living quarters had been condemned as overcrowded and unsanitary. The health visitor reported that the children were constantly exposed to the crude sexual behavior of the parents, especially when the father was drunk, which was fairly frequent. His unemployment, which seemed to be permanent, made him irritable, short-tempered, and brutal. He was brought before the court several times for physically abusing the children, particularly Mary, whom he called "the cripple." The mother was chronically depressed and tired and seemed to have little feeling left inside her for her husband, her children, or herself. A social worker reported that she herself felt depressed every time she made a home visit. When Mary was referred as a child at risk, I was struck by her immediate friendliness. The warm, comfortable, and trustful reaction took me completely by surprise since I was expecting almost the reverse. She was only 9 years old, and yet her experience of life had been dark and dismal. I found myself curiously unsure of how to approach her, but she put me at ease and I soon found myself talking to her with less guardedness than I usually use in a first interview. She herself was quite open when she spoke of her life at home, where sometimes "everyone got in the way" and she had "to keep an eye on the little ones because someone might stamp on them, not knowing they were there." Her dad was "grumpy," but one expected this because he did not have a job. "If he hits us, it hurts a little but then we do something else and we don't feel it anymore." I asked her about her mother and once again she answered with a depth of understanding that was surprising. "We haven't got much money and we all have to eat. I try not to eat too much. Sometimes your stomach hurts and you want to eat more. We don't have too much clothes and some of them have big holes but the holes are not in bad places so you can still wear them." I asked if this made her feel sad and received once again a very matter-of-fact reply, "It doesn't make me feel sad because I'm used to it. But it does make my mom feel sad and she cries sometimes. I help out in the house as much as I can." I wondered how she spent her spare time. Her eyes lit up as she said enthusiastically, "I'm collecting money for the poor children in India. They are starving. They haven't anything to eat and they go to bed hungry. They are always sick and their stomachs get big." I asked what she would want if some kind fairy gave her three wishes, and she considered it very seriously. "First, I want to grow up soon. Then I want to become a nurse. Then I want to go and help look after the poor children in India." And what did she want for herself? Her answer was characteristic for her as I had come to know her in this short time and yet so uncharacteristic for this age of child. "I think I've got everything I want but (and here her eyes sparkled) I'll have a good wish for you if you like. How would you like to go to Disneyland?" I asked whether she had ever been on vacation, but it turned out that she had never actually left the neighborhood except to visit her mother in hospital and to come to the clinic.

In risk research, one attempts to put such human conditions on a rating scale and to reduce them to a set of numbers that can be statistically manipulated. One attempts to add the stresses together to derive a score or to arrange them hierarchically in order of disadvantage. It is difficult for clinicians to observe such life experiences being reduced to a figure without feeling clinically affronted; on the other hand, it is equally difficult for the researcher to be confronted with an unwieldy mass (or mess) of fantasies, feelings, facts, fictions, and fears without feeling the need to quantify the material and to institute proper scientific controls. Researchers do their best to conduct elegant research on data that they often vulgarly refer to as "crap." Clinicians, for their part, are accustomed to "crap" as part of their daily experience with patients, but researchers, in general, prefer things to be a little more rigorous and objective.

Case 1 (Dora) is representative of the extremely vulnerable child where prevention, with any hope of success, needs to be put into effect before conception. The two parents were not only ill equipped for parenthood but created offspring with a high genetic risk for serious disorder. In the second case (John) the loss of the beloved father brought about conditions conducive to depression, often latent during childhood but ready to emerge at any stage of adult life as a depressive illness. In this child, the susceptibility became operative when he lost his best male friend through a road accident in late adolescence and developed enough suicidal ideation to require a short period of hospitalization. The third child (Mary) seemed really to be made of steel since everything that she said and did gave out, in the most mysterious way, the beautiful sound of invulnerability. One would want to study her and to learn from her how she came through her experiences so successfully and to find out, through application to others, whether her techniques were generalizable.

International Aspects of Risk and Vulnerability

It has taken us 4 years of international cooperation to animate the three dolls with which we started and make them into children; it has taken the same number of years to do what Kierkegaard would have us do—complicate our simple and naive initial notions to the point of confusion, ambiguity, and contradiction that make them so much closer to and characteristic of life. It will take perhaps another decade of diligent, systematic work to strike a happy balance between the qualifiable and the quantifiable.

What arguments can be produced to warrant an international

approach to psychiatric problems in children? In the first place, there is no doubt that we all tend to become enclosed and encrusted within our national borders and, for linguistic or chauvinistic reasons, to pay little attention comparatively to work being done elsewhere. To quote Rousseau, knowledge does not travel well and by the time it reaches a distant shore, it is often grossly distorted and out of date. In these days, when the earth is shrinking, we too need to establish more rapid modes of communication between countries and to share our collective knowledge. Coming together in an international arena is not only secure for insularity but also educates the participants in the variety of human experience. The nature of risk, for example, and the amount of risk differ in relation to the state of development of the country concerned, and new risks open up new vulnerabilities and new attempts at mastery. The role of such universal exchange is, as Piaget puts it [2], "to mark precisely, stage by stage, the new orientations, and from one Congress to the next, each can decide if there is stagnation or fresh parts to be explored or expected." Nations can thus monitor one another's progress in this way.

There is still another level of cooperation that must be considered when exploring a new scientific region. One needs to exchange not only between nations but also between disciplines and professions. Each discipline, like each nation, brings a particular point of view that refreshes the perspective of others. Again, to quote Piaget [2], "The future belongs to interdisciplinary work and research, yet because of its reciprocal and often systematic ignorance, this is, in fact, difficult to organize." There is a warning contained in these words that we should heed; unless each of the allied professions makes it its business to know what its neighbor is doing, our total efforts will remain small, disorganized, and ineffectual. We must learn not only to talk across the world but to talk to one another in our own countries.

In considering primary prevention, it is also not enough to concern ourselves with immunizing only our own territory. How can we live on our respective islands or island continents when countless numbers of children are annually becoming victims of *kwashiorkor* and marasmus with their hideous manifestations in bloated bellies and shrunken hulks, when 80 percent of children

in nomadic groups populating sub-Saharan countries long op-
pressed by drought are currently acutely undernourished, when
in India alone nearly one million children die each year because of
malnutrition, and when large numbers of preschoolers in
Guatemala are killed by diarrheal disease. In 1970 a child born in
the United States had an 11 times better chance and a 14 times
better chance of reaching the age of 5 years than did a child born
in India and Africa, respectively. In parts of Latin America cler-
gymen failed to register children until they reached the age of 2
years "because so many die before that it isn't worth it."

What UNICEF has called a "quiet emergency" is the fact that
ten million children all over the world, at any given point in time,
are suffering from starvation. To paraphrase the famous remark
of Brecht, you have to fill stomachs before you practice psychiatry.
In 1959 the General Assembly of the United Nations approved a
Declaration of the Rights of the Child that says, among other
things, that "The child shall have the right to adequate nutrition,
housing, recreation, and medical services." Without these basic
requirements, all children are at risk.

Future Perspectives on Risk and Vulnerability

Are we creating a brighter, safer, and happier world for our
children? Are we diminishing risks, decreasing vulnerability, helping to enhance mastery and coping skills? Are we producing more
competent parents and reproducing less disturbed children? It
would be gratifying to answer all these questions in the affirmative, but if we look at the international scene, it does not seem as if
utopia is around the corner; life around the planet still appears to
carry an inordinate amount of risk for the developing child. It is
certainly true that infant mortality and morbidity have been reduced in some countries, but this is by no means true for the
underdeveloped areas. It is certainly true that child-guidance
clinics have mushroomed almost overnight in some countries, but
this is by no means the case in parts where the majority of the
inhabitants are still struggling for physical survival. Even in those
places where the mental-hygiene movement is flourishing, the
problems keep pace with the solutions; the more clinics we have,

the more we fill them up and the more interminable do the waiting lists become.

A new kind of social historian has recently begun to look into the obscure everyday lives of ordinary people in past centuries and has come up with information that is reassuring to our collective parental egos. Ariès [3] has informed us that we are far more conscious of childhood than the parents of the Middle Ages who scarcely credited their children with any individuality; Langer [4] has reminded us that the murder and abandonment of children prevailed throughout antiquity until about the 4th century A.D. and that from the 4th to the 14th century, parents gave their children over to wet nurses not only to suckle but to "lie upon," expose to the elements, and even to sell into servitude. From the 17th to the 19th century, according to Kellam [5], children were battered into submission and grossly abused by the majority of the adult population. In fact, it was not until the mid-19th century that European governments attempted to legislate against infanticide, child abuse, and child labor. DeMause [6] summed up this historical evolution by remarking that "the history of childhood is a nightmare from which we have only recently begun to awaken. The further back in history one goes, the lower the level of child care, and the more likely the children are to be killed, abandoned, beaten, terrorized and sexually abused." In the opinion of these authorities, the very last thing that anyone would want to be prior to the 20th century was a child, or, if one desired to become a human adult eventually, the only thing to do was to get over one's childhood as soon as possible. In fact, Gratien, in 1646, wrote in his Treatise on Education that "only time can cure the person of childhood." Even allowing for the fact that psychohistorians are liable to be biased in favor of their own age, it would appear as if we had made a remarkable progress since history was first recorded. We have even gone overboard in our recognition of the "little people." The 20th century is "the century of the child," at least in the West, which has apparently become obsessed by the physical, moral, and sexual problems of children. It is not only a child-oriented world but a child-centered one. Today's children not only speak for themselves but are listened to and, in the middle classes, are listened to with respect; they are not told what to do but asked what they might like to do, and when they have a tantrum they are not considered naughty, but neurotic. Parents, at least middle-class Western ones, saw themselves as devoted and dedicated to their children.

It was Rexford [7] who has helped to prick this bubble. It was certainly true that we are much less openly murderous than our predecessors in antiquity, but we are covertly more ambivalent and balance, somewhat uneasily, positive and negative attitudes and behavior. She documents for us the sad fact that the adult person, both parent and professional, are victims of this ambivalence and that although we say that we want the best for our children, we often end up by withholding what would add to their welfare. Often we seem to treat our children with envy and jealousy as if they were our younger siblings.

The ambivalence may take yet another form. The growing disinterest in child rearing among young adults in our society and the trend toward the postponement of having children is increasingly evident. Not only are fewer children being produced in almost all the developed countries, but these are turned over to the care of others while parents go out to work. Some have seen this as questioning the existance of an innate drive toward parenthood or of a developmental phase of parenthood, but it may well be that social and cultural factors have a much greater impact on our innate behavior than we have hitherto realized. It may even be that in our child-rearing methods we are raising children who no longer care to raise children. I would thus agree with Rexford that one of the major risks to children of this century in the Western world, where material aspects are well taken care of, is the ambivalence of adults. This is the large psychological hammer hanging over the heads of the children, and the more vulnerable ones among them find this hard to withstand. Our own self-absorption makes it difficult for us to give to the child and therefore difficult for us to model a caring and considerate role. Here again, we are setting our children at risk by rendering them incapable of altruism and devotedness to others. When everyone is more for himself, the child is more for himself and grows up to become an adult parent who is more concerned with himself than with his children. The roots of parenthood are laid down through strong identifications in the toddler phase of development, and it is with this phase that the current trends are interfering with most. We must be careful not to take our progress for granted and not to mistake psychohistory for absolute truth. According to Becker [8], even history written by historians is often a blend of truth and fantasy, fact and interpretation.

Some historians have raised the question not as to whether we have changes (for better or worse), but whether we can change. Risk and vulnerability seem to be built into the human condition and the basic, enduring elements of the human personality. However, as much as we may modify the risks around the growing child, the genetic aspects of vulnerability may limit our capacity to bring about a better outcome. Let me try and illustrate this point.

An Insect Fable for Our Times

A great fire had broken out in the forest and all the creatures were rushing wildly to the river to get across to safety. From the banks, a water beetle was preparing to take off when a scorpion stopped and pleaded with him. "Let me ride on your back across the river or else I will burn to death here." The water beetle was aghast at the idea; "How can you suggest such a thing," he said, "when in the past you have always attacked us on sight and stung us to death?" "But the situation is radically different," argued the scorpion desperately since the fire was slowly creeping up; "Would I be so crazy as to sting you to death when my own life is at stake? Environmental factors are prepotent under such conditions." The water beetle pondered this and agreed that it was highly logical. They were both at such high risk that specific vulnerabilities could be ignored. So he agreed, whereupon the scorpion jumped on his back. Halfway across the river, the scorpion, alas, stung the water beetle. As they were both dying, the water beetle said reproachfully, "How could you do this to me when I was saving your life?" "Don't blame me," cried the scorpion, "blame my genes. Environment is important as long as the stress is there; remove the stress and the genetic endowment becomes the determining influence." Then they both drowned!

The moral of this story is the moral of the theme of this book;

the vulnerable child must be taught very early not to enter into situations of risk unless his level of competence is great enough to take care of all vicissitudes.

This, together with the previous volume in this series, *Children at Psychiatric Risk,* must be considered as preliminary and somewhat tentative explorations in the new scientific region of risk and vulnerability. We need to educate ourselves in this new area and learn to think preventively as well as therapeutically. It will not be easy to change our clinical habits because, as Nietszche once said, "Mankind has a bad ear for new music," but as clinicians, we need to listen carefully for the sake of our children.

References

1. Kierkegaard, S. Concluding unscientific postscript to the "philosophical fragments." In *A Kierkegaard Anthology,* R. Bretall, Ed. Random House, New York, 1936.
2. Piaget, J. *Biology and Knowledge* (translated by B. Walsh). University of Chicago Press, Chicago, 1971.
3. Aries, P. *Centuries of Childhood.* Knopf, New York, 1962.
4. Langer, W. L. Infanticide: A hisorical survey. *Hist. Childhood Quarz.,* V. 1 (Winter 1974).
5. Kellam, W. Quoted in the article by DeMause.
6. DeMause, L. The evolution of childhood. *Hist. Childhood Quart.,* V. 1 (Spring 1974), 503–575.
7. Rexford, E. Children, child psychiatry and our brave new world. *Arch. Gen. Psychiat.,* 20 (1969), 25–37.
8. Becker, C. L. *Everyman His Own Historian: Essays on History and Politics.* Appleton-Century-Crofts, New York, 1935.

Developmental Genesis of Human Vulnerability: Conceptual Reevaluation

Eleanor S. Wertheim, Ph.D. (Australia)

Introduction

The title of this chapter implies that development may take a course potentially damaging to the individual's chances of further normal development and adaptation, rendering the individual "vulnerable." We propose a model of psychosocial development from which a model of vulnerability of developmental origin can be derived, making explicit the causal and predictive assumptions involved. The approach is normative.

Recent decades have contributed research evidence on early development that challenges many established ideas and practices [1–3]. Neither learning theories [4, 5] nor psychoanalytic schools of thought [6] can accommodate the data. Escalona [5] noted that available theories lack a link to real life. She herself anticipated many major conceptual issues, but there are differences between her position, as outlined in *The Roots of Individuality* [5], and that taken here.

An adequate picture of any organism must take into account at least three types of time scale [7]: (1) a short-term scale that deals with the organism's current situation, (2) A medium scale, pertaining to its own individual history, and (3) a long-term scale, linking the organism to its evolutionary, species-specific history. For the present purpose, these time scales labeled the *situational time scale, the ontogenetic time scale,* and *the phylogenetic time scale,* respectively, provide a framework for the present discussion. Only early development in relation to general principles is considered. The proposed conceptual reevaluation draws on general systems theory [8] and on Piagetian tradition, within a broad evolutionary framework [9].

Situational Time Scale

Here we look at some of the more recent empirical data bearing on typical situations that are normally part of the experience of all infants, such as being born and cared for and interacting with people and the physical world. Escalona already reviewed the evidence dealing with intrinsic organization of human infants' behavior and relationship to the environment, as related to their physiological "states," which regulate the infants' internal and external responses, to their unexpected sensory and cognitive capacities, rhythmic patterns of behavior, spontaneous interest in social and physical surroundings, attentiveness to novel and complex stimuli. Escalona emphasized the importance of early mother-child interaction and of their sensory "match," as well as the active contribution of infants to the shaping of their social and material world. Our aim is to consider some of the new findings from the point of view of common features in mother-child interactions, as revealed by macro- and microbehavioral studies [1–3, 10–30]. The term "mother" is used as synonomous with the person(s) assuming the mothering role *vis-à-vis* the infant.

DIFFERENTIAL RESPONSES OF INFANTS TO HUMAN AND NONHUMAN STIMULI

Human infants have been shown to have an intrinsic ability to discriminate very early between human and nonhuman sensory stimuli, to possess rudimentary sensory and motor systems that are differentially mobilized in response to these two classes of objects, and to initially prefer human to nonhuman stimuli. Detailed spectographic and microvisual/auditory studies of infantile crying, eye-to-eye contact, smiling, and happy vocalizations, contributed to the recognition of their signaling function as these behaviors become available to human babies for social communication, according to an invariable order, prior to the onset of speech proper. The differential aspect of early sensory and motor organization and its more specific theoretical significance have been dealt with elsewhere [1–3].

INTRINSIC REGULATION AT THE INCEPTION OF MOTHER-INFANT SYSTEM

Mother-infant interactions show organized, predictable, formal patterns of reciprocal regulation. In this context the previously neglected issue of the formation of the mother's bond to the baby, as complementary to that of the infant's tie to the mother, has been raised. Systematic information on the origins of the maternal bond continues to be sought. The available data suggest that the formation of this bond may be a gradual process, with distinct prenatal phases, followed by the experience of delivery, then immediate, intimate, physical, postnatal contact with the baby, and further postnatal transactional milestones. It is now thought that obstetric procedures and medication that interfere with normal childbirth, the mother's awareness of its course, and her and the infant's responsiveness in the immediate postpartum period may disrupt this particular phase of the bonding process for both partners. Under natural, normal conditions of delivery, mothers have been observed to react with elation at the first sight of the baby, shared by those present, and to display, with some variations, a predictable pattern of sensory and motor behavior in the first contact with it. For their part, the babies remain alert for several hours after birth prior to first postnatal sleep. When placed on the mother's body, skin to skin, they respond with visual regard, and search for the breast. Licking and sucking of the breast are said to activate hormonal secretions that accelerate uterine contraction, reduce maternal blood loss, and enhance milk flow. If when spoken to and if alert and mobile, newborns were shown in another context to respond microbehaviorally with successive patterns of body movements, synchronized with the time structure of words, irrespective of language used. Comparisons of mother-infant systems allowed immediate contact ("early contact" group) with those managed conventionally ("late contact" group), showed both short- and long-term differences up to 4 years. Mothers in the "early contact" group were judged to behave in ways indicative of a stronger maternal bond, as expressed in the response to and management of the infant's distress during early medical examinations, duration of breast feeding, feeding competence, amount of mutually pleasurable tactile and visual contact during feeding, and later in the quantity and quality of speech to the child.

TEMPORAL ASPECTS OF REGULATION IN MOTHER-INFANT SYSTEMS

An intriguing aspect of the complementary nature of mother-infant transactions is the precise temporal synchrony or alternation observed in the behavior of both partners. In their organizational principle such biosocial rhythms are reminiscent of biological periodicities characteristic of lower levels of individual, physiological functioning [31].

Temporal entrainment of mother and infant, of which the mother is usually unaware, occurs microbehaviorally during breast feeding, in the regulation of eye-to-eye contact, during the infant's visual exploration of surroundings while in the mother's lap (but without direct visual contact between them), and in vocal-linguistic and other playful exchanges. Such intuitive, temporal microcoordination is embedded within more macroscopic patterns of temporal regulation that become gradually established as mother and infant learn to adapt to each other's activity rhythms. Their first transactional crisis, which marks an initial turning point in the mother-infant relationship, is said to occur after the first few days of life, with initial signs of early, reciprocal "fitting in" around the 4th postnatal day. A transactional "steady state" in regard to the infant's physiological regulation and its circadian patterning is usually accomplished by about 3 months. Even under normal conditions this adaptive outcome depends as much on the clarity and consistency of the infant's signals and responsiveness to the mother as on the mother's attention to the signals and ability to correctly interpret and contingently respond to them [32]. The temporal aspect of macro- and microbehavioral adult-infant transactions, rather than physical care and satisfaction of physiological needs, appears to be critical in the formation of their reciprocal, affective tie. In the light of the newer knowledge, the significance of breast feeding itself is likely to be due to the complementary nature of the biochemical properties of maternal milk and the infant's nutritional and immunological requirements, as well as to the social opportunities it provides for multisensory, temporally regulated, pleasurable transactions. Under certain conditions even attention to attractive animate or inanimate external stimuli can temporarily take precedence over the infant's internal needs for physiological satisfaction or comfort. This type of evidence suggests that even in very young infants, perceptual [33] and social processes have a primary regulatory function in daily adaptation.

REGULATION OF COGNITIVE TASKS IN MOTHER-INFANT SYSTEMS

Under normal conditions, in their function as a cognitive stimulus, mothers spontaneously adapt the complexity of their stimulation and response to the changing sensory, cognitive, and motor capacities of the infant. With equally spontaneity they endow the infant's often only loosely structured and inarticulate behavior with personally relevant meaning. This is well illustrated by what is often referred to as "mother's speech." This is a pattern of prosodically, semantically, and syntactically simplified verbal input, intuitively adjusted by the mother in form and complexity, in accordance with the infant's cognitive and linguistic progress. In the process the infant is exposed to cognitive and linguistic patterns within his/her capacity and learns that communication has interpersonal meaning. Here too, such intuitive adaptations are embedded in negotiable units of interaction during which at each new stage of cognitive development mothers have to provide a cognitively appropriate environment and respond to the infant's cognitive demands. These interactions call for the caretaker's cognitive, emotional, and regulatory adaptations, as detailed elsewhere [1].

GENERAL COMMENTS

This is a necessarily sketchy review of the research evidence on early development being gathered at the level of the situational time scale. Additional limitations of the review are inherent in the nature of data available, that is, treating the mother-infant system as if it functioned independently of the triadic, mother-father-infant system, or its social equivalent, of the total family, and the wider social network. In some recent studies fathers [34, 35] have been included. There is also an interest in looking more closely at the earliest infant-infant transactions and their role in development [36]. However, it is too early to draw conclusions from this material. As microbehavioral analysis reveals transactional patterns that escape more macroscopic examination, caution is needed in generalizing from only one or other type of material.

Ontogenetic Time Scale

We are now leaving the empirical realm to consider what ontogenetic models would fit the data and allow for testable predictions. Escalona [5] pointed out that models linking developmental outcomes to objective variables, such as type of rearing environment, parental attitudes, or practices, omit account of the infant as an active, selective agent determining the subjective meaning and impact of these factors. She was similarly critical of homeostatic models, based on the untenable assumption that the developing organism is a closed system. Escalona chose a model according to which the child's subjective experience provides the intervening variable between external events and internal structures. This experience, she rightly argued, can be objectified by looking at the infant's ongoing interactions with the environment. However, Escalona used observations of mother-infant interactions for the purpose of deriving from them individual, formal "adaptation syndromes," characterized by specific structural and functional components. On the motivational side, while acknowledging the infant's capacity for goal-directed behavior, Escalona retained the causal-motivational framework of psychoanalytic ego psychology for want of another acceptable model.

TRANSACTIONAL CONCEPTS

The conceptual position taken here differs from Escalona's in two important respects. It marks a shift from a focus on internal, individual structures and functions to that on "transactional structures" and styles of interpersonal adaptation defined in terms of goals-means relationships. This shift is based on the assumption that to survive, children of all ages have to find a *modus vivendi* with the people and objects in the relevant environment. They have to adapt. The evidence reviewed earlier suggests that under favorable conditions human caretakers facilitate the infant's survival and early adaptations by matching their behavior to that of the infant. Given inborn individual differences in babies such mutual adaptations are critical for developmental outcomes. Furthermore, as is detailed later, causal and motivational issues are approached here from a different angle. Both Escalona's and the present framework belong to the category of formal models concerned with structural and functional rather than content analysis.

According to general systems theory [8], individual development can be only understood in the context of larger processes of which it is a part. In the case of early human development, the basic unit of study must, therefore, include the "infant-environment" system. To simplify the discussion, we consider the mother (M)-child (C) system, treating it as a subsystem of a three-person family (FA), the third person being father (F). The MC system constitutes a transactional system defined by a *formal system of relationships between M and C*. In this case M and C are subsystems of MC, but each of them constitutes a system in its own right, defined by a *formal system of relationships between the various components of M* (or C) such as self-perception, cognitive and motivational (conscious/unconscious) structures, and motor skills. *The formal relationships between subsystems MC, FC, and MF* in turn define the system FA. Thus one is dealing with a complex, hierarchically ordered network of dynamic relationships between and within three different levels of biosocial organization, that of the family, of dyadic groupings within the family, and of *dynamic* configurations within individuals [37]. This "dynamic field" can be conceptualized as an intricate control system. At any point in time, events in one part of the field reverberate over the whole field and facilitate, modify, or constrain events in other parts of the field. For example, the father's unemployment and depression may force the mother to go to work and give up breast feeding, leaving daily care of the infant to the depressed father. In this case, reversal of roles in the MF subsystem leads to sudden changes in MC and FC subsystems, to alterations at the higher FA level and at the lower level of individual C, M, and F. However, knowing how MF, MC, and FC function does not help in making accurate predictions about how FA is functioning. Nor is it possible to deduce from individual changes in C and M what these changes will do to MC as a system. It is a fundamental principle of system functioning that the behavior of a system depends on *how its parts fit together,* on *their relationships,* which determine the organization of the "whole," and not on the individual characteristics of the parts. The principle itself is not new. It has been applied by gestalt psychology to perception as the famous dictum that "the whole" is more than the sum of its parts. The same principle can be found anywhere in nature; for example, the properties of the molecule H_2O are different from the properties of the individual hydrogen and oxygen molecules. What is new is the extension of this formal principle to the understanding of psychosocial behavior in man. It follows that C's relationships may be different in the transactional systems MC, FC, and MFC; hence C could be said to have different "properties" in each of them. Some of Escalona's findings provide empirical support for these concepts. For example, the independent variable of "high"/"low" individual activity used in her study was not always predictive of the infant's behavior and was even less predictive of the mother's response to the infant. All mothers tried, more or less sensitively, to accommodate to their infant but the final, mutual adaptation was in no way related to the formal, individual classification of the baby. Differences in social experience were as great within, as between the active and inactive groups of babies.

It follows, therefore, that the stability of C as a "dynamic configuration" depends on the stability of his/her relationships in developmentally significant systems of which C is a member. The type and degree of system stability can be gauged from an examination of the rules that regulate the relationships between the members. The concept of "rule" is fully discussed elsewhere [38]. Briefly, "rules" are sanctions that prescribe and limit the range of desirable and permissible behaviors across all intra- and extrasystemic sectors of interaction in a given system. Rules are consciously or unconsciously constructed and/or validated at the level of the system as "a whole." As a member of MC, FC, and MFC, "C" from the start contributes to the elaboration of rules in these systems and may follow different rules of relationships in each of them. The rules of a system represent an optimal compromise between the active, adaptive, controlling tendencies of each individual member including "C." The total rule network determines the organizational structure and functioning of the system. It is assumed here that in the course of development children internalize perceived rules and rule networks, as experienced in different system memberships.

PROPOSED TRANSACTIONAL MODEL

Piaget's principle of an adaptive equilibrium of assimilation and accommodation provides an example of the most general rule said to govern the developing infant's relationships with the world, as an "object of knowledge." Stierlin [39] relabeled this rule in the context of mother-infant transactions, referring to the *"doing-undergoing"* dichotomy as one of the principles regulating feedback in an MC system. This principle can be extended to suggest that each of the systems C, MC, FC, and MFC evolves its own system of rules that determines how the balance of "doing-undergoing" is being regulated by the members. The principle of assimilation/accommodation and that of "doing/undergoing" are functionally similar. Only their behavioral universe is different. The latter principle is more specifically applied to balances of transactional control per se. Just as it is impossible not to communicate in a transaction [40], it is equally impossible not to take a stand in relation to reciprocal control. To always "undergo" is tantamount to abdication of one's control in favor of the "other." The "doing-undergoing" dichotomy should not be confused with activity versus passivity. "Activity" and "passivity" denote individual characteristics. "Doing" and "undergoing" are relational concepts, meaning to "regulate others" (self, the physical habitat), and "being regulated by others" (by a part of oneself, by the physical habitat, etc.). At each stage of development C's stability depends on how these two types of regulation are balanced and on the contexts that maintain a given balance. Thus C can be only as stable as are these relational balances, the shared rule systems, and the relevant dynamic fields in which such relational balances are embedded. Theoretically speaking, C's *"transactional space"* includes at least three domains, *the interpersonal, the object-centered, and the intrapersonal* domain. An object-directed domain can be treated as a formal transactional system insofar as physical objects "respond" to actions on them with malleability, textural stimulation, resistance, and so on. The intrapersonal domain can be conceptualized as a transactional system, the components of which are in a dynamic equilibrium as a function of both intra- and extrasystemic processes. The overall stability of C as a system would depend also on the degree of congruence of the rule systems in all three transactional domains.

Development calls for stability as well as change. The "doing-undergoing" dichotomy represents a stable, functional principle that operates throughout development, indeed throughout the life cycle. Only *the balance* between "doing" and "undergoing" shifts progressively. Under normal conditions these shifts are precipitated by the infants' expanding physical, cognitive, and emotional capabilities and skills, signaling new regulatory requirements, to which sensitive transactional partners gradually adapt. Changes over time in the adult partners' own needs and responsibilities, or in the wider political, social, economic, or ecological matrix in which FA is embedded may exert parallel pressures on transactional change in one or all of the C, CM, CF, and MFC systems. Such pressures for change originating in C and/or any of the other systems produce a temporary deviation from established rules of regulation until a new developmentally more appropriate balance of "doing" and "undergoing" is achieved. This reorganization would be at the basis of progressive formal transformations of transactional structures in any system of which C is a member, and because of their dynamic links, also in C. These processes would be homologous with the cognitive reequilibration postulated by Piaget and the resulting progressive formal transformations of mental structures. Like the latter, the transformations of transactional structures would be epigenetically ordered in all domains from simpler, global, to more complex, more highly differentiated and integrated structures, reflecting the gradual changes in the "I-thou," "I-it," and "I-I" relationships taking place in the course of normal development.

Sander [41, 42] empirically derived an outline that was previously adapted [1] as a preliminary, formal, epigenetic model of early transactional development in the interpersonal domain. This shows a graded series of transactional tasks that M and C have to negotiate at successive stages of development, leading to progressive transformations in the "doing-undergoing" balance. The MC system begins with a state of global synchrony and in the end reaches a bipolar state in which the dichotomy of "doing-undergoing" has become integrated both within and between M and C. The total sequence of transactional tasks is prototypical of the whole range of transactional patterns in which human beings engage, specifically, a state of sensory "oneness," reciprocity, joint control, subordination-dominance, and, finally, cooperation, in this order. The transactional transformations shown in Sander's original outline stretch across the sensory-motor period and the transitional stage of emergence of language. If Piaget's concept of vertical decalage, that is, recapitulation of the same formal process at a higher level of organization, should hold for transactional development, one would expect that the epigenetic sequence described by Sander would be repeated on a concrete-operational and later, formal cognitive level. The issue of the temporal relationship between transactional and cognitive stages must be left open for the moment. There are also other questions. For example, would one find horizontal decalage between and within transactional domains at each stage of development? Are there developmentally critical transactional sectors in each domain and for each stage of development? If so, are they the same for each transactional system? What precise processes and mechanisms underlie rule formation and change and determine tolerance of rule deviations in the system or resistance to change [38]? The notion that structural transactional discontinuity is made possible by the operation of a continuous dynamic principle of balanced "doing-undergoing" implies that both "doing" and "undergoing" are part of the human condition. Development merely consists in a formal reorganization of their balance toward greater flexibility in the relationship between the two components, as dictated by demands of reality. This differs from the traditional model of, ideally, linear progression from absolute dependence to absolute independence as a hallmark of increasing maturity. In the proposed transactional model the direction of development is toward the highest form of interdependence and cooperation as the end-point. In the linear model, development moves towards ultimate individual independence and self-sufficiency as its endpoint.

MOTIVATIONAL ASPECTS OF THE TRANSACTIONAL MODEL

Neither "instincts," nor the more neutral concept of "drives," nor that of extrinsic rewards can account for the infant's observed goal directedness. Even very young infants engage in choice behavior, adjusting their response to a desirable end. Research workers have described temporally well-regulated mother-infant systems in which the ebb and flow of pleasurable arousal is patterned on microrhythms of the cognitive transactional feedback in the system. Conversely, temporally divergent MC systems generate negative affect and microbehaviorally apparent attempts by the infant to establish or restore transactional balance in the system, or failing that, to withdraw from transactions by using gaze or head aversion and other strategies. To fit such data the motivational model must allow for the infant's intentional[1] behavior and decision making. The concept of "intrinsic motivation" [43] fulfills this requirement. Whereas Piaget side-stepped the motivational issue in his epistemology, the concept of intrinsic motivation can be built into the formal epigenetic model without any alteration of the concept or the model. In relation to the proposed transactional model, it can be postulated that states of perceived "doing-undergoing" imbalance in the MC system are associated with negative feeling states that motivate one or both partners to find a new transactional balance. Once perceived as satisfactory, this generates a positive feeling state in the system. It is assumed that each transactional stage is associated with an age-sex/culture-characteristic, appropriate balance of "doing-undergoing," which, when perceived as such by both partners, generates an optimal affective state of the system.

The concept of intrinsic motivation is tied to the concept of "cognitive dissonance" said to trigger activity aiming at cognitive adaptation. The latter concept requires the assumption of a discrepancy between schemas of reality encoded in the nervous system and those perceived in the environment. This raises the question of the link between the assumed state of disequilibrium in the nervous system and motivational change. Escalona objected to models tying motivation to brain processes on the grounds that

[1]The precise nature of the observed, early behavioral intentionality is still a vexing issue that cannot be considered here.

such models are reductionist, that is, that they reduce psychological phenomena to the status of epiphenomena of events at a lower, material level of biological organization. The difference between reductionist models and the model proposed here is considered below.

CAUSALITY AND TELEONOMY IN ONTOGENESIS

Reductionist models are based on a static, mechanistic concept of causality. More or less distant antecedents, for example, early hospitalization, or some "fixed" cause such as instincts or specified brain processes, are assumed to influence development and behavior in a direct, linear fashion. In contrast, systems-theoretical concepts are based on the notion of circular, feedback causality operating at a point in time when the behavior occurs. One deals here with "causal configurations" in the relevant dynamic field in which the behavioral system finds itself. Thus, for example, past experience or current conscious/unconscious states of M and C would enter into the determination of causality in a MC system, when relevant, as causal components, together with other relevant components. The causal outcome would be defined by the resultant balance.

General systems theory treats all biological systems as goal-directed and organized; in other words, their behavior always bears some relationship to the final goal. Systems at different levels of organization are dynamically linked and may be formally isomorphic, that is, regulated by similar, formal, governing principles, in the service of such end points. This means that the concurrence of cognitive, motivational, and central nervous system (CNS) disequilibria would be conceptually viewed as an instance of temporal entrainment rather than as a causal chain. In a dynamic field of relations no "causes" can be isolated, only dynamic states of the system.

Phylogenetic Time Scale

It must be assumed that man's phylogenetic heritage includes the capacity to generate culture and the cultural diversity of behavior. The question arises as to whether, over and above culturally diverse phenotypic types of MC and other systems containing

C, there are any formal, species-specific behavioral genotypes that set broad limits to such phenotypic variations. In the light of the apparent lawfulness and precise organization of the MC system (? other systems), the answer may be "yes." The suggested hypothesis states that M and possibly F, older siblings, and other adult members of *Homo sapiens* may be encoded with very general, formal, biological programs complementary to similar encoding of C. Under favorable conditions these programs would provide a basis for the establishment of culturally patterned transactions that ensure the infants' survival and their neurophysiological and psychosocial adaptation to the "environment of birth." The very flexibility of *Homo sapiens* may mean that to become "human beings" the human young must go through an early, relatively prolonged, formally defined period of species-specific psychosocial apprenticeship to fit them into their particular world. Similarly, what is popularly called the "maternal instinct" may actually be a reciprocal MC bond, not "ready-made," but requiring certain conditions for its formation. These are issues for macro- and microbehavioral, transculturally based research. A general, biological bias, shared with Escalona, is thus taken much further and is elaborated here into a bioadaptive model of development, in which the concept of "instincts" is redundant.

Toward a Model of Human Vulnerability of Developmental Origin

The general, formal model of psychosocial development (Model D) as outlined in the preceding paragraphs can be used to construct a model of human vulnerability of developmental origin (model V). Some features of such a V model are considered in the text that follows.

FORMAL PROPERTIES OF THE V MODEL

Vulnerability can be conceptualized in terms of structural and/or functional deviations from normative transactional processes in one or more transactional domains. The focus on formal properties of these transactional processes has several advantages. It allows for the integration of significant internal and external conditions relevant to the adaptation of the "transacting self" at different stages of development and as part of different systems, as reflected in the type and degree of dynamic balance between assimilation/accommodation or doing/undergoing in these systems. The concept of "rule" provides an analytic tool applicable to all transactional systems, irrespective of members' age or number, and of the type, goals, function, or cultural characteristics of the system itself. A comprehensive analysis of the system along the three transactional domains, their most significant sectors, and macro- and microbehavioral functioning would yield a matrix showing the critical goals, and patterns of transactional organization and regulation within and between the different domains and for the system as a whole. Implied in the model is the notion that human ontogenesis proceeds under normal conditions toward biosocial endpoints that ensure survival, biological fitness, and generation of psychosocial meanings without which, in man, the first two may not be attainable.

MULTICAUSAL PROPERTY OF THE V MODEL

In principle, the causal configuration can be conceptualized as a vertically and horizontally ordered casual matrix of varying degrees of complexity depending on the system and its stage of development. All three time scales, each involving a different rate of change, are represented in the matrix. For practical purposes, the infinitesimal rate of evolutionary change means that, short of mutations, the causal contribution of the phylogenetic time scale has to do with biologically determined, formal, species-specific goals, means, and constraints on human development, originally evolved as adaptations to the "environment of evolutionary adaptedness." The rate of change at the level of the ontogenetic time scale is jointly codetermined by the history of a particular transactional system and the rate at which changes in cultural goals, means, and constraints impinge on it and shape or constrain ontogenetic goals and pathways. The ontogenetic time scale bears directly on the situational time scale as cultural trends and shifts interact with idiosyncratically derived goals, means, and constraints in day-to-day family or other relevant institutional transactions. The increasing time lag between the phylogenetic and modern ontogenetic time scales and between the ontogenetic and situational time scales in Western society is currently generating conflicts likely to be causally significant in relation to developmentally induced vulnerability. Boyden [44] coined the term *phylogenetic maladjustment* to draw attention to the thesis that the rapid changes in Western ecology, nutrition, and way of life have by now stretched man's biological coping limits and can be linked to specific forms of ill health. Could it be that modern biosocial engineering of the human newborn's and infant's early transactions with the world has reached similar limits and so contributes to developmental vulnerability? What is, for example, the long-term developmental effect, if any, of missing out on early microbehaviorally regulated, contingent transactions with the caretaker? The more direct causal influences operating on the situational time scale as a function of feedback processes in significant child-mother systems and in the more immediate situational context cannot be considered apart from their dynamic relationship to phylogenetic and ontogenetic time scales.

All epigenetically organized biological systems display certain formal characteristics that further complicate developmental predictions. These can only be hinted at here. Thus, for example, Waddington [7] speaks of the homeorhetic tendency of biological systems, that is, the tendency to stay "on course" developmentally, even if transient disturbances should cause the organism to stray from time to time. The exact mechanism responsible for this adaptive correction is not clear. There is also the fact that chance plays an important part in the epigenetic process itself. Each stage-bound transformation of transactional structures and functions leaves open some, and more or less effectively closes other, potential pathways along which transactions could have been negotiated in the future, had C (or the parent) been party to a different transactional system. These differences may prove irrelevant in that the dissimilar pathways may lead to the same developmental end result. Alternatively, they may result in a more or less irreversible reduction in the future developmental options in one, but not the other, type of transactional system. Such a reduction may not be apparent at first, only for "sleeper effects," that is, delayed consequences of earlier events, to later permanently alter the system's transactional direction, away from the normal course. Thus early transactional traumas may be spontaneously resolved. The nature of the environments with which the child may enter into transactions much later, at critical epigenetic points of change, may reduce or improve chances of favorable developmental outcome. Short-term predictions of developmental vulnerability, or intactness, even if fulfilled, don't necessarily predict long-term outcomes. The complex causal dynamics involved make it obvious that any causally based predictions can at best be only predictions of developmental and adaptive probabilities. This is what Escalona predicted.

Conclusion

In the light of the proposed conceptual reevaluation our task must be broadened to the study and understanding of processes that tie individual "vulnerability," as well as "invulnerability," to the family and social systems in which individuals grow up, *and of which they are an integral part.* There are indications that these are lawful, organized processes. To prevent vulnerability, we must discover the biosocial laws governing these processes. If the proposed model D is valid, the infant's transactions with the world during the first 6 months of life would be critical, insofar as these first months may lay the foundation for the transformation of the human young into a "human being," in the accepted sense of this term. In the world of today, the prevention of vulnerability due to incompleteness of this transformation should head our list of priorities.

Acknowledgments

The original version of this chapter was revised in the light of first-hand study in 1975 of research trends in the United States and Britain, made possible by an International Fellowship of the American Association of University Women, and a Travel Grant in-aid from the Ian Potter Foundation, Melbourne. This support is gratefully acknowledged.

References

1. Wertheim, E. S. Person-environment interaction: The epigenesis of autonomy and competence. II. *Brit J. Med. Psychol.*, 48 (1975a), 95–111.

2. Wertheim, E. S. Person-environment interaction: The epigenesis of autonomy and competence. III. *Brit. J. Med. Psychol.,* 48 (1975b), 237–256.

3. Wertheim, E. S. Person-environment interaction: The epigenesis of autonomy and competence. IV. *Brit. J. Med. Psychol.,* 48 (1975c), 391–402.

4. Kohlberg, L. Stage and sequence: The cognitive development approach to socialization. In *Handbook of Socialization: Theory and Research,* D. A. Goslin, Ed. Rand McNally, Chicago, 1969, pp. 347–480.

5. Escalona, S. K. *The Roots of Individuality.* Aldine, Chicago, 1968.

6. Wertheim, E. S. Person-environment interaction: The epigenesis of autonomy and competence. I. *Brit. J. Med. Psychol.,* 48 (1975d), 1–8.

7. Waddington, C. H. *The Strategy of the Genes.* George Allen and Unwin, London, 1957.

8. Bertalanffy, L. Von. *General Systems Theory.* Braziller, New York, 1968.

9. Lee, R. B. and DeVore, I. *Man the Hunter,* Aldine, Chicago, 1968.

10. Anderson, J. W. Attachment behaviour out of doors. In *Ethological Studies of Child Behavior,* N. Blurton Jones, Ed. Cambridge University Press, Cambridge, 1972, pp. 199–215.

11. Bower, T. G. R. *Development in Infancy.* Freeman, San Francisco, 1974.

12. Brazelton, T. B., Tronick, E., Adamson, F., Als, H., and Wise, S. Early mother-infant reciprocity. In *The Parent-Infant Interaction,* R. Porter and M. O'Connor, Eds. Ciba Foundation, Symposium 33, Elsevier, Amsterdam, 1975, pp. 137–154.

13. Lewis, M. and Rosenblum, L. A. *The Effect of the Infant on the Caregiver.* Wiley, New York, 1974.

14. Condon, W. S. and Sander, L. W. Neonate movement is synchronized with adult speech: interactional participation and language acquisition. *Science,* 183 (1974), 99–101.

15. Collis, G. M. and Schaffer, H. R. Synchronization of visual attention in mother-infant pairs. *J. Child. Psychol. Psychiat.,* 16 (1975), 315–320.

16. Connolly, K. J. and Bruner, J. S. *The Growth of Competence.* Academic Press, London, 1974.

17. Klaus, M. H. and Kennell, J. H. *Mother-infant bonding,* Mosby, St. Louis, 1976.

18. Bullowa, M. When infant and adult communicate, how do they synchronize their behaviors? In *Behaviour In Face to Face Interaction,* A. Kendon, R. M. Harris, and M. Key Ritchie, Eds. Mouton, The Hague, 1975, pp. 95–127.

19. Lipsitt, L. P. Pattern perception and information seeking in early infancy. In *Early Experience and Visual Information Processing in Perceptual and Reading Disorders,* F. A. Young and D. B. Lindsley, Eds. Nat. Acad. Sci., Washington, D.C., 1970, 382–402.

20. Newson, J. Towards a theory of infant understanding. *Bull. Brit. Psychol. Soc.,* 27 (1958), 251–257.

21. Richards, M. P. M. Social interaction in the first weeks of human life. *Psychiat. Neurol. Neurochir.,* 14 (1971), 35–42.

22. Richards, M. P. M. The pros and cons of breast feeding. Unpublished paper presented at a joint meeting of the British Paediatric Association Council and Medical Education and Information Unit of the Spastics Society, Farnham, England, 1974.

23. Sander, L. W. Primary prevention and some aspects of temporal organization in early infant-caretaker interaction. In *Infant Psychiatry—A New Synth-*

esis, E. Rexford, L. W. Sander and t. Shapiro, Eds. Yale University Press, New Haven, 1976, pp. 187–204.

24. Sander, L. W. Infant and Caretaking Environment. Investigation and conceptualization of adaptive behaviour in a system of increasing complexity. In *Exploration in Child Psychiatry,* E. J. Anthony, Ed. Plenum, New York, 1975, pp. 129–166.

25. Stern, D. N. A micro-analysis of mother-infant interaction: Behaviour regulating social contact between a mother and three-and-a-half-month old twins. *J. Amer. Acad. Child Psychiat.,* 10 (1971), 501–517.

26. Yarrow, L. J., Rubenstein, J. L., and Pederson, F. A. *Infant and Environment,* Wiley, New York, 1975.

27. Thoman, E. B. How a rejecting baby affects mother-infant synchrony. In *Parent-Interaction,* R. Porter and M. O'Connor, Eds. Ciba Foundation Symposium 33, Elsevier, Amsterdam, 1975, pp. 177–200.

28. Trevarthen, C. Conversation with a two-month old. *New Sci.,* 162 (1974), 230–235.

29. Tronick, E., Adamson, L., Wise, S., Als, H., and Brazelton, B. T. The infant's response to entrapment between contradictory messages in face to face interaction. Mimeographed copy, Children's Hospital Medical Center and Harvard Medical School, Boston, 1975.

30. Snow, C. E. Mother's speech to children learning language. *Child Development,* 43, (1972), 549–565.

31. Luce, G. G. *Biological Rhythms in Psychiatry and Medicine.* Nat. Inst. Mental Health, Chevy Chase, Md., Public Health Service Publications, No. 2088, 1970.

32. Goldberg, S. Social competence in infancy: A model of parent-infant interaction. *Merrill-Palmer Quart.* (1977), in press.

33. Piaget, J. *Biology and Knowledge,* University of Chicago Press, Chicago, 1971.

34. Parke, R. D. and O'Leary, S. E. Family interaction in the newborn period: Some findings, some observations, and some unresolved issues. In *The Developing Individual in a Changing World,* Vol. 2, K. F. Riegel and J. A. Meacham, Eds. A selection of papers presented at the Second Biennial Meeting of the International Society for Study of Behavioural Development, held at University of Michigan, Ann Arbor, August 1973. International Society for the Study of Behavioural Development, Chicago, 1976, pp. 653–663.

35. Rebelsky, F. and Hanks, C. Fathers verbal interaction with infants in the first three months of life. *Child Devel.,* 42 (1971), 63–68.

36. Lewis, M. and Rosenblum, L. A., Eds. *Friendship and Peer Relations.* Wiley, New York, 1975.

37. Wertheim, E. S. Family unit therapy, The science and typology of family systems. *Family Process,* 12 (1973), 361–376.

38. Wertheim, E. S. The science and typology of family systems. II. Further theoretical and practical considerations. *Family Process,* 14 (1975), 285–309.

39. Stierlin, H. *Conflict and Reconciliation.* Anchor Books, New York, 1969.

40. Watzlawick, P., Beavin, J. H., and Jackson, D. D. *Pragmatics of Human Communication. A Study of Interactional Patterns, Pathologies and Paradoxes.* Norton, New York, 1967.

41. Sander, L. W. Adaptive relationships in early mother-child interaction. *J. Child Psychiat.,* 3 (1964), 231–264.

42. Sander, L. W. The longitudinal course of early mother-child interaction:

Cross-case comparisons in a sample of mother-child pairs, in *Determinants of Infant Behaviour, Vol. IV,* B.M. Foss, Ed. Methuen, London, 1969, pp. 189–227.

43. Hunt, J. McV. Experience and development of motivation: Some reinterpretations. *Child Develop.,* 31 (1960), 489–504.

44. Boyden S. V. *The Impact of Civilization On the Biology of Man.* Univ. of Toronto, Toronto, Canada, 1970.

PHYSICAL ASPECTS OF VULNERABILITY: GENETIC FACTORS, MULTIPLE BIRTHS, HANDICAPS

Editorial

Cyrille Koupernik, M.D. (France)

It seems to me that one should not be satisfied simply to categorize the biological factors of perinatal risk in their chronological order of appearance or through their possible mode of action, as is usually the case. Not only does it present a limited account of the situation, but it repeats itself from one text to another so that in reading it one invariably gets the impression of *déjà lu*. There is a need to look at this whole area in a more innovative way and to try and bring together as an integrated whole prevailing attitudes that seem radically different and opposed to one another but have in common an interest in primary prevention. The juxtaposition of extreme attitudes is not, therefore, intended to serve a polemical but a useful epistemological purpose of furthering our knowledge in this field. To accomplish this it is essential for protagonists to examine carefully the totality of risks involved and to dedicate themselves, irrespective of their theoretical positions, to the health and happiness of the children and adolescents of today who will become the adults of tomorrow. The task of synthesis is not without its difficulties since extremists from both sides have many positive contributions to make, but make them while neglecting the point of view of the other side. The neurologically, obstetrically, pediatrically, and biologically minded, as compared with those having a psychodynamic orientation, focus their entire attention on the *totus puer in cerebro*. It is an objective approach that has made some striking points but that also has its limitations, particularly with regard to its concept of man in his milieu. Yet it cannot be condemned out of hand as pessimistic or fatalistic in its outlook since it is also oriented toward prevention and is relatively realistic in what it feels it can effect in this area. In some respects,

39

its position is unassailable. For example, there is conclusive evidence to suggest that in the presence of toxemia of pregnancy the infant enters life in a precarious state, prone to convulsions and other organic sequelae that punctuate his subsequent development as part of the "continuum of reproductive casualty." It would seem foolish to think that this logical and inexorable concatenation of events had its antecedent not in the toxemia of the mother but in her ambivalence toward carrying him in her womb. However, more rounded studies have indicated that toxemia is a more likely hazard in unmarried teenagers where the pregnancy is fraught with problems and psychological stresses.

The current history-taking methods dealing with obstetrical events are methodologically unsound since not only are the records poorly kept, but a good deal of retrospective distortion can occur. Furthermore, some reliable criteria of stressful birth must be established: the Apgar score is not sufficient. In the absence of these, there is a tendency to make *a priori* statements such as "the condition is of organic origin" and later to assign the child to such diagnostic wastebaskets as "hyperkinetic syndrome," all on the most flimsy and debatable evidence. One finds in the clinical literature of all countries, both European and American, mythical entities, such as Dupre's "motor debility," which is nothing better than a pseudoorganic semiology. What is often overlooked by the pure organicists is that children *without* the slightest indication of a cerebral lesion can nevertheless manifest increased tendon reflexes, poor motor coordination, distractability, irritability, impulsiveness, and hypotonia. They in no way deserve the label of MBD (where D stands for "damaged" or "dysfunction," M for "minimal," and B for "brain"), and even less do they need to be placed on amphetamines.

Now, on the other side, there is a school of clinicians who are almost cultural anthropologists in that they pay no attention at all to the brain and a great deal to relations within kinships—parent-child, grandparent-child, and sibling. This approach owes a great deal to psychoanalysis and to the understanding of emotional factors in the causation of disorder, and for these clinicians the true laboratory for the study of the child is the family.

Each side stresses its claims authoritatively, often promoting beliefs to the level of facts without being too concerned with the nature of evidence of the weighting of data in terms of significance. Of the many examples that would serve to illustrate these points, two have generated the most heat and least light: birth trauma and infantile autism.

For those with a mechanistic viewpoint, every birth is a physically traumatic event. For them, injury ranging from minimal to maximal is expectable since the baby's brain, in passing through the birth passage, is subjected to intense and intermittent pressure. Moreover, there is a critical period when the mother's blood is no longer available as a source of oxygen and energy and the lungs have yet to begin to function adequately. With cesarean section, which is becoming increasingly fashionable, the infant passes from one physiological regime to another with even less time for adjustment. On these grounds, one would anticipate, say the proponents of this view, that every human being is to a greater or lesser extent brain damaged, and as evidence to support this view they cite the existence of blood in the spinal fluid immediately after a normal birth. Whether they recover from it or compensate for it, there is no doubt that the vast majority of human beings pass through this exacting rite of passage without demonstrating any evidence whatsoever of CNS damage or dysfunction and that they work far better and more efficiently than the most sophisticated computers presently in existence. The concept of "reproductive casualty" put forward by the American Pasamanick, carries the organicist's argument to its logical and yet absurd conclusion that these minimal experiences at birth are responsible for the whole range of human behavior, whether healthy, conflictual, or psychopathological. This clearly represents an appeal to principle and not to evidence. On the other side, psychogenesists such as Rank have postulated a psychological birth trauma that can do as much if not more than the physical birth trauma. Lately, the French obstetrician Leboyer has been working toward making birth a completely nonviolent entrance into life by rendering it sensorially as peaceful and as unstimulating as possible. Once again, the rationale is open to a great deal of doubt. In a follow-up study, Leboyer infants did seem to do better developmentally than a matched comparison group, but it is obviously difficult to control for the factor of self-selection.

The conflict over autism is another case in point. The organicists logically connect this drama of child psychiatry to organic factors related to heredity and to neurotransmitters in the brain stem with some postulating hyperarousal and some hypoarousal with little in the way of proof, but with much conviction. The psychogenesists have implicated the parents, describing them in the most negative terms so that not only do they suffer the pain of having an abnormal child but also the guilt for being responsible for it. In recent years, the parents of autistic children have fought back by pointing to the acknowledged fact that they have other normal children and that twin studies have indicated some degree of concordance for autism.

A third point of view has arisen more recently to muddy the causal question even further. This approach has emphasized the socioeconomic dimension. There appears to be good evidence that prematurity, brain damage, and brain dysfunction is connected with the vicissitudes of social class and to such concomitants of the subculture of poverty as malnutrition, poor maternal health, inadequate prenatal care, and a cycle of deprivation. The ghettos of big cities with their filthy conditions, overcrowding, and lack of privacy have spawned untold numbers of infants at high risk for both mortality and morbidity. Even in a highly developed country like France there are grossly underdeveloped areas that compare in deprivation with the poorest and most primitive communities in the world. The neonatal mortality rate is 16 percent, but a more efficient health policy would reduce this by more than half. Currently, there is a high incidence of toxemia among pregnant French women (and consequently a high incidence of morbidity and mortality for such an advanced country) because they work too much and too hard and neglect their prenatal care. This, however, is not the whole story; the physical, social, and psychological factors compound one another. There is a need in Western countries such as France to relearn some of the basic psychosocial lessons regarding the psychology of parenthood, the parent-child relationship, and the family as the crucial unit for the proper care and rearing of the young. One needs to prepare individuals for parenthood, enhance their competence as parents, and back them up with specialist support systems that ensure that they carry out the job well. Only then will we begin to see an appreciable reduction in the complex of disorders stemming from a faulty reproductive process.

Vulnerability Research: A Behavior Genetics Point of View

L. Erlenmeyer-Kimling, Ph.D. (U.S.A.)

The concept of vulnerability to develop a pathological condition later in life has increasingly become a focus of interest in medicine, education, and the social and biological sciences; schizophrenia, the affective disorders, Huntington's chorea, alcoholism, and sociopathic personality—all have been the center of research aimed at picking out, from larger groups at greater than average risk for the disorder in question, those children or adolescents most likely to succumb at later ages. Younger children have been studied in attempts to predict learning disabilities in school, and adults have been followed longitudinally in vulnerability research on hypertension, heart disease, and aging. Considerable efforts have been made to establish the techniques of genetic prenatal diagnosis to detect the fetus that, if born, will develop tragically because of a serious chromosomal anomaly or any of a large number of single-gene conditions with metabolic, and frequently behavioral, consequences. Heterozygote screening for deleterious genes that occur at high rates in certain populations can, in principle, identify couples who risk having offspring afflicted with, for example, sickle-cell anemia or Tay Sachs disease.

The point of vulnerability research is to recognize that a given kind of problem will or may occur well before that problem has

45

actually appeared. Prospective studies of vulnerabilities have two main purposes: (1) preventive intervention and (2) clarification of etiological issues that can be dealt with by examining the natural history of the disorder as it develops.

All research on groups at risk bears a relationship to prevention. Humanitarian ideals, with perhaps an added impetus from the insurance industry, have led us to appreciate that "an ounce of prevention is worth a pound of cure." Prevention by control of nutritional intake in infancy, by special training, by reshaping a life-style, by making it possible for a potential sufferer to remain unborn. The development of preventive measures, through early intervention of whatever form may be indicated—*that* is the rational endpoint for the work on vulnerabilities. It is obviously also one of the chief reasons that high-risk research has become so popular. There is almost a mandate of our times to learn to prevent troubles before they occur. To intervene, however, we must first know who is at risk, and who needs intervention. It is exactly that knowledge that is missing for most of the major psychopathologies, and in fact for most human disease susceptibilities, and it is that knowledge that high-risk, or vulnerability, research seeks to provide.

As I mentioned, the second purpose of many—though not all—of these studies has to do with understanding questions about the origins of a particular disorder. The guidelines for variables that might most profitably be examined in, for example, high-risk research on schizophrenia come from previous observations of functioning in schizophrenic patients and from their recalled histories. As has frequently been pointed out, however, the retrospective work has not been able to distinguish adequately among hypothetical etiological factors.

For schizophrenia, the affective disorders, alcoholism, sociopathy, minimal brain dysfunction, and some of the specific disabilities of learning, it seems quite likely that both hereditary and environmental factors make important and necessary contributions. But for none of these conditions are the genetic patterns of transmission underlying vulnerability perfectly clear; indeed, some workers continue to dismiss them altogether. On the other hand, despite the large numbers of hypotheses advanced about specific features of the environment as causative agents for each of these conditions, respectively, no one variable has yet been definitely determined to differentiate the backgrounds of affected persons from those of properly chosen controls. There is one exception, though, which I return to in a moment.

Even the seemingly straightforward account of the basis for Huntington's chorea has gaps in it. The contingency of this rare but dread disease on a single dominant gene seems to have long been established as fact, and the expected 50-percent risk to the offspring of an affected parent is borne out all too sadly. Nevertheless, there are a number of unanswered questions; for example, why does age of onset range over 40 years or more from one affected person to another, why does the rate of acceleration of the disease course vary substantially in different individuals, and above all, how does the gene act biochemically or neurophysiologically? We are no more capable of differentiating the children who will be tomorrow's victims of Huntington's chorea from their siblings who will remain healthy than we are able to say right now which child of two schizophrenic parents will escape serious psychiatric impairment and which will be among the 40 percent that are expected to incur schizophrenia.

The problem throughout is that single-variable explanations are almost always wrong and that, by and large, investigators have taken a single-variable approach. What is called for are studies that allow the interaction of variables to be analyzed, particularly the interaction of genetic variables and different features of the environment even though gene-environment interactions are unpleasantly difficult to evaluate. In principle, one of the strongest advantages of the prospective vulnerability studies is that they offer the potential for just such analyses. However, many high-risk studies are not being designed to allow that potential to be realized to its full. For instance, if one hypothesizes that a deviant mother-child relationship lies at the root of schizophrenia, it is insufficient simply to make comparisons between the dynamics and outcome of the relationship between schizophrenic mothers and their children as opposed to that between normal mothers and their children. A group of children with normal mothers and schizophrenic fathers must also be evaluated to hold constant the genetic input. Only then can the maternal behaviors be compared. This is merely suggestive of the many design considerations that need to be taken into account in attempting to set up the vulnerability studies so that gene-environment interactions and the problem of covariance may be analyzed [1].

By *interactions* I mean that both the genetic and the environmental variables bear a causal relationship to the development of the disorder or behavioral expression—although neither can produce that outcome alone. By *covariance* I mean that certain genetic and environmental variables tend to be found together because the one is likely to lead to the other. To illustrate, let me refer back to the statement I made a few moments ago about the one differentiating "environmental" variable that has turned up in study after study of the histories of people who showed later psychopathology; the variable is a history of psychiatric disturbance in a parent (and frequently in other relatives as well). Now, to the worker with a strongly psychodynamic orientation, such findings are interpreted to mean that it is the environmental disruption, uncertainty, and so on surrounding the presence of a disturbed parent in the home or the effect of separation from a hospitalized, vagrant, or suicidal parent—which is responsible for the child's later emotional difficulties.

To a genetically oriented observer, however, it is the parent's illness that must first be explained, and then a different kind of interpretation begins to emerge—namely, that the parent's genetic makeup may be involved in his or her own disturbed state of functioning. Such genetic factors—which are presumably transmitted to the offspring, who will later show disturbances also—are partly responsible for creating the environment that the child will experience. The disruption, separation, and so on to which the psychodynamic school attributes the child's difficulties may then be regarded as covariates of the parent's genes and own early environment. Moreover, the child does not play merely a passive role in selecting from and feeding back to his environment, so that his own response proclivities determine to some extent not only the way that he will respond but also what experiences he will have and how his environment will be shaped. If one acknowledges that there may be genetic bases for different response proclivities in different individuals, it will be clear that the gene-environment covariance and interaction are important and difficult issues in the search for explanations of etiology—which is one thing that vulnerability research is about.

A further example can be found in the hypothesis proposed by Kohn [2] to account for the repeated observation that schizophrenia occurs at a higher rate in the lowest social classes than in the middle and upper strata of society. Some workers have considered low social status per se to be significant in the development of the disorder, and others have attempted to account for the relationship of class to schizophrenia strictly in terms of covariance by suggesting that affected persons and genetically vulnerable individuals experience downward social mobility and thus wind up in the lower rungs of the social ladder regardless of where they may have started. Kohn points out that both genetic vulnerability and excessive stress probably do occur at disproportionately high rates in the lower levels of society, but also that the effects of lower social position may tend to impair an individual's ability to cope successfully with stress. It is in the face of such class-correlated impairment, Kohn suggests, that genetically vulnerable persons may be at exceptionally high risk for developing schizophrenia when they encounter severe stress. The model, therefore, is one in which the genetic and environmental variables are thought to be interlocked in both covariance and interactional relationships.

Most of our puzzles in human behavior genetics are likely to require this type of multilayered model, and carefully designed studies of vulnerability may prove to be the best ways to test and clarify the needed models.

References

1. Erlenmeyer-Kimling, L. Gene-environment interactions and the variability of behavior. In *Genetics, Environment, and Behavior,* L. Ehrman, G. S. Omenn, and E. Caspari, Eds. Academic Press, New York, 1972.
2. Kohn, M. L. Social class and schizophrenia: a critical review and a reformulation. *Schiz. Bull.,* No. 7 (1973), 60.

Vulnerability for Infantile Autism in Monozygotic Twins

Paul E. McQuaid, D.P.M. (Ireland)

Introduction

Monozygotic twins concordant for early infantile autism (EIA) are recorded in the literature [1, 13]. There are few reports of twins discordant, and this is seen as important because of the influence of "nurture" and environmental factors [7, 17]. To date, six pairs of identical twins concordant for EIA or infantile psychosis (IP) have been recorded in the literature as far as can be determined. There are probably an additional 18 cases detected but not yet reported [3]. The present chapter constitutes the first report of monozygotic (MZ) Irish twins concordant for infantile autism. A pair of MZ male twins concordant for IP is presented. A distinction is drawn between EIA and IP with associated mental retardation as a guide to prognosis and the necessity to provide suitable social training and education. The relevance of etiology is discussed and the importance of abnormal prenatal history and delivery status, even in cases with strong genetic predisposition, is noted.

CYRIL AND CLYDE

Cyril and Clyde were born on February 22, 1968, after 8 months of gestation, with a birth weight 4 lb 8 oz each. During the pregnancy their mother was grossly overweight (17 stone, or 238 lb) and hypertensive (blood pressure 615/85). She

51

was an irregular prenatal attender, and her twins were undiagnosed because of her gross overweight. Cyril, the first born, was a normal vertex delivery. Clyde had an arm presenting, necessitating a rapid internal version and extraction by breech. He was asphyxiated but recovered rapidly. The placenta was slow to deliver and was removed manually and easily. It was a single piece and did not appear to have two divisions or to be in any way separate.

They are the youngest of five children, with older siblings aged 8½, 7½, and 6½ years. Both had harelips, which were repaired at 3½ months. This involved an 8-week separation from home. Early development was considered to be normal, although some temperature-regulation problems were noted in Clyde, who presented with very cold hands and feet. Both children had mixed sleeping patterns, sleeping during the day and irregularly, and both were thought to be "very dull." Both also rocked their cribs a lot and neither was considered "cuddly," being considered rather "stiff" and "hard to hold." Both children banged their heads against the person holding them as infants on several occasions. Clyde seemed to show some anticipatory behavior to being picked up in the first 4 or 5 months, but not Cyril.

Cyril learned to walk at 2½ years, significantly in advance of Clyde, who started walking at 4. Both children were slow in changing from a crawl to a walk.

Up to the age of about 3 months they were both considered to be "normal," and their mother was sorry that she allowed them to be separated from her for their harelip operations. She was of the opinion that the anesthetic caused "mental retardation" since before the operations they seemed to be normal, and after that they were constantly whining and generally seemed very irritable. At 9 months they were both suspected to be backward, and by 2 years their parents were convinced that they were abnormal. This was because of their generally slow motor development. Clyde was over 1½ years old before he sat up, although Cyril sat at 14 months. At about 3 years Clyde still wanted to be held on somebody's knee, although Cyril was keen to be moving around apparently in a more individual fashion. But for this reason he was considered to be more difficult to train, socialize, and generally manage, and he was thought to be less affectionate than Clyde.

During the children's first 3 years both exhibited a very strong fear of strangers. Both fairly quickly learned the danger of certain situations and objects, such as fire. Both tended sometimes to treat people, including their parents, as objects. Neither child was ever thought to be deaf. It was sometimes difficult to get Cyril's attention because of seeming preoccupation, but neither child became "lost" for any length of time in a type of trance state. Cyril tended to spin or whirl around like a top very often, but not Clyde. Clyde seemed very unsteady in his motor movements, but Cyril seemed unusually skillful. Both seemed a little awkward in doing fine work or playing with small objects and both, generally speaking, appeared "disinterested." Obsessiveness with furniture arrangements did not appear as a feature in either child, nor did either appear to "look through or walk through" people. Both children were significantly destructive, but neither appeared particularly concerned with himself. Both seemed to prefer and to be happiest when left alone. Neither was pliable. In the area of language, Clyde is now making some effort to speak (e.g., "ah, don't shout" and "ah now"). He is constantly screaming and whining, and vocalization is a fairly regular feature. No more formal language is evident. Both children seemed to heed definitive and obvious prohibitive and limiting instructions, particularly from the father. Clyde showed a dislike for large buildings and had a capacity for crying for long periods. He seemed to prefer lying on the ground and manipulating objects to moving around more than did Cyril. The latter had a capacity for banging his head and likewise appeared to be afraid of large buildings [13]. The family history reveals depression in the mother during pregnancy with the twins. The father had convulsions, probably febrile, when he was 6 weeks old. He is also left-handed, and there is a history of two sets of twins on mother's side of the family. Patrick, the eldest sibling, was slow to develop speech. In 1970 both twins were examined by a neuropediatrician who found normal head circumference and CNS.

Physical investigations in July 1971 revealed no abnormality in *audiometry*. Responses were obtained to several very quiet sounds of all frequencies in both children, and Cyril was noticed to vocalize and sing very normally. The reaction of the children to covering of their ears to loud sounds, for example, the passing overhead of aircraft, was further noted. The urinary chromatography, sleep EEG, and serum calcium and Wassermann reaction were normal in both children. However, karyotype analysis showed a modal number of 46 and an apparently normal autosome compliment and an XY sex chromosome constitution in both twins. This is not unexpected in view of the absence of evidence of chromosome aberations reported elsewhere [18]. Serum pholate and skull and bone-age x-rays (April 1971) in both children were normal for their age. Preliminary blood grouping for the children indicates that they are identical for nine different blood-group systems involving up to 16 antigens. Identify to this extent is significant evidence of MZ.

Psychological testing in April 1972 revealed Cyril to be physically more mature looking than his brother and showing no particular defect except for repaired harelip. Concentration was much better than Clyde's, and he was less manneristic and easier to manage. In the test situation he tended to move objects. An infected babble and a tendency to hum were noted. He is left-handed, and he showed more sustained interest than Clyde in the test material. On the Cattell infant intelligence scale he obtained a mental age of 1¼ years, giving him an IQ of 31. On the Vineland social maturity scale he achieved a social age of 1 year, five months, with a social quotient of 34. This indicates intellectual and social functioning at the level of moderate to lower-moderate mental handicap.

Psychological testing in April 1972 revealed Clyde to be a fair-haired, blue-eyed boy looking younger than his actual age. He has a high stepping gait, probably because of only recently developing walking capacity. Clyde is much less advanced looking than his brother. His harelip has also been repaired. No speech is noted, except for spontaneous babble and inarticulate vocalization. He does not seem to know or respond to his name. He may respond to commands such as "get up" but more often ignores such commands when preoccupied. No eye contact is noted except for very brief glances. He likes holding hands and rocking to and fro. Activity is rather aimless, and he has a habit of tapping his fingers on objects. Fleeting cooperation could be obtained during testing, but his facial performances were characterized by a vague irratic response, and he tended to spend much time tapping and poking objects. When the Form Board was placed in front of him he tended to look away. At present he is functioning at the level of severe mental handicap. On the Cattell infant intelligence scale he achieved an IQ of 26. His social age on the Vineland society maturity scale is 1 year, 2 months, giving a social quotient of 28.

The characteristic feature of the twins' family has been mother's tired, unhappy, anxious, and harassed manner. The family is Social Class V (Registrar General, 1970), and the father has been unemployed and at home since 1968 when he had a colostomy carried out for chronic ulcerative colitis. The family subsists on National Assistance, which would barely permit existence at the poverty level. Mother has been unable to adequately cope with the twins, having found them difficult to train in all areas. At the time of follow-up in October 1973 she was expecting her sixth child, having had a stillbirth in January 1973, following which she spent 2 weeks in a mental hospital because of "depression." She is due to deliver January 1974 and is very perturbed about the prospects of having to cope with "three babies." The other siblings are considered to be well and functioning adequately despite the level of domestic stress. The mother would appear to be fond of her children, and observation of interaction would confirm this. The marital situation has remained unsatisfactory because of lack of contraceptive capacity on the mother's part. When she was originally seen in 1972 she was determined not to have any more children, and this resulted in considerable interparental disharmony because of lack of sexual relations. The father appeared to have had a depressive reaction following his surgery in 1968 and has since been irritable, moody, and occasionally aggressive. The maternal grandparents (MGP) were separated because of MGF's drinking, and MGM contracted some form of second liaison from which there was a second family. During pregnancy with the twins the mother suffered from toxemia of pregnancy. They were delivered prematurely by about 6 weeks.

At this time, as reported earlier, Clyde is making some effort to speak and some progress. His behavior is characterized by flicking, tapping, exploratory movements with a lot of noise, and banging of doors. He tends to jump about spasmodically and has to be watched very carefully, as does Cyril because of his interference with cooking utensils and the cook. He is a severe head banger, and this disturbs the mother very much. Cyril is quieter and more manageable and is capable of fleeting gaze contact that is extremely limited, in contrast to Clyde. He seems to be preoccupied with shadows and follows them around. He likes to play with shiny objects in the sun and is generally more in contact than his brother. Neither are toilet trained, and both sleep fitfully. Clyde wakens to bang his head occasionally. They tend to need sleep during the day and are more troublesome if they do not get rest. Both are destructive of anything breakable. Play activity is unconstructive and purely at the sensory motor level. Summertime tends to be better since they can get out to dig. Clyde tends to interact to interfere with Cyril, but neither of them have any contact with other children.

As for separations, the children were in the Mater Hospital for a 3-day period of investigation in 1972, a mental handicap institution in 1973, when the mother was in a mental hospital, and during the summer of 1973 for a month in another mental handicap institution to permit the family to have a break, which was seen as a "holiday." When the children were 2-1/6 years the mother was separated from her husband for a period of 4 months because of her inability to cope with the domestic situation.

As for standard of care, in contrast to other case histories, these children would appear to have been reasonably well cared for and have certainly not been significantly rejected or ignored. The family is not atypical of many rural Irish Social Class V families, and the level of marital disharmony has not been so great as to result in significant breakdown, despite the separation of the parents when the children were just over 2 years old. There is little doubt that the presence of the children in the family creates considerable stress, and the impending arrival of a new baby is likely to impose critical problems. The children are both listed for admission to a residential treatment unit specializing in the care, training, and education of psychotic and seriously disturbed children. Due to the long waiting list and difficulty in replacing children who have reached the limit of developing in the unit, admission is likely to be delayed.

Discussion

The relevance of inheritance in this condition is generally accepted [12]. Kolvin's work [8] clearly distinguishes between three groups of childhood psychoses and notes that "it would appear that late onset psychoses of childhood resembled adult schizophrenia, at least in genetical respects, while infantile psychosis is unrelated to adult schizophrenia or to childhood psychoses of late onset." He found, however, that more parents of children with IP belonged to Social Classes I and II and more parents of children with late onset psychoses to Social Classes IV and V. In addition, he found a high male/female ratio among IP children and a lower but similarly directional trend for late-onset psychotics. This seems important as relating to a developmental deviation in "autistic reaction" in childhood and can be seen in other familial conditions [6].

Menolascino [9] pointed to the multifactorial etiology of the autistic reaction and noted the need to distinguish between the behavioral phenomena and causative factors. He defined eight distinct etiological subgroupings, one of which was described by Kanner as EIA. He does not include a syndrome of EIA or IP associated with significant mental retardation, however. Ornitz and Ritvo [11], in their clinical illustrations, defined a syndrome that they classified as "a more severe manifestation" of the same basic disease called "early infantile autism" and proposed that if the development of the child should remain static, "particularly when speech fails to develop, while the motor and perceptual disturbances gradually abate, he may be relabeled pseudo-retarded."

Irish publications on autistic children [2, 10] prefer a biological explanation to account for the material presented. Crawley [3], however, on the basis of her twin research now supports more the significance of the genetic factors.

Fischer, Glanville, et al. [4] make reference to the "poor" prognosis group and agree with Rutter, Greenfield et al. [14] that these children "will require institutional care for life" in a unit dealing solely with mental retardation. They recognize that with improvement in behavioral status of a great many psychotic children the residual impairment is that of mental retardation primarily, usually associated with some bizarre motor and behavioral characteristics.

The role of inheritance in personality has been examined extensively, and longitudinal studies [16] have shown that the difference between infants as young as 2 months old is obvious, such difference persisting. Infant and childhood responsiveness levels would, likewise, appear to have relevance in terms of inheritance, and the importance to the condition under consideration of such factors has been discussed by Gottesman [5] in suggesting that certain genes or absence of them may predispose to attachment behaviors or lack of, respectively.

Without taking the matter further on the question of classification, it seems fair to include this set of twins in the category of IP with associated mental retardation. It remains to be seen just how damaged the children are and what, if any, residual language function is available. The history of severe obesity with hypertension in the mother, associated with inadequate prenatal care in conjunction with inadequate perinatal preparation and delivery, seems likely to account for the children's defects. It seems further likely that Clyde is more damaged than Cyril in that he reached certain milestones later than his coeval. An assessment of the prognosis for this pair, while dependent on basic levels of intellectual capacity and quality of intrinsic damage, cannot underestimate the relevance of adequate social training and "education" [14, 15]. Clyde and Cyril are on the waiting list for admission to a special unit, St. Paul's Hospital, catering to children residing outside of the Dublin Health Board Area, and it is hoped that they will be admitted within the next year.

References

1. Bakwin, H. Early infantile autism. *J. Pediat.*, 45 (1964), 492–497.
2. Crawley, C. A. Infantile autism—an hypothesis. *J. Irish Med. Ass.*, 64: 415 (1971), 335–345.
3. Crawley, C. A. Personal communication, January 1974.
4. Fischer, I., Glanville, B. W. K., and Browne, I. W. *J. Irish Med. Ass.*, 63 (1970), 49–52.
5. Gottesman, I. I. Genetic variance in an adaptive personality trait. *J. Child Psychol. Psychiat.*, 7, (1966), 199–208.
6. Ingram, T. T. S. *Brain*, 82: Pt. 3 (1959), 450.
7. Kamp, L. N. Autistic syndrome in one of a pair of monozygotic twins. *J. Psychiatia Neurolog. Neurochirurgia* (Holland), 67 (1964), 143–147.
8. Kolvin, I. Studies in childhood psychoses: I–VI. *Brit. J. Psychiat.*, 118; 545 (1971), 381–420.
9. Menolascino, S. Autistic reactions in early childhood: Differential diagnostic considerations. *J. Child Psychol Psychiat.*, 6 (1965), 203–218.
10. O'Moore, M. *J. Irish Med Ass.*, Vol. 65 (1972), 114–120.
11. Ornitz, E. M. and Ritvo, E. R. Perceptual inconstancy in early infantile autism. *Arch Gen. Psychiat.*, 18 (1968), 76–98.
12. Ounsted, C. A biological approach to autistic and hyperkinetic syndromes. *Mod. Trends Paediat.* 3 (1970),
13. Rimland, B. *Infantile Autism.* Appleton-Century-Crofts, New York, 1964.
14. Rutter, M., Greenfeld, D., and Lockyer, L. *Brit. J. Psychiat.*, 113 (1967), 1183–1199.
15. Rutter, M. Psychotic disorders in early childhood. In *Recent Developments in Schizophrenia*, A. J. Coppen and A. Walk, Eds. RMPA, London, 1967, pp.
16. Thomas, A., Birch, H. G., Chess, S. A., Hertzig, M., and Korn, S. *Behavioural Individuality in Early Childhood.* London Univ. Press, London, 1964.
17. Vaillant, G. E. Twins Discordant for Early Infantile Autism. *Arch. Gen. Psychiat.*, 10 (1964) 530–541.
18. Wolraich, M. lack of chromosome aberration in autism. *New Engl. J. Med.*, 5 283 (1970) 1231.

Deprivation and Family Structure with Particular Reference to Twins

Anthony J. Costello (U.K.)

The extremes of inadequate child rearing and the adverse effects of such an experience have been well known since the pioneering work of Spitz and of Goldfarb, although controversy has continued ever since about the nature of the mechanisms at work [26]. Similarly, the ill effects of severe poverty and privation both within and outside the family have been much studied by those concerned with the determination of intelligence and the old nature-nuture controversy. The handicaps following both forms of experience, in the shape of poor attainments, impaired personal relationships, and a variety of behavior problems, are too well known to need repetition here, even though there is still much uncertainty about the incidence and extent of such consequences.

Somewhat surprisingly, the concept of neglect and lack of stimulation within the nuclear family has received little attention, although it is familiar enough to those preoccupied with the nature-nuture controversy. The neglect associated with physical violence to children may have diverted attention from the less obvious but commoner situation of uncomplicated neglect, and of course lesser degrees of neglect tend to be associated with psychopathological mechanisms within the family on which therapeutic intervention is rightly concentrated. But in view of the frequency with which we ascribe maladjustment to extremes of deprivation and privation, within-family neglect deserves more attention than it has received.

The methodological problems are, of course, considerable. One strategy is to investigate families in which the mother is working or caring for the children without the support of a husband. The inference has been that mothers in such circumstances are likely to devote less time to their children. Although this may be true in the case of some working mothers, the problem becomes, as in the case of separation from the mother, one of assessing the nature of the alternative care and the circumstances that lead to the mother's working. On the whole it seems that maternal employment does not by itself lead to any marked intellectual or behavioral disturbances in the children.

Similarly, whereas the handicaps of the children of one-parent families are considerable, they are as likely to be the consequence of economic stress, frequent moves, illness, and all the other difficulties attendant on the situation. Two large-scale surveys in England have shown that children cared for by one parent are likely to lag in attainments early in their school career [9, 12]. The more recent study suggests that this is particularly true of the children of middle-class and skilled working-class families, and in the earlier study it was these children who were most affected by a breakdown of the family situation [13]. It seems possible to infer from both studies that there is a factor in family experience promoting good school achievement, which is greatest in middle-class families and thus most likely to be missed when such a family breaks up.

Within nuclear families of normal structure and situation an alternative approach to the study of the effects of neglect might be to identify abnormal parents. The problem here is that screening for minor degrees of neglect presents almost insuperable difficulties. Neglect is not likely to be tapped by responses to a questionnaire or even to be seen by an observer within the home. Nor are there characteristics of neglectful parents that we can describe with confidence and define operationally so that such parents can

be identified by people such as health visitors in the United King-
dom who have entry into all homes with young children. To identify abnormal children on the assumption that they must have
experienced or at least are more likely to have experienced abnormal patterns of rearing not only begs the question and re-
stricts one to families with one particular class of outcome, but
makes it impossible to collect data prospectively.

An alternative approach that is relatively free of the disadvantages discussed is to look at families so structured that some degree of parental neglect is inevitable, those with many or closely
spaced children. The appropriate measure here is family density
rather than family size, a concept introduced by Waldrop and Bell
[34, 35] that takes into account the interval between births as well
as the total number of children. As in the other approaches outlined in the preceding paragraphs, the density of the family is not
free of associations with other relevant factors, such as social
status, income, and cultural background, all of which influence
the size of the completed family and the intervals between births.
There is also the complicating factor that interactions within the
sibship of an extended family can in theory compensate to some
extent for the inevitable dilution of parental attention.

For these reasons we have chosen to analyze some data collected from the parents of first-born twins. The main aim of this
study, which has been described briefly elsewhere [7, 22], is to
examine the contribution the child's characteristics make to the
pattern of parent-child interaction and to see to what extent the
child's initial behavior modifies or at least sets limits to parental
behavior. The study is prospective, and since the last twins in the
series were only identified at the end of last year it is still too early
to report results on the main hypothesis. However, we already
have, among other data, a detailed breakdown of the distribution
of a mother's time between broad categories of activity over a
24-hour period, collected at intervals of at least one month. The
impact of these data is most striking in the first year when collective interaction between the mother and both children is probably
not meaningful for the children who respond much more intensely to the undivided attention of the mother. At this age few
interactions occur between the children. Even when facing each

other they tend to show little smiling or reaching.[1] The main source of interaction stimulation is thus the mother. There is also evidence from studies of the effects of institutional environments that changes in social responsiveness [16, 17] and language development [4, 28] may occur as the result of severely inadequate care in the first year.

For these reasons I have chosen to analyze the data available from our twin study at the age of 6 months. At this age there is information about 29 pairs of twins. The data presented come from an interview in which the mother is asked to recall the events of the preceding 24 hours. She is asked to describe where each individual in the home was and what he or she was doing for how long to the nearest 5 minutes. Validation studies of this technique, which sounds more formidable than it proves to be in practice, show that although our informants often make errors as to the absolute time at which an event occurred, their estimations of time intervals are reasonably reliable, particularly when summed over a 24-hour period.

The twin sample was collected with the cooperation of hospital prenatal clinics over a large part of London, but it is a volunteer sample in which the middle-class and skilled working-class parents are overrepresented. A control sample of 60 families with a first-born 6-month-old child was identified from a population register of all children under 5 within one London borough. This sample represents 85 percent of those suitable families who were contacted, and although it is thus subject to some volunteer bias, the distribution of occupations among the fathers does not differ significantly from the distribution given by census data for England (and for this area where the distribution closely follows the national pattern). For both samples the measures of maternal behavior show only very small nonsignificant correlations with social class measures based on either the father's occupation or a more refined index derived from the occupation and education of both parents [3]. The parents' mean ages do not differ significantly between the samples, and all the families are living in a similar range of circumstances and housing. One further comment is

---

[1] Our impression is that positive responses to a mirror at 6 months are less common among twins than singletons.

needed before we look at the differences between the samples. Although twinning attracts a lot of attention from friends and relations, for most families the extra help from these sources, which a mother of twins often receives in the first few weeks, disappears by the sixth month. Further, whereas a few twin pairs receive a substantial amount of attention from an adult other than the mother, in the majority of cases the mother has the main burden of caring for the children. Although fathers of twins spend more time with their children than do fathers of singletons, the proportion of total care that they contribute is small.

The mothers of twins and mothers of singletons have very similar waking hours—a mean of 15 hours, 39 minutes for the twins and 15 hours, 21 minutes for the singletons. This is despite the greater time taken to feed the twins, of whom many still have a night feed at this age. Of this time the mothers of twins devote slightly more time to feeding, changing, dressing, washing, and playing with the baby, a total of 275 minutes (SD 105) as opposed to 214 minutes for the singletons [standard deviation (SD) 76]. The range is surprisingly large—80 to 545 minutes for the twins and 40 to 395 minutes for the singletons. It is probably not very meaningful to look at the distribution of time within these broad categories for what one mother may report as play, another may report as washing or dressing, although the content of the activity is equally playful. Some mothers in both groups reported no time at all over a 24-hour period spent in play, which seems unlikely. However, the mothers of singletons reported as much as 240 minutes of play, whereas the maximum a mother of twins reported was 110 minutes (split between the two children).

It seems then that the reasonable assumption that maternal attention is not infinitely elastic is confirmed, and in the early days of twins the limited amount available has to be divided between them. (One measure of the amount attention thus divided is to note the time a child is held by an adult, which is 149 minutes for the singletons but only 85 minutes for each twin.) The next step is to consider how twins are known to differ from singletons. Our own data, from this and from a larger retrospective survey of 215 twins, conducted when they were 2 to 3 years old, and a control sample of 111 singletons, does not conflict with earlier findings.

Twins have long been known to suffer delays in language development [10, 11]. Similar findings have been reported in more recent studies [21, 24, 25]. There is a similar but less marked lag in tests of general intelligence [21, 32] and in tests that measure verbal reasoning [30, 39]. This deficiency might be explained by other factors in twinning than the division of parental attention. The increased hazards of pregnancy and delivery might be responsible, and this explanation appears to be supported by the finding [19, 36] that the smaller twin in an identical pair is the less intelligent. However, this difference is most probably accounted for by the phenomenon of crossed placental circulation in monochorionic twins and in any case needs to be interpreted with caution in view of the lower birth weight of monozygotic twins [6]. Another alternative explanation is that offered by Luria and Yudovitch [23] that the close relationship between the twins absolves them from the need for communication. Luria's experimental separation of twins suffering delayed language is difficult to assess because both children were not given the same treatment after separation. Perhaps the most convincing evidence comes from Record, McKeown, et al. [29, 30], who were able to identify 148 children in a sample of 2164 twins whose twin sib was stillborn or died in the neonatal period. These children had suffered all the physical disadvantages of a twin pregnancy and delivery. Indeed, it could be argued that they were more likely to have been at risk for such factors since one twin had died. Nevertheless, the mean score on a verbal reasoning test of these children was only marginally behind that of the singletons—98.8 against 100.1 and superior to the mean score of 95.7 for twins whose twin sib had survived. This seems to place the responsibility for the effect firmly on psychological rather than physical environmental factors but does not distinguish between the psychological effects of reduced parental attention versus the effects of a special relationship between the twins. Our own prospective study is not sufficiently far advanced to offer more than tentative data on language development, but we were surprised to find that even at 6 months the twin sample is behind on general development, with a mean mental development index on the Bayley [2] scales of 95.3. The mean score on the physical development index is 111.2, but even this is behind the corresponding means for the 6-month controls of 107.9 and 113.1. (The deviations from the published norms for this test in the case of the singletons are probably accounted for by a variation in test procedure, the essential feature of which is that to facilitate comparison within a twin pair, items are presented in a fixed sequence. The effect is to give scores a little higher than usual.) Both samples have been corrected to allow for variations in gestational age [27]. Similar findings were reported by Dales [8] using the Gesell scales. Wilson's [37] data from the Louisville series appears to show a similar effect, although no correction was made for prematurity and a singleton group was not tested by the same investigators. Our own experience suggests that it is unwise to rely on published norms for infant tests since changes in score can arise from minor variations in technique and possibly from different sampling [15]. These lower scores appear at an age when direct twin interaction is unlikely to be important and thus suggest the effect to be mediated by parental behavior.

Although the data are still at an early stage, preliminary analysis of our own prospective study appears to confirm the expectation that when maternal attention is divided it is the favored twin who is more precocious. The direction of effect is, of course, as likely to be that the more advanced child attracts more attention as that increased attention promotes development within such a restricted range of environmental variation.

Dales's data suggest that twins appear to catch up in motor development by the age of 3 years, and using the rather crude indices that are available from retrospective inquiry we certainly could not detect any lag by the second year in our own larger survey. Unfortunately, the information on language development in this survey proved to be inadequate for a comparison between singletons and twins. What did emerge was that on many indices of mothering such as the use of playpens, tolerance of crying, use of confections, and early resort to starchy foods, the twins appeared to receive less adequate care which supports our belief that behind gross measures of attention of the sort observed there are corresponding differences in the more subtle dimensions of early stimulation that Yarrow and others have observed [38].

To summarize so far, there appears to be no doubt that in the early months of twins relative neglect is enforced on the majority of mothers. The early development of twins is delayed, and there is supporting evidence to favor a causal relationship between the two findings. It seems likely that subsequent delays in the general and verbal development of twins are explicable in the same way.

This is in agreement with studies of the effect of birth order and family size. The large English longitudinal studies already referred to are cohort studies, and hence the task of separating social class and other background variables from the effect of family size has to be performed by statistical manipulation.

In the National Child Development Study [9] children with five or more siblings have reading ages about a year behind those of children from sibships of one or two and arithmetic attainment about 2 months behind. In the earlier National Survey [9, 14] the data were analyzed in a slightly different way. The average test scores decline as family size increases. The effect is less marked in the middle than in the manual working class and persists after correction has been made for poor housing, lack of parental interest, and poor schooling. Verbal scores suffer most [14].

Although these data do not support the supposition that the effect might be due to an association between fertility and low intelligence, so that the depressed scores are determined by poor inheritance, an alternative strategy is to make within family comparisons when information is available on the test scores of all the sibship at the same age. The Record, McKeown, et al. study [29] using this technique shows much the same pattern. The difference between consecutive sibs is greater at low than at high birth ranks and smaller in well-to-do families than in poorer ones. Bayley's [1] own data on 1400 children at 1 to 15 months show only small differences in favor of the first born, which disappear at 8 to 11 months and then reappear. The comparison here is between the 36 percent who were first born and all other birth ranks, and one reason for the small size of the difference may be a small representation of the later ranks, which can only be studied in very large samples. None of these studies take spacing into account, and Waldrop and Bell's work [35] suggests that this might be rewarding.

The position with regard to birth order and family size is less clear for ratings of adjustment. The findings of Davie, Butler, et al. [9] were that at 7 years of age, children in large families were more likely to show poor adjustment on the Bristol Social Adjustment Guide, with an effect for children from families of five or more about as large as the sex differential.

In Douglas's survey the position is a little more complex. In general, measures of neuroticism and neurotic types of maladjustment are not related to family size. Measures dependent on factors such as teachers' difficulty in controlling in class and inattentiveness are clearly positively associated with family size as are delinquency rates. A similar bias in the incidence of neurotic versus antisocial and mixed conduct disorder was evident in an epidemiological survey of children on the Isle of Wight [31], the latter group tending to come from large families.

The data on behavioral abnormalities in twins are rather scanty. Our own retrospective study did not produce any evidence of an unusually high level of behavior problems among the twins, even of jealous and aggressive behavior between the children. Indeed, the twins appeared to show more cooperative play and less parallel or separate play than the singletons did with their peers This was after a substantial proportion of the singleton group had been excluded from this comparison because they lacked any experience of play with other children. However, Kim, Dales, et al. [20] found in a more detailed study of twins and singletons in a nursery-school setting that twins showed more solitary play and less affectional and less aggressive behavior. The differences, though statistically significant, were not large. On more dubious indices of adjustment in 2 to 3-year-olds, such as bed wetting, on which we have data, there is no significant difference between twins and singletons and what difference there is favors the twins.

In older twins, despite the widespread interest in the study of psychiatric disorder in twins to establish the contribution of genetic influences, there is a remarkable poverty of information on the incidence of abnormality in twins as a group. Although the investigation of individual pairs suggests there are problems in personality development arising from the twin situation [5, 39], there is very little evidence that twins are more prone to psychiatric illness or show specific forms of illness. This comes both from a study of whole population twin registers [33] and from a study of consecutive hospital admissions [18].

Despite the rather unsatisfactory nature of the evidence on behavior and personality, it seems reasonable to conclude that the main effect of early parental neglect is on intellectual development and that this is probably most marked in verbal and language skills. Early neglect may be responsible for some minor variations in the pattern of social behavior and possibly may lead in some cases to antisocial behavior and conduct disorder, but it would seem more reasonable to lay the blame for more severe psychiatric disorder in cases of early neglect on the psychopathology in the family that made neglect possible.

Summary

It is argued that the most effective way of studying the effects of neglect within the family is to observe the children of families with many and closely spaced children and twins. Data are presented to show the very marked reduction of maternal attention to each twin in the early months. Several studies, including the author's, show delayed development in twins, most marked in measures of language development. It is argued that this is more likely to be the effect of reduced maternal attention than the effect of intertwin interaction or biological hazards associated with twinning. Corresponding findings are described from large-scale longitudinal studies relating to later-born children in large families. There is relatively little evidence of other behavioral changes in children in these situations, and it is suggested that abnormal behaviors in children who have suffered neglect is likely to be directly associated with the factors that lead to neglect and not with neglect per se.

References

1. Bayley, N. Comparisons of mental and motor test scores for ages 1–15 months by sex, birth order, race, geographical location and education of parents. *Child Devel.*, 36 (1965), 379–411.
2. Bayley, N. *Manual for the Bayley Scales of Infant Development.* Psychological Corporation, New York, 1969.

3. Brandis, W. and Henderson, D. *Social Class, Language and Communication.* Routledge and Kegan Paul, London, 1970.
4. Brodbeck, A. J. and Irwin, O. C. The speech behavior of infants without families. *Child Devel.,* 17 (1946), 145–156.
5. Burlingham, D. *Twins: A Study of Three Pairs of Identical Twins.* Imago, London, 1952.
6. Corney, G., Robson, E. B., and Strong, S. J. The effect of zygosity on the birth weight of twins. *Ann. Hum. Genet.,* 36 (1972), 45–59.
7. Costello, A. J. and Leach, P. J. Electronic recording of behavioral interaction. In *Determinants of Behavioral Development,* F. Monks and J. DeWit, Eds. Academic Press, New York, 1972.
8. Dales, R. J. Motor and language development of twins during the first three years. *J. Genet. Psychol.,* 114 (1969), 263–271.
9. Davie, R., Butler, N., and Goldstein, H. *From Birth to Seven.* Longmans, London, 1972.
10. Davis, E. A. *The Development of Linguistic Skill in Twins, Singletons with Siblings and Only Children from 5–10.* Institute Child Welfare Monograph 14, Univ. Minnesota Press, Minneapolis, 1937.
11. Day, E. J. The development of language in twins. 1. A comparison of twins and single children. *Child Devel.,* 3 (1932), 179–199.
12. Douglas, J. W. B. *The Home and the School.* MacGibbon and Kee, London, 1964.
13. Douglas, J. W. B. and Blomfield, J. M. *Children under Five.* Allen and Unwin, London, 1958.
14. Douglas, J. W. B., Ross, J. M., and Simpson, H. R. *All Our Future.* Peter Davies, London, 1968.
15. Francis-Williams, J. and Yule, W. The Bayley infant scales of mental and motor development. An exploratory study with an English sample. *Devel. Med. Child Neurol.,* 9 (1967), 391–401.
16. Freud, A. and Burlingham, D. T. *Infants without Families.* International Universities Press, New York, 1944.
17. Gesell, A. and Amatruda, C. *Developmental Diagnosis.* Hoeber, New York, 1941.
18. Gottesman, I. I. and Shields, J. Schizophrenia in twins: 16 years' consecutive admissions to a psychiatric clinic. *Brit. J. Psychiat.,* 112 (1966), 809–818.
19. Kaelber, C. T. and Pugh, T. F. Influence of intrauterine relations on the intelligence of twins. *New Engl. J. Med.,* 280 (1969), 1030–1034.
20. Kim, C. C., Dales, R. J., Connor, R., Walters, J., and Witherspoon, R. Social interaction of like sex twins and singletons in relation to intelligence, language, and physical development. *J. Genet. Psychol.,* 114 (1969), 203–214.
21. Koch, H. L. *Twins and Twin Relations.* Chicago Univ. Press, Chicago, 1966.
22. Leach, P. J. and Costello, A. J. A twin study of infant-mother interaction. In *Determinants of Behavioral Development,* F. Monks and J. DeWit, Eds. Academic Press, New York, 1972.
23. Luria, A. R. and Yudovich, F. I. *Speech Development of Mental Processes in the Child: an Experimental Investigation.* Staples, London, 1959.
24. Mittler, P. *Psycholinguistic skills in four-year-old twins and singletons.* Ph.D. thesis, University of London, 1969.
15. Mittler, P. Biological and social aspects of language development in twins. *Devel. Med. Child. Neurol.,* 12 (1970), 741–757.

26. O'Connor, N. Children in restricted environments. In *Early Experience and Behavior*, G. Newton, and S. Levine, Eds. Thomas, Springfield, Ill., 1968.
27. Parmelee, A. H. and Schultz, F. Developmental testing of preterm and small-for-date infants. *Paediatrics*, 45 (1970), 21–28.
28. Provence, S. and Lipton, R. *Infants in Institutions*. Internat. Univ. Press, New York, 1962.
29. Record, R. G., McKeown, T., and Edwards, J. H. The relation of measured intelligence to birth order and maternal age. *Ann. Hum. Genet.* 33 (1969), 61–69.
30. Record, R. G., McKeown, T., and Edwards, J. H. An investigation of the difference in measured intelligence between twins and single births. *Ann. Hum. Genet.* 34 (1970), 11–20.
31. Rutter, M., Tizard, J., and Whitmore, K. *Education, Health and Behavior*. Longmans, London, 1970.
32. Scottish Council for Research in Education. *Social Implications of the 1947 Scottish Mental Survey*. Univ. London Press, 1953.
33. Tienari, P. Psychiatric illness in identical twins. *Acta Psychiat. Scand. Suppl. 171*, Vol. 39. Copenhagen: Munksgaard, 1963.
34. Waldrop, M. E. and Bell, R.Q. Relation of preschool dependency behavior to family size and density. *Child Devel.*, 35 (1964), 1147–1153.
35. Waldrop, M. E. and Bell, R. Q. Effects of family size and density on newborn characteristics. *Amer. J. Orthopsychiat.* 35 (1965), 342–343.
36. Willerman, L. and Churchill, J. A. Intelligence and birth weight in identical twins. *Child Devel.*, 38 (1967), 623–629.
37. Wilson, R. S. Twins: early mental development. *Science,* 175 (1972), 914–917.
38. Yarrow, L. J., Rubenstein, J. L., and Pedersen, F. A. Dimensions of early stimulation: differential effects on infant development. *Symposium: Soc. Res. Child Devel.*, Minneapolis, 1971.
39. Zazzo, R. *Les Jumeaux: le Couple et la Personne*. Presses Universitaires de France, Paris, 1960.

Learning Problems in Quadruplets

Robert Krell, M.C., and M. Coval, M.D. (Canada)

Introduction

The presentation of a set of quadruplets (quads) provides a unique opportunity to evaluate children of a common background. Our case study describes 8-year-old quadruplets, of which the two boys had pronounced academic difficulties while the two girls were progressing normally. Parental concern led to this evaluation of academic abilities and learning performance. Psychiatric and psychologic evaluations were requested specifically by the parents, who stated that they wished "to do everything possible" for the children.

CASE STUDY

The quads were born into an upper-middle-class family. The parents had been married 5 years and had a 2-year-old boy. The mother was 28 years old at the time of the quads' birth, and the father was 32. The parents had suspected a multiple birth when the mother was 7½ months pregnant. After the birth both parents kept the quadruplets as free as possible from publicity, with reasonable success. There had been a news release at birth and a few brief news items since. There had been no exploitation or commercialism of the family.

At the time of the referral the father, who is a hard-working professional man, expressed concern that his ambition for the boys had placed too much pressure on them. The mother expressed the wish that her husband be less demanding of them and presented herself as protective of and anxious about her children. There was no indication in the family history of either parent of mental illness or learning problems.

The quadruplets were delivered simultanously by cesarean section in a hospital with several pediatricians in attendance. Each child had its own placenta. The birth weights were as follows:

Carol (girl)	5 lb, 7 oz	Steven (boy)	5 lb
Jeremy (boy)	4 lb, 5 oz	Pamela (girl)	4 lb, 7 oz

Neonatal development. The quadruplets were hospitalized for 20 days prior to discharge. The birth records clearly identify the boys but the girls were identified as baby girls "A" and "D" without names or birth weights.

Steven's Apgar rating was 9, and he was in good condition. At birth a small placental infarct was noted, and meconium was present in the amniotic fluid. At 1 day of age his color was described as "dusky" in comparison with his siblings, and there was fear of a "fetal aspiration syndrome." He responded to oxygen inhalation and was started on penicillin and streptromycin. Four days after birth his chest x-ray was clear, and he was reported to be doing well. He was circumcised 3 days prior to discharge, and there has been no hospitalization since.

Jeremy's Apgar rating was 10. He received oxygen for 1 hour immediately after birth. There were no complications and he was released 3 days after circumcision. He was readmitted 10 days later with a diagnosis of pyloric stenosis and underwent surgery at age 31 days. Nineteen days later he was discharged, having made a good recovery. His only other hospitalization was an emergency-room evaluation of possible head injury following a fall at age 4. The diagnosis of concussion was made and he was held overnight for evaluation.

Carol and Pamela both had Apgar ratings of 10. Baby girl "A" cried immediately at birth, and the pediatrician in attendance described her as behaving like a "mature newborn." She was somewhat slow to become pink from an initial deep cyanosis. After incubation placement, she soon looked quite well. No respiratory problems were noted.

Baby girl "D" was initially a little pale, but her overall condition was good. In the premature nursery this baby remained pale when compared with her brothers and sister. Waxing and waning of the respiratory rate was noted as "characteristic of a more immature infant." She improved rapidly and moved to the routine-care unit in two days.

Clinical evaluations. Steven was 8 years old at the time of his psychiatric and psychological evaluation. His parents described him as a likeable boy at home. At school he was described as "immature" and with a poor attention span. He repeated kindergarten and started grade 1 at age 7. Steven had developed normally in relation to his sisters, except for his speech. He stammered when he first learned to talk and still does. He was described as nervous and introverted, crying readily and "shaking like a leaf." At age 7½ he was evaluated for his poor academic performance at a clinic that specifically investigates "learning disabilities."

The report from this evaluation described Steven as having immature construction and articulation in his speech. He was a nonreader on the Iowa Word Recognition Test. On the kindergarten part of the test he scored at the 9-month level on the prereading section of the Wide Range Reading Test. On the same test he achieved a grade 1.2 level for spelling and 1.6 for arithmetic. The summary stated that Steven had a very serious learning disability, holding his pencil awkwardly and using immature oral language. He had a fair ability to describe the nonverbal symbols. He had a serious language disability with a developmental lag.

In his psychiatric interview by one of us (R. Krell), Steven presented as a pleasant boy who looked younger than his stated age. He was very anxious, his left arm was tremulous, and he had a pronounced speech defect. Although he talked very slowly and was difficult to understand, there was no stammer or stutter. There was little spontaneous speech, but an attempted response to all questions. His movements were clumsy and he appeared uncoordinated when walking. His three wishes centered on the acquisition of money and toys and he expressed a fear of doctors as his sole fear. In play he showed himself to be right-handed, right-legged, and right-eyed. He was able to tandem walk and stand on one leg either side.

Impression. From his history and the results of his learning evaluation, it appeared that Steven had a serious learning disability. His recognition of poor functioning when compared with his successful sisters, plus his parental expectations, caused him pressure and anxiety. This anxiety manifested itself with trembling, frequent crying spells, and aggravation of speech difficulties already present. The quality of his speech and his poor coordination were suggestive of some diffuse neurologic impairment.

Jeremy was seen 1 week after his brother. He was described by his parents as a more irritable baby. He was fussy about eating and had some allergies. He was taken for desensitization shots because the mother had read there was a possible connection between learning disabilities and allergies in children. Jeremy was reported to have reached developmental milestones at an appropriate age except for bedwetting, which persisted until he was 6 years old. His parents had noted with him, as with his brother, that he was smaller, less adept, and less coordinated than either of his sisters.

Jeremy's learning evaluation report described him as having speech articulation problems and being difficult to understand. On the Iowa Word Recognition Test he scored at a grade 1.1. level. On the Wide Range Reading Test, he was at the grade 1.2 level for reading, at 1.4 for spelling and 1.2 for arithmetic. Jeremy was summarized as a cooperative boy who had learning problems with weakness in transmodal learning, immature speech with occasional clutter, and a tendency to perseveration.

At his psychiatric interview, Jeremy looked small for his age. There was definite physical resemblance to his brother. His speech was slurred, he had a slight lisp and articulation problems, but overall his speech was better than his brother's. He, too, was not spontaneous but responded to questions. Although he was more outgoing, he would not elaborate on any of the information he offered. There was evidence of little anxiety but some motor incoordination during play. He was right-handed, right-legged, and left-eyed and could tandem walk or stand on one leg either side. His fund of information was low, and he was unable to think of three wishes.

Impression. Jeremy presented essentially a similar picture of noticeable speech difficulties, poor motor coordination, and an inability to learn basic skills in reading, writing, and number concepts. He was less anxious than his brother. Jeremy's speech and motoric problems were also suggestive of diffuse neurologica impairment with behavioral immaturity.

Carol, at the time of psychiatric interview, looked physically different from her sister, thinner and fair but bigger than both of her brothers. She was the least anxious and most mature of the quads. Carol was aware of her brothers' learning problems and stated she tried to help them with their work. Her speech was good, and she was well coordinated, bright, and spontaneous. There was no evidence for abnormal thought content or neurologic impairment.

Pamela is now the heaviest of the children. She presented as a fidgety, giggly dark-haired girl. She was anxious and acted silly but soon settled down. Her speech was good, she was spontaneous, and again there was no evidence of poor coordination.

Steven and Jeremy were evaluated for learning problems and subsequently had psychiatric interviews as well. Carol and Pamela had only psychiatric interviews. All four quadruplets underwent psychological testing by one of us (M. Coval) when they were 8[16] to 8⅓ years old. The testing was spaced so that the children were able to communicate as little as possible regarding the testing sessions. All four had the WISC and the Frostig, and three had projective tests. The fourth was not completed when mother withdrew the children for yet another opinion elsewhere.

Psychological testing. During Steven's testing it was noted that he stammered, had bitten his nails, and was right-handed. When asked for his street address, he gave an incomplete number, 350 instead of 3550. His brother had preceded him, and Steven was very concerned during his testing with how his brother had done. He was distractible and dropped almost everything he handled during the testing. On the WISC he achieved a Verbal Score of 97 and a Full-Scale IQ of 97. There was a range in the Performance subtest scores of eight points and five on the Verbal. On the Frostig tests his perceptual age range on the subtest was 5½ to 8¼ years. Projective test results showed a tendency to perseveration, good form level, and indications of anxiety over his impulse control and interpersonal relationships. Steven was confused when trying to verbalize roles and identities of boys and girls and men and women. He appeared to be very concerned over his own achievements.

Jeremy was able to give the street name of his address but gave the phone numbers instead of the house numbers. It was noticed during testing that he was startled by slight noises. Jeremy did not know his father's first name. He too had bitten nails and was right-handed. His hand movements were jerky. He had a tendency to repeat every question or the first few words of it before he gave his answer. Jeremy was more relaxed on the performance items and appeared not to care very much about his results. When he indicated that he particularly wanted to succeed on an item, he became tense and performed poorly. On the WISC he had a Verbal Score of 90, a Performance Score of 92, and a Full Scale IQ of 90. On the Frostig he had a perceptual range from 5½ to 10 plus years. On the projective tests Jeremy's speech became incomprehensible when he tried to discuss some of his family relationships. He had difficulties in expressing himself, a poor self-image, and an acute awareness of his inadequacies.

Carol behaved age-appropriately during testing. Her physical appearance was very different from that of the other quads, even in her skin color. She was somewhat anxious and cleared her throat almost constantly. On the verbal items she repeated the questions and then answered them. She worked slowly and well. On the WISC, she achieved a Verbal Score of 123, a Performance Score of 101, and a Full-scale IQ of 114. Her results on the Frostig Perceptual Test ranged from age 7 to above age 10. Her projective results reflected an ongoing rather intense struggle for self-identification. She also showed slightly more intense oral needs than are age-appropriate.

Pamela behaved immaturely at first, acting silly and giggling constantly. She also repeated all the questions she was asked before giving her answer. On the WISC, she had a Verbal Score of 110, a Performance Score of 107, and a Full Scale IQ of 109. On the Frostig her perceptual age ranged from 7 years to 10 plus. Her projective testing results were incomplete.

Comparison of results of psychological testing. The WISC range for the quads was 90 to 123 on the Verbal Scale, 92 to 107 on the Performance Scale, and 90 to 114 on the Full Scale IQ. Four tests (viz., Comprehension, Arithmetic, Vocabulary, and Digit) of the Verbal Scale revealed a range of more than five scale-scored points. The quads had a range of more than five scale-scored Symbol points on only one subtest of the Performance Scale, the Coding Subtest. On the Frostig the girls ranged from 7 to over 10 years, and the boys ranged from 5½ to 10 years.

Discussion

A case history of quadruplets has been described in which the two males had learning difficulties. In 1963 Rosenthal [6] estimated that monozygotic quadruplets would occur in only one of 10 million births and that in only half of these would all survive into adulthood. The quads under discussion were not monozygotic but certainly rare enough to provide a rather unique opportunity to investigate their development at 8 years of age. Only the boys were showing developmental problems, and these problems were concentrated primarily in their academic progress.

In 1966 Eisenberg [3] classified the sources of reading retardation into sociopsychological and psychophysiological factors. The former include objects in teaching, deficient cognitive stimulation, and (lack of) motivation. The latter include general debility, sensory defects, intellectual defects, and a specific reading disability.

In keeping with these criteria, little evidence could be found to support any sociopsychological variables as the major source of the boys' learning difficulties.

Rosenthal [6] has described how quadruplets can be treated by their family as two sets of twins. In this family, that division could easily have been made by sex. It is accepted that children within the same family do not necessarily have the same environment [1]. Indeed, it has been stated that even monozygotic twins within the same family have different physical problems. One can hypothesize that quads can have differences in their living environment, perhaps even more pronounced than do twins. Our investigation exposed no factors within this family's living environment that showed the boys to have been more deprived in sociopsychological areas and no more pressured in psychodynamic areas [7] than the girls, and hence this might account for learning disabilities in two of the quadruplets. In addition, the older singleton male child had been a success academically.

Of the psychophysiologic factors, the quads do not fit into the first three categories of general debility, sensory defects, or intellectual defects. The fourth category is the best fit if specific reading disability is defined as one in which a child is behind in reading, yet has had conventional instruction, a culturally adequate home, intact senses, and at least normal intelligence. The question of intelligence is an issue since both boys do perform at the lower level of the normal range.

Rutter, Tizard, et al. [7] has stressed that reading retardation does not necessarily mean a lag in reading alone; it may be associated with developmental delays in language, perception, and motor function. Both boys demonstrate such delays as decribed by various investigators. It should be noted that although the girls displayed some immature behavior, it was better controlled and more socially acceptable.

Since it appears that the boys can be diagnosed as having

specific reading disabilities, it seems relevant to examine the various causes ascribed to this syndrome as described in the literature.

Perinatal abnormalities, which are slightly higher in boys, have been linked to reading disabilities, which are much more common in boys [6]. The two have been considered in a cause-and-effect relationship, but it seems more likely that both should be considered as effects of an as yet unknown cause.

Low birth weight has been claimed as a cause of reading disability. Mittler [5] refutes this, feeling that low birth weight has only a "weak association with language skills by the age of four." He also reports that although low language skills are commonly found in twins with a low, rather than average, birth weight, no one has yet accounted for the commonly found linguistic inferiority of twins in general. Tanner [8] has challenged the international criteria of 5½ lb as premature weight, suggesting the importance of distinguishing between low birth weight of a baby of normal and shorter-than-normal gestation. He feels a small child of a short gestation period has greater developmental predesposition to pathology. All quads belong to the category of smaller birth weight but normal gestation period. The birth weight ranged from 4 lb, 7 oz to 5 lb, 7 oz, with the girls the smallest and the largest and the boys in the middle. The only possible connection here is that low birth weight after normal gestation and later developmental problems in reading are more likely to occur in boys than girls.

It might be noted that the boys at age 8 were smaller in height and weight than the girls. This is the opposite of one's expectations from the developmental norms of Tanner [8].

The Apgar ratings were high and satisfactory for these children. Denhoff, Hainsworth, et al. [2], in an investigation of stress factors at birth and during the first year of life, stated that a low Apgar rating alone is not enough to predict later learning disabilities. The high ratings of these quads seems further evidence that this Apgar score alone is not enough.

The quads were delivered simultanously, and each received equal attention from the pediatricians in attendance. Only one boy had some respiratory distress, but not of a serious nature. So far as could be determined, the quads had equal access to nourishment *in utero.* All precautions were taken and none of the quads were truly anoxic at any time.

Cerebral cross-dominance, though it occurs more often among children with reading disabilities, is not considered a source of reading disabilities by many investigators, but rather a description of behavior accompanying it. Eisenberg [4] says incomplete cerebral dominance is more probably an underlying developmental antecedent than a cause of reading disabilities. One of the boys (Matthew) was left-eyed, and all else were right dominant. The girls were not tested.

It seems we are back to examining the learning ability of these quads in relation to sex differences. The literature is in agreement that boys predominate over girls in having problems with learning, although the rates vary with the investigator. Many are asking why boys are more vulnerable to this disability than girls, and our study indicates this as a relevant question. Rutter [7] suggests that boys show a "general delay in development in comparison with girls," and that this may be connected with a "greater biological susceptibility to specific delays and development."

This seems to us to describe the development at 8 years of age of the two boys as compared with the two girls in this set of quads. In this multiple birth, given the same intrauterine environment and birth conditions and reasonably similar socio- and psychodynamic background, the male quads proved more vulnerable for as yet unknown reasons to certain developmental delays and to specific reading problems.

References

1. Allen, M. G., Pollen, W., and Hoffer, A. *Parental, Birth and Infancy Factors in Infant Twin Development.* Chess & Thomas, London, 1972.
2. Denhoff, E., Hainsworth, P. K., and Hainsworth, M. L. The child at risk for learning disorder: Can he be identified during the first year of life? *Clin. Pediat.,* 11, (1972) 164–170. March, Vol. 11.
3. Eisenberg, L. Reading retardation: Psychiatric and sociologic aspects. *Paediatrics,* 37 (1966) 352–376.
4. Eisenberg, L. The epidemiology of reading, retardation and a program for preventive intervention. In *The Disabled Reader,* J. Money, Ed. John Hopkins Press, Baltimore, 1966, pp. 3–20.
5. Mittler, P. *The Study of Twins.* Penguin Science of Behaviour, Middlesex, England, 1971.

6. Rosenthal, A., Ed. *The Genaine Quadruplets.* Basic Books, New York, 1963.
7. Rutter, M., Tizard, J. and Whitmore, K. *Education, Health and Behaviour.* Longman, London, 1970.
8. Tanner, J. M. Physical growth. In *Carmichael's Manual of Child Psychology,* Vol. I., P. H. Mussen, Ed. Wiley, New York, 1970, pp. 77–155

The Family and The Handicapped Child: A Study of Vulnerability and Mastery in the Child with Spina Bifida

Elisabeth M. Wann, M.D. (Australia)

The family into which a child is born and of which he becomes a part will have a marked influence on his development, particularly his personality development, just as he himself will in some way modify the functioning of his total family.

This is true for all children and for all families but is of particular significance for the vulnerable child, especially when the vulnerability is obvious at birth or soon afterward in the form of a congenital abnormality or is the sequel of early serious illness. It is one group of such children and their families that I wish to discuss in this chapter, namely those with spina bifida.

Spina bifida is a condition where the protective bony arches in the baby's backbone fail to develop sufficiently to enclose the spinal cord at some point along the spinal track. The lesion most commonly occurs in the lumbosacral region, resulting in paralyses of the lower limbs, skin insensitivity, and incontinence of bladder and bowel. In some 70 percent of such children there is the additional complication of hydrocephalus.

Neurosurgical procedures developed since the introduction of the Spitz-Holter valve in 1958 have increased the incidence of

81

survival in these children and reduced the extent of brain damage. Nevertheless, those who survive are multiply handicapped children for whom existence will always be different and more hazardous than that of the nonhandicapped.

Such children at birth are vulnerable for they have a less efficient apparatus to use in coping with the many developmental tasks required of them. They are also "at risk" since the handicaps they have mean that they have to face procedures and situations not conducive to healthy development and emotional functioning.

The attendant risks are reduced if the child is born into a healthy family—a family that can work through its mourning for the loss of the normal child who is not and be available to help the handicapped child to some degree of mastery of himself and his world.

Voiland and Associates [1] remind us that the basic human qualities of the family as a group derive from the biological and psychological differences between its male and female heads and the gratification of their respective needs when they become parents. Thus, the father is usually elected for the role of leader, provider, and protector, giving him an acceptable opportunity for the gratification of masculine assertiveness in a socially constructive way, and at the same time permitting his wife to fulfill, in a socially useful and emotionally satisfying manner, the feminine masochism that is part of her natural emotional structure. Such a family attains an identity of its own; that is, each member comes to know "who" his family is, as different from all other families, and generally manifests affection for and loyalty to other family members.

In such a family both parents will want children, considering procreation and child rearing integral parts of family life. The advent of the child will of course reactivate for them almost forgotten childhood memories, both pleasurable and painful, which will influence their attitudes and behavioral responses to the presence of a child and his upbringing, including their concept of parental love and the child's physical care and discipline. But gradually these attitudes and values will be modified to meet the behavior and needs of their particular child. Thus for the healthy husband and wife parenthood offers the opportunity for full realization of their emotional needs for creativity, affection, loving, and being loved. Through their children the parents also may hope to enjoy, vicariously, the benefits, privileges, successes, and pleasures they themselves did not have or failed to achieve; in other words, they attain satisfaction by identification with their offspring in the same manner as the child identifies with the parents in achieving his own identity.

When a child is born with the serious defect of spina bifida the blow to parental hopes is a shattering one, and the ensuing grief has to be "worked through" by each parent in his own way. If they can talk together about their loss and be mutually supportive and understanding and if their medical and other advisers appreciate and tolerate their need to mourn, the grief may not proceed to depression but will be resolved using healthy adjustments that will enable them to see "the child" who lurks behind the handicap as their own child, a child with extra needs because he is handicapped. The medical needs of the child at birth increase the difficult and "at risk" situations for him and his parents, especially the mother. It is usually essential that the infant be transferred to a specialist hospital for urgent treatment while the mother remains in the hospital where she was confined, for very few specialist children's hospitals have facilities for the newly delivered mother. This early separation of mother and baby can have very serious effects for the future of each. The mother needs the baby's presence to help her adjust to losing part of herself, which is what happens at the moment of birth, and the baby needs close contact with his mother if he is to mature from Mahler's "normal autistic" phase of the first few weeks of life toward the symbiotic phase, the phase when some "good mothering" principles are incorporated by the child as part of himself. This is the time when mother and baby get to know and understand one another and learn to adjust to one another's needs, as is so beautifully and simply described by Winnicott [2].

Physicians and other workers involved at this time need to recognize the grief of parents and to tolerate their need to mourn—something not always appreciated in our Western society where the "stiff upper lip" is respected—and to do all possible to foster the physical and emotional closeness of mother and baby, even to the extent of modifying our specialist pediatric hospitals so that the puerperal mother and her child can be accommodated together.

Another problem is the uncertainty in the early days about prognosis. Figures vary as to the percentage of children that survive, but the latest figures at Royal Children's Hospital, Melbourne, indicate that 50 to 60 percent will do so. The task of deciding which children have a chance of surviving with a reasonable quality of life is an extremely difficult one, and many surgeons defer making a pronouncement. Although their predicament can be appreciated, it is a very traumatic situation for the parents who on the one hand cannot give up hope and belief that the child will survive and on the other cannot, without guilt, begin to mourn him, as dying.

A warm, intelligent mother who has mothered two other children successfully recently spoke with me about her feelings in the early days of the life of her spina bifida daughter, now aged 7 years:

"I only held her briefly—she was all wrapped up so I could only imagine what the problem was. Then they took her away and when she was gone I felt so "let down." It had been a hard delivery and I just managed to bear the pain because I knew that when it was over I'd hold my baby close and it would all be worthwhile; and then I did not have her. The days waiting to see her again seemed like eternity but I shall never forget the shock of that first visit to the Children's Hospital when I saw her back for the first time. They kept her a month in the hospital and all I could think was that I wanted her to die. But—I had to take her home and it was then that I held her for the first time—it was just as if I were holding a piece of meat—so different from the other babies who snuggled in and gave me such a feeling of warmth. When I got her home I was afraid to touch her in case I harmed her more—they had told me to be careful of her back and to watch "the shunt." I felt so frightened and helpless when she cried and it took a tremendous effort to do the necessary things for her—even today it takes an effort to show her affection.

I asked her if she was able to talk to anyone about her feelings in those early days, and she replied, "No, I was too ashamed." This mother, capable of warm maternal care, was still depressed but might have been helped at the time of the child's birth had she had closer contact with her baby right from the beginning and the opportunity to talk about her feelings with a professional worker, since her husband was not available to her emotionally.

In the basically healthy family, where the father supports the mother emotionally and shares her grief, where he can protect her by discussing such things as prognosis with the medical team and indicate his understanding of her maternal needs by doing all in his power to ensure that she can be with her baby as much as possible, the distress and depression revealed by this mother need not and do not occur, as evidenced by other mothers of spina bifida children with whom I have talked.

The more available the mother and family is to the spina bifida baby in the early months of life, the better is he prepared for the next stage of development. This, in the normal child, commences in the third quarter of the first year of life and involves the beginning of differentation of the self from the symbiotic mother. This stage is always accompanied by anxiety, and whether considered with Mahler as an intrapsychic signal of danger about fear of the loss of the loved object, or with Bowlby as a behavioral sequel and reaction to physical separation from the mother, it is recognized that the mother must not only be present, but must be emotionally available to her child. Of the two, emotional availability would seem the more important. I have known a few spina bifida children hospitalized for short periods at this critical stage to weather the period without undue anxiety and not emerge as Bowlby's affectionless characters. In this small group the early traumas had been minimized by excellent medical care, short-term hospitalization, and healthy family functioning, and the mothers concerned had a remarkable capacity to interact intuitively with their children. In particular, the manner in which they could tolerate and understand the early demanding behavior of their babies was noteworthy. It was not possible for any of them to be physically present throughout their child's stay in the hospital, but when present they did "give emotionally." It should be noted that this anxiety stage tends to occur rather later in spina bifida children, perhaps as the result of their early vicissitudes and slower-than-average physical and cognitive development. For instance, they are all late in sitting independently, and language development seems specifically retarded, especially for those who have experienced long periods of early hospitalization.

The "toddler stage" is a difficult one for the spina bifida child as most will never "toddle" but will, at 3 or 4 years of age or even later, move clumsily, supported by all kinds of calipers and crutches. Thus he does not have the joyful experience of independent mobility until a much later stage; he cannot relieve his anxiety about his mother's departure by going to seek her, nor can he leave her spontanously to test out *voluntarily for himself* his toleration of her absence. Furthermore, he is unable to respond to his urges to explore his world since what he wants is often out of reach. In contrast to normal children, he is seldom reprimanded for sins of commission; rather, he tends to be blamed for continual infantile demands.

At this stage the normal active toddler sets out to master his world—it is an exciting place, and with the development of intelligence he wishes to discover it. His wishes are often frustrated and his actions punished, for what he wishes to do and does is often at variance with his own safety and the comfort of others. He is angry with those (usually the parents) who frustrate him, and temper tantrums are common. But the parents are also loved and needed, so the anger cannot safely be maintained for too long or expressed too directly. Thus he is often in a state of anxiety and tension because of ambivalent feelings for his parents. In the healthy family parents are sensitive to the child's strivings for independence and mastery at this stage and welcome and encourage his activities as signs of maturation and growth; they begin to expect him to do more for himself but not more than his capacity at any stage. In addition, by setting clearly defined limits regarding what behavior is permitted and what is not and by the example of appropriately controlled and expressed aggression, over several months the child gradually learns what is expected of him and what he may expect of others.

All children at this stage experience hostile as well as loving feelings for their parents. This is recognized and accepted by healthy parents who are able to differentiate between hostile feelings and hostile acts, tolerating the former but not the latter, because they recognize and can tolerate ambivalent feelings in themselves. Such parents instead of feeling unloved, hurt, and rejected in the face of their toddler's angry feelings for them can be firm and provide channels through which he may express destructive impulses in socially useful ways. Thus the child learns to control his hostile feelings without too much protest and without feeling excessively guilty or anxious about his behavior.

It is much more difficult for the parents of spina bifida children to cope with this ambivalent stage of the child's development, perhaps because of unresolved guilt feelings that render them more vulnerable to even mild expressions of anger from their child. This sense of guilt may cause parents to react in one of two ways. Some may find themselves unable to limit the child's demands or behavior in any way so he is given no help in the mastering of his own feelings and impulses but continues to expect the environment to gratify all his wishes and develops no ability to delay or channel gratification or consider the rights and needs of others. Such children acquire an extra handicap, which will later interfere with wider social functioning and learning. Other parents become so frightened and threatened by the child's hostile feelings that they react with rejection and punishment, which at times can be extreme.

It must be remembered that the frustrations of the spina bifida child are greater because of his limited mobility and because in another physical area he has the handicap of lack of sphincter control of bowel and bladder. For normal children toilet training increases the ambivalent feelings every child has to some extent for his parents, because the parents who insist on cleanliness interfere with a very pleasurable activity of the child. But when toilet training is achieved it seems to symbolize the mastery the child is acquiring over his body *and* his feelings—a mastery that brings a sense of pleasure and achievement. This feeling of mastery and its accompanying pleasure is denied to most spina bifida children who remain incontinent of bladder until surgical intervention and of bowel until school age or even later. Apart from medical considerations regarding renal function, it seems very desirable that urinary diversion procedures be performed at about the age the child would normally acquire bladder control.

These operations can for some parents be the most traumatic period in their child's long history of treatment, for attention is focused on genital functioning. At this stage questions as to future sexual behavior and activity are asked, and parents have to accept that, in the vast majority of cases, their sons will be impotent and their daughters, though capable of bearing children, unlikely to do so. At this time, the original feelings of loss experienced by parents are often reactivated, and they may again require help in "working them through." But basically healthy parents are again able to achieve an adjustment that enables them to continue to foster their child's development.

All children need to regress at some stage as they master the many tasks of the early years of life. Temporary regression gives them time to reorganize their resources before moving on again to tackle a task or situation that previously had proved too stressful. Regressive behavior can, however, be threatening for immature parents who fail to appreciate that it is often appropriate for the stage of the child's ego development. These parents become angry and berate the child, adding to the stress that was already too much for him. At the other end of the scale there are parents who are anxious about their child's growing independence, preferring him as an infant, and such parents may unconsciously reinforce regressive behavior. This is not uncommon in spina bifida or other handicapped children, for it is often easier to accept a handicapped infant or younger child than to recognize that the handicapped child will become a handicapped adult.

In this chapter I have discussed some of the difficulties of the spina bifida child and his family as the child moves through the developmental stages of the early years of life.

I have stressed how important it is that the child have the support and understanding of a family that is secure in its relationships and parental roles, unthreatened by the normal stages children pass through as they develop an identity and ego of their own, able to cope with recurring stresses and emerge from them, not only intact but more cohesive than before.

Many areas have been omitted. I hope that those discussed may draw attention to some of the emotional needs of the spina bifida child and his family.

References

1. Voiland, A. L. and Associates. *Family Casework Diagnosis*. New York, Columbia Univ. Press, 1962.
2. Winnicott, D. W. XXX. *The Child and the Family*. London. Tavistock, 1957.

Priorities for Vulnerable Children: The Mentally Retarded

Ann M. Clarke, and A. D. B. Clarke, Ph.D. (U.K.)

The term "mental retardation" does not describe a clearly defined entity but rather a heterogeneous group of conditions characterized by low or very low intelligence. The range of ability within what is really an administrative category is very wide, with at one extreme a small proportion of profoundly damaged individuals and at the other, a majority (75 percent of the whole) with only mild degrees of disability. In effect, there are two distinct populations above and below an IQ of about 50, with the mildly retarded on the one hand and the moderately, severely and profoundly retarded, on the other. These differ to a large extent in aetiology, present status, and prognosis and hence are discussed separately.

In most developed countries prevalence rates are assumed to be about 2 to 3 percent, but these differ according to age and to social policy. The absolute numbers identifiable as "at risk" of being labeled mentally retarded are thus very large, but only a minority of the milder cases are treated as such. Often, too, this is of a transitory nature during the school years.

And now two points about vulnerability. First, this is often regarded as a quality—or lack of it—residing in the child. This seems to be true of only one extreme, for example, the autistic or the severely retarded, and it results from genetic or constitutional factors. But at the other extreme it may also result from social conditions of such severity that *all* children in these situations are without exception vulnerable. Such an example is provided by Koluchova [16] concerning twins who were reared in isolation, neglect, and cruelty for 5½ years before rescue. Any child reared in such circumstances will suffer severe cognitive and affective damage. So vulnerability appears to lie on a continuum with, at one extreme, a very small number of children who for constitutional reasons are highly vulnerable to an ordinary environment and at the other extreme all children, regardless of their constitutional differences, who are vulnerable to very severe adversity. In between these extremes, we find the majority of vulnerable children, where an interaction between constitutional and social factors, whether intra- or extrafamilial, results in damage to some, whereas others escape unscathed.

Second, we tend to talk about vulnerability rather than resilience, possibly because our work directs us to the vulnerable and nonresilient, rather than to the vulnerable and resilient, child. Yet, as we indicated when reviewing literature in 1960, one is as much struck by resilience as by vulnerability in childhood. Nevertheless, we still remain extremely ignorant of the mechanisms of either [3]. There is no doubt, however, that powerful factors can be found at work, in some situations, undoing earlier damage.

The Child with IQ Below 50

Let us now briefly consider the child with IQ below 50, who is vulnerable because pathological processes, whether genetic or biological, have produced irreversible CNS damage. Description of the behavior of such children or adults up the the early 1950s remained at the clinical level, and Clarke and Hermelin [5] summarized contemporary views of their potential as follows: [1] at best they find it very difficult to concentrate and, more typically, seem capable only of involuntary and momentary attention; [2] they are incapable of comparing and discriminating even on the simplest plane and of appreciating cause-and-effect relationships;

[3] they are quite incapable of adapting themselves to anything out of the ordinary; [4] they are able to perform only the simplest routine tasks under constant supervision; and [5] they are therefore unable to contribute appreciably toward their own support. Certain experimental studies challenged this clinical view [5, 7, 8, 21]. Such descriptions were seen as accurate statements concerning the initial disabilities of very retarded institutionalized persons, but inaccurate if appropriate training was provided. Thus manual incompetence could in many cases be transformed into reasonably normal dexterity, or distraction could give way to concentration.

We have recently reviewed five main streams of research on the learning of individuals with IQs below 50. The results of these investigations can be integrated remarkably well. On the basis of this evidence, we have argued that severe brain damage or malformation, characteristic of the IQ range 25–50, results in a relative deficiency in acquiring skills merely from exposure to ordinary situations. Yet appropriate manipulation of the environment can present material in such a way that learning, retention, and transfer are improved. Recognition of these quite simple facts could lead to a diminution of the degree of handicap for individuals. Current pessimism about the very retarded individual is based partly on inferring capacity from initial rather than from final performance. It is as yet far from clear what the limits are for behavioral change in such persons, but it is by no means an unreasonable hypothesis that the main defect might itself be modified by appropriate training. It might even be possible to induce a higher level of cognitive functioning artificially; it is probably no accident that unusually "bright" children (e.g., IQ 60+) suffering from Down's syndrome have without exception been reared in specially stimulating homes, and never in institutions [4].

The main priority for such children appears to be the application of existing knowledge to their education and training. This has hardly been done anywhere. It needs to be approached cautiously, by means of independently evaluated demonstration pilot schemes. One should warn that there exist large numbers of sentimentalists, however, who for the best of misguided motives believe that a diluted form of normal nursery education and "enrichment" is the most suitable approach. Nothing could be farther from the truth. Structured and intensive efforts, concentrating on cognitive and manual skills, represent for the very retarded almost the sole opportunity for improvement. Moreover, the degree to which parents can be successfully used as teachers, supplementing and reinforcing the work of the school, remains to be investigated.

The Mildly Retarded

More than 1.5 percent of the population lies within the IQ 50–70 range. A minority of these people owe their condition to pathological factors of less severe degree than those associated with moderate, severe, or profound retardation. The majority are either normal variants where no special genetic-environmental mechanisms are needed to account for their existence or are culturally deprived people, where it is assumed that the interaction of both genetic and adverse environmental factors is implicated.

Let us first consider the facts. A majority of these children are not officially classified as retarded; instead they may find their way informally into remedial classes. If special help is received, then, as noted, it is normally confined to the school years. All epidemiological studies indicate the highest prevalence toward the end of the school period. Thereafter there is a dramatic drop, often by about half, of the numbers identified. So it seems that many of these conditions are self-limiting; insofar as adverse social factors are involved, society may undo or allow to be undone the damaging effects it induced earlier in life—factors that in childhood appear in some special circumstances to be associated with a decrementing IQ [9]. We have postulated three mechanisms to account for the changing status of some of these persons from adolescence onward: (1) camouflage, which becomes possible because intellectual demands may be less after the school years, (2) prolonged social learning, and (3) delayed maturation, which seems to be a sequel to early adversity and reflects the qualities of resilience mentioned earlier [4].

This picture of actuarial improvement also emerges from long-term follow-up studies [1, 14]. Groups that at school age were markedly homogeneous with respect to intelligence, scholastic handicap, and social status become increasingly heterogeneous, with a minority doing very badly, another minority extremely well, and the majority functioning as rather dull members of society. All these studies describe the natural history of deprived subnormal subjects and do not reflect the results of any special intervention.

All this suggests that calculated intervention might be expected to have profound effects in preventing mild retardation. Before discussing evidence it must be stated that the field is bedevilled by the pervasive mythology that early experience per se necessarily has a crucial effect on later characteristics. This results in the focusing of attention on the early years, at the expense of later development, and suggests that if special treatment occurs during this period, it will have long-term consequences. However, it also leads to a certain pessimism, and hence lowered expectancies, if matters have gone badly in early life. This belief in the crucial importance of the early years is negated by the reversibility of early deprivation and by longitudinal studies that indicate that some degree of individual change with respect to age peers is very common [2]. It is of interest that Kagan, who formerly espoused a belief in strong developmental continuity, has recently changed his views [13].

The works of Skeels [18, 19] and Skodak [20] are classic. The accidental finding that seemingly mentally retarded babies, excluded from a Dickensian orphanage, showed marked improvement when moved to a mental retardation hospital where they were the youngest—and hence favorite—inmates was followed by a calculated experiment. The results were replicated and most of the experimental group of 13 were ultimately adopted into rather average homes. On follow-up 25 years later it was clear that outcome for the experimental and contrast groups was vastly different, with the former functioning normally and the latter mainly retarded and institutionalized. Skeels himself did not fully understand his own results; he entitled his monograph "Adult status of children with contrasting *early* life experiences," whereas he should have referred to "*contrasting life experiences*" (our italics). Small wonder that others should have gone even further and believed that intervention of any sort would produce as dramatic results. So, despite the work of Kirk [15], which exactly foreshadowed what was to follow, in this country Project Headstart got off the ground in 1964. By 1969 Arthur Jensen [12] opened his paper in the Harvard Educational Review with the accurate statement that "Compensatory education has been tried and it apparently has failed."

Even then it seemed obvious, however, to any observer with both common sense and some understanding of human development that the assumptions underlying Headstart were incorrect and that Jensen's belief that environment *only* affected cognitive development significantly if it was far worse than ordinary slum conditions was at least doubtful.

As noted, it is unlikely that the first few years are critical for psychosocial development, although they may be for brain development [6]; the two are not synonymous. Moreover, since evidence suggests that most mild retardation is determined in the home, by either heredity, environment, or both, it must be doubted whether any normal school program of a few hours per day even for 2 years prior to school entry can be expected to compensate.

The failure of short-term intervention studies and the success of life-long intervention fit better a model for human development involving long-term genetic/learning interactions. It is probable that the Skeels' experimental group only became irreversibly different after perhaps 15 years of intervention. Another study, already mentioned, offers for the first time a full documentation of recovery of twin boys from the age of 7 years, after 5½ years of extreme isolation, neglect, cruelty, and malnutrition [16]. It is clear that their mental retardation was reversible, for their IQs doubled in a few years and they are now in normal school and have been adopted. The options still remained open for them at age 7. Then finally, one of several properly conceived Headstart studies might be mentioned. A series of brief reports, and some longer, privately circulated documents have been produced by Heber and colleagues [9–11].

Using a two-pronged approach, Heger developed a program for retarded slum-dwelling mothers and for their newborn babies for whom there was a high risk of mild mental retardation, the degree of which would increase progressively during development. These children were removed from their homes (from age 3 months) for 5 days a week and subjected to an intensive program of perceptual, language, and problem-solving stimulation of a sort never previously undertaken for so long a period (6 years) for a potentially retarded group. With the use of suitable controls, not only was the expected deterioration in the children of the experimental group offset, but their development accelerated to an average IQ of 120–130 up to age 3½ to 4 years [10]. These workers have recently issued further and more detailed reports, when many of the children were aged 6 to 7 and already in school [11]. By this time the intervention program has ceased. As we predicted some years ago, there has been an average decline in IQ of members of the experimental group to 112 at age 6 and 110 at age 7. This roughly parallels the expected average decline in members of the control group, so that the differences between them remain roughly constant. The data are incomplete but, if confirmed, indicate clearly that 6 years of intervention are not sufficient to maintain permanently a very high level of function.

In the few successful Headstart studies there has been either total removal from adverse conditions or removal for so much of the child's waking life, coupled with a systematic program of compensation, that substantial gains could occur.

What priorities, then, must we seek for the child living in a certain ecology within the slum [9] and hence vulnerable for mild mental retardation? A number of social scientists have drawn a red herring across the trial by alleging that the concept of psychological (as opposed to material) disadvantage, with its attendant developmental defects, represents an attempt to impose middle-class norms on a rich, indigenous subculture. Perhaps there is a grain of truth somewhere, but is there anything good in a technological society in being unable to read, or to employ cognitive skills that offer a mastery of the environment and of one's destiny? These middle-class social scientists seem to be expressing sentimental middle-class thoughts that echo the 19th-century concept of the "noble savage."

In the long run society must deal with its own pathologies that have created slums and their attendant miseries. In the short run, it is clear that, for individual children, a radical change in life-style is often followed by a radical change in development. It seems clear that preschool education of the kind now offered to children has a negligible effect on their cognitive development and subsequent school achievement. Although specially devised nursery curricula may bring temporary cognitive gains, these have invariably been lost or increasingly weakened once the program is withdrawn. A mass of evidence pinpoints the home, and not the preschool or school as of primary formative importance for the child's development. Thus the major way of effecting long-term changes in children is either by removing them from adversity (which society is often reluctant to do, even though this may offer them a better chance than being kept with their natural family with social worker support) or by changing the behavior of the parents. But evidence shows that those parents most in need of help are least likely to either seek it or accept it if offered, or indeed to be capable of altering their inadequate behavior.

Although the evidence is not absolutely clear, it is highly probable that a majority of grossly deprived children are unplanned and unwanted. It follows, then, that the first priority should be an attempt to ensure that contraceptive procedures are used, so that this damaging situation (both for parents and children) can be avoided. This should be of top priority for social workers in deprived areas, and it would involve offering advice directly in the home and not merely drawing attention to the existence of family-planning clinics. Where mishaps occur, the first line of defense should be voluntary abortion on social grounds or for the mother's mental or physical health. Failing this, the voluntary offer of the child for adoption should be discussed with the mother. There are, of course, important social, ethical, and political issues involved in this whole problem.

Where the main deficit within the deprived family is cognitive/educational, very prolonged and intensive social and educational programs, working in lockstep with willing and cooperative parents, are likely to prove effective.

One must not underestimate the size and extent of the problem, and it would be easy to be defeatist at the outset. But the

President's Committee on Mental Retardation [17] has stated that, using present techniques in the biomedical and behavioral sciences, it would be possible to reduce by one-half the incidence of mental retardation by the end of the century. The culturally disadvantaged constitute the major retarded group, so the main burden would fall here. Whether this possibility becomes a probability is, of course, another matter. Much depends on the resources that society is prepared to allocate in attacking its own defects. Sooner or later it must take action along many fronts. As influential scientists, it is our responsibility to cause it to be sooner rather than later.

References

1. Baller, W. R., Charles, D. C., and Miller, E. L. Mid-life attainment of the mentally retarded: a longitudinal study. *Genet. Psychol. Monogr.,* 75 (1967), 235–329.
2. Clarke, A. D. B. Learning and human development—the forty-second Maudsley Lecture. *Brit. J. Psychol.,* 114 (1968), 1061–77.
3. Clarke, A. D. B. and Clarke, A. M. Some recent advances in the study of early deprivation. *J. Child Psychol. Psychiat.,* 1 (1960), 26–36.
4. Clarke, A. D. B. and Clarke A. M. Mental retardation and behavioural change. In *Development and Regeneration in the Nervous System,* R. M. Gaze and M. J. Keating, Eds. *Brit. Med. Bull.,* 30 (1974), 179–185, British Council, London.
5. Clarke, A. D. B. and Hermelin, B. F. Adult imbeciles: their abilities and trainability. *Lancet,* ii (1955), 337–339.
6. Dobbing, J. and Smart, J. L. (1974). Vulnerability of developing brain and behaviour. In *Development and Regeneration in the Nervous System,* R. M. Gaze and M. J. Keating, Eds. *Brit. Med. Bull.,* 30 (1974), 164–168, British Council, London.
7. Gordon, S., O'Connor, N., and Tizard, J. Some effects of incentives on the performance of imbeciles. *Brit. J. Psychol.,* 45 (1954), 277–287.
8. Gordon, S., O'Connor, N., and Tizard, J. Some effects of incentives on the performance of imbeciles on a repetitive task. *Amer. J. Ment. Defic.,* 60 (1965), 371–377.
9. Heber, R. The role of environmental variables in the etiology of cultural-familial mental retardation. *Proc. 1st Congr. Internat. Assoc. Scient. Stud. Ment. Defic.,* 1968, pp. 456–465. Michael Jackson, Reigate, England. Richards, B. W., Ed.
10. Heber, R. and Garber, H. Rehabilitation of families at risk for mental retardation. Rehabilitation Research and Training Center in Mental Retardation, Univ. Wisconsin, Madison, 1972.
11. Heber, R. and Garber, H. *Proc. 3rd Congr. Internat. Assoc. Scient. Stud. Ment. Defic.,* D. A. Primrose, Ed. ARs Polona, Warsaw, 1974.

12. Jensen, A. R. How much can we boost IQ and scholastic achievement? *Harvard Educ. Rev.*, 39 (1969), 1–123.
13. Kagan, J. and Klein, R. E. Cross-cultural perspectives on early development. *Amer. Psycholog.*, 28 (1973) 947–961.
14. Kennedy, R. J. *A Connecticut Community Revisited: A Study of the Social Adjustment of a Group of Mentally Deficient Adults in 1948 and 1960.* Connecticut State Dept. of Health, Office of Mental Retardation, Hartford, Conn., 1966.
15. Kirk, S. A. *Early Education of the Mentally Retarded.* Urbana, Ill: Univ. Illinois Press, 1958.
16. Koluchova, J. Severe deprivation in twins: a case study. *J. Child Psychol. and Psychiat.*, 13 (1972), 107–114.
17. President's Committee on Mental Retardation. *Entering the Era of Human Ecology.* Department of Health, Education and Welfare, Washington, D. C., Publication No. (OS) 72–7, 1972.
18. Skeels, H. M. Adult status of children with contrasting early life experiences. *Monogr. Soc. Res. Child Devel.*, 31 (3) (1966).
19. Skeels, H. M. and Dye, H. B. (1939). A study of the effects of differential stimulation on mentally retarded children. *Proc. Amer. Assoc. Ment. Defic.*, 44 (1939), 114–136.
20. Skodak, M. Adult status of individuals who experienced early intervention. *Proc. 1st Congr. Internat. Assoc. Scient. Stud. Ment. Defic.*, Michael Jackson, Reigate, 1968. England pp. 11–18.
21. Tizard, J. and Loos, F. M. The learning of a spatial relations test by adult imbeciles. *Amer. J. Ment. Defic.*, 59 (1954), 85–90.

A PSYCHODYNAMIC APPROACH TO VULNERABILITY

Vulnerability and Role of Stimulation in Psychological Development in Early Life

Humberto Nagera, M.D. (U.S.A.)

I begin with the statement that all children are vulnerable, as many others have done throughout this volume. There are, of course, many unfavorable situations that bring vulnerability to the fore, such as child neglect, under- or overstimulation, child abuse, adoption, disruption of the family organization, and parental death. Hence, I review here some of the developmental needs of young infants, hoping to highlight some of the reasons for their vulnerability. Further, I do so against the background of the present move toward day-care centers so that I can point out what I consider to be their considerable dangers given the vulnerability of children, especially during the first two years of life.

If we consider first the dangers involved in this practice to children in the age group of up to 1½ years of age, we have to examine at least *three distinct sets of variables*. Each one of them plays a fundamental role in the healthy development of the infant ("healthy" implying here not only physical health but including a good intellectual, emotional and psychological development). The first set of variables comes from the child himself. The second is from the type of environment in which the child lives, including those human objects responsible for his care. The third is the resultant of the interaction between the endowment, the genetic

101

makeup of all humans as a species (and that peculiar to each individual), and the environment (including the human objects).

Those variables that concern the infant itself are in part genetically determined and are essential to certain characteristics specific for the development of the human brain. Thus, comparatively speaking, the infant of the human species is born with an extremely immature, unfinished brain, to the point that it takes 1½ to 2 years after birth to reach the level of maturity that is typical at the time of birth in other mammalian species. It is embryological maturational forces that push brain development in the anatomophysiological sense to its completion. To complete their tasks such forces, though genetically determined, need *the collaboration of specific forms of environmental stimulation.* In other words, the genetic developmental embryological forces cannot unfold the anatomophysiological blueprint of the brain to its ideal potential without the essential contribution of environmental factors. This environmental contribution is in the nature of a diversity of stimuli that must reach the brain. The function of that stimuli is to trigger and stimulate those genetic embryological mechanisms to complete its task.

Admittedly, this is still an obscure area, but the current evidence is at least quite suggestive, if not conclusive. Different forms of external stimulation (usually contained in the multiplicity of interactions of the mother with her baby) seem to influence the internal, anatomical-maturational processes by at least three different types of mechanisms.

The first type of mechanism seems to favor significant increases in a progressive and more complex arborization of dendrites during the first few months of life. The importance of this phenomenon should be clearly understood. More dendrites mean increased and more complex pathways in the brain, and more pathways mean more functional capabilities and better possibilities of performance for that brain. Conel's [1] studies of the cerebral cortex of babies demonstrated that although the number of cells (neurons) in the cortex is fixed at birth, complex morphological changes continue for long periods of time. Thus he found progressive arborization of dendritic processes during the few months following birth without quantitative cellular increase. The situation here would be similar to a sophisticated piece of electronic equipment that has been poorly wired, where the connections between the systems are not as many in number as they could have been. Such a situation will naturally restrict unnecessarily the functional capabilities of the total equipment. Richmond and Lipton [2] stated that "since it is now accepted generally that neurons are connected in a network and not merely in a linear series, and that nerve impulses pass about the connections in a circular, more or less continuing fashion, the potential significance of this growing arborization of dendrites for the development of the infant may be appreciated" (p. 80). Thus understimulation of the brain during the first few months of life, for example, may well lead to an inferior quality of brain structure (less dendritization, connections, and functional pathways). Furthermore, such developmental maturational processes as those leading to appropriate dendritization can only occur during a limited period of time after birth. Hence if they do not take place during that critical period, they cannot be brought about at a later date. The damage, in the sense of loss of capabilities and function is permanent.

The second type increases the degree of vascularization in certain anatomical structures of the brain. The relationship between function, functional capacity, and the degree of vascularization of an organ (implying here the amount of oxygen available to the organ) is a well-established medical fact.

The third type favors the process of myelinization. Myelinization and function are very closely related. Here again there is hard evidence from animal experimentation suggesting clearly that environmental stimulation has significant effects upon ultimate structure and function. Richmond and Lipton [2] concluded that these "types of studies seem to give support to the contention that even after the fetal stage, environmental stimulation (or lack thereof) can modify developing structure in the central nervous system" (p. 82).

Since the first 2 years of life seem to be the critical period for all these developments to take place, it follows that if the right kind of stimulation is not provided during this phase, the result may be a structure that, though not necessarily "damaged" (in the sense of brain damage), has certainly not developed to its full potential.

If we take into account the possibility of cumulative effects of this type, leading to inferior development in multiple areas of the brain, it is conceivable that the finished brain is one of "inferior quality" for those unfortunate children whose fate it will be to grow, during their first 2 years of life, under conditions of deprivation and understimulation. Such conditions are typical of a variety of environments including, in my view, most of the existent day-care centers and no doubt those numbered in the thousands, that are to be created.

Provence and Lipton [3] have clearly demonstrated by means of direct observations of infants, the appalling damage to the personality and more especially to ego and intellectual development resulting from growing under conditions of deprivation and understimulation, that is, by lack of sufficient human contacts and interactions during the early stage of the child's development.

Some of such developmental lags can be "undone" by placing such children in a more suitable environment (a good foster home, for example) at the appropriate time. As I said somewhere else [4], "it seems to me that in another sense many such children are irreversible and permanently condemned to perform, in terms of his intelligence, at the lower end of normality. To be graphic, it is the difference between somebody digging holes in a road and somebody with the intelligence necessary for a university education. Thus, though 'normal,' deprivational child-rearing practices may have blunted his original genetic potential to such a point that his best is an IQ of 80, while genetically, and given more favorable circumstances in babyhood, he might have reached an IQ of 120."

Clearly, then, the first step that we must ensure developmentally is that the internal maturational embryological forces unfold as ideally as possible. That, as we have shown, requires external stimulation of the kind and quality contained "usually" in the mother-child relationship. This will ensure the best basic equipment in the form of the best brain that the child's endowment has provided him with. *But that condition, essential as it obviously is, is not enough or sufficient in the human species.* Most human behavior and controls are learned which constitutes a most significant difference from all other species. In the latter most behavior is controlled instinctually. In other words, it is controlled automatically by innate, inbuilt mechanisms in the brain that trigger off adaptive responses after the reception of the significant signals and stimuli from the environment. Self-preservation, mating behavior, preservation of the species, food gathering, and so on are frequently regulated in this manner. Not so with the human infant.

To start with, his brain is enormously superior in functional capabilities to any other species. Evolution has not provided him with the type of instinctual patterns of behavior described in the preceding paragraphs and observed in other species. When the time comes he must—since he is helpless and dependent on parental care and teaching for an inordinate large amount of time—use his intelligence to deal with his environment, with dangers, and with others. His specially developed brain has provided him with the capacity to learn to solve problems in a variety of ways. In other words, he can choose "intelligently" among several alternatives, the most adaptive response in a given set of circumstances. He is not restricted, like other species, to one single stereotyped solution. He has the capacity for language development as a tool of communication. He can and indeed has established innumerable forms of social organizations and cultures. He can store and teach his descendants that culture. He can modify his environment to suit his needs and thus he has to a large measure the greatest capacity for survival, in terms of evolution, of any species known. By the same token he possesses the greatest capacity for destruction intraspecies, interspecies, and of his environment.

All these differences clearly demonstrate that he must start learning from day 1 and at incredible pace at that, if he is going to join in an adaptive healthy manner his social group and its organization. This learning is predicated in an active and constant interaction *from birth onward* with human objects. The intensity of the contact needed to achieve this aim *is generally lacking under the institutional conditions* of foundling homes, orphanages, and most likely in ill-devised day-care centers. To use a comparison, it is not enough to have acquired the best computer possible (the best brain possible for a given child), it is also necessary to program it wisely and efficiently. The best computer, if mishandled and badly programmed, will be an inefficient piece of equipment.

We have enough evidence in the field of human development to state that the best programmer of the human brain and as much of human behavior is a good mother-child interaction in the first few years of life. Once that basic and early programming has been achieved, many others (in the forms of teachers, etc.) can participate successfully in the further programming and teaching of the human brain.[1]

One essential factor in this regard is the *constancy of the object,* the constancy of care of the object ministering to the child. The child's brain, at the same time that is developing and acquiring more complex capabilities, must be exercised. It must be exposed to innumerable experiences, not only so that it receives essential stimuli and continues to grow, *but so that it organizes itself,* learning slowly to distinguish (given its capacity to think) inside from outside, self from object, and the body parts under its control and command, as control is progressively acquired. Similarly, he must go successfully (if normality is to be achieved) through the process of separation-individuation as described by Mahler and must learn to use his ego apparatuses as these become structured as well as to understand the innumerable complexities of its environment. Most important, he must learn to establish very early controls over its own primitive reactions and feelings. To further complicate the problem, all these developments must take place in a situation where the infant is not excessively subjected to undesirable forms of stimuli either. Thus in the earliest stages it is imperative that the child (the child's brain) not be subjected to overwhelming, traumatic forms of experiences that it cannot handle and that are enormously disruptive in terms of personality organization. Such stimuli, capable of overwhelming the necessary homeostatic equilibrium in the child, can come from outside, for example, from excessive handling or mishandling, excessive cold or heat, multiple sources of unorganized sounds and other undesirable stimuli impinging on the baby for prolonged periods of time and enforced separations. It can come from the inside

---

[1] None of this should be taken literally. Programming is a graphic word of some explanatory value, but as a term it possesses connotations that are inappropriate and insufficient to describe human development, still, it expresses graphically some of the problems at hand.

when the baby is left to suffer from hunger or from pain unduly.

Granted the kind of background that is ideal for human and brain development, that is, *neither too excessive nor insufficient stimuli,* but the right happy medium, the child still needs some *constancy of objects* to organize its experiences, to understand its world. *An example may clarify this.* When a newborn baby is sufficiently hungry his pleasure-pain equilibrium, his homoeostatic equilibrium, is disrupted. A disturbing feeling interferes with his well-being. This automatically leads to clear signs of distress on the part of the baby that are picked up by the baby's mother. This, in turn, activates the behavior of the healthy mother, who immediately relates to the baby and his need. Usually, the mother has a very ritualized, stereotyped procedure while going about getting ready to satisfy the baby's hunger and thus alleviate or remove his distress. She might go and see her baby, talk to him, manipulate him to ascertain the cause of the cry or other signals released by the infant (he might be wet or uncomfortable for a variety of reasons). Then she may go to the kitchen to fetch bottles and prepare the baby's milk. All this time the child is receiving a variety of sensory stimulation, the steps of the mother while she moves about, her voice if she talks to him (this tends to be stereotyped, too), sounds produced by opening the refrigerator, closing it, the handling of bottles, glasses, spoons, pans, and so on. The baby, who must have been quite disturbed by his first few and new experiences of hunger, learns that after all this stimuli that reaches him, satisfaction arrives and his hunger and distress disappear.

Naturally, once he has established these links in his mind (after a few good experiences of satisfaction) one can observe how his crying stops automatically as soon as he can hear the noises resulting from the mother's activity in the preparation of his food. Thus at this point the internal distress is not a frightening, disturbing experience of discomfort, but one associated with relief and satisfaction. *In short, despair becomes hope.* Further, he has made in some primitive form the first connections between cause and effect and has learned that control pays, that waiting and being attentive can bring rewards, and so on. Obviously, *these first steps in the organization of the mind and of the inner world* of feelings and affects, of learning and knowing something for the first time, is possible, or more feasible and easier, if the object who ministrates to the child is constant. Her stereotyped and routinized behavior, the sameness of the behavior allows the baby to find his bearings, to know the situation or rather to identify it as similar to previous experiences, and consequently to predict the outcome. A constant change of caretakers with different ways, different manners of ministering to the baby, in short, the lack of sameness at the appropriate times will, I think, make it much more difficult for him to find his bearings, learn about the situation, predict the outcome, acquire early control structures, and be confident and relaxed in the face of the internal distress. Clearly, sameness, familiarity, and repeated similar experiences lead to learning and *to primitive understanding and organization in the mind.* Without these early and primitive processes of organization and integration later learning becomes difficult. Changing constantly the system by means of which we attempt to teach something to any child is disruptive and makes the mastery of the tasks more difficult, confusing, and hopeless.

This simplified example, relating to feeding and its significance for mental organization and structuring, can be multiplied *ad infinitum* in terms of what is happening constantly in the context of the mother-child interaction. Therefore, I believe that in the early stages *of the process of the organization of the mind* the existence of essentially one caretaker for the child, the existence of sameness in certain experiences, though not in all, is of enormous significance. After some time, that is, after the ego structure has achieved a certain level of organization, the child is able to deal with more complex tasks, even if some of the variables involved are changed frequently. The need for constancy of the caretaker still exists at somewhat later stages, but that need is then based on factors other than the need for organization in the mind and for the organization of our first mental processes.

The vignettes I have selected show clearly the close interaction between biological factors and psychological factors. In this dependence lies the superiority of the human infant as well as its vulnerability.

References

1. Conel, *The Postnatal Development of the Human Cerebral Cortex,* Vols. 1 et seq, Harvard Univ. Press, Cambridge, Mass, 1939.
2. Richmond, J. B. and Lipton, E. L. Some aspects of the neurophysiology of the newborn and their implications for child development. In L. Jessner and E. Pavenstedt, Eds., *Dynamic Psychopathology in Childhood,* Grune and Stratton, New York, 1959.
3. Provence, S. A. Lipton, R. C. *Infants in Institutions: A Comparison of Their Development with Family-Reared Infants During the First Year of Life.* New York, International Universities Press, 1962.
4. Nagara, H. Social deprivation in infancy: implications for personality development. In *Handbook of Child Psychoanalysis,* B. Wolman, Ed., New York, Van Nostrand Reinhold Co., 1972, pp. 181–190.

Vulnerability of the Traumatized Preschool Child: Usefulness of Brief Analytically Oriented Therapy

Carlos J. Robles, M.D. (Argentina)

In the process of growing up children are exposed to a variety of stresses and life situations that are potentially traumatic. In some circumstances these traumatic situations lead to the development of a neurosis, a "traumatic neurosis," or what is now referred to as an "interference" with normal development.

A traumatic situation that confronts the prelatency child will provoke unconscious conflicts specific for every stage of psychosexual development and bring about such a marked exacerbation of fantasies and affects that the ego becomes incapable of working through the situation in its habitual fashion. It then resorts to pathological means to protect itself from being overwhelmed by anxiety.

One of the mechanisms primarily used in these extreme circumstances is denial, a defense that prevents play from being used, as it ordinarily is to mitigate pressures, and transforms it instead into a compulsive repetition. Frequently this denial is reinforced by denial on the part of the parents so that a needed experience of mourning is obstructed by the adult's own neurotic needs.

111

Normally the child attempts to "play through" the trauma by converting from a passive to an active role. This procedure, however, may fail:

1. When the stimulus is too intense for the child to master at his particular stage of development.
2. When strong fixation points have been established at earlier developmental stages
3. When denial is used as a main defense.

The clinical picture is varied and manifested by combinations of inhibition, repetitive play, mood changes, sleep disturbances, regressive behavior, free floating anxiety, and at times by well-structured symptoms such as stuttering or phobias.

My experience has shown that most of these children react favorably to a brief therapeutic intervention that enables the ego to work out the traumatic incident. At this early age the relative fluidity of defense mechanisms facilitates interventions that can be further enhanced by the mother's participation. With the completion of the phallic phase of development the subsequent repression of latency consolidates the defense system, thus making a more classical analysis mandatory. But prior to this, and depending on the degree of internalization, the pathological reaction is sufficiently plastic to be influenced by short-term treatment, education, and environmental changes. In general, the earlier the intervention, the more rapid is the resolution and the less likely is the development of a fully developed neurosis. It has been convincingly documented that prelatency children, presenting with recent neurotic conflicts triggered off by known causes, can be successfully treated, using the psychoanalytical model, by the systematic, daily analysis for a few months of defenses, resistances, unconscious fantasies, and transference manifestations. In my own cases (nine patients), although psychoanalytical theory was used in the understanding of the symptoms and the preparation of a working hypothesis, neither defense nor transference was interpreted systematically. Instead the therapeutic effort was directed toward making the child more aware of the repressed affects and fantasies associated with the traumatic incident, by correcting any distortions of reality and by recruiting the mother's help in bringing about necessary environmental changes. The therapeutic goals included the relief of symptoms, the advancement of psychosexual development, and the further maturation of the ego.

When denial is overcome in therapy the affects can reach a conscious level where they can be verbalized, worked through in play, and discussed with and accepted by the mother. Verbalization is of the utmost importance to ego growth because it enables the ego to distinguish clearly between fantasy and reality and thus helps the growth of secondary processes.

With these aims in mind, the therapist must be active in his participation, at times directing the play into cathartic channels (Levy's "release therapy") and at time facilitating ego mastery by turning passive into active.

The prognosis with brief intervention is better:

1. When the child has an ego of adequate strength and has had psychosexual development without major regressions or fixations prior to the incident.
2. When the interval between the precipitating event and the therapeutic intervention is short (under 3 months). The shorter the interval, the better the prognosis.
3. When the mother can participate flexibly in the treatment.

CASE ILLUSTRATION

This case is presented here to illustrate the way in which analytically oriented brief therapy may enable a child to overcome a highly traumatic incident that ended in a mutilating surgical intervention.[1] Omar is an 8-year-old boy who grew up in a shanty town that surrounds the city. Coming back from fetching his brother from school they saw a kite tangled up in high-tension wires. Without hesitation he climbed up the pole and received a violent electrical shock that knocked him down unconscious and burned his right arm. After first aid in the emergency ward it was realized that an amputation at shoulder level would be needed, and the surgical department requested psychiatric cooperation to prepare the child. The mother did not want the child to know the truth of the operation. The father, a laborer, was more farseeing but sad and depressed.

First session. There was time for only one session before the operation, so the goal was to offer the child toys where he could play out the accident and possibly

---

[1] The author is indebted to Dr. Diane Goldberg, the therapist who worked with this patient.

turn the passive into active. The doctor takes the toys and brings them to the patient's bed.

Patient: (with anxiety) "I do not know how to write."

Doctor: "Perhaps you are telling me that now you cannot use your right arm anymore because of the accident. Have you talked about it with your doctor?"

Patient: "Yes. . . ."

Doctor: "What did he say?"

Patient (without any affect): "The doctor said he will have to cut my arm off. The one that is black."

Doctor: "It is not because it is black but, due to the accident, your arm is lifeless and without movement, and this could hurt the rest of your body."

The patient attempts to touch the toys with his other arm but does not follow through. He does not play.

Doctor: "It looks as if you are afraid to play because you have to do it with only one hand. [Probably for him to play with one hand would mean that the other one was missing.] I could lend you my hand and bring you the toys you ask me for."

He picks up the toy stethoscope and listens to his own heart.

Doctor: "Maybe you want to know if your heart will be able to resist the loss."

The patient then lines up three little dolls: one dressed as a doctor, a naked one, and the last one dressed as a nurse.

Doctor: "The boy is surrounded and supported by the doctor and the nurse as you are supported by your parents and myself to face the loss."

This led to his worry about what it would be like after the operation. He said he hoped everything would turn out all right.

Doctor: ". . . but you are concerned about missing your arm after the operation. . . ."

The patient turns his head around and cries. The doctor, understanding this affect, shows him how important it was to lose a part of him that was of no use to save the whole, his life. Omar picks up the stethoscope again and listens to his heart. The doctor remarks once more on his fear of not surviving the operation. Then with the scissors he cuts the doll's arm and the doctor remarks that he is doing to the doll what he knows they will do to him to save his life. He repeated the game several times. Then with a pair of pliers he holds up the severed arm. He drops the arm down and cuts it again with the scissors, then picks up the toy wristwatch, looking at it carefully.

Doctor: "They are going to cut your arm off, and you want to be sure your life will be going on." The patient touches his burned arm and cries again.

Doctor: "It hurts to know that you are going to lose it, but the doctors will take away what is burned and could not be used anyhow."

The boy asks for an orange drink and the doctor helps him with it, remarking that he needs a lot of love to overcome this loss. The toys were left with him so that he could keep on playing at operating on the doll's arm.

Second session. When the doctor comes to the ward the boy's arm had already been amputated. After showing the doctor the things he had been building (erector set) with his mother, he cried a lot, saying it hurt. The doctor showed how he was crying for what he had lost. The patient then proceeded to repeat in play the sequence of the operation several times. His going into the operating room on a stretcher and then coming back to the ward. He played all this out with the help of the doctor and silently.

Third session. When they set the toys up the little doll had disappeared, which made him quite anxious, but finally it appeared. He plays with it, giving it injections in its buttocks. There is verbalization of the pain that he feels with these shots and explanation of what they are for.

He repeats once more the play of cutting the doll's arm off. As he plays this out, the doctor gives factual information about the operation and the fact that the arm is gone forever. The patient touches the stump, saying that they put a dressing on and it hurts. The doctor adds that not only the stump hurts but what he lost as well.

After showing the above, he goes back in a repetitive fashion to the doll, pretending to put a drain tube to the arm, taking the doll to the surgical room where they cut the arm, and so on. As he plays, the doctor furnishes details of what the surgeons did while he was under anesthesia. With this the repetitive play dies down. Unfortunately, he had to have another operation on the stump because an infection would not permit normal healing. He accepts this operation quite well. The children in the ward play with him and he is well accepted by them all.

Fourth session. He greets the doctor, and trying to get down from bed, he slips and almost falls down. He cries, saying he does not want to walk. He again listens to his heart with the stethoscope and the next operation, a plastic one, is explained to him. The session ends with him building a house with little bricks using his left hand and helping himself with his mouth. The therapist also helps him with her hands.

Fifth session. When the therapist arrives Omar is building a large house using the same little bricks and continues while the doctor takes the toys out of the box for him to play. Suddenly he asks, "What's your name?" The therapist answers his question and adds that he is accepting himself without an arm and perhaps this is why he wants to identify her by her name. Up to now she was just "Miss" (this is how the patient used to address the therapist), but in the same way as he now has a new identity he wants to know her own identity. After playing a little while with the toys in front of him he asks for paper and pencil and slowly, with his left hand, writes his name. The therapist is moved by the boy's attempt to overcome his handicap and remarks how pleased she is about it and how he is showing her he can do with his left arm what he used to do with the one he lost. The doctor adds that he has not talked to her about the accident and he goes on to give the details as it was described above.

Sixth session. Omar draws a house, complete, which shows how he is restructuring his body image. Then he writes as a title, "My beautiful school." At this point the mother of another patient next to him who is being discharged comes up to him and kisses Omar goodbye. The therapist remarks to Omar that the hospital is like the beautiful school because here he feels accepted as he is without his right arm and recalls how at the beginning he cried, thinking he was not going to be able to write with his left arm. He announces that he is going to do some sums. First he writes a division and then an addition, but with the sign of subtraction. The therapist remarks that he is going to keep growing but that he will never recover his arm.

Seventh session. The therapist visits Omar following the plastic surgery. After mentioning the pain that afflicted him following the operation, he wonders what he is going to do with the therapist and asks, "Shall I do third-grade sums?" The doctor says this is the third surgical operation that he has undergone and the one that is going to take him out of the hospital too. The therapist suggests that perhaps he is also wondering if he is going to pass to the next grade at school. He says he thinks he will because he got all passing marks, and the session ends by his talking of going to school after his discharge.

A Study of Fantasy Life in Vulnerable Disadvantaged Children

Yvon Gauthier, M.D. (Canada)

In this very wide area of observations made on disadvantaged children, a majority of workers have studied the development of intellectual, cognitive, or language abilities and made comparisons with more advantaged children. In our research work we rather emphasized the fantasy life of 4- to 6-year old children, with the hypothesis that the development and expression of fantasies at that critical period has considerable influence on the approach and experience of formal school learning and that disadvantaged children are particularly vulnerable to learning difficulties, their fantasy-life organization preventing an easy transition to the specific tasks of that situation.

We have described in earlier papers [6–8] the population that we have compared (two groups of 20 children coming from both advantaged and disadvantaged families, attending the same school in metropolitan Montreal), our methodology of observation in nursery school, kindergarten and first grade, and the use of a developmental scale inspired by Anna Freud's [4] concept of developmental lines, more specifically this line of development that goes from body to toy and from play to work. We thus were able from observations of games and various productions to rate the: (1) libidinal organization, that is, the movement from (a) contents focused on the body and its extensions, to (b) preoedipal contents, to (c) contents where male and female tendencies are expressed as well as oedipal situations and (2) ego organization of the child, that is, the movement from the id (very impulsive and badly organized activities) toward the ego (very structured and organized activities). At the end of the 3-year observation we could compare the situations of our two groups and see that the advantaged children as a group are more advanced than the disadvantaged ones at all stages of development, particularly when we note the ego characteristics of their fantasy activity.

Before turning our attention to the specific purpose of this chapter, it might be interesting to look at two figures that permit a visualization of our results, over the 3 years of observation. Figure 1, which illustrates the libidinal organization of our two groups (privileged: $N = 17$; underprivileged: $N = 12$) at ages 4, 5, and 6, strikes us with the fact that group F^1, from age 4 to 5, makes an important step forward (significance, .001), and then almost reaches a level at age 5 to 6, (difference not significant).[2] The degree of maturation between ages 4 and 6 remains, however, very significant at .001. For its part, Group D realized limited but almost constant progress from age 4 to 6. The difference, however, is not significant from one year to the next, but it is so from age 4 to 6, at .001. If we establish a comparison between the two groups, we realize that the difference at age 4 is negligible, but rather it becomes very significant at age 5 ($p < .01$) and remains so at age 6 ($p < .10$).

We were surprised to find that both groups, F and D, had reached sensibly the same level at the time of the first rating, after their first year of nursery school. But we must compare their result with the one reported in a previous paper when both groups had all their members; at the time we observed that the difference between the two groups was quite large. This fact is explained when we look at the ratings of those children who left Group D during kindergarten. Since they all were at the preoedi-

---

[1] F = Privileged group; D = underprivileged group.

[2] It may be possible that our categorizing tool has not been adequate to allow us to give a refined evaluation of the progress accomplished by Group F during the first year of school, which is nevertheless a very rich period of maturation.

pal level, we may be justified to believe that they were among the most underprivileged segment of the group, whose process of maturation was most impaired. The final compilation that had to be done with subjects who had been there *all* 3 years was clearly affected by this change.

If we focus our attention now on the organization of the ego among the children of our two groups, at ages 4, 5, and 6 (Figure 2), it is interesting to notice that among the children of each group in particular the maturation process remains almost stationary from one year to the next and that, from a statistical point of view, it never becomes significant. The situation seems to be that Group F rapidly reaches a very adequate level of ego functioning and then remains at that level, whereas Group D settles itself at an inadequate level of ego functioning and realizes thereafter little progress in that sense. These marks, however, always took the age of the child into account and attempted to compare his actual functioning with an ever-increasing level of ideal functioning. On the other hand, the starting-point mark (at age 4) is much higher

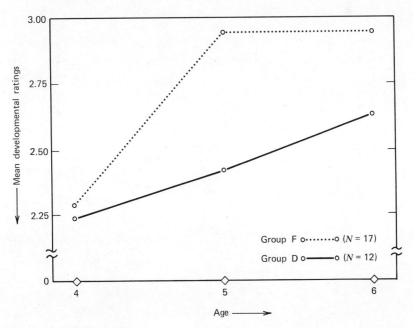

Figure 1 Libidinal organization.

in Group F than in Group D, and that difference reveals a statistical difference of .001. We may assume that the differentiation between the two groups takes place from the start, mostly from the point of view of ego control rather than from the libidinal organization. At ages 5 and 6 the maturation process remains rather stable for both groups, but for each of these periods the difference stays highly significant. This fact reveals that Group F remains, throughout the 3-year period, a better organized group with a more mature structure in its games, activities, and productions than Group D, which even after its 3 years of school, remains a group of often impulsive and poorly organized children.

Fantasy Life of Advantaged Children

Before concentrating our attention on the fantasy life of disadvantaged children, it would be helpful to first summarize some of our conclusions on the development of fantasy life of the advantaged ones.

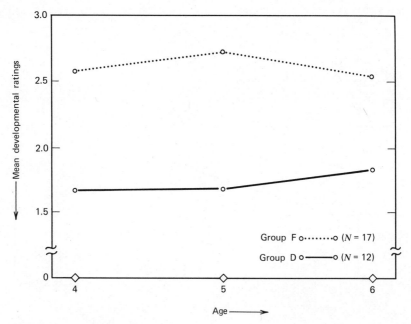

Figure 2   Ego organization.

At age 4 (nursery school), they show very early a very adequate organization of their fantasy life in the predominance of phallic themes; boys demonstrate the importance of being strong and powerful, with the corresponding dangers, while girls naturally illustrate or play out their need to identify to the maternal role; in both we observe indications of involvement in complex family situations.[3]

Their evolution at age 5 continues to be very adequate all through their second year of nursery school. Phallic-oedipal themes are predominant, and the control and organization of their productions strongly indicate the consolidation of ego structure that had already been apparent in the previous year. Themes are varied, and boys and girls clearly show differences in their interests toward the outside world and in their implication in the oedipal situation.

We have been particularly interested in observing the possible changes that occurred after age 5 and before age 7. There is no true solution of continuity in the production of those 2 years. The means the older child uses for the expression of his fantasy life, however, are frequently better organized and show the development of his maturity. Boys continue to organize their fantasy life around competition and fights that often occur in a climate and with instruments of war. Gradually, this whole imagery evolves toward a socialization where sport competition becomes very important. Early scientific knowledge is often used to establish some distance from the dangerous affects that are expressed. Girls also show a continuity of themes in the direction of a deep interest in boys and a happy relationship with them. We frequently encounter in their productions this idealized romantic relationship, which had already been evident during kindergarten.

We have then observed over those 3 years a fantasy life that starts, for most of these advantaged children, at a very adequate level of ego and libidinal organization and gradually evolves and consolidates into a well-organized, structured, varied, and sex-differentiated production where a climate of serenity is most evident. In our observations of the boys we have been impressed by

---

[3] Only drawings spontaneously produced by the children in the class situation were used since they have appeared to us as most revealing of the child's inner life.

this hardly perceptible transition from what could be considered as a dangerous and conflictual phallic situation to the mastery of inside aggression, and then to the gradual control of the outside world through constructions, war, or sportive activities or again through the scientific possessing of menacing elements. The theory of defense mechanisms is abundantly illustrated in this sublimated transformation of aggressive instincts. Our study of girl's productions certainly did not reveal such aggressive contents; as we have been able to see, they are much concerned with an idealized, happy relationship with boys. We may think, with Friend [5], that the decrease of libidinal energies in early latency, at least with boys, could lead to an increase of aggressive energies. In this context learning takes place in a climate of pleasure, and in most cases integration of fantasy and formal learning is easily accomplished.

Fantasy Life of Disadvantaged Children

A very different evolution is observed with disadvantaged children. At the beginning of nursery school (age 4) and for a short time these children first displayed a considerable inhibition in face of the class material. Rapidly, action became the most important instrument of communication of fantasies, which most often did not reach a verbal level of expression. Disorganization of behavior was most frequent, destructive tendencies were often evident; games were sometimes started, but they did not last very long and often led to a complete disorganization of the whole group.

Gradually, however, we noted less disorganization and acting out. The children started building constructions and pursued individual games in which others could be included. They could last longer in the same activities. Expression of their inner life in drawings or paintings became possible, as well as some verbalizations around them. But it was remarkable to note that these plastic productions were much less numerous than in the other group, and even in the better organized children their content was very limited and took much time (until the end of the year) to reach a certain level of organization. Most often these productions revealed to us a primitive, poorly organized perception of the outside world, and their inner life seemed centered around destructive urges, the projection of such destruction onto outside figures, and the image of the preoedipal mother, with its primitive, domineering, and authoritarian characteristics.

It was only late in the year that a good, pleasant image was projected onto the nursery school teacher, who might be beginning to replace and balance the image of the bad mother.

During the second year of nursery school (age 5 to 6) we observed a definite evolution in the fantasy life of these children. Clear indications of the buildings of a positive relationship to the teacher (the same than in the first year) were evident and seemed to be an important element in helping them become more organized and controlled. We noted a marked increase in the number of plastic productions and in the spontaneous verbalizations around them. It became most important for these children to tell a story to the adult around the drawing they had just made, even though there often was no real link of the story to the drawing; the child only needed to be listened to. This marked discordance between a poor development of the form and the appearance of long fantasies that certainly had no evident relation to it, was a frequent observation and suggested to us that verbal abilities and fantasy development seemed to be highly stimulated by this specific activity and somewhat preceded the graphic abilities. Their productions were often centered around the teacher and specially given to her, "It is for you"; "A house for you, you are in the house, you are washing the dishes. You don't see me but I see you." Toward the end of the year we could also observe a better adequacy of the content to the form of the production.

In some of the better organized productions of these children the drawings bring out somewhat late a sense of identification to their house, some interesting expression of the phallic components of the oedipal situation, a striking expression of the ambivalence around growing up, and the wish for security in a stable, working father-mother relationship.

In the production of many of them, however, we were struck by the frequent appearance of early, preoedipal fantasy material, such as the production of early sad feelings about the loss of the mother and the dangers existing within a conflictual relationship with her—with perhaps some hope in resolving the struggle through identification with the mother.

The drawings also expressed the struggle with the preoedipal mother and the attempts to almost take by force from mother the affection one needs and to fight against the father's attempts to make one grow up too fast. But again there was some hope in the final resolution of the plight. In all these drawings no oedipal material, with its characteristic triangular *mise-en-scène,* had been evident as compared with what was seen in the productions of the advantaged children.

On looking at the productions of the children in the first grade (age 6 to 7), this continuity noted in advantaged children, with themes seen in the kindergarten, was even more evident in the production of the disadvantaged children. Conflicts had already started to be solved at the time of kindergarten, for a minority of these children, and their first-grade production already indicated an interesting organization of both inside and outside worlds, as well as interest in—and adaptability to—new tasks.

However, a majority of the productions of the disadvantaged children in the first grade showed an even greater persistence of themes, some of a phallic-oedipal content, but most of them rather poorly solved remnants of earlier periods of maturation. It indicated a fantasy life that was still highly characterized by violence and continuous danger and symbolic images that were frightening because of the pervading aggression and sadness, all at a most primitive level of conflict.

It was a fantasy world still deeply ingrained in the profound conflicts of preceding phases and, specifically, in the web of a pregenital mother-child relationship. If, here and there, signs of calmness suggested an approaching solution to their problems, these were generally precarious, poorly integrated, and soon to be followed by periods of regression. The structuring or defensive role of fantasy in early latency [15] can be readily seen in the privileged child but far less so in the productions of the disadvantaged. One can think of it as a nonprogression, or arrest, or the persistence of a primitive and still very crippling fantasy world rather than a regression.

Vulnerability of Disadvantaged Children

Only late in kindergarten did it seem possible that these children, having progressed in their ego control, might be able to function in a formal learning situation. Our doubts had persisted because of their manifest vulnerability in any unfamiliar situation, especially one requiring still better control of themselves, their fantasies and impulses, and a more focused deployment of their cognitive abilities. On the basis of their improvement it was eventually decided to take the risk of promoting them into the first grade.

The difficulties that such children experience in situations of formal learning have been well documented in numerous publications [3, 14], and our own observations would offer further confirmation. Some authors, like Jensen [10] base their very pessimistic views on compensatory learning on the ceiling imposed by the genetic endowment. In the face of the striking improvement in intellectual functioning in our group over the three years of observation, we would incline more in the direction of the environmental influence in explaining cognitive deficits. Like others [12, 16] we also believe that the usual primary school class situation is not adapted to the specific problems of children like these who have difficulties in verbal communication and often function with a primitive sort of language.

We also believe that an important and much neglected reason for their vulnerability lies in the specific state and development of their fantasy life. At age 4, during the first year of nursery school, action was preferred as the mode of expression of feelings and impulses. Fantasy activity was probably present in such behaviors, but the level of ego differentiation appeared minimal and we were struck by the impulsive characteristics of the few drawings we were able to gather. During kindergarten (age 5 to 6), progress is made, fantasies are beginning to be elaborated, and a structuring influence appears to be at work. Long stories are told by the children, showing an attempt to integrate inner and outer stimuli within the context of a close relationship to the teacher.

We are also struck by the fact that many of these children, at ages 5, 6, and even 7, are still much involved in fantasies of previous developmental levels, indicating a delay in the system of control. Much energy still has to be spent in regressive work or in imaginary fulfillment of early desires. The ego is weak and vulnerable and easily taken over by earlier remnants of a threatening inner life. The findings of Meers [11] in ghetto children with severe ego impediments and a cognitive retardation based on a culture-specific expression of psychopathology are consonant with our observations and results.

The entry into latency becomes a slow and painful process that takes place gradually through this first-grade situation. The tasks usually imposed on them and the demands for conformity to specific rules (so different from the gratifying freedoms and manipulations of nursery school), constitute a difficult new world that reinforces the flight back into a primitive fantasy world, from which they have scarcely taken leave. Our group had the unusual chance of keeping the same teacher throughout the 3 years; with a new teacher, school might have been a still more threatening and regression-provoking place, which is the case in most schools where there is a complete break between nursery school and elementary school.

These observations have several implications for the development of specific resources for such children. Among the several variables that influence the learning situation, the state of development and control of fantasy life appears particularly important, and along with other workers [9, 13, 17], we regret the excessive focus placed with disadvantaged children on cognitive functions and the apparent neglect of the emotional aspects of their development. The role of the teacher in the face of this fantasy life is certainly crucial. The advantaged child builds an important relationship with her, but somehow it does not seem to carry the same affective tone as it does with the disadvantaged. For many of them, fantasy life evokes and revolves around the image of the teacher, through an intensive transferred oedipal relationship that leads to a gradual integration of latency tasks and interests. Through an understanding of the fantasy activity of the child the teacher may be an essential tool in channeling the primitive energy of these childen into more acceptable forms and into more formal learning.

Caldwell and others [1, 2] have come to the conclusion that compensatory education with such children should start very early, in this crucial period of 1 to 3 years. Our observations certainly suggest that there exists severe deficiencies in early mother-child relationships that influence the development of a primitive or fantasy life that continues to be active as late as ages 4, 5, and 6. Such early endeavors appear to us most important, but they are only one link in the immense efforts that should be made at all stages of development, and particularly at this period where fantasy development, social activities, and formal learning do become the daily integrative task of the child's life.

References

1. Caldwell, B. M., Richmond, J. B. The Children's Center in Syracuse, New York. *Early Child Care: The New Perspectives,* L. L. Dittman, Ed. Atherton, New York, 1968, pp. 326–358.
2. Caldwell, B. M. The effects of psychological deprivation on humans in infancy. In *Annual Progress in Child Psychiatry and Development.* Brunner/Mazel, New York, pp. 3–24, 1971.
3. Deutsch, M. *The Disadvantaged Child.* Basic Books, New York, 1967, p. 77.
4. Freud, A. *Normality and Pathology in Childhood. Assessments of Developments.* International Universities Press, New York, 1965.
5. Friend, M. R. The latency period. (Samual Kaplan, reporter). *J. Amer. Psychoan. Assoc.,* 5 (1957), 525–538.
6. Gauthier, Y., Richer, S., Chartier, P., deVisscher, E., Fouchard, D., and Lamy, F. L'Activité fantasmatique d'enfants de 4 ans de milieux favorisé et defavorisé. *Laval Medical,* January (1971a.)
7. Gauthier, Y., Richer, S., Chartier, P., deVisscher, E., Fouchard, D., and Lamy, F., L'Activité fantasmatique d'enfants de 5 ans de milieux favorisé et défavorisé. *Laval Medical,* 42; December (1971b.)
8. Gauthier, Y., Richer, S., Chartier, P., deVisscher, E., Fouchard, D., and Lamy, F., L'Activité fantasmatique d'enfants de milieux favorisé et défavorisé: Evolution de 4 à 6 ans, latence et apprentissage. *Can. Psychiat. Assoc. J.,* 18 (1973), 55–62.
9. Gordon, E.W., Problems in the determination of educability in population with differential characteristics. In: *Disadvantaged Child, Vol. 3, J. Hellmuth, Ed. Brunner/Mazel, New York, pp. 249–267.*
10. Jensen, R. How much can we boost I.Q. and scholastic achievement. *Harvard Ed., Rev.,* 39 (1969), 1–123.

11. Meers, D. P., Psychoanalytic research and intellectual functioning of ghetto-reared black children. *Psychoan. Study Child,* 28 (1973), 395–417.
12. Miller, J. O., An educational imperative and its fallout implications. In *Disadvantaged Child,* Vol. 3, J. Hellmuth, Ed. Brunner/Mazel, New York, 1970, pp. 36–50.
13. Nirk, G. Observations on the relationship of emotional and cognitive development. A psychiatric contribution to compensatory education. *J. Amer. Acad. Child Psychiat.,* 12 (1973), 93–107.
14. Reissman, F. *The Culturally Deprived Child.* Harper & Row, New York, 1962.
15. Sarnoff, C. A. Ego Structure in Latency. *Psychoan. Quart.,* 40 (1971) 387–414.
16. Wilkerson, D. A. Compensatory education: Defining the issues. In *Disadvantaged Child,* Vol. 3, J. Hellmuth, Ed. Brunner/Mazel, New York, 1970, pp. 24–35.
17. Zigler, E. Mental retardation: Current issues and approaches. In *Review of Child Development Research,* Vol. 2, L. W. Hoffman and M. L. Hoffman, Russell Sage Foundation, New York, 1966, pp. 107–168.

Vulnerability to Supernaturalism in Children and Their Parents: A Psychodynamic Appraisal

Jean Livermore Sanville, M.S.S. (U.S.A.)

Around the turn of the century Sir James Frazer [4] wrote, "For ages the army of spirits, once so near, has been receding farther and farther from us, banished by the magic wand of science from hearth and home. . . ." But, said Frazier:

> Far otherwise it is with the savage. To his imagination the world still teems with those motley beings whom a more sober philosophy has discarded. Fairies and goblins, ghosts and demons, still hover about him both waking and sleeping. They dog his footsteps, dazzle his senses, enter into him, harrass and deceive and torment him in a thousand freakish and mischevious ways. . . . Thus it comes about that the endeavour of primitive people to make a clean sweep of all their troubles generally takes the form of a grand hunting out and expulsion of devils and ghosts. They think that if they shake off their accursed tormentors, they will make a fresh start in life, happy and innocent; the tales of Eden and the old poetic golden age will come true again.

Yet today, some 70 years later, it would seem that the army of spirits is returning. Not only are they still haunting the so-called "primitive" world, but they are reluctant to take their departure from rapidly modernizing areas, and tales of their mysterious presences are frequent in the consulting rooms even of our contemporary scientific society. Pattison [9] has spoken of "the widespread renewal of social interest in the supernatural, mystical, magical, and 'irrational' in contemporary western society. . . . The tip of the iceberg of this social revolution of consciousness in our manifest fascination with demonology and exorcism."

Here in the United States, where science has allegedly long banished the spirits, we are currently witnessing an antiintellectual trend. Astrology is widely popular. Patients of all ages see no discrepancy between working in psychotherapy and at the same time religiously scanning the daily newspapers for their horoscopes. ("The fault, dear Brutus, lies . . . in the stars!") Ancient religions have been revived, and many of our young patients engage in meditation or practice vegetarianism on a religious or moral basis. Moreover, there is a new fascination with the devil and with black magic, as is evident by the crowds flocking to the films "The Exorcist" and "Wizards" (advertised as demonstrating the powers of magic over the demons of scientific technology). This chapter attempts to examine the effects of such exposures on susceptible patients already engrossed for psychological reasons in the spiritual world.

CASE 1

"Louise," aged 14 years, was referred by her mother's therapist. It was reported that she was defiant and abusive toward the mother and even came to blows with her at times. This behavior had been exacerbated following a visit to "The Exorcist." She had been frightened by the film and wanted to sleep with her parents the night after seeing it. When they forbade this, she hurled ugly epithets at her mother particularly. In discussing her reasons for hating her mother, she described her as someone who was so deprived by her early background of poverty that she was quite unable to gratify or indulge her material wishes in any way. She hinted at something like a "gnawing interior devil" [3] in the mother since she had systematically undernourished herself to the point of being virtually skin and bones. Her father, however, was somebody that she could manipulate but his frequent indulgence of her wishes incurred the mother's strong disapproval, a fact that added to the gratification. He also encouraged her in her attacks on his wife so that she felt justified in making them.

Prior to seeing "The Exorcist" Louise and a girl friend had played at witchcraft. They had obtained a book from the library purporting to instruct them on how to put a hex on people. For example, they had obtained a hair from a girl whom they disliked and had carefully burned it ritualistically, using candlelight and incantations. They had also tried to work "good magic" on Louise in an effort to improve her grades at school. After seeing "The Exorcist" Louise resolved not to play with magic any more or to talk about the devil, "because if he exists he might punish me." She reported a number of dreams that she associated with "The Exorcist," in one of which she went to see it again with a friend, but this time covered her eyes during the entire performance, as if to say, "I can go through it, yet stop it from entering me." That her own special brand of superstition lurks behind the theme of "The Exorcist" was evident from a later part of the same dream, in which she retreated to "the projection room, which was also like my brother's room, and there, looking out into the hall was a monster rather like a huge pumpkin." This, however, had a Halloween-like aspect and was not so terrifying. Perhaps we can surmise that when there is a father who dilutes the pathology of the mother, the child may find ways to play out fears, ward off those that are too great, and to engage in more overt rebellion. In psychotherapy, Louise was disappointed that the therapist had not yet seen the film and in every hour she would ask her whether she had read the book. Her wish seemed to be for the therapist to be the strong adult who could protect her against the possibility of malignant regression [1]. Although it was early in her treatment, she was already manifesting anxiety over some of her unbridled impulsive behavior.

We see in her play with witchcraft and in her choosing to see "The Exorcist" something of the transitional phenomena, described by Winnicott [14], that was neither "inside" as part of "me" nor "outside" as part of "not me." It appeared to serve the function of mediating between inner and outer. She had an ego strong enough to regulate its own capacity for regression. She could play the witch game or see "The Exorcist" up to the point where it was "too much" and then shut her eyes to it. In her dream she could deal with her own pumpkin apparition. Kris [8] has maintained that one organizing function of ego is its ability to voluntarily and temporarily withdraw cathexis from one area to another, so as to regain improved control later. Thus regression occurs for the sake of progression.

With the younger and more vulnerable child or one with a more fragile ego, this type of "ego exercise" may be less feasible, and the ego can be for a time overwhelmed by exposure to a film such as "The Exorcist." There may not have been sufficient progression for regression to be safe [1].

CASE 2

Sarah, aged 10 years, was an only child whose actress mother took her to see the movie, and it precipitated an acute psychological crisis. The mother claimed that Sarah had always loved scary films and had seen all the Frankenstein ones. In the past she had suffered perhaps a night or two of fears following such exposures, but these had been handled by the mother sleeping with her or the light being left on in the child's bedroom. On the occasion of seeing "The Exorcist" they had left in the middle of the movie; Sarah told the therapist that she had begged her mother to leave earlier, and the mother in turn insisted that it was she who had wanted to leave and the girl who had wished to stay. Following the experience Sarah had become distraught. She had wept hysterically, claiming she was losing her mind, and was inconsolable. She demanded to see a psychotherapist. The mother had had some 4 years of analysis, and the father, from whom the mother was divorced since Sarah was 2½, had also been in psychotherapy, so this was a familiar recourse. (The girl had not seen the end of the film to learn that only a priest could succeed in solving a problem of this sort!)

Sarah brought her mother and father to her first hour and insisted that they tell her story, particularly directing her mother to recall the time when she had · struck her some four years ago, on Christmas day, when Sarah had refused to return home from the house of a friend. It was the first time that she had physically assaulted her daughter, although she acknowledged a chronic bad temper and often took out her bad feelings on Sarah by verbal abuse. Sarah had not known "what got into mother" and had been terrified. Now that she felt herself to be going insane; it was as if "something had got into her." Her father had no temper but did not play with her or spend time with her even when she was at his house.

In her therapy Sarah was disinclined to play and preferred to talk, anxiously, about herself. She spoke of being small for her age and of being picked on and victimized by other children. She had plotted for years to get her mother and father together again, but to her distress her father had married another woman. She visited him every other weekend and often felt frightened while there. Her room was upstairs and when her father and his wife were downstairs with the TV set on, they were not able to hear her. There were noises in her room. She thought of the snake that a friend found under her house. "Snakes can bite and kill you." She worried about death. Her mother's father had died when mother was her age. "But I'm not scared that my father will die," she assured the therapist. Her big pervasive fear was that something would happen to her mother if she were not with her. Someone would break into the house and murder her. She could not sleep because of this concern. After seeing "The Exorcist" she developed fears even of going to school. She found herself unable to think or learn and was sure she was going insane. Her mother's sister had gone insane and was still "in a nut house." "Spirits can make you insane. 'Insane' is when you do things and don't know why, like when Regan (the girl in "The Exorcist") pee-ed on the floor," and like when she "cut herself like this" with the crucifix and blood gushed out (here she demonstrated with gestures, not having a word for masturbation).

Sarah made very much of the mother's not loving her own mother and never seeing her. Her mother had told her that she divorced her husband because she did not love him. One could understand how this child had a special terror about expressing hostility since it could lead to permanent separation; even her autonomous strivings were fraught with danger for they could evoke her mother's uncontrollable rages.

Her mother, in an interview with the therapist, wept guiltily for having "destroyed Sarah's ego." Her rages were so like those of her own mother, whom she had resolved to be unlike. This mother had driven one daughter to suicide and another to an insane asylum. Only the son had escaped. As the youngest of four, she was not herself abused by the mother, but had watched in horror as mother "committed atrocities" on her sisters. She recalled, for example, one scene at the table when her mother forced garbage down the mouth of the sister who is now insane, and "father didn't even intervene!" He was ineffectual while he lived, and he died when she was 9. Her mother had then become even worse, "a Nazi, who relished Hitler's killing of the Jews." When she married a Jew, it was the end of her contact with her mother. Her husband had been a "good" man, of even disposition, but undemonstrative. He always forgot Sarah's birthday, never attended her school events, and was generally not very involved in fatherhood. Yet in her anguish at what she felt to be her own destructiveness, she questioned whether Sarah might not be better off living with her father. She had broached this to the child several times, but Sarah avowed her love for her mother and her wish to be always with her. Weeping, the mother said, "But Betty (the insane sister) loved mother too. Only I did not!"

There were many points of identification that Sarah had with Regan of "The Exorcist"—the actress mother, an affair of the latter with her director, and a father who was mainly absent and whose forgetting of birthdays and such enraged the mother and disappointed Sarah. Her love for her mother was such that it could admit no hostility, for that would jeopardize the dependence she needed. Unlike Louise, she could not permit herself anger at the dangerous mother, for there was no father on whom she could depend for supplies. And so she identified with her mother and with the mother's fears that her daughter would become insane. The spirit of the grandmother, haunting the mother, was the culprit. This spirit would make mother behave in evil ways and would then punish her by giving her a psychotic and possibly suicidal child.

It is not only the "primitive," not only the child, nor only the ignorant or lower-class person who may be intrigued and preoccupied with the supernatural. Let us regard a case involving a family whose house was inhabited by a "malevolent presence." The father in this instance was a professional man and the mother highly intelligent, highly educated, a person who had "dropped out" short of completing her dissertation for a Ph.D.

CASE 3

Alicia's family was referred by the nursery school because their 3½-year-old daughter had recently manifested unusually hostile behavior toward both children and teachers. The director reported that she was unsure whether the mother would follow through, as the latter was inclined to blame the school and to deny any problems in the home. However, she did come and my first impression was of a somewhat paranoid, tense, brittle woman, watchful of my every response. She did indeed blame the teachers, in whose eyes she had observed dislike of Alicia.

She did not deny certain problems at home, however. Her marital relationship was strained, and there had even been a recent "confrontation" about a possible divorce. This had occurred after an episode in which her husband had accused her of getting into his collection of ancient coins. She had been outraged, had burst into a temper, and had thrown eggs at him. Alicia, witnessing this scene, had fled to her room in fright and tears.

In her first therapy session, Alicia got right to her concern by indicating her wish that both her mother and father would join us. During the hour she asked her father point blank, "And will you stay with us?" He agreed to do so. In later hours, she played with clay, and her themes were of dinosaurs who get caught in the tar and die. She could imagine how awful that would be. There was also the theme of poisoned worms, "And if you eat them or touch them, you die." In her transference she was often ingratiating. She would say things like, "You are nice. You have a pretty dress." But then she would add that she could not get over being nervous.

Therapeutic work continued with both mother and child, with the father coming in as often as he could manage. About 2 months after we had begun, the mother came to her session with a degree of embarrassment and told me the following story. One of Alicia's symptoms was that she would get up in the night, and come to her parents' room, wanting to sleep with them. She always expressed a fear of monsters coming up the stairs. The mother said that they lived in a 40-year-old house and that it did indeed have many strange noises. She used to think it was probably just due to cracks from the earthquake. However, they would often hear footsteps mounting the stairs, and on going out would find no one there. She made a point of the fact that her husband had independently observed and reported these phenomena. Her younger brother, who used to babysit for them, refused to babysit any more because of the noises in the house. One day, in broad daylight, the mother had heard the footsteps on the stairs. She went out from her bathroom, and no one was there. Returning to the bathroom, she heard the guitar playing in the child's room. Somewhat angrily she had gone there expecting that Alicia had not stayed down for her nap. Alicia was sound asleep, and the guitar was in place in the closet. However, she felt "a malevolent presence" in the room. She called in a friend, an expert on the occult, and the friend went into Alicia's room. While she was there, Alicia, who was out in the yard playing, let out a bloodcurdling, "inhuman scream." Later she could not say why she had done that. When the mother's friend emerged from the room she was shaken and white, and said that indeed there was a malevolent presence. When she had gone into the closet with the guitar, she had begun speaking in tongues. She recommended that the family call a certain minister. This man came and affirmed the friend's diagnosis. An exorcism took place. The minister came with his Bible, read certain passages, made specific incantations, sprinkled holy water about, and kept admonishing the evil spirit that this was a Christian house in which he would not be permitted to remain. Finally, the minister erected "a ring of guardian spirits" around the property. On finding out that the father had once been Catholic and she Protestant, he asked this couple if they would go for a while to his Fundamentalist Church, and they readily agreed. It was also recommended that they remove all pre-Columbian art from the house. Moreover, the mother was to burn in the barbeque a certain witch doll that Alicia had cherished. She declared that while the doll was burning the barbeque table moved, and that it was not only she who saw this.

The mother reported that all had been well since the exorcism. She expressed her conviction that there had been in all probability two presences, warring over the soul of Alicia, one to make it evil and one to keep it good. At the end of her story she looked at me sharply and demanded to know what I thought. I simply shrugged, feeling that rationality was no solution here. Had I ever heard of such things, she wanted to know. I replied in the affirmative. "From sane people?", she demanded, thus indicating some uneasiness in her "solution." A few weeks after this she ceased treatment, claiming that everything was better. Alicia was sleeping through the night and was no longer so hostile. Moreover, therapy was a financial burden. Several months later she returned with a new array of problems. She expressed frustration with the sexual impotence of her husband, unhappiness at her own confinement to home and children, irritation with Alicia, fear that her irritation with the child was going to harm her, and a concern that she was becoming alcoholic. She was counting on her husband's greater gentleness with Alicia, but also feeling tied to him on this account.

This time she was more ready for real work, having tested me in that initial period and having found me unwilling to label her psychotic. She proceeded to put forth more of herself. Whereas in the first period of treatment she had concealed from me her intense interest and preoccupation with ancient religions and the occult, she now explored these at length together with her many experiences with extrasensory perception, her conversations with a dead grandmother and the friendship with her "witch" friend, whom the minister had advised her not to see. She restored to the house her pre-Columbian art. But then, in October—the second anniversary of the strange events—she had the uneasy feeling that "it was happening" again. The footsteps on the stairs were heard repeatedly. She and her husband had returned after a night out and, smelling smoke, had rushed to Alicia's room to find that the carpet was afire under the child's bed. Alicia had been playing house there and had left a lighted bulb against inflammable materials. This was, said the mother, the kind of behavior that would be promoted by a malevolent being. This time, in the context of a more secure working relationship, the therapist gave her several responses to her question, "What do you think?" She was willing, tentatively, to entertain alternative hypothesis that a fire might result simply from a child's thoughtless play with a light bulb. However, the mother persisted with her own idea, telling me that she had had a dream that she regarded as prophetic and sent by an evil being. In the dream, she was in a bank and saw a man trying to assault Alicia. Alicia did not know what was happening. She rescued her daughter and asked the bank teller the man's name, only to learn that it was "Derek" (a Scandinavian word for knife). Mother was not closed to the gentle suggestion that we could look at her dream in a way other than as prophesying that something evil would happen to her child. The therapist's approach was consistently to interpret the reparative inclination along with the destructive impulse. In this instance she could accept the notion that the hostility of the "Derek" in the dream could be her own but that the wish to save the child and the actual rescue were also hers as well. In other words, the "two presences warring over the soul of Alicia" might both be within her.

This led into a period of intensive work on herself, involving exploration of consequences of her having had a singularly destructive father and a passive, masochistic mother. The mother had become alcoholic, just as the patient was fearing for herself. Rejecting an identification with such a downtrodden mother, she had become in her early years super ambitious. She was a straight-A student, scholarly and puritanical. Just short of her Ph.D. she had "dropped out" to marry her husband precisely because she sensed that she was "too one-sided" and "too rigid." It would appear that then too she permitted herself a degree of regression, that is, being taken care of by a "good father," which she sees her husband to be. She accomplished some repair in that phase but she was increasingly perceiving her husband as sexually and socially inadequate. Her gratitude to him for having been a good source and having provided an ambiance in which she could function made her feel too guilty to contemplate leaving him.

In the last few months she referred her younger brother for a consultation. At 16, he was already alcoholic, but now there was also an acute crisis. The parents, with whom he had been living had finally separated, and "demons had got into him." Suddenly he was behaving with utmost destructiveness to his mother. He was seen just following an episode that terrified him because he found himself acting with mother exactly as his hated father had, actually striking her. He felt invaded by his father, "spooked," and feared he was "going bananas." Classically, the lost object was now felt to be within the self, there was an urgent need to project it onto the mother, to reexternalize this evil.

This three-generational data may permit some speculation about one type of demonic possession in today's world and about its dissolution with the help of psychotherapy. The mother had a patriarchal and malicious father and a pathetic, though benign, mother. She internalized father as a powerful, evil spirit and mother as a good but weak spirit. These two introjects could not fuse, but warred within her. She selected as husband a "tamed" father-figure, and this enabled her to grapple with her still deeper ambivalence toward her mother. Her husband provided her with glimpses of positive, peaceful parenting. When she herself became a mother, the "bad spirit" of her mother erupted within her. In the nursery school the negative aspects of her feelings toward her daughter were projected onto the teacher, in her dreams onto murderous men, and in her fantasies onto malevolent beings. When the school recommended psychological help, she had first to test the therapist to find both the strength of the father and the benign qualities of the mother comfortably fused. When the test was passed, she felt ready to modernize her search for spiritual exorcism, this time through the processes of analytic psychotherapy. Currently, she is shaking off her "accursed tormentors" and is making a fresh start that even Frazer could not forsee—namely, she is becoming that new breed of liberated woman who unites in herself both strong and benign qualities. She has embarked on a satisfying career while carefully attending to the needs of her husband and daughter. She is dealing flexibly with the remnants of her evil spirits.

Just as the mother had felt her child to be endangered by the bad spirit within her, so Alicia herself felt that danger. She had clung to the father's presence as a protection from the witch mother. She had feared that both she and the father could be inundated and swallowed up (the phallic dinosaurs engulfed in mother earth), or poisoned by the "biting tongue" of the snake (the phallic mother). Her newly exorcised mother enabled Alicia to pass more quickly through the heritage of evil spirits.

One way of coping with the evil within is to project it out again onto convenient human objects or onto evil spirits. However, the question still remains as to why a "modern" person needs to conjure up that invisible malicious presence and why other less archaic projections are inadequate. We may not have the answers as yet, but such episodes clearly represent a deeper regression. Perhaps this woman's absorption in primitive religions lent form to her torment. In any event, it would seem that a more powerful father, God himself, was required, so huge was her measure of the evil that lurked within. In the course of therapy the mother progressed from recourse to magical thinking, to religious faith, and finally to an ability to use psychological healing. She could utilize creative interpretation to transform primary process into poetic metaphor [2, 10, 11].

Summary and Conclusions

At this point I think it is appropriate to quote Freud: "The states of possession correspond to our neuroses . . . the demons are bad and reprehensible wishes."

I have been describing a mode of repetition compulsion extant today, in which "civilized" peoples are involved in certain recapitulations both ontogenetically and phylogenetically. We observe regressions not only to those phases of individual life in which magical thinking prevailed, but to those stages in the evolution of human society in which magic and faith are used to overcome the evil spirits. To the extent that this regression is a cultural phenomenon it would seem to be made possible precisely by the "progress" we have attained [1]. The descent can be safe only when the "sense of that height clings [13]."

Clinically, we ask to what extent for each patient can the regression be benign. My data suggest that children in intact families, whose parents have a "good enough" relationship, may utilize play, fantasies, and dreams and even exposure to scary films such as "The Exorcist" to good advantage. They experience a sense of choice in this, deliberately confronting the fearful so as to master it. When there is even one strong and benevolent and protective parent, the prognosis tends to be favorable for a separation from the witch mother or the witch father, as the case may be. The child must be capable of some hostility toward the "bad" parent or the "bad" aspects of the parent if he is to "place the object outside the self" as Winnicott [14] has pointed out; such destructiveness plays a part in developing a reality sense. For this to happen, however, "the object" must fulfill two conditions; he or she must not retaliate and must survive. The children whom I have described as suffering the most jeopardy to their sense of reality were those who dared not be hostile lest they invoke the retaliative wrath of a parent or be abandoned by that parent altogether.

These are sobering considerations in a society in which there are more and more single-parent families. Women alone with responsibilities for supporting and caring for young children are quite likely to feel deprived of good sources, and unprotected in their own functioning. It is easy for them to reexperience that maternal deprivation that Freud [6] has suggested we all feel to some extent, and for oral rage to be a common response to demands on a felt scarcity of supply. In day-care centers for children of working mothers one became familiar with the frequent complaints that mothers are forever screaming and scolding, even when not actually physically abusive. But battering too appears on the increase, and the phenomena described herein are pertinent to that.

It is not being suggested that it is only, or even mainly, single parents who abuse children psychologically or physically. Women who are beginning to experience their wife-mother roles as inferior may go through a phase of neglecting or rejecting their offspring as veritable jailers. However, as they move forth and find satisfactions in their own functioning they become even better mothers, not needing to take out their resentments on their children.

There are implications, however, for society in this transitional period. There must be readily available good child care centers to supplement the family. We do know enough about the mental health needs of children so that we can—with adequate financial support—provide centers to assure that such needs be met [7].

What can we, as clinicians, learn from the "regressive" phenomena of the invasion of the spirits into our "scientific" consulting rooms? It is that in our efforts to make psychotherapy a "science" we have gone astray and created metaphors that are singularly inept. We speak of "object-relationships" and of internalized "objects." Now an object is, by definition, something tangible, visible, or stable in form. It is a person mainly with reference to the impression made on the mind or feeling of the observer. Perhaps we can speak of a person as an object toward whom we direct thought or action, but we do not take him or her inside of us. What we introject is not even a substance, which would still be matter or material, although some analysts [1] have suggested this as a better term. What we introject is in fact "spirit," a vital principle, incorporeal, of a particular character—"good" or "bad." As the word comes from *spinare,* the Latin verb "to breathe," both literally and figuratively it would seem to symbolize better what we endeavor to connote. The infant's first oxygen supply is through the umbilical cord, and much of what it "takes in" after birth from the mother is by way of words and actions that entail breathing of different qualities depending on whether, for example, the mother is elated or depressed, her "spirits" high or low. Neither the breast (an object) or the milk (a substance) can be perceived as good if the mother's pervasive attitude (spirit) is negative.

When the tormented mothers described here discover that they have been goaded to actions that they regret, it is by spirits, essences emanating from "bad" internalized aspects of an original parent, insufficiently countered by "good" internalized aspects. The frightened children are correct in perceiving that "something has gotten into them" and that they need a good spirit to battle the scary one. Both parent and child do need exorcism, and if we are to practice that, we have something to learn from the "primitives."

References

1. Balint, M., Progression for the sake of regression. In *Thrills and Regressions* International Universities Press, New York, 1959, pp. xxx.
2. Caruth, E. and Ekstein, R. Interpretation within the metaphor: further considerations. *J. Child Psychiat.,* 53 (1972) 531–539.
3. Erikson, E. *Young Man Luther.* Norton, New York, 1958, p. 244.
4. Frazer, Sir James George. *The Golden Bough* (abridged ed.). Macmillan, New York, 1951.
5. Freud, S. (1922). *A 17th Century Demonological Neurosis. Standard Edition,* Vol. 22. Hogarth Press, London, 1964.
6. Freud, S. (1932). *Femininity. Standard Edition,* Vol. 22. Hogarth Press, London, 1964.
7. Heinicke, C. The organization of day care: considerations relating to the mental health needs of child and family. *Amer. J. Orthopsychiat.,* 43:1 (1973), 8–22.
8. Kris, E. On preconscious mental processes. In *Organization and Pathology of Thought,* Columbia Univ. Press, New York, 1951. Ed. D. Rapaport 474–93.
9. Pattison, E. M. Psychosocial interpretation of exorcism. *J. Operat. Psychiat.,* 8:2 (1977). Pp. 5–21.
10. Reider, N. Metaphor as interpretation. *Internat. J. Psychoan.,* 53 (1972), 463–469.

11. Roland, A. Imagery and symbolic expression in dreams and art. *Internat. J. Psychoan.*, 53 (1972), 531–539.
12. Shor, J. Two principles of reparative regression: Self-traumatization and self-provocation. *Psychoan. Rev.*, 59 (1972), 259–281.
13. Stanford, A. *The Descent.* Viking Press, New York, 1970.
14. Winnicott, D. W. *Playing and Reality.* Basic Books, New York, 1971.

THE VULNERABLE INFANT

Differential Vulnerability and Coping in Boys and Girls at Birth

Justin D. Call, M.D. (U.S.A.)

Introduction

The study of the human newborn infant is undergoing a resurgence and offers a new hope to students of behavior in providing clues to the solution of the ever-recurring puzzle of interacting inherited and environmental variables in normal and deviant development. This is not the first such resurgence of interest, nor is it likely to be the last, considering man's preoccupations about his origins. The current chapter of those engaging in pursuit of baby-watching follows a great tradition. Our great-great-grandfather was Charles Darwin, who in 1877 published a paper entitled "Biographical sketch of an infant [22]." Like his trip on the Beagle, Darwin kept a daily diary on the development of his first-born son, summarizing his observations from birth to age 2 years, 7½ months. His thought was that through such observation one might gain some understanding of the development of expressions in man [21]. It is interesting historically that these observations on his son were made in the years 1840 to 1842, during which time he was also writing up his now famous voyage that so unsettled the world.

Each newly discovered functional capacity or deviation in the young infant's behavior raises basic questions concerning its origin, whether it is: (1) the infant's orientation, attachment and social responsiveness to the mother, (2) the capacity for discrimination, learning, problem-solving, and language function, or (3) the adaptive responses to change in the external and internal environment subsumed under the term "ego" or the psychic change underpinning the development of psychopathology, such as the development of anxiety, depression, inner conflict, or defense mechanisms.

Freud said in 1905 [26] that "The direct observation of children has the disadvantage of working upon data which are easily misunderstandable; psychoanalysis is made difficult by the fact that it can only reach its data, as well as its conclusions, after long detours. But cooperation by the two methods can attain a satisfactory degree of certainty in their findings . . ."

The focus of this congress is on the vulnerable child. I present some observations on normal infants over the first four days of life, focusing specifically on sex differences observed in response to breast and bottle feeding. The increased vulnerability of males to various physical, psychological, and learning difficulties and certain differences in the mental abilities and skills between the sexes already well documented in the literature are viewed within a psychoanalytic and psychobiological theory of early development suggested by these and other studies of infant development.

Aims of the Study

The specific focus of this study was to assess the influence of interacting experiential and constitutional variables in the earliest phases of postnatal development, that is, to observe the effect of feeding on patterns of arousal and activity in boys as contrasted with girls during the first 4 days of life, to determine the relative significance of the sex variables in relation to other variables on the behavior chosen for study.

Selection of Variables

It was decided to identify some biologically available movement patterns and reflexes in boys and girls and to study the effects of feeding upon these behaviors. Hand-face contacting was selected because: (1) this behavior is often interpreted as indicating hunger, (2) it has been studied quantitatively by others, [37], (3) it is quantifiable at birth, and (4) movements of the hand toward the face and mouth are a part of one of the earliest identifiable ego functions, the eye-hand-mouth unit of functioning described by Hoffer [38].

In preliminary work reported by Constas and Call [20] it has been shown that sex differences in intensities of hand-face contacts to the snout and parasnout areas could be ascertained and might be present and that it might also be worthwhile to control for right, center, and left head position. Analysis of data for the first ten cases of the present study confirmed the earlier finding [16, 60].

If it could be shown with a larger sample and better control of variables that differences in the frequency and location of hand-face contacts do exist between boys and girls, one could infer a basic variation in congenitally available ego equipment.

Three reflex activities were selected for study—rooting, the hand-mouth reflex, and sucking. Rooting was selected because it is one of the means by which the infant makes its earliest orientation and anchorage to an object [17]. Also, it has been shown in previous studies that certain aspects of rooting behavior may become exaggerated by preferential stimulation to specific components of rooting by the mother. This, together with the way the mother holds the infant, the way she establishes visual, auditory, and kinesthetic reciprocity with her infant as shown in feeding, care, and play, constitutes her style [18]. Rooting activity is utilized in establishing the earliest anticipatory functions that the infant can make to the environment [15]. Benjamin and Tennes [8] have shown that pathological head nodding in infancy may be derived from patterns of rooting stimuli offered by the mother. Spitz [55] has shown that rooting behavior underlies the first semantic "no" and "yes." Rooting, of course, has great significance because of its biological ubiquity in other mammals. Intensity of rooting to standard stimuli can also be quantified.

The hand-mouth reflex, first discovered by Babkin [3], consists of the infant's opening his mouth, sometimes protruding the tongue, and turning his head to the midline when both palms are pressed firmly by the examiner's thumbs. It also is quantifiable. It reflects the basic neurological integration of hand and mouth functions. Also, it occurs in other mammals and reminds us that hand and mouth functions are not far apart biologically and psychologically.

Sucking was utilized as a reflexive activity for study because its survival value and psychological significance has been studied and written about for decades. Freud [26] specifically designated sucking as one aspect of oral drive. A most interesting and important theoretical question presents itself for study, specifically, whether the behaviors that the mother usually interprets as indicating hunger—such as crying, sucking, increased activity, hand-face contacting and more intense rooting activity, a manifestation of hunger and/or oral drive—at first simply reflect an increase of non-specific general physiological arousal and only later become organized as part of the signal-response system between mother and infant in relation to hunger and oral drive as a result of early learning. If so, what is the nature of that learning process and how does it evolve from the basic physiology?

Recent studies [51, 62] have called attention to nonnutritive sucking in quite a different context, namely, as a manifestation of underlying CNS microrhythms. Reuben Kron [40, 41] in Philadelphia, has reported some elegant studies on individual differences in sucking behavior of infants and also has demonstrated the operant aspect of sucking behavior in learning during the early days of life. Thus these behaviors, observable in the newborn, provide focus for lively discussion among infant psychiatrists, psychoanalysts, and psychologists interested in learning.

In my opinion the infant's level of sleep and wakefulness defined as the "state variable" has proved to be, in all of the recent studies of infant behavior, much of the recurrent hope for bringing greater order into the data derived from newborn observation. This is because, when the state variable is controlled, some consistency of results in terms of spontaneous behavior and responsiveness of the infant to stimuli became possible. Thus the infant's spontaneous behavioral response to stimulation must be qualified with respect to the state of arousal at the time of observation. The state variable may be utilized as either an independent or dependent variable. I think it is methodologically important and historically interesting that the various subclassifications within the wakeful state were made possible when Peter Wolff [61] and others defined one such state within this continuum, namely, alert inactivity. The subclassifications of sleep were made possible by the fact that one such state, namely, rapid eye-movement (REM) sleep in infancy was defined by Roffwarg, Dement, et al. [50]. This made it easier to define a whole continuum of sleep states. Thus by defining one specific state within each of the general categories of sleep or awake it has been possible to define more clearly an entire series of states. The series presented in this study and found most useful in considering the infant's spontaneous behaviors is by no means the only suitable classification and it is by no means "complete."

The choice of feeding variables (breast vs. bottle) allows us to evaluate the effects of calories on behavior because the bottle-fed infant receives significantly more calories during the first 4 days.

Methods

The sample of infants studied consisted of four major groups: 10 exclusively breast-fed boys (Group I), 12 bottle-fed boys (Group II), eight exclusively breast-fed girls (Group III), and nine bottle-fed girls (Group IV). Each subject was selected within 7 hours of birth according to the following criteria:

1. A medically uncomplicated pregnancy and delivery.
2. An Apgar rating of 7 or above at 3 minutes.
3. A minimum of analgesia and sedation during labor.
4. A healthy, neurologically intact infant.
5. Permission of parents and attending physician to make the study.
6. Birth at a time when observation schedule permitted new cases.

The composition of the experimental groups can be summarized as follows:

1. The average age of the mothers was 24 for both breast- and bottle-fed boys and 25 for both breast- and bottle-fed girls.
2. One out of 10 breast-fed boys was a first child, three out of 12 bottle-fed boys were a first child, three out of eight

breast-fed girls were a first child, and two out of nine bottle-fed girls were a first child.

3. One male bottle-fed child was admitted to the study even though his mother had had a convulsive disorder and was on Dilantin. His Apgar score was 10 at birth, and he showed no evident depressive reactions. Another male bottle-fed child was admitted to the study whose mother had undergone surgery for a bowel obstruction secondary to regional ileitis in the 5th month of pregnancy. This child was also normal at birth, with an Apgar score of 8. One breast-fed boy was admitted to the study whose mother had a umbilical herniorrhaphy in the 6th month of pregnancy. This child was obviously well at birth also. One breast-fed girl was admitted to the study whose mother had migraine headaches. Otherwise, the maternal health record of the mothers before and during pregnancy was excellent. None of the mothers had a history of bleeding during pregnancy.

4. The average gestational age of the sample was 40 weeks, with no more than $\frac{1}{2}$ week variation between groups.

5. Fortunately for this and other studies, very little medication was given to the mother during labor on the Obstetrical Service of the UCLA Center for Health Sciences. One-third of the group in this study received as much as 73 to 100 mg of Demoral or Visterol no more than one hour before delivery. This was equally distributed among the breast- and bottle-fed boys and the bottle-fed girls. None of the breast-fed girls received this much medication. About half of the total sample received no medication whatever other than local anesthetics to the perineal, cervical, spinal, and caudal areas.

6. The socioeconomic status of patients in the various groups could be determined on the basis of them being UCLA clinic cases, county welfare cases, and private patients. A few more private patients were found in both the male and female breast-fed groups than in the bottle-fed groups. Otherwise the distribution of social classes was equal in each of the groups.

7. The smallest infant admitted to study, a bottle-fed girl,

weighed 2600 g, and the largest was a breast-fed boy weighing 4100 g. The average weight of all the boys was 3450 g, while that of the girls was 3160 g. There were no significant variations in the distribution of birth weight or the average of birth weight in the breast- and bottle-fed girls.

8. Most of the Apgar scores were in the 9–10 range. One breast-fed boy with an Apgar score of 7 was accepted for study because this boy appeared to be active and alert 5 minutes after birth. Two of the bottle-fed boys, one of the breast-fed girls, and three of the bottle-fed girls had Apgar scores of 8. The remainder of the sample had Apgar scores of 9 or 10.

Thus the four groups of infants did not vary from each other with respect to maternal (24–25 years) age, parity, maternal health during pregnancy, medication received during labor, gestational age, or Apgar score (7–10). The girls in general were 300 g lighter than the boys, and both male and female breast-fed infants showed a slightly greater number of infants coming from higher socioeconomic levels.

STATE CLASSIFICATION

Medical students utilized as research assistants were trained to identify and time the spontaneous occurrence of each of the states of arousal as follows:

1. Regular sleep. This refers to quiet sleep, respirations regular, eyes closed, minimal activity.
2. Irregular sleep. Eyes closed, REM not observed, lid movements may be present, respirations irregular, moderate activity present.
3. Rapid eye movement sleep. Sleep with REM observed under the eyelids. Other facial and bodily activities are usually present.
4. Drowsy. In this state the eyes are opening and closing. The infant may be yawning or the eyes may be rolling about without obviously looking at anything with eyelids open. Rapid eye movements are not present.
5. Awake attentive. The eyes are open and can fix on an object

and follow its movements. There is a glistening quality to the conjunctivae. There may be some general activity of low intensity.

6. Awake and active without crying. The eyes are open and not fixed. The infant is moving about but not crying.
7. Whimpering.
8. Good cry.

Students were also trained to identify and record hand-face contacts. Three head positions were distinguished, right when the head was turned more than 45 degrees to the right, left when the head was turned more than 45 degrees to the left, and center when the head was in the midline or less than 45 degrees in either direction. All hand-face contacts were recorded with respect to right or left hand used and whether the contact was to the snout or parasnout area. The snout area of the face was defined as the area of the face bounded by an imaginary line connecting the tip of the nose, the nasolabial folds and the midchin. All other areas of the face and head were designated as the parasnout area. When the infant's hand made contact with any part of the face, this was designated as one contact. The next contact would not be counted until the infant's hand left the prior contact area and recontacted the face. The duration of each contact was not studied. Often when the infant contacts the snout area with the hand, sucking activity can be observed. The number of sucks in such circumstances was recorded. These data were all recorded on an Esterline Angus Recorder proceeding at a constant rate so that intensities and location of hand-face contacting before and after feeding with each given state and head position could be measured.

ROOTING RESPONSE

Observers were also trained to test and rate sucking, hand-mouth, and rooting reflexes as follows:

1. Stimulus. The bare index finger lightly placed at the corner of the mouth when the infant is not mouthing spontaneously or making hand-mouth contacts. The finger is held steadily if head moves.
2. Response ratings. This was graded as follows:

0 No response to stimulus
1 Slight opening of mouth
2 Moderate opening of mouth
3 Wide opening of mouth
   Tighter closing of mouth

Other aspects of response such as movement of the head to midline, tonguing, and other mouthing movements may occur, but rating was based only on the above-listed criteria.

Sucking was tested by placing the gloved, small finger of the observer in the center of the infant's two lips and then into the mouth itself as the lips opened. The number of sucks in each series or burst of sucking was recorded over a 1-minute period. Data on sucking are analyzed with regard to the total number of sucks, the number of sucking bursts, average number of sucks per burst, and burst with the most sucks in the 1-minute period.

Interrater reliability was studied using two simultaneous Esterline Angus recordings, one for each observer. Ninety percent or greater agreement was obtained on all measures following the training period. Ninety-five or higher percent of agreement was obtained on the rating of rooting, hand-mouth, and sucking reflexes.

Procedure

The first prefeeding observation was made when the infant was about 8 hours of age, always before 12 hours of age, and prior to any feeding whatsoever. The clothed infant (shirt and diapers) was placed gently on his back in his basinet such that his arms were free. Noise, light, and temperature level were recorded. The infant's head position, changes in head position, and hand-face contacts were recorded during each 20-minute period of observation, using the Esterline Angus Recorder at the cribside. The baby's rooting, sucking, and hand-mouth reflexes were then tested three times, separated by an interval of at least 1 minute. The infant was given distilled water by the nurse on the first feeding. At the termination of feeding the infant was again observed supine in his crib for a period of 20 minutes, as noted above. Reflexes were tested as before the 20-minute period of observation and again tested after the 20-minute period of observation, first without outside stimulation and then with artificial stimulation if the infant was asleep.[1] The same series of observations was repeated on day 2 after birth, except that the infant was given to the mother to feed on the days 3 and 4. Ten infants were born during July and August of 1964, 14 in July and August of 1965, and 15 in July and August of 1966. Most of the infants were born between midnight and noon and most of the observations were made during the morning and afternoon hours, a few in the early evening.

Variables quantified in the observational setting were as follows:

1. The average age in hours for each of the observations on each of the 4 days of life at the time of the prefeeding run did not vary significantly from one group to the other. The first observation occurred on the average at 7 hours of age and was followed 26 hours later at 33 hours of age for the second observation. The third observation followed the second by 21 hours and took place at 54 hours of age, and the fourth observation followed the third by 22 hours, taking place at age 78 hours.
2. The number of hours since the last feeding prior to the one observed was 4 on the second, third, and fourth observations. This did not vary between the breast- and bottle-fed male and female groups.
3. The environmental temperature varied from 77 to 81 degrees during the first three observations for all of the groups, with overall average of 80 degrees. The average was 77 degrees for the fourth observation. This lower figure for the fourth observation was probably related to the fact that almost all fourth observations for all of the infants in each of the groups were made in the home rather than the hospital.
4. Light conditions did not vary between the groups for the first three observations, averaging 14-ft candles. On the

---

[1] Methods of stimulating the infants included noise, moving legs and arms, and gently stroking chest and body. Stimulation was used only when infant was in lower state of arousal than when reflexes were tested immediately after feeding.

fourth observation the average was 17.5-ft candles (at home).

5. The noise level in the environment was likewise fairly uniform for the four observations and for all the groups. The lowest noise level was 37 decibels, and the highest noise level average was 53 decibels, with an overall average for all four observations in all groups of 46 decibels.

6. Total time with the mother averaged 21 minutes for the first observation, 39 minutes for the second, 26 for the third, and 23 for the fourth. Breast-fed girls spent slightly more (not statistically significant) time with the mother than bottle-fed girls, but this difference was not present with breast-fed boys.

7. Actual time spent nursing at the breast or bottle was 25 minutes for all four groups on day 1 and varied according to whether the infant was breast- or bottle-fed on days 2 and 3, with breast-fed infants spending about half the time nursing that bottle-fed infants spent (i.e., 10 minutes as contrasted to 15 or 20 minutes). On day 4, however, breast- and bottle-fed infants spent about the same amount of time actually nursing (15 minutes).

8. The actual amount of formula taken varied with sex in the following way: 20 cc for both sexes on day 1, 37 cc for both sexes on day 2, 47 cc for boys and 41 cc for girls on day 3, and 63 cc for boys and 60 cc for girls on day 4. In contrast, breast-fed infants obtain about 2 cc on day 2, 44 cc on day 3, and 20 cc on day 4 (per feeding) [24].

In summary, the environmental variables did not differ significantly between the four study groups with respect to temperature, light, noise, and location of the observation. The environmental temperature in the infant's home was on the average 3 degrees lower than in the hospital when the observation was made on day 4. Breast-fed boys and girls spent about half as much time actually nursing on days 2 and 3 than did bottle-fed boys and girls. Breast-fed infants obtained far less milk than bottle-fed infants.

The actual holding style, play, hand-to-hand contact, visual attentiveness was filmed at the home visit on day 4 and has been the subject of a separate paper.

Results

As shown in Figure 1 (percent time in each state), about 50 percent of the time is spent in various sleep states (S1, S2, and S3), 8 percent in state "drowsy" (S4), approximately 20 percent in "awake-attentive" (S5) and "awake-active" (S6), and another 20 percent of the time spent either whimpering (S7) or crying (S8). Henceforth in reporting results each state is designated as S1, S2, S3, and so on. If the entire sample is combined for all 4 days, it is seen that there is an increase in S2, S3, and S5 and a decrease in S7 and S8 after feeding. These differences are not great and, as will be shown later, vary considerably with each group.

As shown in Figure 2, the percent time spent in S1 through S8 was charted for each day for all 39 infants. Sleep states, S1, S2, and S3, all decrease over the 4 days; drowsy, S4, stays about the same, and awake states, S5, S6, S7, and S8, all increase; thus the infant progresses to a more wakeful state during the first 4 days of life.

Figure 3 shows the effect of breast and bottle feeding on the percent of total time spent in S1 plus S2 plus S3 in boys and girls before and after feeding for each of the 4 days. Both boys and girls who are bottle-fed increase the amount of time spent asleep after feeding on each of the 4 days. The effect of breast feeding is not uniform. Breast-fed boys spend less time asleep after feeding on days 2 and 3 and more time asleep after feeding on day 4, whereas breast-fed girls spend about the same amount of time asleep after feeding on day 2 and slightly more time asleep after breast feeding on days 3 and 4. It is obvious that caloric intake profoundly influences behavior during each of the first 4 days of life.

In Figure 4 it can be observed again that breast-fed girls tend to shift away from awake states (S5 + S6 + S7 + S8) after feeding on day 3, whereas breast-fed boys do not shift away from awake states after feeding until day 4. Bottle-fed boys and girls shift consistently away from awake to sleep states on all 4 days. The amount of shift to awake states is greater in breast-fed boys than in breast-fed girls, and the amount of shift away from awake states is much greater in bottle-fed girls than in bottle-fed boys. Caloric requirements for sleep would appear to be less for girls than boys.

State*	Total	Prefeeding	Postfeeding
1	6	6	7
2	30	26	33
3	15	13	17
4	8	9	7
5	13	10	15
6	7	7	6
7	9	11	8
8	11	18	8
	99	100	101

Figure 1 Percent time in each state — 39 infants (data for days 1, 2, 3, 4 combined). State 1 — regular sleep, state 2 — irregular sleep, state 3 — REM sleep, state 4 — drowsy, state 5 — awake and visually attentive, state 6 — awake active, not visually attentive, state 7 — soft crying, state 8 — loud crying.

Figure 5 shows that breast-fed girls spend more of their awake time in S5 on days 3 and 4 before and after feeding than do boys. A study of the average duration of time which an infant spent in a given state once having gotten there was also made. This can be referred to as "average time in state." No significant sex differences were observed for average time in states 1, 3, 4, 5, 6, 7, and 8 when other appropriate variables (breast vs. bottle, days 1, 2, 3, 4, pre- and post-feeding) were controlled. Bottle-fed girls spent a higher average time in state 2 than did bottle-fed boys. Breast-fed boys showed a higher average time in S2 than breast-fed girls, both before and after feeding. The average duration of time in S3 (30 to 90 seconds) shows S3 to be the most consistent of all states. It is not influenced by sex, type of feeding or day of life.

Figure 6 shows increased duration of crying episodes over the 4 days and increased duration of crying episodes on each of the 4 days after feeding. Sex and type of feeding differences were not remarkable. Differences in duration of crying over the first 4 days may have been due to changes in physiological adjustment after birth. The longer duration of crying episodes after feeding on all 4 days is compatible with the notion that increased energy from feeding may have made it possible for the infant to sustain crying for longer periods.

Exclusively breast-fed infants generally receive very few calories during the first 2 days of life. On day 3, breast-fed infants

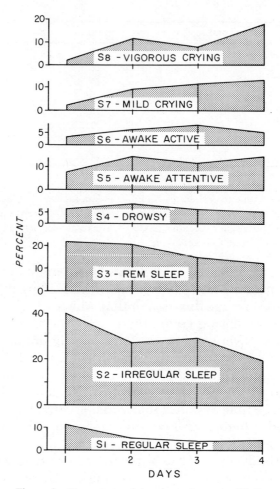

Figure 2   Percentage of time in each state—all infants.

receive approximately 4 cc of feeding (17 calories) and on day 4, 30 cc of feeding (120 calories). If one wishes to determine the behavioral effect of inadequate caloric intake in an infant who had recovered from the birth process, an evaluation of the breast-fed infant's behavior after feeding on day 3 would offer an optimum situation. Therefore, we calculated the average amount of time during 20 minutes of observation each group of infants spend in each of the eight states on day 3. Breast-fed boys are contrasted with breast-fed girls after feeding on day 3. The results of this are

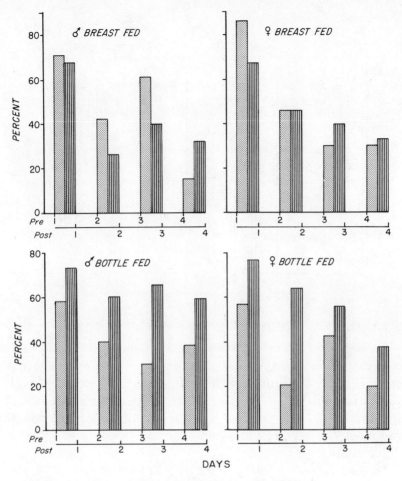

Figure 3 Percentage of time in sleep states (S1 + S2 + S3).

shown in Figure 7, which demonstrates that the boys and girls spend about equal amounts of time in the sleep states. Girls spend a great deal more time in the awake attentive state, whereas boys spend a great deal more time crying. Similar differences between breast-fed boys and girls were found on day 4 as well.

HAND-FACE CONTACTS

Three basic questions may be raised concerning the data on the frequency of hand-face contacting: (1) the influence of state on

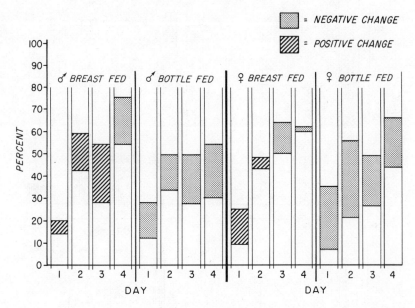

Figure 4   Percentage of change to active-awake states (S5 + S6 + S7 + S8) after feeding.

the frequency and location of hand-face contacts over the first 4 days of life, (2) the influence of type of feeding (breast vs. bottle) on the frequency and location of hand-face contacts when the state variable is held constant, and (3) sex differences in rate and location of contact present when state and feeding variables are held constant.

The data from the four groups of infants with respect to these questions can be summarized as follows:

1. The frequency of hand-face contact gradually increases from S1 to S6 in all four groups. This is shown in Figures 8 and 9.
2. In S7 and S8 the rate of hand-face contacts continues to increase for breast-fed girls but decreases for all other groups (see Figure 9).
3. In S6 (Figure 10) where the frequency of hand-face contacts is uniformly high, bottle-fed boys show higher prefeeding rates than bottle-fed girls. Both boys and girls show a significant decrease in frequency of hand-face contacts after

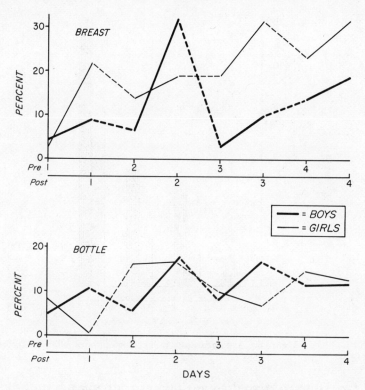

Figure 5 Percentage of time in state 5 before and after feeding.

bottle feeding. In state 2 (Figure 10) breast-fed girls show a diminution in hand-face contacts after feeding on days 3 and 4 (after the milk has come in), whereas boys do not show such a decrease. Also in Figure 10, bottle-fed girls show a lower rate of hand-face contact before and after feeding than bottle-fed boys, but boys show a uniform decrease in the intensity of hand-face contacts on day 2.

4. Both breast- and bottle-fed girls show a preponderance of hand-face contacting to the snout area in states 3, 4, 5, and 6. Snout and parasnout contacts are of equal intensity in these states for both breast- and bottle-fed boys except in state 6, where snout contacts are greater than parasnout contacts. These findings are illustrated in Figure 8.

5. Bottle-fed girls show a significantly lower intensity of hand-

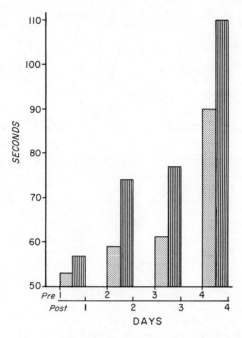

Figure 6   Average duration of crying episodes (all infants).

face contacts than does any other group in each state. This is true for all states and is shown in Figure 8. Bottle-fed girls show an obvious preponderance of hand-face contacts to the snout area as compared to the parasnout area in all states.

In summary, the frequency of hand-face contacting is increased with increasing arousal. There are significantly more snout contacts than parasnout contacts in all groups when the infant is in state 6 (awake-active). This ratio of snout to parasnout contacts reverses in states 7 and 8, except in breast-fed girls. Girls show a preponderance of snout contacts over parasnout contacts as compared to boys in states 3, 4, 5, and 6.

Caloric intake (bottle-feeding) diminishes the frequency of hand-face contacts when the state is held constant, but the effect of calories in diminishing the frequency of hand-face contacts is greater on girls than boys.

When compared in the same state, rooting and sucking re-

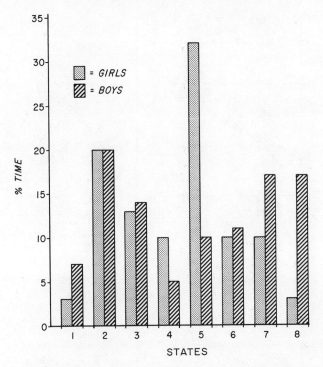

Figure 7 Percentage of time in each state for 10 boys and 8 girls after breast feeding on day 3 (20-minute observation period).

sponses were more intense before feeding than after. The diminution in intensity of sucking and rooting responses was greater in bottle-fed than in breast-fed infants.

The fact that bottle feeding produced a consistent pattern of sleep and diminished intensity of hand-face contacts over the first 4 days of life, while breast feeding did not produce this change until day 3 in girls and until day 4 in boys would come as no surprise to mothers and nurses attuned to the hunger needs of the small infant.

In view of the apparent effect of calories on behavior at this early age, it seems appropriate to review the pertinent metabolic variables involved. Adamson [1] has shown that oxygen consumption is 4.6 to 4.8 ml per kg per minute in the immediate postnatal period and increases to 6.75 ml per kg per minute at 24 hours of age. Graham and Shanks [30] estimate basal caloric needs at 55

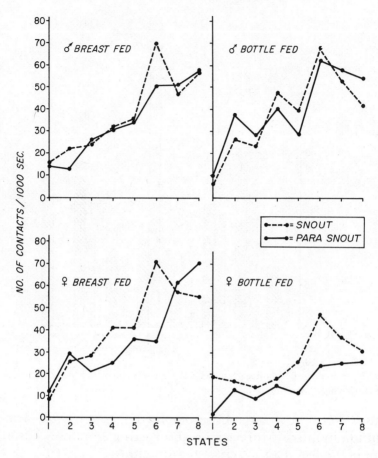

Figure 8 Hand-face contacts by states (pre-, post-, and days combined).

calories per kg for 24 hours, with total caloric requirement, including growth needs and loss from excreta, at 100 calories per kg per day. Smith [54] emphasizes that caloric requirements may increase by 100 percent if the infant is active. Differences in caloric requirements to maintain these various physiological processes for boys versus girls in the neonatal period have apparently not been studied. Lewis, Duval, et al. [42] have demonstrated that males show a consistently higher basal metabolism between the ages of 2 and 15 years, through adulthood and into senescence [53]. Garn and Clark [29] have shown that boys have a higher oxygen consumption per kilogram of body weight than girls of

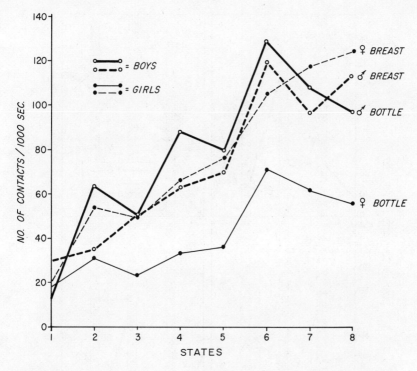

Figure 9 Snout and parasnout contacts by state (pre-, post-, and days combined).

the same muscular mass and suggest that this difference may be related to anabolic steroid hormones. Such factors may account for some of the differences in the response of boys and girls to breast and bottle feeding. Actual calories from breast feeding first become available in small quantities when the milk comes in (replacing colostrum) on the third day. Most women know that the best way to a man's heart is through his stomach and also that keeping an adolescent boy well fed and satisfied is often three times more costly than feeding a girl. The present study suggests that these differences are present at birth.

Summary

Four separate groups of infants, 10 breast-fed boys, 12 bottle-fed boys, eight breast-fed girls, and nine bottle-fed girls, were compared with each other on each of the first 4 days of life, both

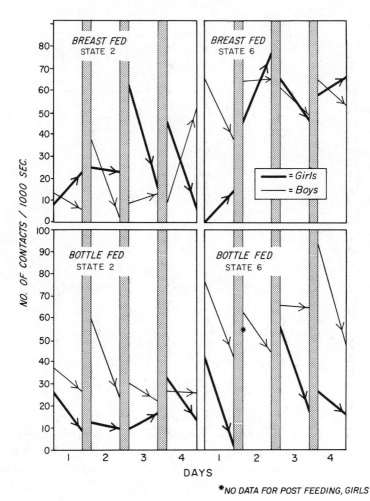

Figure 10   Hand-face contacts by state, sex, and feeding.

before and after feeding. The infants were all normal at birth. Their mothers had been well during pregnancy, had received minimal medication during labor, and were willing to cooperate in the study.

It was shown that after bottle feeding the infants slept more, showed fewer hand-face contacts, less intense sucking, and less intense rooting activity than before feeding when these activities were quantified during the same state of arousal before and after feeding. This effect was not observed in breast-fed infants. It is confirmed that hunger is a specific internal psychophysiological state at birth, which is relieved specifically by food. Thus hunger may be considered a *primary* motivation of behavior in the newborn.

Three major differences between boys and girls are suggested by the data: First, hunger drive is more easily reduced in girls; second, girls spend more time and progress more frequently to the state of alert-attentiveness than boys before and after low caloric feeding (under similar circumstances boys spend more time and gravitate more frequently to whimpering and crying than girls); and third, girls tend to make fewer hand-face contacts than boys but make more such contacts to the snout area. The shift to sleep states was quantitatively greater in bottle-fed girls than in bottle-fed boys. Girls also showed longer sleep intervals than did boys. Breast-fed girls showed a shift to sleep after feeding on days 3 and 4, whereas boys did not show this shift until day 4. These findings again suggest that hunger needs are more easily satisfied in girls than in boys.

The fact that girls spend a greater percentage of time in awake-attentive states and boys spend a greater percentage of time in whimpering and crying when hunger needs have not been satiated, as in the case of breast feeding on days 3 and 4, suggests that under conditions of increased hunger girls may be capable of responding to environmental stimuli more discriminantly than boys. This would suggest that the behavior of boys may be more motivated by appetitive internal forces and that the behavior of girls may be more motivated by stimulus hunger. Thus the behavior of boys may become more drive-dependent and thus more drive-organized, whereas that of girls may be less drive-dependent and more environmentally cued. These, of course, are relative matters.

The increase in hand-face contacting while crying and in a high state of physiological need (hunger) in breast-fed girls suggests a greater capacity for behavioral control during periods of diffuse unpleasure in girls than in boys.

The greater tendency of girls to target the hand-face contacts to the snout area while awake suggests a higher degree of neural organization in girls for hand-mouth functioning. This, coupled with the greater capacity of girls to maintain the state of awake-attentiveness also found in a small sample by Boismier [11], may predispose girls to higher levels of integration of eye-hand-mouth function. Korner [38] has shown greater oral tactile sensitivity in girls.

The implications of these sex differences observed in the human neonate are widely ramifying. A comprehensive review of the current research activity on normal infant development is reported by Stone, Smith, et al. [58]. A review of gender differences, including some recently developed theory, is reported by Ounsted and Taylor [43]. A correlation of sex differences noted at birth with social behavior and learning shown at age 3 is reported by Bell, Weller, et al. [6]. What are some of the implications of these studies for an understanding of high risk and coping? I mention only a few possibilities. There are implications for the greater incidence of psychotic reactions and other psychopathology in boys than in girls and for greater disturbances in learning ability in boys. The differences found at birth suggest a constitutional basis for differences in rates of development found in boys and girls, with girls proving more rapid. There are implications also for differing child-rearing roles for parents of boys as contrasted with girls and for the biological contribution to gender identity.

And finally, these studies point to the necessity of controlling the interaction of sex and feeding variables with age when other behaviors as environmental events are being studied.

A final word of caution concerning what was not found or studied may be in order. The sex differences are probably not as great as individual differences between infants. These studies make no assertion concerning the processes of identification in men and women. The sex differences studied here are not qualitatively or quantitatively of sufficient magnitude to warrant them being called "etiological" for any later illness, character trait, or ability. No comment can be made regarding the desirability of breast versus bottle feeding based on these data.

Acknowledgment

I am grateful for the help provided in making the infant observations to Robert Constas, Robert Settlage, Richard Rawson, Ross Frank, Tom Trott, Catherine Wechsler, and Michael Kurtz, who were supported by Fellowship funds for medical students, provided by the U.S. Public Health Service and the California State Department of Mental Hygiene. Don Gilbertson gave volunteer assistance in the development of computer programs for the preliminary data analysis. Dr. Edward Forgy and Tom Perser, also supported by fellowship funds, developed computer programs for the final analysis of the data and statistical evaluation, utilizing the UCLA Health Sciences Computer Center.

This research was also supported by a grant from the Mahone Fund of the Los Angeles Psychoanalytic Society and Institute.

References

1. Adamson, J. The role of thermal factors in foetal and neonatal life. *Pediat. Clin. N. Amer., The Newborn, I,* 13 (1966), 599–619.
2. Ainsworth, M.D. Patterns of attachment behavior shown by the infant in interaction with his mother. *Merrill-Palmer Quart.,* 10 (1964), 51–58.
3. Babkin, P. S. The establishment of reflex activity in early postnatal life. In *Central Nervous Systems and Behavior* (transl. from Russian). Josiah Macy, Jr. Foundation, New York.
4. Bell, R. Q. and Costello, N. S. Three tests for sex differences in tactile sensitivity in the newborn. *Biologia Neonatorum,* 7 (1965), 335–347.
5. Bell, R. Q. and Darling, J. F. The prone head reaction in the human newborn: Relationship with sex and tactile sensitivity. *Child Devel.,* 36 (1965), 943–949.
6. Bell, R. Q., Weller, G. M., and Waldrop, M. F. Newborn and preschooler: Organization of behavior and relations between periods. *Monogr. Soc. Res. Child Devel.,* 36: 1–2 (1971), serial No. 142.
7. Beller, E. K, and Neubauer, P. B. Sex differences and symptom patterns in early childhood. *J. Amer. Acad. Child Psychiat.,* 2 (1963), 417–433.
8. Benjamin, J. D. and Tennes, K. A case of pathological headnodding. Paper read at the Los Angeles Society for Child Psychiatry and at the American Psychoanalytic Association, 1958.
9. Benjamin, J. D. and Tennes, K. Prediction and psychopathology theory. In *Dynamic Psychopathology in Childhood,* L. Jessner and E. Pavenstedt, Eds. Grune and Stratton, New York, 1959.
10. Blauvelt, H. H. Capacity of a human neonate reflex to signal future response by present action. *Child Develop.,* 33 (1962), 21–28.
11. Boismier, J. D. A Markov analysis of behavioral arousal in the human infant. Unpublished Master's thesis, George Peabody College, Nashville, Tennessee, 1970.
12. Bower, T. G. R. Stimulus variables determining space perception in infants. *Science,* 149 (1965), 88–89.
13. Bowlby, J. The nature of the child's tie to his mother. *Internat. J. Psychoanal.,* 39 (1958), 350–373.
14. Brazelton, T. B., Scholl, M. L., and Robey, J. S. Visual response in the newborn. *Pediatrics,* 37 (1966), 284–290.

15. Call, J. D. Newborn approach behavior and early ego development. *Internat. J. Psychoan.*, 45 (1964), 286–294.
16. Call, J. D. Some sex differences in behavior of newborn babies. Presented at UCLA Medical Society Meeting, Neuropsychiatric Institute, Los Angeles, 1965.
17. Call, J. D. Lap and finger play in infancy, implications for ego development. *Internat. J. Psychoan.*, 49 (1968), 375–378.
18. Call, J. D. and Marschak, M. Styles and games in infancy. *J. Amer. Acad. Child Psychiat.*, 5 (1966), 193–210.
19. Cameron, J., Livson, N., and Bayley, N. Infant vocalizations and their relationship to mature intelligence. *Science*, 157 (1967), 331–333.
20. Constas, R. and Call, J. D. Spontaneous hand-mouth activity, rooting and hand-mouth reflexes as related to state in the newborn infant. Presented to the Society for Research in Child Development, University of California, Berkeley, 1963.
21. Darwin, C. *The Expression of Emotion in Man and Animals*, Appleton, New York, 1873.
22. Darwin, C. (1877). Biographical sketch of an infant. *Mind, A Quarterly Review of Psychology and Philosophy*, No. 7, 1877.
23. Dayton, G. O., Jones, M. H., Steel, B., and Rose, M. Developmental studies of coordinated eye movements in the human infant: II. An oculo-graphic study of the fixation reflex in the newborn. *Arch. Ophthalmol.*, 71 (1964), 871–875.
24. Evans, F. R. and McKieth, R. *Infant Feeding and Infant Difficulties.* Churchill, London, 1951.
25. Fantz, R. L. Pattern vision in newborn infants. *Science*, 140 (1963), 296–297.
26. Freud, S. (1905). *Three Essays on the Theory of Sexuality. Standard Edition*, Vol. 7. London: Hogarth Press.
27. Fries, M. E., Brokaw, K., and Murray, M. D. The formation of character as observed in the well baby clinic. *Amer. J. Dis. Child.*, 49 (1935), 28–42.
28. Fries, M. E. and Wolff, P. Some hypotheses on the role of the congenital activity type in personality development. *Psychoan. Study Child*, 8 (1953), 48–62.
29. Garn, S. M. and Clark, L. L. The sex differences in the basic metabolic rate. *Child Develop.*, 24 (1953), 215–224.
30. Graham, S. and Shanks, R. A. *Notes on Infant Feeding.* Livingston, Edinburgh, 1960.
31. Harlow, H. F. and Harlow, M. Learning to love. *Amer. Sci.*, 54 (1966), 244–272.
32. Hendry, L. S. and Kessen, W. Oral behavior of newborn infants as a function of age and time since feeding. *Child Develop.*, 35 (1964), 201–208.
33. Hershenson, M. Visual discrimination in the human newborn. *J. Comp. Physiol. Psychol.*, 58 (1964), 270–276.
34. Hershenson, M., Munsinger, H., and Kessen, W. Preference for shapes of intermediate variability in the newborn human. *Science*, 147 (1964), 630–631.
35. Hess, E. H. and Polt, J. M. Pupil size in relation to mental activity during simple problem-solving. *Science*, 143 (1964), 1190.
36. Hoffer, W. Mouth, hand and ego integration. *Psychoan. Study Child*, 3:(1947), 49–56.

37. Kessen, W., Williams, E. J., and Williams, J. P. Selection and test of response measures in the study of the human newborn. *Child Develop.*, 32:(1961), 7–24.
38. Korner, A. F. Sex differences in newborns with special reference to differences in the organization or oral behavior. *J. Child Psychol. Psychiat.*, 14 (1973), 19–29.
39. Kris, E. On preconscious mental processes. *Psychoan. Quart.*, 19 (1950), pp. 540–60.
40. Kron, R. E. Instrumental conditioning of nutritive sucking behavior in the newborn. In *Recent Advances in Biological Psychiatry*, Vol. 9, J. Wortis, Ed. Plenum Press, New York, pp. 295–300.
41. Kron, R. E. The effect of arousal and of learning upon sucking behavior in the newborn. In *Recent Advances in Biological Psychiatry*, Vol. 10, J. Wortis, Ed. Plenum Press, New York, .
42. Lewis, R. S., Duval, A. M., Iliff, A. Standards for the basal metabolism of children from 2 to 15 years of age, inclusive. *J. Pediat.*, 23 (1943), 1–18.
43. Ounsted, C. and Taylor, D. C., Eds. *Gender Differences: Their Ontogeny and Significance.* The Whitefriars Press, London and Tonbridge, 1972.
44. Owen, G. M., Jensen, R. L., and Fomon, S. J. Sex-related difference in total body water and exchangeable chloride during infancy. *J. Pediat.*, 60 (1962), 858–868.
45. Parmelee, A. H., Jr., Wenner, W. H., and Schulz, H. R. Infant sleep patterns from birth to 16 weeks of age. *J. Pediat.*, 65 (1964), 576.
46. Parmelee, A. H., Wenner, W. H., Akiyama, Y., Schultz, M., and Stern, E. Sleep states in premature infants. *Devel. Med. Child Neurol.*, 9 (1967), 70–77.
47. Prechtl, H. F. R. The directed head turning response and allied movements of the human body. *Behaviour*, 13 (1958), 212–242.
48. Provence, S. and Lipton, R. D. *Infants in Institutions.* International Universities Press, New York, 1962.
49. Rapaport, D. On the psychoanalytic theory of motivation. In *Nebraska Symposium on Motivation*, E. Jones, Ed. Univ. Nebraska Press, Lincoln, 1960.
50. Roffwarg, H. P., Dement, W. D., and Fisher, C. Preliminary observations of the sleep-dream patterns on neonates, infants, children and adults. *Monographs on Child Psychiatry No. 2*, Pergamon Press, New York, 1964.
51. Sander, L. W. Regulation and organization in the early infant-caretaker system. In *Brain and Early Behaviour*, R. J. Robinson, Ed. Academic Press, New York, 1969, pp. 311–333.
52. Schaefer, E. D. and Bayley, N. Maternal behavior, child behavior and the human sleep-dream cycle. *Science*, 152 (1963), 604.
53. Shock, N. W. Metabolism and age. *J. Chronic Dis.*, 2 (1955), 687–703.
54. Smith, C. A. *The Physiology of the Newborn Infant.* Charles C. Thomas, Springfield, Ill., 1959.
55. Spitz, R. A. *No and Yes: On Beginnings of Human Communication.* International Universities Press, New York, 1957.
56. Spitz, R. A. *A Genetic Field Theory of Ego Formation.* International Universities Press, New York, 1959.
57. Stechler, G., Bradford, S., and Levy, H. Attention in the newborn: Effect on motility and skin potential. *Science*, 151 (1966), 1246–1248.
58. Stone, L. J., Smith, H. T., and Murphy, L. B., Eds. *The Competent Infant.* Basic Books, New York, 1973.

59. Tauber, E. S. and Koffler, S. Optomotor response in human infants to apparent motion: Evidence of innateness. *Science,* 152 (1966), 382–383.
60. Trott, T. Sex differences in the behavior of neonates. Presentation to West Coast Conferences of Medical Student Research Projects, University of Oregon Medical School, Portland, 1966.
61. Wolff, P. H. Observations on newborn infants. *Psychosomat. Med.,* 21 (1959), 110–118.
62. Wolff, P. H. and White, B. L. Visual pursuit and attention in young infants. *J. Amer. Acad. Child Psychiat.,* 4 (1965), 473–484.

Infant Risk Factors in Developmental Deviancy

Arnold J. Sameroff, Ph.D. (U.S.A.)*

The ability to identify children early in development who later exhibit behavioral deviances appears to be much akin to the medieval search for the philosopher's stone that would turn lead into gold. Constitutional approaches have vied with environmental approaches in attempts to define characteristics that place a child at risk. Among the more prominent of the constitutional characteristics has been the "continuum of reproductive casualty" postulated by Lilienfeld, Pasamanick, and Rogers [10], which related complications of pregnancy and delivery to later intellectual and emotional disturbance. Others [13] have argued for the value of neurological signs in the prediction of later deviancy. More genetic orientations have been found in the work of Mednick [11] and Rosenthal [14] in the prediction of risk for schizophrenia based on maternal psychopathology.

However, reviews of the evidence for these approaches [12, 15] have found little support for the existence of such causal chains that would permit prediction of later outcome from early constitutional characteristics of the child. The study of perinatal anoxia is a good example of such research. It would appear logical

* Supported by USPHS-NIMH Grant No. MH-16544 and the Grant Foundation.

173

to assume that cerebral oxygen deprivation early in development would produce later deficits in intellectual functioning. A large longitudinal study was designed to test this hypothesis using a sample of 300 anoxic infants in St. Louis, Missouri. As expected, when these infants were examined during the first days of life they did show some impairment resulting from their anoxia [7]. These same infants were seen again at three years of age and tested with a battery of cognitive, perceptual motor, personality, and neurological tests [6]. The group of anoxic infants scored lower than controls on all tests of cognitive function, had more positive neurological findings, and showed some personality differences. At 7 years of age these infants were again tested [4]. Paradoxically significant IQ differences had disappeared between the anoxic group and the control population. Of the 21 cognitive and perceptual measures only two tasks seemed still to be deficient in these children. The results of this study indicated that although anoxic infants do poorly on newborn measures and may still show some signs of deficit at 3 years of age, by 7 years of age they were performing almost as well as nonanoxic controls. These results typify most of the longitudinal studies of perinatal complications.

The focus on environmental factors in development has resulted in much greater predictive efficiency. Werner, Bierman, and French [19] were led to the conclusion based on data from their 10-year longitudinal study of the influence of perinatal factors that "ten times more children had problems related to the effects of poor early environment than the effects of perinatal stress." The poor environments found in the Werner study were characterized by mothers with low socioeconomic status, poor educational background, or unstable family emotional climate.

Again, however, the identification of a poor early environment in itself does not appear to directly predict to later deviancy. From the worst imaginable social, emotional, and economic situations children have emerged with the best possible adaptation to life [5]. The research on the battered child provides us with some interesting evidence to support this point. Even though we can differentiate the personalities of parents who abuse and neglect their children from those who do not, not all parents with these characteristics neglect or abuse their children [15].

Given the lack of efficiency in predicting risk from either constitutional or environmental factors alone, some combination of the two might provide a more useful guide to developmental prognosis. Thomas, Chess, et al. [18] have suggested such a model in their longitudinal study of the temperamental characteristics of children from early infancy. They suggested that it was the relation between the infant's characteristics and the adaptive style adopted by its parents that was significant. A child's behavior taken alone was not predictive unless the parents could not adapt to the extraordinary caretaking demands of the child. Parent's childrearing attitudes taken alone were not predictive unless the temperament of the child was taken into consideration.

This view has great merit in explaining the research mentioned earlier on perinatal complications and child abuse. Although there is no connection between birth complications and later deviancy in middle-class children, children with such problems raised in lower-class environments show deficits of 20 to 40 IQ points. One must conclude that it is not the birth complication that caused the later deviancy, but the inability of parents from impoverished environments to adapt to the increased caretaking demands required by their child.

Similarly, although the battering parent does not abuse all his children, the ones that get battered are those requiring the most caretaking demands. There appear to be many more premature or ill children among those who are battered than among those who are not [9].

What conclusions can be drawn about identifying early risk factors from this analysis? It appears that the characteristics of neither the child nor his parents taken alone are predictive of later deviancy. The characteristics of the combination must be considered. So far we have identified a number of environmental risk factors based on low social class and family emotional instability. The infants who require more adaptive responses from their parents have been mentioned. How can we better typify these infants?

To better describe the characteristics of such children, Thomas, Chess, et al. [17] launched a longitudinal study of temperament from early infancy to 10 years of age. Although individual differences had frequently been recognized and assessed in the literature, these assessments have traditionally been unidimensional, for example, active versus passive, sensitive versus insensitive, and positive mood versus negative mood. Thomas and his associates made an effort to provide a more differentiated view of individuality in infancy. Through parental interviews beginning when the child was 3 months old they were able to identify nine categories of infant reactivity: (1) activity level, (2) rhythmicity, defined as the regularity in time with which behaviors such as feeding and sleeping occurred, (3) approach or withdrawal, defined as the nature of the response to a new stimulus, (4) adaptability in responses to new or altered situations, (5) intensity of reaction as expressed in the energy level of a response, (6) threshold of responsiveness, defined as the strength of stimulation necessary to evoke a response, (7) mood quality, whether happy or unhappy, (8) distractibility, defined as the effectiveness of extraneous stimulation to alter ongoing behavior, and (9) persistence in behavior.

From these nine behavioral categories several clusters emerged that appeared to define distinguishable infant temperaments. The three most prominent clusters were labeled the "difficult baby," the "slow-to-warm up baby," and the "easy baby". The "difficult" baby was characterized as irregular, nonadaptive, low in initial approach, and having intense reactions of negative mood, in contrast to the "easy" baby, who was regular, positive, adaptive, approaching, and low in intensity of response.

Several studies have demonstrated that difficult infant temperaments are related to both current and later developmental problems. Thomas, Chess, and Birch, [18] reported that whereas only 10 percent of their longitudinal sample were categorized as having been difficult children, 70 percent of these had later behavioral disturbances accounting for 25 percent of the disturbances found in the whole sample. Carey [2] developed a shortened procedure for the temperament assessment in the form of a self-administered questionnaire for use in clinical pediatric practice that assessed the same nine characteristics that the Thomas study [18] assessed through extensive interviews. Carey [3] found a significant relationship between difficult temperaments as measured by his questionnaire and colic in infants seen in his clinical practice. In addition, he found that difficult babies, while having no more illnesses than easy babies, did have more lacerations.

The identification of a difficult temperament in infants combined with poor environmental factors provides us with an interactional model for identifying risk factors in infancy. The interactional model not only provides better predictive efficiency, but makes a lot better sense than the simple linear models found among those who take either side of the nature-nurture controversy. Yet there are some major problems remaining in the assumptions underlying this interactional model. The central problem is the static nature of the interactional model. It ignores the dialectic nature of the interplay between organism and environment in which both mutually alter each other across time. The interactional model requires that the environmental factors, that is, family social circumstance and emotional climate, be independent of the constitutional factors, that is, the infant's temperamental characteristics. Thomas and his associates explicitly did not concern themselves with the origins of the infant's difficult temperament; they merely pointed out that having it made greater problems for the parent. Recent research, however, is beginning to make a case that the infant's temperament is not independent of the characteristics of his environment, but rather may be strongly influenced by it.

In a longitudinal study of parent-child relationships, Wessel, Cobb, et al. [20] were able to identify 48 "paroxysmal fussers" from a sample of 98 infants whose mothers were interviewed when the infant was 1 year old. A fussy infant was defined as "one who, otherwise healthy and well-fed, had paroxysms of irritability, fussing or crying lasting for a total of more than 3 hours a day and occurring on more than 3 days in any one week."

The most important contributing factor to the fussiness appeared to be family tension. In the group of infants rated as having high family tension, 72 percent were fussy, compared to only 26 percent in the group of infants in which family tension was not seen as prominent. The records of these families were examined to determine if the tension was an antecedent or a consequent of the infant's fussiness. The tension was noted both before and after the weeks in which the infant was fussy.

Carey [1] followed up on the work of Wessel et al. [20] to determine some of the antecedents of infantile colic. He interviewed 103 mothers during the lying-in period and recorded the number of times that each mother indicated she was anxious about something. Forty of the 103 women expressed anxiety and were placed in the anxious group. Carey followed these women and their infants in his clinical practice for the following year, and 13 babies were found to be colicky as defined by the Wessel study [20]. Of the 13 fussy infants, 11 had mothers who had been placed in the anxious group during the postpartum period. Carey concluded that although anxiety in the mother does not produce colic in every child, nor does every child with colic have an anxious mother, it is possible to use maternal anxiety to identify a group of infants at high risk for such a disorder.

Rochester Developmental Psychopathology Study

At the University of Rochester, Melvin Zax and myself have been engaged in a longitudinal study of the offspring of women with a variety of psychiatric disorders to: (1) determine whether the psychiatric status of the mother had any effect on the constitutional characteristics of the offspring and (2) identify characteristics of these offspring that would be predictive of later emotional disorders in these children. The women in the study were assessed psychometrically and with a psychiatric interview during their pregnancy. After their infants were born they were examined in the newborn nursery with a variety of neurological psychophysiological and behavioral tests. At 4 and 12 months of age observers went into the home of these infants and using a time sampling technique recorded the mother-infant interactions for periods of 4 to 6 hours. At 4, 12, and 30 months of age the infants were brought into our research laboratory and tested with the Bayley developmental scales as well as a number of other psychometric instruments. Since the study is still under way I cannot present you with complete data. At 4 and 12 months we have seen 240 and 170 infants, respectively, whereas only 60 infants have passed through the 30-month assessment.

The most important variable that seems to have emerged from

our data is related to the temperamental characteristics of the child described earlier. When the infants were 4 months of age their mothers filled out the Carey [2] questionnaire described earlier to assess the temperament of the child. The children were scored on the basis of how closely they approximated the difficult child described by Thomas and his associates [17, 18]. We then attempted to discover the antecedents in either the infant or the mother of the difficult temperament. Our first effort was to discover if the psychiatric characteristics of the mother played a role in the temperament of the child. Four groups of 26 women, each having diagnoses of either schizophrenia, neurotic depression, personality disorder, or no disorder were matched for age, race, socioeconomic status, and marital status. When the temperament scores for these women were compared no significant differences were found. To sharpen the psychiatric distinction, the group of schizophrenic women were compared only with the normal controls. Again no differences were found in temperament between the infants of the schizophrenic women and those of the control subjects. It was apparent from these data that psychiatric diagnosis per se was not a primary determinant of infant temperament.

In an earlier study [16] of perinatal complications, Melvin Zax and I had compared the same groups of women to determine if there were any differences in birth or delivery complications. As with our temperament data, no differences were found between these groups in pregnancy and delivery complication histories. However, in that earlier study we found that if the women were divided on the basis of severity of mental illness rather than specific diagnosis, there were observable differences. When a high pathology group of women who had many hospitalizations and psychiatric contacts were compared with a group of women who had few psychiatric contacts and no hospitalization, it was found that the more chronically ill group had a greater number of pregnancy and delivery complications. It was thought that this same breakdown might show similar findings for the temperament data.

When the temperament scores of the offspring of a high pathology group consisting of neurotic depressives and schizophrenics were compared to the scores of a low pathology group consisting of situational and personality disorders and to a control group of normal mothers, significant differences were found. Severity of mental illness did appear to be a contributor to difficult temperament in the infants. However, the major differences were between the normal controls and the two psychiatric groups, rather than between the two pathology groups. Psychiatric diagnosis appeared to be a weaker differentiator than we had suspected. Luckily, a number of other variables were available that could be related to the level of difficult temperament in the child. Among these were the prenatal psychometric scores on our anxiety and maternal attitude questionnaires in addition to the demographic variables of race and social class, these four maternal variables were found to be reliably correlated with the difficult temperament of the child ($p < .001$; $r = 0.37$ for anxiety, .33 with poor attitudes to pregnancy, .41 with race, and .42 with socioeconomic status). To differentitate which of these factors were making the largest contribution to the child's temperament, a multiple regression analysis was performed. The regression analysis showed that the mother's anxiety score measured before the child's birth had the greatest influence on his temperament at 4 months of age. Social class and race were close behind. Maternal attitudes did not affect the outcome independently of their relation to the other three variables. A fifth variable did enter the picture, however; the more previous children a woman had borne, the more her current child tended to have a difficult temperament. When examined alone, each of these factors—anxiety, race, social class, and number of children—correlated with temperament at 4 months of age. What is of sociological interest is that whereas these characteristics taken separately all contribute to producing difficult temperaments during infancy, thereby increasing developmental risk, they are usually found in combination, that is, with low socioeconomic status, poor education, many siblings, and Black race, producing superrisk.

Now that we have discussed some of the variables that contribute to producing a difficult temperament in the child, let us examine some of the consequences of this difficult temperament. In our study we have not yet analyzed the behavioral and mental status data for the infants at 30 months of age. The only criterion score we can point to is their Bayley IQ scores from the psychometric testing. With the 50 subjects for which we have complete data, an extremely interesting pattern of correlations appeared. The correlation between the infant test scores on the Bayley at 4 months of age and the Bayley scores at 30 months of age was .18, typical of the low correlations found between these age periods. However, when we correlated the difficult temperament score obtained at 4 months of age with the Bayley IQ score at 30 months of age we found a highly significant correlation (.49; $p < .01$). Our two other psychometric assessments at 30 months of age, the Peabody and Binet Vocabulary Tests, also correlated strongly with the 4-month difficult-temperament assessment.

Again we performed a multiple regression analysis to determine what were the most significant contributors to the 30-month Bayley IQ score. Socioeconomic status and race still were very high on the list. But the mother's prenatal anxiety score, which contributed so much to the child's difficult temperament at 4 months, made no significant contribution to the 30-month developmental score. Instead it was replaced by the difficult temperament itself. What we must conclude from this data is that if one wants to predict an infant's IQ score at 30 months of age from a child's behavior at 4 months of age, a much more reliable prediction can be made based on his temperament than on his intellectual functioning. Although psychometric assessments at 30 months of age do not provide a very differentiated view of psychological functioning, it is all that we can discuss in this preliminary view of our data.

Risk Factors

What can be concluded from our study related to early risk factors and later mental and emotional illness? We have identified a constellation of variables that predict to a difficult temperament in the infant early in the first year of life. However, this constellation of variables is not found in the infant, but rather in the mother. It is a constellation which focuses on a poor emotional state expressed in high anxiety accompanied by poor attitudes toward her own pregnancy and the child that will be a product of that pregnancy. This combination is predominantly found among social groups with low economic status and poor education. If one wants to seek risk factors in development, it is clear that this is the population on which to focus.

Of more consequence for the identification of risk factors is our view of what the developmental process is all about. In this day and age where so much emphasis is being placed on intrinsic factors of the child such as the poor genes that Jensen and Herrnstein argue predispose the infant toward low IQ, or that Rosenthal [14] and Heston [8] argue predispose the infant toward schizophrenia, it is well to remember that environment still plays the major role in producing the diversity of behaviors found among humankind. However, rather than accepting the simplistic environmentalist views of the 1930s, we now are able to see the environment in intimate connection with the characteristics of the child. It is the transactions between the constitutional characteristics of the child and the emotional and social characteristics of his environment that will produce the ultimate outcome for that child. It is neither in the environment alone nor in the child alone that we can find factors that will be predictive of later deviancy or normalcy. In our specific study the low IQs at 30 months are produced by neither the difficult temperament of the child nor the anxiety and poor attitudes of the mother, but are the result of a complex process over time of which these two variables are a part.

The transactional model that we see begins with a mother stressed emotionally, socially, and economically who produces a child to whom these stresses are communicated, producing in that child a difficult temperament. Where the anxiety of the mother may have no direct connection with later outcomes, such as the child's competence at 30 months, it does have an effect mediated by the child's temperament. The negative characteristics of the child provides little reinforcement for his parents and consequently, unless they are free of other social stresses, they do little for the child in turn. The child's resulting relative incompetence at 30 months does little to elicit more positive treatment from his parents, and so it goes—a reciprocal process by which the child and his parents march down the road to a less than positive developmental outcome.

Although the model of infant risk that I have proposed is clearly more complex than the simpler understanding of developmental outcomes based on single etiological factors, it provides in turn a large number of points in time at which remedial intervention can occur. The role of the psychiatrist may be secondary to the role of the obstetrician in attempting to reduce anxiety and promote positive attitudes in his patients and to the role of the pediatrician in helping parents understand and adapt to infants who may have difficult temperaments.

When one pessimistically views development as the determined expression of genic properties, there is little room for accepting or treating deviancy. When development is seen as the outcome of continuous transactions between a child and his environment, one is permitted the optimism that we can find myriad points at which interventions can act to normalize both the child and his environment.

References

1. Carey, W. B. Maternal anxiety and infantile colic. *Clin. Pediat.*, 7 (1968), 590–595.
2. Carey, W. B. A simplified method for measuring infant temperament. *J. Pediat.*, 77 (1970), 188–194.
3. Carey, W. W. Measuring infant temperament. *J. Pediat.*, 81 (1972), 414.
4. Corah, N. L., Anthony, E. J., Painter, P., Stern, J. A., and Thurston, D. L. Effects of perinatal anoxia after seven years. *Psychol. Monogr.*, 79 (1965), (3, whole No. 596).
5. Garmezy, N. Vulnerability research and the issue of primary prevention. *Amer. J. Orthopsychol.*, 41 (1971), 101–116.
6. Graham, F. K., Ernhart, C. B., Thurston, D., and Croft, M. Development three years after perinatal anoxia and other potentially damaging newborn experiences. *Psychol. Monogr.*, 76 (1962), 3, whole issue No. 522.
7. Graham, F. K., Pennoyer, M. M., Caldwell, B. M., Greenman, M., and Hartman, A. F. Relationship between clinical status and behavior test performance in a newborn group with histories suggesting anoxia. *J. Pediat.*, 50 (1957), 177–189.
8. Heston, L. L. Psychiatric disorders in foster home reared children of schizophrenic mothers. *Brit. J. Psychiat.*, 112 (1966), 819–825.
9. Klein, M. and Stern, L. Low birth weight and the battered child syndrome. *Amer. J. Dis. Childr.*, 122 (1971), 15–18.
10. Lilienfeld, A. M., Pasamanick, B., and Rogers, M. Relationships between

pregnancy experience and the development of certain neuropsychiatric disorders in childhood. *Amer. J. Publ. Health*, 45 (1955), 637–643.

11. Mednick, S. A. A longitudinal study of children with a high risk for schizophrenia. *Ment. Hyg.*, 50 (1966), 522–535.

12. Parmelce, A. H. and Haber, A. Who is the "risk infant?" *Clin. Obstet. Gynecol.*, 16 (1973), 376–387.

13. Prechtl, H. F. R. Prognostic value of neurological signs in the newborn infant. *Proc. Roy. Soc. Med.*, 58 (1965), 3.

14. Rosenthal, D. *Genetic Theory and Abnormal Behavior*. McGraw-Hill, New York, 1970.

15. Sameroff, A. J. and Chandler, M. Reproductive risk and the continuum of caretaking casualty. In *Review of Child Development Research*, Vol. 4, F. D. Horowitz, M. Hetherington, S. Scarr-Salapatek, and G. Siegel, Eds. Univ. Chicago Press, Chicago, in press.

16. Sameroff, A. J. and Zax, M. Schizotaxia revisited: Model issues in the etiology of schizophrenia. *Amer. J. Orthopsychiat.*, 43 (1973), 744–754.

17. Thomas, A., Chess, S., Birch, H. G., Hertzig, M. E., and Korn, S. *Behavioral Individuality in Early Childhood*. Univ. London Press, London, 1963.

18. Thomas, A., Chess, S., and Birch, H. *Temperament and Behavior Disorders in Children*. New York Univ. Press, New York, 1968.

19. Werner, E. E, Bierman, J. M., and French, F. E. *The Children of Kauai*. Univ. Hawaii Press, Honolulu, 1971.

20. Wessel, M. A., Cobb, J. C., Jackson, E. B., Harris, G. S., Jr., and Detwiler, A. C. Paroxysmal fussing in infancy sometimes called colic. *Pediatrics*, 14 (1954), 421–434.

Infant Developmental Distress Syndrome and Subsequent Health

Wallace Ironside, Ph.D. (Australia)

The Problem

The Royal New Zealand Society for the Health of Women and Children Incorporated, or as it is more commonly known, the Plunket Society, is now New Zealand's organization for the care of the preschool child from the time mother returns home with it from the maternity hospital. As part of its service the Plunket Society has six hospitals, all named Karitane, for the diagnosis, treatment, and management of infants who have difficult problems of rearing from whatever cause. The hospitals have mothercraft sections to which mothers may be admitted for training in appropriate methods of infant care. Nearly all the children admitted to the Karitane Hospital in Dunedin, New Zealand, where the work I report on began, are less than 1 year old, most of them a few weeks to a few months of age.

An analysis of the admissions to the hospital demonstrate that just over 70 percent of the babies under 12 months of age do not suffer from any discernible somatic pathology (Table 1). These admissions are dictated by what on the surface appear to be problems of growth and function as described by the nurses' diagnostic categories, which are the ones used (Table 2). It is perhaps easier to appreciate the dimensions of the child-care problem presented

185

by the babies admitted without discernible somatic pathology if their numbers are seen as a proportion of the live births of the area mainly served by the Karitane Hospital. For the years 1968, 1969, and 1970 the admissions amount to approximately 10 percent of the live births (Table 3). I should add here that the high rate of admissions to Karitane Hospital of babies without discernbile somatic pathology who were not premature, and that they were a substantial percentage of live births in the area, were findings that confirmed what at first were the clinical impressions that prompted me to take a closer look at the babies themselves and the families they came from. What were the true difficulties of rearing and nursing that had led to the admissions of the infants to hospital and often their mothers as well? What were the immediate effects of hospitalization? What progress did the babies make after they left the hospital? Such were the questions for which answers were sought.

Methodology

Details of the methodology of the study have been published elsewhere [1], so I do not dwell on them here. Suffice it to say that the babies were observed systematically and neurologically examined to exclude minimal brain damage. Their parents, espe-

Table 1　Infants Admitted to Karitane Hospital, Dunedin
for Years 1968, 1969, and 1970

	No Primary Somatic Pathology		Primary Somatic Pathology		Premature ($< 5\frac{1}{2}$ lb)		Totals	
	N	%	N	%	N	%	N	%
1968	262	70.2	30	8.0	81	21.8	373	100
1969	246	70.3	13	3.7	91	26.0	350	100
1970	248	72.9	25	7.4	67	19.7	340	100
Grand Totals	756[a]	71.1	68[b]	6.4	239[c]	22.5	1063	100

[a] Includes 22 sets of twins.
[b] Includes 1 set of twins.
[c] Includes 22 sets of twins & 1 set of triplets.

Table 2   Nurses' Diagnostic Categories

Behavior problem
Sleeping disturbance
Irritability, crossness, screaming
Colic
Poor feeder
Vomiting and/or spilling
Upset motions
Establishment of breast feeding
Establishment of artificial feeding
Failure to thrive
Weakling care

Table 3   Infants (under 12 months) Admitted with no Somatic Pathology Expressed as Percentage of Live Births in Area Served by Karitane Hospital

Year	No Primary Somatic Pathology	Number of Live Births	Percentage
1968	262	2580	10.2
1969	246	2515	9.8
1970	248	2441	10.1

cially the mothers, were psychologically examined in detail. After a preliminary study of 30 babies, a small group of eight randomly selected infants was taken into a detailed study, the results of which form the basis of this lecture. For comparative purposes it was felt that it would be helpful to do a parallel study of eight infants who had not been admitted to the hospital and who were matched, with their mothers, for eight variables (Table 4). The ages of the babies ranged from a few weeks old to almost 10 months (Table 5). The follow-up of their progress is now some 3 years, 9 months in duration, and a further follow-up will be conducted in about 6 weeks' time.

An inevitable shortcoming of this kind of work is that subjects are lost to the study. One of the Karitane babies and her parents have returned to Scotland and to all extents and purposes have thus been removed from the study. Despite such losses, the follow-up will continue as long as practicable. The findings have led to more precise formulations of problems for study and directions for research that are now being implemented in Dunedin.

The Infant Developmental Distress Syndrome

At the level of clinical observation the syndrome can be described as having six major components. Four of them concern the behavior of the infant, the fifth the infant-mother relationship, and the sixth the response to therapy.

First is an excessive of crying. From this one could infer that there is a disturbance of affectivity. The crying is loud, prolonged, often inconsolable, although feeding or comforting may temporarily relieve it. However, it does not necessarily occur at night as well as during the day. In the Karitane Hospital a diagnosis of a recent admission of a baby with an infant developmental distress syndrome (IDDS) could be made, sight unseen, on the basis of its crying echoing from the nursery through the corridors.

Second are the feeding difficulties. These have to do with problems of breast suckling or taking the bottle if the child has been weaned. Frequent interruptions of the feeding process, usually ending with the infant crying, make for short intervals between meals. Other associated problems are excessive spilling or positing

Table 4   Matching Factors for Selection of Comparison Group

Infants	Mothers
Age	Age
Sex	Parity
Weight	Confinement
Apgar rating	Postpartum physical health

Table 5   Infants' Ages when First Examined

	1		2		3		4		5		6		7		8	
Pairs	E	C	E	C	E	C	E	C	E	C	E	C	E	C	E	C
Age in weeks	2	4	8	11	2	2	2	3	35	38	13	16	13	19	4	5

Code: E — Experimental group
         C — Comparison group

of milk and vomiting, which in some instances is projectile in quality and at first usually suspect of pyloric stenosis. Infants obtained enough milk on the whole to satisfy their nutritional requirements and hence were not underweight.

Third, sleep rhythm is disturbed. Nurses' reports confirmed the impression that the affected infant spent many waking hours crying and restless, to which the nurses would respond by lifting and rocking. If successful the infant would sleep for 1 or 2 hours, only to wake up and begin crying again.

Fourth is hyperresponsivity. Startle responses are frequently observed even when the infants are asleep. The handling of the baby occasioned by the neurological examination was a good test. Hyperresponsivity was demonstrated by the infants reaching a Stage 5 (see Prechtle and Beintema [2]) level of distress sometimes even after only a few minutes of examination. Thus the examination had to be spread over several days to complete it.

Fifth is the infant-mother relationship. The mother herself is distressed with manifest symptoms of anxiety and depression. These are associated with ideas of herself as inadequate and a failure, of destructive impulses toward the infant, or of the infant being deliberately provocative and calculating in its behavior. The overall impression the mother gives is one of desperation, at times reaching a level that can only be described as frantic agitation. At this point I must draw attention to the clinical principle that infant behavior should always be considered in terms of the infant-mother relationship in addition to other assessments.

A variety of the infant developmental distress syndrome is characterized by apparent apathy, sleepiness, but nevertheless in the circumstance of the neurological examination, for example, displaying hyperresponsivity. The infant gives the clinical impression of being withdrawn in the manner that Engel has labeled as conservation-withdrawal. He suggests that this is a biological defense for the purpose of garnering resources to deal with difficulties posed by the environment. This variation of the IDDS was seen relatively infrequently, and only one of eight experimental clinical babies fell into that category.

Quite distinct from the five presenting features of the syndrome just described is the sixth, which is worth pausing for a moment to consider at somewhat greater length. This is the effect of admission and subsequent management and care in hospital on the IDDS. *The younger babies, say, under 10 weeks of age, recovered from the signs of their distress syndromes within 72 hours of admission.* The older babies up to several months of age took somewhat longer, and the oldest babies, those approaching 1 year of age, could be discharged from the hospital with residual distress behavior still evident. One of the babies in the long-term follow-up study fell into the last category.

What did the management and the care of the IDDS consist of? First, the infants received a great deal of attention from the nurses. They were young girls to each of whom a baby was specifically allocated for nursing whilst it was in hospital. However, because of the daily three-shift system, each baby had two other nurses who would not pay quite as much attention to it. This system of allocating babies to specific nurses for general management and care meant that they were seldom left crying for long. Lifting, rocking, and consoling the infant was very much a feature of the general management. Because of the routine functioning of the ward, feeding was given at specific periods during the 24 hours. While by no means rigid, the tendency was to adhere to the feeding schedules. If the nurse felt a baby should have something in between, it was usually sweetened water. For bottle-fed babies there might be alteration of milk formula and making the mixture either thicker or thinner. For the breast-fed babies nurses gave the mother instructions on how to conduct breast feeding. For the mothers who stayed in the hospital with their babies, a simple training program of mothercraft was provided. As a practical measure it was useful, but it also had the effect of general reassurance for the mother herself had participated in the successful therapy. Last, I should mention that Phenobarbitone in small doses was often prescribed. As it was not a feature of the research to attempt to demonstrate that other methods of treatment were either more or less efficacious, I cannot say whether excluding the prescription of Phenobarbitone from the therapeutic regimen would have made any difference. With recovery from the distress syndrome the infants were kept on Phenobarbitone for 2 or 3 weeks and then the dose reduced to nil over a few days.

The treatment of the babies who had the withdrawn version of the syndrome followed the lines described in the preceding paragraphs. Because they did not cry much they did not receive the handling and comforting that the babies with the overt distress were given. Nor were they prescribed Phenobarbitone. Sometimes these babies were labeled as "weakling." This had little reference to variables such as birth weight or stature, but was a description of the infant's apathy, low-intensity crying, and tendency not to respond to stimuli. Even so, the general therapeutic regimen had the effect on the infants of producing spontaneity and responsiveness. This took longer and was, in comparison, not as dramatic as recovery from the active version.

The important significance of treatment of the IDDS is the demonstration that it is rapidly reversible with younger infants. The oldest infants who had suffered from the syndrome for months did not respond with the same degree of success. In other words, this is yet another example of the principle that therapeutic intervention at the proper time produces the best results.

It has been remarked that the response of the babies to admission to hospital was a consequence of separation from the mother. However, it made no difference whether the infants came into hospital on their own or with their mothers. The results were the same.

Results

BABIES AT INTAKE

There are five female pairs and three male pairs of infants. In this respect the sample is not representative of the infant population admitted to the hospital. The female-male ratio of babies admitted to the hospital was 100 to 117, considerably in excess of the slight preponderance of male children born over females in the population as a whole. Undoubtedly in a study involving a larger number of infants, this skewing of the sample would be rectified. I do not think that the distortion in any way affects the general conclusions to be drawn. It is of little consequence whether the baby is male or female when it is suffering from the IDDS and its sequelae.

Let us now look more closely at the findings of the study in detail of eight babies with the IDDS and the parallel group of eight babies studied in exactly the same way for comparison purposes (Tables 6 and 7). The features listed refer only to the most prominent ones. Two of the comparison babies (1 and 2) had had feeding difficulties prior to intake, but in each instance the mother had coped without resort to hospital admission and the babies had recovered.

MOTHERS AT INTAKE

Now let us consider the mothers. First of all I would like to give you some idea of their responses to having been pregnant and given birth to their babies (Tables 8 and 9). A trend toward more effective adjustment, both biologically and emotionally during the latter part of the puerperium on the part of the mothers of the comparison babies, would seem to be the case. Only a study of a large number of mothers will demonstrate whether the capacity for adaptability is indeed a relevant factor. When the comparison mothers, if I can call them that, came into the study, two of them had already demonstrated their ability to cope successfully with their infants' feeding behavior disorders.

Table 6   Features of Infant Developmental Distress Syndrome at Intake

Pairs		Syndrome
1 (M)	Exp	Crying, severe feeding difficulty, easily distressed
	Comp	Difficulty with breast feeding days 4–14; now recovered (5th week)
2 (F)	Exp	Crying, severe feeding difficulty, not sleeping (later scalded)
	Comp	None
(3) (F)	Exp	Crying, screaming, severe feeding difficulty (later battered)
	Comp	None
4 (F)	Exp	Crying, screaming, severe feeding difficulty, not sleeping
	Comp	None

Code:	M	— Male
	F	— Female
	Exp	— Experimental group
	Comp	— Comparison group

Table 7   Features of Infant Developmental Distress Syndrome at Intake

Pairs		Syndrome
5 (F)	Exp	Crying, screaming, severe feeding difficulty, not sleeping
	Comp	None
6 (M)	Exp	Crying, screaming, severe feeding difficulty
	Comp	None
7 (M)	Exp	Crying, severe feeding difficulty
	Comp	Feeding difficulty 7th to 13th week; now recovered (19th week)
8 (F)	Exp	Easily distressed, alleged weakling (later grossly deprived, then battered)
	Comp	None

Code: M — Male $N = 3$ pairs
F — Female $N = 5$ pairs

FATHERS AT INTAKE

To study family relationships that could influence the infant-mother relationship, at the time of intake the fathers were examined in detail in a similar manner to that of the mothers. Their perception of and emotional adjustment to their wives' pregnancies were assessed (Table 10). Only one of the fathers of the comparison babies showed some emotional upset when he learned his wife was pregnant but quickly worked through it. On the other hand, three of the fathers of the clinical experimental babies had emotional disturbances, especially when their wives were confined. Indeed, one of them showed a classical couvade pattern. Only by seeing a much larger sample of fathers will it be possible to decide whether this trend is significant.

FINDINGS AT FOLLOW-UP APPROXIMATELY 3 YEARS, 9 MONTHS AFTER INTAKE INTO STUDY

The infants and their families were followed up at approximately 6 months and again at 12 months after intake. Since then they have been followed up annually. To date five follow-ups of the babies and their families have been conducted.

Table 8   Maternal Biological Adjustment to Gestation, Parturition, and Puerperium

	Conception		Pregnancy		Birth		Puerperium(a)[c]		Puerperium(b)[d]	
	Exp[a]	Comp[b]	Exp	Comp	Exp	Comp	Exp	Comp	Exp	Comp
Difficulties	3	3	2	3	3	3	4	3	5	1
No difficulties	5	5	6	5	5	5	4	5	3	7

[a]Experimental group ($N = 8$).
[b]Comparison group ($N = 8$).
[c]One to 14 days.
[d]Fifteen to 28 days.

Table 9   Maternal, Emotional Adjustment to Gestation, Parturition, and Puerperium

	Conception		Pregnancy		Birth		Puerperium(a)[c]		Puerperium(b)[d]	
	Exp[a]	Comp[b]	Exp	Comp	Exp	Comp	Exp	Comp	Exp	Comp
Difficulties	3	1	2	3	3	3	6	2	7	3
No difficulties	5	7	6	5	5	5	2	6	1	5

[a]Experimental group ($N = 8$).
[b]Comparison group ($N = 8$).
[c]One to 14 days.
[d]Fifteen to 28 days.

The follow-up examinations are conducted in the homes of the babies. The interviewing technique is open-ended and directed at covering the ground listed in Tables 11 and 12. After the follow-up examination the information obtained is immediately recorded, and predictions as to what might eventuate during the following year are made. These predictions have been checked at subsequent follow-up sessions.

Table 13 is a synopsis of how the infants were at intake and at the last follow-up in October 1971. Seven out of the clinical experimental children suffered from what I term "developmental disorders." One was well by the standards used in this research. Two of the comparison babies also had developmental disorders. Stated baldly as I have just done, you will not fully appreciate the significance of these findings. For example, four (Nos. 1, 2, 3, and 5) had each suffered from what can be stated as threatening

Table 10 Paternal Emotional Adjustment to Gestation,
Parturition, and Puerperium

	Conception		Pregnancy		Birth		Puerperium(a)[c]		Puerperium(b)[d]	
	Exp[a]	Comp[b]	Exp	Comp	Exp	Comp	Exp	Comp	Exp	Comp
Difficulties	1	1	1	0	3	0	1	0	2	0
No difficulties	6	7	6	8	4	8	6	8	5	8

[a]Experimental group ($N = 7$).
[b]Comparison group ($N = 8$).
[c]One to 14 days.
[d]Fifteen to 28 days.

traumata. Two (Nos. 3 and 8) had been battered, one scalded (No. 2) and the fourth (No. 1) involved in a severe motor accident that resulted in 3 months of hospitalization. A fifth (No. 6) suffers repeated head injury, some of which have caused concussion and scalp wounds requiring surgical suture. At the last follow-up his face had several deep scratches. None of the comparison group have had that kind of experience. The two comparison children with developmental disorders were considerably less crippled by them than the clinical experimental children. However, the clinical experimental child who was well was one of those who was severely battered before she was 6 months old and had spent 3 months in a hospital, one of them in a neurosurgical ward. I refer to her later. The difference between the two groups is clearer if we take each pair one by one (Tables 14–21).

Let us now turn to the health of the mothers as they were at the follow-up in October 1971. The mothers then were not the same as at the beginning of the study. The first battered baby was transferred when 6 months old to the care of foster parents who eventually adopted her. The second battered baby was transferred when 6 months old to the care of foster parents prior to the battering. The foster mother was responsible for the injuries. The baby was then transferred to the care of another foster mother, and just after the last follow-up the foster mother suddenly resigned from her role. Thus at the next follow-up that child will have yet another surrogate parent with whom she will have established a relationship. Despite these changes of experimental mothers I believe that it is constructive to take a closer look at both groups (Tables 22–25).

Table 11   Follow-up Check List (1)

Physical health history and current status
   This should be thorough and will need direct questioning to clarify
   and cover all systems

Developmental history
   Feeding
   Elimination
   Sleep
   Speech   —   language and understanding
                                       expressive speech
                                       style of speaking
   Locomotor behavior   —   general activity
                                       itemized activity
                                       milestones
   Body image   —   interest in
                                       awareness of
   Intelligence   —   task perceiving
                                       task solving
                                       nursery books and counting
                                       purse and coin test
   Psychosexual   —   phase
                                       interest and expression
   Adaptability   —   new situations
                                       current demands
                                       speed and grasp
   Separations
   Responsiveness
   Sociability relationships   —   mother
                                       father
                                       siblings
                                       friends
                                       strangers
                                       animals
                                       object relations
   Temperamental affective characteristics

Current and continuing family and marital situations
   How things are now, whether old difficulties continue and what is
   or is not being done to cope.

Table 12 Follow-up Check List (2)

Father's account (if possible) when not available for joint session
    His observation may add perspective to wife's

Problems leading to admission to karitane
    Recall of and report on progress

Other problems
    Any new problems arising and continuing (or not)

Problems past and present
    History of what has been and is happening
    Current understanding of them
    Coping methods (etc.)

Physical status

Symptoms	Developmental Deviations
Skin	Sensory
Musculoskeletal	Motor
Alimentary	Speech
Respiratory	Cognitive
Cardiovascular	Affective
Genitourinary	Social
Central Nervous system	Psychosexual
Special senses	Integrative
Endocrine	Other
Other	

Current and continuing family and marital situations
    How things are now, whether old difficulties continue, and what is
    or is not being done to cope.

Six (Nos. 1, 2, 5, 6, 7, and 8) of the mothers of the clinical experimental children still experience difficulties in their relationships with the children or have emotional disturbances sufficiently serious to influence the relationships. One (No. 4) of the original experimental mothers was rated as well, although it is interesting to note that when her child had an upper respiratory tract infection some months previously she had become anxious because of her fear that the child would choke and suffocate. She was the mother who sought help originally because of her infanticidal impulse, which she fantasied as putting a pillow over the baby's face and suffocating her.

Table 13 Health of Infants at Intake and at Follow-up Approximately 3³/₄ Years Later

Pairs		Intake Feb.–May 1968	Follow-up Oct. 1971
1	Exp	IDDS	DD
	Comp	Well	Well
2	Exp	IDDS	DD
	Comp	Well	Well
3	Exp	IDDS[a]	Well
	Comp	Well	Well
4	Exp	IDDS	DD
	Comp	Well	DD
5	Exp	IDDS	DD
	Comp	Well	Well
6	Exp	IDDS	DD
	Comp	Well	Well
7	Exp	IDDS	DD
	Comp	Well	DD
8	Exp	IDDS[a]	DD
	Comp	Well	Well

Code: Exp — Experimental group
      Comp — Comparison group
      DD — Development disorder present, 7 exp and 3 comp (total)
[a] Babies who were battered.

Table 14 Health of Children at Follow-up 3³/₄ Years Later (First Pair)

Gregory: 3³/₄ Years, First Child	Carl: 3³/₄ Years
Major accident—fractured left femur, hospital 3 months	Active
Reckless disregard of traffic despite training	No developmental deviations
Negativistic behavior	Relates well to brother
Bad temper	Mother—accepts maternal role fully now; no problems with gestation, etc. of 2nd child.
Obsessional	
Mother—rejects maternal role; no more children	

Table 15   Health of Children at Follow-up 3³/₄ Years Later (Second Pair)

Tracy: 3³/₄ Years, Second Child	Kerri: 3⁵/₆ Years
Food refusal and vomiting	Physically large—42¹/₂ in tall
Constipation	No developmental deviations
Scars on face and neck from severe scalding	Mother—no difficulties
Sedatives for sleeping	
Tonsilectomy	
Enuresis	
Mother—a battle with feeding; fear Tracy will waste away; could choke her—fears she may lose self-control	

Table 16   Health of Children at Follow-up 3³/₄ Years Later (Third Pair)

Tania: 3²/₃ Years, Fourth Child	Lisa: 3²/₃ Years
Was battered in first year	No developmental deviations
Some food refusal recently; otherwise no developmental deviations	Some shyness with strangers
Relates well to brother	Mother—no difficulties, but predisposition for depression
Mother—no difficulties with Tania; no problems with her first gestation, etc.	

Table 17   Health of Children at Follow-up 3³/₄ Years Later (Fourth Pair)

Carmen: 3²/₃ Years, First Child	Sonya: 3²/₃ Years
Speech mostly unintelligible—dyslalia, condensations, omissions, etc.	Slight feeding difficulty
Otherwise development without deviations	Severe separation anxiety
Accepts sister	Enuresis
Mother—phobic about Carmen's recent URT[a] infection—would choke and suffocate—ref. postpartum infanticide impulse; gestation of second child—no difficulties	Accepts brother
	Mother—rapprochement with own mother; gestation of second child—no difficulties

[a]URT = upper respiratory tract.

Table 18 Health of Children at Follow-up 3³/₄ Years Later
(Fifth Pair)

Lynn: 3½ Years, First Child	Christine: 4¼ Years
Eczema (mother also has)	Slight speech difficulty
Has "wind"	Jealous of sister
Sleep disturbance	Height 43 in
Phobias	Mother—no difficulties with gestation
Easily hurt by slight physical trauma	of second child; marital relationship
Mother—pregnant—no difficulties but	improved
has "wind"	

Table 19 Health of Children at Follow-up 3³/₄ Years Later
(Sixth Pair)

Craig: 3⁵/₆ Years, Third Child	Mark: 3⁵/₆ Years
Many injuries, especially headstitches,	Some separation anxiety
face has severe lacerations	Full nocturnal bladder control not yet
Multiple URT infections	established
Food refusal	Mother—no difficulties ascertained
Severe separation anxiety and panic	
Mother—depressive episodes improved;	
now no need for antidepressants	

Table 20 Health of Children at Follow-up 3³/₄ Years Later
(Seventh Pair)

Dean: 3³/₄ Years, Second Child	Mark: 3³/₄ Years
Severe eczema	Slight hydrophobia
Enuresis—diurnal and nocturnal	Persistent infantile speech
Stuttering, dyslalia, condensations,	Adjusted well to new brother
omissions	Mother—no difficulties ascertained
Height 37½ in	
Sleep disturbance	
Low frustration threshold	
Good relationship with older and	
younger sisters	
Mother—separated from husband; en-	
raged by Dean's enuresis	

Table 21   Health of Children at Follow-up 3³/₄ Years Later
(Eighth Pair)

Karen: 3¹/₂ Years, Fifth Child	Nicola: 3¹/₂ Years
Severely deprived with developmental retardation first year	Inhibited with strangers, especially doctors; otherwise no developmental deviations
Battered third year	
Scarring left ear, upper lip, chin for cosmetic surgery	Mother — no difficulties ascertained
Developmental therapy for 8 months	
Severe speech defect	
Severe regression on brief separation from foster mother	
Passive withdrawal frequent	
Insensitive to pain	
Foster mother — suddenly resigned prior to interview	

I have already referred to the two foster mothers, one of whom (No. 3) proved stable and healthy from the beginning and the other (No.8) who clearly had a serious personality disorder, the seriousness of which was not appreciated by the researchers on the occasions they interviewed her though she was diagnosed as having neurotic problems. The third foster mother clearly had severe personality and object relationships difficulties. Thus it comes as no surprise that she suddenly relinquished her foster mother role.

Three (Nos. 2, 5, 6) of the experimental group mothers had made gains in health, as reflected in improved marital relationships and less severe crippling by neurotic difficulties. One (No. 7) of the experimental mothers had separated from her husband who was, at the outset of the research, recognized as having major personality difficulties. He had been disturbed by his wife's pregnancy and confinement and had the utmost difficulty in relating comfortably to his children.

Two (Nos. 1 and 5) of the mothers of the comparison group children had signs and symptoms of emotional disturbance at intake. The quality of these is of significance. They were both contained, controlled, and less severe than those suffered by the clinical experimental-group mothers. At the time of the last follow-up both of the mothers had shown considerable growth and maturity. One had now accepted completely and unambivalently her role as a mother. At previous follow-ups she had displayed increasing strengths as a mother. The difficult marital relationship of the other mother had considerably improved.

For a moment I would like to pause to consider the infant-mother relationships of the battered babies. The one who did well (No. 3) was, when she was 6 months old and had recovered from the physical effects of the battering, fostered to a surrogate mother, a stable and healthy woman who had a sound marriage, though childless. At the age of 1 year the baby had recovered

Table 22   Health of Mothers at Intake and at Follow-up
Approximately $3^3/_4$ Years Later

	Experimental Group	Comparison Group
First pair intake	Exhausted, tense, no more babies	Depressed, feels inadequate as mother
Follow-up	Working full-time; another woman in mother role	Now confident in maternal role; no difficulties with second child
Second pair intake	Extreme tension, pedophobia	No admitted or detected difficulties
Follow-up	Ambivalence (+ +) to daughter; marriage improved	Continues well

Table 23   Health of Mothers at Intake and at Follow-up
Approximately $3^3/_4$ Years Later

	Experimental Group	Comparison Group
Third pair intake	Depressed, desperate, screaming at infant	No admitted or detected difficulties
Follow-up	Foster mother well; no difficulties with own first child	Continues well
Fourth pair intake	Depressed, desperate, infanticidal impulse	No admitted or detected difficulties
Follow-up	Well; no difficulties with second child	Continues well; no difficulties with second child

Table 24   Health of Mothers at Intake and at Follow-up
Approximately 3³/₄ Years Later

	Experimental Group	Comparison Group
Fifth pair intake	Depressed, desperate, hypochondriacal projection	Depressed, anxious, marital difficulties
Follow-up	November 25, 1970 — improved but remains anxious; pregnant	Well; no difficulties with second child; marriage improved
Sixth pair intake	Acute anxiety, helplessness	No admitted or detectable difficulties
Follow-up	Depressive episodes, tricyclics; improving	Continues well

Table 25   Health of Mothers at Intake and at Follow-up
·Approximately 3³/₄ Years Later

	Experimental Group	Comparison Group
Seventh pair intake	Helplessness, angry with infant	No admitted or detected difficulties
Follow-up	Overt hatred for son; separated from husband	Continues well
Eighth pair intake	Severe personality disorder	Anxiety-depressive states in past but no current difficulties detected
Follow-up	Two foster mothers with severe personality disorders	Continues well

from her developmental retardation. Subsequent follow-ups showed healthy gains and, at the last one, her behavior as well within the normal limits for a bright girl of her age. This, surely, must be an outstanding example of highly successful but fortuitous therapy. When she had recovered from the effects of the battering, most pediatricians and child psychiatrists would have predicted, as did the researchers, a poor developmental prognosis.

The other child (No. 8) who was battered has proved to be the one with the most severe developmental disorder. At the age of 6 months she was transferred to the care of a foster mother because of gross neglect and deprivation by her biological mother. Her development was so retarded that it was on a par with an infant of 8 to 10 weeks rather than 6 months. At the age of 11½ months, when seen at the second follow-up, she had made a developmental spurt and was among the most advanced of the younger babies. One year later it was noted that she was somewhat reserved, had not gained as had been predicted, and had an injury of the right hand that the mother explained as an accidental burn. According to the mother, the child did not suffer from pain. Subsequently, I felt that it would be worthwhile looking more into the pain insensitivity for I thought it might be a consequence of the gross deprivation she had suffered in the first 6 months of her life. It was then discovered that the family had suddenly moved from Dunedin without letting anyone know. They were located in a far-distant town where the local health officer finally had eventually made contact with them. Suspicions arose of battering, and some months later this was confirmed. When seen at the follow-up in 1970 the child was severely retarded, with a vocabulary less than she had had at 1 year old, a teetering, infantile wide-stanced gait, and a striking conservation-withdrawal response in the presence of strangers. She has since undergone plastic surgery to her lips and nose, and there is more to come. In February 1971 she was taken into Associate Professor Lewis's developmental treatment center for 5 hours of daily therapy 5 times a week. At the last follow-up she had made gains, but the conservation-withdrawal response in the face of a stranger was readily evoked, her vocabulary was limited, and she had major difficulties in relating to others. It seems likely that she has suffered permanent damage to her personality development.

Etiology

To begin with, a consideration of the etiology must be confirmed to the babies and their mothers who were the subjects of this study. Later I make some speculative generalizations. Seven of the experimental mothers had major problems with mothering. Two had severe personality disorders and were unable to establish a nurturing role with their children. One of these battered her child, and the other grossly neglected her. The quality of the personality disturbance hinted at psychosis for neither of them recognized the unreality and inappropriateness of their perception of their babies and their responses to their babies' needs. Two other mothers (Nos. 1 and 2) had major overt problems with mothering, but they recognized this to be the case. One of these has now entirely given up the maternal role and transferred it to her own mother, so the child is now being reared by his grandmother. The relationship between the mother and her own mother has been directly observed, so it is not merely a matter of speculation from retrospective history to state that although the two women superficially appear to relate satisfactorily to each other, there is in fact a good deal of antagonism embedded in their independent-dependent relationship. The other mother, whose child suffered a severe scald in her second year (her elder child had been severely burned in his second year!), felt that she had a constant battle with her daughter. She had overt feelings of hatred for her own mother.

Two (Nos. 5 and 6) other mothers were recent immigrants to New Zealand. Both were extremely dependent on their own mothers and the question can rightly be asked why they had traveled so far from Britain if that was the case. It turned out that one was acting out her father's wish to immigrate to New Zealand. Although dependent on her mother, she nevertheless had not been able ever to confide matters of deep emotional import. The other immigrant mother has since returned to Scotland. She could not establish a supportive network in her new surroundings. In her childhood she had been hospitalized for 18 months for the treatment of severe burns. Of this hospitalization her most vivid memories were of the arrivals and the departures of her visiting mother and her great distress when her mother went away. Her childhood memories end there.

Of the remaining two mothers, one (No. 4) had had a hostile and angry relationship with her mother for many years. This was not severe enough to exclude communication between the two. This was the mother who, shortly after she returned home from the maternity hospital, had an impulse to suffocate her baby when she did not stop crying. The last (No. 8) of the eight mothers at first appeared to have no serious problems in her relationship with her own mother. She was an only child and stated that she was unable to discuss matters of personal moment with her mother. Apart from that, she appeared to have a good relationship. For support in her mothering role, however, she sought help from her husband. But he, an adopted child, was the last person able to give it. The marriage has now broken up. Her relationship to her son is at times one of overt hatred, associated with fantasies of assault that are so intense that she fears she might act them out.

In contrast to the experimental mothers, only one (No. 4) of the comparison mothers had difficulties in the maternal role that approached in severity those of the experimental mothers. However, she had the resource of being able to establish a supportive network of relationships. Her mother-in-law was a good mother surrogate. She also had a strong mutually supportive relationship with another young wife. At the time of intake, both were sharing a house and supporting each other in the rearing of the babies that they each had just had. It is significant that this mother has managed to achieve a rapprochement with her own mother at the time of the last follow-up.

In terms of etiology it would appear that the experimental mothers had difficulty in the maternal role, partly as a consequence of their own rearing and upbringing. Stating it in that way is oversimplifying the issue because a large number of processes inevitably are involved in the adult capacity of the woman to be a competent mother. The incapacity to act comfortably in the maternal role was reflected in misperceptions of the infant's needs and, indeed, of perceiving the infant as an infant. The more the infant expressed its distress, the more difficulty the mother had in her efforts to alleviate it. In this manner a self-reinforcing cycle of action and reaction was established. Hospitalization certainly had the effect of breaking the cycle, temporarily at any rate.

In spite of the respite provided by the hospital, the data obtained from this study suggest that the relationship between mother and her child had been sufficiently strongly established prior to admission that the maternal components of it tended to remain fixed. Whereas hospital intervention meant that the infants' behavior disorders were strikingly alleviated, this could not be stated of the mothers. I have already said enough to emphasize that there has thus far persisted in the mothers' relationships with their children processes that contributed to the original difficulties that brought about their hospitalization. It seems as if the persistence of these components in the infant-maternal relationship has contributed to the developmental disorders from which the experimental babies are now suffering.

The etiological concept that I have presented is, of course, one that is used widely. In the present context it is one that nevertheless fits the information obtained.

The IDDS babies had mothers who themselves had impairment or incapacity to assume the maternal roles that would have enabled them to cope with the developmental needs of their children. Both retrospective and observational data point strongly to the maternal incapacity as having been the consequence of developmental difficulties that the mothers had suffered in their early years.

Discussion

The signals of infant distress have been widely studied, and excellent reports exist on the sleep, feeding, crying, and other aspects of infant behavior. On the other hand, to my knowledge, the concept of the infant developmental distress syndrome has not been described and presented by others.

A previous contribution by Associate Professor Lewis and myself evoked the criticism that the IDDS is no more than behavior in the normative range. That has an element of truth in it. The retrospective data suggest that at first the behavior of the infant is within the normative range. With the mother unable to respond and to satisfy the infant's immediate and developmental needs, a mutually shared distress state is rapidly reached in which the mother suffers severe emotional disturbance and the infant distress behavior becomes chronic at a level Prechtl and Beintema [2] would rate as Stage 5—that stage of infant distress in which it is impossible to conduct a neurological examination. The point that I wish to make is that the normative behavior of the infant imperceptibly becomes pathological, and this in turn impedes developmental progress. It indicates a persistence of difficulties in the infant-mother relationship due to depleted or not yet existent maternal resources. There is also the probability that the interactions between the infant and mother become stereotyped so that a subsequent developmental disorder is apparent in later childhood. Moreover, because of chronic distress behavior, infants numbering approximately 10 percent of live births in the area served by the Karitane Hospital are admitted to it for treatment. I think, therefore, that it is justifiable to refer to the observable constellation of signs of chronic infant distress behavior as a syndrome with implications for developmental disorder.

In India the babies have sleeping and feeding difficulties and at times cry a lot without apparent reason, and some infants are much more easily distressed than others. But in the Hindu extended family system this creates no problems. Firstborn babies are often handed over to the more experienced mother-in-law to take care of, for it is felt that the young mother is insufficiently experienced and mature for the important task. (Half of the babies in this study were firstborns.) Moreover, the extended family system provides several mother surrogates who can be turned to with confidence when any problem of infant rearing occurs. The young mother has a strong supportive social network. Another feature of Hindu society that differs from ours is that it is intensely child-centered. It would seem then that the IDDS is a culture-bonded syndrome. It so happened that I saw no infants in New Delhi who suffered from it.

Considering the IDDS as a culture-bonded syndrome puts it into a different perspective. Mothers are usually regarded as blameworthy in our society when their contribution to infant developmental pathology is discussed. By thinking in terms of cultural attitudes toward child rearing and the sources of help within a society for a mother in distress, a less judgmental approach and hence a more satisfactory understanding of what is happening can be achieved. In New Zealand a system of helping mothers is now well established. I do not think it is as effective as the Hindu extended family, but it does provide relief to both infants and mothers.

Regarding a syndrome as culture-bonded has crucial meanings for prevention. In the present state of our knowledge, and the theory that stems from it, a culture-bonded syndrome should be 100 percent preventable, although we all understand that the complexities of the biological, social, and cultural circumstances of human beings do make prevention a difficult matter in practice. There have been many reports on how impervious to change are cultural and social attitudes even though they are demonstrably irrational. Child rearing as one of the fundamental biological processes has its fair share of irrational attitudes, even in our scientific and technologically competent society. Nevertheless, the IDDS theoretically should be completely preventable. Even if it turns out that the syndrome is less prevalent than this study suggests, efforts at primary prevention are, in my opinion, still justified.

Prevention also implies recognizing vulnerability. An infant who has developed the IDDS would seem to be vulnerable to subsequent developmental disorder. Treatment is indicated. The effectiveness of early hospital intervention has already been described. But clearly this needs to be followed up with ongoing therapy over a long period if subsequent developmental disorder is to be avoided. Thus the IDDS is a sign of the *vulnerability of the infant at risk*.

The vulnerability of the mother also needs assessment. The data of this research suggest that the mother who has persistent problems in adopting the maternal role, especially if this is related to her own rearing, if there is a lack of supportive figures in her social network, if there is evidence of marital difficulties, and if the later part of the puerperium has been characterized by biological and emotional maladjustment, then it is likely that the *mother is vulnerable and at risk*.

By assessing the vulnerabilities of infant and mother it would seem that it is clinically feasible to recognize the *nursing couple who are at risk*.

To turn again to the IDDS proper I would suggest that it is a harbinger both of later developmental disorder and life-threatening traumata. To regard the syndrome as merely evidence of incompetent mothering to which infants respond in the only ways open to them, implying that the behavior is within the normative range, is to adopt a value-judgment approach to what appears to be a rather common pediatric problem in our society. If further research confirms the hunches that the disorder is indeed wisespread but unrecognized, there will be tremendous possibilities for all those involved in maternal and child-health services to participate in early recognition and prevention of the more unfortunate sequelae.

Conclusions

What I have attempted to do in this chapter is to draw the reader's attention to a syndrome I have named the *infant developmental distress syndrome*. It has an incidence of approximately 10 percent of the live births of the location where the clinical study was conducted and is responsible for approximately 70 percent of the admissions to an infant-care hospital. The syndrome presents as excessive crying, hyperresponsivity, and disorder of feeding and sleeping patterns. It occurs in association with extreme maternal distress. Its response to hospital, nonspecific therapy is rapid.

The mothers have difficulty in accepting and adjusting to the maternal role. Their personal histories suggest that they themselves had difficulties in their relationships with their mothers.

Following hospital discharge of their infants the mothers continued to have problems in coping. The outcome of this after nearly 4 years is that the infants, now children, have developmental disorders. Of the eight experimental children, four were exposed to life-threatening traumata during those years in comparison with none of the parallel group of matched children who had not suffered the IDDS.

The one experimental clinical child who did not have a developmental disorder at the last follow-up had been battered with a severe head injury. She had been transferred to the care of foster, later adoptive, parents who provided a stable and loving upbringing.

Circumstantial evidence suggests that the IDDS is culture-bonded; theoretically, this has the implication that it is 100 percent preventable. Primary prevention would involve a drastic change in attitude culturally and socially toward the infant and the maternal role. Secondary prevention would involve recognition of vulnerable infants and mothers, the nursing couple at risk, and the provision of long-term supportive and therapeutic measures for the nursing couple. To achieve this would entail changes in the structure and functioning of maternal and child-welfare services and especially in the training of personnel, both medical and paramedical.

References

1. Lewis, P. J., Ironside, W., McKinnon, P., et al. The Karitane project: psychological ill-health, infant distress and the postpartum period. *N. Z. Med. J.* 79:1005-9, 12 Jun 74.
2. Prechtl, H. and Beintema, D. *The Neurological Examination of the Full-Term Newborn Infant,* The Spastics Society Medical Education and Information Unit, London, 1964.

VULNERABILITY AND PARENTHOOD

The Positive Value of Parents

Clare Claiborne Park, Litt.D. (U.S.A.)

Ten years ago I would not have dared to speak to you on the positive value of parents—nor would I have been invited. I am the parent of a child diagnosed at 3 as suffering from early infantile autism, one of the most disabling psychiatric conditions known. To say this 10 years ago would have been to display myself as a "refrigerator parent," whose emotional emptiness was demonstrated by the indubitable fact that I observed my child's abnormal behavior, and tried to do so objectively. I even went so far as the mothers described by a renowned clinician of infantile autism who observed their children "as if they were clinical subjects" and "compiled detailed notes and diaries on them."[1].

My daughter, at 3, was a classic case, without speech or verbal comprehension, absorbed in objects and patterns rather than to people, but with characteristic isolated areas of high cognitive ability (she and our family are described in detail elsewhere)[2]. She was the youngest of four children, of whom the older three were and still are notably bright, beautiful, plucky, and trouble-free. My autistic child is now 16, and I am here because competent professionals, who have watched my daughter and me, together and apart, visited our home and met our family, have concluded that as parents I and my husband have done a good job.

One of these, Elizabeth Irvine, has cited our experience in a previous volume in this series[3]. It is her conviction that many

214

parents can "do more than any professional can to help their children contend with their handicaps without psychiatric damage" that has led to this presentation.

Except for diagnosis, she has never been hospitalized; she has never lived anywhere but in her own home; she has never gone to a special school. She can now function in a special class in a public high school. She rides the bus and takes gym, art, typing, math, and home economics with normal children. Her behavior, though by no means uniformly normal, is sufficiently under control to make all this possible, and her winning, if childlike, personality draws many people to her. Follow-up studies on severely autistic 3-year-olds have been very discouraging; my daughter has done better than most. Perhaps the objectivity, the diaries and notes, have contributed; they were intended to.

Because we live in a rural area far from sophisticated mental-health facilities the only therapy that she has had for 16 years has been what we, her family, have given her, joined later while she developed by teachers and by resourceful and devoted young companions who functioned as cotherapists. Such therapy has been only an intensification and prolongation of the teaching and loving interaction that goes on in most families of small children.

Professionals have been intensely aware of parents' capacity for doing things wrong. Let me quote from a few of these negative assessments:

1. In 1973 a book written by a well-known psychiatrist appeared with the title *Are Parents Bad for Children?* with the strong implication that the answer was "yes."[4].
2. The precipitating factor in infantile autism is the parent's wish that his child should not exist [5].
3. Studies show a large measure of agreement on characteristic maternal attitudes. A pertinent summarized description from Tietze is quoted: "All mothers were over-anxious and obsessive, all were domineering . . . all mothers were found to be restrictive with regard to the libidinal gratification of their children. Most of them were perfectionistic and over-solicitous, and more dependent on approval by others than the average mother." So many mothers of these children are emotionally detached and seeking gratification from intel-

lectual sources rather than from contact with people . . . it can
be said that many of the mothers surround their infant in a
scientific aura and emotional void which are very striking . . .
they apply literally the rigid and the mechanistic rules that
they are quick to seize on as ways and means of rearing the
perfect child [3].

4. If the parents were not difficult or peculiar, it is unlikely that
   the patient would be schizophrenic [6].
5. The parents of autistic, childhood schizophrenics, we sur-
   mised, have forms of behavior which would rebuff, impair,
   and interfere with the very beginnings of relationships that
   they might have with the child and would continue to do so
   later . . . Cynical outlook: Approximately 70% of the CS parents were in this group. They expect the worst possible
   motivation in people. They sound embittered, disen-
   chanted, and describe warmth, closeness, and tender moti-
   vations with contempt, skepticism, or scorn. Often their
   criticism conveys an active, destructive quality with a sadistic
   finality about people leaving one another . . . others convey
   resignation, withdrawal, disinterest, and avoidance . . .
   [others] treat everything in a superficial "surfacey" way . . .
   Facetiousness appears particularly in the tests of parents who
   might be classed as either cynical or superficial . . . Some
   parents convey a sense of disaffiliation via detachment and
   intellectualized distance. When parents with these intense,
   disaffiliating, distancing, and unempathic tendencies have
   an infant with a low innate capacity to elicit appropriate
   responsiveness, transactional failures crippling to ego development will necessarily begin at birth [7].

Today there is a frail willingness to recognize the capacity of
parents for doing things right; to see us as contributors to our
children's adaptation rather than their maladaptation, their independence rather than their dependence, and their strength rather
than their weakness. It is so easy to find what one is searching for
psychologically. When incompetence and guilt are assumed in
parents they are easily found, not to say thereby created. However, now there are professionals (like Fenichel of the League
School and Schopler [8,9,10] of the Parent Training Project in

North Carolina) who are apparently willing to make the important initial assumption that parents can help their children to grow and develop; that they will work night and day at this task and call up every reserve of feeling and intelligence that they have. This means that professionals are recognizing that parents have their particular kind of expertise that can be brought into the service of treatment. Besides the immemorial techniques of affectionate family living, parents of "vulnerable children" begin with a significant advantage that professionals can only obtain with time and difficulty—a total familiarity with the child's past and present history, his physical and emotional environment, and his verbal and nonverbal language. In addition, many of these parents are intensely motivated by the conviction that their children can grow and develop and that it is their task to help him to go as far as he can.

What then can one say to the arrogance, and willingness to hurt, implicit in the question, "are parents bad for their children?" Can it be answered? Can it be answered by a psychiatrist with his attention focused on the clinical? Of all types of success, the most widespread is successful parenthood, the species survives because this is so. It is also the least conspicuous. It is precisely the parents who successfully pilot their children through illness and crisis who never come to professional attention. When the illness is so grave, the crisis so acute, that we are driven to seek professional help, too often the doctors appear to ignore our successes while assuming that whatever failure is all ours. This attitude is changing, as is evident from Appleton's article [11]. It will change even further. In the mean time, I would like to leave you with one question relating to all that I have said: How was it possible for so many professionals, wise observers of the human condition, dedicated before all else to the principles of *primum non nocere*, so to misperceive us?

References

1. Despert, J. L. *The Functionally Disturbed Child: An Inquiry into Family Patterns.* Doubleday-Anchor Books, New York, 1970.
2. Park, C. C. *The Seige: The First Eight Years of an Autistic Child.* Atlantic Little Brown, Boston, 1972. (Translations in French, German, Dutch, Swedish, Danish, and Japanese.)
3. Irvine, E. E. The risks of the Register: Or the management of expectation. In

The Child in His Family, Vol. III: Children at Psychiatric Risk, E. J. Anthony, and C. Koupernik, Eds. Wiley, New York, 1974.

4. Blaine, G. *Are Parents Bad for Children?* Coward, McCann & Geohegan, New York, 1973.

5. Bettleheim, B. *The Empty Fortress.* Free Press, New York, 1967.

6. Lidz, T. "Family Studies and Treatments of Schizophrenia," in *Progress in Group and Family Therapy.* Branner/Mazel, New York, 1972.

7. Singer, M. T., and Winne, L. C. Differentiating characteristics of parents of childhood schizophrenia, cs, childhood neurotics, and young adult schizophrenics. *Am. J. Psychiatr.* 120(1963).

8. Schopler, E. Parents of psychotic children as scapegoats. *J. of Contemp. Psychotherapy,* 4, 1(1971), 17–22.

9. Schopler, E., and Loftin, J. Thought disorders in parents of psychistic children: A function of test anxiety. *Arch. Gen. Psychiatry,,* 20(1969) 174.

10. Schopler, E., and Reichler, R. J. Parents as co-therapists in the treatment of psychotic children. *Ann. Progress in Child Psychiatry and Child Development.* S. Chess and A. Thomas, Eds. Brunner/Mazel, New York, 1972.

11. Appleton, W. S. Mistreatment of patients' families by psychiatrists. *Am. J. Psychiatr.,* 131(June, 1974).

Concerning Parental Vulnerability: Issues Around Child and Infant Loss

Beatrice Cooper, M.S.W., and Rudolf Ekstein, Ph.D. (U.S.A.)

We are concerned with the meaning of infant loss to a vulnerable woman at the critical moment of giving birth. Our interest was mobilized through the mother of one of the children studied in the Research Project on Childhood Psychosis.[1] This mother was born in an impoverished black ghetto but moved into an educated, middle-class milieu during her adulthood and marriage. The child's conception was planned and cherished by parents whose marriage was stable, although there were relatively normal tensions and differences after five previous pregnancies had terminated in miscarriage or stillbirth.

When she looked into the face of her live, full-term baby, this mother saw him for a moment as her stillborn son. Vincent Van Gogh's mother might have had such an experience before naming her newborn baby Vincent, the name of a child she lost after birth the very same day a year earlier. Our mother had no knowledge of, nor was she concerned with, the type of handling this child would require to enable him to exist for himself rather than as the weak substitute for the idealized dead baby. Yet she projected her

[1]Reiss-Davis Child Study Center, Los Angeles, California.

vulnerability on to her live son, perhaps the same vulnerability that she saw in that lifeless extension of herself, her dead son. Was it then surprising, when he was evaluated as severely emotionally disturbed at the age of 5 years, that she continued to identify him with the dead child?

Many questions arise about these vulnerable parents' oscillating capacity to allow a child to develop a separate existence rather than be the extension of that dead part of the parents' selves that they need to have confirmed. This child is additionally burdened by having to exist as a substitute for the dead child. He must struggle against overwhelming confusion and fusion as he reaches for individuation, the development of a separate and alive self. He is unable to provide his mother with the feeling that he is genuinely alive. She senses that he is not attuned to her, that he is a separate being whom she must psychologically bring to life.

Added to the horror of her many miscarriages and stillbirths, which robbed her of the promise of life and motherhood, she is now faced with a psychotic child. Thus her vulnerability places her in the position of experiencing a double loss. She contemplates the future without the hopes and goals she would enjoy in raising a normal child. She wonders about his safety if she allows herself to care for him. We realize that she feels crushed and unable to cope because of her overwhelming vulnerability.

The professional literature concerns itself more frequently with children who experience the loss of a parent than with parents who experience the loss of a child or infant. Cain's paper [1] calls attention to the case of a disturbed child who was deliberately conceived as a replacement shortly after the death of another child. The author discussed the circumstances of conception, the constellation of parental attitudes that may cloud the child's upbringing, and the potentially severe pathological consequences of these influences on the child's emotional development.

The mother of our patient could only start to resolve her mourning meaningfully later in her child's development; that is, during the course of his psychiatric treatment. Because of the tragic circumstances surrounding his birth the child was overvalued. Usually the latency child develops the fantasy of the family romance—of being the child of important parents. In this case, however, the parents developed the inverted or reversed family-romance fantasy that their child, not really theirs, was a genius who would bring fame and fortune to himself as well as to them. (Laius and Jocasta later did think of Oedipus as somebody else's son.) He was living proof of their projected, primary narcissism. He was to replace the idealized dead babies, outdo the scholarly father, compete successfully with the white culture, and cure his psychotic illness—an impossible plot to live up to. The mother must maintain the fiction—it can be done—while also seeing in him her dead babies.

Generic to most of our work with parents of severely disturbed children, we find in the underlying reversed family romance a pathological exaggeration of parental love. Because the parents are encouraged by what they are convinced is great promise, they feel capable of sustaining the endless responsibility required for the care and treatment of such a child. The parents' adaptive use of the reversed family romance myth enables them to maintain the support and treatment for years notwithstanding the frequent lack of adequate community assistance for the treatment of mental disorders. They must deny, or at least postpone, their awareness of the reality that, should the treatment be successful, their child may develop into a mere ordinary person, not a super genius.

We are frequently invited, and are tempted, to enter into collusion with parents who need us to reinforce their romantic notion, sometimes illusion, sometimes delusion, that they have a very special, psychotic child. The special values they secretly harbor encourage them to feel that the child is worthy of the time, personal investment, and immense sacrifice required for a continuing, perhaps successful, therapy process. The concept of the child's omnipotentiality [7] suggests that all choices are open, that everything is possible, but it leaves unspoken the underlying terror, the danger of negative outcome. The emphasis is on the pathological hope that the potential of this highly valued, gifted child is infinite, but it also implies the underlying potential for negative, destructive impulse by means of which the child will destroy the parents and himself. (Did not Paul Bunyan destroy his parents?) The mother not only dreams that he will be the substitute for the dead babies, she also feels that he may die, be injured, or be impaired. The hope then turns into despair both merging and continuing, outside and inside, as in a möebius strip [2].

We are familiar with the way children unconsciously forge their personal history when they first vaguely realize that their parents are not the outstanding and powerful people that they were perceived and idealized to be in early childhood. In their fantasies they replace their real parents with more acceptable parents and are thus enabled to endure the reality of their ordinary family situation while maintaining a sense of omnipotence. This expression of the child's longing is discussed by Freud [4] as a longing for the happy, vanished days when father was the strongest and noblest; it is an expression of regret that these days are gone forever.

Such forgeries actually are mutual, although the parents reconstruct the past quite differently. They, too, need the family-romance fantasy. When the child no longer sees him as omnipotent, the father may dream, or actually say, "My son in reality is a genius." What father has not looked into the face of his newborn child and viewing the miracle of life seen the omnipotential of the child? This omnipotentiality is seen as hidden omnipotence such as when we say, "He may be the president some day. He can be anything he wants to be and I, as the parent, will facilitate it. I will make it possible." If the child cashes in on the potential, then the omnipotentiality is given up as one possible commitment is selected and concentrated on. Retaining the *omnipotentiality* may be *underlined* by the feeling that life now might last forever since *all still lies ahead.* The parent gives up his own sense of omnipotence by transferring it to his child; he can project his primary narcissism on to the child for whom he will go to any lengths to enable him to develop his potential. The child, on the other hand, attempts to identify with the more famous, fantasied father. He develops into a more successful, mature person and thus resolves the prelatency conflict he experienced with his parents. Both parent and child need to have a separate, private mythology to maintain their omnipotence, at least as omnipotential; they must hope for the future. The parent, through the miracle of birth, the giving of life to another, is able to sacrifice himself and accept his mundane, limited life experiences by endowing the child with the promise of a more fulfilled life. Thus in each new generation is born the hope that it can do and be better than the last. This certainly holds true for developing rather than static societies.

What should be examined more closely is how the parents of a psychotic child become vulnerable when faced with the insurmountable gap between fantasy and reality. In our experience with psychotic children we find that parents, particularly mothers, are able to dedicate themselves to long-term treatment. They maintain their children in a therapeutic process despite external obstacles that frequently arise in the family situation. The fathers' involvement is usually not as extensive as the mothers'.

Lidz's [5] studies were directed toward the failure of parental nurturance, not necessarily from overt rejection but frequently because of deficiencies within the mother's own development. His data support, rather than refute, the hypothesis that intrafamiliar environment plays a critical role in the etiology of schizophrenia. However, we are not directing ourselves toward the cause of the illness, but rather to the cause of the cure [3]. What is the specific nature of, and what is required in, the recovery process of these kinds of cases? The parents collaborate with us in working to help their child toward adaptation and recovery.

Our mother, depressed at the time of the birth experience, was literally unable to give words to her child. The nature of their relationship was that she held him in her arms and drew pictures for him. She gave him drawings, images; she maintained a silent communion with him while she drew pictures to illustrate, entertain, and bring to him the larger world. As a result of this form of communication he became a very skillful, precocious cartoonist at a very early age. In his beginning therapy hours he drew a cast of characters for this therapist. It was soon discernible, however, that he was unable to develop a plot for the characters, a script that would lead somewhere, to some denouement or solution [6]. He followed the inverse of Jewish religion, as if he believed one may make images of the deity but is forbidden, discouraged, to express what one sees in thoughts or through the spoken word.

Because of the mother's innermost fear that she had been too biologically immature to produce live children, she felt the need to protect her son from her own inability. She encouraged the father to become the substitute mothering figure. The father tried in vain to relate to the remote, often unresponsive infant. The father spoke with words, not pictures; he relied primarily on communication, while the mother relied primarily on communion.

The mother sought white women with whom she could have a close relationship. Her closest friend was a crippled, white librarian whom she experienced as a giver of knowledge, the provider of intellect. This was the only woman she would allow to assume the substitute mothering role for her son. We are reminded here of the lyrics in the current musical "Jesus Christ Superstar" in which Mary Magdalane says, "I don't know how to love him," a haunting appeal to the audience to appreciate, satisfy, and nurture Christ, whom she realized was miraculously brought to earth for some reason, as yet unknown, but of immense impact and meaning to her. Bewildered by the responsibility of being the purveyor of Christ, she then appealed to the audience to take him in, nurture him, be nurtured by him, and sustain him within the intrapsychic self. In some such way our mother appealed to our clinic to rescue her child from the destructive black mothering, to recognize that damaged part of herself that she felt could only be repaired by the white clinic, the white doctor, the white social worker. She created for herself a duality that was experienced at times as insurmountable.

This mother was seen in the testing situation as a remote, distant person, apologetic, tense, and uneasy, which masked a defense of childlike helplessness related to expression of strong affect. She is a woman in constant pursuit of self-perception. Deliberation, articulation, and thought-before-action, have become explicit values for her in and of themselves, as well as the means by which she organizes her internal and external life. Implicit is her assumption that the work of the intellect can offset base, primitive, and consistently unacceptable feelings and impulses that she seeks to suppress. The wish for spontaneous communality with others is perceived as loathsome. To this wish she reacts by using the organizing force of reason as a means of warding off the impulsive pull toward instinctual gratification. Beneath the conflict surrounding impulse expression lies the more malignant and persistent difficulty that she experiences concerning her integrity as a person, her doubt and compulsive defenses. Often she struggles with a sense of vacancy, an empty vessel in which the origins of her being are experienced as vague and therefore anxiety-provoking. In one sense her pursuit of knowledge becomes a way of attempting to verify the past and in that sense the very origin of self. Not unlike the creative artist who literally gives birth to a work of art in his struggle for perfect artistic expression, this mother struggles to give birth to herself by discovering who and what she should be through study and portrayal of what she has learned to become. The consequence of this struggle to attain selfhood is the inconstant and inconsistent way in which this mother experiences and expresses affect. Typically, she is unable to assess the appropriateness, the means of expression, and the value of what she feels. The relationships between objects and feelings become indistinct and at times confusing for her. Therefore, the consequences of strong feelings or interpersonal commitments are to be distrusted for her in the sense that they may lead to an unpredictable outcome. For this mother the struggle to acquire authentic selfhood has been lifelong and remains her most persistent pursuit. She seems to be engaged in a mission to discover how she might become whoever she should be.

The father is a thick-set man who appears much older than his age. At the outset he appears passive and compliant and maintains an open, low-keyed relationship. He frequently complains of weariness. However, when working with this man the degree of pervasiveness and intensity of disruptive anxiety that he experiences can be easily discerned. Frequently his tension is evidenced in physical symptoms, including faltering speech, perspiration, and occasional gastric discomfort. When his customary distancing devices and defenses fail to maintain anxiety at a tolerable level he sought to flee from the testing material to neutral intellectual topics and then ultimately to flee from the examiner as well. Throughout all these maneuvers he maintains a cooperative attitude of passive compliance. Principally, his anxiety seems related to conflict involving the recognition and expression of intense affect. He prefers to contend with chronic, moderate-level depression rather than deal with more intense feelings. He has organized his life by means of modulating and distancing devices. Driven by a need to gain knowledge to control an explosively turbulent inner world, knowledge and power are synonymous for him. Often angered by a feeling that people single him out for messy jobs and dirty work, he is then able to project feelings of distrust, disgust, hatred, and rage on to an external world that he distrusts. He maintains an image of himself as an overburdened hero or victim, in need of sympathy and support from his perceived persecutors. He is further beset by unresolved, infantile concerns. Leaning heavily on the fact of an upbringing in a father-absent household, he maintains a particular, peculiar version of "the family romance" in his fantasy that his father was a great military man, a hero of battle. This romantic notion has been one way he could distance himself from the rage he continues to harbor toward the missing father who failed to act as a foil for the demands of the mother. Separation from the mother has been a most arduous and painful process involving partial identification with the fantasized soldier-hero father, perhaps a projection of an invention of the ego ideal. Frustration and rage, as well as feelings of helpnessness and ineffectuality, have been displaced on to medical doctors seeking to treat the mother who presumably had lost a bout with a terminal illness. Anger toward the unreliable but powerful man is also displaced on the would-be healers and confirms the father's open distrust of the entire healing profession. He feels particularly helpless to aid his son and does feel responsible for the boy's condition. Somewhat identified with the damaged boy, he presumes that the father-like sons are participants in a futile struggle to make their way in a world which moves too quickly for them. If only they had received the proper nutriments early in their development then they would have less difficulty making their way. Women have somehow escaped this dilemma; they have resources that men do not have. His masculine sexual identity has been hard won; he has been plagued by a sense of inadequacy and imminent failure. Throughout these many struggles, however, he does not lose the capacity for adequate reality testing, although self-observation and impulse control become tenuous under stress.

To the nonclinical eye he would appear the ideal upward-bound self-made man. However, he frequently relies on impulsive diffuse action as an outlet for acutely disruptive anxiety experiences. His capacity to recover from such surges of tension is variable and to a degree dependent on the amount of support he can muster from his immediate environment.

Knowledge of these dynamics was ascertained during the early period of the treatment process. In our actual clinical work we were confronted with the parents' covert vulnerability in carrying the role of restoring functioning to their vulnerable child, that damaged part of themselves they wanted so much to protect. They could outwardly accept that the child was in a treatment process but could not acknowledge that they themselves were also in a parallel treatment process. This process made them feel even more vulnerable to exposure to self and therapist. The father did not want the white woman to know about his inner, intimate, tumultuous feelings, the doubts about his self-identity. The closer he came to self-disclosure, the more threatened he felt. He considered it paramount to maintain a psychological distance, as was evidenced by the time sequence by which he kept his appointments. On the other hand, the mother's more positive relationship with white women enabled her to deal with her initial distrust. She always felt that her control of the relationship would prevent it from getting out of hand. Underlying all this were the parents' memories and scars of poverty and hunger, so that in their present affluence they feel the way to show love for a person is to overfeed him. It became clear that the therapy process was likened to a feeding relationship in which both parents could accept that what *they* could not feed their child could perhaps be fed to him elsewhere; it did not necessarily render them more vulnerable. Involvement not only exposed these parents to greater vulnerability but also to loss of their projected omnipotence. Intellectually they understood the treatment approach would not necessarily be a detriment, or result in a decline in their child's intellectual functioning; emotionally they felt it would. There was a time when the boy was able to tell on what day of the week in the future a certain date would fall and could make accurate weather predictions, like an almanac. Now they complained that he was losing some of this magic, some of his omniscience. The mother felt that her miscarriage of the twins and the loss of his parental grandmother, both events occurring when he was 4½ years old, had had a deeply adverse effect on him. He regressed in school, losing interest in his intellectual pursuits. He seemed preoccupied with death and obsessively drew little coffin-like boxes into which he drew the outline of a baby. Although the faces were not delineated, he labeled them "dead boy" or "dead girl." The mother recalled that he was present while she was aborting the twins and was with her when she arranged a medical school to accept the bodies because she could not afford a funeral or burial services. While she poignantly described the trauma that she and her son had suffered, it seemed evident that she was accusing society, which we appeared to represent, of not being sensitive enough to take that dead part of her and treat it with dignity and appropriate reverence. It was clear that in working with her we would have to accept her projection of hatred of, disappointment in, and frustration with herself for her inability to carry full-term children and for not ridding her of that part of herself that malfunctioned. The parents felt that treatment in the clinic had very little meaning for their child, just as time had no meaning. They saw him suspended in timelessness and unreality; they felt that only they could bring him down to earth so that he would be less vulnerable, be less frightened, and thus would choose to identify with the more prosaic, everyday, ordinary world. Our involvement with the child caught us in a double bind; we had taken over where the parents left off; we would now have to regard him as special, as omnipotential. Since we were investing so much in him, it was implied that we expected something very special to emerge when the therapy process terminated. The parents could not believe that we had no specific expectations or preconceived goals as to what the child would accomplish with the therapy. He was frequently used as a mirror to see the feelings they were experiencing but could not see as their own feelings. These parents very clearly described the way in which they needed external structure to function and resist and struggle against it. Whenever the child was not in school, the mother did not have a class at the college, or the father was not involved in some kind of professional activity they were confronted with lack of structure and a kind of empty, unlimited freedom that terrified them.

In this clinical situation we were faced wth the back-breaking task of working with a family who had experienced repetitive loss of children representing also their self-concept as emptied-out people who could give birth to nothing. When they actually produced a surviving child he was seen as that living confirmation of the deadness, the emptiness, the damaged self that had no right to survive. The vicious circle was completed when the most precious thing they could give to their child, their own sense of intellectual omnipotence, was seen as not even sufficient to satisfy a school setting. This then confirmed their innermost fears that he was a dead child and thus required intensive psychiatric treatment. He could no longer fool the community by masquerading as a precocious, intellectual functioning, totally human being when, in fact, he was a robot-like child. Thus they became extremely vulnerable to what they considered to be the community's confirmation of their innermost fears.

Summary

This case study offers a magnified version of the clinical team's technical task; namely, the transference dilemma of the therapists in initiating a therapy process away from the point of hopelessness toward possible acceptance of emotional growth. The psychotic child, the living symbol of biological incompetence, is also seen as the projection of the parents' "deadness," or biological and emotional impotency. The therapists and the clinic are seen as ths last desperate hope that may reverse the process. Projected onto them are the unconscious aims of perfection, impossible to achieve, and also the despair that requires the family to believe no heavenly or earthly power will promote a new fertility.

In addition to the usual technical problems, we must learn to cope with the countertransference fantasy, double-edged as it is, that requires of us that we accomplish a miracle or surrender to doom.

In his effort to communicate with the therapist the child currently develops an endless cast of characters who are ready for the show but have no play, no plot. Thus, like the six characters in search of an author, he asks that we develop a theme, a process. The current characters are almost as dead as the infants are lost. We, the therapists, cannot be the authors of this family's life story; we can only initiate a new process to help them move from paralysis toward development.

Some of the most recent experiences, such as the birth of a normal child, or the improved socializing capacity of the sick child indicate that we are beyond the overture and move into the first act of recovery. The parents' emphasis on and push for, precocious development is now seen as their need to push against the inherent psychological weakness.

References

1. Cain, Albert C. On replacing a child. Presented at the meeting of the American Orthopsychiatric Association, March 1962.
2. Caruth, E. The onion and the moebius strip: Rational and irrational models for the secondary and primary process. In *The Challenge: Despair and Hope in the Conquest of Inner Space*, R. Ekstein, Ed. Brunner/Mazel, New York, 1971.
3. Ekstein, R. and Friedman, S. Cause of the illness or cause of the cure? *Internat J. Psychiat.*, 3 (1968), 224–229.
4. Freud, S. (1909) Family romances. *Standard Edition.* Hogarth Press, London, 1959.
5. Lidz, T. *Schizophrenia and the family.* International Universities Press, New York, 1965.
6. Liebowitz, J. Story-telling in search of a plot. *Reiss-Davis Clin. Bull.*, 2 (1972), 112–115.
7. Pumpian-Mindlin, E. Omnipotentiality, youth, and commitment. *J. Amer. Academy Child Psychiat.*, 1 (1965) 1–18.

A Conceptual Model for Study of Some Abusing Parents

Henry P. Coppolillo, M.D. (U.S.A.)

After Kempe, Silverman, et al. presented their paper on battered children in 1962 [1] the medical and lay world expressed a somewhat hypocritical reaction of amazement and outrage. I say "somewhat hypocritical" because the cries of anguish of tortured children could have been easily heard by anyone willing to hear; heard in the voices of Ambroise Tardieu [2] from France, Charles Dickens from England, Balestrini [3] from Italy, and Caffey [4] from the United States, as well as others who told of children who were neglected, abused, or killed by parents. But the hypocrisy of society toward children may be the subject for another study. A number of workers overcame or had no time for outrage. Among these were Brandt Steele and Carl Pollock [1, 5], who laid the groundwork for the psychological study of abusing parents. Leaning heavily on their pioneering work and on that of Benedek, I should like to propose a model for the study of some abusive parents. This model attempts to integrate various issues of abuse into a single field of forces.

In the course of successful child rearing the mothering person's investment in her child is enormous. Her attention, devotion, and energy, especially during the child's infancy, are almost entirely vested in the little being. We have focused a good deal of attention on how the child thrives in this period of "emotional symbiosis" [6]. It would seem that for our purposes an equally legitimate question might be that of the mother's psychological survival and equanimity during this period of intense investment of psychic energy. Where does she find the strength and replenishment? What protects her from exhaustion and depletion? Benedek has done extensive work in this area, and many of the answers to this question can be found in her writing [6–9].

The mother's output of care, concern, devotion, and attention that flow from her to the child (as depicted in Figure 1 by the heavy arrow from M to Ch) is replenished by several mechanisms in the optimal situation. As the mother nurtures, cares, and attends she unconsciously relives the gratification experienced as she was lovingly enveloped by her own mother [7]. In addition, she is gratified and supported by virtue of achieving oneness with her ego ideal of motherliness (Figure 1a). Furthermore, in the course of the pregnancy and during the child's infancy the father assumes a supportive, maternal role toward the mother (Figure 1b). Finally, both because of her identification with the child [7] and the sheer joy at seeing the child thrive, the mother experiences gratification, tenderness, and fulfillment rather than depletion as she devotes herself to the task of mothering (Figure 1c).

I should like to dwell for a moment on this last section and offer a slightly more microscopic model of mother-child transactions. From some of our own preliminary observations and from reviewing the work of Bowlby [10] we offer an ethological model of the vicissitudes of bonding between the human infant and his mother.

In a perfect situation (Figure 2a), which we must speculate never exists, the child (Ch) is equipped with an armementarium of signals that act as stimuli (or releasers) for the mother. This repertoire of signals consists of his cries, his reflexes (sucking, rooting, buccinator), and as suggested by Balikov [11], his helplessness, his size, and so on. In the ideal situation, each signal the child emits falls onto maternal terrain that is sensitive and responsive. The maternal response gratifies the child, and both the infant's stimulus and the maternal response leave behind, in each member of the thriving team, memory traces that prepare them for a more vigorous and gratifying effort the next time need tensions arise in the system. A series of these memory traces lay the groundwork in

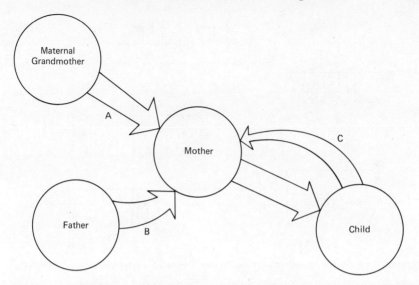

Figure 1   A model of the interrelationship maintaining homeostasis in early parenting.

the child for that trait which has been variously called hope [12], confidence [13], and optimism [14].

Very likely a perfect system of communication between mother and child exists only in theory. In life, although a large number of the signals emitted by the child bring a satisfying response from the mother, there is a small but important number of those that do not. Who has not known of, or experienced directly, the situation in which father returning from work hears mother say "Thank God you're home, George. The baby has been impossible all afternoon. I simply don't know what he wants (Figure 2*b*)." By being forced to tolerate a state of need tension for a longer than usual period of time, the child not only increased his tolerance for frustration but also experienced the intrusion of that often painful awareness we call "reality." Thus suffering somewhat prolonged periods of frustration may well be necessary for the development of reality sense and frustration tolerance in the growing infant.

Needless to say, the situation is not always so felicitous. There are instances where the communicative mechanisms break down. To use the graphically descriptive phrase of Renee Spitz [15], "the derailment of dialogue" can occur in a number of ways.

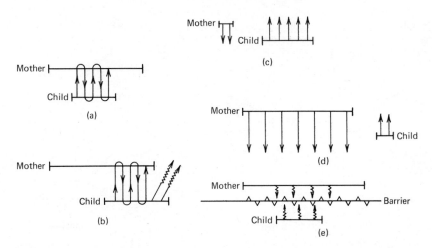

Figure 2   The various possibilities in established and derailed mother-infant "dialogues."

Referring to Figure 2*c*, we can imagine those situations in which the child has a perfectly valid set of signals, but for whatever reason (physical illness, depression, or temperament), the mothering person is either unable to respond or responds in a nongratifying way. As an example, we can think of those mothers who have been obtended to the point of stupor by being tranquilized and then thrust or abandoned in a situation in which they must care for their child without help. We may one day want to discuss with those of our colleagues who care for adult patients whether it is indeed a therapeutic triumph to send a young woman patient home from the hospital on massive doses of tranquilizing drugs.

On the other hand, there are those times when the mother's capacity and readiness to become motherly lay distressingly fallow because of the infant's inability to stimulate or respond to her (Figure 2*d*). Examples of this condition can be found in Brazelton's important description of the rapidity with which the "derailment of dialogue" can occur between newborns who have been born sedated and their anxious mothers [16]. Some of the precursors of this condition are described by Thomas, Chess, et al. in their studies of "temperament of children" [17].

Finally, it behooves us to recognize that another situation exists that can lead to destructive interference with mother-child bonding. This condition is all the more regrettable because there are instances in which it is iatrogenic and could be avoided by enlightened, progressive management. I refer to those situations in which the capacity to achieve mutuality is initially ample and adequate in both mother and child but is subsequently destroyed by barriers imposed by external agencies. Klaus and his coworkers, taking advantage of an experiment in nature, have definitive data on the subject (18–20). They demonstrate, with rich and carefully scrutinized data, that in those cases where mother and child had to be separated during the critical newborn period there exists the possibility of serious damage to the mother's capacity to attach herself and become sensitive to her child. These noncontact mothers' caretaking performance and the number of incidents of battering, failure to thrive, and abandonment, as compared to a control group of mothers who had free access to their children, was striking. These studies strongly support the thesis that there is a phase of development of the mother-child symbiosis that is critical. The mothering person and the child must be available to each other during this critical period, and hopefully there are no gross *intrapersonal* impediments to the bonding process in either partner, as well as no *interpersonal* barriers (e.g., plate-glass windows, overly intrusive grandmothers, obstructive nurses or doctors, books with poorly conceived, poorly articulated, and poorly tested edicts on how to mother, etc.) that interfere with the bonding process.

However, this raises another question! Surely we have all known about numbers of adopted children who were denied access to their biological or adoptive mothers during this critical period and were subsequently raised with little or no difficulty in achieving a mutually gratifying symbiosis with the subsequent mothering person. Similarly, we have known of successfully raised children who were separated from their mothers by the necessary or unnecessary regulations of a nursery where they were kept for weeks on end by illness. How can this be explained? From talks with successful adoptive mothers and those who have overcome the barriers imposed by separation during the critical period of bonding, important differences emerge. These latter mothers remained *confident* and *aware*. Because of their own past experiences or because of environmental support (or probably both), these mothers, even though they may not have been able to articulate it, were able to recognize that there had been a disturbance in the development of the symbiosis and even more importantly, that the disturbance was not due to their inadequacy or badness. But note what happens in less fortunate circumstances; let us take the potentially abusive mother as an example. She has no such reserve of confidence and is *not* aware of what had constituted the barrier to bonding. Because of her painful experiences in being mothered she is prone to unconsciously conceive of mothers as depriving and withholding. As Benedek [7] describes, the hate that is experienced for the depriving mother, through identification, spreads to the self. It then corrosively reaches into the future to taint her offspring. Grinker put it aptly in describing this three generation spread of hate. He said [21] "at the same time (as the future mother was developing hate for herself and her own mother), (she) he develops a precursory hatred of the subject that needs." In this way, driven by hate and unprotected by confidence, she must remain convinced that she is a hateful ogre who has spawned a detestable child. To conceive of compensating for the breach in the development of the symbiosis, as the confident mother does, is as impossible for her as it is to conceive that she can change the past.

To return now to the proposed model (Figure 1) we should be authorized to conceive of the potentially abusive situation as one in which *one factor* is the state of *subjective psychological depletion* of the mother. I say "one factor" because I am convinced from clinical inferences that the environment in which the mother finds herself with her child takes complimentarity in permitting the abuse, through its inattention, and the conspiracy of silence that surrounds the precursors to serious abuse. With O'Neill, Meachem, et al. [22], I refer now to the soft-tissue injuries and unexplained "accidents" that often leave the physician's office or the emergency room without further investigation. I would add to this the outbursts of temper and other demonstrations of exasperation toward the child that the nonabusive parent frequently ignores. We, and others, have noted this environmental conspiracy of silence (usually as represented by the nonabusive spouse) in another situation of damage to the child. We have seen it in virtually every case of incest that we have had the opportunity to study.

In summary, then, we feel that physical child abuse occurs when the environment leaves the mothering person alone with a normally demanding child and when she is in a state of subjective depletion. This state of depletion occurs when: (1) the unconscious reliving of her own experience at her mother's breast is painful rather than gratifying and evokes images of motherliness that are venemous and ugly rather than gratifyingly serene, (2) because of the encrusted inability to relate and because of the kind of mate an isolated person would pick, the mothering person finds herself alone and without succour in the presence of the normally tyrannical demands of the child and (3) situations obtain, as described in the preceding paragraphs, in which the mother cannot perceive or the child cannot emit comprehensible signs of need and gratification that stimulate and reward the mother's motherliness. It is when all three of these sources of replenishment break down that the mother finds herself prey to a syndrome of depletion. Feeling empty, inept, and without succour and probably because of the negatively tainted identification with the needful child, the mother can scarcely tell who stimulates and who is stimulated. All she knows is that more stimulation is intolerable, and driven by the chronic rage (around unsatisfied wishes for comfort) that she has harbored since her own childhood [11], she turns to destroy the source of the stimulus. With it, all too often she destroys that which she also loved—her own child.

It is my conviction that this model is useful because it enlarges the field of inquiry somewhat and conceptually permits us to study the interplay of forces on the participants in a potential tragedy. I believe the hypotheses that emerge from this model can be tested and if proven, may lead us to more varied and more effective forms of intervention. And intervene we must, if we would limit the spread of child abuse in future generations. We should intervene not only to calm the cries of children who have from birth known little other than pain, but also to respond to the anguished cries of help of that child from the past still present in the mother.

References

1. Kempe, C. H., Silverman, F. N., Steele, B. F., Droegemueller, W., and Silver H. K. The battered child syndrome. *J. Amer. Med. Assoc., 181* (1962), 17–24.
2. Tardieu, A. Etude medico-legale sur l'infanticide. J.-B. Bailliere et Fels, Paris, 1868.
3. Balestrini, R. *Aborto, Infanticidio ed Esposezione d'Infanti.* Bocca, Torino, 1888.
4. Caffey, G. Multiple fractures in the long bones of infants suffering from subdural hematoma. *Amer. J. Roentgenol.,* 56:2 (1946), 163–173.
5. Steele, B. F. and Pollock, C. B. A psychiatric study of parents who abuse infants and small children. In *The Battered Child,* R. Helfer and C. F. Kempe, Eds. Univ. of Chicago Press, Chicago, 1968.
6. Benedek, T. *Psychosexual Function in Women.* Ronald Press, 1952, New York.
7. Benedek, T. Toward the biology of the depressive constellation. *J. Amer. Psychoan. Assoc.* 4 (1956), 389–427.
8. Benedek, T. Psychobiological aspects of mothering. *Amer. J. Orthopsychiat.,* 26 (1956), 272–278.
9. Benedek, T. Parenthood as a developmental phase. A contribution to libido theory. *J. Amer. Psychoan. Assoc.* 7 (1959), 389–417.
10. Bowlby, J. *Attachment and Loss,* Vol. 1. Basic Books, New York, 1969.
11. Balikov, H. Personal communication of unpublished data.
12. French, T. M. *The Integration of Behavior,* Vol. 1. *Basic Postulates.* University of Chicago Press, Chicago, 1952.
13. Benedek, T. Adaptation to reality in early infancy. *Psychoan. Quart.,* 7 (1938), 200–215.
14. Erikson, E. *Childhood and Society.* Norton, New York, 1950.
15. Spitz, Renee. *The First Year of Life.* International Universities Press, New York, 1965.
16. Brazelton, T. B. Observations of the neonate. *J. Am. Acad. Child Psychiat.,* 1 (1962), 38.
17. Thomas, A., Chess, S. and Birch, H. *Behavioral Individuality in Early Childhood.* New York Univ. Press, New York, 1963.
18. Klaus, H. and Kennell, J. H. Mothers separated from their newborn infants. *Pediat. Clin. N. Amer.,* 17 (1970), 1015–1037.
19. Fanaroff, A. A., Kennell, J. H., and Klaus, M. Followup of low birth weight infants, the predictive value of maternal visiting patterns. *Pediatrics,* 49, 2 (1972), 287–290.
20. Klaus, M. H., Jerauld, R., Kreger, N. C., McAlpine, W., Steffo, M., and Kennell, J. Maternal attachment. *New Eng. J. Med.,* 286 (1972), 460–463.
21. Grinker, R. R. Quoted in Benedek [7].
22. O'Neill, J. A., Meachem, W. F., Griffin, P. P., and Sawyers, J. L. Patterns of injury in the battered child syndrome. *J. Trauma,* 13:4 (1973), 332–339.
23. Green, A. H., Gaines, R. W., and Sandgrund, A. Child abuse: Pathological syndrome of family interaction. *Amer. J. Psychiat.* 131:8 (1974) 882–886.

The Abusing Parent: Perceptions, Memories, and Pathological Identifications as Precipitants in the Attack

Frank I. Bishop, M.D. (Australia)

Published literature on the subject [2] indicates that parents who sporadically but violently attack their offspring usually do so under pressure of intolerable psychic stress. Objectively, this stress may appear to be a minor one but may reach intolerable proportions when imposed on a personality structure that has developed along a deviant pathway in a setting of repeated psychic or physical trauma in an emotionally empty, unrewarding, or adverse environment.

Studies of laboratory animals have similarly shown that parents will attack offspring under what appear to be only minor stresses in special circumstances [3]. In the cases we observed, frequent precipitating causes were minor stresses imposed on a parent who was already suffering loss of self-esteem and emotional isolation with unsatisfied dependency needs, coupled with the task of caring for a child who was perceived as damaged, unrewarding, unloving, rejecting, or as a potential aggressor.

CASE 1

A 28-year-old, attractive but depressed mother of two children was referred for assistance when her son, a red-headed, gray-eyed, slightly built, pale, eden-

239

tulous 4-year-old, who had previously been admitted in infancy for failure to thrive, was found to be still thin, underweight, and maltreated. Despite the absence of any serious physical injuries he had been punished frequently, severely, and inappropriately. More than once he had been thrown across the room after the mother had screamed at him, threatened to kill him, and hit him repeatedly about the head and face. The mother complained that he was cheeky, defiant, aggressive, uncontrollable, and always made her give in in the end, so that he always got what he wanted.

At interview and in therapy he proved to be an intelligent, alert, pleasant child who quickly made a warm, trusting relationship with a female therapist but was clinging, dependent, perseveratively demanding, and whining with the mother.

The mother's own life history was unusual in that she perceived herself as having been given away by her mother to a maternal aunt who had no children. This occurred when her own mother came to the aunt's house to collect her on the way home from the maternity hospital with a new baby, a girl, when the mother was aged 7 years. For the next 21 years the mother had tried desperately to be a perfect child for a maternal aunt and uncle. As a hairdresser she often helped her younger sister in her salon on busy days.

Her perception of her son as revealed in treatment was that his behavior was just like her in-laws, who constantly upset her, especially her husband's brother, who was always insultingly rude even to her neighbors. Worse still, her son reminded her of the "red-haired bitch" whom she remembered having intercourse with her father on a couch in the loungeroom while her mother prepared the evening meal. She was a preschool child at this time. In the interview she observed at this point, "What a complete bitch she must have been when she knew Mum was in the next room cooking the tea!" When asked what would happen if her son's hair color were changed, the mother commented that she had often thought of doing just that. Further, she admitted she dyed her hair because, despite its ash-blond color, it had a reddish tinge in colored photographs and she just couldn't bear it. That she identified herself to some extent with this woman is suggested by her relating in the same interview how her mother had become extremely angry when she returned home with her overalls on back to front after a visit to the park with a neighbor's son.

It seems that this boy was perceived as an aggregate of parts of at least two people who have considerable emotional significance for her and that this aggregate, which she has projected onto the child, is totally unacceptable yet continues to control and dominate her.

CASE 2

A 30-year-old paranoid schizophrenic mother was seen when her son, aged 6 years, was referred for admission by a practicing child psychiatrist who saw clearly that the child's life was in danger. The boy was of medium build with blue eyes and black curly hair. He was extremely anxious and had grave difficulty talking about his feelings, becoming pale, tremulous, nauseated, and on one occasion, vomiting. His reality testing was poor, and it was noted that when the mother visited she was perserverative in her attempts to invalidate his appropriate reality judgments. The history obtained was alarming. The mother's father was a plausible but aggressive psychopath who had verbally and physically attacked her throughout her life so that as a young adolescent she became shaky, frightened, and nauseated whenever she heard her father's car in the driveway. Despite having lived always in large cities she had married a farmer by whom she had two children, the presenting child and a daughter 2 years younger. She had left her husband, who had beaten her severely 3 years prior to referral, and for 1 year had lived with a de facto husband.

The little boy had suffered a series of severe injuries: three head injuries including one fractured skull, a fractured humerus, severe bruising of the scrotum and penis, and finally a severe laceration of the right wrist that cut all structures superficial to the volar aspect of the radius and ulna. The mother became very angry, describing how he always injured himself when he absconded from home at night, and how he could undo any locks or bolts; thus he was now put into a "bag-jacket" at night with a drawstring around the neck. The mother was still angry, describing how he screamed and fell face forward onto the floor when he jumped out of bed as a result of night terrors. She described also his black angry moods when he was out of control, attacking her as her father had done; of his senseless cruelty to his younger sister, reminding her of her exhusband's treatment of her; and of his complete failure to respond to her needs, just as her de facto husband failed her despite the fact that she loved him.

Finally, she talked about her own black moods with the anger and hostility she experienced and how she knew when one would ensue because they always followed the onset of the same changes in her son. Some 5 months later when his parents tried to persuade him to go home with them from the hospital, the child told the staff of his fear of returning home "in case there was another accident."

Here the child seems to have been perceived as a complex aggregate of parts of his grandparents, his father, his mother and more illogically, of his de facto father. Here all these angry attacking aspects were clearly mother's own angry, hostile, unacceptable impulses, and her child-rearing behavior was such as would ultimately validate these gross perceptual distortions.

CASE 3

A 22-year-old mother, who did no serious harm to her first adopted male child, killed her newly adopted daughter when the infant was 8 weeks old. The mother described her own unsatisfactory parenting experience, including the constant hostility she had received from her own parents, especially her mother, and how difficult it had been when she was constantly chosen to do all the unpleasant tasks. She had been repeatedly beaten by her mother since the results of her efforts were never up to standard, whereas her younger siblings were rarely beaten. The mother also said how extremely fortunate she was to have such a good, considerate husband.

Later in this single interview she described her anguish when she found 1 year prior to this tragedy that she had been conceived out of wedlock to a male who was not the person she had always understood to be her father. She then talked about her attack on the child, explaining how she had been completely unable to stand the baby's crying. Finally, with the house in complete disorder and with no hope of completing even the simplest of household tasks, she had listened to the baby screaming but heard her mother screaming at her. She felt frightened at first and then extremely angry, and instead of changing the infant she threw it from the doorway of the nursery into the basinet, but missed. The baby hit the wall behind the basinet and then slid down into it, where it "looked odd and did not move."

Here it would appear that this psychotically depressed mother had, for a brief period of time, perceived the infant as being her own mother, abusing and threatening her for her complete lack of competence as a housekeeper and mother.

Discussion

Maurice Merleau-Ponty [1] poses a question in general but, to us, very cogent terms:

We want to know how, by its own vitality . . . consciousness can, in the course of time, modify the structure of its surroundings; how at every moment, its former experience is open to it in the form of an horizon which it can re-open . . . in an act of recollection . . . which then immediately provides the perceived with a present atmosphere and significance.

This question clearly involves consideration of perceptual memory and the translocation of memories in time and their utilization in what may be misperceptions of the object.

Clinically we find that consideration of this aspect suggests that we are dealing with problems of feeling, auditory, and visual memory and the resulting perceptual analyses and constructs that are frequently based on condensation to a part-object level. Then a gesture, expression, action, or a piece of behavior exhibited by the child evokes in the parent feelings that, by association, re-create situations that the parent, as a child, found intolerable. The child then becomes the parent's own parents, attacking them, and they react with all the venom and fury they experienced when they were deeply hurt but too small, helpless, and weak to retaliate. As adults their physical capacities are no longer so limited and if, by these processes, the child becomes their parent, they then attack their child with all the repressed infantile and hence uncontrollable fury.

We are dealing, then, with a situation where the "child," who is now a parent, no longer needs to displace his homicidal attempts or wishes onto himself (as in childhood suicide) but has presented to him, through feelings linked to these painful memories and the accompanying perceptual distortions, the object of his original hatred. In other words, it is as if with his full adult power he were confronted by the object that aroused not only all his anger and hatred but that intensifies these since he was, on previous occasions, impotent and helpless.

This concatenation of psychic insults produces in the parent a sudden massive regression with loss of control associated with what is essentially a momentary psychosis based on a transference phenomenon in which primary process thinking and primitive psychical organization are paramount.

In the cases described we found that the mother had failed to perceive her infant or child as a unique individual and had instead projected onto the child what she perceived as the unacceptable, bad aspects of the personality and behavior of people emotionally significant to her. These projections onto the child were clearly part-object perceptions, which by projection have produced pathological identifications of the child.

These pathological identifications produced either transient or fixed misperceptions of the infant or child. There was in each case a total failure to perceive the child as a unique individual and a total incapacity to respond to his needs.

Numerous other cases have indicated the same distressing patterns of pathological identification with grossly inappropriate responses. For instance, a child's forceful hunger cry may recreate for the mother her husband's ill-temper and shouting, her father's anger and criticism, her own mother's demands on her for comfort, or affection or assistance with younger siblings—all preventing the gratification of her own needs.

A sobbing child may activate feelings of sadness, loneliness, emptiness, and loss. If unable to comfort the infant, the mother may become aware of her own unmet dependency needs and her helplessness so that she feels deeply hurt and then very angry.

A baby who refuses to suck, or who vomits, turns away, or avoids contact may reactivate the mother's feelings of inferiority and low self-esteem since she feels unable to mother her child adequately or doubts the quality of what she supplies. Similarly, an infant's early attempts at ambulation and exploration may permit her in fantasy to see the child grown older, leaving her as she was previously deserted or rejected. These same poorly coordinated motor efforts may produce anxieties about control and stir up fantasies of what could happen if she lost control or how difficult this child may be to manage when older. It may activate memories of episodes of loss of control on her part or of violent behavior directed against her until in fantasy she can see the child becoming her parent attacking her. Thus for a very brief moment or over a more protracted period a small infant or child may be perceived to be an aggregate of the bad parts of persons emotionally significant to the parent. Any or all of these parts of the child may produce a pathological identification completely antithetical to the parent's hopes and expectations, and it is hardly surprising that a child so identified may become a hated object, all the more so since the greatest needs these parents display is their tremendous need for love and approval from the child.

In extreme cases every unacceptable impulse experienced by the parent may be perceived as arising from the child with disastrous consequences to the parental perception and identification of the child.

To answer Merleau-Ponty's question, then, we can state that perceptions occurring in the prelogical stage of child development are especially associated with feeling states and that under conditions of severe psychic stress, consciousness has "this former experience" forcibly and brutally opened to it so that it quite illogically and pathologically "provides the perceived with a present atmosphere and significance."

Conclusion

It appears almost axiomatic then that only when we can appreciate the meaning of the child's behavior to the parent *at the actual moment of maltreatment* can we really comprehend and thereby explain why this particular child was maltreated at that particular moment. It is this level of understanding that enables us to treat the equally unfortunate parent in the established case and to prevent attack where the parental life experience and the parental identification of the child render it vulnerable.

It is noteworthy that these pathological identifications of the child do not differ from the parents' self-concepts and identifications as elaborated by Steele and Pollock [2].

References

1. Merleau-Ponty, M. Associations and the projection of memories. In *Phenomenology of Perception*, Colin Smith, Transl. Humanities Press, Atlantic Highlands, N.J., 1962.
2. Steele, B. and Pollock, G. In *The Battered Child*, R. E. Helfer and C. Henry Kempe, Eds. Univ. of Chicago Press, Chicago, 1968.
3. Wright, E. A. *Symposium: The very young. Proc. Roy. Soc. Med.*, 61 (1968), 23–25.

Vulnerability and Incest

M. Joyce Grant, M.S.W. (Australia)

CASE STUDY

Brian, aged 2 years, was referred to the hospital because of severe constipation, involving impacted feces. When first seen he was so frightened and withdrawn that mental retardation or autism was queried and a full assessment of him and his family commenced.

It soon became obvious that within Brian's family of two parents and six older siblings (a son and two daughters by the mother's first marriage and three daughters and Brian by her second marriage) there was tremendous deprivation, both material and emotional, with family malfunctioning at every level and a pattern of family disintegration in the face of severe internal stress and reintegration in the face of perceived threats from a seemingly hostile world. In short, this was what could be labeled a multiproblem family.

In the midst of the almost unceasing series of small crises came considerable concern when the two youngest girls, aged 6 and 8, were sexually interfered with by a middle-aged neighbor. The father characteristically isolated himself emotionally from the situation, and the mother expressed shock, distress, and anger at this incident and the resultant confusion and legal action. Almost immediately afterward 17-year-old Sharon, the second eldest daughter, always a somewhat disturbed girl, developed an acute psychiatric illness with agitated depression and phobia. This resulted in her immediate admission to a general hospital, followed by admission to a psychiatric hospital and many months of in-patient treatment. She attributed her "breakdown" to the fact that the involvement of her younger sisters in this sexual attack reactivated her memories of her stepfather forcing intercourse on her during her mother's confinement in the hospital for Brian's birth, 2 years earlier. Again the mother expressed shock, distress, and anger when learning of this incident. However, she volunteered the information that her husband had over a period sexually interfered with both her

247

daughters by her first marriage. She had known of this situation when the family was living in England and also when the family was on the trip out to Australia, but she had been convinced that this had ceased over the last 6 years—the period since being in Australia. Her attitude was initially of shocked disbelief at this new revelation, but she maintained a passivity about initiating any action, as she felt all this was in the past. She was adamant that her younger daughters could not be involved in an incestuous relationship with their own father. Needless to say, soon afterward the elder of the two young girls revealed that both she and her younger sister were currently involved sexually with their father and had been for several years. At last the mother had to face this fact, but she was still somewhat reluctant to take any action until it was forced on her by her teenage daughter, Sharon, insisting that the mother make a choice between her and the husband, as Sharon refused to return home from the hospital while her step-father was present in the home. Finally, the mother left her husband, not to protect her younger daughters, but to meet the wishes of her demanding, dependent older daughter. The father refused all professional contacts and remained unaccessible to any help. Here was a family containing five daughters, all at risk because of the incestuous behavior of the disturbed, isolated, violent father with poor impulse control, and yet none receiving protection from a mother who could deny to herself what was occurring over a long period of time in a small flat. The mother's own background had been one of severe deprivation, with a permanently disabled father and a chronically psychotic mother, who perceived sex as something violent, to be endured if necessary, but to be avoided at almost any cost, even at the cost of her daughters. The five girls reared in this family, exposed to much of the same dangers, resembled the three dolls mentioned in the introductory paragraph of our congress program. The second elder girl, Sharon, and the youngest daughter, 6-year-old Ruth, were the glass dolls who shattered. Sharon had a long psychiatric illness, clung to her mother in a hostile dependent relationship, and showed little possibility of ever forming a heterosexual relationship. Ruth, at 6, was a poorly functioning child, with chronic encopresis, shallow affect, no evidence of guilt or shame, and a capacity only for superficial relationships and appeared very much at risk for sexual acting-out behavior in the future. The eldest daughter, Carol, had married young to escape from her home and was struggling to maintain a balance between the demands of her young, rather domineering husband and the excessive demands of her mother. She and the second youngest daughter, 8-year-old Rose, who was having school difficulties, showing poor peer relationships, and giving indications of some aggressive acting-out behavior, were like the plastic dolls, probably permanently scarred by their stressful experiences. Mavis, the middle daughter, the first born of the second family, was the only daughter who convincingly maintained that she had not been involved incestuously with her father and was, in fact, the only member of the family who had any kind of positive relationship with this man. She was the daughter who could view both parents with unexpected maturity and compassionate tolerance and was reserved and loyal in speaking of them. Despite leaving school early, she took the initiative in seeking further training, finally developed a positive relationship with a boy from a stable family with a higher socioeconomic background, and was warmly accepted by this family, but she did not break her bonds with her own family. She, who had faced and mastered various difficulties within her family was, indeed, like the doll of steel who emitted a fine ringing sound.

Discussion

Possibly the children of this family may have had the potentials for normal healthy development, but the family psychopathology had distorted this development. On the other hand, there are those children where physiological factors and genetic inheritance have constituted risk factors within the children and the stability and healthy positive attitudes of the families may be important determinants as to whether such children achieve mastery over their inherent defects. This can occur in the basic determinant of gender itself. Studies undertaken by John Money and others and work undertaken at the Royal Children's Hospital, Melbourne, have indicated that a definite gender identity fostered early, and firmly reinforced by a warmly supportive family, have assisted in the establishment of stable gender identity in some hermaphrodites despite uncertain and conflicting aspects of anatomical structures and chromosomal pattern.

The importance of the family's attitudes to sex, sexual development, and sexual behavior can be noted in other types of handicapped children—the physically handicapped or the mentally retarded child. No doubt the attitudes of the family may frequently reflect those of the community, but often these are further distorted or modified by individual parental psychopathology. Too often, the physically handicapped child is treated as if sex or sexual development is something that does not exist or must be denied by the parents. Sometimes it is as if the child with a physical disability is no longer a child with the same curiosity, phases of sexual development, conflicts, and needs as the healthy child. Perhaps it is this denial of normal sexuality in childhood that leads to so many intense conflicts in adolescence among this group of children with physical handicaps, which so greatly increases the risk factor in an already vulnerable group.

Only recently are professional workers beginning to give more attention to this important area of development.

Conversely, among the families of mentally retarded children there is so often an exaggerated emphasis on sexual factors, especially in boys, as if mental retardation is synonomous with sexual perversion and normal sexual development. This may be a phase appropriate with the general development within the child, but is often seen in more sinister terms. This general attitude may become still further distorted with individual parental psychopathology. Ronald, aged 15 years, was a mildly retarded boy with a conscientious, concerned, caring, middle-class mother who carried most of the family responsibility. One day she asked if Ronald could have a vasectomy. This request did not arise, as one might first suspect, from a fear of Ronald becoming sexually dangerous in the community, as the mother anticipated that he would develop physically and emotionally into adult life and reach the point of fathering a child. It was to prevent the birth of a retarded child such as Ronald that this mother wished the operation, although there was no evidence of genetic factors in the etiology of this retardation. The complexities of this mother's problems became more obvious when it was noted that she appeared unaware, or at least to deny, how much her son resembled his father in general physical appearance. The father was a passive man whom his wife was determined to protect from stress, even to the extent of making most of the decisions regarding the family. Her normal calmness was shattered and she became distressed and angry at the suggestion that her husband might be permitted to share more of the family responsibilities. Hence Ronald was a vulnerable boy because of a degree of mental retardation, but his striving to mastery was hampered by his mother's over concern, which also concealed a wish to castrate physically the son of the man she was castrating emotionally.

Within the normal developmental patterns of the average family there is need for the child to identify with each parent and, in particular, to identify with the sex role of the parent of his or her own sex. When such a role in the family is at variance with the sex role acceptable within that particular community, such a child is much more at risk for not achieving healthy development, whether he lives within a primitive society or an industrial culture. If the parental roles are too confused or distorted by individual parental psychopathology, the child can so easily move on toward homosexuality at one extreme or any lesser degree of confused sexual behavior. Apart from the gender and sex-role identity, for healthy development each child needs to have an accepting family environment for the experimentation and mastery of the balance of expressions of positive and negative feelings essential for the achievement of satisfactory social relationships, and especially for the achievement ultimately of mature adult heterosexual relationships.

In summary, abnormal and unhealthy parental attitudes to sex, whether overtly or covertly expressed, can seriously distort normal child development, although each child may vary greatly as to how he or she is effected, because of the many other factors involved in individual personality development. Nevertheless, even the most vulnerable child born with severe sexual abnormalities can be helped toward mastery of these handicaps by the healthy, well-motivated, stable family. Some children with other disabilities can be hurt further by unhealthy parental attitudes to sexual behavior, attitudes that often reflect those of society but are further distorted by individual parental beliefs. Confusion of sexual identity can result from a sex role within the family being incongruent with that acceptable to the current society in which the family lives. The normal child needs to be free to satisfy his natural curiosity, explore his world, test out his relationships, healthily express both his love and hostility, and finally seek a stable sex identity before he can move on to a satisfying heterosexual relationship. Yet after all these centuries questions are still being asked regarding what a child should be told about sex and when, how, and by whom?

Conflicted Parents: High and Low Vulnerability of Children to Divorce

Gudrun Brun, M.D. (Denmark)

The Custody Battle

In most divorce cases in Scandinavian countries, parents agree on the placement of the children, usually deciding that custody be given to the mother, at least when the child is below school age. They also generally agree that siblings should stay together. Only in a comparatively few cases are the parents unable to solve this problem, and it is then left to the court to decide. As the divorce rate increases more custody battles occur, accompanied by disturbing conflicts between the parents from which the children receive little protection.

Gradually the idea has emerged that the overriding consideration should be the child's best interests and that this cannot be expressed in terms of rigid rules. The judges today, at least in the Scandinavian countries, are more apt to give the custody of a child to the father than they were 10 years ago. The fathers express more interest in their children, and in many cases the husband's standard of living and the wife's are very much the same, which means that both parents are equally capable of providing the child with food, clothing, and medical care. The emotional ties existing between the parents and the child can then be decisive factors.

In those instances where custody is disputed, a psychiatric-social-psychological examination of the parties and of the children may be obtained, and it is becoming more common for the court to ask for such an examination. For various reasons child psychiatrists are reluctant to participate in custody disputes, taking the position that these matters should not be handled in court and that it is difficult to be an advocate for the child, independently of the parents, when the child is part of the family and when his fate is equally dependent on the reactions of the losing and winning parties. The psychiatrist often feels that a filed recommendation with expressions such as "reliable," "unreliable," "strong," "weak," "capable," or "less capable," may leave the losing party stigmatized by society as "unfit." Furthermore, the whole custody procedure in the courts with its adversary system has a tendency to exacerbate the conflicts still further so that any prospect of reconciliation becomes remote.

The examination takes place when the parents are passing through a critical period and thus are very likely functioning less adequately than under normal circumstances. At such times it is difficult to predict how the parties will function in the future. It is the task of the psychiatric examiner to find possible alternatives that meet the best interests of the child while at the same time taking into consideration the positive and negative impact of a recommendation with which both child and parents have to live. Family or supportive therapy may help some parents to decide among themselves as to the best solution for the child without taking the matter to court and intensifying the acrimony.

Anna Freud [1] has concluded that "children need party status in any court proceeding concerned with their fate. They need to be represented, independently of the adults, *as persons in their own right.*" But whether represented independently or not, it is difficult for many children to maintain positive emotional ties with parents who are hostile to each other without falling a prey to severe loyalty conflicts. In every case, considered on its own merits, it is very important, to quote Goldstein [2], "to find the least detrimental alternative for the child."

General Aims of the Research

The general aims of the research were:

1. To study the impact of *contested divorces* on the mental health of the children.
2. To find if any principles might be elicited that could serve to guide the court on the disposition of custody and visiting rights.

In this study the term "divorce" was taken to cover a period of time involving three stages: the planning for the divorce, the actual proceedings of the court, and the fight over visiting rights (a process that can last for months and even years).

Specific Aims of the Research

The aims were to consider:

1. To what extent divorce represents a risk for the development of emotional disturbances in children.
2. To what extent vulnerability from this risk varies with age and sex of the child.
3. To what extent disturbed parents generate disturbed divorces that generate disturbed children, and that the disturbances in the children antedate the divorce process.
4. To what extent divorce courts are influenced by expert psychological opinion regarding custody, especially with respect to those cases where paternal custody is advised.

Methodology

The data were derived from a standard questionnaire coded for computer programming. Both parents and children were psychiatrically examined, and psychological tests were carried out on small samples of the children (CAT on 183, TAT on 60, DAP on 197). In addition, play observations were made on 60 children aged 4 to 11 years.

The sample was representative of the social groups that stratify the Danish population and consisted of 322 families, with 500 children (aged from 3 to 16 years).

The period of study covered 10 years (1961–1971) and was cross-sectional. As no follow-up investigation has been undertaken as yet no conclusions regarding long-term outcome are currently available. Many of the disturbances reported may well have been transient and "situational." It should be emphasized that both parents were required to give consent for participation in the study, both for themselves and for their children.

Results

The following trends were observed during the study:

1. Psychiatric evaluation of the parents was carried out on at least one of the partners in 200 out of 322 pairs. Thirty-six fathers and 44 mothers were found to be psychotic (40 percent)! Other diagnoses included character disorders, alcoholism, neurotic disorders, borderline cases, and mental retardation. The psychotic cases tended to show paranoid reactions, but none of them had previously undergone a psychiatric examination. In the 140 traumatized children without previous symptoms, 93 had parents with a psychiatric diagnosis. In the 112 children for whom divorce proved an advantage, 90 had parents with a psychiatric diagnosis. In 172 healthy children for whom divorce seemed to have no appreciable affect, 118 had parents with a psychiatric diagnosis. There was a nonsignificant tendency for the divorce to prove advantageous for the children when the parents were psychiatrically disturbed.
2. Psychiatric evaluation of the children (500) revealed the sex distribution over the age range to follow the normal pattern. Character disorders (moderate to severe) were found in 15 cases, two of whom had been institutionalized. Neurotic disorders (moderate to severe) occurred in 188 cases (38 percent). Borderline and psychotic states were present in 13 cases (four of whom manifested *folie a deux*).
3. The immediate disturbing effects of the divorce process on the children were not easily separated from preexisting dis-

orders or from disorders that continue following the termination of the divorce. The children are expected to accept
the court's decision on custody despite their struggle with
distorting interpretations, guilty feelings regarding the disruption of the parental union, shame at being children of
divorce, grief at the loss of a parent, an inner refusal to
accept the reality of the situation, resentment of the parent
to whom they are "given," and idealization of the lost parent.
As a result, they become aggressive and disobedient, anxious
and insecure, or inhibited and withdrawn. The children are
also expected to accept the court's decision on visitation
rights and to relate to the absent parent in a positive way.
The visits can be traumatic since the parents may haggle
over money, resurrect past grievances and recriminations,
and continue to blame each other in front of the children,
who are torn between the two loyalties. The risk for the
children of becoming disturbed is thus a complicated product of parental loss, parental warfare, the visitation
dramas, and the decision making of the court and its experts. The interaction between these risks and the vulnerability of the children influences the outcome of the divorce
stress decisively. Of the 500 children, 140 were traumatized
(28 percent).

4. On the other hand, the outcome can prove advantageous.
   The children may find a more stable environment free from
   daily conflict that may give them the opportunity to master
   the trauma and revert to a more healthy development. Of
   the 500 children, 142 appeared to improve (28 percent).

5. A sizable group of children (218, or 44 percent) seemed not
   to be affected one way or the other. This last group comprised those with a low vulnerability as well as those using
   denial as a defense; the former continued to do well whereas
   the latter had subsequent difficulties in establishing emotional ties.

6. Among the group of children manifesting symptoms were
   those who had suffered from emotional problems since
   early life and for many years preceding the divorce.

7. As far as age and sex were concerned, the stressful effects of
   divorce were significantly greater for *latency children* than for

preschool and adolescent children. They were also significantly greater for latency boys than for latency girls; no such sex differences occurred with preschool or latency children. For boys the stressful effects are equally distributed throughout the period of latency, whereas for girls the effects were significantly greater during the first phase of latency (6–8 years), when in psychoanalytic terms the oedipal attachment to the father is still undergoing resolution. There was also a statistical tendency for divorce to be more advantageous for girls than for boys.

8. The consensus between court and "expert" was reasonably good (although this would not necessarily have any generalizability outside a particular court and particular psychiatrist). The court's decision agreed with the expert's advice on custody in 321 out of 333 children and on visitation rights in 156 out of 167 children. There was a statistical tendency to give custody of children under 6 years to the mother, but the father was not disfavored for girls under 6 years. This was true also for the whole sample in which 113 children were given in custody to the father and 220 to the mother. Nine mothers and 53 fathers were denied visiting rights.

9. The test results uncovered feelings of lonliness, helplessness, and insecurity and a great deal of anxiety and aggression especially by children in the latency period. In connection with the testing about 10 percent of the children associated to a *dream* mostly of the night before the examination, the manifest content of which was similar to that presented in the test material and reflected the conflicts between the parents and the child's own conflict of loyalty and his rescue impulses. A typical example is, "I hear my father crying for help. I run in order to rescue him, but all of a sudden a big iron wheel is moving toward me."

Conclusion

To be a useful advocate for the child, it is not enough to find the "least detrimental alternative." Many children undergo characteristic loyalty conflicts that may be exacerbated by the custody examination when they feel under pressure of choice. The interviewer must, therefore, be sensitive to the child's feelings of guilt and try to relieve them as much as possible. It is his task to decide what is best for the child, even when this is in opposition to the child's stated wishes. It is important to bring out the real feelings rather than conforming ones; this demands a measure of trust and confidence in the face of the child's knowledge that every written word can be read afterward by the parents and could be used against him. As a 7-year-old put it, "I dare not tell them where I want to live. If I stay with Daddy, Mommy will be sad, and if I stay with Mommy, Daddy will be sad—couldn't we make it our secret?"

After the decisions have been made the child will continue to need support in many cases. Postdivorce turbulence between the parents can mean emotional trouble for the child requiring the special skillfulness of those engaged in the total process.

Despite the many and varied matrimonial experiments in current operation (open marriages, group marriages, contract marriages, "parent swapping," etc.), generally speaking, children still seem to find their greatest security within a compatible and steady nuclear parental relationship. This was best formulated by a 10-year old girl who said:

When I was a baby my father said this screaming brat is going to make trouble and I need peace, and so he left. In the beginning he came to visit us now and again, but then we did not see him any more. My father for the moment is No. 4. My mother is very much in love with him and he is very friendly with me. It is damned unfair and hard going to keep replacing one father by another. If you like him you miss him very much afterwards when he goes away, and you never know if he will. I think I am too little to go through all that. When I am a grown-up and have a husband and small children of my own, I'll have just one family, always. I like it best that way and I believe it is the best for the children too.

References

1. Freud, A., The child as a person in his own right. *Psychoan. Study Child,* 27(1973), pp. 621–625.
2. Goldstein, J., Finding the Least Detrimental Alternative. *The Psychoan. Study Child,* 27(1973), pp. 626–641.

VULNERABLE CHILDREN OF MADNESS

A Program of Studies on Children at High Risk for Schizophrenia

L. Erlenmeyer-Kimling, Ph.D. (U.S.A.)

Everyone agrees that the roots of schizophrenia are to be found somewhere in the developmental histories of the affected individual. Just where they should be sought and how they are composed remain matters of speculation, however, even after many years of intensive efforts devoted to understanding the "cause" and nature of this disorder. Infancy, early childhood, the latency period, adolescence? When do prodromal signs begin to emerge—if, in fact, there are any—and when do critical periods of vulnerability take place—if, in fact, there are critical periods? What are the villains? Damage occurring in the birth process, distorted patterns of familial communication patterns or role playing, exceptional or unexceptional social stresses, the unfolding of a genetic predisposition, or complex combinations of factors? There are still no definitive answers.

The problem is that schizophrenologists have backed into the study of development. They have examined the childhoods of thousands of schizophrenic patients but almost always from a distance, from backward glances long after the traces of important formative influences have become obscured and recall, a shaky affair at best, has been colored by the knowledge that eventually a failure had occurred. As Garmezy and Streitman [2] have noted,

"To suggest that case history information gathered in the present is an accurate reflection of the past . . . only confuses the scientific effort to untangle causation in psychopathology." Equally capable of misleading are attempts to identify primary disturbances in psychological or biological functions from observations of abnormalities in schizophrenic patients. Yet until comparatively recently, the early years of those who would later become schizophrenic, and all the adverse things that were supposed to be taking place in those years, were known only from retrospective reports.

In the wave of studies on populations at risk for schizophrenia that has surfaced in the past several years [2] there are for the first time opportunities to observe the schizophrenic-to-be as a developing organism rather than as an endproduct of a chain of malignant forces. With the prospective approach, life-history experiences and their impact can be evaluated directly at the time of occurrence. In particular, these studies—given a reasonable amount of time for longitudinal follow-up—can be expected to elucidate the characteristics of children at risk, thus allowing a sharp distinction to be made between antecedent and consequent features of the illness, as has not been possible heretofore. Early identification of vulnerability is the other shared goal of most of the ongoing investigations because early identification is obviously a necessary first step in the formulation of effective programs of preventive intervention.

In many other ways, the several prospective studies differ considerably from each other, as is apparent in this symposium and the one that follows tomorrow. They differ in theoretical orientation and the variables selected for study; they differ in design, sample size, age range of the subjects, and sometimes in the criteria used for selecting the populations at risk.

The program of research that I would like to discuss is one of two prospective studies that my colleagues and I are conducting at the New York State Psychiatric Institute. We have been carrying out the pilot phase of this program during the past 3 years. It is truly a developmental study in the sense that it involves sustained inquiry into a great many facets of day-to-day life and assessment of a variety of psychological, social, and biological processes over a period of several years. Beginning with children aged 7 to 12, we hope to be able to map the entire span from 7 to 20 years of age through both longitudinal and age cross-sectional evaluations. The relatively large numbers of subjects scheduled for inclusion in this program are selected because they are considered statistically to be at high, very high, or low risk for manifesting schizophrenia at some time during their lives. What we hope to be able to observe through careful comparisons of these graded risk groups is the emergence of a genetic vulnerability to schizophrenia and the ways in which environmental variables play on that predisposition for good or bad—that is, as buffers or as triggers to psychopathology.

Subjects

The age range of the subjects at initial observation was chosen as 7 to 12 years because this range offers a relatively economical way of maximizing the sample size. It allows us to study, at the one extreme, children who are just beginning to cope with school demands and independence from the family, and at the other extreme of the target age range, children who are entering puberty, facing the transitional years of junior high school and all of the attendant turmoil of that period. Then, with follow-up, the youngest children will have gone through the grade-school years and will be entering early adolescence themselves, while the oldest children will have passed into adolescence and will already be in the early years of the schizophrenia risk period.

Many prospective studies concentrate their attention on children of affected mothers. We have included the children of schizophrenic fathers as well. The level of risk is expected to be the same in both groups, according to previous studies on adult offspring of schizophrenics, and there should certainly be an equal number of genetically vulnerable individuals in each group unless a rather unlikely mechanism of sex linkage were operating. It is obvious, however, that exposure to many types of environmental influences may be quite different from the prenatal period onward for the youngsters in these two groups. Comparisons between the mother and father groups may therefore allow us to evaluate hypotheses about maternal factors, both psychological and biological, that have been proposed in etiological speculations about schizophrenia.

We also include a group of children at very high risk for schizophrenia. They are offspring of two affected parents. Based on previous studies of risk in such groups, we would expect about 40 percent of these subjects to develop a schizophrenic psychosis [1]. Inclusion of both the two-parent and one-parent groups makes it possible to compare subjects at different levels of risk and to use the very high-risk groups as a means of cross-validating our observations in the high-risk groups.

There are two types of "low-risk" groups. First is the offspring of psychiatrically normal parents, which should provide baseline data for comparison with the children at high risk. In passing, let me note that one valuable byproduct of the program will be the wealth of data about normal development that can be derived from this group. We expect to be able to obtain information about long-term patterns of growth and change in respect to, for example, school functioning or mental health ratings, as well as normative developmental data on a number of psychophysiological, psychophysical, attentional, and other response processes for which such data are currently very scanty or even lacking entirely.

The second "low-risk" group is composed of children whose parents have other psychiatric disorders, chiefly, the affective psychoses. These subjects may actually be at high risk for other conditions, but we do not expect them to develop schizophrenia. If the diagnoses of the parents in this group turn out to be sufficiently homogeneous, we may also learn something about children at risk for that particular disorder. The purpose of including the "other psychiatric" group, however, is to enable us to distinguish variables that may be specific to children of schizophrenic parents, as opposed to variables that simply set apart the children of psychiatrically ill parents in general from children of normal parents.

We include only those families in which we can examine two or more siblings in the target age range. Sibling comparisons will be of particular value in attempting to analyze gene-environment interactions. For example, differences in environmental treatments can be compared in sibling pairs that turn out to be discordant versus pairs that turn out to be concordant for mental health outcome. We are also interested in determining whether some families within the risk groups produce more, and others fewer, vulnerable offspring and whether such differenes, if found, are correlated in any way with differences in severity of the parent's illness, psychological assets and liabilities of the presumably well spouse, the background family histories of the parents, and so on.

Children in the three risk groups and in the "other psychiatric" group are located by screening consecutive admissions to mental hospitals in the greater metropolitan area and identifying patients who have two or more children in the target age range, have intact marriages, and meet other criteria of the study, which are that both parents be white and English speaking. (These criteria were set for the purpose of simplifying logistics of the study.) Blind diagnoses are made of the parents' case records by two, or usually three, independent reviewers, and those cases in which there is diagnostic agreement are accepted for the study. The "low-risk" normal control subjects have been located by canvasing two large school districts in which the majority of the high-risk subjects reside. Families in which either parent is found to have had a history of psychiatric hospitalizations or treatment are eliminated from the study.

The sample of children[1] examined during the pilot phase of the program consists of: (1) 67 subjects with one schizophrenic parent (44 mothers, 23 fathers), (2) 13 subjects with two schizophrenic parents, (3) 25 subjects who had either a mother or a father with a psychiatric diagnosis other than schizophrenia, and (4) 100 subjects whose parents had never had psychiatric treatment. Of these children 108 have been reexamined in a second round of home and laboratory visits approximately 2 years after they were first seen. We hope to reexamine the remaining subjects in the near future and to add a new, larger sample composed of each of the several subgroups.

---

[1] In addition, there were three children with a schizophrenic mother and manic-depressive father, one mentally retarded child with a schizophrenic mother, and one child of unknown biological parentage adopted by normal parents.

Collection of Data

HOME VISIT

Our first contact with the subjects takes place in a visit to their own homes, during which a 2 to 3-hour structured interview is conducted with the well parent, or the more intact of the two if both parents are schizophrenic. In the normal control families we randomly select the mother or father as the interviewee. The interview covers: (1) personal and family histories of both parents; (2) pregnancy, birth, developmental stages, and physical health, and (3) behavioral, peer, and school histories of all children in the family, as well as the parent's assessment of the impact of the spouse's psychiatric illness and hospitalization upon each of the children. Such data have been collected on 47 younger and 75 older siblings of the study children, in addition to 205 study children themselves.

During the home visit the MMPI (Minnesota Multiphasic Personality Interview) is administered to the parents, and the Bender-Gestalt, Draw-a-Person, and Family Drawing tests are administered to each study child. A structured interview is also conducted with the children. The two interviewers (one for the parent and one for the children) independently complete ratings on the quality and condition of the home and neighborhood.

LABORATORY VISIT

Shortly after the home visit the study children came to our laboratory for a series of tests and measures lasting about 6 hours. Members of the laboratory staff do not have access to information about the children and do not know whether they are risk or "control" subjects.

Most of the procedures for the laboratory visits were selected because they were considered to reflect functions that have been found to be disturbed in schizophrenic patients—or at least in some subgroups of schizophrenic patients—and at the same time they were believed to show developmental continuity over a wide span of ages. The laboratory procedures are focused quite heavily on measures of attention, distractability, response latency, neurological functioning, and psychophysiological responsivity. The WISC and several experimental psychological tests are given also, and a structured interview is videotaped to provide a permanent record of the child at that point in time. In the planned expansion of the program we use the videotaped session for a formalized psychiatric interview, which will be viewed and rated by Dr. Clarice Kestenbaum and members of the Child Psychiatry staff at St. Luke's Hospital in a double-blind procedure.

FOLLOW-UP CONTACTS

At 6 month intervals subsequent to the first laboratory visit we conduct brief follow-up interviews by telephone to ensure that we maintain contact with the families between test sessions and, equally important, that we secure a running documentary of the life experiences of the study children and their siblings.

REPEATED HOME AND LABORATORY VISITS

As I mentioned earlier, over one half of the pilot subjects have been seen in a second round of testing. The second visit to the home allows us to update the histories on all family members, to conduct a mental status interview with the presumably well parent and to retest the study children. Because the second visit to the laboratory includes many of the same measures that are administered in the first test round it will be possible to study longitudinal changes and rates of changes in a number of response processes. During the pilot study we had an opportunity to add several procedures between the first and second laboratory visits; these measures, which include electroencephalogram (EEG), evoked potential recordings, and measures of stimulus intensity tolerance, will form part of the basic laboratory battery to be used in the future.

PLANNED EXPANDED STUDY

Our research goals over the next several years call for a final sample of over 500 study children, including the pilot subjects who will, of course, continue to be followed. All of the children will have been examined at least twice during a 5-year period. In addition to the home and laboratory procedures that I have described, rather sketchily, and the maintenance of telephone interviews throughout the entire study, school record data and teacher's evaluations will be collected in the forthcoming phase of the program to complement the parents' reports, children's self-reports, and our own observations of behavior. Dr. Norman Watt of the University of Massachusetts will be collaborating with us on this phase of study [6].

Finally, we expect that biographical data will have been collected and kept up to date on a sizable number of younger and older siblings of the study children.

Findings in the First Round of Testing

The first round of testing of our pilot sample has produced a number of findings, a few of which I would like to summarize very briefly. Because the psychiatric control group and the group with two schizophrenic parents are quite small, I refer at present only to the data on the children with one schizophrenic parent and the normal control group.

First, the neurological examination, administered by a qualified pediatric neurologist, shows no significant differences (ANOVA) between our normal control subjects and the children of schizophrenic parents with respect to an overall impairment score, nor does a multivariate discriminant function analysis show a difference in the patterning of the separate items on the examination. What is interesting, however, is that for the 7 to 10-year-old boys—and only for them—we see a weak trend, with the children of schizophrenic parents doing worse. Although this finding is not very strong at all, it is reminiscent of the report by Dr. Joseph Marcus [4] on an Israeli sample in which the difference between risk and control subjects on the neurological examination was seen only in the younger-aged males.

If the standard clinical neurology examination does not clearly differentiate the groups in our study, the modified Lincoln-Oseretsky Motor Test, which is designed to tap gross and fine motor coordination, does show significant differences ($p \leq .05$) between the risk and control children at all ages. Girls do better than boys in all groups, and the between-group differences are slightly greater for males than for females. Item analyses show very different patterns of performance in the risk and control subjects and suggest that the children of schizophrenic parents are especially poor in tasks requiring fine motor coordination.

The Bender-Gestalt test also shows highly significant ($p \leq .001$)

differences between the groups at all ages and for both sexes, and a multiple discriminant function analysis correctly assigns 78 percent of the subjects to their own groups.

Second, a different type of measure administered in the laboratory is a modification of the Continuous Performance Test (CPT) used by Mirsky and Kornetsky [5] and others to study attentional processes in schizophrenic patients. In our version of the CPT, the subject is asked to respond—keypress—as rapidly as possible when two identical stimuli in a row are presented on a visual display. Four blocks of 80 trials each are presented with auditory distraction and four blocks are without distraction. A 100 percent correct score would produce 10 responses per block. Rather to our surprise, we find no significant between-group differences in reaction time. A signal detection analysis shows, however, that in both the distraction and no-distraction conditions, the risk subjects are significantly less able to discriminate the stimuli than the controls.

Five of the 152 subjects (59 risk and 93 normal controls) who were tested on the CPT made no responses to the target stimuli during at least one full block of the eight blocks. Interestingly, these subjects all turned out to be children with schizophrenic mothers; they all had poor developmental scores on the modified Lincoln-Oseretsky and on the Bender-Gestalt. Three of them were considered by the examining neurologist to show some neurological impairment, and all were reported by their parents to show some type of emotional problem or to have serious difficulties in school. Failure to perform on the CPT may, therefore, be a relatively good differentiator of a special subgroup of the children at risk.

These are not the only children, however, who were reported to have difficulties during the pilot study. At latest follow-up, 22 percent of the children with one schizophrenic parent (20 percent of those with schizophrenic mothers and 26 percent of those with schizophrenic fathers) were receiving some type of help for emotional or school-related problems. Thirty-eight percent of the small group of children with two affected parents were also receiving help, but only 4 percent of the subjects in the psychiatric and normal control groups were reported to be receiving or in need of help. The problems reported range from hospitalization for a frank psychotic breakdown to remedial difficulties in school. We do not believe that all of these are related to the eventual likelihood of developing schizophrenia. Instead, they suggest, as did the data of Heston [3] on children adopted away from their schizophrenic mothers, that children of schizophrenic parents may be at unusually high risk for many types of behavioral and emotional problems and that the task of sorting out the children who are really at risk for schizophrenia will not be easy and probably cannot be done in a single round of assessments.

References

1. Erlenmeyer-Kimling, L. Studies on the offspring of two schizophrenic parents. In *The Transmission of Schizophrenia*, D. Rosenthal and S. S. Kety, Eds. Pergamon press, New York, 1968, pp. 65–83.
2. Garmezy, N. and Streitman, S. Children at risk: The search for the antecedents of schizophrenia. *Schiz. Bull*, No. 8 (Spring 1974)
3. Heston, L. L. Psychiatric disorders in foster home reared children of schizophrenic mothers. *Brit. J. Psychiat.*, 112 (1966), 819.
4. Marcus, J. Neurological and physiological characteristics of the children of schizophrenic parents. *Seventh Congress of the International Association of Child Psychiatry and Allied Professions*, Jerusalem, 1970.
5. Mirsky, A. E. and Kornetsky, C. On the dissimilar effects of drugs on the digit symbol substitution and continuous performance test. *Psychopharmacol.*, 5 (1964), 161.
6. Watt, N. F. Longitudinal changes in the social behavior of children hospitalized for schizophrenia as adults. *J. Nerv. Ment. Dis.*, 155 (1972), 42.

From Birth to Breakdown: A Prospective Study of Vulnerability

E. James Anthony, M.D. (U.S.A.)

Recent decades have seen the rapid evolution of methodologies designed to throw a clearer clinical light on the natural history (or should one term it the "unnatural history") of serious mental disorder within the spectrum of psychosis. These new procedures have permitted us to observe at first hand the vicissitudes of an underlying psychotic process through different phases of the life cycle. As a result of such prospective studies some new knowledge has been obtained regarding the premorbid developments of psychosis. The so-called short-term longitudinal design—the Lewinian interplay of forces within a particular life space and life time [2]—has made it possible to span a longer period of developmental time than previously and to focus more intensively and exclusively on the event structures and functions within a particular developmental environment. Not only, therefore, can one now observe the acute or gradual unfolding of a schizophrenic disturbance and monitor the rise and fall of the various disordered components, but one can also watch the interplay of vulnerable and resilient elements within the personality.

All the facts at our disposal at the present time would point to the conclusion that children with a 10 to 20 percent expectancy of developing psychosis as adults, as compared with the general population, are at even higher risk for a variety of disturbances during childhood and adolescence. We have educed from our data that such disturbances stem from three sources:

1. At times they represent antecedents of later psychosis, psychosis in the making and psychosis in the miniature (as novelist Virginia Woolf referred to her own childhood disturbances).
2. At other times the disturbances resemble, to a greater or lesser extent, the classical *folie a deux* observed when dominant psychotic figures are in intimate contact with submissive ones.
3. And reactive disorders that seem to be a direct consequence to the frustrations, mystifications, and irritations that come from living in a chaotic, disorganized, and irrational milieu.

Our further studies have indicated that the total risk to which a child is exposed may vary within the same family since birth, health, and environmental experiences are never the same for every child. To compound the problem further, we became aware that even the children at highest risk (our high-risk group, as we call them) were not all equally susceptible to these different disturbances and that an additional factor of vulnerability had to be called in to explain some of the variance. To clarify the relationship of risk to vulnerability, we began to make the global assumption that risk is a function of experience and vulnerability a function of inherence. Although we subscribed strongly to an epigenetic point of view that conceived of the organism as developing in a continuously emergent fashion through an interaction between gene and environment, there seemed to be no method available to us to disentangle the factors of inheritance, inherence, and environment.

Such fundamental ignorance on our part could not deter us from constructing heuristic models and putting them to the test of our longitudinal experience. We devised elaborate measures for assessing risk and vulnerability and on applying these criteria to our sample of offspring of psychotic parents, we extracted a subgroup, designated HRHV (high risk, high vulnerability) that scored highest in tests of risk and vulnerability. With unwarrantable presumption, considering the embryonic state of the field, we next proceeded to predict, not without some trepidation, the life history of an HRHV subject from birth to breakdown, bearing in mind the possible negating effects of intervening experiences.

The Feeling of Vulnerability

Quite early in our studies we made what was for us a significant discovery on a phenomenological plane. We found that an appreciable number of our HRHV subjects spontaneously expressed feelings of vulnerability. The sense of vulnerability appeared to stem from a cluster of phenomena—perceptual, cognitive, affective, and relational, that is, the major ingredients that constitute humanness. In more dynamic terms, there frequently appears to be a failure in the psychological process of hatching, as described by Mahler [4] as leading to a merging of child and adult pathology within the symbiotic encapsulation. One form of vulnerability appears to grow out of this shared delusional state [1], but there is another form, of a more autistic nature, in which the child-individual can never seem to confirm his own reality. At times he seems to be aware of a real reality beyond that of his own psychic reality, but there is sufficiently often awareness for him to perceive that he is living in a different world and perceiving it in a different way. In the creatively disordered individual, the phenomenological experience is even more accentuated so that they exist with bifocal perspectives of reality and unreality. Kafka was a "superphrenic" in this respect and records in a fragmented autobiography his perception of this discrepancy:

He is a small child taking a nap in the afternoon on a warm summer's day and drowsily listening to his mother calling to a neighbor from the balcony: "What are you doing, my dear? It's so hot." The other woman, from her garden, replies: "I'm having tea outside."

It was this perfectly ordinary exchange that haunted Kafka for the rest of his life. It seemed to him that somewhere out there beyond him there was a world of ordinary people interacting in an ordinary way. To someone like him, who had never been able to conceive of anything approaching an "average expectable environment," such experiences seemed unbelievable. His own environment was characterized by menace and automatically transformed any scene that came under his scrutiny into a vague apprehensiveness coupled with threat. Later on in his life he was to remark pathetically, "I have always wanted to see things as they are before they show themselves to me." For him there was always persecution latent in the fabric of the universe.

One of our subjects, with no pretense at creativity, remarked that he seemed to have different compartments in his mind. "In one of them, the "hullo" section, I can say in a very ordinary way, "Isn't it nice today" or "We could have rain later on in the evening," but at the same time in another compartment there is a feeling of something dreadful about to happen as if it contained a poisonous gas that was "ready to enter the world and put an end to everything."

Whatever engenders it in the first place, this peculiar feeling of vulnerability, this transformational capacity, or this ability to hold the visible world together in one piece hovers constantly and fills the background of attention.

Whatever engenders it in the first place, this feeling of vulnerability incipiently becomes a way of life, a state of mind, and a mode of looking at the environment through a heightened sensibility. Thereafter there is a built-in expectation that an inner disintegration or an outer disaster of an unknown nature is lying in wait around the corner, and often elaborate strategies are developed to hoodwink possible persecutors.

"The Vulnerability Complex"

The dynamic world is too full already of complexes to add still another one, but there does seem to be some justification from our material to warrant the use of such a term. I can best illustrate the complex from an actual case history. A paranoid schizophrenic man in his early 30s began to write a book describing his unusual life experiences. He prefaced his manuscript with the comment:

I am sure many people will say that I do not really hear my "voices" and that I am just crazy; perhaps I am, but there have been a lot of coincidences in my life regarding these voices. All I can do is to relate things as best I can and those who do not believe will probably not buy the book anyway and read it. My first known contact with the spirit world was through automatic writing. It began soon after reading Ruth Montgomery's book explaining the process and the Karma rules. I soon began to find out the hard way just how much the third world of spirits was responsible for much of the suffering taking place on our physical world. I soon kept getting mental thoughts to get my Uncle Harold to a hospital for the alcoholic's cure before it was too late and he drank himself into the grave. Yet, another spirit voice kept telling me not to try and save him as I would be needing him to help me from the third world. Things really began to happen after his funeral. Uncle Harold began talking to me in a voice that was exactly as it was when he was alive and on earth. This third world, a spirit world, begins to program the individuals on earth and compels them to say or act in some manner that is completely unlike their normal selves. This is the cause of many divorces and was the main reason why my wife and I have pulled apart. Now there are also good souls in the third world that try to prevent such rotten programming and have occasionally helped to smooth out the marriage each time arguments have started. The third world, therefore, contains both good and bad spirits and both have been using my mind as a focal point for coordinating their programs. (Thus I was implicated in the assassinations of John Kennedy, Bob Kennedy and Martin Luther King). There is one strange thing about the third world of spirits. The good ones seem slow and almost embarrassed to come forward and speak to me so that I can hear them: the lousy ones speak much more clearly and loudly. As I became more and more involved in the third world, I became their representative on earth and was able to predict the California earthquake. I was dismayed that this could have happened to America and I asked God why this couldn't have happened to Russia, who are our worst enemies. Apparently the earthquake force was aimed at Russia but hit us instead but I asked for them to keep aiming at Russia.

This manuscript was terminated suddenly when the author shot himself to death for reasons that were not very clear except that his wife had decided to take her two boys and leave him. She was concerned because their father was involving them increasingly in "third-world" activities. They not only helped with the preparation of the manuscript, the bibliographic research, and so on, but both boys, aged 8 and 10 years, were deeply involved with their father. I had an interview with them after he had shot himself:

Jim says, "I'm hungry. When I am hungry I am angry with everybody. I almost feel like killing everybody. It's like having a dagger in my stomach." I say, "It sounds as if you were angry at me for not stopping bad things from happening to you." Bob says, "Since we started coming, lots of things happened. Mom and Dad separated and then we lost Daddy." Jim says, "Perhaps if we hadn't come none of this would have happened. I don't think you did it. I think it is the building." Bob says, "We can do two things. We can knock down the whole building or we can not come anymore." Jim says, "Knocking down the building would be difficult. Not coming is practical." I say, "You still want to blame the building and not to blame me; you still want to destroy the building and not to hurt me. How can you be angry at stones?" Bob says, "We have a list of building complexes." I ask what this means. Bob says, "It means always imagining that something is the matter with you but something is not the matter with you but something is the matter with people and people make you think that something is the matter with you. Our mother thinks we need help. I don't need help. My father can help me from the other place. This place is making us sick. We don't want to come. We lost our father." I say, "Both of you have had a very bad time and it will be hard to get over it without being helped. You seem to have this complex where everything bad is always going to happen to you." Jim says slowly, "I guess we call it the Lister Building Complex but it's everywhere. It's like the world complex. We just feel different from all other kids. They just have fun. Things don't happen to them like they happen to us."

What one is observing here is the underlying process that gradually corrodes the sense of security and safety and leads inevitably to malevolent expectations of the world.

To examine the proposition more carefully, we contrived a little experiment based on the assumptions of naive psychology systematically advanced by Heider [3]. The child attempts, even more than the adult, to construct a commonsense psychological viewpoint that stands him in reasonable stead for all practical purposes in everyday life. Where this viewpoint is inclined to fail is in novel or unusual situations in which past experience is of no help. An encounter with a stranger in a strange environment may overtax the resources of the child's naive understanding and compel him to fall back on guidelines derived from parental attitudes and behavior. In the experiment the subject is confronted by a stranger presenting two sets of objects that are, by childhood standards: (1) attractive, delectable, and need-satisfying and (2) repulsive, unpleasant, uninteresting, and functionless. Two questions were then put to the child, "Which of the two sets of objects is the stranger likely to offer you? If the stranger has to give himself one of the objects and offer the other to you, which object would you expect to receive?" For the average control child from "an average expectable environment," there was not much doubt about the first question. The strangers of the world are collectively regarded as benignly disposed toward children and motivated only by good wishes and intentions. The same anticipated benevolence determined the average child's response to the second question. It was again tacitly assumed that adults, as a collective, tend to place the child's welfare ahead of their own. It was difficult for any child in the 7 to 12-year range to admit that ignorance of the stranger's background and credentials made it impossible for him to predict the stranger's intentions. He could not admit having sufficient information to reach a valid conclusion. Both normal and disturbed children attempted, therefore, to make conjectures. The experiment did not significantly differentiate the children of psychotic parents as a whole from those of nonpsychotic parents, but it did elicit some extreme individual reactions and abreactions from some of the children. This small group had parents who had been hospitalized more than once with paranoid schizophrenia and were from a lower social class. The difference from control subjects was significant. Within the inquiry, the basic mistrustfulness of these children was clearly demonstrated. As a group they insisted that they could not depend on people or trust them and that unless they were very careful, they nearly always got "the dirty end of the stick." In their dismal picture of the human condition, adults often ruthlessly exploited children for their own selfish ends. Certainly for this type of child the experiment had a moderate degree of "seriousness."

FROM BIRTH TO BREAKDOWN: THE CASE OF LAURA

I have selected one of our HRHV cases because I have known her from birth and have monitored her whole development. She is now 16 years old and belongs to the first family that we began investigating in depth. What was special about her and her two siblings was that both her parents were schizophrenic, which placed the genetic expectancy for adult schizophrenia somewhere at 25 to 30 percent. To make things worse, the developmental environment provided by the parents was among the most chaotic, disorganized, confused, mystifying, and incoherent that I have ever encountered.

Laura's family history, observed through four generations, was riddled with schizophrenic psychosis. The maternal grandmother died in a state mental hospital; the maternal uncle was resident in the same hospital, and her mother had received psychiatric care that had been consistently diagnosed as undifferentiated schizophrenia from the age of 16 years. Since the age of 8 the mother had a history of incestuous relationships (unfortunately common in our peculiar sample) with two of her brothers and an uncle. Even during states of remission, she was grossly pathological and was described as promiscuous, untruthful, and thieving. She inconsistently battered, abused, neglected, rejected, and pampered the three children. During the postpartum phase she developed strong impulses to kill the infants, and after watching Laura in contact with her I came to the conclusion that physical survival was preferable to any emotional damage resulting from mother-infant separation. Two of the mother's siblings were ambulatory schizophrenics, and two others seemed eccentric even for the rural part of Missouri from which they came.

The father was the only child of orthodox Jewish parents who had been discharged from the army because of periodic hallucinatory and delusional spells. His mother-in-law, who never minced her words, dismissed him as a "crazy slob." They met in a mental hospital and fell in love with each other's delusions. "I thought that she was really a princess in disguise and she showed me a royal birthmark on her thigh." She, for her part, accepted his reincarnation from Moses since he had been left in a laundry basket outside a posh house on Fifth Avenue. The central figure in this developmental drama was the maternal grandmother. To describe her as a matriarch would be to understate her overwhelming impact on the extended family group that she ruled with a rod of iron. She anticipated and prepared for each psychotic breakdown in her family and took over the care of the children. Laura thus became her baby. "As long as she stays with me, she will keep well," said this matriarch. "It was when her mother left home that she broke down. My children know where they are when they are with me. When they leave me, they get lost."

Her daughter, Laura's mother, put up a feeble struggle against submergence but eventually died in the process. In one letter she wrote: "I don't relish writing this letter to you because I don't know what to think of you. Instead of helping me or trying to get me home you have plunged me headlong into a mess. To say the least, I am bitter about what you have done to my children. I know because I am incarcerated in this institution with my husband that you believe us both mad and that no matter what we did or said you would still doubt our sanity. I have never come up to your standards but regardless of what I may have done in the past, I think myself a better person than you because I believe I could eventually forgive you for what you have done to me but I doubt whether you will ever be able to forgive me for being so imperfect as to become mentally ill."

The matriarch showed me her reply to this tormented letter. She made no reference to the emotions or the accusations but talked factually in terms of financial arrangements, schooling, the price of food, the need to mow the lawn, and the dilapidated state of the roof.

There were two reasons for my decision to remove Laura immediately from the care of the parents: (1) she was already showing withdrawal symptoms under minimal stress, apathy, disinterest in objects and people, and a low autonomic functioning and (2) a psychotic constellation was gradually being established between mother and infant, which I observed from time to time and found both alarming and upsetting. For instance, on one occasion I observed the mother feeding Laura, who gagged and spat up the food. The mother immediately hit her, saying, "Don't do that." The feeding got rougher and ended with the baby being pulled out of the chair with one of her legs still caught in it, screaming with pain. The mother said to her, "What are you trying to do to me? Trying to make me crazy?" She raised the baby to her face and said, with mock grief, "I am sorry, baby, I am sorry." As the baby stopped crying she abruptly began calling her "naughty" and "bad" in a loud attacking voice and the baby started to cry again. Once again the mother started to laugh, lifted her up and said, almost maliciously, "I am sorry baby, I am sorry." And once again the baby stopped crying. This cycle, which was repeated many times, and offers a striking example of what Winnicott refers to as "tantalizing behavior" in cases of deviant mothering. Such cycles are particularly pathogenic since they create inevitable sequelae of pleasure and pain that the individual finds later difficult to separate.

At this point in Laura's life the mother disappeared and the grandmother took over with a completeness that soon had Laura shadowing her and looking disconsolate and confused when outside the immediate matriarchal orbit. She would toddle obediently in the wake of her grandmother, looking to neither left nor right and showing little curiosity and exploratory zeal. The matriarch would remark with enormous satisfaction, "She really can't do without me; just try and get her away and you will hear her howl." In watching her eat I was reminded of a remark of Freud that "when we observe a behavior of a patient, we do not see the trauma he experienced but how he coped with it." The grandmother was still feeding her with a spoon "because she liked it that way and because it's quicker." Laura was holding the food in her mouth tucking it away into corners of her cheeks but without swallowing it. The grandmother would then say, "I know her tricks" and put her thumb over her mouth while squeezing her cheeks. The toddler would then swallow convulsively the look of panic appearing in her eyes. Once it was down, the grandmother praised her inordinantly and she beamed happily. Grandmother remarked: "She's such a funny kid; she both enjoys eating and hates eating. At times you would think I was doing her harm and she looks at me as if I was feeding her poison. But then, at other times, she wants to kiss me everytime I put food into her mouth. What can you say about a child like that?"

At the age of 6 Laura came in for her regular follow-up. In the interim her mother had remarried but then had died quite unexpectedly. I tried to explore any element of grief but she dismissed the matter abruptly, saying, "My grandmum's my mom. She's the only mum I've got." I said gently that it was sad to lose somebody even when things had not gone too well with them, but she turned her back and said, "I didn't know her." We talked about school, and she said she did not like it and preferred to be at home. I wondered why. "My grandmum wouldn't let anyone do anything to me. She'd see them off." I asked who might want to harm her. "Nobody. It's just a feeling I've got. When I look at people after a while they begin to look bad." I asked whether she felt the same about me and she smiled; "You're quite kind and I don't think that you would want to do anything bad to me."

She suddenly fell silent and looked troubled, and I wondered aloud what had frightened her. Did it have something to do with me? For a while she continued to be silent and then said that it sometimes happened like this even at home. "I begin to feel afraid that something very bad is going to happen and then everything goes far away and looks different and strange. It makes me feel wierd." She asked if I could do anything to stop it. I said that we could try and understand what made her afraid and that might help to stop it.

On testing, her rating for vulnerability was still extremely high as well as her score on the prepsychosis checklist. Her level of competence was average, and her coping and defense systems appeared to be holding up. I wrote the comment that the underlying psychotic process was showing evidence of minor eruptions and my prediction was that she would struggle through the rest of childhood with some increasing micropsychotic episodes and then, because of her high vulnerability, become a candidate for breakdown in early adult life.

At the age of 10 she asked to see me outside the usual follow-up time. I found her more than usually nervous. Her school achievements over the past few years had been fluctuating, but currently she was doing a little less than average work. Her test IQ was 110. I asked her why she had come and she said it was because of school. She said that a month ago she had begun to have difficulty understanding the teacher or sometimes even her friends when they talked to her. "Their words seem to get jumbled up and this makes me feel very nervous. I don't understand them properly when they speak. Sometimes it's because I get those funny feelings I told you about before and then everything gets mixed up." As she talked she seemed extremely jittery. I told her that listening was sometimes difficult for everyone because they might be thinking of other things or because they might be anxious. Quite suddenly she said, "Do you think I'll go crazy?" This was followed by a traumatic silence on both our parts, and I felt a wave of sympathy for her going through me. I said very definitely that her tests showed no indication of any craziness (which was true). However, her Rorschach test was later given to an independent judge, who detected elements of thought disorder. I asked her to be sure to keep in touch with me and to call me whenever she felt more than usually anxious, which she did from time to time.

For the next 2 years she seemed much better in school and her competence and vulnerability scores improved. On the Academic Progress Chart the developmental curve was now above the average line. She was now 12, well developed, and quite beautiful when her face was untroubled. She had started her periods, but they were not quite regular. Her grandmother complained that she was lazy, uncooperative, sloppy, and somewhat careless about her personal grooming. She seemed unusually interested in horses. She was now making failing grades at school, and what infuriated her grandmother even more was that she was stealing from home. Moreover, she was mixing with a very dubious bunch of girls who were non-church-goers and whose mothers looked like prostitutes rather like her own mother. During the summer Laura told a friend that she was planning to run away from home because she felt stifled, and when her grandmother heard about this she warned her that this was what her mother had done and "look how she had suffered from it."

When she came to see me, I reminded her that she'd always said that home was the safest place in the world, and she admitted that this was still true, though when she was there she could hardly breathe. At times she felt terribly scared of her grandmother especially when she got angry. "Her face changes and becomes large and horrible, full of lumps and her eyes look like holes and I almost feel that she could kill me." She felt trapped. She could neither leave nor stay. I arranged for her to come in once a week, and this seemed to tide her over the crisis. Her school work began improving again and she had stopped stealing.

At 14 there was a sharp rise in the vulnerability score, a higher rating on the prepsychotic checklist, a falling off in competence, and a new despondency. There were no overt signs of psychotic development, and I was anxious and revised my prediction, feeling that her breakdown would come somewhere during adolescence.

Toward the end of her 14th year her grandmother wrote to say that the principal had called her with a disturbing piece of news. He said that Laura was claiming to be a witch and to be able to cast spells on the other children. She had told them that her dead mother frequently talked to her and would do anything that she asked her to do. If anyone hurt Laura, she could harm them. I received an urgent letter from the grandmother, "I do not feel that my daughter's condition especially that she is now dead, could affect Laura in any way. She was never around her mother except in infancy. Yet, she does seem to be so much like her in many ways and now she seems to be feeling and thinking like her. She also misrepresents facts in the way that her mother did before she became mental. I am very worried about this witch business. My God, Doctor, how can we help this child? She seems to be going the same way as her mother and father and nothing I am able to do can stop it. God bless you for all you've done so far."

When I saw her there was a new distance between us, and she looked at me evasively, allusively, and mistrustfully. Previously I had always felt confident of coaxing her back with me to reality, but now I was far from sure. She talked freely about her dead mother and her close identification with her and asked me to tell her everything about her since I was the one who knew her so well. "I can get to know her through you." I asked her what she wanted to know in particular and she replied, "I want to know whether she loved me and whether she went crazy because of me and whether she wanted me and just couldn't get me away from my grandmom. She is my real mom and I want her back." I asked her to tell me how she was feeling and she said, with a very strange expression on her face, "If you knew my mother, you would be knowing how I'm feeling." A manifest schizoaffective disorder had begun.

Conclusion

To follow a child from birth to breakdown is both a fascinating and disturbing experience, fluctuating between hopefulness and helplessness. If this child had gone into intensive psychotherapeutic treatment, I am not sure whether the breakdown would have been staved off, although the interplay between high risk, high vulnerability, low competence, and a pathogenic environment appeared to load the dice against her. Even though one is so conscious in this work of the impact of the parents illness on the child, I am in agreement with Winnicott's statement that "a child's illness is his own" and not merely reactive or reflective of environmental disturbances.

I am reminded of a much more articulate individual, Virginia Woolf, who became conscious quite early of her "skinlessness," her extreme vulnerability from early childhood. Her description of her 13-year-old breakdown "in miniature," as she later referred to it, comprised a sense of depersonalization and loss of self, a blankness of mind, a wish to be completely alone, and to have no pleasure in life whatsoever. In this period, following the death of her mother (whom she never forgave for dying on her), she retreated into a dream world that was full of "voices." Every detail of life stuck out in her mind as if she were in a play. She found herself observing quite dispassionately, almost as if she was pretending, afraid that she was not feeling enough. She could notice the raindrops sliding down the windowpane. She was dazed, wooden, with the "substance gone out of everything." Later she was able to describe this first breakdown with greater objectivity. "It was like watching life, a long way off, unreal, through the wrong end of the telescope." Toward the latter part of adolescence, at the time of her second breakdown, she declared that she had never been able to become part of life. "It was as if the world is entire and I am outside of it, crying, 'Oh save me from being blown forever outside the loop of time!' Other people seemed to live in a real world but I often fall down into nothingness. I have to bang my head against some hard door to call myself back to the body." But it was only through this shutting-out process that she was able to create a coherent inner world for herself. However, what is most striking about all the characters in her books is their separateness. Their minds seem lost in a dream world from which they hear in the distance the sounds of other people moving about in the world. When the other person is forced on their attention they feel a shock of surprise.

Here we have Kafka's experience and also the experience of many of our HRHV subjects whose worlds, though not so articulately described, seem populated by persons living on a distant but normal planet.

References

1. Anthony, E. J. The influence of maternal psychosis on children—Folie á deux. In *Parenthood*, E. J. Anthony, and T. Benedek, Eds. Little, Brown, Boston, 1970, pp. 571–593.
2. Anthony, E. J. The influence of a manic-depressive environment on the developing child. In *Depression and Human Existence*, E. J. Anthony and T. Benedek, Eds. Little, Brown, Boston, 1975a, pp. 279–315.
3. Anthony, E. J. The use of the "serious" experiment in child psychiatric research. In *Explorations in Child Psychiatry*, E. J. Anthony, Ed. Plenum Press, New York, 1975b, pp. 383–414.
4. Mahler, M., Pine, F., and Bergman, A. *The Psychological Birth of the Human Infant*. Basic Books, New York, 1975.

The Invisible Children

Selma Fraiberg, M.D. (U.S.A.)

Dr. Anthony's beautiful and disturbing essay says so much in its compact 22 pages that it needs to be read several times, I have found, to get the full import of his work and his findings. Research into the natural history of mental disorder is not only an imperative need in psychiatry, but we, as clinicians, responding to this research, must consider the implications for our work with the psychotic patient and his family.

In the largest number of mental hospitals, or in outpatient treatment, the children of schizophrenic parents are invisible. They may not appear in the case record, except as names. They are a kind of ghostly presence in the treatment of the parent. I thought I might entitle my remarks "The invisible children."

It is my hope that Dr. Anthony's paper and his studies will stimulate us to reflect on our practices in adult psychotherapy and consider the ways in which a mental health team approach can bring help to the imperiled children as well as the parents. Once the children become visible there are ways in which psychiatry can bring its resources to these children, and it is possible that we can prevent grave disorder in a large number of cases.

I would like to begin by bringing into focus the risk and vulnerability factors that are at the center of Dr. Anthony's paper. In the case of offspring of one schizophrenic parent, the genetic expectancy for adult schizophrenia is somewhere around 10 per-

cent. In the case of the child who is the offspring of two schizophrenic parents, the genetic expectancy as cited by Dr. Anthony is
25 to 30 percent. In either case, the children of schizophrenics are
as a group identifiable as a *risk* population, even if they were being
reared in "an average expectable environment." Dr. Anthony has
chosen to use the term vulnerability for the inheritance factor and
uses the term "risk" as a function of experience. I try to keep to his
definitions in what follows.

This brings us to examine with Dr. Anthony the loading of risk
factors in the *experience* of the child of a schizophrenic parent who
is reared by that parent. Genetic vulnerability may be compounded by erratic and abusive child-rearing practices or by the
experience of being caught up in the delusional world of the
parent during the formative years in which a child must constitute
a stable sense of objective reality.

Since my own experience with the children of psychotic parents
is largely with infants and children under the age of 3 years, I
have selected from Dr. Anthony's material and our own experience at the Child Development Project the risk factors as I see
them in the early years. Dr. Anthony's case report, Laura, can
serve us very well in this respect.

Laura, when we first meet her in Dr. Anthony's account, is a
baby, 8 months old, conceived in a mental hospital, the child of
two schizophrenic parents. She is living with her mother and we
are witness, with Dr. Anthony, to a chilling display of maternal
cruelty, alternating with mock apologies to the terrified baby, in
which we see sadistic intention.

A child under the age of 18 months must be considered vulnerable in the psychological sense, even under all favorable circumstances in child rearing. It is during the sensorimotor period
that the child must accomplish two central tasks in development.
He learns to love, trust, and value his human partners, and by 18
months he also achieves the concept of a self and an object world;
this achievement is by no means independent of the first developmental task, the achievement of human bonds.

If either of these two central tasks of the sensorimotor period is
impeded or imperiled through environmental circumstance, we
find that the child, even *without* genetic vulnerability, will show the

effects through instability in ego organization. He need not become psychotic at any time, but he will be susceptible to affective and cognitive disorders. In the case of Laura and, I think, many other children who come into the world with genetic risks of many kinds, the scale may be tipped in the direction of adaptive incapacity when the early ego organization is assaulted. The shaky constitution of a self and an object world, the deprivation of human experience that builds trust and the judgment of "what is real" are then imposed on the constitutional vulnerabilities, and risk is compounded.

If all this were not enough, there are still other events that can imperil the early ego organization of normal children and that certainly increase the risks for the children of a psychotic mother. For all children the experience of prolonged separation from a mother during the early years of life can create disturbances in the affective sphere, anxiety, depression, and a disturbance in the perception of reality. Whether such experiences of separation and loss are damaging to early development depends on the quality of substitute mother care available to the child during the period of loss. In the case of the children of schizophrenic mothers, there will typically be repeated hospitalizations. Who is providing substitute mother care for these children who are already suffering from the effects of erratic or even abusive mothering? Most often, in our experience, it is "anyone handy," and the nightmare is compounded by multiple and indifferent caregivers.

In the case of Laura, Dr. Anthony had to make another kind of decision in the best interest of the child. The psychotic mother *was* at home, we gather, and we do not know if there were hospitalizations during the period that the mother was caring for the child. But the abuse of the child by her mother left Dr. Anthony with the only possible decision, that Laura had to be removed from her mother's care. He was thoroughly mindful of the meaning of separation to a child of Laura's age and he would also be able to say, I know, that even the child of an abusive mother has a kind of attachment to the mother, even though that attachment might be morbid. So Laura needed to be removed from her mother's care. And, where Laura's slim hope of survival in the psychological sense would now be dependent on good mothering in a stable home, this care could only be provided by a grandmother whose own instability and erratic child-rearing practices tipped the scales once more.

When we last see Laura in Dr. Anthony's report we share his own pain. Laura is moving toward a psychotic break. We meet her again in a mental hospital.

Can we, as clinicians, intervene at any point in this morbid process for the children of schizophrenics? At several points? Is there hope for psychiatric intervention on behalf of the children?

I think there is. If we understand the implications of Dr. Anthony's research, there *are* variables in the environment and experience of these vulnerable children that have provided a different outcome for a sizable percentage of this population. Thus if the genetic expectancy for the offspring of schizophrenic mothers is 10 percent, we still have to account for the 90 percent of this population that does not become schizophrenic. It is possible that there are specific genetic variables that do or do not dispose toward schizophrenia, but it is also possible, and this seems to be supported by Dr. Anthony's work, that the effect of a morbid environment on the adaptive capacities of the young child may narrow and finally close off the adaptive routes.

Not all schizophrenic mothers are as malevolent and dangerous as was Laura's mother. But most schizophrenic mothers are to some extent disabled in their capacities to mother and must have support and guidance from experts to nuture their children. Even the children of schizophrenic mothers who do *not* themselves become schizophrenic may show the effects of erratic mothering through grave emotional instability.

The implications for our own work in psychiatry are sobering, but they may lead us to develop a rational approach to the treatment of schizophrenics and their children. This means that psychiatrists, social workers, and psychologists need to view the children of schizophrenic parents as their patients, even though the hospital registry lists only the mother or the father as "patient." The invisible children in the patient's record need to become visible. And then the following questions arise. Who is taking care of the baby and the older children? Where are the children? What is the *quality* of child care provided during hospitalization? Are the children damaged? Are they in danger? Can this mother, with expert help, care for her children, or are the children endangered if they continue to live with her? If they are endangered, how can we work toward stable foster care plans? It means also that the hospital does not discharge its responsibility to the mother and her children with discharge from the hospital. It means reshaping our philosophy of patient care, both in- and out-patient, and this can be done, I believe, as soon as the invisible children become visible.

Family Interaction: An Alternative Starting Point for Evaluating Risk of Psychosis

Lyman C. Wynne, M.D., Ph.D. (U.S.A.)

In his recent comprehensive review Norman Garmezy [1] has delineated four major research approaches to the study of antecedents. Type I studies are those that employ *clinical retrospective* methods; Type II studies involve the method of *follow-back* in which the starting point is the disordered adult, and premorbid status is evaluated retrospectively from reports based on society's records; Type III studies utilize *follow-up* procedures for evaluating the adult adjustment of disturbed children who, initially, are likely to be selected from data available in the files of child guidance clinics; and Type IV studies use the *follow-through* (or longitudinal-developmental) method to study children at risk.

In this chapter I argue that methodological difficulties and, more fundamentally, conceptual prejudgments, have far too prematurely restricted the actual research strategies used in the study of the origins of psychosis. I assume that by now everyone agrees on the basic scientific principle that the explicit formulation of alternative, competing hypotheses, each of which is potentially disconfirmable, is a requirement for rapid scientific progress [2]. Nevertheless, with very few exceptions this principle has not been manifest in most studies of the psychoses, especially schizophrenia. Risk studies thus far have not included procedures for

293

evaluation of family interaction hypotheses. I attempt to spell out what I believe to be the rationale and need for including in such studies procedures that will permit the testing of a set of alternative hypotheses (in addition to genetic, biochemical, and psychological hypotheses) in which schizophrenia is explicitly assessed in terms of indices of family relationships and family interaction.

I need not belabor the now familiar point that the Type I clinical retrospective methods may generate significant hypotheses but cannot reach etiologic conclusions. Thus studies of family relationships and family interaction have generated hypotheses for etiologic research, but like other contemporaneous observations made after illness has emerged, family data, no more than contemporaneous biochemical or individual psychological data, cannot establish antecedents.

The Type II follow-back studies could conceivably evaluate etiology, but unfortunately do not provide suitable data for the study of family interaction. Obtained in an earlier era, records provided by schools and child guidance clinics have typically not centered on analysis in depth of the family as a social unit, and not in a single study have they supplied data that could provide an adequate test, whether negative or positive, with respect to *family interaction* hypotheses. Wahl [3] and Rutter [4], for example, have examined the effects of parental loss on children, but it is not unexpected that such a gross factor should elicit a gross conclusion, namely, that parental loss is related to a diversity of outcomes.

The Type III follow-up studies are those in which children considered at risk are selected through records of facilities, such as child guidance clinics. These records are then examined in relation to an evaluation of contemporary status of the children when seen some years later. Robins and O'Neal [5] have pointed out that child patients are, after all, patients, and the history of events preceding the symptoms is still subject to retrospective bias, even though they are seen as closer to the onset of the disorder. Child guidance clinics have been oriented to the developmental history of the individual child rather than the development of the family as a system. Therefore, follow-up risk studies, like the follow-back studies, have not provided data about family interaction or the details of family relationships. Only gross factors, such as parental illness and foster replacements, which vary widely in their meaning and effect and depend on a host of unexamined variables, have been studied with this approach.

Thus because of the lack of relevant data, hypotheses concerning family patterns simply have not been evaluated. Even historical data about family relationships are often unavailable. In recent years, although conjoint family therapy has in some agencies provided the potentiality for a more balanced picture of the family, most clinics and most families continue to focus on the identified, presenting patient in family therapy or fail to provide detailed observations about family interaction. Therefore, family therapy records remain suspect as the data base for evaluating family hypotheses. Although it is possible to take excerpts of tape recordings of family therapy for the blind evaluation of family communication patterns [6], deriving usable data from therapy tapes is methodologically cumbersome as one must search long and diligently for excerpts that illustrate family interactions that are not heavily focused on the patient's symptoms.

Thus we are perforce pushed toward the admittedly difficult and expensive longitudinal prospective studies that Garmezy calls Type IV, or follow-through research. Garmezy's comprehensive review reflects the state of this field, namely, that these prospective studies largely involve the "children of mentally ill parents." I have previously [7] proposed a broader approach to the study of risk in which family characteristics *other than psychopathological ones* would be selected as predictor variables, and not those requiring the presence of mental illness in a parent, to define a child as being at risk. For example, I proposed that samples be selected on the basis of measures of parental communication as an alternative to selection on the basis of diagnosed and manifest parental or child psychopathology. Even within our own research setting at the University of Rochester, I have found that "risk" researchers are hesitant to risk working with such "nongenetic" criteria. Therefore, in our Rochester study a combination of criteria has been adopted in which family interaction measures can be examined as independent variables even though parental psychopathology serves as the *initial* starting point for entry into the family.*

It is my impression that our traditions of thinking are deeply ingrained with the view that schizophrenia and its more specific behavioral components, such as irrationality, arise only through a process of transmission from one generation to the next, especially the transmission of genetic endowment. This way of thinking was made explicit in the title and text of the well-known conference volume, *The Transmission of Schizophrenia* [8]. Similarly, psychoanalytic and other dynamic theorists of child development have tended to emphasize the processes of identification that would lead to *similarities* between parents and their offspring, with parent and child considered in dyadic relationships.

A family-systems approach, in contrast, looks at the matrix of relationships and roles, the function of shared family myths and values that help maintain the relationships, and the outward manifestations of these relationships in recurrent communication patterns. This viewpoint makes explicit the expectation that the family members will differ from one another, not only because of their presumed biologic differences but also because of their differing psychosocial place within the family and their differing contacts with influences beyond the family boundary.

Clearly, a family systems point of view can encompass and incorporate both genetic and traditional psychodynamic processes because it moves onto a different level of conceptualization beyond, but not ignoring, individual and dyadic analysis (biological and behavioral). However, it is not surprising that the organ orientation of medicine and the personality orientation of psychiatry and psychology are more familiar ground than a family-systems approach. Child psychiatry is only beginning to emerge from this constricting individual conceptual frame of reference.

In addition to the conceptual logic of a family systems view-

*The University of Rochester Child and Family Study is supported by NIMH Program Project Grant MH22836, Lyman C. Wynne, Principal Investigator. Team leaders in this program are Alfred Baldwin, Michael Chandler, Robert Cole, Lawrence Fisher, Fredric Jones, James E. Jones, Howard Iker, Ronald Kokes, Stephen Munson, Barry Ritzler, John Romano, Leonard Salzman, and John S. Strauss.

point in risk research, a variety of data also suggest the need for investigations on the family level. First of all, 88 to 90 percent of schizophrenics do not have a schizophrenic parent. Among acute reactive schizophrenics with whom preventive or prompt therapeutic measures may be especially valuable, the proportion without diagnosed, overt symptomatology in a parent is probably higher. Thus, the diagnosis of parental schizophrenia will, at best, miss most of the children who are potential schizophrenics. Even if these children do become schizophrenic, the fact of parental schizophrenia makes them unrepresentative of schizophrenics more generally.

One way to circumvent this problem is to change the ground rules, to become interested in a much broader group of outcomes than clinical schizophrenia, to include parents with so-called schizophrenia-spectrum and borderline cases as well as those identified as "inadequate personality" [9]. I personally feel that this broadened approach is likely to be highly fruitful, but it must also be recognized that it does not involve study of risk for schizophrenia with clearly defined boundaries. It calls instead for either a new concept of psychiatric illness in which a dimensionalized rather than a categorical approach to psychiatric disturbance is the keystone [10].

Another strategy for increasing the risk has been proposed by Erlenmeyer-Kimling [11], who has worked with children of two schizophrenic parents whom she regards as at "high" risk in contrast to children of one schizophrenic parent, whom she describes as having "intermediate" risk. However, because so few schizophrenics have two schizophrenic parents, it seems likely, both on genetic and psychosocial grounds, that the children of dual-mated schizophrenics, even when they do become schizophrenic themselves, are indeed unlikely to be representative of the broader population of schizophrenics.

It should be noted in passing that recent reports from the Danish high risk studies suggest that, in the families of children selected as at high risk because of one schizophrenic parent, mainly the mother, actual psychiatric examination of the spouses has not been reported as yet. Mednick [12] has found that after a hospital record check of the husbands of the original Mednick high-risk Danish sample, a number of families now need to be reclassified as dual-mated rather than as single-schizophrenic-parent families. According to Schulsinger [13], the direct interviewing of spouses who do not have a psychiatric record reveals that an unexpectedly high incidence of psychopathology is found in the spouses. If a pattern of assortative mating is confirmed, this may change the genetic interpretation of the adoptive and high-risk Danish studies. Thus research in which children are selected on the basis of hospital, or register diagnostic data about their parents, needs to be consistently reassessed in the light of direct research interviewing of other, non-index, family members.

These findings are consistent with observations made for some years by Lidz and Lidz [14], Alanen [15], Wynne and Singer [16], and others, who have been reported after more intensive family studies that peculiar, difficult-to-assess features are found in parents of schizophrenics even though these parents usually have not been diagnosed as psychiatric patients. I emphasize that the family as a unit has not yet been examined in detail even with respect to parental psychopathology in prospective high-risk research.

Dr. Margaret Singer and I [17] have found in our cross-sectional studies of a diversity of families with schizophrenic offspring as well as a variety of borderline, nonschizophrenic and normal offspring, that multivariate statistical techniques permit a differentiation between measures of parental psychopathology and parental communication deviance. Although these two measures are correlated, communication deviances retain a considerable differentiating power, even when the degree of parental psychopathology is "held constant" by means of an analysis of covariance and related statistical techniques.

With results of prospective risk studies still pending, our present data so far have the traditional limitations of other data obtained after a family member has become psychiatrically disturbed. Nevertheless, their relevance for prospective longitudinal research is clear; they suggest that one need not, or perhaps should not, rely on parental mental illness, whether severe or mild, as the sole factor for selecting families on the assumption that there will be increased risk of schizophrenia or psychosis in an offspring.

For many years Margaret Singer and I have taken the position that the various components of schizophrenic disorder need to be examined not only in terms of direct transmission of psychopathology and genes but also from the vantage point of the impact of persons in the family social unit on one another. We have been concerned with the formative processes evolving in the development of vulnerability through the reciprocal impact of enduring patterns of interaction and communication [18].

We continue to assume, and our own evidence supports, the traditional view that parents and children, whether in disordered or normal families, do share some things in common. However, we believe that this traditional viewpoint is inadequate to explain the phenomena of observed differences between parents and children, differences that can be predicted from data obtained by observing and analyzing parental forms of communication. This point of view depends on a systems concept, within which the psychological boundaries of the family and other key relationships provide a theoretical framework in which the shaping of behavior patterns, both adaptive and maladaptive, can take place.

Furthermore, and of great importance for the assessment of risk, the potentially pathogenic impact of one parent may be either actively corrected, augmented, or passively allowed to go unchallenged by the other parent [18]. We now believe that modes of interaction can best be assessed by direct observation of parents in active communication with one another, rather than by individual testing. However, we also have found value in examining the style with which individual parents give attention to the task of interpreting the meaning of Rorschach cards. This process, we have hypothesized, has a broad and pervasive counterpart in the style with which a parent shares foci of attention with a growing child and interprets or reasons about unfamiliar percepts. In this work we have found that the frequency of communication deviances in *both* parents successfully predicts the contemporaneous severity of psychiatric illness in an offspring. However, it is only recently in our current Rochester research program that we have been able to apply these family methods to a prospective, longitudinal sample of families, prior to the appearance of any prodromal signs in the biological offspring.

Here a fascinating research opportunity presents itself. Even though the families were selected because *one* parent had a history of either schizophrenic or depressive illness, we are able to make assessments of risk that vary within each subgroup of families, that is, to make predictive distinctions based specifically on family interactional data rather than only on the diagnosis of the disturbed parent. Thus this approach permits examination of both genetic risk variables and family interaction risk variables.

Additionally, by examining directly the psychologic, neurologic, and psychophysiologic response dispositions of a child (prior to possible psychiatric disturbance), we can consider the extent to which these variables mediate between this pair of parents and the development of a child of a given sex, age, and maturational level.

Quite clearly, how and whether the various members of a family are or are not the focus of communicational difficulties, is a function of complex factors, of which the variety or degree of symptomatic psychopathology in either parent, currently or in the past, is but one component. Thus the concept of impact, of parent on child and vice versa, is a complex one involving the multidirectional processes of family life and evolving over time in ways that can best be examined in prospective longitudinal research.

It may be well for me to underline that I am not advocating dismissing an assessment of psychopathology in parents and other family members. Rather, after having spent many years in helping to develop improved standardized diagnostic methods, I believe that symptomatic and personality manifestations need more detailed, multidimensional scrutiny rather than being summarized in single labels. Improved assessment of symptoms will help in evaluating the appropriate weight given to genetic factors if studies are carried out on appropriate samples. Viewing symptoms in a family interaction context, they have usually been regarded as a manifestation of disorder in the family system, but, in addition, certainly have an impact upon the family system once they have emerged or have threatened to emerge.

Neither am I setting aside the importance of biologic, biochemical, and neurophysiologic investigations in my emphasis on family-systems hypotheses. Rather, each of these approaches can provide specific variables whose significance can be compared and may be additive with family variables, preferably studied in the *same* sample of families. I emphasize the latter point because there has been a tendency to conclude that evidence of a particular factor, studied separately, establishes an etiologic picture. For example, in oral discussions, if not in writing, a number of people have spoken of a genetic etiology of schizophrenia as having been established. In my observation, this generalization frequently has been misunderstood. More precisely, the genetic evidence indicates that there is a contributing factor of predisposition in *some* degree in *some* of the persons designated as schizophrenics. The important genetic data cannot be placed in scientific perspective if they are inflated into *comprehensive* etiologic conclusions for all schizophrenics.

Similarly, studies of family relationships and communication, as they are brought into prospective longitudinal studies of risk, obviously will not account for all the variance in developmental outcomes. I do hypothesize that such variables will account for a significant portion of the variance. Unless these variables are explicitly included in risk research, as well as in adoption and twin studies, they can not be disconfirmed—a minimal scientific goal. Further, in its emphasis on developmental processes, I expect such research to pave the way for more effective prevention and intervention in families who have one or more children at special risk for serious psychiatric disorder.

References

1. Garmezy, N. Children at risk: The search for antecedents of schizophrenia. Part I: Cconceptual models and research methods. *Schiz. Bull.,* no. 8 (1974), 14–90.
2. Platt, J. R. Strong inference. *Science,* 146(1964), 347–353.
3. Wahl, C. W. Some antecedent factors in the family histories of 568 male schizophrenics of the United States Navy. *Amer. J. Psychiat.,* 113(1956), 201–210.
4. Rutter, M. Parent-child separation: Psychological effects on the children. *J. Child Psychol. Psychiat.,* 12(1971), 233–260.
5. Robins, L. N., and O'Neal, P. L. The strategy of follow-up studies, with special reference to children. In *Modern Perspectives in International Child Psychiatry,* Howells, J. G., Ed. Oliver & Boyd, Edinburgh, 1969, pp. 785–804.
6. Morris, G. O., and Wynne, L. C. Schizophrenic offspring and styles of pa-

rental communication: A predictive study using family therapy excerpts. *Psychiatry,* 28(1965), 19–44.

7. Wynne, L. C. Family research in the pathogenisis of schizophrenia. Intermediate variables in the study of families at high risk. In *Problems of Psychosis,* Doucet, P., and Laurin, C., Eds. Excerpta Medica, Amsterdam, 1971, pp. 401–423.

8. Rosenthal, D., and Kety, S. S., Eds. *The Transmission of Schizophrenia.* Pergamon Press, New York, 1968.

9. Kety, S. S., Rosenthal, D., Wender, P. H., and Schulsinger, F. The types and prevalence of mental illness in the biological and adoptive families of adopted schizophrenics. *J. Psychiat. Res.,* 6(suppl.) (1968), 345–362.

10. Strauss, J. S. Diagnostic models and the nature of psychiatric disorder. *Arch. Gen. Psychiat.,* 29(1973), 445–450.

11. Erlenmeyer–Kimling, L. Studies on the offspring of two schizophrenic patients. In *The Transmission of Schizophrenia,* Rosenthall, D., and Kety, S. S., Eds. Pergamon Press, New York, 1968.

12. Mednick, B. R. Breakdown in high-risk subjects: Familial and early environmental factors. *J. Abn. Psychol.,* 82(1973), 469–475; and Mednick, S. A., Schulsinger, F., Higgins, J., and Bell, B. F., Eds. *Genetics, Invironment and Psychopathology.* American Elsevier, New York, 1974.

13. Schulsinger, F. Personal communication, 1974.

14. Lidz, R. W., and Lidz, T. The family environment of schizophrenic patients. *Amer. J. Psychiat.,* 106(1949), 332–345.

15. Alanen, Y. O. The family in the pathogenesis of schizophrenic and neurotic disorders. Munksgaard, Copenhagen, 1966.

16. Wynne, L. C., Singer, M. T. Thought disorder and family relations of schizophrenics. *Arch. Gen. Psychiat.,* 9(1963), 191–198.

17. Singer, M. T., and Wynne, L. C. Principles for scoring communication defects and deviances in parents of schizophrenics: Rorschach and TAT scoring manuals. *Psychiatry,* 29(1966), 260–288.

18. Wynne, L. C. Methodologies and conceptual issues in the study of schizophrenics and their families. *J. Psychiat. Res.,* 6(suppl.) (1968), 185–199.

19. Singer, M. T., and Wynne, L. C. Thought disorder and family relations of schizophrenics, IV: Results and implications. *Arch. Gen. Psychiat.,* 12(1965), 201–212.

00. Goldstein, M. The study of families of disturbed adolescents at risk for schizophrenia and related conditions. Presented at International Association for Child Psychiatry and Allied Professions, Philadephia, July, 1976.

Study of Families of Disturbed Adolescents at Risk for Schizophrenia and Related Conditions*

Michael J. Goldstein, Ph.D. (U.S.A.)

Systematic research on adolescents who may be at risk for schizophrenia is particularly important since it is directly concerned with the ultimate development of effective early intervention programs that hold promise for either preventing or reducing the severity of adult schizophrenia. Any intervention model presupposes three things: first, that we know which individuals are in special need of such preventive services; second, that we have sufficient knowledge of the critical attributes of such individuals, which, if modified early would affect the base rate of the development of adult psychopathology; and third, that we know the type of intervention likely to be effective in modifying these attributes.

In the case of the first issue, there are certain clues recurring in studies of high-risk children and suggesting distinctive behavioral characteristics that differentiate the prepsychotic child or adolescent from other less vulnerable groups of the same age. However, these clues are fragmentary and relate primarily to a certain class

*Supported by NIMH Grants MH-08744 and MH-13512

of prepsychotic child, namely, those whose mothers have also had schizophrenic episodes. It appears that before we mount large-scale primary prevention programs designed to minimize the likelihood of a schizophrenic episode later in life, we need to specify more clearly the types of high-risk children who require this intervention and those attributes that should be the targets of a useful intervention program.

The project, described in a previous paper [5], has been conducted by a group working with my colleague Eliot Rodnick and myself. It followed the tripartite strategy in the preceding paragraph and was designed to identify aspects of familial interaction and adolescent psychopathology that were particularly related "to the spectrum of schizophrenic disorders in adulthood" [3]. Our focus has been twofold: first to identify family interaction patterns correlated with subsequent schizophreniform reactions and, second, to identify aspects of behavioral disturbance in adolescence that relate to this pattern of adult psychopathology. It may be that the two are so linked that either one is useful as the other to identify the child vulnerable for subsequent schizophrenia. However, we have attempted to hedge our bets on this issue as it may prove more effective to identify high-risk children on the basis of familial patterns than on manifest psychopathology of the child. Although there is some evidence from our findings to date that the two are correlated, to some extent we continue to have an open mind about the relative utility of either criteria for selecting vulnerable children.

It may be helpful to know something of the strategy underlying our project so that the data that I present here can be seen in proper context. In this project we have restricted our attention to adolescence, the developmental period immediately prior to the peak onset of schizophrenia. We have defined our high-risk sample as disturbed adolescents who manifest behavioral problems during this age period that are sufficiently marked to merit professional assistance. It appears that those individuals who have serious emotional difficulties during adolescence represent a more vulnerable group for subsequent psychopathology than do well-functioning teenagers.

Development of Adolescent Behavior Problem Groups

To generate comparison groups, we have subdivided our sample of disturbed adolescents into four subgroups based upon the manifest presenting problem. These four groups are as follows:

GROUP 1: AGGRESSIVE ANTISOCIAL

This group is characterized by poorly controlled, impulsive, and acting-out behavior. Some degree of inner tension or subjective distress may be present but is clearly subordinate to the aggressive patterns and poor impulse control, which appear to be the predominant behavioral characteristics. These were manifest across a broad range of interpersonal functioning, for instance, in peer relationships, in the family, in school, and in conflicts with the law.

GROUP 2: ACTIVE FAMILY CONFLICT

This group is characterized by a defiant, disrespectful stance toward parents, belligerence and antogonism in the family setting, and often signs of inner distress or turmoil, such as tension, anxiety and somatic complaints. In contrast to Group 1, there are few manifestations of aggression or rebellion to authorities outside of the family.

GROUP 3: PASSIVE, NEGATIVE

This group is characterized by negativism, sullenness, and indirect forms of hostility or defiance toward parents. In contrast to Group 2, overt defiance and temper outbursts are infrequent, and there is a superficial compliance to wishes of adults. School difficulties are frequent, typically described as underachievement with little evidence of disruptive behavior.

GROUP 4: WITHDRAWN, SOCIALLY ISOLATED

This group is characterized by marked social isolation, general uncommunicativeness, few if any friends, and excessive dependence on one or both parents. Gross fears or signs of marked anxiety and tension are often present. Much of the unstructured time of these adolescents is spent in solitary pursuits.

These groups demonstrate quite contrasting styles of coping with stress that allow for meaningful comparisons among the groups. Some of these modes of coping can be seen to contain components of the coping style of the schizophrenic, such as withdrawal and social isolation. Others, such as acting out and passive aggression, seem only indirectly related, if at all, to the manifest complex of behaviors that we call schizophrenia. Our emphasis has been on whether consistencies exist between particular attributes of intrafamilial relations and adolescent coping style across a broad spectrum of patterns of adolescent psychopathology.

Our emphasis in this project has been on differentiating among these four groups on measures assessing various aspects of the family system, but we have also attempted to define certain general dimensions implicit in this fourfold grouping. First, there is the dimension of the locus of the conflict—whether the behavioral difficulties of the adolescent are restricted largely to relationships within the home or whether they are manifested outside the home as well. The aggressive antisocial and passive negative groups (Groups 1 and 3) are both similar along this dimension as both exhibit significant behavioral difficulties outside the home. The active family conflict and withdrawn groups (Groups 2 and 4) are similar in that relationships within the home are seen as central.

Second, the groups can be viewed in terms of the activity present in the adolescent's problems. The aggressive antisocial and active family conflict is similarly active in interpersonal relationships, whereas the other two groups are distinctly more passive. These two dimensions of *locus* and *activity* have served as useful guides in analyzing our data. Not only has it been possible to search for differences in family patterns between the four problem groups, but we could also collapse the data from different groups along either the locus or activity dimension to determine whether familial patterns related to these more general aspects of adolescent psychopathology.

Basic Project Procedures

The project has focused upon intact families with a disturbed adolescent seen at the UCLA Psychology Clinic. There were no special criteria for inclusion in the study except willingness to participate in the six-session family assessment procedure. The six sessions are spaced at weekly intervals and are designed to provide comprehensive data on each family member and his mode of interacting with the others. Special emphasis has been placed on studying social influence and communication patterns within the family. Suffice it to say that extensive data are collected on each family in the project, which varies from individual test performance to reactions to videotapes of a highly charged confrontation among family members. Much of the data analysis carried out to date has been largely cross-sectional in nature as we have searched for relationships between adolescent behavioral difficulties and concurrently observed family interaction patterns. The number of these relationships found to date has been gratifying, and our data suggest that distinctive patterns of familial interaction are correlated with each of our four subgroups of adolescent disturbance. However, our long-range goal has been to relate these data to the patterns of psychopathology that might emerge and be noted subsequently during the adult years of the target cases. As we are interested in schizophrenia, we were particularly interested in which members of the sample showed some type of schizophreniform reaction or adjustment during early adulthood so that we could examine the earlier data for predictive clues.

Use of Transactional Thought Disturbance Index

The fourfold grouping of the adolescent behavior pattern has proved extremely useful not only in revealing distinctive patterns of intrafamilial relationships, but has been found to relate as well to adjustment during the young adult period [1]. However, we still felt a need to utilize measures that have been found useful in the work of others in differentiating parents of schizophrenics from parents of other psychopathological groups. The work of Wynne and Singer [6, 7], with their concept of transactional thought disturbance, provides a meaningful way to connect our prospective study with earlier work. Therefore, we attempted to utilize their concept and applied it to TAT data available on the parents of the disturbed adolescents. James Jones [2], a member of our research group, recently developed a scoring system for transactional thought disturbance for the TAT, with the kind assistance of Margaret Singer, and developed factor patterns which discriminated among the members of the families in our sample. It was particularly gratifying that these factor-pattern profiles discriminated parents of schizophrenics from parents of other psychiatric groups in a sample utilized in the original Singer-Wynne research. These profiles suggested three levels of risk for schizophrenia—high, intermediate, and low—based on the probability that a particular profile was associated with a schizophrenic offspring. These profile decision rules were then applied to the parental data available from our sample of disturbed adolescents, and the parents were grouped according to these three risk levels.

These risk levels were then related to the form of the behavior problem manifested by the teenager and can be seen in Table 1. These data indicate that subjects from the high-risk category— that is, the category with a high probability of schizophrenic offspring—are located primarily in Groups 2 and 4. You will recall that these are the groups previously identified as within-home locus problem groups. The data are even more striking when the sex of the adolescent is considered as there is *not* a single male adolescent from Groups 1 and 3 (outside-home locus groups) whose parents fall in the high-risk category. Thus all male cases in the high-risk group come from either the active family conflict or withdrawn, socially isolated groups. These findings are particularly interesting as preliminary 5-year follow-up data on these male cases carried out by another member of our research team, Frederick Jones [1], also revealed that these two groups were at considerably greater risk for severe early adult psychopathology than were the outside-home locus groups (Groups 1 and 3). These data are particularly interesting as the follow-up sample overlapped only to a small extent with the James Jones sample.

Intervention and its Utilization

Research on intervention with high- and low-risk families was not originally included as part of our research program. How-

Table 1 Relationship Between Parental TAT Estimate of Transactional
Thought Disturbance and Form of Adolescent Disturbance[a]

Risk Category	Adolescent Problem Group			
	I[b]	II[c]	III[d]	IV[e]
High	3	6	1	7
Intermediate	4	3	3	4
Low	4	3	4	2

[a] Taken from James Jones [2].
[b] Aggressive antisocial.
[c] Active family conflict.
[d] Passive negative.
[e] Withdrawn, socially isolated.

ever, it became obvious that the family assessment procedures developed were not merely effective for revealing intrafamilial dynamics but created a readiness for therapy on the part of family members. Because our project was oriented toward the family as a system and because our procedures serve to increase a family's readiness for intervention at that level, we have utilized family-oriented therapeutic procedures with high- and low-risk families.

We have come to recognize that a family's capacity to absorb intervention services is one indicator of the difficulty in modifying that family system. Thus the utilization of therapeutic services by a family serves as a criterion variable against which to relate other predictor variables. We arrived at a quantitative index of therapy utilization by considering both the number of therapy sessions and the number of family members treated at each session to yield a therapy-absorbtion index that varies from 0 to 25.

We have attempted to relate this therapy-absorbtion score to numerous variables, but of greatest interest was the transactional thought disturbance index described in the previous section. The relationship between the estimate of risk and the therapy-absorbtion score is presented in Table 2. These data indicate that the number of cases in the high-risk group who absorbed extensive therapeutic services far exceeds the frequency found in the other two risk groups. Therefore, those families identified as high risk, based on parental transactional thought disturbance scores, require large amounts of therapy—individual, group, and family—before showing signs of behavioral change in both the

Table 2   Degree of Therapy Utilization by Cases in Each Risk Category[a]
($N = 44$)

Density Index (Range 0-25)	Low	Intermediate	High
0-3	6	6	2
4-6	3	4	3
8-25	4	4	12

[a] Taken from James Jones [2].

family system and the identified adolescent patient. It is important to note that there was no knowledge of risk status with regard to schizophrenia at the time these families were in therapy.

Pilot Studies of Family Therapy Process in High- and Low-Risk Families

These large differences in therapy absorbtion, particularly of family therapy, raises the question of why these high-risk families make them so resistant to change. Is it the transactional thought disturbance manifest in the parental TAT stories that becomes manifest in a similar form in the transactions of family therapy? Or is the transactional thought-disturbance index merely a sur- face indicator of many aspects of family functioning that impede communication in familial transactions at many levels? One way to approach these issues is to analyze in detail the actual process of family therapy with families of high and low risk according to the TAT index. One of our students, Julia Lewis [4], has recently conducted a pilot study contrasting audiotape transcriptions of an early and late family therapy session with two high- and two low- risk families. Lewis coded these sessions using measures of: (1) who talked, (2) the responsiveness of family members to each other's remarks, (3) the number of interruptions, and (4) the man- ifest affect in each statement. She found quite distinctive differ- ences between the two high-risk and two low-risk families on most of these measures.

In the high-risk families there is a shift from early to later therapy sessions in speaking patterns as the identified teenager patient drops out of the interaction as mother, father, and therapist increase their rate of interactions. In the low-risk families this realignment was not noted and the adolescent remains an active participant in the family sessions. All families in Lewis's sample increased the rate of acknowledgment of their responses to others' remarks, but the high-risk families showed less of a change in responsiveness than did the low-risk cases. As might be expected from the responsiveness data, all families declined in their rate of interruptions, with the high-risk families showing less decline.

The affect rate was particularly revealing of interactional differences in this small sample of four families. In the low-risk families, early and late family therapy sessions are generally distinguishable by a drop in negative affect in all family members. In the high-risk families this is not true for the mothers in particular, as they show a shift from relatively neutral affect in early sessions to increasing negative affect in later sessions.

Generally, Lewis's pilot data suggest that it is difficult to distinguish high- from low-risk families in their early family therapy sessions. It is the contrast with the later sessions that is most revealing. These contrasts suggest that high-risk families show the greatest structural realignment as seen by the gradual reduction of the adolescent's participation in the therapy session. This suggests that high-risk teenagers, coming (as we know) from inside-home locus family groups, gradually escape the focus of family attention and embroilment. The affect changes in the high-risk mother also indicate that they enter therapy either denying their anger and frustration or expressing their feelings covertly and that as therapy progresses, they become more direct and open in expressing their feelings. If these findings should hold up on larger samples, they would suggest that high-risk families in contrast with other types of disturbed families, do manifest a number of the qualities hypothesized by earlier writers to be characteristic of schizophrenic families; for example, overinvolvement with a particular offspring, a low ability to acknowledge the meaning of others' statements, and a denial of affect, particularly of negative feelings. These conclusions, should they continue to be supported by larger samples, would be particularly meaningful as they arise from a *prospective* study of intrafamilial relationships in which there is no psychotic offspring to cloud the meaning of the data. Thus the interactional patterns of high-risk families can be seen to exist prior to the onset of a psychotic episode, and we can rule out the hypothesis that they arise as reactions to the existence of a severely disturbed, psychotic offspring in the family. This gives greater weight to theories that emphasize the etiological significance of intrafamilial processes in the development of schizophrenia and schizophrenia-like disorders.

References

1. Jones, F. H. A four-year follow-up of vulnerable adolescents: The prediction of outcomes in early adulthood from measures of social competence, coping style and overall level of adjustment. *J. Nerv. Ment. Dis.* (1974), in press.
2. Jones, J. E. Transactional style deviance in families of disturbed adolescents. Ph.D. dissertation, University of California, Los Angeles, 1974.
3. Kety, S. S., Rosenthal, D., Wender, P. H., and Schulsinger, F. The types and prevalence of mental illness in the biological and adoptive families of adopted schizophrenics. In *The Transmission of Schizophrenia*, D. Rosenthal and S. S. Kety, Eds. Pergamon Press, New York, 1968, pp. 345–362.
4. Lewis, J. An empirical investigation of process in family therapy. M.A. thesis, University of California, Los Angeles, 1974.
5. Rodnick, E. H. and Goldstein, M. J. A research strategy for studying risk for schizophrenia during adolescence and early adulthood. In *The Child in His Family: Children at Psychiatric Risk*, E. J. Anthony and C. Koupernik, Eds. Wiley-Interscience, New York, 1974, pp. 507–526.
6. Wynne, L. C. and Singer, M. T. Thought disorder and the family relations of schizophrenics I and II. *Arch. Gen. Psychiat.*, 9 (1963), 191–206.
7. Wynne, L. C. and Singer, M. T. Thought disorder and the family relations of schizophrenics III and IV. *Arch. Gen. Psychiat.*, 12 (1965), 187–212.

Study of Children at Risk: Use of Psychological Test Batteries*

Lois Franklin, Ph.D., Julien Worland, Ph.D., Loretta Cass, Ph.D., Larry Bass, Ph.D., and E. James Anthony, M.D. (U.S.A.)

In recent years studies of the etiology of schizophrenia and other psychiatric categories of disturbance have increasingly turned to the development of children at high risk because of schizophrenic parentage. The origin of the method of observation of the high risk or vulnerable group is credited to Mednick and his research group [8, 9], who have engaged in a longitudinal study of high-risk children of schizophrenic parents in Denmark. These subjects, at genetic high risk for schizophrenia, are studied with a variety of measures, including tests of intelligence and personality, psychophysiological measures, psychiatric interviews, and school reports.

Other studies that investigate the adjustment of children of psychiatrically disturbed parents include those of Anthony [1], Beisser, Glasser, et al. [5], Garmezy [4], and Rolf [11].

Rolf [11], following Garmezy's methodology [4], identified children rendered vulnerable by reason of their mothers' mental disturbance. One group consisted of children of schizophrenic

*Supported by NIMH Grants MH12043, MH14052, and MH24819.

mothers, and a second group was selected on the basis of mothers with neurotic depressive reactions, all with internalizing symptoms. He also included two groups of already disturbed children without history of psychiatrically disturbed parents. These children were dichotomized into internalizers and externalizers. Children of all four target groups were matched with two control children within their classroom. Measures of psychosocial competence were used, that is, sociometric measures in the classroom and a teacher's rating scale. Relatively low competence of the children of schizophrenic mothers and the unsocialized aggressive children (externalizers) was reported.

Beisser, Glasser, et al. [5] report on 240 children of schizophrenic mothers. Children of neurotic and normal mothers served as controls. The measures were scores on behavior ratings by parents and teachers. Schizophrenic mothers rated their children as more disturbed, with boys more severely disturbed than girls. The sex difference was not significant for fathers' ratings. Differences of parents' ratings were significant for pathological and normal groups, but not between the schizophrenic and neurotic. The correlation of mothers' and teachers' ratings was 0.27, significant at the .01 level. The authors' findings lend support to their hypothesis of greater maladjustment in children of schizophrenic mothers.

Rutter [13] studied children admitted to the hospital for psychiatric disturbance and dental care. More of the psychiatrically disturbed children had psychiatrically disturbed parents than did the control group. The children of psychiatrically disturbed parents were also more severely disturbed.

Landau, Harth, et al. [7] used clinical psychological measures (Wechsler Intelligence Scale for Children, Bender-Gestalt, and human figure drawings) as well as teacher ratings, parents' reports, and interviews with children to study 250 children of psychotic parents. They found lags in speech development, greater frequency and seriousness of physical illness and primary habit disorders, and significant differences in interpersonal relationships and sexual identification when the research group was compared with controls. Children of psychotics were lower in WISC scores, with significant differences for the Information, Arithmetic, Comprehension, and Digit Span subtests.

Anthony [1, 2] delineated precursive, symbiotic and induced types of disturbance in children of psychotic parents. The latter two, having to do with the child's relationship with the parent or reaction to the environmental situation, are considered amenable to change with separation from the parental psychosis, while the former, the precursive symptoms, is viewed as more unyielding to intervention. Anthony's [1] investigation, of which the present study is a part, includes extensive clinical and experimental investigation.

Presented here are preliminary results from the total sample of children, reporting clinical psychologists' ratings of psychological adjustment comparing children of psychotic parents (CPP) and children of normal parents (CNP). Traditional clinical batteries of tests were used in evaluating each child. It was felt that the use of these batteries could, when evaluated by experienced clinicians, provide a thorough description of the personality of children at risk.

The basic hypothesis was that CPPs would show greater disturbance than children of CNPs.

Hypotheses

The specific hypotheses were derived from an earlier pilot investigation on a subsample of the same subjects studied here (Cass, Franklin, Bass; manuscript in preparation). It was predicted that: (1) ratings of psychological disturbance would correlate with teachers' ratings of school adjustment, (2) that CPP would be rated more pathological than CNP, (3) despite higher referral rates for psychiatric services for boys than girls, male and female children would not differ, (4) Black children would be rated higher, and (5) latency-aged children would be rated as less pathological than either prelatency or adolescent children.

Method
SUBJECTS

A total of 246 children served as subjects in this study. Of these, 133 were CPP, and 113 were CNP. All were from intact families in which there had been no significant separations in the family history other than hospitalizations. The children ranged in age from 4 to 19 years.

The children in the CPP group came from 48 families, in which 27 mothers and 19 fathers were hospitalized in a psychiatric setting with a diagnosis of schizophrenia ($N = 31$) or manic-depressive psychosis ($N = 17$) at the time the families volunteered to participate in this research. The CNP children were from 37 families whose parents had been contacted through schools and had volunteered to participate. Neither parent in the CNP families had a history of psychiatric illness or prolonged physical illness. In all groups there was a somewhat uneven distribution for race and socioeconomic class (see Table 1).

To establish validity for the measures used, results from two additional analyses are reported in the following paragraphs. First, a subsample of 90 children was studied in relation to their school adjustment. For this sample 51 CPP and 39 CNP subjects were studied, of whom 47 were white and 43 black. Second, the parents of CNP and CPP children were tested and rated in the manner reported as follows for their children.

VARIABLES

The major focus of this study was to determine if clinical psychology test batteries would indicate any disturbance in children's emotional adjustment as a result of psychotic parentage. Two different rating scales were available for determining such effects: (1) ratings of psychological disturbance by clinical

Table 1   Cell Frequencies in Design

Group	Race[a]	Class[b]	n
CPP	White	MC	52
CPP	White	LC	34
CPP	Black	MC	9
CPP	Black	LC	38
CNP	White	MC	67
CNP	White	LC	6
CNP	Black	MC	12
CNP	Black	LC	28

[a] Hollingshead Two-Factor Index of Social Position (Hollingshead, 1957).
[b] Forty-four ≤ middle class; 45 ≤ lower class.

psychologists from psychological test results and (2) ratings by teachers on the child's school adjustment.

Clinical psychologists' ratings were made from the results of individually administered batteries of psychological tests, including the WISC, figure drawings, Rorschach, and the TAT. The adults' battery was identical except the Wechsler Adult Intelligence Scale (WAIS) was used. Twelve psychological variables were rated on 5-point scales of psychological disturbance. The variables were: (1) thinking (logicality), (2) reality testing, (3) concreteness, (4) anxiety, (5) object relations, (6) identity, (7) impulse control, (8) emotionality, (9) aggressivity, (10) efficiency of defenses, (11) coping, and (12) pathology of content. The results from clinical psychologists' ratings, reported in the following paragraphs, are based on the sum of these 12 ratings, with a possible range of from 12 to 60.

The teachers' ratings were based on a rating scale devised for this study for the purpose of providing a measure of the subject's adjustment in a real-life situation. The ratings were made by one interviewer who talked to the teachers of each subject. Seven ratings were included on the teachers' rating scale: (1) task orientation (self-motivation and attitudes toward learning), (2) school achievement, (3) relationship with teacher, (4) relationship with peers, (5) emotional adjustment, (6) motor control (perceptual-motor problems, clumsiness, motor activity level), and (7) social conduct and delinquency. The results reported here are based on the sums of the seven ratings, rated on 5-point scales, with a possible range of 7 to 35. Teachers were assessed by the interviewer on their knowledge of the home situation and whether they had specific knowledge of any hospitalizations among their students' parents.

PROCEDURE

Protocols of psychological testing on all subjects were scored by the testers. Then levels of adjustment on the 12 variables were rated blindly by one of three other psychologists. The only identifying information provided the raters was age and sex of the subject. All testers and raters were white. Raters were all clinical psychologists with experience in childhood assessment. School ratings were made by an interviewer blind with respect to the hypotheses of the project and having no information other than the name of the subject and his or her school. Interviews with teachers were conducted in the school, and the interviewer's ratings were based on information provided by the teachers, including their behavioral description.

Results

To establish validity for the clinicians' ratings, three preliminary analyses were done. First, ratings of psychotic and nonpsychotic adults were compared to determine if psychologists could blindly differentiate these two groups. Psychotic adults (median 37) received significantly higher ratings than control adults (median 27) (Mann-Whitney $U = 1230, z = 4.23, p < .001$) and their nonpsychotic spouses (median 28) (Wilcoxon $T = 61.5, z = 4.88, p < .001$).

Second, clinicians' ratings of children were compared to those of the children's teachers. It was hypothesized that children rated most disturbed by clinicians would have the greatest impairment in school achievement and peer relations. This hypothesis was borne out. Overall, ratings correlated at a moderate level ($r_s = .32$), which was nonetheless significant ($N = 90, t = 3.20, p < .005$). Subgroup correlations varied between $-.12$ (not significant) and $+.47$ (see Table 2). Interrater reliability on the teachers' ratings independently established the stability of those ratings ($N = 21, r_s = .89, t = 8.50, p < .001$).

Table 2   Correlations of Teachers' Ratings and Clinicians' Ratings
of CPP and CNP

Group	N	r_s	t	$p <$
Total	90	.32	3.20	.005
CNP	39	.22	1.14	NS
CPP	51	.29	2.15	.025
CNP White	23	.47	2.46	.025
CNP Black	16	$-.12$	$-.45$	NS
CPP White	24	.37	1.89	.10
CPP Black	27	.39	2.12	.025
White	47	.42	3.10	.005
Black	43	.33	2.23	.025

Third, clinicians' ratings were assessed for reliability by comparing the raters with one another on the number of agreements in individual ratings (thinking, reality testing, etc.). The percentages of exact agreement varied between 79 percent and 88 percent, and the percentages of agreement within one scale step were between 98 percent and 99 percent. This agreement was a significant improvement over chance ($\chi^2 = 187.16, df = 3, p < .001$). These three preliminary analyses provided confidence that the clinical ratings could give reliable and consensually validated information about children.

Two different methods of assessment are provided by the clinicians' and the teachers' ratings. Using one-tailed tests of significance, teachers' ratings reliably differentiated between CNP and CPP subjects (Mann-Whitney $U = 604, z = 3.17, p < .0008$). Considered by racial subgroups, teachers could correctly differentiate white CPP and CNP ($U = 112, z = 2.61, p < .0045$) and black CPP and CNP ($U = 189, z = 1.85, p < .0322$). It should be noted that better differentiation was made in the black group, for whom fewer teachers had information about parental illnesses (53 percent of teachers of white CPP and 7 percent of teachers of black CPPs). These results are summarized in Figure 1.

Clinicians' ratings involved a larger n and uneven distribution of cell frequencies, so the analyses of group, class, and race differences on clinicians' ratings were carried out by a three-way

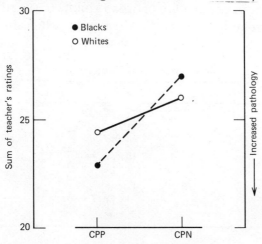

Figure 1 Teacher's rating of pathology.

analysis of variance for unequal *n* values [3]. The ANOVA results, showing only a significant racial effect, are summarized in Table 3 and Figure 2. They demonstrate that the clinicians could differentiate CPP and CNP subjects who were white and middle class ($t = 1.72$, $df = 117$, $p < .05$, one-tailed), but did not differentiate children in other racial and class groups. They also demonstrate that clinicians rated black children higher (more disturbed) than white children.

Further analyses of sex and age differences determined that male and female children did not differ from one another in either the CPP ($U = 2282$, $z = .34$, NS) or in the CNP ($U = 1320$ $z = -1.05$, NS) groups.

The predicted age effect was that latency-aged children would be rated lower than pre-latency-aged or adolescent children. This was not found, and there were significant differences between these three age groups, with latency-aged children receiving the highest ratings in both groups (Kruskal-Wallis $H = 42.7$, $df = 8$, $p < .001$). See Table 4 for median scores.

Discussion

Interpretation of these results can procede along two mutually exclusive avenues. Since the investigation is exploratory, we have only theoretical rather than empirical reason to suspect that there are differences in personality between children reared by psychotic and nonpsychotic parents. Consequently, when differences are

Table 3   Analysis of Variance Results

Source	MS	F
Group (A)	232.93	3.32[a]
Class (B)	55.65	.79
Race (C)	907.20	12.92[b]
A × B	184.77	2.63
A × C	63.63	.90
B × C	126.46	1.80
A × B × C	48.74	.69
Error	3853.92	

[a] trend, $p < .10$.
[b] $p < .0001$.

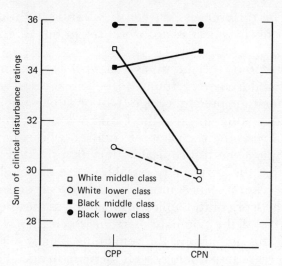

Figure 2 Sum of clinical disturbance ratings for white, black, middle-class, and lower-class children of psychotic (CPP) and normal (CNP) parents.

**Table 4   Median Sums of Clinical Disturbance Ratings
for Three Age Groups of CPP and CNP**

	Age					
	Prelatency[a]		Latency[b]		Adolescence[c]	
Group	*n*	Median	*n*	Median	*n*	Median
CPP	16	34.5	82	38	35	30
CNP	19	29	68	35	26	28.5

[a] Aged 71 months.
[b] Ages 72 to 143 months.
[c] Aged 144 months.

found between these two groups the interpretation could be that real differences do exist and were correctly assessed by the clinicians, or that real differences do not exist and the apparent differences are due to biases in the judgments of the clinicians. Of course, the fact that the clinicians correctly could differentiate normal and psychotic adults provides confidence—but not assurance—that they could correctly assess pathology in children.

Of all the groups studied, we would expect that negative bias would be least evident in the assessments of white middle-class children. The differences between CNP and CPP found in this group most likely reflect real differences in our sample populations.

There are four specific areas that call for attention. First, latency-age children were found to be more disturbed in both groups than either prelatency age (<6) or adolescent (>12) children. The low ratings given to the 4- and 5-year-old children were an artifact due to the exclusion of children who either were unable to complete the full clinical battery or provided so little information that the personality variables were not ratable according to our criteria. Since more 4- and 5-year olds had to be excluded, the score of the subjects remaining at those ages are not representative of the populations from which they were drawn. Eliminating this age group, the remaining data would suggest a gradual decrease in pathology with increase in age. The correlation between chronological age and clinical disturbance ratings was −.39. Raters were, of course, aware of the age of children, on the assumption that they could make appropriate corrections for developmental improvements in articulation and integration of responses to projective material. But the most parsimonious interpretation of the results would be that appropriate age corrections were not made and inappropriately mature criteria were applied to the younger children.

Because of unequal sampling, age differences might also have accounted for the lower (healthier) ratings given to lower-class white CPPs, and higher (more pathological) ratings given to middle-class white CPPs. But the percentage of latency-aged (more disturbed) children was higher in the lower-class (healthier) group. This difference, therefore, cannot be explained in terms of sampling artifact. This surprising result raises many questions about the applicability of our tests to disadvantaged groups.

The more disturbed ratings given to black subjects come as no surprise when considered in the light of the considerable recent attention given to how poorly minority groups fare on these culturally biased tests [6, 10]. Considering these recent findings on the limited applicability of traditional psychological tests for intelligence, learning, perception, and personality, the traditional battery is not recommended for further studies involving interracial group differences. However, clinicians were able to differentiate white middle class CNPs from CPPs. This may imply that there is impairment in personality development as a result of psychotic parentage in other class and racial groups as well but that we are only capable of quantifying it with traditional instruments in white middle-class children.

The implication of this study is that risk researchers relying on traditional psychological methods of assessment must remain aware of changes in the status of their instruments resulting from research in other areas of investigation. Since the designing of the present study in 1965 the effects of class and race on projective and cognitive test performance have gradually been studied and quantified. At the present time, methods of personality measurement accurate across race and class are difficult, if not impossible, to discover. This leaves us with few options. We can delay our risk research until better clinical methods are devised or we can limit ourselves to studying white middle class children at risk. This latter suggestion, however, excludes a large number of children who have been described as at high risk for reason other than parental psychosis [12].

Another resolution would be to rely on tests requiring less interpretation between observed behavior and reluctant evaluation, that is, to emphasize methods that directly measure the behavior of our research subjects (e.g., see Rolf [11]). The good showing of teachers' interview material reported here which was based on observed school behavior supports this suggestion.

At a research design level, this study points out that in long-term longitudinal studies a serious problem is the confounding effect of time not only in changing social and political realities correlated with our dependent variables, but also in the professions and their techniques that are employed to investigate those dependent variables.

References

1. Anthony, E. J. A clinical evaluation of children with psychotic parents. *Amer. J. Psychiat.*, 122 (1969), 177–184.
2. Anthony, E. J. The developmental precursors of adult schizophrenia. In *The Transmission of Schizophrenia*. D. Rosenthal and S. Kety, Eds. Pergamon Press, Oxford, 1970.
3. Finn, J. D. *Multivariance: Univariate and Multivariate Analysis of Variance,*

Covariance, and Regression: A Fortran IV Program, Version V. National Educational Resources, Ann Arbor, 1972.

4. Garmezy, N. Vulnerable children: Implications derived from studies of an internalizing-externalizing symptom dimension. In *Psychopathology of Adolescence,* J. Zubin and A. Freedman, Eds. Grune and Stratton, New York, 1969.

5. Beisser, A., Glasser, N., and Grant, M. Psychosocial adjustment in children of schizophrenic mothers. *J. Nerv. Ment. Dis.* 145:6 (1967), 420–440.

6. Katz, I. A critique of personality approaches to Negro performance, with research suggestions. *J. Social Issues,* 25 (1969), 13–27.

7. Landau, R. Hearth, M., Othnay, M., and Sharfhertz, M. The influence of psychotic parents on their children's development. *Amer. J. Psychiat.,* 129:1 (1972), 38–43.

8. Mednick, S. and Schulsinger, F. Some premorbid characteristics related to breakdown in children with schizophrenic mothers. In *The Transmission of Schizophrenia.* D. Rosenthal and S. Kety, Eds. Oxford: Pergamon Press, Oxford, 1968. pp. 267–291.

9. Mednick, S. and McNeil, T. Current methodology in research on the etiology of schizophrenia: Serious difficulties which suggest the use of the high-risk group method. *Psychol. Bull.* 70 (1968), 681–693.

10. Rohwer, W. Learning, race, and school success. In *Annual Progress in Child Psychiatry and Child Development,* S. Chess and A. Thomas, Eds. Brunner-Mazel, New York, 1972. 237–257.

11. Rolf, J. The social and academic competence of children vulnerable to schizophrenia and other behavior pathologies. *J. Abnorm. Psychol.,* 80:33 (1972), 225–243.

12. Rolf, J. and Harig, P. Etiological research in schizophrenia and the rationale for primary intervention. *Amer. J. Orthopsychiat.,* 44:4 (1974), 538–554.

13. Rutter, M. *Children of Sick Parents: An Environmental and Psychiatric Study.* Oxford University Press, London, 1966.

14. Hollingshead, A.B., *Two-Factor Index of Social Position.* (Printed privately), New Haven, Conn. 1957.

A Measure of Vulnerability to Risk of Parental Psychosis

Harriet S. Lander, M.S., E. James Anthony, M.D., Loretta
Cass, Ph.D., Lois Franklin, Ph.D., and Larry Bass, Ph.D.
(U.S.A.)

One major aim of risk research in schizophrenia is to devise
means for identifying those children in high-risk families (with
one psychotic parent) who are most vulnerable to the parental
psychopathology and thus most in need of psychiatric intervention. Beisser, Glasser, et al. [3] and others have shown that the
range of adjustment in such families is quite wide, varying from
normalcy to extreme psychopathology. Anthony [1] and Mosher,
Pollin, et al. [8] have examined several factors which seem crucial
in identifying the most vulnerable children. Anthony, in his study
of the *folie à deux* phenomenon, emphasizes the lack of psychological "placement barrier" between the susceptible child and the
psychotic parent that permits pathological ideas and perceptions
to pass from one to the other. The vulnerable child is seen as
having inherent deficits in ego functioning (e.g., lack of self-
determination, control, and confidence) and developmental
deficits in separation-individuation. Mosher and his colleagues
studied 11 pairs of identical twins, one of whom was schizophrenic, and found that in 10 pairs the psychotic twin identified
with the "sicker" parent. The schizophrenic twin also tended to be
more submissive.

325

The present study was designed to test the hypothesis that a group of highly vulnerable children could be identified on the basis of: (1) their close involvement and identification with the psychotic parent and (2) personality traits of submissiveness and suggestibility. These factors, it was felt, would make the child more likely to internalize, at least in part, the distorted perceptual and cognitive world of the psychotic parent. The child who is highly involved with a disturbed parent and who shows, in addition, personality traits of submissiveness and suggestibility would lack psychological distance and adequate defense against the psychotic ideation in the home. It was hypothesized, then, that children with these traits would show more psychopathology than their nonvulnerable or less-vulnerable siblings and would look, psychologically, more like the ill parent. They would be at higher risk for adult psychosis, and would, therefore, be most in need of psychiatric intervention.

Method

The subjects were 141 children from 45 families in which one parent had been hospitalized with a diagnosis of schizophrenia or manic-depressive psychosis. All subjects and their parents have been evaluated extensively, as part of a larger on-going research project. This evaluation included structured, in-depth psychiatric interviews and a standard battery of psychological tests (appropriate WISC or WAIS, Rorschach, TAT, and Draw-A-Person).

VULNERABILITY RATING SCALE

All children in the study were rated by the psychiatrist (E. James Anthony, M.D.) on the following eight items that made up the "vulnerability rating scale":

1. identification with ill parent.
2. credulity about parental delusions.
3. influence of parental illness.
4. undue submissiveness.
5. undue suggestibility.
6. involvement with ill parent (three wishes test).
7. involvement with ill parent (three houses test).
8. involvement with ill parent (three dreams test).

Items 1, 2, and 3 were rated on the basis of interview information from both the well parent and children. "Undue submissiveness" was measured by the child's willingness to perform certain unusual acts without prior explanation, such as, "Put your finger in your nostril," or "Lie down on the floor." The child's response to suggestions about body sway (Rombergism), eye closure and fist closure determined his rating on "undue suggestibility." The first of the three tests of involvement, the "three houses test," assessed the child's expressed desire to live with the ill parent; the others tapped his inclusion of the ill parent in his wishes and dreams. Subjects received one point for each factor rated present; possible scores, then, ranged from 0 to 8, with the higher scores indicating more involvement, submissiveness, and so on.

Two groups of subjects were then drawn from the total number, one group at the highest end of the vulnerability scale and one at the lowest end. The groups were designated as follows: (1) *highly vulnerable children* ($N = 19$)—those who received a score of at least five on the eight items of the "vulnerability rating scale" and (2) *low vulnerable*, or less vulnerable, children ($N = 21$)—those who received a score of 0 or 1 on the vulnerability rating scale. Table 1 shows descriptive data on the two groups.

DEPENDENT VARIABLES

Each subject was rated blindly by a team of three clinical psychologists on a quantitative "psychological rating scale." The scale was developed to assess various areas of psychological functioning using not only formal scores, but also more complex data such as content, sequence, and balance of responses from the test protocols. The scores, which reflect clinical judgment, were made on a scale ranging from 0, denoting no indicators of disturbance for that variable, to 4, denoting incapacitating disturbance.

Fourteen variables were rated by the clinical psychologists:

1. diagnosis.
2. severity of disturbance.
3. logicality of thinking.
4. reality testing.
5. concreteness.
6. efficiency of defenses.

7. coping.
8. pathology of content.
9. object relations.
10. anxiety.
11. identity.
12. impulse control.
13. emotionality.
14. aggressivity.

It was hypothesized that some of the variables would reflect more sharply the impact of the disorganized, primitive thinking of the psychotic parent on the vulnerable children. These were the areas that tapped distorted perception and ideation, such as items 3 and 5, and some that assessed the child's overall level of psychological functioning, such as items 2, 6, and 7. The starred variables were those predicted to show differences between the high and low vulnerable groups.

For each variable the subjects were cast into a 2 × 3 table, and data were analyzed statistically using the chi-square (χ^2) method.

Results

As shown in Table 2 and Figure 1, the "high vulnerable" group did show significantly more disturbance than the "low vulnerable" group in all of the predicted areas of psychological functioning as well as in several others. Diagnoses made by the clinical psychologists placed five of the 19 "high vulnerable" children, or 26 percent, in the category "borderline psychotic or psychotic." In contrast none of those in the "low vulnerable" group were diagnosed in this way. This difference as assessed using the χ^2 method was significant at the .025 level.

Further, whatever their diagnostic category, the children in the "high vulnerable" group tended to be seen as showing more disturbance. Thirty-seven percent of this group were rated as showing "serious or incapacitating disturbance," whereas only 9 percent of the "low vulnerable" subjects were placed in this category. Conversely, 43 percent of the "low vulnerables" and 21 percent of the "high vulnerables" were rated as showing either good adjustment or only mild pathology.

Table 1   Vulnerable and Low Vulnerable Groups: Descriptive Data

	Low Vulnerable $N = 21$	High Vulnerable $N = 19$
$\overline{X}$ Age in months	137.19	131.42
Full-scale IQ	108.28	102.63
Number of male subjects	12	6
Number of female subjects	9	13
Number of subjects with mother psychotic	15	9
Number of subjects with father psychotic	6	10
Parental diagnosis: schizophrenia	14	12
Parental diagnosis: manic-depressive psychosis	7	7

Table 2   Psychological Ratings: Significant Differences Between High Vulnerable and Low Vulnerable Groups

Variable	$\chi^2 \ (df = 2)$	Significance Level
Diagnosis	7.11	.025
Severity of disturbance	4.80	.05
Logicality of thinking	5.54	.05
Reality testing	5.18	.05
Efficiency of defenses	11.73	.005
Coping	9.38	.005
Impulse control (superego)	5.95	.05
Aggressivity	10.49	.005
Sum of disturbance ratings[a]	$U = 137.50$	
	$Z = -1.68$	$.01 < p < .05$

[a] Mann-Whitney U test.

The factor of reality testing was of particular interest in this study since it seemed basic to the more complex cognitive and psychological functions. Vulnerable children of a psychotic parent were hypothesized to be particularly susceptible to internalizing the parental distortions in perceiving reality and difficulties in differentiating between reality and fantasy. This rating, which was based mainly on Rorschach, TAT responses, and WISC content, showed the serious dysfunctions to which the "high vulnerable" group seemed particularly prone. The "vulnerable" children were

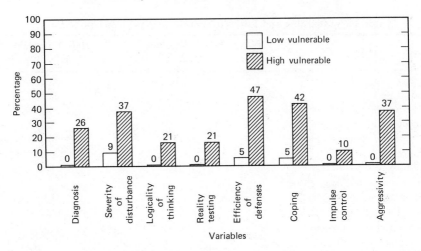

Figure 1 Psychological ratings: percent of high and low vulnerable subjects. Rated as showing serious pathology.

characterized significantly more often as showing "severe departures from stimulus accuracy with low $F+$ percent (20 to 30 percent below age norms), frequent tangential associations even on structured tests, percepts based on autistic thinking, and stimuli seen on the basis of the patient's inner needs, conflicts, and anxieties." None of the "low vulnerables," but over 20 percent of the "vulnerables," received this rating. Similarly, significantly more of the "low vulnerable" children than the "vulnerable" were rated as having "creative and original responses, but with high fidelity to the stimulus; elaborations, creative but not fluid or illogical; accuracy on Rorschach within 10 percent of age norms; if inaccuracies are given, patient is aware of them."

A pattern similar to this is apparent on the other variables listed as well. In each case, significantly more of the "high vulnerable" children than the "low vulnerable" children were rated as showing serious or incapacitating pathology, and significantly more of the "low vulnerable" children were rated as showing no or only mild pathology.

When disturbance scores from all categories of the psychological ratings were summed, the "high vulnerable" group scored significantly higher than the "low vulnerable" group; that is, the "vulnerable" children were rated as more disturbed across all 14 of the ratings.

Psychiatric evaluations were also made on all subjects, and the data are shown in Figure 2.

There were six psychiatric categories, each scored on a 6-point scale with high scores indicating more serious degrees of pathology. The categories were:

1. risk of disturbance in childhood.
2. actual disturbance in childhood.
3. risk of disturbance in adulthood.
4. risk of psychosis in adulthood.
5. global rating of vulnerability.
6. global rating of adjustment.

The two groups differed markedly on all categories with the "high vulnerable" group showing more pathology on each measure than the "low vulnerable" subjects.

Another psychiatric variable, "category of clinical disturbance in childhood," again demonstrated the marked difference be-

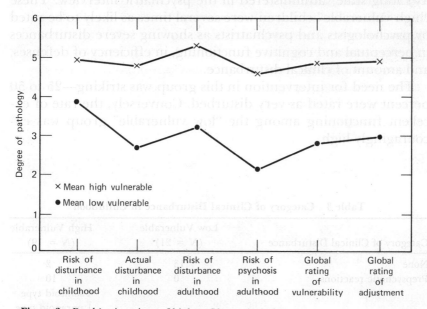

Figure 2 Psychiatric ratings of high and low vulnerability.

tween groups. None of the "low vulnerable" children were seen to have prepsychotic symptomatology; in contrast, 10 (> 50 percent) of the "high vulnerable" group were rated as showing some prepsychotic symptoms. Of these, four were classified as schizoid type, one as paranoid type, and five as depressed type (see Table 3).

Conversely, the number of well-adjusted children in the "low vulnerable" group is encouragingly high—13 of 21, or 62 percent. Only two of the "high vulnerable" children, or 10 percent were seen as showing no disturbance on psychiatric evaluation.

Discussion

The results of this study support the view that the impact of parental psychopathology is measurably greater for those children designated as "high vulnerable." These are the children who were most involved and identified with the ill parent and who showed personality traits of suggestibility and submissiveness. They were readily identified by means of the 8-point "vulnerability rating scale" administered in the psychiatric interview. These "high vulnerable" children were several times as likely to be rated by psychologists and psychiatrists as showing severe disturbances in perceptual and cognitive functioning, in efficiency of defenses, and amount of clinical disturbance.

The need for intervention in this group was striking—25 to 50 percent were rated as very disturbed. Conversely, the rate of excellent functioning among the "low vulnerable" group was encouragingly high.

Table 3   Category of Clinical Disturbance in Childhood

Category of Clinical Disturbance	Low Vulnerable ($N = 21$)	High Vulnerable ($N = 19$)
None	13	2
Prepsychotic reactions	0	10
		4 schizoid type
		1 paranoid type
		5 depressed type

Garmezy [7] and others have urged a search for the areas of competence characteristic of the "invulnerable" children in high-risk families. Several factors emerged in this study as being of value in protecting the child from the impact of parental psychosis; these include the ability to distance psychologically from the ill parent and to defend against the kind of submissive, receptive involvement with a psychotic parent that can lead to internalizing, disturbed thought processes. Personality traits of confidence, nonsubmissiveness, and a kind of healthy skepticism seem of considerable importance.

As Newman and San Martino [9] point out in their papers on children of seriously disturbed parents, "A child learns his parents' version of reality, a mythology which enables him to organize his life and set his goals. . . . The child is a playwright, reworking the script which has been played out before him. . . . At the last curtain, his final resolution will be his own."

References

1. Anthony, E. J. *Folie à deux.* A developmental failure in the process of separation-individuation. In *Separation-Individuation,* International Universities Press, New York, 1969, pp.
2. Anthony, E. J. A clinical evaluation of children with psychotic parents. *Amer. J. Psychiat.,* 126 (1969), 2.
3. Beisser, A. R., Glasser, N., and Grant, M. Psychosocial adjustment in children of schizophrenic mothers. *J. Nerv. Ment. Dis.,* 145: 6, (1967), 429–440.
4. Garmezy, N. Vulnerability research and the issue of primary prevention. *Amer. J. Orthopsychiat.,* 41 (1971), 101–116.
5. Garmezy, N. Models of etiology for the study of children at risk for schizophrenia. In *Life History Research,* Vol. V, Ed. M. Robb, L. N. Robbins, and M. Pollack, Eds. Univ. Minnesota Press, Minneapolis, 1972, pp. 9–23.
6. Garmezy, N. The study of competence in children at risk for severe psychopathology. In *Child in His Family: Children at Psychiatric Risk,* Vol. III of International Yearbook of the International Association for Child Psychiatry and Allied Professions. John Wiley, New York, 1974, pp. 77–97.
7. Mosher, L. R., Pollin, W., and Stabenau, J. Families with identical twins discordant for schizophrenia: Some relationships between identification, thinking styles, psychopathology, and dominance-submissiveness. *Brit. J. Psychiat.,* 118 (1971), 29–42.
8. Newman, M. and San Martino, M. R. The child and the seriously disturbed parent. Patterns of adaptation to parental psychosis. *J. Amer. Acad. Child Psychiat.,* 10 (1971), 358–374.

Teacher Ratings of Children Vulnerable to Psychopathology

Sheldon Weintraub, Ph.D., Diane E. Liebert, Ph.D., and John M. Neale, Ph.D. (U.S.A.)

Children spend almost half of their waking hours in school—an environment representative of the work, competitive and social demands with which they will later have to cope. Teachers, as educators and parent surrogates, are in a unique position to assess how a child copes with these demands and to compare his adjustment with that of his classmates. Considerable evidence exists that teachers are able to appraise a child's current adjustment with considerable reliability and validity [4, 17, 19]. Lambert and Bower [4], for example, found that 90 percent of elementary-school pupils rated as emotionally disturbed by teachers were so labeled by experienced clinicians following individual assessment. In predicting later maladjustment, teachers were even more successful than clinicians. As part of the longitudinal project of Schiff and Kellam [8] teachers rated 2000 children on social contact, maturation, and global adaptation. These same children were independently evaluated by clinical psychologists on six symptomatic scales (flatness, depression, anxiety, hyperkinesis, bizarreness, and global mental health). There was significant agreement between the teachers and clinicians' ratings, but over time the teachers' ratings were better predictors, not only to later adaptational ratings by teachers but also to later clinical assessment.

335

Teacher ratings have also been used in the search for precursor patterns to adult maladjustment. Watt [18] and Bower, Shellhammer, et al. [2] in follow-back studies of adult schizophrenics found them to be more maladjusted than their normal classmate controls as rated by their teachers. Several studies employing the high-risk method [1, 5, 7] have also reported differences in teacher-rated school behavior of high-risk versus normal children. Mednick and Schulsinger [5], for example, found that although the high-risk subjects were as a whole doing adequately, their teachers saw them as being easily upset and reacting to excitement by withdrawal. Further, they were seen as loners, passive in peer relations and classroom activities, and nervous.

The purpose of this chapter is to compare teachers' ratings of the adjustment of vulnerable, high-risk children with either a schizophrenic or depressed mother to ratings of control children.[1] Although teachers' ratings are the only data we have thus far analyzed, they constitute only part of our assessment battery designed to provide a complete description of the characteristics— both positive and negative—of vulnerable children. Additional procedures include parent ratings, peer ratings, and self-ratings. We also utilize information already available in the child's school records such as grades, achievement, aptitude-test scores, attendance records, and teachers' comments. The child's health, social, and psychiatric history is obtained from both parents. And finally, several laboratory tasks, designed to test more specific variables which may be crucially important in normal childhood development and in the etiology of schizophrenia, are being investigated with these children.

Method

SELECTION OF CHILDREN

Four groups of children, grades kindergarten through ninth, are being investigated: two target groups with a mother diagnosed as schizophrenic or depressed and two control groups whose parents have been screened for psychopathology. The two control

---

[1] Children with schizophrenic and depressive fathers are also included in the project to analyze the role of sex of parent, but the sample size at this time does not warrant their inclusion in this analysis.

groups are selected once target children are located in their classrooms. One of these is a same-sex but otherwise randomly drawn child from the same classroom; the other is matched to the target child on sex, age, race, social class and IQ. The two control groups are necessary since on the one hand, matching is desirable to control for potential confounding (e.g., the differences between high- and low-risk subjects could be due to social class differences rather than to vulnerability per se) while on the other hand, variables that are matched may not be merely peripheral correlates of schizophrenia. For example, matching on social class involves the tacit assumption that social class is "not really" relevant to the development of schizophrenia. This assumption may not be warranted; hence a random control group becomes desirable [6].

SELECTION AND ASSESSMENT OF PARENTS

All psychiatric new admissions from inpatient or outpatient mental health facilities with school-aged children are considered for selection. All inpatients hospitalized for reasons other than alcoholism, drug abuse, or central nervous system impairment are approached for selection into the study. Outpatients are additionally screened, and only those patients who appear to have psychotic or severe depressive symptomatology are approached.

The parents of control children selected in the school are contacted and requested to participate in an investigation "to determine what aspects of family life help children to grow up to be well-adjusted, successful adults." No mention of parental psychiatric status is mentioned, but the full extent of the family's participation is explained and their permission and consent obtained.

The assessment procedures consist of the following measures: (1) Current and Past Psychopathology Scales (CAPPS) [9], (2) MMPI, (3) Patient Adjustment Scale—Spouse Informant, and (4) Spouse Adjustment—Patient Informant. This assessment battery is administered to the patient, spouse, and controls and includes not only information obtained by self-report, but also information as perceived and reported by the spouse. All interviews are administered during home visits as well as at the hospital and are tape recorded.

All of the diagnostic information—case history, official diagnosis, behavioral and diagnostic evaluation, spouses' ratings, social and psychiatric history information, computer diagnosis based on the CAPPS, and tape recordings of the diagnostic interview—is independently evaluated by two trained diagnosticians, blind to any information about the children, who must agree on the classification of a patient as schizophrenic or depressive.

Sample

The data reported here are based on a sample of 58 children with a schizophrenic mother, 43 children with a depressive mother, and 58 matched control and 56 random control children (see Table 1). The mean number of children per family in study and education and occupation of the head of the household is presented in Table 2. Occupation and education were coded by CAPPS scales; occupational ratings range from 1 (higher executive, proprietor of a large concern or major professional) to 8 (adult not working at a job) and education ratings from 1 (professional: M.D., M.A., M.S., M.E., B.Ms., Ph.D., L.L.B.) to 7 (under 7 years of school).

Measures

The instrument selected to obtain teachers' ratings is the Devereux Elementary School Behavior Rating Scale [11]. The scale consists of 47 behavior items that the teacher rates either on the basis of frequency of occurrence ("How often does the child . . . initiate classroom discussion?") or on a 7-point scale indicating the degree of behavior ("To what degree is the child . . . unwilling to go back over his work?"). The time to rate each child averages about 10 minutes. Factor scores are then obtained through simple

Table 1   Distribution of Children by Sex, Grade,
and Mother's Diagnosis

Children	Mother Schizophrenic		Mother Depressive		Mother Normal	
	Kind.–5th	6th–9th	Kind.–5th	6th–9th	Kind.–5th	6th–9th
Males	19	9	16	8	38	17
Females	20	10	8	11	39	20

Table 2 Demographic Characteristics of Sample

Group	Number of Families	$\overline{X}$ Number of Children per Family in Study	Head of Household	
			$\overline{X}$ Education[a]	$\overline{X}$ Occupation[b]
Schizophrenic	25	2.3	4.153	4.25
Depressive	17	2.5	4.41	4.12
Matched Control	58	1.0	N/A[c]	4.18
Random Control	56	1.0	N/A[c]	3.81

[a]*Education scale:* highest grade completed: 1—advanced degree, 2—college graduate, 3—some college, 4—high-school graduate, 5—some high school, 6—7 to 9 years, 7—under 7 years.

[b]*Occupation scale:* 1—major professional or executive, 2—lesser professional or business manager, 3—administrative personnel, law enforcement, or minor professional, 4—clerical or sales worker, 5—skilled manual employee, 6—semiskilled, 7—unskilled, 8—not working.

addition of the scores of the three or more items contributing to that behavior dimension. The 11 factors are:

1. Classroom disturbance. Extent to which child teases and torments classmates, interferes with others' work, is quickly drawn into noisemaking, and must be reprimanded or controlled.

2. Impatience. Extent to which child starts work too quickly, is sloppy and hasty in its performance and is unwilling to review it.

3. Disrespect-defiance. Extent to which child speaks disrespectfully to teacher, resists doing what is asked of him, belittles the work being done, and breaks classroom rules.

4. External blame. Extent to which child says teacher does not help him or never calls on him, blames external circumstances when things do not go well for him, and is quick to say the work assigned is too difficult.

5. Achievement anxiety. Extent to which child gets upset about test scores, worries about knowing the "right" answers, is overly anxious when tests are given, is sensitive to criticism or correction.

6. External reliance. Extent to which child looks to others for direction, relies on the teacher for direction, requires pre-

cise instructions; and has difficulty making his own decisions.

7. Comprehension. Extent to which child gets the point of
   what is going on in class, seems able to apply what he has
   learned, and knows material when called on to recite.
8. Inattentive-withdrawn. Extent to which child does not pay
   attention and seems oblivious of what is happening in the
   classroom, is preoccupied, or is difficult to reach.
9. Irrelevant responsiveness. Extent to which child tells
   exaggerated stories, gives irrelevant answers, interrupts
   when teacher is talking, and makes inappropriate comments.
10. Creative initiative. Extent to which child brings things to
    class that relate to current topics, talks about things in an
    interesting fashion, initiates classroom discussion, and in-
    troduces personal experiences into class discussion.
11. Need for closeness to teacher. Extent to which child seeks
    out the teacher before or after class, is friendly toward the
    teacher, offers to do things for him or her, and likes to be
    physically close to the teacher.

Test-retest reliabilities over a one week period range between
0.85 and 0.91 for all DESB factors, with a median test-retest
coefficient of 0.87 [11]. Interrater reliability between teachers and
teacher aids ranged between .62 to .77, with a median rater reliability coefficient of .70. Regarding validity, each of the 11 factors
correlate significantly with grades, controlling for IQ in both
normal American and French children [10, 14–16] and among
groups of problem children [10]. In summary, the following features make the Devereux Scale particularly desirable [12]:

1. The teacher rates overt behavior of the child rather than
   making inferences about personality traits.
2. Ratings can be completed on a child in 5 to 10 minutes.
3. The use of a rating scale rather than present-absent judgments increase the instrument's sensitivity.
4. The scale has adequate reliability and validity.
5. Extensive normative data have been collected.
6. Factor analytic methodology was used in the scale's construction.

7. The scale provides multiple behavioral factors.

Procedures

Since much of our assessment is conducted in the schools, a plan was worked out so that the confidentiality of subjects and their family is maintained. The reason for our choice of children is concealed from those teaching personnel who have daily contact with them. These persons are told only that this study is concerned with the academic and social competence of school children in the county and that subjects are selected on a random basis. To further ensure the anonymity of the target child, the teacher completes a very brief child behavior rating form on all of the boys or girls in the class, depending on the sex of the target child. The teacher is told that we are comparing the utility of this brief behavior-rating procedure with the considerably longer Devereux Scale, which she is asked to complete on just three children who were selected "randomly" (target child, matched control, random control).

Results

The first step in the data analysis was a comparison of the matched and random control groups on each of the 11 Devereux factors. No significant differences were found, allowing these two groups to be combined in subsequent analyses. The data for each of the Devereux factors were then analyzed by a "3 (groups: children with a schizophrenic, depressed, or normal mother) × 2 (sex) × 2 (grade level: kindergarten–fifth, sixth–ninth)" analysis of variance. Group effects were analyzed by using two planned, orthogonal comparisons: (1) target (children with either a schizophrenic or depressive mother) versus controls and (2) children with a schizophrenic mother versus children with a depressive mother. Interactions were evaluated via simple effects analyses followed by appropriate contrasts. The results were as follows:

1. Classroom disturbance. A significant main effect was obtained for sex ($F = 16.53$; $df = 1/203$; $p < .01$); girls were

rated lower on classroom disturbance than boys. The children of schizophrenic and depressive mothers did not differ significantly, but together were rated higher than the controls ($F = 6.15$; $df = 1/203$; $p < .02$).

2. Impatience. There was a significant main effect for sex, with boys being rated as more impatient ($F = 19.14$; $df = 1/203$; $p < .01$) and a groups × sex interaction ($F = 3.80$; $df = 2/203$; $p < .05$). For boys the targets differed from controls ($p < .01$) with most of the effect being contributed by those with a depressive mother. For girls the targets again differed from the controls ($p < .01$), but this time the effect was primarily due to those with a schizophrenic mother.

3. Disrespect-defiance. Target children were rated higher on this scale than control children ($F = 7.54$; $df = 1/203$; $p < .01$), but children with a schizophrenic mother did not differ significantly from those with a depressed mother.

4. External blame. No significant effects were obtained.

5. Achievement anxiety. No significant effects were obtained.

6. External reliance. No significant effects were obtained.

7. Comprehension. The target groups were rated significantly lower than the controls ($F = 6.48$; $df = 1/203$; $p < .02$), but there were no significant differences between the two target groups.

8. Inattentive-withdrawn. A significant groups × sex interaction was found ($F = 4.30$; $df = 2/203$; $p < .05$). For boys the target groups differed from the controls ($p < .01$), with sons of depressive mothers being most inattentive-withdrawn. For girls the target groups again differed significantly ($p < .01$) from the controls, but the daughters of schizophrenics were rated highest.

9. Irrelevant responsiveness. There was a significant main effect for sex ($F = 6.83$; $df = 1/203$; $p < .01$,) with boys rated higher than girls.

10. Creative initiative. There was a significant main effect for grade ($F = 5.10$; $df = 1/203$; $p < .05$). Younger children were rated higher. Target groups were rated significantly lower than the controls ($F = 10.49$; $df = 1/203$; $p < .002$), but the two target groups did not differ.

11. Need for closeness to teacher. A significant main effect was found for grade (F = 15.21; df = 1/203; p < .01), with younger children rated higher than older ones. Target children were rated significantly lower than controls (F = 7.09; df = 1/203; p < .01), but the two target groups were not significantly different.

Discussion

The results quite strikingly indicate that children with either a schizophrenic or a depressive mother are perceived by their teachers as more deviant than their classmates with normal parents. The target groups differed from the controls on seven of the 11 Devereux factors, exhibiting relatively high levels of classroom disturbance, impatience, disrespect-defiance, and inattentiveness-withdrawal. They also show relatively low comprehension, creative initiative, and relatedness to teacher. This pattern is quite similar to a profile type found by Spivack, Swift, et al. [13] in their profile analyses of classroom behavior. They describe children with such a profile as presenting a major behavioral disturbance. They manifest acting-out and impulsive behavior and are in conflict with the behavioral demands of the classroom. They seem unable to make productive use of the classroom and achieve poorly. Such children, the authors comment, "will more than challenge the best of teachers" (Spivack, Swift, et al. [13], p. 288). These target children with either a schizophrenic or depressive mother may indeed be described as vulnerable.

Focusing now on only the children of schizophrenic mothers, the pattern of results is consistent with other studies which compared such children to offspring of normal parents. Garmezy's [3] review of studies pointed to a wide range of psychopathology in such children. Previous [6, 18] studies have viewed such findings as being specific to schizophrenia. Our data challenge this interpretation. Teachers did not perceive differences between the children of schizophrenic or depressive mothers; on no scale was there a significant difference between them. Similar results using different measures have been found by Rolf [7] and Beisser, Glasser, et al. [1].

Therefore, without a control group of children of parents with nonschizophrenic psychopathology, one cannot properly interpret differences between children of schizophrenic parents and those of normals as due *specifically* to schizophrenic genes or rearing patterns.

References

1. Beisser, A. R., Glasser, N., and Grant, M. Psychosocial adjustment of children of schizophrenic mothers. *J. Nerv. Ment. Dis.*, 145 (1967), 429–440.
2. Bower, E. M., Shellhamer, T. A., and Daily, J. M. School characteristics of male adolescents who later become schizophrenic. *Amer. J. Orthopsychiat.*, 1960, 30, 712–729.
3. Garmezy, N. (with the collaboration of S. Streitman). Children at risk: The search for the antecedents of schizophrenia. Part I. Conceptual models and research methods. *Schizo. Bull.*, 8, (1974), 14–91.
4. Lambert, N. and Bower, E. *Technical Report on In-school Screening of Emotionally Handicapped Children.* Educational Testing Service, Princeton, N. J., 1961.
5. Mednick, S. A. and Schulsinger, F. Some premorbid characteristics related to the breakdown of children with schizophrenic mothers. In *The Transmission of Schizophrenia*, D. Rosenthal and S. S. Kety, Eds. Pergamon Press, New York, 1968, pp. 267–291.
6. Meehl, P. E. High school yearbooks: A reply to Schwarz. *J. Abnorm. Psychol.*, 77 (1971), 143–147.
7. Rolf, J. E. The academic and social competence of children vulnerable to schizophrenia and other behavior pathologies. *J. Abnorm. Psychol.*, 80:3 (1972), 225–243.
8. Schiff, S. K. and Kellam, S. G. A community-wide mental health program of prevention and early treatment in first grade. *Psychiatric Research Report*, No. 21, Amer. Psychiatric Assoc., April 1967, pp. 92–102.
9. Spitzer, R. and Endicott, J. *Current and Past Psychopathology Scales (CAPPS).* Evaluations Unit, Biometrics Research, New York State Department of Mental Hygiene, New York, 1968.
10. Spivak, F. and Swift, M. The Devereux Elementary School Behavior Rating Scale: A study of the nature and organization of achievement related disturbed classroom behavior. *J. Spec. Educ.*, 1 (1966), 71–91.
11. Spivack, G. and Swift, M. *Devereux Elementary School Behavior Rating Scale Manual.* The Devereux Foundation, Devon, Pa., 1967.
12. Spivack, G. and Swift, M. The classroom behavior of children: A critical review of teacher administered rating scales. *J. Spec. Educ.* 7, (1973), 55–89.
13. Spivack, G., Swift, M., and Prewitt, J. Syndromes of disturbed classroom behavior: A behavioral diagnostic system for elementary schools. *J. Spec. Educ.*, 5 (1972), 269–292.
14. Swift, M. and Spivack, G. The assessment of achievement-related classroom behavior. *J. Spec. Educ.*, 2 (1968), 137–154.
15. Swift, M. and Spivack, G. Clarifying the relationship between academic success and overt classroom behavior. *Except. Childr.*, 36 (1969), 99–104.

16. Swift, M., Spivack, G., DeLisser, O., Danset, A., Danset-Leger, J., and Win-nykamen, F. Organization of children's disturbed classroom behavior: A cross-cultural investigation in France and the U.S.A. *Except. Child* 38:492–3, Feb. 72.
17. Ullman, Charles A. Teachers, peers and tests as predictors of adjustment. *J. Educ. Psychol.*, 48, (1957), 257.
18. Watt, N. F. Childhood roots of schizophrenia. In *Life History Research in Psychopathology*, Vol. III, D. F. Ricks, A. Thomas, and M. Roff, Eds. Univ. Minnesota Press, Minneapolis, in press.
19. Zax, M., Cowen, E., Izzo, L. and Trost, M. Identifying emotional distur-bance in the school setting. *Amer. J. Orthopsychiat.*, 34 (1969), 447.

Role Taking, Referential Communication, and Egocentric Intrusions in Mother-Child Interactions of Children Vulnerable to Risk of Parental Psychosis

Michael J. Chandler, Ph.D. (Canada)

This chapter is intended primarily as a brief for a more transactional and developmentally oriented approach to the study of emergent childhood psychopathology. The central point to be elaborated is that during the course of their development children employ a series of qualitatively different modes of cognitive organization, each of which is generally less complex than the adult-oriented social environment with which they must cope. As a consequence, children who are unable to draw on the resources of persons more cognitively mature than themselves are necessarily slated for a series of inevitable social failures. It seems, therefore, incumbent on the adults, who normally set standards of social complexity, to mediate this environment for young persons less competent than themselves.

Two different sets of skills seem required to fulfill this mediating function. The first involves the recognition that children conceptualize the world in ways that are qualitatively different from that characteristic of most adults. The second concerns the ability to author alternative presentations of social situations, tailored by

347

an accurate understanding of the child's current cognitive capabilities. In the absence of caretakers capable of fulfilling these important mediating functions, the child is abandoned to a social environment with which he is developmentally unsuited to cope. Social organization based on principles that are "over one's head" is no organization at all, and extended exposure to such incoherence is seen in this view to make a potential contribution to the development of serious psychopathology. Any factors that compromise the success with which a child's caretakers are able to identify and take into account systematic developmental changes in his cognitive organization are thus seen as potentially active ingredients in the etiology of subsequent disorder.

The purpose of the research, about which this chapter is intended as a preliminary report, has been to assess the effectiveness with which parents of varying mental health status are able to accurately assess the cognitive-developmental level of their children and interact with them in ways that reflect and draw on this awareness. *The general hypothesis under study is that parents who, because of their own emotional difficulties, are unable to recognize or take into consideration important developmental differences between themselves and their children are handicapped in their role as mediators of the adult social environment and through their failures, seriously jeopardize the adaptational efforts of their children.* More specifically, this research has involved an attempt to assess the relative skill with which both psychiatrically disordered women and their children differentiate themselves from one another and come to appreciate that each possesses qualitatively different, age-related modes of cognitive organization.

Although the ability to accurately infer the character of another person's cognitive organization is undoubtedly dependent on a variety of different skill dimensions, one necessary prerequisite to all of these is the ability to distinguish between one's own thoughts and feelings and those of others and to successfully take roles and perspectives other than one's own. This set of abilities, which Piaget [12] has characterized as falling along an egocentrism-perspectivism dimension, has been shown to vary as a function of age [11] and to exercise control over the development of a variety of social interactional competencies. Other investigators [2, 5, 6, 8], concerned with the extention of developmental theory into the study of childhood psychopathology, have demonstrated that persistent developmental delays in the acquisition of role-taking skills are closely associated with a variety of more general failures in social adaptation. Whether interpreted as cause or effect, the measurement of role-taking skills in disordered populations has, however, most commonly had as its limited purpose the demonstration that persons who express other forms of social pathology are also persistently egocentric as well. When viewed in a more interpersonal context, however, knowledge of the role-taking skills of both children and their parents may serve as a barometer of their abilities to engage in effective mutual interaction and may provide important information regarding the manner in which social incompetencies reverberate across generations.

Egocentrism among intellectual peers involves a faulty attribution process, but the thoughts and feelings that are misassigned at least tend to be on a kind of conceptual par with those ideas for which they are mistaken. Parents, on the other hand, who think egocentrically about their children and who ascribe to them thoughts and feelings that are actually their own, perpetrate a double disservice. Their egocentric attributions are not only mistaken, but because adult conceptualizations are typically more complex, the ideas that they project also tend to be adultomorphic or otherwise developmentally out-of-step. In the context of parent-child interactions, therefore, egocentric thought tends to ride roughshod over existing developmental differences and to interfere with the capacity of adults to recognize and mediate the conceptual confusions of younger generations.

For their part, children are somewhat more within their developmental rights when they egocentrically assume a mistaken communality between their own and their parents' thoughts and feelings. Under normal circumstances, however, profound egocentric errors gradually give way to a more perspectivistic orientation, and by the middle childhood years young persons typically come to recognize the largely privileged character of their own and others' internal states. Their gradual shift toward a more objective, socially decentered view is assumed by Piaget [13] to develop as a result of social interaction with persons who insist on the private and independent character of their own thoughts and feelings. Parents are assumed to play a major role in this educational process and, unless prevented from doing so by their own persistent egocentric confusions, actively instruct their children in the notion that thoughts are the private property of those who think them. Precisely what egocentric children do not need, however, are caretakers who are themselves confused about such matters and who, because of their own persistent egocentricism, iron out the differences of opinion that must be brought to the child's attention if he is to make effective developmental progress. Children who lack this kind of opportunity to learn perspective-taking skills and whose childhood egocentricism persists beyond the normal tenure further aggravate the problems in understanding that face their parents. To the extent that their own development is anomalous, they compound the diagnostic problem confronting their parents and invalidate whatever normative developmental standards their caretaker may attempt to apply to them. Beyond the fact of their atypical developmental course, persistently egocentric children are by definition less alert to differences between themselves and their parents and are thus less likely to militate in behalf of their own independent attitudes and beliefs or to force a recognition of their separate existence.

For all of these reasons, egocentric thinking has the particularly perverse characteristic of being self-validating in that it creates conditions that are its own justification. Egocentric parents adultomorphically misascribe their own thoughts and feelings to their children, whose efforts to overcome their own age-appropriate egocentricism are consequently impaired, creating developmental deviation that ensures that their parent's egocentric attributions will continue to overestimate their children's cognitive capabilities. No one who is locked into this self-justifying and self-fulfilling prophecy is able to gain the distance required to detect the fallacies on which it is based, and a maladaptive system is created that is ideally suited to echo across succeeding generations.

To collect information that might support or challenge this developmentally oriented, transactional view of emergent childhood psychopathology, three kinds of data are required. The first and second of these consist of independent measures of the role or perspective-taking skills of both parents and their children. Beyond these individual assessments, some third and more interactional measure is required, in the context of which it is possible to determine the manner in which both child and parent assess one another's perspectives and attempt to employ this information in cooperative ventures. The research on which my colleague Norman Garmezy and I are collaborating is an attempt to obtain such data on a study population composed of 4-, 7-, or 11-year old children whose mothers have a history of serious psychiatric disorders. This project, which is a component part of the larger University of Rochester Child and Family Study, is in an early stage of data collection, and no clear conclusions can as yet be derived from these preliminary findings. It is possible, however, to describe some of the assessment strategies that we are employing and outline in a tentative way the apparent direction of some of our findings.

Of the several different procedures employed in this study to individually evaluate the role- or perspective-taking skills of both the child and adult subjects, only one is briefly described here in an effort to illustrate the general assessment approach being used. This procedure, described elsewhere in more detail [6], hinges on a measurement strategy developed by Flavell, Botkin, et al. [9] and Chandler [3, 5, 6] in which subjects are asked to describe stimulus drawings from both their own perspective and the viewpoint of other persons who are provided access to less information than themselves. Intrusion of priviledged information into the accounts intended as descriptive of another individual's point of view are scored as evidence of egocentric errors in distinguishing public from private information.

The actual stimulus materials employed in this procedure are a set of cartoon drawings that can be presented either in their entirety or masked in such a way that only fractional parts of the original design are visible through a small hole cut into the overlay. This masking procedure provides such a narrow window onto the total drawing that an observer who is provided only this keyhole view could not reasonably guess the subject matter of the entire cartoon. One of these drawings, for example, depicts a ship coming to save a drowning witch. Once the overlay has been superimposed on this drawing all that remains visible is a square frame from which two triangles, made up of the tip of the witch's hat and the prow of the ship, extend inward from the side and bottom borders.

Other drawings in this series each show all or parts of a camel behind a fence, two elephants smelling a grapefruit, a bear climbing a tree, and a boy playing a trombone in a telephone booth.

The procedure is individually administered to both the children and parents of our study and proceeds in two steps. The child or adult subject is first shown the completed drawing and asked to describe and caption these pictures. Following these descriptions the drawings are masked, exposing only the narrow keyhole views onto the larger scenes. The respondents are then asked to indicate how these limited, fractional parts of the original drawings would be interpreted by their own child or parent. What this procedure accomplishes is to install in the subject pieces of private and highly privileged information that must be entirely set aside if one is to successfully take the point of view of someone who has access to less information than himself. Any attribution stating or implying that an only partially informed witness or bystander would know, as the subject legitimately knows, details of the larger unabridged scene, constitutes a clear and unambiguous egocentric error and demonstrates a serious flaw in the ability to set aside one's own point of view and step into the role or perspective of someone else.

Data resulting from the application of this procedure are currently available on approximately 40 mothers and children who have served as subjects in the University of Rochester Child and Family Study. Two sorts of tentative conclusions are supported by these preliminary findings. First, these vulnerable children appear generally slower to abdicate their own egocentric assumptions than do comparable samples of their age mates, selected at random from public school settings. Particularly among the older of these subjects there have been numerous instances in which these children have evidenced marked delays in the development of age-appropriate role- and perspective-taking skills, and these repeated instances of egocentric error seem comparable to those previously observed in populations of already seriously emotionally disturbed children [3, 6]. Second, the results obtained with the mothers of these children also suggest that many of these women egocentrically attribute information to their children that is legitimately known only to themselves. Although comparable normative data are less readily available, these instances of profound egocentric error are inconsistent with standards of normal adult functioning and parallel the results of Feffer [8] and others who have presented evidence of major deficits in the role- and perspective-taking skills of psychiatrically disordered adults. Although not available at this early phase in our longitudinal study, collateral data from other facets of the University of Rochester projects will eventually permit a determination of whether this evidence of persistent egocentric errors in the thinking of both children and their parents will be related to present and future disorders among the members of this vulnerable study population. Whatever the future consequence of the deficits in role- and perspective-taking skills observed in the individual assessments of these children and their parents, such failures in understanding clearly have important implications for the quality of current interactions. The assessment of these anticipated interactional difficulties has constituted the second focus of this longitudinal research effort.

The particular feature of parent-child interaction on which this research has focused has been the relative skill with which both parties are able to identify one another's informational needs and phrase helpful communications that take these needs into account. This ability dimension, referred to as *referential communication skill*, was selected for study for a number of interdependent reasons. First, it is precisely this nexus of intergenerational communication that a number of theorists [14] have identified as the most likely point at which the pathologies of parents are visited upon their children. Second, it is in the formulation of effective referential communications that the ability of both parents and children to identify important differences in one another's roles and points of view is put to their most serious test. Finally, existing research has clearly demonstrated that referential communication skills systematically improve during the course of normal development [10], are seriously compromised in children with manifest emotional difficulties [6], and are often sharply impaired in schizophrenic and other seriously disordered adults [7]. As previously discussed, it is precisely when this set of three conditions is met that one is most justified in suspecting some cross-generational link in the etiology of childhood disorder.

On the basis of a similar chain of reasoning Alkire [1] has investigated the referential communication skills within the families of both normal and disturbed adolescents. The results of this study indicate important referential communication deviancies in the cross-talk of families with disturbed children and suggest that the kinds of faulty communication patterns employed may be related to the type of symptom pattern exhibited by the child.

The general assessment strategy employed in this and previous studies of referential communication consists of the presentation of various arrays of stimulus objects that one member of the communications dyad must describe to the other in such a way that the other participant is able to determine which of the various objects is being discussed. Failures in the communication of such details are generally interpreted as the result of egocentric errors in the assumptions made about what others already know and still need to know in order to understand.

The stimulus materials most commonly employed in previous studies have been readily distinguishable and easily dimensionalized objects, whose relevant features can be tallied up and set as a standard against which the adequacy of various communications about them can be compared. For comparative purposes the present study has included materials and procedures similar to those just described. To this end, the children and parents of this study are required to communicate with one another about the size, shape, color, and coordinates of geometric objects located in a 3 × 3 matrix.[1] In an effort to focus attentions on issues of more affective and interpersonal relevance, however, these subjects are also required to make referential communications about a series of photographs that differ only in the affective expressions portrayed. In each of these procedures both parent and child are required to reciprocate information to each other. In addition, both are required to first describe these materials to a nonfamily member, and the results of these less inbred referential communication efforts are then compared with the parent-child interaction data.

---

[1] This procedure is a modification of the test described in S. Greenspan, C. Barenboim, and M. J. Chandler, A matrix test of referential communication ability in children (manuscript in preparation).

The analyses of these data tend to become quite involuted, and only a few very general and sketchy trends and details have as yet begun to emerge. The most striking of these is the extremely broad range of competencies observed in the referential communication skills of these family members. The failures routinely observed in the performances of the youngest of the children studied were anticipated on the basis of previously published norms and thus are of limited interest. Similar failures observed among the older of the child subjects are much less normative and parallel other data based on the study of already seriously disturbed children [6]. More significant still are the multiple instances in which mothers have been observed to communicate to their children in ways that reflect profound egocentric confusions about the sorts of information that clear communication demands.

When comparisons are made between the kinds of communications that these mothers direct toward other adults and toward their own children, two quite interesting results seem to emerge. First, these mothers, all of whom are to one degree or another psychiatrically disturbed, seem generally alert to the fact that communications directed toward children require some degree of special care and attention. With only one or two exceptions, all of the mothers have more to say and say it with more precision when they are attempting to instruct their children. These data seem to suggest that, despite their history of disorder, these women are reasonably alert to the fact that some sort of developmental differences exist between children and adults and that these differences demand that children be afforded special handling in referential communication situations. The available data regarding the particular kinds of efforts exerted by these mothers in behalf of their children is, however, somewhat less encouraging. For example, when these mothers attempt to describe affect-laden facial expressions to their children they frequently shift to a strategy that avoids the use of affect terms and rely instead on entirely physicalistic descriptions of head positions or facial contours. Whereas these more concrete descriptions reflect a concern over possible differences between the conceptualization of children and adults, they also often reflect serious misperceptions regarding the kinds of information their children are capable of processing. For example, in one of these families studied the mother described the series of pictures of facial expressions by providing lengthy anecdotes that recalled situations in which she had once worn similar expressions. Much to her embarrassment, her 10-year-old son described his own series of photographs by making concise and highly sophisticated reference to the affective tone that uniquely characterized each picture. In another family a mother concluded that her son did not know the terms "circle," "square," and "triangle" and attempted to describe a large red circle by explaining that it was "a big fat Mars." In her concern that geometric terms might be beyond his comprehension she tended to ignore the fact that not every 8-year-old knows that Mars is the large red planet. In both of these examples, and many others that are available as well, there is mounting evidence that these disturbed mothers recognize that something special is required in dealing with young children. The difficulty that they seem to experience is in knowing what that something might be, and in their efforts to be helpful they seem to frequently seriously misjudge the kind of help that is really needed. They seem, in this sense, to be particularly ineffective in helping to mediate environmental complexity in a way that is well suited and to meet their child's changing developmental needs.

References

1. Alkire, A., Goldstein, M. J., Rodnick, E. H., et al. Social Influence and counterinfluence within families of four types of disturbed adolescents. *J. Abnorm Psychol.* 77:32–41, 1971.
2. Anthony, E. J. An experimental approach to the psychopathology of childhood autism. *Brit. J. Med. Psychol.*, 32 (1958), 19–37.
3. Chandler, M. J. Egocentrism and childhood psychopathology: The development and application of measurement techniques. Paper presented at the biennial meeting of the Society for Research in Child Development, Minneapolis, 1971.
4. Chandler, M. J. Egocentrism in normal and pathological child development. In *Determinants of Behavioral Development*, F. Monks, W. Hartup, and J. DeWitt, Eds. Academic Press, New York, 1972.
5. Chandler, M. J. Egocentrism and antisocial behavior: The assessment and training of social perspective-taking skills. *Devel. Psychol.*, 9 (1973), 326–332.
6. Chandler, M. J., Greenspan, S., and Barenboim, C. The assessment and training of role-taking and referencial communication skills in in-

stitutionalized emotionally disturbed children. *Devel. Psychol.*, 10 (1974), 546–553.

7. Cohen, B. and Camhi, J. Schizophrenic performance in a word-communication task. *J. Abnorm. Psychol.*, 72 (1967), 240–246.

8. Feffer, M. H. The cognitive implications of role taking behavior. *J. Personality,* 27 (1959), 152–168.

9. Flavell, J. H., Botkin, P. T., Fry, C. L., Wright, J. W., and Jarvis, P. E. *The Development of Role Taking and Communication Skills in Children.* Wiley, New York, 1968.

10. Krauss, R. and Glucksberg, S. The development of communication: Competence as a function of age. *Child Devel.*, 40 (1969), 255–266.

11. Looft, W. R. Egocentrism and social interaction across the life span. *Psychol. Bull.*, 78 (1972), 73–92.

12. Piaget, J. and Inhelder, B. *The Child's Conception of Space.* Routledge & Kegan Paul, London, 1956.

13. Piaget, J. Piaget's theory, In *Carmichael's Manual of Child Psychology*, P. Mussen, Ed. Wiley, New York, 1970.

14. Wynne, L. C. Communication disorders and the quest for relatedness in families of schizophrenics. *Amer. J. Psychoan.*, 30 (1970), 100–114.

Piagetian Egocentrism, Empathy, and Affect Discrimination in Children at High Risk for Psychosis

Bruno J. Anthony, M.A., M.Ph. (U.S.A.)

Introduction

In the last 8 years our ongoing longitudinal research in St. Louis on the child at risk for parental psychosis has produced an almost overwhelming amount of data. At times of despair, we have estimated that we have collected, scored, and coded 495,000 bits of information from 114 families containing 335 children. This data wealth has been accumulated by the four main sections of the project: (1) psychiatric, (2) clinical, (3) social, and (4) experimental. The vast and very complicated task of analysis has begun. The following is a report on one small section within this broad and promising design. Aided by many others I have been involved with the analysis of a battery of tests contained in the experimental section of the study tapping the cognitive development of our subjects aged 6 through 11 years.

The original hypothesis formulated for this area of our risk project predicted different cognitive and affective experiences for the child in a normal household from that of a child in a family containing a psychotic parent. Parents, when seen as programmers of the young person's experiential world, influence the way the child perceives and deals with the environment. Because of the sometimes abnormal behavior of the psychotic parent, his contribution to the child's development could be significantly different from that of a normal parent.

One of the central constructs we utilized to tap for any apparent abnormalities in a child's normal mental growth was Piaget's [16] concept of egocentrism—one component of his theory of developing decentration. He proposes that a child at the preoperational stage should be less able to separate his point of view from that of others than when concrete operational behavior appears.

The child below 7 years, according to Piaget, is midway between two types of thought: (1) "autistic" or incommunicable and (2) logical, which frees the child to adapt his thought to that of others. I might add that this developmental sequence is only one of three decentering processes in the Piaget scheme; the others occur in infancy and adolescence (see Appendix).

Our research employed a number of measures to test for the child's ability to decenter his focus. We attempted to learn the extent to which our subjects were able to perceive the external environment through the eyes of others, to think what another may be thinking, and to feel what another might feel.

One of the instruments in our cognitive battery was developed by our St. Louis research group and was labeled the Affect Discrimination Test (ADT). We hoped that it would efficiently examine the empathic understanding necessary to predict how another might feel, which we thought could serve as one indication of the extent of decentration of thought.

The format of the test can be divided into four components: (1) subject, (2) facial expression, (3) emotional situation, and (4) prediction. By asking children to pick out the photograph of an actor's face corresponding to an emotion evoked by a certain situation, it was hoped that differences in the ability to connect feeling with expression would correspond to differences in empathy or the ability to predict the emotional behavior of another. We felt that any disturbance in this empathic development could effect the character of a child's social interaction and adaption.

Izard, [11] states that "facial expression, as the public aspect of emotion, constitutes the cornerstone of social-responsiveness, emotional attachments, and meaningful interpersonal affective ties." That the ability to connect situations with emotional expression is a prerequisite for empathic understanding was recognized as far back as 1873 by Darwin [8], the first great investigator into emotional expression. He wrote, "The movements of expression give vividness and energy to our spoken words. They reveal the thoughts and intentions of others more truly than do words which may be falsified." The relationship of empathy and facial expression is also pointed out by Gilbert [10], who found a relationship between items describing an emotionally expressive and aware child and a battery of cognitive tests based on the affective knowledge of the child, including the sorting of facial expression and the ability to define emotion words. Even more important for our study is her finding of a significant correlation between the child who is affect-aware and the teacher rating of empathy in that child. We concluded that the child who is unable to comprehend emotion from a face, as a result of a feeling aroused by a set of events, is at a loss in attempts at sending and receiving interpersonal communication.

This inability to empathize with another's experience would be very evident in egocentric children for they would have difficulty in looking outside themselves and comprehending the feelings of others. Thus we were aware that the extent to which the inability to empathize would hamper performance on the ADT would be a function of the validity of the test in distinguishing egocentric from nonegocentric children. Before attempting to measure the influence of variables relevant to our sample on ADT performance, therefore, we felt our first task was to evaluate the test in its capacity to measure the empathic understanding of a child.

Validity Study

The first question we asked was do we have the necessary ingredients for a study of empathy. The four components of the ADT mentioned earlier—subject, facial expression, emotional situation, and prediction—correspond to the vital factors of any study of interpersonal perception proposed by Gage and Cronbach [9] in their excellent criticism of previous studies on empathy.

The first component mentioned by these two researchers is the judge—the individual whom the experiment is attempting to measure. Our large bunch of judges could be divided into two groups of children aged 6 to 11 years: (1) 77 children from families with one parent a diagnosed psychotic personality and (2) 65 children with parents professing no history of any type of mental or physical illness. Besides these divisions, our subject pool also spanned both races, the middle and lower class and both sexes. (see Chart 1).

It is obvious that to obtain a measure of empathy from a subject, the experiment must include somebody to empathize with. Gage and Cronbach [9] label this component the other. In the

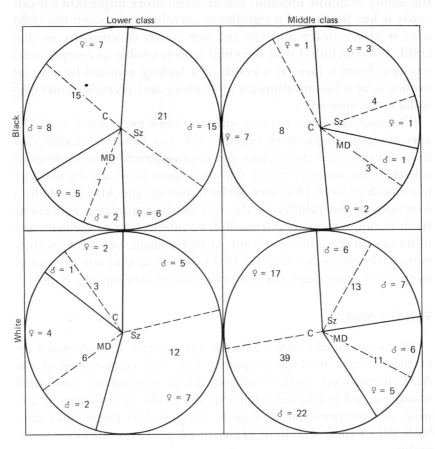

Chart 1 Sample breakdown by race, social class, sex, parental health, and parental diagnosis.

ADT a child was asked to feel like somebody in a photograph. These stimuli were chosen from 43 facial shots of professional actors asked to produce nine different emotions—"happy," "sad," "surprised," "angry," "pleased," "disgusted," "afraid," "suspicious," and "worried." Out of the total number of pictures, adults and children participating in the development of the test were given the task of sorting the photographs into categories corresponding to the nine target emotions. The one picture most often placed under each emotion was then used as the test stimuli. In the final version of the ADT the subject was presented with a set of the nine most representative photographs from both sexes and asked to examine each one.

The experiments then presented what Gage and Cronbach [9] call the "input," or "information concerning the other which is available to the judge." This digestion of material is the first stage in understanding another person. The input given to each subject on the ADT consisted of short descriptive situations containing the target emotion such as "This person is sad because his best friend is sick, or this person is angry because someone has wrecked his new car."

These situations were also a result of a pilot study conducted in public grade schools throughout St. Louis. Children were asked, "What can you think of that would make you feel sad or happy?" Their responses were written down verbatim and those occurring most frequently were used in the final procedure.

With the pictures before him and the information from the situational description in his mind, the child is ready for the second and most important stage of the empathic process—the interpretation of the information and the arrival at predictive statements about the other. Here, in our test, the predictive statement is nonverbal. The child's task is to point to the face in a picture that best represents the way the *other* should react in a given situation. This last component of any study of empathy is the behavior that can be objectively measured and, in the Gage and Cronbach system, [9] is referred to as the "outtake."

Thus I have tried to show that the ADT contains the basic structure of a study on interpersonal perception. Continuing with the investigation of the validity of this test, we were concerned by the fact that our instrument was somewhat similar to Borke's [3] test of perspectivate thinking in which she found that children as young as 3 years could abandon their egocentric attitudes and take the point of view of others. This finding is in opposition to Piaget, who feels that social egocentrism begins to wane at about age 6 or 7.

Chandler [5, 6] has criticized Borke's method as measuring stereotyping and projection rather than empathy or insight. He felt that using her procedure, both egocentric and nonegocentric subjects could be expected to perform in an identical fashion. Using a method where the child evaluated another point of view whose information was clearly different from his own, Chandler concluded that "in early age children, anticipation of the affective responses of others was accurate but that assuming perspectives different from one's own is a late-arriving developmental accomplishment." We felt that our measure required the child to use more empathic decentered thinking than Borke's. In her study the child was coached as to which pictures represented which emotion before being asked to make situation and facial expression and thus did not have to deal with faces at all. Although the ADT also asked the child to connect a situation with an emotional reaction, it also required an understanding of the relation between feeling and human facial expression gained from the environment, which we feel develops simultaneously with the knowledge that emotions in others exist separately from one's own. Thus we felt that the prediction of affective responses *from the human face* is not an early-arriving phonomena, but that this empathic ability as measured by the ADT develops later in the child, assisted by increasing decentration.

Our hypothesis was born out by the discovery of a significant developmental trend in the ADT within the years 6 and 12 (see Figure 1), shadowing the development away from egocentrism. However, we had reservations about the significance of this trend. Others have shown that certain photographs of expression are misleading. Because we employed nine photographs, each portraying a different emotion, we wished to determine whether a low-scoring subject was actually lacking in empathy or whether his errors were a result of ambiguities in the picture itself, causing blends of facial expression that could easily be classified as more than one emotion.

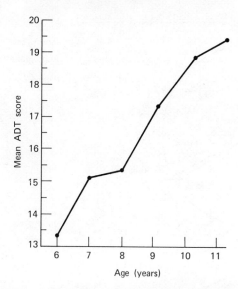

Figure 1   Mean ADT scores as a function of age.

In trying to untangle these alternate explanations, we divided the number of times each response was given into three categories: (1) *correct*—the right response to the right stimuli, (2) *appropriate*—incorrect response-stimuli pairing but one given more than 10 percent of the time by our normal population, and (3) *inappropriate*—incorrect response-stimulus pairing; one given less than 10 percent of the time by our normal population. An example is provided in Chart 2.

Even though we felt that appropriate errors could be evidence for lack of refined empathic skills, we decided to investigate only inappropriate errors as indicating a real deficit in empathy. If empathic abilities were not measured by the ADT, we should see the same number of inappropriate errors across our age range, possibly arising from random error. We have found this not to be the case. A definite developmental downward trend in inappropriate errors appears for the total sample and for each separate response. We feel that this fact adds support to the notion that egocentric and nonegocentric children perform differently on the ADT (see Figure 2).

Dealing further with the relevancy of the ADT, we felt that a valid measure of empathy should distinguish the well-functioning

Surprise responses to male stimuli

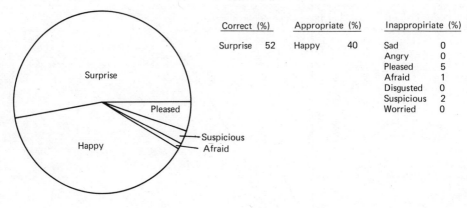

	Correct (%)		Appropriate (%)		Inappropiriate (%)	
	Surprise	52	Happy	40	Sad	0
					Angry	0
					Pleased	5
					Afraid	1
					Disgusted	0
					Suspicious	2
					Worried	0

Surprise responses to female stimuli

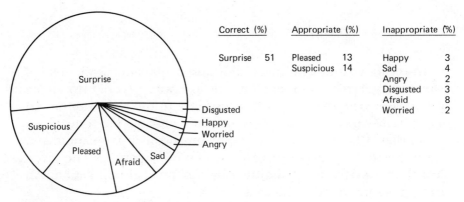

	Correct (%)		Appropriate (%)		Inappropriate (%)	
	Surprise	51	Pleased	13	Happy	3
			Suspicious	14	Sad	4
					Angry	2
					Disgusted	3
					Afraid	8
					Worried	2

Chart 2   Example of division of total number of times a response was elicited into correct, appropriate, and inappropriate categories.

child from one less socially skilled. Others have shown that the concept of egocentrism does differentiate children with asocial types of childhood psychopathology from those with normal development. Thus we also felt that another measure of the accuracy of our tool would be the ability to distinguish our least socially healthy from those who appear better adjusted.

We felt that a child rated as more disturbed from ratings derived from the clinical battery used in the study [4] would be less socially adaptable, partially as a result of a lack of empathy in his behavior, than a more well-adjusted child. Thus we determined

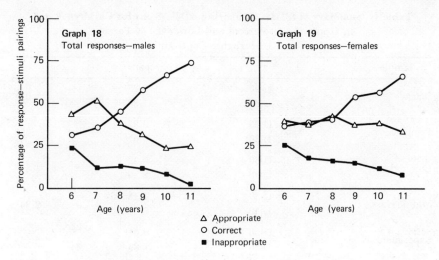

Figure 2 Comparison of correct, appropriate, and inappropriate response-stimuli pairings for total responses on ADT.

those children rated in approximately the top and bottom 30 percent on a disturbance continuum and compared their mean adjusted scores on the ADT (see Table 1).

The results showed that the test seems to distinguish disturbed from nondisturbed children regardless of the way the sample is broken down.

As an outside criterion to measure the social adaptability, we examined the ratings of the school behavior of each child garnered from interviews with each individual's teacher. Agreeing with our sum of disturbance rating, the upper 25 percent and lower 25 percent of children judged from the school rating of adjustment were significantly differentiated by their ADT score ($t = 2.30$; $p < .025$). If these children's disorders, judged from clinical ratings and school behavior, can be traced in part to delays in affective role taking, causing them to be centered in their interpersonal interactions, the ADT seems to illuminate this egocentric nonempathic attitude.

Finally, our cognitive battery included the Piagetian Three Mountains Test (TMT) and the Children's Embedded Figures Test (CEFT). Both have been shown [12, 15] to examine the child's ability to organize his world, placing himself in a field sepa-

Table 1   Summary of *t*-Tests Comparing ADT Means for Children Rated
in Upper (U) 30 Percent and Lower (L) 30 Percent
on a Disturbance Continuum

Sample		Means	t
Blacks	U-30	0.27	2.01[a]
	L-30	−1.88	
Whites	U-30	0.97	1.92[a]
	L-30	−0.61	
Lower class	U-30	−0.47	1.86[a]
	L-30	−2.24	
Middle class	U-30	1.13	2.24[b]
	L-30	−0.45	
Experimentals	U-30	−0.04	2.25[b]
	L-30	−1.85	
Controls	U-30	1.56	3.51[C]
	L-30	−1.14	
Males	U-30	0.69	2.74[c]
	L-30	−1.31	
Females	U-30	1.05	2.99[c]
	L-30	−1.70	

[a] $p < .05$.
[b] $p < .025$.
[c] $p < .005$.

rate from the environment. We hypothesized that the same basic skills are necessary for functioning in all three tests, realizing, though, that other factors contribute differentially to successful performance in each task. Keeping this in mind, we expected mild correlations between all three tests, which was borne out (see Table 2). From our study of the relevancy of the ADT, the phenomenon we believe we have tapped can be stated as the ability of children to recognize that an expression or the face of another different from themselves connotes something about the way he is feeling and is a result of a certain set of circumstances. We call our phenomenon *predictive empathy*. It is our opinion that a child's performance on the ADT is aided if he realizes, nonegocentrically, that there are other points of view than his own that he gains from an awareness of others and their actions in the world. It appears that the skill is developed in the child between 6 and 11 years of age as he decenters and that variations in that development are allied with disturbance in the child.

We now felt somewhat more comfortable in using the ADT in the study of children at risk for parented psychosis.

Effect of Independent Variables

If the ADT functions as a true barometer of the empathic level of a child, we hypothesized that it would show that a child brought up in a home dominated by the presence of a diagnosed psychotic parent is unable to perform at an adequate level on our measure because of the unusual affective environment and interaction. This egocentric behavior would be in contrast to a child brought up in a normal household where the learning of affective recognition and role taking is a simpler matter. The effect of the delay or nonappearance of socially decentered thought could be a significant factor in the development of later pathology. We thus looked for differences between our experimental children from families with one psychotic parent and our control children from normal families on our measure.

Our experimental group was comprised of children with parents diagnosed as both schizophrenic and manic depressive. We felt that the vast differences in the type and amount of affect displayed by these two groups of parents could influence the social learning of their children. It was our opinion that the flatness of emotion and the passivity displayed by the schizophrenic would be much more of a deterrent to the normal development of the child than the exaggerated behavior of the manic depressive. Thus, besides investigating overall differences between our ex-

Table 2   Correlation Matrix between Various Measures Tapping Differentiation

	CEFT	TMT	ADT
CEFT	—	.490[b]	.431[b]
TMT	—	—	.216[a]
ADT	—	—	—

[a] $p < .01$.
[b] $p < .005$.

perimental and control population, we hoped to uncover any effects related to the wide variance in behavior covered under the broad heading of psychosis.

Besides our interest in the effect of parental health on the affective role-taking abilities of the child, we had also to be concerned with other variables because of the complicated makeup of our sample that spanned class, race, and sex. We were interested in corroborating a pilot study on the ADT that reported significantly diverse performances by middle-class children over lower-class children as well as females over males (7).

From Kohn's [14] work, we hypothesized that the type of interpretations of the world passed on by the lower-class family engendered the same developmental trends as those encountered in the family of a psychotic. Feelings of impotence and lack of control over the environment present in the lower class could prolong the autistic types of behavior in children, hampering their development of empathic spirit.

Besides the variables of social class and sex, our sample included both races. We acknowledged the vast differences between cultures but could not justify the conclusion that the ability to decipher emotion felt by others should be significantly different between Whites and Blacks. However, we were concerned with the types of stimuli used in the test. The actors who posed for the photographs portraying the different emotions were all White; this fact, coupled with the middle-class White bent to the situations provoking the emotions, would perhaps hamper the performance of black subjects. We thus hypothesized no differences in ADT scores between races but were aware that the test design could include built-in biases.

Our analysis of the ADT in its role in research on the child at risk for psychiatric illness thus focused on hypotheses discussed in the preceding paragraphs. We now turn to the analysis of the effects of these various environmental and genetic factors relevant to the children in our study that we believe could influence their empathic abilities and thus their susceptibility to deficits in social adaptability. From prior analyses we felt that the greatest amount of information about the independent variables would derive from a breakdown of the total sample into three age groups: Group I—6 to 7 years, Group II—8 to 9 years, and Group III—10 to 11.

The first hypothesis we considered was that females will perform better than males. All evidence indicates that there is no difference between the sexes, which does not coincide with the earlier work by Clack. (7). We next considered the three variables of the parental health of each child, the class, and the race. Because of the inequalities in the cell composition of our sample (see Chart 1) it was impossible to perform three-way analyses to determine the relative effects of our independent variables. A series of two way ANOVA's were performed, however, combining the four main independent variables to discover their influence on ADT performance at each critical age group (Table 3). From an analysis of the *total* sample, the effect of a diagnosed psychotic parent did not appear to significantly hamper the decentering process in his children.

Table 3   Summary of Two-Way ANOVAs Matching Four Independent Variables for Total Sample and at Three Age Levels

Pairing	Total Sample	Group I $x \leq 96$ Months	Group II $96 < x \leq 120$ Months	Group III $x > 120$ Months
Parental health/race	3.37	7.30[b]	0.01	0.02
	8.11[b]	0.95	7.87[b]	0.18
Parental health/social class	1.19	6.69[a]	0.91	0.00
	8.65[b]	0.05	12.39[b]	0.98
Parental health/sex	4.35[a]	8.43[b]	0.19	0.03
	0.04	1.67	0.86	0.07
Social class/race	3.53	1.35	5.49[a]	—
	0.82	1.97	2.54	—
Social class/sex	12.14[b]	0.88	12.93[b]	1.05
	0.17	1.52	1.04	0.07
Race/sex	9.40[b,c]	1.53	9.80[b]	0.30
	0.03	0.00	1.85	0.12

[a] $p < 0.05$.
[b] $p < .01$.
[c] Interaction significant, $p < .05$.

The prior finding, however, is misleading. These same analyses, when broken down into groups corresponding to the youngest, middle, and oldest children in our sample, produce a pattern indicating that there is an initially large influence of parental health on the social skills of a child that abates as time passes. Children under 8 years of age, of a psychotic parent, do significantly worse on the ADT than those children with two healthy parents. At younger ages this factor accounts for a greater proportion of the variance than either race, social class, or sex. In older children (Groups II and III), parental health becomes less of a factor in ADT performance, and no significant differences appear between the two groups.

We found that in Group II the effect of parental health, as a deterrent to successful role-taking in the child, loses its power. At this time, social class appears to emerge as the most important differentiator. In both younger and older children, social class does not effect performance on the ADT to any significant extent. The uneven influence of social class and parental health during the development of the child's capacity for empathy can be seen from a graph of the means of four divisions of our sample— lower-class experimental and control children plus middle-class experimental and control children (see Figure 3).

At ages 6 and 7 the control children of both classes group together at a higher level than experimental children of both classes. However, in Group II lower-class controls fall sharply, whereas, conversely, middle-class experimentals rise at a similar sharp rate. Within that age group lower-class experimentals differ significantly from their middle-class counterparts ($t = -1.92; p < .05$), likewise, lower-class controls differ from middle-class controls ($t = -3.74; p < .01$).

In Group II we also find that race accounts for significant proportions of the variance when matched against parental health and sex, but race cannot account for the social class difference (see Table 3). Social class thus remains as the most important factor in determining ADT achievement in children between 8 and 10, indicating that a lower-class environment in some way hinders normal development of empathic skills.

The last hypothesis states that children with a manic-depressive parent will score higher on the ADT than children with a schizo-

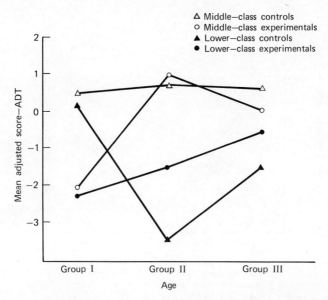

Figure 3 Comparison of means of Groups formed by combining variables of "class" and "parental health."

phrenic parent. Figure 4 plots the mean ADT scores for control children, the offspring of manic-depressive parents, and the children of schizophrenics as a function of our three age groups. The dichotomy within our experimental population, evident from this graph, seems to confirm our hypothesis that the affective environments in the two types of psychotic households produce different sequences of affective role-taking development.

We have seen that the significant contrast in means between experimental and normal children is due mainly to differences in the younger age group. However, the poor performance registered by our experimental children in Group I arises more from the scores of children with a schizophrenic parent than those of children from a manic-depressive household. The affective disorder of manic-depressives does not interfere greatly with their children's ADT performance in comparison with our normal population for Group I, whereas the children of schizophrenics score lower than controls at the .05 level (see Table 4).

During development the ability to feel as another feels rises dramatically in the children of manic-depressives, surpassing the

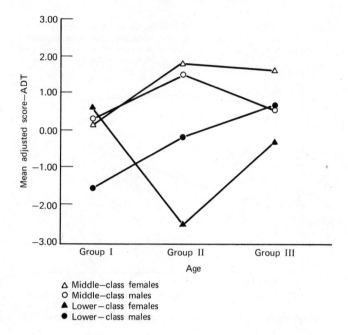

Figure 4 Comparison of mean ADT scores between children differing with respect to parental diagnosis at three age levels.

performance of controls in our two older age groups. In Group III the two sections of experimental children are so split on their levels of ADT achievement that they are significantly different at the .1 level.

Thus we see that the racial and sexual makeup of our sample is relatively unimportant in determining the empathic abilities of children. However, parental health, especially the presence of a schizophrenic in the home, remains the most important factor for ADT ability in children below 8 and is a detriment throughout development. In the middle childhood years, 8 to 10, social class accounts for the largest amount of variance.

Discussion

We had hoped that the concept of predictive empathy could tap part of the developing social behavior of the child as he moves from Piaget's preoperatory level to the concrete operations of

Table 4 Summary of *t*-Tests Comparing Means for Children
Differing in Respect to Parental Diagnosis

Diagnosis	Total Sample	Group I	Group II	Group III
Manic depressive vs. normal	−.02	−1.17	.38	1.28
Schizophrenic vs. normal	−2.23[b]	−3.11[c]	−.91	−.93
Manic depressive vs. schizophrenic	−2.27[b]	−1.00	−.96	−1.66[a]
Experimental vs. normal	−2.09[b]	−2.73[c]	−.45	−0.13

[a] $p < .1$.
[b] $p < .025$.
[c] $p < .01$.

thought. Piaget and Inhelder ([17], p. 116) distinguish two types of affective social realities present at this time in the relationships between the parent and the child and the child and his peers. The parent is foremost the transmitter of culture and specific feelings (specifically moral feelings):

Second, there are also the social relations among the children themselves, and in part between the children and the adults, but as a continuous and constructive process of reciprocal socialization and no longer simply a unilateral transmission.

We believe that the extent of the child's cognizance of this second social reality, based on the acknowledgment of the other's point of view, can be affected by his genetic and environmental milieu (especially the type of information the parent provides in the didactic type of social situation) causing differential achievement on the ADT.

In our analysis of the ADT we were primarily interested in the influence of a psychotic personality on the empathic ability of children in social exchange. However, we also found it necessary to extract the effect of various relevant variables because of our sample makeup.

Unlike Clack [7], who found young females to perform better than young males, we could find no distinctive differences at any age. Our sample was heavily loaded with Black lower-class children and White middle-class children causing class and race effects to be difficult to untangle. However, in our Group II, where

Black-White differences appeared most apparent, we were able to show that class effects could successfully account for the disparate performance of the two races. Even though there seemed to be a trend toward lower scores for Black children, we felt they were at a disadvantage because of the type of stimuli employed rendering any inference invalid.

The factors that we found to be meaningful influences on ADT performance were the presence of a psychotic parent in the home and the social class of the family. Lower-class children in our Group II scored significantly lower than middle-class children, whereas those children exposed to a sick parent were hampered on the ADT in Group I. Furthermore, within our experimental group the children of manic depressives scored no differently than did controls and dramatically split from the children of schizophrenics, performing significantly higher in Group III. Children in homes dominated by a schizophrenic parent scored far lower in the early years and were at a disadvantage throughout our age range.

The coupling of schizophrenia and lower-class status as detrimental to the normal development of social behavior coincides and lends support for Kohn's theories [13] concerning the higher incidence of schizophrenia in the disadvantaged economic groups. He believes that lower-class families transmit to their children a view of social reality consonant with their own experiences. The system passed on is conformist, limited, rigid, and supportive of feelings of being at the mercy of the world. Similarly, schizophrenia, a failure to interpret social reality, "is essentially a disorder of orientation—a severe deficit in man's ability to accurately comprehend the world about him. If one looks at it clinically, it is a caricature of precisely the outstanding features of the conformist orientation—an over-simple and rigid conception of reality, fearfulness and distrust and a lack of empathic understanding of other peoples' motives and feelings."

We believe that our study supports the idea that similar systems of social reality are passed on to the child of the schizophrenic and the child of the lower class and that it presents a severe obstacle to the development of empathic understanding.

Whereas the child of the schizophrenic appeared hampered

throughout the development from ages 6 to 12, the effect of social class was felt primarily in Group II (8 to 10 years old). Since the differences disappeared between lower class and middle class in the oldest children, their deficit in role-taking ability appears not to be the long-term deficit of the children at risk for schizophrenia.

The presence of a diagnosed manic-depressive in the home does not lower performance on the ADT in their offspring as it does when the sick parent is schizophrenic. The thought disorders in schizophrenics, characterized by rigidity, discontinuity, ambivalence, autism, and impotence thrust on the child and interfering with the normal course of social-relations development, are not present in the manic-depressive. Rather, the bipolar nature of the affective disturbance causes swings from euphoria and extreme feelings of omnipotence to extreme depression and lack of self-esteem. We feel that it is perhaps easier for the child to recognize the unreality of the sick parent's private view "and that his megalomania, or extreme self-depreciation is not guided by a realistic appraisal" [2].

To examine this proposal, we extracted a measure of sick parent involvement for each of our experimental subjects, using the Bene-Anthony Family Relations Test [1]. As can be seen from Figure 5, the amount of involvement with the sick parent increases with age for the children of schizophrenics, whereas it decreases in the children of manic depressives. Although this result is only a preliminary analysis, it suggests that the children of manic-depressives are able to remove themselves from the unreality manifested by their disturbed parent and develop normal empathic feelings to aid them in their social relations. The world of the schizophrenic, however, is more difficult for a child to shed, and its influence on him and his view of reality remains a factor throughout his social development.

Appendix

Our investigation dealt with only the second of the three decentering processes suggested by Piaget and Inhelder (16). We acknowledge that the first differentiation occurs during the sen-

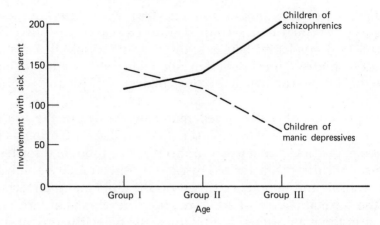

Figure 5 Comparison on involvement with sick parent between children differing with respect to parental diagnosis.

sorimotor period where the child separates the effects of his own actions from the qualities of external objects, situating his own ego in the organized field. However, we were concerned with the return of egocentric behavior due to the appearance of the symbolic function that expands the child's feelings of omnipotence to great proportions. At this time (age 5 to 6) the ego and the points of view of others are fused, and only when the child reaches the stage of concrete operations (7 to 8) is he able to structure relationships that enable skills to develop in interindividual relations, that is, social cooperation.

The structuring of formal thought in adolescence again forces the reappearance of the centered perspective. Where egocentrism in the infant is manifested as the inability to see oneself as separate in a field and in the preoperational period as the nondifferentiation of another's viewpoint from oneself, the adolescent egocentrism stems from the adoption of adult roles and the failure to distinguish his goals and the realities of society.

Even though the tasks of decentration vary during childhood, Piaget ([18], p. 345) emphasizes that "Essentially, the process, which at any one of the developmental stages moves from egocentrism toward decentering, constantly subjects increases in knowledge to a refocussing of perspective."

References

1. Anthony, E. J. An experimental approach to the psychopathology of child-hood autism. *Brit. J. Med. Psychol.*, 32 (1956), 19–37.
2. Anthony, E. J. The influence of manic depressive environment on the developing child. In *Depression and the Human Existence*, E. J. Anthony and T. Benedek, Eds. Little Brown, Boston, 1975.
3. Borke, H. Interpersonal perception of young children. *Devel. Psychol.*, 5 (1971), 263–269.
4. Cass, L. K., Franklin, L., and Bass, L. Psychological disturbance in children of psychotic parents as compared to the children of non-psychotic parents. Currently under editorial review.
5. Chandler, M. J. The picture Arrangement subset of the WAIS as an index of social egocentrism: A comparative study of normal and emotionally disturbed children. Unpublished manuscript.
6. Chander, M. J. and Greenspan, S. Ersatz egocentrism: A reply to H. Borke. *Developmental Psychology*, (1971).
7. Clack, G. S. Effects of social class, age and sex on tests of perception, affect discrimination and deferred gratification in children. Unpublished doctoral dissertation, Washington University, 1970.
8. Darwin, C. *The Expression of Emotion in Man and Animals*, Appleton, New York, 1873.
9. Gage, N. L. and Cronbach, L. J. Conceptual and Methodological Problems in Interpersonal Perception. *Psych. Review*, Vol. 62, 1955, pp. 411–421.
10. Gilbert, D. C. The young child's awareness of affect. *Child Devel.*, 40 (1969), 629–640.
11. Izard, C. E. *The Face of Emotion*. Appleton-Century-Crofts, New York, 1971.
12. Karp, S. A. and Konstadt, N. L. *Manual for the Children's Embedded Figures Test*. Cognitive Tests, Brooklyn, New York, 1963.
13. Kohn, M. L. *Class and Conformity: A Study in Values*. The Dorsey Press, Homewood, Ill., 1969, pp. 199–200.
14. Kohn, M. L. Class, family and schizophrenia: A reformulation. *Social Forces*, 50 (1972), 295–313.
15. Piaget, J. and Inhelder, B. *The Child's Conception of Space*. Routledge and Kegan Paul, London, 1956.
16. Piaget, J. and Inhelder, B. *The Growth of Logical Thinking from Childhood to Adolescence*. Basic Books, New York, 1958.
17. Piaget, J. and Inhelder, B. *The Psychology of the Child*. Basic Books, New York, 1969.

VULNERABILITY AND THE
DISADVANTAGEOUS ENVIRONMENT

Behavior Problems in Infant School Children in Deprived Areas

Maurice Chazan, Ph.D. and Susan Threlfall, M.A. (U.K.)

Between 1968 and 1972 the Schools Council Research and Development Project in Compensatory Education, based at the University College of Swansea, was engaged on a number of enquiries involving infant school children in several areas of England and Wales. The main aims of the project were, briefly: (1) to provide screening techniques to enable children in need of compensatory education to be identified on entry to school, (2) to make longitudinal studies of infant school children in "deprived" areas, and (3) to produce language materials that may be used to help deprived children at the infant school stage (for an outline of the scope of the project, see Williams [10]). As part of the work carried out in connection with the second of these three aims, information was gathered about the prevalence of behavior problems in a number of infant schools serving the catchment areas differing widely in socioeconomic level, mainly to ascertain whether schools in "deprived" areas faced greater problems in connection with emotional and behavior disturbance than those in areas where there was little or no evidence of deprivation. In addition to the general survey approach, an intensive study was made of those children in the "deprived" area schools who presented relatively severe behavior problems in class in their first year at school, in order to discover which home background factors were associated with poor adjustment in these children, what progress they made in the infant school, and to what extent behavior problems persisted throughout the 3 years of the infant school. The views of both parents and teachers were also sought on ways of dealing with behavior problems in infant school children. This paper summarizes the findings of the project on these questions and makes some practical suggestions for helping poorly adjusted children in the infant school. A full account of the studies is found in Chazan and Jackson, [3, 4] and in Chazan, Jackson, et al. [2].

Prevalence

The general survey sample initially consisted of 725 children (335 "deprived", 309 "control," and 61 rural) attending 26 urban and 11 rural infant schools. The urban sample was taken from London and two local education authorities in Wales, and the rural sample came from one county in Wales. In the urban areas the local education authorities selected 14 schools serving catchment areas that could be described as "deprived" and 12 schools serving predominantly "middle-class" and "settled working-class" areas. In the rural area, where this kind of division was not applicable, a representative sample of 11 schools was selected.

The "deprived" areas in each of the four boroughs consisted not only of conglomerations of old, dilapidated, and usually overcrowded houses, but also of council house estates, early and more recent, where various demographic data, including family size and the percentage of the population in the lower occupational classes, indicated at least relative deprivation. The "control" areas were almost entirely residential, and their population statistics showed a higher proportion of professional or "white-collar" occupations, more owner-occupiers, and smaller families. Ratable values of private dwellings in these areas were also higher (considerably so in some cases). The rural area (RA) chosen was a relatively small Welsh county, mainly agricultural and with only a small amount of light industry. The nearest sizable town was over 40 miles from some of the homes. Although four of the 11 schools were situated in an urban district, all of them served a scattered community with some isolated farms up to 8 miles or more from the school. Public transport services were minimal, and the few towns within the county were fairly small; the population of the whole county was less than 20,000.

Data on aspects of the emotional and social development of the whole sample were obtained at intervals throughout the period of 3 years during which the children attended the infant school. In particular, information relating to the prevalence and nature of behavior problems was provided by the class teachers toward the end of the first and final years of infant schooling. In addition to making an overall rating of the child's level of adjustment, based on that used by Schaefer as part of a Classroom Behavior Inventory that he developed in the United States (unpublished to date), the teachers completed Stott's six adjustment pointers [9]. Without undue trouble to the teacher, these pointers enable a general picture to be obtained of the number of children in a given school or class whose response gives some cause for concern. The head teachers and class teachers were also asked about the problems they faced in dealing with emotional or behavioral difficulties shown by their pupils.

In the first year, according to the class teachers, as much as 24 percent of the total sample, aged 5 years to 5 years, 7 months, showed *some* indication of behavior deviating from the desirable norm, and approximately 13 to 14 percent appeared to be presenting problems to an extent warranting attention, although only about 1 percent were considered to need specialist help. Withdrawal and restlessness were the most common problems in the total sample, the boys presenting considerably more problems than the girls, particularly in respect of restlessness and aggressiveness. Similar results were obtained in the third-year survey, which involved 602 children (279 "deprived," 265 "control," and 58 rural).

On both occasions, approximately 27 percent of the "deprived" area children scored at least one adverse Stott pointer, and 16 percent were rated as "somewhat" or "very" disturbed. In the first year there was very little difference in the prevalence of behavior problems between the DA ("deprived" area) and the SWC (small Welsh community) children, but significantly more of the DA group presented problems than did the middle-class sample (of whom 16 percent scored 1+ Stott pointers, and 6 percent were rated as "somewhat" or "very" disturbed). The DA children tended to display more aggressiveness and unsociability than the other children, and it was with problems arising from restlessness and aggressiveness that the DA schools stated they were particularly concerned. However, at this stage the differences in behavior between the DA and other groups were not as great as might have been expected. There was a tendency, though not a very marked one, for the gap between the DA children and the "control" area (CA) group (as a whole) to widen over the infant school period, in that the DA children were rated as displaying more extreme behavior than the CA children to a greater extent on the second occasion than the first. This seemed to reflect the tendency of the SWC group to be showing fewer gross behavior problems at 7+ than at 5+, as, surprisingly, the gap between the DA and middle-class children was not as wide in the second survey as in the first. Although few significant differences emerged on either occasion between the urban and rural samples, there was a widening of the gap on most items between these groups also, with the rural sample having few children with really severe problems.

All the head teachers (14 DA, 12 CA, and 10 RA) and class teachers (19 DA, 18 CA, and 11 RA) attached great importance to the development of emotional and social maturity in their pupils, placing this above other educational aims such as the development of language skills or creativity, or scholastic progress. The estimates given by the head teachers of the prevalence of children in their schools presenting emotional, social, or behavioral problems, either mild or serious, varied widely, ranging from 0 to 30 percent in the case of mild problems and from 0 to 18 percent in the case of more serious difficulties. These estimates suggested, to a rather greater extent than the schedules completed by the class teachers, that the DA schools faced more serious problems relating to behavior disturbance than did the CA or RA schools.

The teachers in the different areas, asked to rank six types of problem behavior in order of frequency of occurrence in their classes, all placed *restlessness* first, but whereas urban teachers ranked *aggressiveness* next, rural teachers felt that *shyness/withdrawal* was second in frequency, and DA teachers placed *dis-*

ruptive and *unruly* behavior higher than *nervousness* (e.g., timidity, tearfulness), which came at the bottom of their list. The DA and RA teacher heads largely confirmed the ratings of the teachers in their schools, although the CA heads considered that *nervousness* rather than *restlessness* or *aggressiveness* was a particularly common problem.

Both the head teachers and the class teachers found most difficulty in coping with restlessness, aggressiveness, and antisocial behavior (e.g., lying, stealing, destructiveness). It would seem, therefore, that not only did the DA class teachers have a somewhat higher incidence of behavior problems than did the other groups, but the types of behavior that occurred most frequently were the ones generally found most difficult to deal with.

Adjustment and Home Background

Home background factors associated with poor adjustment in the infant school were examined, mainly through an intensive study of 39 "poorly adjusted" (PA) children (22 boys, 17 girls) selected from the total initial sample of children living in "deprived" urban areas on the basis of their showing the most behavior problems according to the Stott and Schaefer ratings. These children were compared with a control group of 42 "well-adjusted" (WA) children (24 boys, 18 girls), chosen from the same schools, who presented the fewest behavior problems in the DA sample. The age, sex, and social-class distribution of the two groups (PA and WA) was similar. Completion of the Rutter Behavior Scales [6, 7] by both teachers and parents confirmed that there was a highly significant difference in adjustment between the two groups at home as well as at school, even though the parents' and teachers' ratings showed considerable differences for many individuals.

Information on the children's early development and home background, as well as on the parents' use of services, was obtained through three home visits. In most cases it was the mother who was interviewed as the level of cooperation and interest in the project was high. All the WA group had both parents at home, whereas five PA children had only one parent.

Few differences between the groups emerged in respect to their early development. Slightly more of the PA group had been "unwanted" or at least unplanned babies, and significantly more fathers in this group had been away from home for long periods. More of the PA children had speech difficulties, but the health problems of the two groups were similar. The PA children were more often unwilling to go to school.

Each home was rated on a 4-point scale on 10 items, five relating mainly to material deprivation, and five mainly of a cultural nature. Material factors rated were income, cleanliness of the home, housing conditions, play space, and the mother's care of the child. Cultural factors covered the mother's education, social class (based on father's occupation), provision of play materials and books, use of external stimuli, and level of parental interest in the child's education. The comparison between the PA and WA groups showed that the PA children had a significantly more deprived background, both materially and culturally. The mothers of the poorly adjusted children had to manage on lower incomes, tended to be in poorer physical health, and coped less well with looking after the home. They had had more restricted educational opportunities themselves and thus showed less interest in their children's school progress. The PA children were less well provided with books and toys as well as play space within the home. Their parents read to them less, and although every family had a television set, the PA children watched with less discrimination. The PA group, too, was less often taken on outings to such places as the park, cinema, or zoo, and their parents had fewer interests or hobbies in which they could participate. There were thus fewer opportunities in the homes of the PA group for the children to keep themselves "out of mischief" and to be stimulated intellectually.

As would be expected, the PA children were more demanding at home than were the WA children, and the parents were more indulgent and more likely to give in to the children "for the sake of peace." No significant differences were recorded between the groups in the methods of rewards and punishment used by the parents. The majority of parents used smacking at least occasionally, and "being sent to bed" was another commonly employed punishment or threat. Few of the parents in either group seemed to feel any responsibility for the child's behavior or to realize that this might in some way be related to their own mood or actions. Rather more than half of the parents from each group promised their children a reward for good behavior or helpfulness or gave the child an unexpected reward after good behavior. The PA parents, however, were less consistent in their handling of their children.

In summary, the PA parents provided a much less secure, happy, and settled home background for their children. While only six of the WA group came from homes that seemed not to be completely secure, well over half of the PA group came from homes rated as insecure in respect to both financial factors and the relationship between the parents. The PA mother, too, tended to be less emotionally stable.

Adjustment and School Progress

On entry to the infant school the WA children were rated by their teachers as significantly ahead of the PA children in skills such as writing one's name or drawing simple objects. Later schedules showed a marked difference in favor of the WA group on many items relating to school achievement, such as prereading and reading skills, number skills, creative work, and patterns of speech. This wide gap in attainments was consistently shown by the schedules throughout the 3 years of infant schooling and was confirmed by the scores on the final test battery (Table 1). The results of the standardized tests given in the third year revealed highly significant differences in mean scores between the groups in tests of reading, spelling, vocabulary, and mathematics. The PA children were a year or more behind the WA group in all these aspects of school attainment, and many of them had made very little progress at the time of testing.

Although the differences in the school progress of the two groups were very marked—and it is of interest to note how well the WA children, all living in deprived areas, were doing—it is difficult to know to what extent they can be attributed to differences in adjustment. There is a complex interaction between attainment, adjustment, and general ability (or intelligence), which factor, as measured by standardized tests, is an important one in school success, particularly in primary school. Children of low

Table 1 Comparison of PA and WA Group Scores on Final Test Battery

Group	N	Mean Age	Burt Word Recog.	Neale Accuracy	Neale Rate	Neale Comp.	WISC Vocab.	Daniels-Diack Spelling	NFER Basic Maths (Maths Score)	NFER Picture Intell. A (Standardized Score)
				Mean Attainment Ages (Years, Months)						
Poorly adjusted	36	7, 6	5, 4	6, 9	7, 2	6, 8	5, 10	5, 10	15	91
Well adjusted	41	7, 6	7, 8	8, 2	8, 1	8, 2	7, 6	7, 2	25	103
General survey sample	542	7, 6	7, 4	7, 11	7, 11	7, 6	7, 6	7, 0	21	100
Deprived area sample	277	7, 6	6, 7	7, 6	7, 9	7, 3	6. 10	6. 5	19	97

Note: all differences between the mean scores of the PA and WA groups are significant at the 0.1-percent level or beyond.

intelligence may, *as a result of their difficulties with school work*, become restless, aggressive, or withdrawn in class. It is relevant to ask, therefore, to what extent differences in intelligence in the two groups played a part. The PA group did, in fact, have somewhat lower scores than the WA children on the Raven's Colored Progressive Matrices test and the NFER Picture Test "A," both of which may be regarded as nonverbal measures of intelligence. However, the mean scores of the PA group in these tests were within the average range, and statistical procedures adopted to control for intelligence indicated that the differences in the school performance of the WA and PA groups could not be attributed wholly to differences in general ability. Even on the basis of the scores actually obtained on the nonverbal intelligence tests, it seemed that the PA children were underfunctioning to a considerable extent. Furthermore, it must be borne in mind that in the case of PA children, scores on intelligence tests tend not to give a true reflection of potential, since these children may not adapt easily to the test situation. Therefore, although the findings of this study concerning the school progress of the two groups need be interpreted with caution, they suggest that children showing marked behavior problems in their first year at school, even if they are of normal ability, are likely to be at risk of continued school failure.

Persistence of Behavior Problems

Behavior problems in young children may well be transient, and poor adjustment is not necessarily a long-lasting handicap. It was of interest to ascertain to what extent the initial ratings of children presenting relatively severe problems were confirmed in their final year at infant school, and also whether those children whose problems did persist throughout the 3 years differed in any way from those whose problems appeared to have been resolved by the time they reached the end of their infant school career.

In the total survey sample, when the persistence and development of poor adjustment was looked at in individual cases, it was found that although a number of children improved in adjustment over the period, as many as 34 out of 80 children (42.5 percent) who were rated as "poorly adjusted" at 5+ on fairly strict criteria and remained in the sample throughout still presented behavior problems at 7+ years. In the intensive study, of the 36 children in the PA group rated again in their last year, 17 remained "poorly adjusted" on the original criteria (3+ adverse Stott pointers *or* a Schaefer rating of "very" or "somewhat" disturbed); 40 out of the 42 "well-adjusted" children were again rated in this category. Thus while the WA children remained a stable group, some of the PA children seemed to have resolved their problems by the third year.

The "persistent" members of the PA group had exhibited a greater number of problems or more severe difficulties at the earlier stage than had those children who improved in adjustment. The main differences in the background of the "persistent" and "nonpersistent" members of the PA group were on variables most directly related to school activities (e.g., use and provision of play materials and books, extent to which parents read to or played with the child, whether parents encouraged curiosity, and degree of contact between home and school). Those items relating to the more material factors in the home and, surprisingly, those reflecting its emotional atmosphere showed only small differences between the groups. These findings confirm that a lack of parental encouragement and a paucity of intellectual stimulation at home make it particularly difficult for a child to come to terms with the demands of school life.

Use of Services

THE SCHOOL

The general survey showed that, when asked to rate their pupils systematically, teachers identified a considerable number as presenting behavior problems. Yet as many as 80 percent of the class teachers stated either that they did not need any help in dealing with these problems or that they were satisfied with the assistance already available. In most cases they felt that problem behavior could be dealt with internally, sometimes in consultation with colleagues or parents. Although some would welcome advice on coping with problem behavior from outside agencies concerned with child welfare, referral to such agencies (e.g., the school psychological service) tended to be seen as a last resort.

Only two children in the PA group were said to have received help from a child guidance clinic.

Some of the head teachers saw the need for more efficient liaison with existing services and more help from the social services, but on the whole the head teachers confirmed the view of the teachers that they would prefer to cope with behavior problems by means of internal school resources, including aides and extra teachers, rather than by enlisting outside help. Although the rural schools in particular felt the lack of an educational psychologist on whom they could call if necessary, over a third of the heads were quite satisfied with the help available to them, which included the child guidance service, school medical officer, welfare officer, school nurse, and social services.

Despite the reluctance on the part of the school to seek expert help for children with behavior problems, it cannot be said that the teachers felt that the problem behavior that they observed in the child's early years was likely to be resolved easily. In the third year, 19 "poorly adjusted" children were assessed as "almost certain to face difficulties in the junior school" because of behavioral and other difficulties.

THE PARENTS

Although many of the parents, particularly in the PA group, reported behavior problems of various kinds at home, few were really worried about the behavior or development of their children. Many parents, however, seemed to be very uncertain about what behavior problems or habits were "normal" at this age and frequently sought reassurance from the interviewer about this. About half of the total sample of parents, too, were rated as rather less than confident about the way they handled questions of discipline or problem behavior. Many asked the interviewer about various methods concerned with bringing up children and expressed doubt as to whether they as parents were doing "the right thing." Yet few parents had actually sought or received any help or advice on bringing up their children and, when specifically asked, only seven parents (three PA and four WA) felt that any extra advice on handling children was necessary. Many of the families had little or no knowledge of the sources of help available in a crisis; for example, 26 PA and 21 WA parents were not aware of the service provided by child guidance clinics.

Implications For Action

The inquiries undertaken by the project were not designed to discover or evaluate any procedures to alleviate problems of behavior at the infant school stage. However, the information obtained from these investigations, which emphasize that a wide variety of attitudes and practices is to be found within the "working class", may serve as a basis for making suggestions about the kinds of action needed to help infant school children with problems of adjustment. Apart from measures designed to deal with behavior difficulties when they occur in the classroom, the association between poor adjustment and deprivation found in the project's inquiries suggests that helping children from deprived backgrounds to make an easy transition from home to the school setting will help to reduce the incidence of behavior difficulties. The discussion here considers how both parents and school may be given help and support, with particular reference to the role of the psychological services.

PARENTS

Home-background factors have been shown to be related to the child's initial adjustment to school. It is relevant to ask, therefore, how parents can be helped to provide an environment that will prepare the child socially and emotionally for life at school. Undoubtedly, there are many parents who already provide their children with an appropriate environment, and in addition there are many who, though they may not provide what educationalists or psychologists would regard as the "ideal" setting for the child's fullest development, are quite unaware of any need for help. The number of parents who actively seek help or feel an unmet need for help is surprisingly small. Two main approaches seem desirable here. One is to provide, more systematically than at present, "education for parenthood," beginning on a formal basis in the secondary school and continuing to be available in the adult years. The other is to make access to the various helping agencies easier and more rewarding.

Education for parenthood starts early in the child's life, when he observes his own parents' actions, and the way in which the child (and later the adolescent) is handled by his parents is probably the most important factor in his preparation for being a parent himself. However, the secondary school can contribute to this preparation by encouraging discussions, for example, about adolescence and issues worrying adolescents. Older secondary-school pupils can benefit from a practical study of the child and his development, such as by visiting nurseries, play groups, and nursery schools. Courses on child rearing organized in colleges of further education or university extramural departments are valuable, as are classes and discussions arranged at pre- and postnatal clinics. Psychologists and psychiatrists can contribute to this work by taking the initiative in organizing experimental courses, giving talks and leading discussions, acting as consultants, and helping to train group leaders.

Although considerable progress has been made in providing help and guidance for parents in bringing up their children, much more remains to be done, not the least in making existing services more effective. Apart from the provisions for financial assistance and free school meals, the functions of the various auxiliary services are not widely or accurately known by parents in deprived areas. Services such as child guidance or speech therapy are not known to many parents, not even to some of those who have experienced a definite need for help. It is important, therefore, that the local authority should by all possible means ensure that the facilities available to families in need are widely known, and it is also desirable that parents should not be made to feel embarrassment or undue frustration when seeking help from the social, medical, or psychological services. In addition to the diagnostic and treatment services provided by child guidance clinics for the more serious problems of adjustment referred to them, there is a need for a comprehensive counseling service for parents, with the emphasis on preventing developmental difficulties and enabling parents to understand how they can support their children's efforts in school. It would be appropriate that a counseling service of this kind have very close links with nursery and infant schools. This would help to bridge the gap between home and school, which contributes to the poor adjustment of some children in deprived areas. Children may present problems in school without the parents being aware of any difficulties or at home without the teachers knowing, and regular discussions between parents and teachers—sometimes together with a psychologist or psychiatrist—will bring to both a better understanding of a child's development.

THE SCHOOL

The inquiries conducted by the project have shown that, with systematic screening procedures, even of a simple kind, teachers can identify infant school children at risk of both maladjustment and school failure. Although it is important that the significance of behavior problems at this stage should not be exaggerated and that infant school children should not be "labeled" in any rigid way, the fact that a number of children not only remain poorly adjusted throughout the 3 years of infant school but are also at risk of continued learning difficulties suggests that more attention should be given to their problems. To this end, teachers need more guidance in recognizing signs of poor adjustment, dealing with behavior problems in the classroom, and knowing when to request outside help.

It has been shown that teachers frequently regard calling on external agencies as a "last resort." This is probably in part because they wish to deal with the problems of their pupils themselves and do not want to acknowledge an inability to cope with these, but also because the outside agencies are often viewed as somewhat remote from the school. For example, the British Social Services Department, which is administered separately from the local education authority, may not have close links with the schools, and the school psychological service may be able to devote only a very limited amount of time to infant schools. If they are to be effective the auxiliary agencies must be seen by the schools to be real partners. They must also be prepared to work within the school as well as outside it. With the development of the school psychological service in Britain, there has indeed been a tendency for the psychologist to make his base in the school rather than in the office or clinic; but, as previously stated, because of pressures from junior and secondary schools, few educational psychologists are able to devote much time to infant schools. At present with the reorganization of the health services in Britain, there are indications that child guidance clinics will strengthen their links with other community services. Useful models of comprehensive and community-centered approaches to prevention and treatment of developmental difficulties have been provided by projects in the United States during recent years, for example, in South Carolina [5] and Woodlawn, Chicago [8].

Within the classroom, infant school teachers are usually well aware of the desirability of giving more individual attention to children with problems, but large classes make this difficult. Apart from a reduction in the size of classes, particularly necessary in schools in deprived areas, additional paraprofessional staff such as teachers' aides considerably help here.

Some children will need rather more attention than can be given by the class teacher, even with an assistant to help her. Although some teachers may not welcome even specialist aid within the classroom, the availability of peripatetic teachers specifically trained in dealing with problem children may help to reduce pressures when a class contains a number of difficult children. Several local education authorities in Britain have begun experiments in providing teachers of this kind, as well as in establishing special classes or nursery-type units for children who do not fit into infant school life. The Inner London Education Authority, for example, has set up "nurture groups" designed for very immature children, particularly in inner city schools. These groups are run on a semidomestic basis, and the principles of care are those of the mother with her young child, though with the aim of orienting the children toward a return to normal school life [1]. Experiments of this kind, which aim at providing help for children with difficulties yet are firmly based in the ordinary school, merit wide replication.

Conclusion

The problems of poor adjustment at the infant school stage should not be exaggerated. Children are very adaptable and the majority, coming from all kinds of home background, enjoy and benefit from their infant schooling, even if the process of adjustment takes a little time. Nevertheless, a not negligible minority of children, especially those from disadvantaged homes, fail to adjust to the infant school. We need to know much more about how to help this group. It would be valuable to observe the effects of early screening procedures used in the infant school, followed by guidance to both teachers and parents of children identified as "at risk." We also need to increase our knowledge, about the effects of different approaches on children with different kinds of behavior problems. However, it is suggested here that a great deal can be done, through the collaboration of home, school, and the auxiliary agencies, to prevent serious problems of emotional and social adjustment from developing at the infant school stage, or at least to minimize their effects.

References

1. Boxall, M. Nuture Groups. *Concern (National Children's Bureau)*, 12 (1973), 8–12.
2. Chazan, M., Cox, T., Jackson, S., and Laing, A. F. *Studies of Infant School Children. II—Deprivation and Development*. Basil Blackwell (for Schools Council), Oxford, in press.
3. Chazan, M. and Jackson, S. Behaviour problems in the infant school. *J. Child Psychol. Psychiat.*, 12 (1971), 191–210.
4. Chazan, M. and Jackson, S. Behaviour problems in the infant school: changes over two years. *J. Child Psychol. Psychiat.*, 15 (1974), 33–46.
5. Newton, M. R. and Brown, R. D. A Preventive Approach to Developmental Problems in School Children. In *Behavioral Science Frontiers in Education*, E. M. Bower, and W. G. Hollister, Eds. Wiley, New York, 1967, Chapter 21.
6. Rutter, M. A children's behaviour questionnaire for completion by teachers: preliminary findings. *J. Child Psychol. Psychiat.*, 8 (1967), 1–11.
7. Rutter, M., Tizard, J., and Whitmore, K. *Education, Health and Behaviour*. Longmans, London, 1970.
8. Schiff, S. K. and Kellam, S. G. A community-wide mental health program of prevention and early treatment in first grade. *Psychiatric Research Report* No. 21, American Psychiatric Association, April 1967, 92–102.
9. Stott, D. H. *The Social Adjustment of Children* (Manual to the Bristol Social Adjustment Guides, 3rd edition). Univ. London Press, London, 1966.
10. Williams, P. The Schools Council Research and Development Project in Compensatory Education. In *Compensatory Education*, M. Chazan, Ed., Butterworths, London, 1973.

Discontinuity between Home and School as a Hazard in Child Development

Discontinuity between Home and School as a Hazard in Child Development

Betty H. Watts, Ph.D. (U.S.A.)

Before we can examine the need for continuity between home and school, we should reach some agreement on the purposes and goals of the education programs we develop and offer to young people. I would suggest that a working statement of these goals might be something like the following. Schools aim through their personnel and program to help children develop in an optimal fashion to enable them to achieve greater happiness, satisfaction, success, self-realization, sense of purpose, and enjoyment of learning during the years of their childhood and adolescence and to develop their imaginations and joy in living and so that they might develop a concern and appreciation of others and a concern for social justice. We would hope further that they might also, on leaving school, find a meaningful and secure place in the wider community and make appropriate contributions to the well-being and development of that community.

If we take this view of education and its goals, then obviously education is not a matter for the school alone. The school and home must work cooperatively together if these goals are to be achieved. Indeed, Havighurst [1] has written of an implicit contract between home and school:

> The parents contract to prepare their child for school entrance both cognitively and affectively. They further contract to keep him in school and to make

399

home conditions appropriate for his success in school. The school contracts to receive the child, teach him as well as it can, taking account of his strengths and weaknesses and the ways in which he can learn most successfully. Very little of this contract is put into legal codes but the education of the child is successful only when both parties carry out their obligations fully.

The home has an undoubted influence on the way in which children respond to the school environment and the degree of success they achieve in this new setting. Several studies [2,] have shown that the home is, in fact, more important than the school in determining how well children do at school.

We must ask why this is so. A partial answer lies in the cumulative nature of child development. Children base later learnings on earlier learnings. As a result of their home experiences, they bring to school certain concepts, skills, and knowledge, and these are the bases on which they respond to what the school has to offer. They also bring to school, as a result of their home experiences, certain orientations, expectations, and attitudes; these help determine how they will perceive the school and hence the influence the school will have on their further development. Also as a result of home and community experiences (both before school entrance and during out-of-school hours) they have developed certain values, certain behaviors; certain rewards and sanctions have become meaningful to them and others have no significance for them.

As a result of these experiences, then, children are ready to respond differentially to what the school has to offer and will consequently profit differentially from these offerings. The home has provided the first major teaching for the child and will throughout his life, at least the early years of his life, inevitably continue to act as an educator.

Adams [6] and colleagues, in a discussion of community development and teacher education, cite a story that they believe to be probably apochryphal, which reports a small child saying to its parent, "If you and the teacher are both trying to bring me up, isn't it about time you got together?"

This small child shows a recognition of the complementary roles of home and school; he sees the need for a partnership. Are the adults in his world—his parents and teachers—equally insightful? We must plan for a fruitful partnership between teachers and parents, with each showing a respectful recognition of the other's contribution. We need to examine in some detail the particular roles of parents and the particular roles of teachers; we need to determine where these overlap and where they differ. If there is to be a fruitful partnership, a further need must be satisfied; teachers must understand the expectations that parents have of schools and parents must know what expectations teachers hold of them.

What are the specific contributions that the home makes to the educational development of children once they are at school? (They have, of course, almost complete responsibility for the early learning and cognitive development of their children.) I would suggest that these include the following:

1. They provide the major emotional climate in which children grow and develop. Parents are normally more significant in the child's eyes than are his teachers, and it is his parents' values, attitudes, and beliefs that he is likely to incorporate. Because of the child's personal attachment to his parents, the learning situation in the home is a highly emotional one.

2. Because of this climate, the parents are a major force in helping to determine the young child's goals. The goals he adopts shape his behavior in and out of the classroom.

3. The parents provide an individual learning situation for the child, almost a tutorial setting. They can offer almost instant feedback to him in his learning endeavors; they can manipulate experiences and explanations to suit the individual child.

4. They provide a great variety of learning experiences for the young child—in the home, via the mass media, and through the whole range of activities conducted by the family outside the home.

5. They have an intimate knowledge of the child within the home setting because of the many opportunities provided for observation. Thus they know him as a person—his likes and dislikes, his reactions, the things that prove attractive to him, the rewards that are perceived by him as rewarding, and the ways of learning he prefers. This knowledge is to some degree necessarily subjective.

6. They know how the child reacts to the school program and

school events and can help him in a one-to-one situation to examine and profit from these reactions.

7. They can provide a setting, which the school cannot, for the child's application of his school learnings to his out-of-school life.

What are the specific contributions which the teachers bring to the child's learning?

1. In a sense, they view the child from a much wider vantage point than can the home. They see the child within the context of his age group, and they see him also in settings where in some ways he is more free to be himself than is the case in the home.
2. They are able to make a more objective appraisal of the child, and his strengths and weaknesses than can the home.
3. The teachers, of course, bring to the situation professional pedagogical skills, insights, and knowledges that they can use to tempt the child to make steady progress toward the objectives of the educational program.
4. Teachers also offer themselves as adults other than parents as role models for the children.

It would then seem obvious that if the child is to profit from both groups of teaching adults, there is an urgent need for communication between the home and the school and a marked degree of continuity between school and out-of-school experiences. Dottrens [5] has argued that "It is not the school which is the center of the child's life, but his family, his friends, his house, his street, his village and the relationships which all this implies. Any educational system or curriculum which cuts the child off from the sources of his experiences and emotions stands self-condemned."

I think, in many ways, because of the lack of communication between school and home and because of the failure of the school to recognize and value the specific contribution of the home, we have cut many children off from the sources of their experiences and emotions. In the beginning when schools were planned, the view of learning that prevailed and the educational objectives that were held led to the creation of buildings. The children's learning experiences were planned to occur within the four walls of the school. At the same time fences were erected around the school and over time the effect was gradually to hedge the school off from the community it served and to see education as the school's business and as a process that occurred within the school complex. Gradually there developed, among some teachers at least, a view that they were the experts and that they alone could and should provide the learning settings for the children. Education was the school's business.

This has perhaps had minimum adverse effects on some young children, but the adverse effects on many children have been extreme. I am thinking here of the children whom today we describe as "culturally different." These are the children from homes and subcommunities whose values and styles of life differ in some ways from the values of the school, which is essentially a mainstream culture institution. It is to the situation of these children that the remainder of this chapter is addressed.

Obviously there are some areas of overlap between home and school for most children; there is probably rarely complete overlap, even in the case of mainstream middle-class children. For these latter the situation might be seen as:

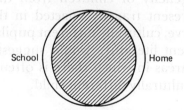

For many culturally different children the area of overlap is much slighter:

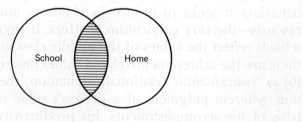

Although the magnitude of the overlap is of importance, the most significant issue is the content of the areas where there is no overlap. Some incongruities between the home and school experiences of the child are probably of little import; all children can (and need to) tolerate a degree of dissonance, a degree of conflict. But there are some areas of the child's life situation where dissonance between home and school experiences has a major debilitating effect on his educational and personal development and fulfillment.

The existence of differences between culturally different groups must be emphasized. Some writers on the contemporary scene display a tendency to see all ethnic minorities as essentially similar; this is particularly noticeable when most of these groups are economically or culturally or socially disadvantaged. The disadvantage is overgeneralized and the uniqueness of subcultural profiles is forgotten. Thus poor Blacks, poor American Indians, poor Puerto Ricans, poor Mexican Americans, and poor Australian Aboriginals are discussed in some of the literature as if their ethnic membership were of little import. Equally important are the differences within groups. Differences within any one group are vast, and failure, particularly by the school, to recognize (and value) the heterogeneity of children from the one subculture exacerbates the present tragedy enacted in the schools, which serve, or should serve, culturally different pupils.

A survey of recent literature would suggest the following as highly significant areas in which there is often home/school discontinuity for the culturally different child.

Values

The values of the school determine its goals, its priorities, the behaviors it seeks to induce in children, and the behaviors it rewards—the very curriculum it offers. It would seem that most schools reflect the values of the middle-class mainstream culture; these are the achievement-related values described by Kluckhohn [6] as "*individualistic* relational orientation; the *achieving* orientation, wherein judgment of a person's value is primarily on the basis of his accomplishments, his productivity; the *man-against-*

nature, or rational-mastery orientation; and the definition of human nature as evil but perfectible."

Many cultural minorities, however, reveal a different profile of values; for some, group goals have primacy over individual goals. In some communities, a person is judged in terms of what he is rather than what he has achieved. These are the affiliative rather than the achievement subcultures, and members of these groups interact with their children in the light of their value systems.

Child-rearing values vary, too, by sub-culture and social class. Kohn's studies [7–10], for example, have shown working-class parents to value obedience, neatness, and cleanliness, whereas middle-class parents ascribe greater importance to characteristics such as curiosity, happiness, consideration, and self-control. His and other data suggest also a social-class difference in respect to the valuing of self-direction and conformity to external authority; discontinuity between school and home with regard to these values has strong implications for the minority child's feelings of security.

Do home and school place equal value on success? Certainly the school wishes pupils to succeed academically. My own experience with cultural minority groups in Australia suggests a vast majority of parents want their children to succeed. It may be that success is desired as a means to the end of a better job, "a better life than I had", but success is a goal.

Motives

Ausubel [11] suggested that achievement motivation in school settings has three components: (1) a cognitive drive that is task-oriented (the need to know), (2) an ego-enhancing component concerned with achievement as a source of primary or earned status, and (3) an affiliative component, oriented toward achievement as a way of ensuring continued status. He pointed out that varying proportions of these components are normally represented in achievement-motivation, depending on a number of variables, including culture and ethnic origin. Many schools emphasize components (1) and (2). These motives are not, however, strongly characteristic of a significant proportion of some minority groups; in their case it is often the need for affiliation, which is the regnant motive. If the school makes no attempt to engage this affiliative motive at least initially in the service of classroom learning, many youngsters fail to find sources of satisfaction in the classroom and the discontinuities between their in-school and out-of-school lives are heightened.

Rewards

Rewards and reinforcements for learning are an accepted element of most teaching strategies. The critical question, in relation to the motivation of minority children is, "What rewards are attractive to them?"

Verbal praise is viewed by many teachers as a reward. Gallimore, MacDonald, et al. [12] show that this is not always true, at least for one minority group:

Among Hawaiian youngsters, however, many the social-influence techniques which are verbal in nature are ineffective since children seem largely indifferent and inattentive to adult talk, unless it is deliberately entertaining, or directed at them individually. They do not know what to make of verbal praise; it is at best meaningless to them. Protestations of affection, or the withdrawal of affection, are not understood.

Havighurst [13] argues strongly the need for teachers to recognize that reward-punishment systems are rooted in particular cultures and learned by the children as they are socialized:

Human learning is influenced by a variety of rewards, which are themselves arranged in a culturally based reward-punishment system which is learned.

This requires us to examine the nature of rewards. We cannot simply assume that "a reward is a reward and that is it," as we might be tempted to do if we were studying the learning behaviour of cats, or pigeons, or rats. It was more or less obvious to researchers that reward systems might vary with social class, or with ethnic sub-culture.

He has devised a model of the human-reward-punishment system, showing a development trend from satisfaction or deprivation of physical-physiological appetites (age 0 to 4 years), through praise-disapproval from outside persons and approval-disapproval from superego (age 5 to 10) to approval-disapproval from ego (age 10 to 15). He suggests that different subcultures carry their children along this evolutionary path at different rates and in different ways; there are thus differences in the reward systems taught to children.

Modes of discipline in general may be discontinuous from home to school. The school may adopt modes of control that are oriented toward rational considerations involving antecedent conditions and consequent effects and/or modes oriented toward the subjective states of individual persons. Some homes are more likely to institute modes of control governed by status or position [14]. Bernstein [15] captures the insecurity of such a child:

. . . a child socialized by controllers who favor positional or imperative procedures becomes highly sensitive to specific role relations in the context of control. Such a child may be bewildered, initially, when placed in a context of control where personal procedures are used, since he may lack the orientation and the facility to take up the different options or alternatives which this form of control makes available. Person-oriented forms of control may induce role strain where the child has been socialized through imperative or positional forms of control.

Locus of Control

Schools must proceed on the assumption that children believe that outcomes are contingent on their own behavior and that success is due to their own efforts, that is, that they have an internal locus of control. Research among certain culturally disadvantaged groups has shown many to perceive the typical achievement situation as externally based and controlled rather than a function of their own behavior [16–20].

While children continue to believe that luck, fate, or other external agencies determine their future, school learning is hardly likely to become personally important in their eyes. To become involved, the child needs to feel that there is a high probability that his own actions can lead to the attainment of his goals.

Many members of disadvantaged minorities could be expected to show evidence of external locus of control, to show evidence of a sense of powerlessness.

Lessing [21] argues:

. . . racial discrimination, with the attendant denial of rewards for individual achievement or self-discipline facilitate the development of a sense of futility and

powerlessness, and a perception of the self as at the mercy of external forces. . . .
The child is then realistically even less able to control his own life and has even
less reason to delay impulse gratification for the sake of future rewards that he
does not have the skills to obtain.

Linguistic Systems

The linguistic system of the school is primarily what Bernstein
[22] has called the elaborated code, that is, a code oriented toward
receiving and offering universalistic meanings, a code where the
speaker makes his intentions explicit verbally, a code that requires
a longer time dimension of verbal planning. This is the language
of teacher and of textbook.

It is not, however, the language of all pupils. Some learn, as
they are socialized in their own distinctive linguistic communities,
a restricted code of language, one that is more context-bound and
oriented toward particularistic meanings.

Bernstein examines the source of difficulty for those working-
class children who are more accustomed in their out-of-school
lives to a restricted rather than an elaborated code:

> The school is necessarily concerned with the transmission and development of
> universalistic orders of meaning. It is concerned with making explicit and
> elaborating, through language, principles and operations as these apply to ob-
> jects . . . and to persons . . . One child through his socialization is already sensitive
> to the symbolic orders of the school, whereas another child is much less sensitive
> to the universalistic orders of the school. The second child is oriented toward
> particularistic orders of meaning which are context-bound, in which principles
> and operations are implicit,and toward a form of language use through which
> such meanings are realized. The school is necessarily trying to develop in this
> child orders of relevance and relation as these apply to persons and objects which
> are not initially the ones he spontaneously moves toward.

In the past, some schools have reacted adversely to the inability
of certain groups of children (e.g., inner-city Blacks) to speak
standard English. Linguists, psycholinguists, and sociolinguists
have recently been concerned to emphasize the linguistic integrity
of the various dialects. These theorists have analyzed the differences between nonstandard and standard forms of English; these
differences are phonemic, syntactical, and semantic. Thus for
some children there is a discontinuity between home and school in

linguistic system, in orientation toward the use of language, and in the form of social relations in which the language system is rooted.

Where the child speaks a form of English other than standard, a major area of discontinuity between school and home exists; this is an area of high emotional significance to the child and, *as schools are currently operated*, a major cause of academic failure.

Cognitive Development

The research literature of the 1940s, 1950s, and 1960s documents the lower-IQ, below-average school performance, high illiteracy rates, and high drop-out rates among many of the culturally different groups, especially those where a majority of the members live in depressed socioeconomic conditions.

Explanations of these limited achievements have been sought in the home circumstances of the children. Correlational studies have linked diminished achievement with membership of large families, overcrowded homes, poor nutritional status, lack of a stimulating environment, and lack of pressure for language development and for achievement motivation.

Factors such as these are undoubtedly obstacles to the academic progress of many children. But it may be that these "explanations" are too simplistic in their approach. They focus on discontinuities between home and school, but in a one-sided fashion—the home does not promote the development of abilities the school believes important. But does not the home promote the development of other abilities? What are these other abilities, and why does the school not make use of them?

The school favors the abstract, conceptual style. Studies have shown that some culturally different groups develop different cognitive styles. Differences, documented with varying degrees of precision, include, for example, impulsivity versus reflection, less abstract conceptualization and categorization of stimuli, more concreteness and inflexibility in intellectual functioning, and motoric preference.

The child's cognitive style determines his utilization of his intellectual abilities. Sigel [23] states that "Styles of categorization may be an important intellectual dimension to determine how intelligence operates. An individual's 'style' dictates the cues he will use, but not necessarily determines the level on which he performs. The style of categorization sets the direction but not the level on which an individual's intelligence might function." If the school does not capitalize on the culturally different child's preferred cognitive style, the result may be underperformance. An increasing number of theorists express the view that culturally different children are often judged as incompetent, whereas, in reality, it is their performance, not their competence, which is deficient. The gap between competence and performance is attributed to inappropriate situational cues—inappropriate because they fail to stimulate the child to action [24–26].

A further area of home/school discontinuity for the culturally different child lies in the types of experiences provided at home and in his ensuing store of concepts. These are often very different from those of his middle-class counterpart. They are not in themselves, however, less valid as bases for further learning.

Consequences of Discontinuities

Likely consequences of discontinuities such as those outlined in the preceding paragraphs are:

1. A lack of understanding by parents of goals of the school program, its curriculum, methodology, and relevance to the children's futures.
2. A lack of understanding by teachers of pupils' home circumstances, parental aspirations for the children, and nature and extent of the children's out-of-school learnings.
3. An alienation of the child from the school, and perhaps from the mainstream culture, in view of its perceived irrelevance to his life and a diminished self-concept.
4. An alienation of the cultural minority from the institutions of the mainstream culture (including the school) and a perpetuation of their socioeconomic disadvantage.

PARENTAL UNDERSTANDING

Where parents have no clear understanding of the school program, there is often a tendency for them to regard themselves as unable to help their children. This tendency is heightened by their own past educational history, which was frequently one of failure, limited educational opportunity, and drop-out. In fact, many such parents could, if they knew what the school was about, were reassured of their own competence, and were helped to adopt attitudes of responsibility for their children's learning, provide considerable assistance for their children. This assistance could most valuably take the form of an informed interest in their children's work, of rewards for school achievement, and of active support for the school.

The past decade has seen notable changes in the schools—in their aims and in their methodologies, in the types of learning situations they create, and in the curriculum offered. Even many mainstream parents feel somewhat bewildered about these changes and may, if the school does not take pains to inform them about its goals and programs, decide to leave the whole business of education to the schools. This tendency may become even more marked in the case of culturally different parents.

Children are motivated in their endeavors by the attitudes of those who are significant to them; in the vast majority of cases a child's parents hold greater significance for him than do his teachers. If his parents are apathetic about or antagonistic toward the school program, do not reward his school activities, or do not enquire into and actively try to encourage his school progress, he is likely to judge school to be of little personal importance to him and may turn his energies to other activities that seem more consonant with the values of home and/or peer group.

If parents are to take a vital interest in the school progress of their children, then obviously they must not only understand the school and its program but must also accept it—particularly its priorities and its methods. One must wonder if such acceptance is possible in the absence of a parent voice in the determination of the school's goals. If programs are developed by school personnel and imposed without consultation, parental understanding and endorsement seem highly improbable.

The school is essentially a mainstream culture institution, but it serves a culturally pluralistic society. Different groups in the community have different values and orientations to life. Is the school, with its particular orientation, to determine by itself the objectives of the program or is this a matter for the community in collaboration with the school? Grotberg [27] lists two criteria she would use in assessing programs of early childhood education, concern for the whole child and parental involvement. With respect to parent participation, she argues that "The defence for this position rests on moral grounds as well as research evidence. It does not seem possible for society to morally justify the encouragement of parent abdication. Parents must be involved in decisions affecting their children and their role in influencing early development must be recognized." She goes on to say, "The degree to which parents participate in both the decision making process and the educational program of an institution may well determine the level of the effectiveness of the institution."

Through dialogue the different groups can define an agreed role for the school as providing part of the total education of the child that will facilitate his development, a role for the school that will not present the young child with inconsistencies and incongruities between his two worlds that he cannot yet handle. At a later stage in his development, during the years of adolescence, he will be able to handle such dissonances and determine the pattern of his own future development. But the young child learns as a whole being; he looks for consistency among the adults of his world and what they ask of him.

TEACHER UNDERSTANDING

Teachers from middle-class mainstream culture have an intimate knowledge of the preschool and out-of-school learnings of their middle-class pupils. Armed with this knowledge and supported by curriculum guides that are, in the main, developed to meet the needs of middle-class children, teachers can plan learning situations that capitalize on the child's developed concepts, understandings and skills and that lead him forward to new learnings from a secure base.

Teachers of the culturally different are themselves disadvantaged in their educational planning because they frequently lack a close knowledge of the child's previous learnings. This makes it difficult for them to ensure that the child is ready for new learnings and it makes it extremely difficult for them to capitalize on the learnings and interests that the minority child has already achieved. They lack knowledge, too, of the child's preferred cognitive style, values and goals, learned modes of interacting with others, and the expectations he holds of others, of the rewards that are meaningful to him. They frequently do not understand his linguistic system (its content or its potency) and are unaware of the demands they make when they expect him to operate in standard English; they do not appreciate the sociolinguistic interference from the contrasting communicative demands in and outside the school [28]. Consequently, the child's motivation is impaired, he sees himself presented with almost insuperable obstacles to his academic progress, school learning seems unconnected with his real life, seems of no personal importance, and often failure is the logical end point.

Increased home-school communication is necessary to help teachers acquire this understanding of their pupils and the home and community forces which shape the attitudes and orientations of their pupils. Such communication can afford help to teachers in yet another area.

Most teachers are members of the middle class. As such, they have had no opportunity to understand the cultures of the various minority groups. Lack of understanding tends to lead to a lack of appreciation; we cannot appreciate what we do not understand. Neither is it easy for us to respect a way of life—a style of life—that is different from our own and known to us only superficially. Many of us know, for example, only the "liabilities" of the culture of poverty; only intimate acquaintance can help us to understand its strengths and assets.

It is this lack of understanding, breeding a lack of appreciation and respect, that in my opinion has led to the view of culturally different children as deficient rather than different. The tragic educational and social consequences of this view as well as its sheer illogicality are being emphasized by an increasing number of writers, notably Passow [29], Fantini [30], Bernstein [31], Labov [32], Baratz [33], Williams [34], White [35], and Cole and Bruner [36]. Such writers emphasize the negative evaluation of cultural minority groups that accompanies the deficit position. Torrey [37], for example, states that:

> . . . the main impact of Afro. American dialect on education has not been its structural differences from standard English, not its relative intrinsic usefulness as a medium of thought, but its function as a low status-stigma and its association

with a rejected culture. The attitudes of teachers toward this dialect and of dialect speakers towards the teachers' language have affected the social relationships of children with the schools in such a way as to make education of many children almost impossible.

Most teachers of culturally different pupils are mainstream culture members. Most have demonstrated, through their own educational history, the particular cognitive styles, values, and motives our schools have always been able to use effectively. The challenge to these teachers now is to help children with abilities and orientations different from their own to learn. Guiding the learning process involves highly personal and intimate transactions between teacher and pupil. There must be instantaneous appreciation by the teacher of the child's perception of a situation and the cues in a given situation that are significant to him. He must be able to sense the value the child is exacting from a particular experience if he is to guide him; he must know each child's distinctive preferred cognitive style.

Not only is it important that teachers recognize diversity in their pupils, it is critical that they value these alternative styles and see them as educationally viable and valid. Otherwise, even if appropriate strategies are developed and made available, there may be little demonstrable gain: the strategies, if used, will be used unwisely, without insight and without expectation of success. In contrast, the teacher who prizes this diversity will, in his day-to-day interactions with his pupils, be alert to recognize a variety of talents and to use these to tempt his pupils forward toward optimal development.

Mood [38] lists some 50 attributes of teachers "that might conceivably be as important to learning as understanding the meaning of words." He groups these under five headings: (1) dedication to the educability of all children, (2) ability to communicate, (3) ability to motivate, (4) ability to organize and manage a class, and (5) ability to create learning experiences. Particularly in the case of ethnic minority pupils, ability (5) cannot flourish if ability (1) is not marked.

Disadvantage and deficit do exist among some members (perhaps a majority) of certain cultural minorities. However, if these are the major characteristics an educator notes, he is led to a negative view of the child, to an expectation of learning difficulties, to an approach aimed at overcoming the child's weaknesses, and also inevitably to a negative valuation of the child's background and culture which produced the deficits.

An orientation to cultural difference would define the school's task quite differently. It would require the school, courteously and realistically, to accept the minority child as he is and his home and community as emotionally and cognitively significant to him. It would also require educators to understand how these children might learn most effectively and to devise strategies that would capitalize on their distinctive learning styles, strengths, and orientations. That is, the school would attempt to fulfill its side of Havighurst's contract described earlier. Educators would at the same time hopefully be led to recognize, appreciate, welcome, and value the cultural diversity of their pupils.

The deficit approach is likely to lead teachers to see the seeds of failure in the child and his home, and the difference orientation is likely to lead teachers to accept the professional challenge of creating effective and satisfying educational experiences for these children.

PUPIL ALIENATION

The minority child is frequently asked to live in two almost completely non-overlapping worlds, the home and the school. He sees little or no connection between the two—little or no connection of adults and little or no connection of ideas or values. What is rewarded in the one is either ignored or punished in the other. The social distance between his home and the school is enormous. Much of what the school teaches is foreign to his orientations to life. Under these circumstances, the home becomes for him a more successful pressure group than the school.

If he could see the adults in these two worlds in closer communication, if they could show him a meeting ground between these two worlds, his position in both worlds would become more tenable. He would not feel that espousal of the one would mean rejection of the other. If these things could happen, it is at least likely that his orientation to the school and what it has to offer would become more positive.

If, in addition, the school capitalized on his strengths and assets, academic success would be less elusive. As Williams [34] says:

The culturally different child has typically progressed normally, hence schools should be able to build upon what he does know, rather than starting from scratch. Building upon what he does know will avoid the cultural depreciation and eventual self-depreciation (or total alienation) now promoted by the schools. Making schools polyculturally oriented will be the first step in the reformation of a now—polycultural society with monocultural opportunity.

Furthermore, if increased dialogue between home and school led to increased mutual respect, teachers would be able to enhance the minority child's feelings of self-esteem. Educators need to help minority children to develop favorable feelings about themselves and positive feelings of ethnic identity. If they succeed in this task, likely consequences for the children will be: (1) an expectation of success and a mobilization of effort to turn the expectation into reality, (2) a desire to meet challenges, (3) a feeling of competence that allows them to bear occasional failures and not to be defeated or engulfed by them, and (4) an expectation that others will like them and think well of them. Such children are likely, other things being equal, to meet success in the school situation; this success will reinforce their feelings of self-esteem.

ALIENATION OF THE CULTURAL MINORITY

Continued failure by the social institutions of the mainstream culture to ensure the full development of minority children's capabilities will lead inevitably to certain consequences:

1. The socioeconomic well-being of the group will continue to be threatened as adolescents continue to leave school and find open to them, because of their school achievements, only occupations on the margin of the surrounding affluent society.
2. In turn, this means a perpetuation for the oncoming generations of the conditions of poverty with its associated difficulties for developing children.
3. The minority groups, particularly probably the young, will become increasingly alienated from the larger society, which simultaneously excludes them from participation and denigrates their identity.
4. The majority society itself becomes weakened through denying itself the opportunity of enriching its own way of life through the respected contributions of its minority members.

References

1. Havighurst, R. J. Minority subcultures and the law effect. *Amer. Psychologists,* 25: 4 (1970), 313–322.
2. Coleman, J. S. *Equality of Educational Opportunity.* Washington, U.S. Government Printing Office, Washington, D.C., 1966.
3. H.M.S.O. *Children and Their Primary Schools.* London, 1967.
4. Adams, R. S. *Community Development and The Training of Teachers of the Disadvantaged.* Univ. Missouri, College of Education, Columbia, 1966.
5. Dottrens, R. *The Primary School Curriculum.* UNESCO, New York, 1962.
6. Kluckhohn, F. Dominant and substitute profiles of cultural orientations: their significance for the analysis of social stratification. *Social Forces* 28 (1950), 376–393.
7. Kohn, M. L. Social class and parental values. *Amer. J. Sociol.,* 64 (1959), 337–351.
8. Kohn, M. L. Social class and parent-child relationships: and interpretation. Amer. J. Sociol., 68 (1963), 471–480.
9. Kohn, M. L. and Pearlin, L. J. Social class, occupation and parental values: a cross-national study. *Amer. Sociol. Rev.,* 31 (1966), 466–479.
10. Kohn, M. L. and Schooler, C. Class, occupation and orientation. *Amer. Sociol. Rev.,* (1969), 659–678. Vol. 34.
11. Ausubel, D. P. *Educational Psychology: A Cognitive View.* Holt, Rinehart and Winston, New York, 1968.
12. Gallimore, R., MacDonald, W. S., and Boggs, S. Education. In *Studies in a Hawiian Community: Na Makamaka O Nankuli,* R. Gallimore and A. Howard, Eds. Pacific Anthropological Records, No. 1. Bernice P. Bishop Museum, Honolulu, Hawaii, 1968.
13. See Havighurst [1].
14. Olim, E. G. Maternal language styles and cognitive development of children. In *Language and Poverty,* F. Williams, Ed. Markham Press, Chicago, 1970, pp. 212–228.
15. Bernstein, B. A sociolinguistic approach to socialization: with some reference of educability. In *Language and Poverty,* F. Williams, Ed. Markham Press, Chicago, 1970, pp. 25–61.
16. Battle, E. S. and Rotter, J. B., Children's feelings of personal control as related to social class and ethnic group. *J. Personality* 31 (1963), 482–490.
17. Piven, F. Participation of residents in neighbourhood community action programs. *Social Work,* 11: 1 (1966), 73–80.
18. de Charms, R. Motivation change in low income black children: A step beyond reinforcement theory. Paper presented at AERA Conference, 1970.
19. Bartel, N. R. Locus of control and achievement in middle class and lower class children. Paper presented to AERA Conference, 1970.
20. Maehr, M. and Sjogren, D. Atkinson's theory of achievement motivation: First step towards a theory of academic motivation. *Rev. Educ. Res.,* 41 (1971), 2.
21. Lessing, E. E. Racial differences in indices of ego functioning relevant to academic achievement. *J. Genet. Psychol.,* 115 (1969), 153–167.
22. See Bernstein [15].
23. Sigel, I. E. How intelligence tests limit understanding of intelligence. *Merrill-Palmer Quarterly of Behavior and Development,* 9 (1963), 39–56.
24. Wallace, J. What units shall we employ? *J. Consult. Psychol.,* 31 (1967), 56–64.

25. Labov, W. The logical non standard English. In *Language and Poverty*, F. Williams, Ed. Markham Press, Chicago, 1970, pp. 153–187.
26. Cole, M. and Bruner, J. S. Preliminaries to a theory of cultural differences. In *Early Childhood Education*, J. J. Gordon, Ed. N.S.S.E. 71st Yearbook, Part II, 1972.
27. Grotberg, E. H. Institutional responsibilities for early childhood education. In *Early Childhood Education*, I. J. Gordon, Ed. N.S.S.E. 71st Yearbook, Part II, 1972.
28. Cazden, C. B. The neglected situation in child language research and education. In *Language and Poverty*, F. Williams, Ed. Markham Press, Chicago, 1970, pp. 81–101.
29. Passow, A. H. Education in depressed areas. In *Education of the Disadvantaged*, A. H. Passow, M. Goldberg, and A. J. Tannebaum, Eds. Holt, Rinehart and Winston, New York, 1967.
30. Fantini, M. D. Beyond cultural deprivation and compensatory education. *Psychiat. Soc. Sci. Rev.*, 3 (1969), 6–13.
31. See Bernstein [15].
32. See Labov [25].
33. Baratz, J. C. Teaching reading in an urban negro school system. In *Language and Poverty*, F. Williams, Ed. Markham Press, Chicago, 1970, pp. 11–24.
34. Williams, F., Ed. *Language and Poverty*. Markham Press, Chicago, 1970.
35. White, W. F. *Tactics For Teaching The Disadvantaged*. McGraw Hill, New York, 1971.
36. See Cole, and Bruner, [26].
37. Torrey, J. W. Illiteracy in the ghetto. *Harvard Educ. Rev.*, 40 (1970), 2, 253–259.
38. Mood, A. M. Do teachers make a difference? In *Do Teachers Make A Difference*. U.S. Department of Health, Education, and Welfare, Washington, D.C. 1972.

Vulnerability of Children from Minority Groups: Scholastic Learning Problems of Skolt Lapp Children

Leila Seitamo, Ph.D. (Finland)

The problems faced by the Lapps today are global ones—economic, social, and cultural. Basically, the crisis arises from the collision of two different cultures. The Finnish culture, similar to the Western cultures, leans on private ownership, and the Lappish one leans on common ownership. Traditionally, the sources of livelihood among the Lapps—hunting, fishing, and raising of reindeer—were located over vast land areas that were the common property of the family or village. At present the Lapps have no judicial rights over land or water areas. Their economy has changed considerably and can no longer ensure them a decent living, which in turn has had social consequences [9, 10].

An important cultural factor is the linguistic difference between the Finnish and the Lappish languages; whereas both are Finno-Ugric languages, they are only remotely related and are not mutually intelligible. The differences between the dialects or the languages of the three Lappish groups—the Skolt Lapps, the Fjeld or Reindeer Lapps, and the Fishing Lapps—make efforts at unification very difficult.

The Lappish culture is becoming assimilated to that of the Finns, chiefly as a result of changes in the economy of the Lapps and the influence of the Finnish school system.

The Lappish language is not an official language in the Nordic countries, so it does not have the same official position of a native language in the Finnish school system as is accorded to Finnish and Swedish. Finnish is used as the language of instruction in schools in the Lappish area; the Lappish children are taught in the same manner as the Finnish children, and according to the same curriculum. For example, Lappish children who are native speakers of Lappish receive a grade for Finnish as their native tongue. For these purely linguistic reasons and because of differences in culture, most of the Lappish children do not progress in their academic performance as well as Finnish children might [10, 14]. During the last 4 to 5 years the problems of the Lappish children have at long last received serious attention and improvements are under way.

The present chapter has a dual purpose: (1) to study the educational problems of the Skolt Lapp children and (2) to discuss the official plans for improving education among Lappish children in Finland. The data have been selected from a study undertaken by the writer as a member of the IBP/HA research group and as an investigator of the National Board of Education in Finland.

The theoretical frame of reference is based on learning theory [1, 3, 4, 15].

Aim of the Study

The purpose of this chapter is to study to what extent the cross-effect of the traditional Skolt culture and the Finnish schooling system results in difficulties in schoolwork for the Skolt Lapp children. The problem is to define the degree to which: (1) cultural factors affect the educational readiness of the Skolt Lapp children in intellectual functions and school motivation and patterns of work habits and (2) these factors affect school achievement.

Sample and Method

The subjects were the whole school-age group of Skolt children in Sevettijärvi ($N = 81$) and in Nellim ($N = 30$), age range 6 to 15 years. The control group was a sample from Northern Finland:

the two villages nearest to the Lappish area, Sassali in Sodankylä and Tanhua in Savukoski ($N = 68$). Because of the difficulty of the task, several measures were used: (1) intelligence tests, (2) scales rated by the teachers, children and parents, (3) childrens' drawings, (4) projective tests, (5) half-open interviews and observations.

In this connection, the WISC test, including Block Design as a measure of culture-free performance for eliminating the effects of cultural factors, was used as much as possible to discover the problem areas in all groups. This definition is more a practical evaluation of potential learning ability than it is a fair culture-free estimate. In the Sevettijärvi and the Northern Finnish groups, the groups of intensive study, the following measures were used:

1. Teachers' ratings of the personality traits of the children (5-point numerical scale, Cattell-Pitkänen), Children's ratings: the question: Do you like to go to school (yes-no).
2. School achievement—school grades, the percentage of those who failed to progress from one grade to the next, follow-up and retrospective study during first 3 school years (grades I–III).

CULTURAL SITUATION

The traditional Skolt community as compared to the Finnish schooling society is described by means of certain major characteristics (Table 1). These are derived from the writer's earlier studies by means of observations, interviews and from the Inventory "Children's Reports of Parental Behavior" (Schaefer's Scale [13]). These characteristics concern Sevettijärvi. The culture in Nellim can be seen to be markedly more acculturated to the Northern Finnish culture.

STATISTICAL ANALYSIS

The correlative analyses are not yet completed. In this connection significance of differences of means by t-test and discrimination analysis are available.

General Hypothesis

On the basis of the cultural characteristics, we can assume that in the Sevettijärvi group there is:

Table 1   Characteristics of Skolt Culture
(Compared with Northern Finnish Culture)

Stimulus—environment
  Deprivation in stimuli encountered in schooling society
  Dominance of stimuli related to nature

Language
  Dominance of Skolt language

Norms—traditional
  Freedom—living among nature important
  Efficiency not valued
  Good human relationships valued

Education
  Parents—warm, tender, permissive, helpful, comforting, indulgent
  Schooling of parents poor
  Rational explanations rare—irrational usual
  Poor control over school achievement
  Fathers more permissive toward boys; less control over school achievement

1. Underdevelopment in verbal intellectual functions and in nonverbal intellectual functions typical of the schooling society, but a high degree of development in functions typical of the Skolt culture.
2. Poor motivation on all levels of school performance and underdevelopment in the work habits needed for school work.
3. Poor school achievement.

Poor performances (1, 2, 3) are assumed to concern most markedly the Sevettijärvi boys. The assumption is based on abrupt changes in role playing for the males in Sevettijärvi and on the lesser degree of guidance and control exercised on the boys by their parents. The Nellim group is assumed to be rather similar to the Finnish group.

Readiness for School: Intellectual Functions

Differences between the culture groups (Table 2) are observed as follows:

1. On the Block Design there are no significant differences between the culture groups. We can conclude that the intel-

Table 2 Means, Standard Deviations, and Significance of Differences between Means on Nonverbal Tests

Test	1 Sevetti ($N = 81$)	2 Nellim ($N = 30$)	3 N. Finland ($N = 68$)	T = Test 1:3	1:2	2:3
WISC:KOHS	11.51	12.27	11.74	0.63	1.49	1.04
Cubes (BD)	(2.24)	(2.75)	(2.13)			
Picture	11.69	12.43	10.43	3.32[b]	1.40	3.62[c]
Completion (PC)	(2.31)	(2.93)	(2.33)			
Picture	6.96	8.10	8.29	3.22[b]	2.41[a]	0.34
Arrangement (PA)	(2.27)	(2.02)	(2.79)			
Object	10.47	11.70	10.76	0.65	2.12[a]	1.50
Assembly (OA)	(2.78)	(2.53)	(2.77)			
Coding (COD)	6.48	7.93	7.41	2.07[a]	2.24[a]	0.95
	(3.07)	(2.97)	(2.29)			

[a] $p < .05$.
[b] $p < .01$.
[c] $p < .001$.

lectual levels of these groups are equal when the effect of cultural factors is eliminated as much as possible.

2. On the Picture Completion Test the Skolt groups score significantly higher than do the Finnish group. The importance of exact perceptions when living in the wilds and a cultural pattern that reinforces perceptual functions have been assumed to account favorably for these abilities. The results are in accordance with the hypothesis of the high degree of development in functions typical of Skolt culture.

3. On the Picture Arrangement Test the Sevettijärvi group scores significantly lower than did the other groups. Deprivation in the physical stimulus environment is assumed to account for this difference.

4. On the Object Assembly Test the Skolt groups score similarly to the Finnish group.

5. On the Coding the Sevettijärvi group scores significantly lower than the other groups. The most important component of this test is speed and accuracy in reproducing one's perceptions with the pencil. Lack of training, motivation, and speed efficiency in this type of function, typical of the schooling society, is assumed to lead to this difference.

6. On most of the verbal tests (Tables 3 and 4) the Sevettijärvi group scores significantly lower than the other groups. On vocabulary tests the differences are very marked. The Nellim and Finnish groups are very close together. Poor ability in Finnish and deprivation of verbal stimuli are assumed to be the causes of the inferiority of the Sevettijärvi group in the verbal intellectual functions.

The following sex differences are observed:

1. Boys from Sevettijärvi tend to score lower than other groups on several culturally linked tests (Tables 5a and 5b).
2. On most of the verbal tests the levels of the Sevettijärvi boys are significantly lower than those of the boys from the Nellim and Finnish groups. The differences between the Sevettijärvi boys and girls point in the same direction, but not significantly. Within the other groups an opposite trend is found between the two sexes: a tendency appears for the boys to attain a better level.
3. The differences between the nonverbal performances, especially on the Coding, are very marked. In this subtest the Nellim group resembles the Sevettijärvi group more than it does the Finnish group. The inferiority of the Skolt boys in this and other performance tests may be explained by cultural and neurophysiological factors. The nondirective educational attitudes of the parents toward the Skolt boys do not offer proper opportunities for training in perceptual and fine motor coordination (e.g., in handicrafts). The girls, however, develop fine motor abilities by participating in the handwork of the women from their early years. They are also generally guided and controlled more than the boys. According to biosocial theory [2], the boys suffer more than the girls from the disadvantageous environment, malnutrition, and so on, which have an unfavorable effect on their physiological maturity, motor development, and spatial learning ability.
4. The IQs of the Sevettijärvi boys are significantly lower on every scale than those of the other boys, but lower than that of the Sevettijärvi girls only on the Performance Scale. Thus

Table 3 **Means, Standard Deviations, and Significance of Differences between Means on Verbal Tests**

	1 Sevetti (N = 81)	2 Nellim (N = 30)	3 N. Finland (N = 68)	t = Test		
				1:3	1:2	2:3
Vocabulary (V)	7.95	9.97	9.84	3.97[c]	1.87	1.27
	(2.89)	(2.48)	(2.88)			
Information (I)	9.07	9.76	10.37	2.51[a]	1.05	0.95
	(3.06)	(2.57)	(3.23)			
Comprehension	10.36	12.43	11.46	2.09[a]	3.19[b]	1.38
(C)	(3.07)	(2.98)	(3.34)			
Similarities	10.54	10.33	11.24	1.49	0.34	1.36
(S)	(2.70)	(3.23)	(2.93)			
Arithmetic	8.48	9.50	8.41	0.21	2.30[a]	2.71[b]
(A)	(2.16)	(1.81)	(1.85)			
Age	10.83	10.88	10.73	0.08	0.23	0.23
	(2.43)	(2.50)	(2.50)			

[a] p < .05.
[b] p < .01.
[c] p < .001.

Table 4 **Means, Standard Deviations, and Significance of Differences between Means of IQs on WISC Scale**

Scale	1 Sevetti (N = 81)	2 Nellim (N = 30)	3 N. Finland (N = 68)	t = Test		
				1:3	1:2	2:3
Verbal	95.31	101.27	101.43	2.68[b]	2.05[a]	0.05
	(14.02)	(12.26)	(13.72)			
Performance	95.83	103.30	97.32	0.70	2.59[a]	2.11[a]
	(13.46)	(13.54)	(12.63)			
Full	95.20	102.43	99.43	1.97	2.57[a]	1.08
	(13.36)	(12.57)	(12.74)			

[a] p < .05.
[b] p < .01.

the inferiority of the Sevettijärvi boys appears especially clearly in nonverbal functions, though the cross-cultural differences between the Sevettijärvi Skolt and Finnish boys are still clearer on the Verbal Scale than on the Performance Scale.

Table 5a Means, Standard Deviations, and Significance of Differences of Means on Intelligence Test: Sex Differences
(F—Girls; M—Boys)

Tests	Sevetti F(39)	Sevetti M(42)	Nellim F(16)	Nellim M(14)	N. Finland F(33)	N. Finland M(35)	Girls versus Boys Sevetti df = 79 t	p<	Nellim df = 28 t	p<	N. Finland df = 66 t	p<
BD	12.0 (2.1)	11.0 (2.3)	12.4 (2.7)	12.1 (2.9)	11.5 (2.2)	12.0 (2.1)	1.92	.1	.34	NS	−1.04	NS
PC	11.8 (2.4)	11.6 (2.2)	11.8 (2.5)	13.1 (3.3)	10.0 (2.2)	10.9 (2.4)	0.48	NS	−1.21	NS	−1.56	NS
PA	7.4 (2.3)	6.5 (2.2)	8.0 (1.6)	8.2 (2.5)	8.0 (2.2)	8.6 (3.2)	1.71	.1	−0.28	NS	−0.91	NS
OA	10.8 (2.8)	10.2 (2.8)	12.1 (2.4)	11.3 (2.6)	10.7 (2.7)	10.8 (2.9)	1.0	NS	0.81	NS	−0.1	NS
COD	7.9 (3.1)	5.2 (2.4)	9.4 (2.6)	6.3 (2.6)	8.0 (2.3)	6.9 (2.2)	4.39	.001	3.18	.01	1.96	.1

Nonverbal IQ	99.9 (14.2)	92.0 (11.6)	105.2 (10.9)	101.1 (16.2)	96.4 (11.2)	98.2 (14.2)	2.73	.01	0.78	NS	−0.59	NS
V	7.9 (2.5)	8.0 (3.3)	7.8 (1.6)	10.6 (2.5)	9.1 (2.8)	10.5 (2.8)	−0.16	NS	−3.62	.01	−2.09	.01
I	9.3 (3.1)	8.9 (3.0)	9.1 (2.4)	10.4 (2.7)	9.8 (3.6)	10.9 (2.8)	0.06	NS	−1.36	NS	−1.33	NS
C	10.5 (2.7)	10.2 (3.4)	11.3 (2.9)	13.7 (2.6)	11.2 (3.5)	11.7 (3.2)	0.5	NS	−2.29	.05	−0.5	NS
S	10.7 (2.3)	10.4 (3.1)	10.3 (2.5)	10.4 (4.0)	11.4 (3.3)	11.1 (2.6)	0.62	NS	−0.03	NS	0.42	NS
A	8.9 (2.4)	8.1 (1.8)	9.4 (1.9)	9.6 (1.8)	8.1 (1.9)	8.8 (1.8)	1.77	.1	−0.19	NS	−1.37	NS
Verbal IQ	96.7 (13.2)	94.0 (14.8)	97.3 (10.5)	105.8 (12.8)	98.9 (15.1)	103.8 (12.1)	0.86	NS	−1.94	.1	−1.44	NS
Full-scale IQ	98.1 (13.5)	92.5 (13.8)	101.1 (10.3)	104.0 (15.0)	97.4 (13.1)	101.3 (12.3)	1.89	.1	−0.61	NS	−1.26	NS

Table 5b   Significance of Differences of Means on
Intelligence Tests: Subgroups[a]

	Differences between Girls						Differences between Boys					
	I:III		I:II		II:III		I:III		I:II		II:III	
	$df = 70$		$df = 53$		$df = 47$		$df = 75$		$df = 54$		$df = 47$	
Test	t	p<	t	p<	t	p<	t	p<	t	p<	t	p<
BD	1.06	NS	−0.63	NS	1.33	NS	−1.85	.1	−1.32	NS	0.09	NS
PC	3.29	.01	0.01	NS	2.55	.05	1.34	NS	−1.99	.1	2.63	.05
PA	−1.02	NS	−0.9	NS	0.04	NS	−3.28	.01	−2.37	.05	−0.39	NS
OA	0.1	NS	−1.55	NS	1.65	NS	−0.96	NS	−1.29	NS	0.52	NS
COD	−0.11	NS	−1.65	NS	1.9	.1	−3.18	.01	−1.45	NS	−0.79	NS
Nonverbal IQ	1.15	NS	−1.29	NS	2.56	.05	−2.1	.05	−2.25	.05	0.61	NS
V	−1.88	.1	0.21	NS	−1.74	.1	−3.57	.001	−2.65	.05	0.03	NS
I	−0.6	NS	0.2	NS	−0.65	NS	−3.02	.01	−1.7	.1	−0.54	NS
C	−0.94	NS	−0.91	NS	0.08	NS	−1.91	.1	−3.51	.001	2.09	.05
S	−0.96	NS	0.6	NS	−1.13	NS	−1.08	NS	0	NS	−0.74	NS
A	1.57	NS	−0.74	NS	2.27	.05	−1.54	NS	−2.62	.05	1.5	NS
Verbal IQ	−0.65	NS	−0.14	NS	−0.39	NS	−3.09	.01	−2.63	.05	0.52	NS
Full-scale IQ	0.22	NS	−0.77	NS	0.96	NS	−3.03	.01	−2.73	.01	0.62	NS

[a] *Code:*   I—Sevettijärvi, II—Nellim, III—N. Finland.

5. The differences between the girls are rather small. In the verbal functions there is a slight tendency toward a higher level in the Finnish girls, but no significant differences appear. On the Vocabulary Scale the difference is somewhat clearer reaching the level of a tendency ($p < .1$). On the Picture Completion Test the Skolt girls score significantly higher than do the Finnish girls.

The function of age is observed as follows:

1. Amongst the Sevettijärvi group most verbal functions improve significantly more than the expected norm values as a function of age (Table 6).
2. The improvement is more marked among the boys. Thus the readiness of the Sevettijärvi boys in verbal intellectual functions is very poor in the lower classes, but it improves markedly as a function of length of school career.

Table 6 Correlations of WISC Verbal Test Scores with Age

Test	Sevettijarvi			Nellim			North Finland		
	T[a]	F	M	T	F	M	T	F	M
	(81)	(39)	(42)	(30)	(16)	(14)	(68)	(33)	(35)
	r			r			r		
Vocabulary	.19[b]	.08	.28[b]	−.24	−.39	−.09	−.03	.09	−.14
Information	.44[e]	.39[c]	.51[e]	.24	.16	.41	.17	.20	.14
Comprehension	.42[e]	.46[d]	.41[d]	.17	.18	.30	−.03	.00	−.06
Similarities	.35[d]	.28[b]	.42[d]	.34[b]	.27	.42	.23[b]	.34[c]	.12
Arithmetic	−.06	−.16	.09	−.20	−.26	−.11	.03	.25	−.17
Verbal IQ	.37[e]	.29[b]	.46[d]	.12	.05	.29	.10	.23	−.02

[a] Total for subgroup.
[b] $p < .1$.
[c] $p < .05$.
[d] $p < .01$.
[e] $p < .001$.

Table 7 Attractiveness of School[a]

	Sevettijärvi Percent Yes	North Finland Percent Yes
Girls	58	87
Boys	24	65

[a] Question: "Do You Like to Go to School?" (yes-no).

Readiness for School: School Motivation and Patterns of Work Habits

Motivation to attend school is significantly lower for the Sevettijärvi group, especially for the boys, than for the Finnish group (Table 7). The differences between the Skolt and Finnish boys also show up very clearly in the teachers' ratings. The differences between the girls' groups are small. Significant differences also appear between the Skolt boys and girls.

The Sevettijärvi boys may be distinguished significantly from the girls by a discriminator consisting of attitudes toward schoolwork (Table 8). Low scholastic motivation, poor work habits, hostile attitudes toward school and teachers, and traits of imbalance

Table 8 Significance of Differences of Means on Teachers' Ratings and Discrimination Analysis: Sevettijärvi girls (I) versus boys (II)

Ratings	$p <$ on Group Rated Higher I	II	Correlations between Discriminating Functions and Variables
Busy	.1		−.34
Impolite		.001	.59
Balanced	.1		−.3
Ambitious	.05		−.36
Malicious		.01	.39
likes to go to school	.001		−.6
bear tales	.05		−.35
Effective	.05		−.38
Hard-working	.01		−.46
Stubborn		.05	.35
Cooperative	.1		−.32
Friendly	.05		−.39
Unpersevering		.05	.42
Noisy		.05	.39
Excitable		.1	.29
Undependable		.01	.49
Insolent		.001	.57
Hostile		.001	.57

Eigenvalue	Percent	χ^2 I xx 2	NDF	Prob.	Canonical Correlations
1.030	100.0	38.22	18	.996	.71

Wilks λ	F		Prob.
.492718	(18,45) = 2.574		.9948

Discriminating functions			Estimated pairwise overlap probabilities		
Group	Mean	SD	I	II	
I Sevetti girls	1.673	1.116	I 1.0	0.1136	= 4/31 girls
II Sevetti boys	3.671	0.878	II 0.1816	1.0	= 5/33 boys

are characteristic of the Sevettijärvi Skolt boys. "Avoidance" behavior, manifested as fearfulness, ineffectiveness, and dislike for school, characterize the Skolt boys, whereas "approach" behavior in the form of activity is typical of the Finnish boys (Table 9). These discriminating traits increase significantly as a function of school career.

Table 9 Significance of Differences of Means on Teachers' Ratings and
Discrimination Analysis: Sevettijärvi Boys (I) versus Finnish Boys (II)

Ratings	$p <$ on Group Rated Higher		Correlations between Discriminating Functions and Variables
	I	II	
Sad	.1		−.33
Dependent	.1		−.37
Impolite	.1		−.37
Retiring	.1		−.34
Flexible		.05	.43
Attention seek-ing		.05	.34
Likes to go to school;		.01	.47
talkative		.05	.43
Effective		.01	.55
Active		.05	.41
Hard-working		.1	.34
Relaxed		.1	.33
Unpersevering	.05		−.42
Short-tempered		.1	.38
Shy	.01		−.61
Domineering		.05	.4

Eigenvalue	Percent	χ^2 1 xx 2	NDF	Prob.	Canonical Correlations
.6559	100.0	27.74	16	.966	.6294

Wilks λ	F	Prob.
.603884	(16,47) = 1.927	.9584

Discriminating functions			Estimated pairwise overlap probabilities		
Group	Mean	SD	I	II	
I Sevetti boys	−0.1035	0.9687	I	1.0	0.2052 = 7/33 Sevetti boys
II N. Finland boys	1.492	1.032	II	0.2199	1.0 = 4/31 N. Finland boys

Achievement in School

The annual percentage of those who fail to progress from one grade to the next is enormously high in the Sevettijärvi group (Table 10), with most of the failures occurring during the first 3 years and more often among boys than girls. In reading, writing, and mathematics the achievements of the Sevettijärvi girls are poorer than those of the Finnish boys (Table 11). The mean grades of the Sevettijärvi boys in these and other theoretical subjects, as given in their school reports, are significantly lower than those of the girls. The pupils remaining in the same class for 2 years are included in these calculations. Thus the longer school career of the Skolt boys does not serve to raise their achievements to the same level as those of the other groups. The same differences also appear in the achievement tests. Continuation to more advanced schooling is rare, and the interruption of education is common.

Table 10   Percentages of Pupils Remaining in Same Class: Follow-up and Retrospective Study during First 3 School Years

	I		II		III		I–III	
	(FR)	%	(FR)	%	(FR)	%	(FR)	%
Sevettijärvi girls	(3)	8	–	–	(2)	5	(5)	11
Sevettijärvi boys	(9)	21	(1)	2	(1)	2	(11)	26
N. Finnish girls	–	–	(1)	3	–	–	(1)	3
N. Finnish boys	(1)	3	(1)	3	–	–	(2)	6

Table 11   Means, Standard Deviations, and Significance of Differences of School Marks[a]

Test	I, F (37)	I, M (43)	II, F (34)	II, M (35)
Reading	7.29	6.74	7.64	7.2
	(1.46)	(1.12)	(0.99)	(0.88)
Writing	7.13	6.23	7.26	6.77
	(1.11)	(1.25)	(0.97)	(0.86)
Mathematics	6.54	6.23	6.79	6.97
	(1.46)	(1.27)	(1.23)	(1.4)
Mean	7.32	6.78	7.3	7.06
	(0.92)	(0.89)	(0.8)	(0.82)

t-Test between	I, F : I, M		II, F : II, M		I, F : II, M		I, F : II, M	
	t	$p<$	t	$p<$	t	$p<$	t	$p<$
Reading	1.88	.1	1.93	.1	−1.14	NS	−1.93	.1
Writing	3.32	.01	2.19	.05	−0.51	NS	−2.12	.05
Mathematics	0.99	NS	−0.54	NS	−0.77	NS	−2.40	.05
Mean	2.58	.05	1.20	NS	0.05	NS	−1.42	.2

[a] I—Sevettijärvi; II—N. Finland, including pupils remaining in the same class.

Summary

Summarizing the main results, it is found that the Sevettijärvi group occupies the least favorable position in intellectual and motivational readiness for schoolwork in terms of the Finnish school system. These factors aggregately comprise an unfavorable accumulation of cultural consequences for the Skolt children. According to the hypothesis, this concerns especially clearly the Sevettijärvi boys' group. The collision of two different cultures with abrupt changes in role playing for the males—and a very important factor—the shortcomings of the Finnish school system result in poor scholastic achievement. This in turn prevents the boys from finding school rewarding, lowers their motivation and self-confidence, and leads to behavioral disturbances. Deprivation of firm continuous contact with men while living in dormitories during their school years increases the difficulties of the boys. Because of feelings of inferiority, the Skolt boys are very unwilling to undertake further vocational training. These difficulties also have very far-reaching consequences for the maintenance and development of the Skolt culture.

The difficulties of the other Lappish groups are similar to those of the Skolts.

References

1. Bloom, B. S. *Stability and Change in Human Characteristics.* Third Printing. Wiley, New York, 1966.
2. Dawson, J. L. M. Theory and research in cross-cultural psychology. *Bull. Brit. Psychol. Soc.,* 24 (1971), 291–306.
3. Hansegård, N. E., *Tvåspråkighet eller Halvspråkighet.* Aldus/Bonniers, Stockholm, 1968.
4. Hunt, J. McV. *Intelligence and Experience.* Ronald Press, New York, 1961.
5. *Komiteanmietintö,* Helsinki, B 63 (1971).
6. *Komiteanmietintö,* Helsinki, 46 (1973).
7. *Komiteanmietintö,* Helsinki, 88 (1973).
8. Korhonen, M., Mosnikoff, J., and Sammallahti, P. *Koltansaamen Opas.* Castrenianum. No. 4, Helsinki, 1973.
9. Nickul, K. *Saamelaiset Kansana ja Kansalaisina.* SKS, Helsinki, 1970.
10. Nuorgam-Poutasuo, H. The current state and future of the Lapps. Paper read at CCC Symposium on The Connections between the Teaching and Learning of the Mother Tongue and the Teaching of Other Modern Languages. Turku, Finland, 1972.
11. Sammallahti, P. *Aabbâs Säämas.* Mimeographed, 1972.

12. Sammallahti, P. *Aabbâs Jiännkiell.* Mimeographed, 1973.
13. Seitamo, L., Das elterliche Verhalten in der Wahrnehmung der Kinder. Paper read at International Seminar on Man in the Arctic, Kiel, 1970. Abstract in Bericht über das 4H Internationale Symposium Der Mensch in der Arktis. *Anthrop. Anz. Jg.* 33: 2 (1971), 114–131.
14. Seitamo, L, Intellectual functions in Skolt and Northern Finnish children with special references to cultural factors. *Inter-Nord,* 12 (1972), 338–343.
15. Wolf, R. M. The identification and measurement of environmental process variables related to intelligence. Dissertation, Department of Education, Chicago, Illinois. Microfilmed by Department of Photoduplication, the University of Chicago Library. Thesis No. T-106442, 1964.

Separation, Loss and Surrogate Mother-Child Relationship

Sidney Z. Moss, M.S.W., A.C.S.W., and Miriam S. Moss, M.A. (U.S.A.)

The theme of this chapter is concerned with the way new attachments are made after a child has lost his biological mother through separation or death. The focus is on interaction between surrogate mother and child as each strives to create an emotional unity without a biological base.

Two terms deserve comment at the outset; *biological mother* denotes the woman who gave birth to the child, and *surrogate mother* is the woman who carries the maternal functions, but is not the biological mother. The authors do not assert that there is one "real" mother, despite King Solomon's choice or the delineation of a psychological mother by Goldstein, Freud, et al. [6].

Millions of children today are being raised by other than their biological parents. In 1970 alone there were 175,000 children adopted [9] and over a quarter of a million in foster care [13]. This is a reflection of population growth, and is compounded by the increase in divorce and remarriage. It has been estimated that one in every nine children in the United States is a stepchild and further, that one in five of all persons has lived in a stepfamily [22].

Although some authors have explored the process by which a mother and child develop a bond [2, 11, 23, 26], little systematic

435

attention has been given to reattachment with a new mothering object [2, 4, 18]. How have the millions of children and their surrogate mothers developed their relationships? What are the dynamics of this process? Steps toward mastery of the reattachment experience between child and surrogate mother are the subject of the following discussion.

The first section focuses on the child and the second on the surrogate mother. This separation is artificial, for ease in presentation. The complexities of their interactions emerge throughout.

A surrogate mother may carry any of a number of roles—stepmother, adoptive mother, foster mother, or other family member who is a regular caretaker. This discussion focuses primarily on those who have a *permanent* commitment to the child. Additionally, the central concern here is with the young child who has had some knowledge and experience of his biological mother before he comes to the surrogate. It cannot be ignored, however, that fetal bonds or very early infantile relations may have a significant influence on the creation of later ties with a surrogate.

Although the overall schema of this chapter is applicable to any situation of a surrogate mother and a child, its limitations are extensive. It does not explore the profound differences between a surrogate mother who is a stepmother (i.e., married to the biological father) and an adoptive mother (whose husband is not the biological father). It also does not discuss: (1) the surrogate who has borne her own children prior to or after the onset of her mothering this child, (2) the double-surrogate family—to which each parent brings children from a prior marriage, (3) the implications of culture and the social network of the family, (4) the age factor for both mother and child, (5) sex differential, (6) personality of each, or (7) the all-important influence of the father.

The Child

When a child joins his surrogate mother, they may be strangers. How does he view the loss of his biological mother? How does he perceive himself? How does the surrogate mother appear to him? How does he perceive the situation and respond to it?

This section explores these questions.

PERCEPTION OF LOSS

In other animals, loss of the mother is often devastating [7, 8], as it is for humans [24, 25]. Without considering the dynamics of separation from the biological mother, one cannot understand the dynamics of reattachment to the surrogate mother.

Loss and separation are the basic variables affecting new attachments. Separation of young children from their mother is analagous to a mourning experience. They react with anger and protest, despair, and threat to self [12]. The surrogate mother should be aware of this trauma of loss and the child's need to resolve his grief.

The failure to complete mourning [10] may exacerbate reactions to losses later in life. Indeed, unresolved grief can affect the child's later parenting of subsequent generations [16]. When a child has begun to work through some of these feelings, he may then reach out to his surrogate mother.

The child creates an assumptive world [15], explaining to others and hopefully himself the reasons for the separation from his biological mother.

PERCEPTION OF SELF

A child's personality plays an important role in how he perceives himself at the time he begins with a surrogate mother. There are, however, significant situational determinants.

The identity of the child is threatened when he is shifted from one mother to another. One of his first questions is whether he will be accepted as he is, or whether he will need to change himself. Since the surrogate mother has power to give or withhold love and care, the child may be under much pressure to change. He is weakened by the thought that if he were lovable he would not have lost his biological mother. Thus he is doubly motivated to adjust to the surrogate mother's ways.

An important issue for the child is the conflict over loyalty and belongingness. He asks, "Who is my real mother? Who will take care of me? If I listen to this mother will I be disloyal to the other? How do I reconcile two different views or expectations of me? Why didn't my mother love me, and keep me?" As a result of the painful confusion over belongingness, a child may have the deep loneliness of a marginal person.

The above issues are woven into the fabric of genealogical bewilderment or a confusion over identity [17]. In spite of a child's attempt to reach out, he may never be able fully to give up his investment of his biological mother. Clinical evidence indicates that the feelings remain underground and erupt around adolescence or later life when separation issues arise. These painful feelings are a reflection of the loss of continuity and of an opportunity to identify with a family history of people, events, and myths. The child is deprived of knowledge of the source of his biological uniqueness and of an opportunity to participate in his biological family's destiny.

If a child sees himself as being attacked in this new situation, he will defend himself against the risk of losing his self. Not being lovable and without an identity may be worse than death. The terror of being annihilated has profound effects on the relationship between self and others. A child may see himself as rejected and abandoned. Feeling unloved and unwanted, dispossessed only to be repossessed by a stranger, creates low self-esteem and may weaken a child's ability to develop new attachments. A child may dread being replaceable, just as his biological mother was. Will he do something bad and need to be sent away? Is he destined to be deserted again? The shock of replacement may seem like dying and being reborn. An older child may feel stigma in not belonging. He may feel that he is different from others because he does not have a biological tie to his surrogate mother. If his biological mother is living, he may feel ashamed for her failure to keep him with her. He may perceive himself as an undesired stranger, an unwanted child.

PERCEPTION OF SURROGATE MOTHER

How does he see his surrogate mother? In comparison to the biological mother, the surrogate mother looks, feels, and is different. She behaves in unexpected ways. She is, in effect, a stranger. The child's past relationship with his biological mother may in some complex ways determine his response to the surrogate mother. On the one hand, the child may so idealize his earlier tie that he initially rejects a substitute; on the other hand, the child may have found a haven and sense of real mothering for the first time.

If the primary relation was close and warm, the child may risk a new relationship because he knows it can be good. He may, however, see the surrogate mother as the cause of his loss, or he may shrink back because the earlier tie was aborted and he can neither risk further abandonment nor fully trust again.

If the earlier tie with the biological mother was tenuous or conflictual, the child may have so little experience with good mothering that he withdraws. Deprivation may, however, be a spur to create a tie with the surrogate mother.

Of course, the way the child perceives the surrogate is in considerable part a reflection of the attitudes and behavior of the surrogate mother herself. The child's perception of the surrogate mother is colored by the fact that someone else, not she, is his biological mother. This view will continue to be of significance during the child's lifetime.

PERCEPTION OF THE SITUATION AND RESPONSE TO IT

His whole universe is tinged with uncertainty. The child has basic needs for protection, nurturance, learning, and autonomy. He does not have the stable, supportive environment that can assure him that his needs will be met.

The child must simultaneously respond to the changes in the nonhuman environment and in the interpersonal sphere. It is not just habit or familiarity he gives up, but a source of at-homeness through identification and emotional support with the physical surroundings. He seeks a coherent picture of where he is and how he is expected to behave. He tests out each aspect of the situation to learn guidelines for his behavior and boundaries for the relationship.

When a child leaves the old and comes to the new he brings his old ways, and they may be maladaptive. He may see adults as not to be trusted and find evidence that he is correct. The child's response to the surrogate may include many kinds of resistances such as distrust, indifference, masking, withdrawal, and overt hostility.

Normal human distrust and discomfort with a new situation is exacerbated in the child-surrogate mother relationship. There is a fear of trusting the future since the past has been so unreliable. If the surrogate mother is unable to accept the child's past, this is tantamount to not accepting him. Besides, how can he trust that her love, even if genuine, could melt his anguish?

A child may open up with grief and mourning. Unless the surrogate mother is able to accept the child's feelings—not to deny them, play them down, or avoid them—the child's grief may be reinforced. The child may seem indifferent as a defense against the surrogate mother's failure to accept his grief. He may think it is better to insulate and deaden himself than to bare his feelings and meet rejection.

If a child accepts the situation readily, it may be a form of denial. Masking of true feelings may be so pervasive that it leads to the creation of a pseudoself. Geared toward approval rather than acceptance, he begins to give up the side of himself that is displeasing to the new mother. Denial of one's identity to fit into another's expectations can lead to a false security and vulnerability to later stresses. Giving up one's potential may be cause for much guilt. Perhaps a child, hiding his true self, unknowingly begins to accumulate an existential guilt and becomes afraid of life.

A child who withdraws remains aloof rather than risking further rejection. He fears any intimacy that comes on too quickly. Withdrawal may be a way of returning to an earlier state of dependency so as to hold on to the past and to undo the loss. Withdrawal, therefore, is a means of coping with attachment difficulties. Regression, however, represents unsuccessful coping. In some cases children lose control over toilet training, show speech difficulties, including mutism, and at the extreme, exhibit autism. These serious withdrawal behaviors are forms of psychic numbing utilized by a child as he seeks some control over his life.

Hostility may also be expressed. It may spring from self-hate as well as be a reaction to a spectrum of responses from the surrogate mother. The child may show rebelliousness and anger in protesting a situation that was thrust on him. Angry at both mothers, the child may be unable to cope with his confusion and feeling of loss. Fearing further abandonment, he may flay out against a sense of helplessness and hopelessness. He may provoke an unwary surrogate mother to reach out only to create a quarrel to keep her away as if testing her capacity to love and showing his power. This tends to keep the surrogate mother on guard and maintains an emotional barrier. The child wants the surrogate mother to respond empathically to his suffering. He may test repeatedly—often to the limit—the surrogate mother's capacity to accept him.

Although the child may resist the surrogate mother in many of these ways, he has a strong need to develop a bond with this new mother figure. It is ironic that through this transition he desperately needs a mother, yet only has the surrogate mother whose problematic presence is part of the reason for his upset. He needs connectedness and independence, and a consistent view of the world and his place in it. The child will try to satisfy these needs through his relationship with his surrogate mother.

The Surrogate Mother

Using the framework described in the previous section that focused on the child, this section explores how the surrogate mother views herself, the child, and their situation—and how she responds in line with these perceptions.

PERCEPTION OF SELF

The presence of the child—whether adopted or stepchild—has an impact on the surrogate mother's self-perception. She sees herself as a stranger. She may feel the absence of any historic tie, of the familiarity that is a key to mutuality. The initial pressure to create a bond exacerbates the feeling of strangeness and exacts a shift in her sense of identity.

Caught by the immediate responsibilities of parenting, the surrogate mother may feel uncertain about her ability to meet the child's demands. If she is buttressed by a good experience with her own mother, her ability to risk herself in mothering the child is enhanced. If she had previous satisfying personal experiences with a surrogate parent, she may find the new role of surrogate mother more easy to assume.

The mother wants to gain a feeling of belongingness with the child. She wants to adapt to the child but simultaneously fears the need for change in her self. She hopes that her intrinsic worth as a person will be accepted, and she feels threatened by the possibility of rejection.

She may feel the lack of the biological unity that fosters the achievement of separation-individuation [11] or that lays the groundwork for symbiosis even prior to birth [1].

Guilt may enter in a number of ways. It can result from the idea that she has taken the child away from his biological mother and is rearing him as her own. She may feel unequal to the biological mother in not being able to love as much or in the same way. She may feel that she has rejected or sacrificed her own yet-unborn child, substituting a less worthy surrogate in its place. She may in some deep sense be reacting to the loss of the unborn child and mourning it as she attaches herself to the surrogate child.

A surrogate mother may suffer from feeling stigma in her role. This is particularly true of the stepmother, whose negative image is reflected throughout literature. Basically, the surrogate mother sees herself as a substitute—and her relationship with the child is forever mediated by that fact.

PERCEPTION OF THE CHILD

The surrogate mother sees the child as representing the genetic past over which she has no control. If she can accept this existential fact, she may be able to accept her role in the child's present and future.

Depending on the surrogate mother's knowledge of the conditions under which the child came to her, the surrogate mother may see him as in need of rescue from a bad fate. A neglected or deprived child may be viewed in terms of his condition rather than for himself.

The surrogate mother may see the child as a gift—a possession that proves her own personal worthiness. This again is a depersonalization of the child and a stance that views him primarily in relation to her and her needs.

The child's face, build, coloring, and energy are basically hereditary. The surrogate mother may have certain preferences and may have difficulty accepting the child as he is.

The surrogate mother's perception of the child is colored by her perception of his biological mother. The child is not viewed in isolation. There is a third party to the mother-child dyad, one who may be dead or unseen. Although the biological mother's presence is never erased, there is danger of seeing a child's problematic behavior as linked to his heredity and to his past, and disowning any responsibility for it.

SURROGATE RESPONDS TO SITUATION

This section presents and discusses many of the early and continuing responses of the mother as she enters into a relationship with the child. As the surrogate mother begins with the child, she is confronted by the fact that there are no special rituals or guidelines that will facilitate the development of this relationship. Even the physical arrival of the child is generally not formally announced or celebrated. She may have had little opportunity to work through many of the things that are facilitated in the 9 months of pregnancy.

The surrogate mother generally is not relocated from a familiar physical environment to a strange new home and neighborhood. She does not have to learn to negotiate an alien world, as does the child. However, she needs to view her life space quite differently—sharing some very private sectors of it with the child and relinquishing others.

The surrogate mother's tie with the child may be viewed as a triad—including the biological mother. Simmel[21] has told us that in a triad each person is an intermediary between the other two. This chapter emphasizes that much of what takes place between the surrogate mother and the child is influenced by their perceptions of the biological mother. The surrogate often has strong feelings of guilt, hostility, and jealousy toward the biological mother [22]. Each of these feelings plays a strong role in her developing relationship with the child.

Two questions recur in the interactions between surrogate mother and child: (1) how they can deal with the losses that have occurred and (2) how they can develop a new bond.

Surrogate mothers vary in their willingness and ability to deal with the past. In general, a burden of secrecy stands as a barrier to an open relationship.

The mother may avoid thinking and talking about the child's past, particularly the fact that the child is not biologically hers. A surrogate mother may feel the need to destroy or avoid the past as if it stands in the way of mothering. A mother may refuse to discuss the child's past, deny it existed, and behave as if the child were biologically her own.

Surrogate mothers may seek biological similarities in the child and underscore the validity of similarities perceived by others. They may fabricate birth data. A mother may fear that intrusions of thoughts of the biological mother will reduce the viability of her relationship and her claim on the child. The surrogate mother may feel that the biological owning of the child tightens the bond and reduces the risks of the child's resistance to her parenting. She may fear that the child will say, "I will not do as you want because you are not my real mother" or "My real mother would not treat me this way." She fears that the child will not offer her unconditional love.

When the child is clearly aware that his surrogate mother is not his biological mother, he wants to know who his biological mother is. Where is she? To some extent there are real limitations on how much the surrogate mother can tell the child. There may be much she does not know or does not want to know. Surrogate mothers often carry forever the uncertainty of an absolute claim on the child. They may often be plagued by the anxiety that the biological tie is stronger and that the biological mother will assert this tie.

There has been a growing organized concern of adult adopted children to search for their biological parents. They claim that the adopted person has a right to know when he reaches adulthood and to decide what if anything he will do with this knowledge [5, 14]. The threat of this knowledge to surrogate parents is intense. The potential threat to the biological parent is also present; however, the value to the adopted child may be significant.

The child wants to know not only who his mother was but why she gave him up. Each time the surrogate mother gives information to the child, she may feel that she is in some sense sharing the child himself with the biological mother and bringing him closer to the biological mother. This may well engender fears on the surrogate's part of rejections, abandonment, and loss. She may wish to root out the biological mother and claim the child as her own.

The child must be ready and supported emotionally to handle information about his past. He must integrate this shattering knowledge into his identity and create a new world view. In so doing, he reevaluates his relationship with his surrogate mother and with the image of his biological mother. He may try to protect himself from further realization of fears of loss and abandonment—two of the most dreaded fears of childhood.

The child's vulnerability to his past losses, combined with the surrogate's fear of losing the child, sets a theme of fear of separation in their relationship. In their attempts to maintain the bond, each may overtly or unconsciously threaten the other with abandonment, with the surrogate mother saying, "You're not my child; I can always send you back," and the child crying, "You're not my mother; I will go back."

Warm empathic mothering by the surrogate is related to how she copes with losses in her own past and in her child's past. She must be aware of the impact of these factors on the child as she reaches out.

The surrogate mother has certain expectations of the child, and these expectations determine her initial responses. As the mother tentatively offers the child what she feels he should have, she is sensitive to his responses. She tries to accept his uncertainties, resistances, and lack of familiarity with her ways. Slowly, each responds to the other. They must together negotiate the fine line between being too close and too distant. The basic ingredient that each is seeking is a firm sense of commitment at the outset; the surrogate tie continually pursues it.

A mother may try to establish a bond through control and possessiveness. She may expect the child to conform completely to her expectations and use subtle or overt threats of abandonment to enforce his compliance.

Individuation of the child may be thwarted rather than facilitated by the lack of a biological tie. Often the child is cast into the mold of the unreal expectations of the surrogate mother. She may need to have the child succeed and thus prove her adequacy as both a person and a mother. The net effect may then be less autonomy for the child.

Thus the mother may see the child in terms of her own needs, rather than accept him as he is. Perhaps this may in part be a response to the child's high expectations of the surrogate mother, whom he feels should compensate for his deprivations and surpass his idealized image of his biological mother.

The surrogate mother may exact demands in return for what

she has given to the child. A mother may say that "I wanted only *you*," or "I gave up others in order to have you." Built into these claims is the demand for reciprocity. Children are expected to be grateful. The child may feel that his gratitude can never equal the surrogate mother's gift [20]. Critical or negative responses on the part of the child are thwarted; "how sharper than a serpent's tooth it is to have a thankless child" [19].

The surrogate may try to prove in her commitment to the child that she is superior to the biological mother. If she says, "I will not leave you like your mother did," there is a double message, implying a threat of another abandonment.

If the surrogate sees the child as an object to be pitied and she sees herself as a rescuer, gratitude is again fostered on the part of the child, and the debt becomes impossible to repay. Bound together by the overwhelming expectation of gratitude, a symbiotic tie may be created that is very difficult to dissolve.

It takes time and understanding to develop mutuality in expectations, dependency, and affection. Identification of surrogate mother and child as separate but related in an emotional unity is basic for good parent-child relations. The surrogate mother has to be truly therapeutic to support the child through this crisis. Weathering the transition may add maturity to both.

Summary and Implications

In summary, a surrogate mother and her child need to work through the meaning of loss and reattachment. This process is central to the development of a viable bond.

Variations on this separation-attachment schema are found in many other areas of family life—the person who has separated from his divorced or deceased spouse and begins a new marriage, the in-laws who have a new pseudo-parent-child relationship, the child who has a stepsibling or a halfsibling, or the parent who has a child after another one has died.

The dynamics of the surrogate relationship occur in a wide variety of human interactions—the substitute teacher, the counselor at a summer camp, the change to a new therapist, or an institutional caretaker for the young, criminal, ill, or the aged.

Each of us has suffered the loss of a parent or a significant other person and has developed some form of relationship with a surrogate. Our attitudes and those of the surrogate are forever mediated by the image of the original significant figure.

References

1. Benedek, T. Parenthood as a developmental phase. *J. Amer. Psychoan. Assoc.*, 7: (1959), 389–417.
2. Bowlby, J. *Attachment and Loss*, Vol. 1. *Attachment*. Basic Books, New York, 1969.
3. Bowlby, J. *Attachment and Loss,* Vol. 2. *Separation*. Basic Books, New York, 1973.
4. Deutsch, H. *The Psychology of Women*, Vol. II, *Motherhood*. Grune and Stratton, New York, 1945.
5. Fisher, F. *The Search for Anna Fisher*. Arthur Fields, New York, 1973.
6. Goldstein, J., Freud A., and Solnit, A. J. *Beyond the Best Interests of the Child*. Free Press, New York, 1973.
7. Goodall, J., *In the Shadow of Man*. Houghton Mifflin, Boston, 1971.
8. Harlow, H. F., Harlow, M. K., Dodsworth, R. D., and Arling, G. L. Maternal behavior of rhesus monkeys deprived of mothering and peer associations in infancy. *Proc. Amer. Phil. Soc.*, 110 (1966), 58–66.
9. Kadushin, A., Child welfare: adoption and foster care. *Encyclopedia of Social Work*. Vol. I, NASW, New York, 1971.
10. Lindemann, E., The symptomatology and management of acute grief. *Amer. J Psychiat.*, 101 (1944), 141–48.
11. Mahler, M. S. On the first three subphases of the separation-individuation process. *Internat. J. Psychoan.*, 53 (1972), 333–338.
12. Moss, S. Z. and Moss, M. S. Separation as a death experience. *Child Psychiat. Human Devel.*, 3 (1973), 187–94.
13. NASW, *Statistics on Demographic and Social Welfare Trends*. NASW, Washington D.C., 1973.
14. Nemy, E. Frustrating search for identity—who are their real parents? *The New York Times,* July 25, 1972.
15. Parkes, C. M. *Bereavement: Studies of Grief in Adult Life*. International Universities Press, New York, 1972.
16. Paul, N. The use of empathy in the resolution of grief. *Perspect. Biol. Med.*, 11 (1967), 153–69.
17. Sants, H. J. Genealogical bewilderment in children with substitute parents. *Brit. J. Med. Psychol.*, 37 (1964), 133–41.
18. Schechter, M. D. About adoptive parents. In *Parenthood*, E. J. Anthony and T. Benedek, Eds. Little, Brown, Boston, 1970.
19. Shakespeare, W., *King Lear*, Act 1, Scene 4.
20. Simmel, G., Faithfulness and gratitude. In *Theories of Society*, T. Parsons, Ed. Free Press, New York, 1961.
21. Simmel, G., The isolated individual and the dyad.
22. Simon, A. W. *Stepchild in the Family*. Pocket Books, New York, 1965.

23. Spitz, R. *The First Year of Life.* International Universities Press, New York, 1965.
24. Spitz, R. Hospitalism. *Psychoan. Study Child,* 1 (1945), 53–74.
25. Spitz, R. Anaclitic depression. *Psychoan. Study Child,* 2 (1946), 313–342.
26. Winnicott, D. W., *Collected Papers: Through Pediatrics to Psychoanalysis.* Basic Books, New York, 1958.
27. Wolff, K. H. *The Sociology of George Simmel.* Free Press, Glencoe, 1950.

The Vulnerable Child and the Healing Environment

Martin Wolins, Ph.D. (U.S.A.)

Cultural deprivation, academic failure, and personality problems are conditions that most societies try to remedy. The affluent have tended to approach such problems on an individual level and to hang intervention on interpersonal processes between old-timer and newcomer, tutor and pupil, therapist and disturbed. Such an approach, whatever its theoretical base (Freud, Jung, Adler, Rogers or their most recent followers), assumes that the individual relationship between the helper (read: therapist) and the helped (read: patient) is of paramount importance. It is assumed in such therapeutic undertakings that through the medium of transference the needed change is effected, the problem reduced or eliminated.

Honored as this approach has been, it did not withstand well the test of time and experience. This has apparently occurred for two reasons:

1. Many subjects did not change to any degree greater than similar but untreated individuals [9, 16].
2. The one-to-one approach even if assumed to be effective did not lend itself to mass application due to shortages of manpower, extremely high per capita costs, and the reluctance of subjects to become involved in a treatment (as contrasted with a socialization) experience.

It was to be expected that these problems would for either or both of these reasons soon become the province of group-care intervention. Increasing numbers of needy subjects, considerations of cost and, even more significantly, cost/benefit led naturally in this direction. But here too lay disappointment. Aggregations of the deprived, uneducated, disturbed, when kept in closed isolation of institution, school, hospital, or other setting fed upon each other's problems and quickly converted the newcomer. As Polsky [17] had observed in the delinquents' institution, these settings not only did not help the problematic children, but even subverted staff whose function it was to treat them. At best, such settings filled with candidates for help did little or nothing for them [2] unless the environment consisted primarily of a population partaking of the attributes to be achieved.

Here, however, several new and difficult issues arose. If we begin with an assumption that a population with the attributes to be gained is a necessary precondition of success, then we may ask:

1. Do such populations in aggregates exist and where may they be found?
2. Will they be amenable to the introduction of problematic subjects?
3. What is the tip-over point where the problematic begin to establish and enforce normative behavior?

Numerous alternatives have been attempted in regard to question 1. Jones [14] and others have established an expanded "therapeutic community" one including patients, staff, and some members of a nearby English town. Gmeiner [11] and his co-workers have used the social structure of Austrian villages as adjuncts to their open Kinderdörfer. Feuerstein and Krasilowsky [7] grafted a group of seriously disturbed youth onto the healthy body of a youth village for "normal" wards. Gottesmann [12] and Wolins [21] have described the introduction of "culturally deprived" into the normal lifestream of the Israeli *kibbutz*. In brief, the settings could be found.

In regard to question 2, the answer seems generally positive, but with reservations. In every instance the experimenters describe some friction between the "healthy" environment and the "treatment groups" of subjects. To be sure, even some extreme conditions of banishment of the treatment groups in the *kibbutzim* and of the experimenters [5] have been recorded. This should come as no surprise. No "normal" population wishes to be identified with the problematic, nor does it express a great urge to become a therapeutic medium. Why should it? Furthermore, if the process of change is based on the theoretical foundations of modeling and reinforcement [1], it always contains the possibility of moving from the sick to the well rather than what is intended, (i.e., the other way around). Polsky [17] has illustrated this beyond doubt, although a recent report [6] gives reason to believe that the movement need not necessarily be in a negative direction.

Thus the issue of receptivity of "normal" groups to the introduction of problematic members remains an open one and so do the reciprocal effects of the two groups. To considerable measure this is related to the question of tip-over-point, that is, the balance of forces between the supposed changers and those to be changed. We know little about the phenomenon except at the extremes of the continuum and/or under rather simplistic laboratory conditions. Because we know little, professional opinion has been cautious about mixing normal with problematic populations, with their fear of negative outcomes outweighing their hopes of positive change. In any case, the normal reluctance of a population to be associated with deviant, troublesome individuals is usually reinforced by professional behavior that on theoretical as well as practical grounds finds it easier to operate segregated rather than integrated educational and therapeutic establishments.

However, various research findings shed some light on what might be anticipated in the placement of problematic populations within "normal" settings. These may be formulated in a series of propositions.

First, any kind of deviance on the part of a newcomer will hinder group functioning and as such will be resented. The determined, unconventional individual is disruptive because he fails to behave in a predictable manner [13]. The same kind of negative influence is also effected by those who are overly anxious to achieve results as they tend to lower group goals [24].

Second, the problem of the deviant will be particularly acute in highly cohesive groups since they provide less room for maneuver than groups with undefined memberships, objectives, or means [23].

Third, certain conditions of the person or task(s) that predispose the individual to group influence will ease the pains of integration and increase the likelihood of a normal dispersion of newcomers (or "deviants") among the old-timers (or "normals"). In regard to the populations in question, age and sex will be determining attributes of persons and specificity will be determining as to tasks.

Preadolescent females—due to the higher probability of their conforming to group expectations—should have least adjustment difficulties and adolescent males should have most [4].

Low specificity and measurability of tasks and their performance will yield greater conformity and allow for less painful integration. Thus integration of "deviants" will be more rapid and easier if the tasks required of their groups are more general and less prone to objective evaluation (see discussion of this issue in Shaw [18], pp. 250–251.)

Fourth, group members', relative competence *vis-à-vis* the majority should be reflected in sanctioned performance. For example, Costanzo, Reitan, et al. [3] have found that increases in perceived majority group competence are correlated with conformity in minority members' behavior.

Finally, the group should lead to an increase in the venturesomeness of new members as it accepts them and provides a feeling of security. In fact, members should be expected to compete at risk-taking to the degree that they feel challenged by goals and accepted by their peers [15].

In brief, certain types of group environments—while posing difficulties—should nevertheless be conducive to achievment for deprived (or other "deviant") children. These should offer considerable acceptance and initial laxity, have a high proportion of young (and female) members among the deprived, a considerable majority of apparently competent others, and demands that include numerous, often generally described, and basically immeasurable criteria.

Given these conditions as background, it is clear why some current attempts to deal with cultural deprivation through the placement in "normal" institutions should arouse considerable interest. At this moment we are able to report on only one such group and in only one setting. Admittedly, we will not produce nor will we claim to provide definitive data. We can, however, explore some aspects of this phenomenon.

Nitzanim is a youth village. Founded at about the birth of the country, it is as old as the State of Israel—25 years at the time of the experiment. Like the State of Israel, it is also an experiment in absorption. For the first 20 years of its history it was mainly a cultural gateway, an entry point to the society for new arrivals from the various countries of the Diaspora. In the past few years, though, the problems of internal absorption have increasingly come to the forefront in Israel and in Nitzanim. A new population of young people—*T'unei Tipuach* (TT)—has increasingly received the attention and interest of child-care professionals, educators, psychologists, social workers, and others.

Now, *T'unei Tipuach* is a term worth understanding since it carries value connotations above and beyond its gross translation of "culturally deprived." Literally, the words mean "loaded, charged with fostering or cultivation." In short, not the negative term of deprivation, but the positive one of opportunity, characterizes this phenomenon. Nevertheless, the youth who is thus designated is still deviant—in both the country and the youth village. Most young people his age are learning—but he is not. Most have clear and realistic vocational objectives—but he does not. Most have families which encourage and nurture their aspirations—but he does not. Most (almost all boys and nearly all girls) plan to enter the Armed Forces following middle school, but he is not in middle school and there is a high probability the Armed Forces will not accept him.

Forty eight TT children were placed in Nitzanim in the fall of 1972. Although a few such children had been in the institution before, the new group by virtue of its size and assumed deprivation level was qualitatively different from the "normal." The "normal" population of Nitzanim, some 300 young people 14 to 18 years old, is predominantly immigrant—those who are in Israel without parents (some 30 percent) and those whose parents are in the country but either need social assistance or whose children need assistance in acquiring the language, subject matter, and values of Israeli youth (some 60 percent).

This immigrant population is highly mixed, consisting of some 40 different national backgrounds. Within the immigrant millieu two other, much smaller groups have lived for the past few years—about 20 to 25 TT children referred by the Welfare Ministry and an equal number of children with various backgrounds placed privately by their parents. The TTs thus deviate not only by virtue of their academic retardation, but also because they are "Israelis." In fact, this is the way they are referred to in the youth village.

With regard to this type of placement, two directions of inquiry are appropriate: (1) the impact of the setting on the TTs and (2) the reciprocal (i.e., the impact of the TTs on the youth village). In this brief and preliminary study we focus only on (1). Even that is somewhat problematic since the data available are largely the result of tests administered about 6 to 7 months (and again at 20 months) after the placement occurred. Our general conclusions: The TTs are doing well at Nitzanim and—so far as we can tell—Nitzanim was not negatively affected by them, although the process was demanding and even painful at times. Negative anecdotal material abounds from the wards, "Why did you bring *them* here? and from the staff, "How do you deal with *them*?" But the situation about 6 to 7 months after placement seemed stable, quite positive, and creative.

At 29 months after intake (May 1974) the report of the group leader (*madricha*) of this group was almost glowing. They had been merged with a group of immigrants from the Soviet Union with whom the TTs had initially been involved in constant misunderstandings and even conflict. Their ability to lead a group existence had grown. They were reasonably serious in school. However, most important to the life of the village was the marked reduction in verbal and physical antisocial behavior. In a more enthusiastic moment the group leader and also some other staff of the village concluded that these former TTs were nearly ready to absorb and positively acculturate newcomers. To be sure, the situation was still precarious, as occasional "backsliding" (bad language, thefts, etc.) showed, but, on the whole there was considerable satisfaction among staff, and in informal conversation among the village elite one could detect a sense of accomplishment. "We did it," said one of the graduating wards to the investigator, "but it was rough at the start."

Perhaps one reason for the relatively positive conclusion is in the state of the entrants. From the evidence at our disposal it is proper to assume that they were not severely deprived. First, their families whom we interviewed and observed in their homes using the Geismar-La Sorte [10] family-assessment scale are generally well, and this appears to be true along all seven of the dimensions noted (see Table 1).

Clearly, these are largely families who provide good physical care for their children, are generally based on good emotional relations, and are socially integrated into their communities. The statistical analysis disguises, however, some serious cases of social and familial difficulties. For example, the visitor who interviewed case 6 described it as follows:

The family of seven lives in (X Town) in small one-story two-room house in an unpaved side street. One enters through the kitchen where one finds a large iron bed with side rails (like a cage) in which the family keeps the badly retarded oldest child. The mother was in bed (at time of visit) together with two younger children while a boy of 12 was washing the floor under her supervision. The

Table 1   Family Functioning along Seven Specified Dimensions[a]

Dimension	Condition of the Family (in Percent of Families)			
	NA	Adequate	Marginal	Inadequate
1. Social activities[b]	4	55	38	3
2. Health conditions and practices	4	52	34	10
3. Role enactment parents and children	4	55	38	3
4. Physical care of children	4	83	10	3
5. Emotional relations	4	67	26	3
6. Income and budgeting	4	58	31	7
7. Property management	4	69	24	3

[a] The number of families in the sample was 28. Of the 48 students who initially entered, 13 had either left the program or were erroneously included in our sample. For another six we could not obtain interviews on most items for the family and child and dropped them from the sample. As far as could be ascertained nothing distinguished the NAs from the 29 children-families in the sample. For one family, there was no interview.

[b] For definitions, see Geismar and La Sorte [10], pp. 205-222.

mother excused herself saying, "I've been ailing since the last childbirth six weeks ago."

Despite this particular case, there seemed to be a warm relationship between the mother and children, who were helpful and attentive to the younger ones. They all seemed well nourished. Furthermore, the mother was anxious to include the father in the interview and requested that the interviewer "return later in the day." In fact, all of the families in the sample are heir to personal or familial problems—a prerequisite to the children's admission into the program.

More significantly, but obviously related to this general state of fairly positive family conditions, the value orientation of these families is quite in line with the institution's expectations. Using a 5-factor inventory [20] we compared the responses of parents with those of the institution's select pupils ("elite"). By and large, we found them compatible. Several rather interesting distinctions do appear, however, between the elite's position and that of the parents. First, the elite has learned to discriminate between competitive and controlled achievement, whereas the parents have not. They value achievement highly, though—an asset the youth village can utilize in its work with their children. Second, and related to earlier, the families may be somewhat less concerned with helping others—doing things for others at one's own expense than are the institutional elite; this is something that one should probably expect from adults in general. Third, the parents value conformity—a virtue in this instance since this helps the modeling and reinforcement assignment of the institution in relation to the TT children. Finally, we have the matter of rejecting detachment, which the elite comes close to doing and the parents do not.

The overall impression regarding parental values conveyed by Table 2 is thus positive, with some reservations. Parents appear to push (at least verbally) in the direction of achievement and conformity, which should stand the institution in good stead. The somewhat defficient support of social involvement (shown in Factors I and V), while problematic, is nevertheless secondary in the short run given the primary, educational objectives of placing the TT in the youth village. In the long run, though, these and the parental inability to discriminate between controlled and competitive achievement should prove troublesome as they might lead to isolation, egoism, and aggression.

What about the children at time of admission? Anecdotal reports depict them as dull, academically deficient, and socially problematic. Apparently, the anecdotes correctly depicted the situation, at least insofar as academic performance and cognitive skills are concerned. The initial Primary Mental Abilities (PMA) test [19] (in Hebrew Translation) scores for tests administered in September 1972 had a mean of 154.4 [range 112–187 and standard deviation (SD) 17.3] closely comparable to scores for 14-year-olds in one of the deprived [i.e., low Socioeconomic strata (SES)] schools in Jerusalem whose eighth graders obtained 155.0 (SD 27.52 *sic*). First grading period marks fully support the anec-

Table 2   Parental Values Compared with Institutional Elite
(Low Values Reflect Acceptance; High Reflect Rejection)

	Factors	Parents Mean	S.D.	Elite Mean Value	S.D.	Range of Possible Responses	Cutting Point + −
I.	Other orientation (e.g., "wants to devote his life to helping other people")	12.6	3.0	11.8	2.6	6–24	15
II.	Achievement (controlled) (e.g., "tries to be best in whatever he does")	10.9	2.2	9.7	1.9	5–20	12.5
III.	Competitive achievement (e.g., "enjoys competing with others to find who is best")	11.4	1.9	12.3	2.0	5–20	12.5
IV.	Individualism (e.g., "would rather be different from others rather than just like them")	16.4	3.3	14.8	2.1	6–24	15
V.	Detachment (e.g., likes to be left alone to do just what he wants to do)	16.2	2.7	17.5	2.5	7–28	17.5

dotal reports showing the TTs to be highly deficient in language and mathematics.

Two positive features of this population should be noted before proceeding with an analysis of what happened to the children in the youth village. First is the close ties they continue to maintain with their families. Visiting is normal (as defined by the youth village)[1] for all but one child. This should be anticipated given the state of family functioning we noted earlier. Second, the relatively low standard deviation of this group on the PMA as compared with low-SES subjects shows a selectivity that should positively affect institutional behavior even though we do have a number of cases low on the scale (four cases below 140—112, 133, 133, and 139, to be specific). In short, the wards are in the upper-range TT populations as to both familial environment and cognitive functioning. Yet these are also academic failures—children who have not done well in school, and were not ready to progress into normal secondary or vocational education.

On arrival in the village the children were deliberately integrated with other (i.e., non-TT) wards. For various reasons the distribution in the living groups was by no means ideal. It would have been desirable to have predominant majorities of "normals" along with sizable minorities of TTs, the former to give a strong positive character to the groups, and the latter to give the TTs a measure of strength so that they do not feel totally overwhelmed from the outset. Out of living groups of approximately 40, the TTs in our sample constituted eight in E_1 (Pine—an agriculturally-oriented group) and 21 in E_2 (Wave—a vocationally-oriented group specializing in merchant marine subjects).[2]

During September 1972 through May 1973 these children lived in the regular groups and received usual academic and work assignments, with one exception. They were eligible for an enrich-

---

[1] The child goes home once every three weeks and on holidays, and the parents have visited in the village at least twice between September 1972 and April 1973.

[2] For a more detailed description (in English), see Report of the Select Subcommittee on Education, Committee on Education and Labor House of Representatives Ninety-First Congress, Second Session, U.S. Government Printing Office, Washington, D.C., 1970. For additional information about the youth village in Israel, see Wolins and Gottesmann [22].

ment program designed and supervised by Feuerstein.[3] Tests at the conclusion of less than one full school year showed progress in several areas but also some stability of negative aspects. Positive change occurred in relation to cognitive growth and social adjustment. There was no apparent positive movement in the value area.

The changes noted in Table 3 are not large but are uniformly positive in several respects. First, there is a modest increase in the mean of right responses with a corresponding reduction of the standard deviation mainly by a rise in the lower range of scores. Second, there is a reduction in the number and range of wrong answers. This despite the fact that the *total* number of responses rose. This rise constitutes third point to be noted. The 24 children made 657 additional decisions (27.4 per person), showing an increased measure of risking. And not all the risk was wasted, as the mean gain shows. Finally, the rather positive results are well distributed over the full range of PMA items (see Table 4).

Thus in every category we note a slight improvement for about two-thirds of the cases, by both an increase in the number of answers right and a decrease in the wrongs.

Academic performance also gives reason for cautious optimism. Spring term 1974 grades were available for 25 of the 28 subjects originally in the study. Table 5 shows their distribution by academic subject aggregates (in categories of language, mathematics, and vocational subjects).

Table 3 Primary Mental Abilities Scores for TT Children Times I and II (N = 24 for Whom Both Times I and II Tests were Available)

Time	R(ight) Range	Mean	SD
I	112–187	154.4	17.3
II	123–188	159.0	14.0
	W(rong) Range	Mean	SD
I	16–68	38.6	11.7
II	13–61	30.0	10.1

[3] For a description, see Feuerstein [8]. We cannot analyze the effect of the enrichment program per se due to inadequate sample—only some TTs participated in the program.

Table 4   Comparison of Wards at Times I and II in Regard to
Changes in Right and Wrong Responses
(*N* = 24)

Type of Material	Right Answers (Numbers of Children)			Wrong Answers		
	Rise	Drop	No Change	Rise	Drop	No Change
Verbal	13	7	4	6	18	0
Numerical	17	6	1	6	16	2
Grouping	20	3	1	8	11	5
Total	19	4	1	10	14	0

Table 5   Distribution of Mean Grades in Three Subject Categories (May 1974)

Subject	Grades (on a scale of 4-10)					
	4 (Failure)	5	6 (Satisfactory)	7	8 (Good)	Total
Language	1	6	11	4	3	25
Mathematics	7	3	10	3	2	25
Vocational	1	1	12	6	5	25

As the table shows, there are still some problems in mathematics, and the bulk of wards are earning satisfactory but not good or excellent (9s and 10s) grades. However, we should remember that these are the former school failures for whom satisfactory school achievement is indeed an accomplishment.

Regarding social integration the results we have are also encouraging. It was to be anticipated that the usual population of Nitzanim would reject the TTs from the outset. Anecdotal materials indicate that such a rejection did indeed occur at the start. Yet when we administered sociometric tests in May 1973, the TTs appeared evenly distributed as to status within their respective groups. Two types of questions were asked—one indicating preference, and the other rejection in four social situations. For example:

1. With whom among the members of the group would you like to share a room? (Name three persons.)

And immediately following the reverse:

2. With whom from the group would you not like to share a room? This is followed by three spaces.

Both the positive and negative choices were then rank-ordered within the living group (Pine and Wave) and each child received a score combining the two attitudes. The score was computed as follows:

Rank of Person in Positive Choice	Rank in Nega- tive Choice	Summary Score
1–5 high on list	Not mentioned	1 star
1–5	7–13 low on list	2
6–9	Not mentioned	3
1–5	1–6	4
6–9	7–13	5
6–9	1–6	6
Not mentioned	Not mentioned	7 isolate
Not mentioned	7–13	8 reject
Not mentioned	1–6	9 severe reject

Table 5 shows that as of the end of the first school year the TTs had generally done well socially but also that some danger signs were up. In regard to every question there were TT stars or near stars but also some rejects and even severe rejects. First, to the positive side, the TT children were, as a group, well accepted by the others in regard to social, vocational, and academic contacts. To be sure, they themselves comprised a considerable proportion of the *choosers,* but they were also selected by the non-TTs in their groups.[4] On the negative side, it should be a matter of some concern (and an issue for intervention) that a number of children appeared in categories 7, 8, and 9 (i.e., isolation, rejection, and severe rejection). It requires little professional competence or even plain common sense to realize what such a social status means for a child anywhere and more especially for one in a youth village. Distant from his parents, siblings, and neighborhood friends and rejected by his institutional peers such a child has no

---

[4] By May 1974, that is, at the end of 20 months in care, most of the TTs are fully integrated with the immigrant Russians. Staff reports on their sociometric position are generally favorable.

one to turn to except the staff. One can only hope that the staff has the insight, time, and good will to respond properly.

By comparison with cognitive growth and social integration in a dynamic environment, value acquisition is a complex and slow process. This holds not only in regard to behavior but even for expression. If we assume that the value position of the TT children at intake was similar to their parents' and set as our goal in Nitzanim the behavior and values of the elite, then by the end of the first academic year (Table 6) the TTs appear to have gained little but confusion. On four of the five factors they seemed to be moving away from the elite or overshooting it. The situation was particularly blatant in regard to controlled achievement (i.e., competing against yourself) and individualism (i.e., the desire and ability to be different).

It is reasonable to propose that in regard to the former the children lacked comprehension and in the latter they acted as blind converts. Neither is a particularly positive trait. The two possibly bright aspects in the whole matter were the slight movement in Factor V and the rejection of competitive achievement. Even these two were accompanied by rejection of controlled (read: good) achievement as well. And, the progress in detachment—which is, to be sure, an asset in group care—may nevertheless in this instance reflect a fear of isolation still based on earlier insecurities.

The whole matter of values is most difficult. Unlike cognitive development or social relationships, there is no good *end* here. Rather it is a particular position along a continuum that is most desirable. That position is known only to models and reinforcers. It takes time to learn where to find and how to land on this small island in the broad expanse. This is done by successive approximation in which "reversal" and "overshooting" are logical preliminary steps.

In May 1974 (some 20 months after placement) it was possible to secure some additional data on the TTs. These included grades (Table 7) and a re-test on value inventory. The value data are of greatest interest as they reflect the group leaders' satisfaction with their charges. Briefly stated, there occurred positive changes on each dimension. The new data are as follows (N = 21):

	Factor	Mean	SD
I.	Other orientation	12.2	2.8
II.	Controlled achievement	10.2	2.0
III.	Competitive achievement	12.5	2.1
IV.	Individualism	15.3	2.4
V.	Detachment	17.3	2.8

This means that on every one of the variables the TT expressed values have come closer to those of the elite. In part, the change in group means and reduction in SDs is due to the dropping out of several more problematic wards. However, subject by subject comparisons of parent scores and ward scores of May 1973 and May 1974 show substantial changes in *individuals who remained in the program.*

In summary, we have here a fairly successful case of group impact on culturally deprived adolescents. They exhibit positive changes in cognition and social integration even after only a brief period (7–9 months) of care. Little impact is noted in regard to values in the first year but much more in the second. While the achievement is commendable and should lead to further placement of such children in settings like Nitzanim, the cautious selection that was employed (as evident in the status of families and of most children at time of placement) precludes any conclusions regarding the impact of such an environment on more severely deprived, that is, the most needy potential consumers of such a rehabilitation approach. Thus, whereas Youth Aliyah and Nitzanim have cause for pride in that achievement, there is reason to wish that the experiment will become more adventurous, more bold, and hence more risky and potentially more significant. To be more specific, Nitzanim and similar settings should be encouraged to accept some more difficult children, but they must also maintain a substantial and well-rooted elite to cope with the socialization difficulties such children will undoubtedly pose.

How well did our observations follow the theoretical propositions stated earlier? Given sample size and the measurements used, it is improper to draw theoretical conclusions. Rather, we may divide the propositions into two groups, those who, given the

Table 6 Sociometric Position of TTs and Their Groupmates in Pine and Wave Groups at End of One School Year

| | Summary Values | | | | | | | | | |
	1 Star	2	3	4	5	6	7 Isolate	8 Reject	9 Severe Reject	Total
Group					Number of children in category					
Living in the same room										
Pine TTs	1	2	1	—	2	1	—	2	—	9
Pine others	3	2	2	1	3	4	—	1	1	17
Wave TTs	7	2	4	1	6	3	—	3	2	28
Wave others	2	—	3	—	3	1	—	—	2	11
Eating at same table										
Pine TTs	—	5	1	1	1	—	—	1	—	9
Pine others	—	3	2	1	4	5	—	—	2	17
Wave TTs	5	5	2	1	5	9	—	1	—	28
Wave others	2	—	—	—	5	2	—	—	—	9[a]
Doing homework jointly										
Pine TTs	1	1	—	1	2	2	—	1	1	9
Pine others	1	1	1	4	7	3	—	—	—	17
Wave TTs	7	2	3	1	9	3	—	—	4	29
Wave others	1	2	1	—	2	2	1	—	1	10
Working together										
Pine TTs	1	2	1	—	1	1	1	2	—	9
Pine others	1	4	3	2	4	2	—	—	1	17
Wave TTs	4	4	4	2	5	3	1	3	2	28
Wave others	4	—	—	1	4	—	—	1	1	11

[a] Slight variations in N due to absence of responses on some negative items.

Table 7   Mean Value Position of Parents, Children, and Elite (May 1973)
(Low N = Acceptance; High N = Rejection)

	Factor	Parents		Elite		Children		
		Mean	SD	Mean	SD	Mean	SD	Change
I.	Other orientation	12.6	3.0	11.8	2.6	12.8	3.2	Reversal
II.	Controlled achievement	10.9	2.2	9.7	1.9	12.1	2.5	Reversal
III.	Competitive achievement	11.4	1.9	12.3	2.0	12.9	2.3	Overshoot
IV.	Individualism	16.4	3.3	14.8	2.1	17.3	2.8	Reversal
V.	Detachment	16.2	2.7	17.5	2.5	16.6	3.8	Progress

conditions at Nitzanim, seemed to facilitate individual achievement, and those who hindered. Facilitating the adjustment and
advancement of wards were the unspecific numerous demands,
the sex-mixed group (Pine), the acceptance by staff and ultimately
by the other children and the high proportion of competent,
praised peer-level others. Hindering achievement was the inevitable deviances of the TTs from institutional norms that led to
initial rejection, making staff work exceptionally difficult and important. To a degree the existing cohesion of an elite made initial
entry more difficult, but a large village has many subgroups and
considerable accommodation can occur. On balance, however, it is
clear that the forces toward positive change were dominant. What
should improve the balance further is a larger proportion of
females, and it would seem (perhaps unbelievably) the prior experience with TTs that will make the behavior of following groups
less bizarre-looking and hence more tolerable. Perhaps of most
significance in this project is the fact that the powerful environment of the institution functioned positively. Because the institution (village in this case) is such a powerful instrument, the risk
involved in its use is considerable. On the one hand, the likelihood
of rejection by the elite always hovered over the TTs. Vulnerable
as they were due to past rejection and failure, a further negative
experience in this closed environment would have been devastating indeed. Midway in the first year it became clear that the institution did not have such an impact; this is a credit to the staff,
the elite, and the multipurposive nature of the environment.
However, the TTs were not the only vulnerable children in this
experiment. The elite and other children in the village were also

at risk; they too were vulnerable. Yet, vulnerability is a constant of a living, growing, functioning individual and social system. The task is to turn vulnerability from problem to challenge to solution.

References

1. Bandura, A. *Principles of Behavior Modification.* Holt, Rinehard and Winston, New York, 1969.
2. Coleman, J. S. *Equality of Educational Opportunity.* U.S. Office of Education, Washington, D.C., 1966.
3. Costanzo, P. R., Reitan, H. T., and Shaw, M. E. Conformity as a function of experimentally induced minority and majority competence. *Psychonomic Sci.,* 10 (1968), 329–330.
4. Costanzo, P. R. and Shaw, M. E. Conformity as function of age level. *Child Devel.,* 37 (1966), 967–975.
5. Cumming, J. and Cumming E. *Closed Ranks,* Harvard Univ. Press, Cambridge, Mass., 1957.
6. Feldman, R. A. Prosocial and antisocial boys together. *Social Work,* 18: 5 (1973), 26–37.
7. Feuerstein, R. and Krasilowsky, D. The Treatment Group Technique. In Wolins and Gottesmann [22].
8. Feuerstein, R. The development of the socio-culturally disadvantaged adolescent in group care. In Wolins and Gottesmann [22].
9. Fisher, J. Is casework effective? A review. *Social Work,* 18: 1 (1973), 5–20.
10. Geismar, L. L. and La Sorte, M. A., *Understanding the Multi-Problem Family.* Association Press, New York, 1964.
11. Gmeiner, H. *Die SOS Kinderdörfer.* SOS-Kinderdorf Verlag, Innsbruck, 1960.
12. Gottesmann, M. An immigrant youth group and its absorption in a Kibbutz. In Wolins and Gottesmann [22].
13. Haythorn, W. W. The influence of individual members on the characteristics of small groups. *J. Abnorm. Soc. Psychol.,* 1953, 48 (1953), 276–284.
14. Jones, M. *The Therapeutic Community,* Basic Books, New York, 1953.
15. Levinger, G. and Schneider, D. J. Test of the "risk is a value" hypothesis. *J. Personality Soc. Psychol.,* 11 (1969), 165–169.
16. Levitt, E. E. Psychotherapy with children: A further evaluation. *Behav. Res. Ther.,* 1: 1 (1963), 43–51.
17. Polsky, H. *Cottage Six.* Russell Sage Foundation, New York, 1962.
18. Shaw, M. E. *Group Dynamics: The Psychology of Group Behavior.* McGraw-Hill, New York, 1971.
19. Thurstone, L. L. and Thurstone, T. G. *Primary Mental Abilities Test, (P.M.A.).* Science Research Associates, New York, 1962 (administered in Hebrew).
20. Wolins, M. Group care: Friend or foe? *Social Work,* 14: 1 (1969), 35–53.
21. Wolins, M., "The Kibbutz as foster mother," in Wolins and Gottesmann [22].
22. Wolins, M. and Gottesmann, M., Eds. *Group Care: An Israeli Approach.* Gordon and Breach, New York, 1971.
23. Wyer, R. S. Effects of incentive to perform well, group attraction, and group acceptance on conformity in a judgmental task. *J. Soc. Psychol.,* 4 (1966), 21–26.

24. Zander, A. and Wulff, D. Members' test anxiety and competence: Determinants of a group's aspirations. *J. Personality,* 34 (1966), 54–70.

LIFE HISTORY OF THE VULNERABLE CHILD

Editorial

Colette Chiland, M.D., Ph.D. (France)

One can easily enough, in general terms, define parameters of risk that are external and statistical. If one thinks of *risk* as an antecedent state determined by various circumstances and events, such as heredity, pregnancy, the perinatal experiences, physical illnesses, social class, pathology in the parents, and vicissitudes of family life, then *vulnerability* can be regarded as a consequent state manifested by the child at risk. At any moment during development when an assessment is made, the conclusions do not carry any weight beyond the point of evaluation. For instance, an apparent resistance to increased risks at a particular point does not permit us to conclude that no further trouble is to be expected later on, especially at so-called "critical periods" of development such as entering school, reaching puberty, becoming adult, or grappling with any of the psychosexual stages. These "critical periods" may constitute in themselves factors of risk or may aggravate risks that have made their appearance earlier. A similar state of vulnerability may exist or be reactivated following on traumatization even when the subject appears to have come through the exposure unscathed.

The parameters of vulnerability are even more difficult to discern than those of risk. Risks do not operate on a passive or inert individual. At all levels of risk and vulnerability, the subject actively organizes what happens to him. For example, in the area of

471

genetics the presence of pathological genes and a knowledge of their mode of transmission, whether dominant or recessive, do not allow us to draw direct conclusions as to the nature of the disturbance being observed. The manifestation of disorder is modulated by the gene groupings, their spatial proximity, their degree of penetrance and expressivity, and other variables. The utilization of innate potential is also a function of environmental relationships, of the way in which the child is cathected by the parents and the parents by the child. What is commonly ascribed to factors of constitution may well be an instance of "benevolent narcissism," as the French say, where the subject cathects himself positively for a condition of intense and rigidly defensive narcissism. The disentanglement of genetic, constitutional, and early environmental factors is far from being an easy clinical exercise, and yet we jump to some conclusion in our everyday practices.

The vulnerability of the child also depends on his entire developmental history, which cannot be described only from the outside as a series of observable events but even more importantly as a subjectively experienced chain of circumstances where the significance of events is determined by the impression that they make on the individual, and which may have no relation at all to their external objective importance. A commonplace fact of everyday life is the way in which the carelessly spoken and quickly forgotten words of a parent can have a structuring role on the child's fantasies that can in turn influence the child's behavior. For such reasons the vulnerability of the child can, in the most propitious cases, be better understood by psychoanalytic than by objective external investigations that do not attempt to get below the surface or probe into the essence of the internal state.

An 18-Year, Prospective, Longitudinal Study of Adopted Boys

Michael Bohman, M.D., Ph.D., and Sören Sigvardsson, B. A.
(Sweden)

Stimulation for studies on the process of adoption has come mainly from two quarters: (1) genetic research and (2) the child-welfare activities of the community. For genetic research the adoptive situation presents a ready-made experiment at base for testing hypotheses concerning the importance of heredity versus childhood environment in the development of certain types of mental disturbances or diseases (e.g., schizophrenia, primary affective disease, psychopathic personality). The goal of the social research on adoption is to determine which factors in the child, the adoptive parents, and society influence the adoptive process and to what extent this process can be predicted at the time of the child's placement. The general idea behind both these kinds of research is the hope of being able to work out practical models for the prediction and the prevention of diseases and social maladjustment. As a tool in social-political research, the "adoption method" offers a unique opportunity to analyze the triple hypothesis that inequalities of occupational status and income result from the effects of genetic inheritance, family background, and schooling.

The present chapter summarizes some findings in a longitudinal study of male adoptees who were investigated at different ages from birth to 18 to 19 years of age when they were enlisted for military service and also briefly discusses some implications of these findings for our understanding of the variations of social and intellectual abilities among people in our society and for the consequences of child-welfare policy.

Some Methodological Considerations

Prospective or anterospective longitudinal studies with reference to personal development are taken here to imply that the same individuals are continually observed in adequate studies or behavioral assessments at regular intervals during their childhood and adolescence.

A great deal of the knowledge about children's development has been derived from cross-sectional investigations of representative samples of different age groups. Thus the data obtained on different occasions have not originated from the same individuals, but from groups of different children at different ages. This kind of investigation has some inherent limitations regarding the possibilities of making predictions about individual development. When studying relations between previous observations and subsequent events with a view of constructing a model for *prediction,* the only resort is to make several observations of the same group on children at different points of time.

The principle of the longitudinal follow-up, which is gaining increasing practical currency in connection with preventive child care, is that progression, regression, and deviant development at certain ages is assessed in relation to the initial situation together with achievement during earlier stages [4].

Subjects and Methods

The investigation presented here originated in a cohort of 624 children born in 1956–1957. They were born after unwanted pregnancies, and at the time of their births their mothers had reported to an adoption agency that they wanted them adopted. Subjects, family background, and so on have been described at length elsewhere [1, 2], and only a short description is given here. Of the original cohort, 168 children were placed in adoptive homes before the age of 1 year (Group I), 208 returned to their biological mothers (Group II), most of them shortly after birth, and were brought up by them, and 203 children (Group III) were placed in foster care, most of them before 1 year of age. In these cases there was no clear decision about the legal status of the child from the beginning, but most of these children grew up with their foster parents. However, after some years many of the children were legally adopted. Accordingly, the three groups represent three alternative models of placement for unwanted children. From the very beginning of our study it was clear to us that these three alternative subjects provided us with an excellent opportunity to compare and evaluate the results and influences of child-welfare decisions on the social and personal development of the subjects. The adopted children (Group I) were placed in homes, which had been thoroughly prepared for this task through a series of interviews before placement. Among the adopted parents there were many of good social, educational, and economic standing. Of the adoptive fathers 68 percent had professional or intermediate occupations, as compared to only 28 percent in a representative control group. The children in the other two groups had less favorable placement conditions. The *biological mothers* who took care of their children themselves despite their earlier decision to have them adopted (Group II) were predominantly young, unmarried or alone, mostly unskilled or semiskilled, and had unsatisfactory places to live. About half of them already had one or several other children. In general, their financial and social opportunities were limited.

The foster parents in Group III were on the average older than the adoptive parents. Their education and occupational status were similar to those in the general population. In contrast to the children in the other two groups, these children grew up in small communities or in rural areas. These parents were seldom prepared for their task as nonbiological parents, as were the adoptive parents in Group I. Payments from the child-welfare organization were also the rule, at least at the beginning of the placement.

When one compares the outcome of the placement of the children in these three groups, it must be borne in mind that the process of placement itself involved a certain amount of selection in respect to the children. Children in Group III, more often than those in Groups I and II, had a negative social heritage, parents with criminal records or alcohol problems, or mothers who suffered more frequent complications during pregnancy or delivery. They had also a relatively longer stay in infants' homes before their placement, compared to other children in the cohort. Through the collection of much social and medical background data we tried to make it possible to check for such selective factors in our future analyses.

General Design of the Study

The study was planned as a longitudinal ex-post-facto experiment, starting at the time of pregnancy. The children in Groups II and III have served as a basis for comparison with the adopted children in Group I. The results of studies at 11 and 15 years of age have been reported elsewhere [1, 2, 3].

To date we have also completed a study of the boys at 18 years of age regarding information about the medical and psychological investigation at the time of their enlistment for military service. In the present chapter we intend to summarize some of the pertinent findings from these three studies at 11, 15, and 18 years of age concerning the male-cohort focusing on the changes with time.

Methods

At 11 and 15 years of age information was collected from official records, interviews with teachers, questionnaires, school marks, and school health cards. By 18 years of age we had access to medical and psychological data from the military enlistment procedure. The data-collection methods have consequently been somewhat different at the various ages of observation. Figure 1 illustrates the various steps in the investigation over the years.

The results of the interviews with teachers at the study at 11 years showed that the adopted boys manifested a high rate of nervous and behavioral disturbances compared to class controls. Twenty-two percent were classified as "problem children," compared to 12 percent among their class controls. There were, however, very few among either the subjects or the controls that could be classified as antisocial.

Cohort of 329 Boys Born 1956–1957

	Group I Adopted	Group II Restored to Biological Mother	Group III Foster Children
Birth	$N = 93$	$N = 118$	$N = 118$
11 Years: teachers' interviews, school marks	$N = 93$	$N = 106$	$N = 69^a$
15 Years: teachers' questionnaire school marks	$N = 89$	$N = 109$	$N = 113$
18 Years: military enlistment procedure	$N = 79$	$N = 93$	$N = 91$

[a]One year group only.

Figure 1 General design of the study.

The adjustment of the adopted boys appeared to be fairly independent of the various background variables investigated, such as perinatal complications, age at placement, economic status of adoptive parents, or registered information such as criminality or alcohol abuse about the biological parents. Our conclusion was that the adoptive situation in itself was a stressful experience for both children and parents, which accounted for the high frequency of disturbances among the adoptees.

Furthermore, a comparison with the other two groups showed the same rate of disturbances as among the adopted boys, with 20 percent for Group II and 22 percent for Group III. These results contradicted our hypotheses as we had expected fewer disturbances among the adoptees, who had been brought up in much better socioeconomic circumstances than the children in the comparison groups. The disturbances were, however, more pronounced in Groups II and III than in Group I, even if antisocial behavior was seldom found.

Four years later, when the boys were attending the 8th class of the 9-year Swedish comprehensive schooling, we sent a questionnaire to their class teachers. The instruments used in this study were rating scales, in which the adjustment and behavior of the pupils were scored on 7-point scales. This study showed that the differences between adopted children and their classmates were by now of little consequence. There was still, admittedly, a slight tendency for them to have lower scores for adjustment in different variables and to have lower mean marks compared with their controls, but these differences were very small and only occasionally significant. On the other hand, a considerable proportion of the boys in the other two groups now displayed yet stronger tendencies of maladjustment than were found at the age of 11.

Among the adopted boys 5 percent were classified as socially maladjusted, compared to 6 percent among the controls. Among boys in Groups II and III the corresponding figures were 14 percent and 15 percent (differences statistically significant at 1-percent level). The term "social maladjustment" here stands for cases displaying for instance repeated criminality, truancy, abuse of alcohol or drugs, and so on.

Correlations between Adjustments at Ages 11 and 15

One of the aims of a prospective longitudinal study is to gain some knowledge about behavior and symptom persistence over a period of time. Such knowledge is essential for adequate assessment of the value of current observations concerning the individual child.

As was expected the various symptoms and syndromes of behavior among the adopted boys and their comparison groups showed positive correlations between the two ages of observation. These correlations were highest among the comparison groups (II + III); that is, symptom persistence was highest in these groups. In this context, only correlations concerning maladjustment at 11 and social maladjustment at 15 are discussed. As was mentioned earlier, the two classifications do not correspond completely. "Maladjustment" or "problem" at 11 implies that the boy had a certain number of symptoms and exhibited behavior that was disturbing to himself or his surroundings. At 15 the term "social maladjustment" implies

Table 1   Correlations between Classifications of Adjustment at Ages 11 and 15

		Group I			Group II			Group III		
		15 Years								
		A	B	C	A	B	C	A	B	C
	1.	2	13	5	8	8	3	6	7	3
11 Years	2.	2	17	11	3	20	4	—	10	6
	3.	—	19	20	2	27	29	2	23	11
		$\chi^2 = 7.95$			$\chi^2 = 29.05$			$\chi^2 = 13.69$		
		$c = 0.29$			$c = 0.47$			$c = 0.41$		

Code: 1 — "Problem child"   A — Social maladjustment
          2 — Moderate symptoms   B — Fair adjustment
          3 — Few or no symptoms   C — Good adjustment

behavior such as truancy, running away, criminality, abuse of alcohol, or drugs.

In the adopted group from among 20 maladjusted "problem boys" at the interview at 11, only two were classified as "socially maladjusted" at 15 ($c = 0.29$; $x^2 = 7.95$; p = NS). But of the 19 "problem boys" at 11 years of age in Group II, eight were "socially maladjusted at 15 ($c = 0.47$; $\chi^2 = 29.05$). In Group III, six out of the 16 "problem boys" at 11 were "socially maladjusted" at 15 ($c = 0.41$).

The risk of a "problem boy" at 11 being classified as socially maladjusted 4 years later was consequently very low among the adopted boys in Group I, but much higher among children with other placements. However, from a purely practical point of view the observations at 11 were not very useful as predictors for social adjustment at 15 for any of the placement groups.

The predictive power at the "positive end" of our rating scales may be said to be somewhat better. Very few of those boys who were judged to be "symptom-free" or have "moderate symptoms" were classified as socially maladjusted at 15 (none in Group I, two in Group II, and two in Group III).

Considering the somewhat different modes of data collection and the different classifications of the variables at 11 and 15, there was a fairly good agreement between the two studies. For instance, such variables as aggressivity, ability to concentrate, and intellectual capacity showed high correlations between ages.

It may be justifiable to conclude that high aggressivity, lack of concentration, or lower than average intellectual capacity did not lead to social maladjustment among the adopted boys in Group I. It is conceivable that it did do so in the comparison groups, although our data do not permit us to analyze this at present.

Boys at 18: Investigation at Military Enlistment Procedure

In Sweden there is general conscription for all men between the ages of 18 and 47. The aim of military conscript training is that male citizens be selected for training in one of the branches of the armed forces. Officially, the objectives of enlistment procedures are as follows:

1. To test a conscript's fitness for service in the armed forces and his suitability for training prior to posting within the military organization.
2. To make decisions concerning exemption or possible alternative service during the period required of the conscript if he is to fulfill his service commitment.
3. To decide about enlistment and postings.

In other words, the aim of the enlistment procedures is partly an analysis of each individual's capacity to fulfill the requirement of military service and partly a preparation of conscripts for appropriate postings within the defense system.

Since 1968 about 90 percent of all male youths have been required to undergo a 2-day intensive medical, psychological, and social examination, which leads to the establishment of a personal health and capacity profile. The following enlistment procedure variables are used in the analysis of this series:

1. Intellectual capacity. This is measured on a 9-grade Stanine scale and is based on four tests that include logic-inductive, spatial, linguistic,and technical factors.
2. Psychical function capacity. This is analyzed during a semis-tructural interview with a psychologist and aims at giving a complete picture of a youth's education, occupational experience, social background, interests, personality and social functions, and so on. This is used as a basis for assessing his

military suitability and potential for leadership. The operative time for the psychological test element is 175 minutes, and the result is summed up in a psychological profile.
3. Medical examination. This consists of anamnesis, a physical examination and laboratory tests on blood and urine, x-rays, electrocardiogram, and so on. The results of these examinations are not discussed in this chapter.
4. Assessment of leadership capacity. The leadership capacity of about 60 percent of those with the highest intellectual evaluation was assessed. The basis of this appraisal is measures of adjustment and function in school, employment, leisure time, and home and emotional stability, which implies that these are also the variables that are of interest for civilian leadership capacity.

Subjects and Drop-outs

Every male subject from the original cohort of 329 boys was identified according to his birth data and identity number, available from the official population register. For every subject a male born on the same day was selected as a control. When the list of subjects and controls was checked against "persontapes" of the military enlistment data, 22.8 percent of the subjects and 15.8 percent of the controls had dropped out for various reasons. This attrition rate is higher than was expected for both subjects and controls. Otto [5] found, for instance, that only 8.7 percent of the 1953 cohort for military enlistment was missing, as a result of death, emigration, or exemption in advance because of illness or handicap or for other reasons. The attrition rate was about the same for adopted boys (Group I) as for their controls (17.2 percent and 18.3 percent, respectively), but was higher in Groups II and III. According to our analyses the higher attrition among these groups was due to emigration and exemption for sociomedical reasons. Thus we were left with 263 boys who had all passed the military enlistment procedure. The somewhat higher attrition among our controls compared to the 193 cohort may be connected with a tendency at present to exempt more youths from military service than in previous years.

Results of Military Enlistment Investigation

INTELLECTUAL CAPACITY

Intellectual capacity was, as mentioned, assessed by four different tests, including logic-inductive, linguistic, spatial, and technical abilities. Means among subjects and controls are given for the different subtests in Table 2. Differences were assessed by t-tests (one-tailed). The standardization of the tests and assessments were changed between 1956 and 1957, which implies that means were different between these years. This does not, however, affect the comparison between subjects and controls in our series as every subject had a control born on the same day. In Groups I and III there were about as many subject-control pairs born 1956 as in 1957. In Group II, on the other hand, there were more subject-control pairs born in 1956. As the Stanine values were higher that year, means for the whole group is elevated. This is the reason why the controls in Group II are somewhat higher than in the two other control groups. Consequently, comparisons should be done only between subjects and controls in every group, not between groups.

In all four partial tests (verbal, logical, spatial, and technical) there is a good agreement between subjects in Group I and their controls. In Groups II and III, however, there are strong significant differences between subjects and controls; specifically, the subjects as a group had a much lower intellectual capacity than did their controls as measured in these tests.

PSYCHICAL FUNCTION CAPACITY

Table 3 summarizes the results of the psychologists assessments of the conscripts "Psychical function capacity" during the interviews. As can be seen, there is a fairly good agreement between the adopted subjects and their controls matched by age. Subjects in Groups II and III, on the other hand, have lower means. These differences are, however, statistically significant only for Group II.

LEADERSHIP CAPACITY

As many adopted boys as controls were chosen for assessment of "leadership capacity" (ca. 68 percent). The controls as a group were rated a little higher, but the difference between the groups was not statistically significant. On the other hand, subjects in

Table 2   Intellectual Capacity: Means for Subtests

	Group I			Group II			Group III		
	Sub-jects	Con-trol	*p*	Sub-jects	Con-trols	*p*	Sub-jects	Con-trols	*p*
Subtest	$N=79$	$N=74$		$N=90$	$N=102$		$N=87$	$N=99$	
Logic-inductive	5.24	5.46	NS	4.87	5.62	.005	4.44	5.28	.005
Linguistic	5.18	5.15	NS	4.86	5.58	.005	4.52	5.35	.005
Spatial	5.53	5.30	NS	5.34	5.98	.01	4.77	5.61	.005
Technical	4.96	4.91	NS	4.40	5.13	.005	4.22	4.77	.05

Table 3   Psychical Function Capacity According to Psychologist's Assessment: Means

Group I			Group II			Group III		
Subjects	Controls	*p*	Subjects	Controls	*p*	Subjects	Controls	*p*
$N=79$	$N=72$		$N=91$	$N=102$		$N=85$	$N=97$	
5.19	5.15	NS	4.84	5.47	.005	4.76	5.08	NS

Groups II and III were less often selected for assessment on this item than their controls (58 percent in Group II, 49 percent in Group III as against 68 percent and 64 percent among controls). The two comparison groups (II and III) had significantly lower means than their controls for this item.

To summarize, then, the interviews, tests, and investigations during the military enlistment procedure have confirmed our observation at 15 years of age in all three groups. The adopted cohort shows much the same achievements in different tests and assessments as in their age-related controls, and we have not found any clear tendencies toward a positive or negative deviation in this group. The drop-out was of the same magnitude as in the control group, and the adopted boys were taken out and screened for military leadership in the same proportion as the controls. Subjects in Groups II and III, on the other hand, had relatively high frequency of drop-outs compared to controls and did not reach the same level of achievement as their controls or as subjects in Group I on all subtests and assessments.

Discussion

It is obvious from our results that the deviations and nervous disturbances, which we found at age 11 in all three groups, were to a large extent overcome among the adopted boys. Their social prognosis has evidently been no better or worse than for boys in general. Their intellectual capacity, as it was measured and classified during the enlistment procedure, showed about the same distribution as their age-matched controls.

As mentioned earlier, adopted boys were placed in homes belonging mostly to professional and intermediate occupations (i.e., Swedish Social Class III). Controls, on the other hand, were randomly distributed, and thus it is conceivable that their parents' education corresponded to the distribution in the general population.

In his study of the 1953 cohort of Swedish conscripts, Otto [5] showed a high correlation between social class and intellectual capacity. Measured on military enlistment, boys from Social Class I were greatly overrepresented among the highest evaluations, and those from Social Class III were the least represented. Thus it may be concluded that the adopted boys could be expected to have higher means for intellectual capacity than do their controls. There may be various reasons for this failure to keep up with their social class level. It may be that the adoptive situation in itself is fraught with complications, which has an impact on the general level of achievement. One explanation could be the influence of genetic factors from the biological parents. As we have no certain data at present about the intellectual capacity of the biological parents, this hypothesis is difficult to either prove or discard. At the age of 11 we found, however, no association between childrens' school marks and the education of their biological parents [1]. Among boys reared in their biological homes or in foster homes, the high risk of maladjustment and underachievement that we have found both at 11 and 15 seems to persist.

Looking at the negative social heritage for the whole cohort of these unwanted children, the conclusion is warranted that the intervention and decisions made by parents, social-welfare authorities, and the adoption agency at the time of the child's birth has had a very decisive influence on later life opportunities and careers, in both positive and negative directions.

Many of the boys who returned to their natural mothers experienced a childhood fraught with social and emotional handicaps. Most mothers were ambivalent in their attitude toward their child and were not quite sure if they wanted to keep him. They were often alone, without any support from the child's father or from relatives, and their economic circumstances were often poor. It is quite obvious that these boys ran a considerably higher risk of becoming socially maladjusted. The same is true of those boys whom either the social authorities or whose mothers decided to place in foster care. It is conceivable that both the children and the foster parents felt that their relationship was insecure. In fact, we found this when we broached this question in personal interviews with many foster parents at the 11-year follow-up. Furthermore, the foster parents were seldom as prepared in advance for taking on the difficult task of bringing up a foster child, as were the adoptive parents. The high rate of maladjustment and underachievement among the foster boys may be partly explained by this lack of security during their upbringing.

These comparisons between groups presuppose that all groups were all alike at the beginning and that no selective factors had influence on any direction. As we have already mentioned, there were such selective factors at the beginning. For instance, there were more pregnancy complications among children in Groups II and III, as well as more social complications among the biological parents (criminality, alcohol abuse) compared to Group I. In our analyses [2] we have not been able to show that such background factors have had any significant influence on the boys' careers. Such influences have been limited and marginal and cannot explain the big differences between the adopted boys and the boys in the other two groups. We have so far no support for a hypothesis that genetic factors accounted for the differences between the groups.

Our results are in line with those of an English investigation recently published by Tizard [6] concerning children from institutions who had been placed during their preschool years in adoptive and foster homes or had been restored to their natural mothers. Although the sample was small and selective, Tizard's results and conclusions point in the same direction as ours. Placement with adoptive parents, ready to accept the child as their own, is a much better proposition in terms of the child's development and social adjustment than is an insecure fostering or being returned to an ambivalent mother living under social and emotional pressure. The implication of our study for the general policy of child care is, of course, *not* that adoption is always the best solution for a child with a social handicap. Rather, the conclusion must be that *early* preventive work is important, regardless of what decision is made for the child's future.

References

1. Bohman, M. Adopted children and their families. A follow-up study of adopted children, their background, environment and adjustment. Proprius, Stockholm, 1970.
2. Bohman, M. A comparative study of adopted children, foster children and children in their biological environment born after undesired pregnancies. *Acta Paediat. Scand. Suppl.*, 221 (1971).
3. Bohman, M. Fifth Hilda Lewis Lecture: "Undesired" children—a prognostic study. *Child Adoption*, No. 2, 1973.
4. Klackenberg, G. A prospective longitudinal study of children. *Acta Paediat. Scand. Suppl.*, 224 (1971).
5. Otto, U. Male youths. *Acta Psychiat. Scand. Suppl.*, 264 (1976).
6. Tizard, B. *Adoption: A Second Chance.* Open Books, London, 1977.

Follow-up Psychological Studies of Abused Children

Pierre Strauss, M.D., and M. Rouyer, M.D. (France)

Twenty children were examined by our team from 2 to 12 years after abuse, either in the placement (foster family, specialized institutions) or at school when the child was still in the family. In all cases, routine contacts were established with child guidance clinics and other institutions in charge of the child before or after abuse.

Nearly all the children suffered from severe and prolonged emotional deficiencies due to pathological emotional relationships with the parents and that were aggravated by multiple caretaking changes during the first years of life, such as placement in various institutions, in foster homes distant from the natural family, and in the care of day nurses, often of poor quality and frequently alternating.

From the psychological point of view, these children have many characteristics in common, at least until they reach the age of 5 years. After this age the specific decisions taken concerning the child—keeping contact with the family, placement, or psychotherapy—play a large part in shaping variations of personality.

Before 5 years of age, more or less marked behavior disturbances are observed that include emotional instability, poor attention span, dependency, demandingness, difficulties in peer adjustment, and provocative attitudes toward other children. In spite of normal intelligence in most cases, there are delays in the acquisition of drawing, speaking, and motor activity.

In all cases the intellectual decline toward pseudoimbecility is associated at the same time with the disappearance of most of the striking behavior disturbances. Becoming more passive, the children are better tolerated at school and may be admitted to special classes for the retarded or to boarding schools without any psychological help being given.

Ten of the children, aged 8 to 10 years, show passive and inhibited qualities with an IQ of no more than 80 and are thus regarded as educationally subnormal and placed in special classes. Learning is a major problem. The behavior disturbances reported by preschool and elementary-grade teachers are suggestive of psychosis concealed by retardation.

Only early help prior to elementary school has any chance of being effective. The instability prevents learning, and this disability persists. If speech problems are not dealt with before 6 years of age, these also tend to remain unchanged.

The more striking the symptomatology at the onset, the greater is the warning to everyone concerned with the child. But the danger is that such marked manifestations may not correlate with the gravity of the psychological disturbances and that children more passive but as deeply disturbed fail to receive any help because they do not upset the class.

Children cared for before age 5 by a good foster family seem to have a better intellectual development, but with an emotional dependency on and a strong fixation to the foster parents. Cognition is also less impaired in the few cases where the child and the family have received psychological help over a prolonged period. Only a follow-up into adult life would demonstrate whether the measures adopted have had lasting therapeutic and beneficial effects.

The personality of a child is modeled on the parental image. Physical abuse, as studies of abusing parents show, induce several attitudes ranging from identification with the aggressor to perverse or moral masochism. These severe personality disturbances come to light, often in a striking way, only at the adult stage in relation to object choice and to parental behavior toward children.

It would be of great interest to follow up our cases into adolescence. Their future is perhaps not too compromised. Among the foster families who took care of these abused children, there were adults who underwent the same difficulties during childhood; their capacity for love, warmth, and their tolerance for difficult children is very evident.

Vulnerability of Hyperkinetic (MBD) Child to Subsequent Serious Psychopathology: A Controlled 7-Year Follow-Up

Hans R. Huessy, M.D., and Alan H. Cohen, B.S. (U.S.A.)

Many clinicians and investigators have devoted considerable attention recently to the hyperkinetic child syndrome. This syndrome, alternatively referred to as the *hyperactive behavior syndrome, postencephalitic behavior disorder, minimal cerebral dysfunction,* and *minimal brain damage,* has been used to group together children who exhibit a variety of related behavioral disorders and/or learning disabilities. Although many authors often use highly personalized criteria to identify "hyperkinetic" children, there has been a recent trend to standardize diagnostic procedures. The following characteristics, all of which are not necessarily seen in a given child, are common features of the hyperkinetic child syndrome: (1) hyperactivity, (2) emotional overreactivity, (3) temper tantrums, (4) short attention span, (5) impulsiveness, (6) difficulty with groups, (7) deficits in the subtle use of language, and (8) coordination and learning problems.

Hyperkinetic children are described by their parents as being uncooperative, restless, noisy, destructive, and unpredictable. They do not finish projects, listen to directions, sit still at meals, stay with games, or respond to discipline. Elementary-school

491

teachers consider these youngsters immature, moody, inattentive, aggressive, nervous, careless, distractable, excitable, stubborn, and inconsistent. Girls often are described as slow workers or daydreamers when in grade school.

Although the word "syndrome" implies a specific disease entity, a single verifiable etiology of the hyperkinetic child syndrome has not yet been established. It is highly probable that the children who display the characteristic behaviors enumerated above represent an etiologically heterogeneous group. Investigators have demonstrated that associations exist between minimal brain dysfunction (MBD) and the following: (1) prematurity and low birth weight, (2) complications of pregnancy and delivery, (3) anoxia during the first few days of life, (4) multiple minor congenital anomalies, and (5) innate personality characteristics of infants (i.e., genetics). There is also some evidence that socioeconomic class and the family environment may alter the long-term course of hyperkinesis.

A common belief held by many clinicians, educators, and parents is that MBD is a benign, self-limiting disorder of childhood with a favorable prognosis. The unfounded notion that hyperactive children outgrow their illness is based on clinical anecdotes and studies without long-term followups. Many early reports claimed that these childhood problems disappeared with maturation. For example, Laufer and Denhoff [13], in their classical description of the hyperkinetic behavior syndrome in children, stated that "In later years this syndrome tends to wane spontaneously and disappear." They reported that this disorder did not persist in those patients whom they followed into adult life and concluded that it may disappear at any age from 8 to 18.

The natural course and development of the hyperkinetic syndrome is beginning to receive increasing attention. Several recent follow-up studies of hyperkinetic children suggest that the prognosis for these youngsters may be far graver than previously suspected. These reports demonstrate that although hyperactivity per se may diminish or disappear with age, serious academic, social, and psychological problems may persist into adolescence and even adulthood. The magnitude of the problem at hand can be appreciated better if we realize that anywhere within 3 to 20 percent of the school-age population manifest the features of the hyperkinetic syndrome. Many of the follow-up reports in the literature are retrospective studies that lack suitable control groups and were conducted on skewed samples of rather severely affected children seen in psychiatric clinics. We have recently begun investigating adult hyperkinetics and find them to apparently respond to pharmacotherapy similarly to hyperkinetic children. The present investigation was undertaken to delineate more clearly the natural course of the hyperkinetic syndrome.

To determine the prevalence and stability of this syndrome, an initial study of 501 second-graders enrolled in "normal" classes in a number of small town and rural school systems in Vermont was conducted in 1966. Hyperkinetic children were identified by a psychiatric questionnaire filled out by their teachers. As described in a previous paper, scores above the 80th percentile placed a child in the study group. The original population was restudied in 1968 and again in 1969. The last follow-up distinguished a group of hyperkinetic pupils stable over 4 years (Group G) from six other groups of hyperkinetics in whom the behavior pattern of hyperkinesis was not stable over this same period of time. It was proposed that the prognosis for these different groups might be significantly different. The present study was designed to evaluate the current academic performance and social adjustment of the children identified as hyperkinetic at least once in the past three studies and to compare their outcome with that of two control groups drawn from the original population of 501 second-graders. One control group (H) consists of those children who had three consecutive low scores on the hyperkinesis questionnaire, and the second control group (J) consists of those pupils who had three consecutive moderate scores. The hyperkinetic and control groups were all matched for sex.

To evaluate the youngsters' academic performance and social adjustment in the classroom, we carefully examined their school records and obtained the following information:

1. Date of birth.
2. Grade of enrollment during 1972–1973 school year.
3. Number of grades repeated.
4. Final grades in English, mathematics, science, and social studies for the 1971–1972 and 1972–1973 school years.

5. Academic level of courses taken, i.e., advanced, average, slow (remedial).
6. IQ scores (grades 5–8) (Otis-Lennon, Kuhlman Finch, SCAT).
7. Achievement test scores.
8. Comments about poor social adjustment and disciplinary problems.

In addition, the records of various community mental health centers throughout Vermont were checked by their staff members in an attempt to determine whether any subjects received psychiatric or psychopharmacological treatment during the past 8 years.

Results

At the present time we have located 140 of the 175 subjects selected for the study (or 80 percent), including 95 of the 118 hyperkinetics (or 80 percent) and 45 of the 57 controls (or 79 percent). The hyperkinetic group located includes 72 percent boys and 28 percent girls compared to the 67 percent boys and 33 percent girls in the control group located.

The average age of the control group at follow-up was 15.3 (with a range of 14.6 to 16.3), whereas that of the hyperkinetic population was 15.5 (with a range of 14.6 to 17.5).

Eleven percent of the hyperkinetics were no longer enrolled in regular classes, including four boys who had dropped out of school, two who were placed in special education classes, two who were enrolled in a school for the retarded, one boy who was institutionalized in a correctional school, and one psychotic girl who is now receiving private tutoring at home. In contrast, one boy (or 2 percent of the control group) was no longer in a regular class, being placed in a correctional institution.

The mean IQ of the hyperkinetic population was 95.3 (range 74–123; median 96.0), whereas that of the control group was 107.3 (range 84–131; median 108.3). Most of the reports in the literature mention that the IQ range of hyperkinetics is comparable to that of controls. However, our report clearly demonstrates that the mean IQ of hyperkinetic children is indeed significantly lower than that of the control group. This finding has been confirmed recently in a report by Stewart's [26] group in St. Louis, who found that hyperactive children in suburban elementary schools had a mean IQ that was 15 points lower than that of their fellow classmates. Although several factors may be operating, we believe that the short attention span, distractibility, and perhaps perceptual-motor disturbances of the hyperkinetic child are important factors leading to poor performance on almost any kind of test, especially group examinations, such as the IQ tests commonly given in schools.

Our control group was impressively more successful in academic performance as compared to the hyperkinetic children. The mean grade-point average for the hyperkinetic group was 1.90, whereas that of the control group was 2.76. Almost 75 percent of the control group achieved good or excellent grades as compared to less than 25 percent of the hyperkinetic group. In addition, 16 percent of the controls did poor or very poor work as compared to 56 percent of the hyperkinetics. Group H (our low controls) had the highest grade-point average, and Group G had the lowest averages.

Achievement test scores were substantially lower for the hyperkinetic group in comparison to the controls. Furthermore, a much higher percentage of the hyperkinetic population was enrolled in remedial classes and had repeated one or more grades.

Regarding social adjustment, we found that 35 percent of the hyperkinetics were considered to be discipline problems with poor or very poor social adjustment, whereas only 7 percent of the controls were viewed as discipline problems. Many hyperkinetics were suspended, placed on social probation, and/or assigned numerous detentions. Some of their offenses included truancy, tardiness, smoking in school, cutting classes, forging passes, stealing, discharging fire extinguishers, disrupting classroom lessons, and defying school authorities. Teachers considered a substantial portion of the hyperkinetic population to be loud, inattentive, uncooperative, lazy, sneaky, immature, annoying, inconsiderate, defiant, easily discouraged, and easily distracted. Furthermore, teachers noted that many of the hyperkinetic children daydreamed, fooled around constantly, disturbed others, desired attention, responded poorly to discipline, and were unable to sit still, concentrate, and/or follow directions. None of the records of the control population contained comments similar to these descriptions. There were twice as many boys as girls identified as hyperkinetic in the second grade. By the fifth grade the ratio was four to one. Girls had fewer poor outcomes. In a just completed study by Perault and Novotny [22], our questionnaire showed a positive correlation with the more commonly used teacher questionnaire developed by Conners [4].

Discussion

The data that we have collected appears to confirm the notion that children who are identified as being hyperkinetic in grade school are at risk for developing academic as well as social adjustment problems in adolescence. In comparison to our control group, our hyperkinetic children had substantially lower mean grade-point averages, achievement scores, and IQ scores. Furthermore, the hyperkinetic population was much more likely than the control group to be in slow or remedial classes in school, to exhibit poor or very poor social adjustment, and to have repeated one or more grades. An examination of all of the data reveals that Group H (the low controls) had a remarkably good prognosis. It is interesting that those pupils who were designated as being hyperkinetic only in second grade also had a relatively good outcome as adolescents. The fact that this group had the highest percentage of girls may be significant. On the other hand, those pupils who were identified three consecutive times in previous studies as being hyperkinetic had a particularly grave prognosis. In addition to achieving the lowest grade-point average, these pupils were most likely to be in both English and mathematics remedial classes and to display poor or very poor social adjustment.

There is increasing evidence that supports our finding that hyperactive children do not necessarily outgrow their symptoms. Minde's [18] group in Montreal reported on a prospective 5-year follow-up study of 155 hyperactive children (mean age at follow-up 13.3 years; range 10 to 18) and demonstrated that although hyperactivity and excitability tended to diminish with age, a significant proportion of their children manifested emotional immaturity, inability to maintain goals, and low self-esteem. These authors concluded that distractibility remained a disabling problem for their subjects, and accounted, at least in part, for severe underachievement in school.

Mendelson's [16] study of 83 children (aged 12 to 16) diagnosed as hyperactive 2 to 5 years previously showed that many children were involved in delinquent behavior such as fighting, stealing, running away from home, and truancy. Chronic low self-esteem appeared to be a serious problem in the children with poor outcomes.

Even more alarming is the accumulating evidence that the hyperkinetic child syndrome may be associated with various psychiatric disturbances of adulthood. Morris' [19] group conducted a 20 to 30-year follow-up of hospitalized children with symptoms suggestive of MBD and discovered that 20 percent were doing well, 16.6 percent were psychotic, and the remainder displayed a spectrum of psychopathology.

In a follow-up study of 524 child guidance clinic patients, many of whom were most likely hyperkinetic children, Robins [24] found that a significant proportion of these youngsters became sociopathic or psychotic as adults. At follow-up, 34 percent of the patient population had disabling symptoms, as compared with 8 percent of the control group.

Menkes's [17] group reevaluated 14 hyperkinetic children who had been referred to a child psychiatry clinic at a mean of 24 years previously and found that hyperactivity was still present in three (21 percent) of the 14 subjects. Furthermore, at the time of reexamination, four (29 percent) of the subjects were psychotic, three (21 percent) were retarded, and three (21 percent) had been institutionalized for a criminal offense or delinquency. This research group was unable to find any correlation between the patients' social adjustment as adults and either their early home environment or the amount of treatment they received.

Finally, Huessy's recent follow-up of 84 hyperactive children (ages 9 to 24) who had received pharmacologic therapy presents further evidence that hyperkinetic children are at risk for developing later difficulties. The rate of institutionalization in a facility for delinquent youths, the rate of psychiatric hospitalization, and the school drop-out rate for their population 8 to 10 years after the diagnosis of hyperkinesis were considerably higher than the expected rates of the state of Vermont as a whole. As in Menkes's study, Huessy was unable to relate drug response or length of psychopharmacological therapy to final outcome.

In contrast to these long-term follow-up studies, our investigation identified only a small proportion of the hyperkinetic population as being institutionalized in a correctional facility or hospitalized in a psychiatric hospital. In addition, the drop-out rate of our subjects was not very remarkable—4 percent for the hyperkinetic group and 2 percent for the control population. We must realize, however, that the mean age at follow-up of our hyperkinetic children was 15.5 years, which is considerably lower than that of the subjects who were followed in these other studies. Thus we anticipate that our hyperkinetic children may develop more serious problems such as psychosis or delinquency over the ensuing years. Only one of the hyperkinetic boys was seen in a mental health clinic. We plan to continue following our subjects and to reevaluate their social, educational, and psychological status as adults.

It is extremely important that more emphasis be placed on the early identification and treatment of hyperkinetic children in the hope of modifying what appears to be a more serious prognosis than is generally suspected. Primary prevention through improved pre- and perinatal care should become a widespread practice. In addition, modified or supplementary education, psychopharmacological therapy, and parental guidance should be considered at an early age. Recent evidence suggests that hyperkinesis pharmacotherapy may be beneficial if extended into adult life. It remains to be seen whether such long-term medication will alter adult outcomes significantly. Evaluations of treatment must deal with our finding that 65 percent of our children had outgrown their gross difficulties without treatment. Perhaps some of the poor adult outcomes, even in the face of good response to pharmacotherapy, are due to our inability to overcome the child's early years of subtly or grossly being able to control his or her parents. In any event, the search for more successful therapeutic interventions must be pursued vigorously.

Appendix

Table A.1 Children Identified as "Hyperkinetic" in Previous Studies by Scores above 80th Percentile

Study No.	Grade[a]	Children (N)	Boys (N)	Boys (%)	Girls (N)	Girls (%)
1 (1966)	2	64	44	69	20	31
2 (1968)	4	66	49	74	17	26
3 (1969)	5	63	51	81	12	19

[a] Refers to grade in which most of children studied were enrolled.

Table A.2 Subgroups of Hyperkinetic Children According to Previous Study in Which They Were Identified

Group	Study	Children (N)	Boys (N)	Boys (%)	Girls (N)	Girls (%)
A	1 (1966)	20	12	60	8	40
B	2 (1968)	18	11	61	7	39
C	3 (1969)	19	14	74	5	26
D	1, 2	17	11	65	6	35
E	1, 3	13	10	77	3	23
F	2, 3	17	16	94	1	6
G	1, 2, 3	14	11	79	3	21
Total		118	85	72	33	28
Controls						
H	3 consecutive scores, 0–30 percentiles	28	20	71	8	29
J	3 consecutive scores, 31–70 percentiles	29	21	72	8	29

Table A.3 Percentages of Boys and Girls in Selected versus Located Populations

	HK[a] + Control					HK					Control				
	Total	Boys		Girls		Total	Boys		Girls		Total	Boys		Girls	
	N	N	%	N	%	N	N	%	N	%	N	N	%	N	%
Selected	175	126	72	49	28	118	85	72	33	28	57	41	72	16	28
Located	140	99	71	41	29	95	69	73	26	27	45	30	67	15	33

[a] Hyperkinetic.

Table A.4 Boys and Girls Located According to Group

Group	N	Boys (N)	Boys (%)	Girls (N)	Girls (%)
A	17	10	60	7	40
B	14	8	57	6	43
C	17	13	76	4	24
D	13	8	62	5	38
E	10	7	70	3	30
F	14	13	93	1	7
G	10	10	100	0	0
H	22	15	68	7	32
J	23	15	65	8	35

Table A.5 Mean IQ Scores According to Group
(Number of Subjects in Parentheses)

J(23)	HK(90)	Con(45)	A(10)	B(14)	C(17)	D(11)	E(9)	F(13)	G(9)	H(22)
100.7	95.3	107.3	97.8	97.3	98.4	90.0	83.9	96.9	90.0	114.1

Table A.6 Mean IQ Sources According to School
(Number of Subjects in Parentheses)

	School 1[a]	School 2[b]	School 3[c]	School 4[d]	Misc. Schools	Total
Hyperkinetics	90.3(18)	91.3(18)	102.0(20)	95.4(26)	99.3(8)	95.3(90)
Controls	106.7(7)	106.0(13)	109.1(13)	107.8(11)	97.0(1)	107.3(45)

[a] Scat, grade 7.
[b] Otis-Lennon, grade 5.
[c] Kuhlmann-Finch, grade 8.
[d] Otis Lennon, grade 7.

Table A.7 Grade-point Average According to Group
(Number of Subjects in Parentheses)

HK(90)	Con(45)	A(17)	B(14)	C(17)	D(11)	E(9)	F(13)	G(9)	H(22)	J(23)
2.76	1.90	2.22	1.89	1.93	1.95	1.90	1.68	1.48	2.97	2.55

Table A.8   Grade-point Average (GPA) Distribution According to Group
(Results in Percentage of Group)

	HK	Con	A	B	C	D	E	F	G	H	J
Excellent (GPA 3.01–4.0)	7	31	24	14	0	0	0	0	0	36	26
Good (GPA 2.51–3.0)	11	38	12	7	18	18	11	8	0	50	26
Average (GPA 2.01–2.5)	26	16	18	36	29	36	22	23	11	14	17
Poor (GPA 1.51–2.0)	30	16	41	7	24	18	44	38	44	0	30
Very Poor (GPA 0.00–1.5)	26	0	6	36	30	27	22	30	44	0	0

Table A.9   Mean Grade-point Average of Hyperkinetics versus Controls
According to IQ
(Number of Subjects in Parentheses)

	71–80	81–90	91–100	101–110	111–120	121–130	131–140
Hyperkinetics	1.41(9)	2.05(22)	1.87(28)	2.04(21)	2.83(2)	3.07(1)	SRA[a]
Controls	SRA[a]	2.50(5)	2.42(5)	2.60(15)	2.86(16)	3.38(2)	3.75(1)

[a] SRA, percentiles.

Table A.10   Achievement Test Scores According to School
(7th-Grade Results)
(Number of Subjects in Parentheses)

	School 1[a]	School 2[b]	School 3[c]	School 4[d]
Hyperkinetics	13.4(18)	5.3(18)	35.4(20)	6.0(26)
Controls	38.7(7)	6.8(13)	72.2(13)	7.8(11)

[a] SRS, percentiles.
[b] California Achievement, grade equivalents.
[c] California Achievement, percentiles.
[d] Iowa Skills, grade equivalents.

Table A.11 Children in Remedial and Advanced Sections According to Group (Figures Refer to Percentage of Group)

	HK	Con	A	B	C	D	E	F	G	H	J
Remedial											
Mathematics	38	2	47	25	31	45	44	33	44	0	5
English	42	14	24	16	50	18	55	75	67	5	23
Both	24	0	24	8	25	9	33	33	44	0	0
Advanced											
Mathematics	5	27	6	17	0	0	0	0	0	36	18
English	1	23	6	0	0	0	0	0	0	32	14
Both	0	7	0	0	0	0	0	0	0	14	0

Table A.12 Children Who Repeated One or More Grades According to Group (Figures Refer to Percentage of Group with Number of Subjects in Parentheses)

HK(90)	Con(45)	A(17)	B(14)	C(17)	D(11)	E(9)	F(13)	G(9)	H(22)	J(23)
50	11	47	43	29	82	67	62	33	0	22

Table A.13 Children with Poor or Very Poor Social Adjustment According to Group (Number of Subjects in Parentheses)

	HK	Con	A	B	C	D	E	F	G	H	J
Poor											
Number	17	1	0	1	5	2	0	5	4	0	1
Percent	19	2	0	8	29	17	0	38	40	0	4
Very poor											
Number	15	2	0	2	5	1	2	2	3	0	2
Percent	16	4	0	15	29	8	20	15	30	0	9
Poor or very poor											
Number	32	3	0	3	10	3	0	7	7	0	3
Percent	35	7	0	23	59	25	20	54	70	0	13

Table A.14 Children Rated in Top 20 Percentiles on Teacher Questionnaire in 9th Grade According to Group (Number of Subjects in Parentheses)

	HK (38)	Con (33)	A (8)	B (4)	C (6)	D (8)	E (3)	F (5)	G (4)	H (17)	J (16)
Number	12	2	0	1	1	4	0	2	4	0	2
Percent	32	6	0	25	16	50	0	40	100	0	13

References

1. Bradley, C. Characteristics and management of children with behavior problems associated with brain damage. *Paediat. Clin. N. Amer.*, 4 (1957), 1049–1060.
2. Cantwell, D. P. Psychiatric illness in the families of hyperactive children. *Arch. Gen. Psychiat.*, 27 (1972), 414–417.
3. Childers, A. Hyperactivity in children having behavior disorders, *Amer. J. Orthopsychiat.*, 5 (1935), 227–243.
4. Conners, C. K. A teacher rating scale for use in drug studies with children. *Amer. J. Psychiat.*, 126 (1969), 884–888.
5. Huessy, H. R. Study of the prevalence and therapy of choreatiform syndrome or hyperkinesis in rural Vermont. *Acta Paedopsychiat.*, 34 (1967), 130–135.
6. Huessy, H. R. and Gendron, R. Prevalence of the so-called hyperkinetic syndrome in public school children in Vermont. *Acta Paedopsychiat.*, 37 (1970), 243–248.
7. Huessy, H. R., Marshall, C., and Gendron, R. Five hundred children followed from grade two through grade five for the prevalence of behavior disorder. *Acta Paedopsychiat.*, 39 (1973), 301–309.
8. Huessy, H. R., Metoyer, M., and Townsend, M. Eight to ten year follow-up of 84 children treated for behavioral disorder in rural Vermont. *Acta Paedopsychiat.*, (1974), 40 (6):230–5, 1974.
9. Huessy, H. R. Minimal brain dysfunction in children (hyperkinetic syndrome): Recognition and treatment. *Drug Ther.* (1973), 52–63.
10. Huessy, H. R. The adult hyperkinetic. *Amer. J. Psychiat.*, 131 (1974), 724–725.
11. Kenny, T., Clemmens, R., and Hudsen, B. Characteristics of children referred because of hyperactivity. *J. Pediat.*, 79 (1971), 618–622.
12. Laufer, M. W. Psychiatric diagnosis and treatment of children with minimal brain dysfunction. *Ann. N. Y. Acad. Sci.*, 205 (1973), 303–309.
13. Laufer, M. W. and Denhoff, E. Hyperkinetic behavior syndrome in children, *J. Pediat.*, 50 (1957), 463–474.
14. Mackay, M., Beck, L., and Taylor, R. Methylphenidate for adolescents with minimal brain dysfunction. *N.Y. State J. Med.*, 73 (1973), 550–554.
15. Mellsop, G. Psychiatric patients as children and adults: Childhood predictors of adult illness. *J. Child Psychol. Psychiat.*, 13 (1972), 91–101.
16. Mendelson, W., Johnson, N., and Stewart, M. Hyperactive children as teenagers: A follow-up study. *J. Nerv. Ment. Dis.*, 153 (1971), 273–279.
17. Menkes, M., Rowe, J., and Menkes, J. A 25-year follow-up study on the hyperkinetic children with minimal brain dysfunction. *Pediat.*, 39 (1967), 393–399.
18. Minde, K., Lewin, D., and Weiss, G. Hyperactive child in elementary school: A five-year controlled follow-up. *Except. Child.*, 38 (1971), 215–221.
19. Morris, H., Jr., Escoll, P., and Wexler, R. Aggressive behavior disorders of childhood: A follow-up study. *Amer. J. Psychiat.*, 112 (1972), 55–72.
20. Oettinger, L. Presentation given at the Claremont Reading Conference, Claremont, California, February 9, 1973.
21. Pasamanick, B., Rogers, M. E., and Lilienfield, A. M. Pregnancy experience and the development of behavior disorder in children. *Amer. J. Psychiat.*, 112 (1956), 613–618.

22. Perault, P. and Novotny, M. Early diagnosis of minimal brain dysfunction in children. 1974.
23. Report on Conference on Use of Stimulant Drugs in Treatment of Behaviorally Disturbed Young School Children. Sponsored by the Office of Child Development and the Office of the Assistant Secretary for Health and Scientific Affairs, Department of Health, Education, and Welfare, Washington, D.C., 1971.
24. Robins, L. *Deviant Children Grown Up*. Williams and Wilkins, Baltimore, 1966.
25. Rogers, E., Lilienfield, A. M., and Pasamanick, B. Prenatal and paranatal factors in the development of childhood behavior disorders. *Acta Psychiat. Neurol. Scand.*, Suppl. 102 (1955), 1–157.
26. Stewart, M. Hyperactive children. *Sci. Amer.*, 222 (1970), 94–99.
27. Thom, D. A. and Johnston, F. S. Time as factor in solution of delinquency. *Mental Hygiene*, 25 (1941), 269–287.
28. Thomas, R., Chess, S., and Birch, H. *Temperament and Behavior Disorders in Children*. New York Univ. Press, N.Y., 1968.
29. Waldrop, M. and Halversen, C. Minor physical anomalies and hyperactive behavior in young children. In *The Exceptional Infant*, Vol. II, J. Hellmuth, Ed. Brunner/Mazel, New York, 1971.

Fate of Child Psychiatric Risk Groups:A 10 to 15-Year Follow-up

Katri Malmivaara, M.D., E. Keinänen, Ph.D., and Marja Saarelma, M.D. (Finland)

When the children in this report were patients in the child psychiatry ward during 1956–1962 there were some 470,000 inhabitants in Helsinki, the capital of Finland. Urbanization was lively, and there were considerable housing problems. Three child guidance centers had been functioning with limited resources in the city before the period under study. Child-welfare activities were expanding and developing their psychiatric services. Child psychiatry was very young at that time, and the child psychiatrists of our unit are among the first in the country. The child psychiatry unit in Aurora Hospital (a general hospital owned by the city) was founded in 1952 and was the first, and during the time of the study, the only, psychotherapeutically oriented child psychiatry unit in Helsinki.

From the beginning, we have systematically made the whole family join the treatment of each child. At the present there are about 50 child psychiatry beds between five hospitals for the needs of the inhabitants of the city, although some of these also serve the province. In Finland, hospital treatment is almost totally under public subsidy. The daily fee for a child patient at hospital at that time corresponded to $1, and many families were relieved from paying it. Thus economic status differences do not have much influence on our patient population.

In the full-time ward of the unit 16 children of age 4 to 14 years can be treated. The most referrals come from the child guidance centers and the pediatric wards of the same hospital where we do consultation work on a regular basis.

Aim and Outline of the Study

The aim of the study is to find out how our 323 former patients were doing by the end of 1972 (i.e., 10 to 15 years after treatment), with special reference to needs of mental health services and disciplinary action to society. Who was helped by treatment, who was not, and why? How should treatment methods be developed? A closer look is taken of a subsample of 87 long-term patients—drawn from the total of 323—who were invited for two follow-up sessions in 1971–1972. Seventy-four young adults aged 18 to 24 years turned up for a psychiatric interview and 72 for a psychological testing session. Their general mental health status and working ability were assessed and are reported here with some other preliminary findings.

Basic information about the child and his family was coded from clinical records of all patients (323). These include the following facts: (1) age at admission to treatment, (2) sex, (3) sibling position, (4) social class, (5) family structure, (6) hereditary psychiatric factors, (7) indicators of MBD, (8) concrete deprivations at early age, (9) duration of treatment and the manner of terminating it, and (10) recommendations for further treatment. Estimations included are diagnosis, intelligence level, parent-child relationships, parents' psychopathology, family problems seen both as interaction within the family and as adjustment to society, family's motivation for treatment, result of treatment, and prognosis at the termination of treatment.

In diagnosis classification the prognosis is seen as serious in two directions—psychosis and asociality. Frijling-Schroeder's definition was the basis for our "psychotic and borderline" category (25 cases). The other risk group, "asocial" category (85 cases), consists of children with asocial behavior (dishonesty, physical aggressiveness, truancy, running away) and an immature personality with serious contact disturbances.

"Organic" category, only 12 cases, includes epilepsy, gross neurological disturbances, and mental deficiency. Because of small size and heterogeneity, this group is not studied further but is included when "all patients" are spoken of. Minor signs of brain dysfunction are found in all diagnostic groups. Dysfunction was not always detected because possibilities for running an electroencephalogram were limited during these early years and psychological tests were not as developed as they are now.

The bulk of our population is children who cannot be diagnosed within the categories mentioned here. They are called "neurotics" (201). Psychosomatic symptoms are mostly found in this group.

Some Characteristics of the Population

Tables 1–5 show that two-thirds of the population are boys; that the most numerous age group at admission is from 7 to 10 years; that the major part of the population is diagnosed as "neurotics"; that brain-dysfunction indicators are mostly found in psychotic patients and psychosomatic symptoms mainly in neurotic patients; that hereditary psychiatric factors are most common in the psychotic patients; and that the intelligence distribution is skewed toward higher intelligence levels and the distribution of social classes toward higher social groups.

Table 1   All Patients by Age at Admission to Treatment

Age	Girls	Boys	Total
5–6	34	63	97
7–10	44	93	137
11 +	30	59	89
Total	108	215	323

Table 2   Long-term Patients by Age at Admission to Treatment and Sex

Age	Girls	Boys	Total
5–6	10	16	26
7–10	19	42	61
Total	29	58	87

Table 3   Psychosomatic Symptoms and Diagnosis
(N—"Neurotic," P—"Psychotic," A—"Asocial," O—"Organic")

Psychosomatic Symptoms	N	P	A	O	Total
Not present	185	24	85	12	
Present	16	1	0	0	
Total	201	25	85	12	323
Not present	92%	96%	100%	100%	
Present	8%	4%			

Table 4   All Patients by Minimal Brain Dysfunction and Diagnosis
(N—"Neurotic," P—"Psychotic," A—"Asocial")

Brain Dysfunction	N	P	A	Total
Not present	173	19	72	
Present	28	6	13	
Total	201	25	85	311
Not present	86%	76%	85%	
Present	14%	24%	15%	

Table 5   All Patients by Intelligence and Social Class

| | Social Class | | | | | | |
	I	II	III	IV	Not Known	Total	Percent
Above average IQ	31	27	34	6		98	30%
Average IQ	42	47	67	11		167	52%
Below average IQ	6	9	21	6		42	13%
IQ not estimated	8	2	5	1		16	5%
Total	87	85	127	24		323	
Patient population 1956–1962	26%	27%	40%	7%	0%	100%	
Total Helsinki population 1960	20%	22%	39%	14%	5%	100%	

Statistically Significant Differences between Diagnostic Categories

SEX

At the preschool age (5–6 years) there are as many girls as boys in the asocial category; at puberty the number of asocial boys is triple that of girls. In all other diagnostic categories there is one girl to two boys.

SOCIAL CLASS

The majority of our psychotic or borderline children belong to Social Class I. The percentage of asocial children rises with descending social class.

MOTHER'S PSYCHOPATHOLOGY

Mothers of psychotic and asocial children have distinctly more psychiatric disturbances than do those of neurotic children. Mothers of psychotic children are or have been psychotic in more cases (16 percent) than others (1–3 percent), whereas immaturity is more common in the mothers of asocial children (18 percent) than in other mothers (4–9 percent); the differences are highly significant.

FATHER'S PSYCHOPATHOLOGY

This nearly doubles percentage-wise, highly significantly going from neurotic to psychotic to asocial children. Immature fathers are common in families of asocial children, and only 39 percent have no notes on the father's psychopathology.

FAMILY PROBLEMS

Interaction seems chaotic in nearly half (47 percent) of asocial children's families, which is twice as often as in neurotic and psychotic children's families. Adjustment problems give a similar picture; from "maladjusted families" come 46 percent of the asocial, but 16 percent of the psychotic and 21 percent of the neurotic children. Significance of differences is high.

Development of Prognostic Classification

A closer look at the long-term patient population consists of an evaluation scheme (see Table 6) of about 100 items on various information on the child and his family. The descriptive items of this scheme are designed to differentiate between the three diagnostic categories—"neurotic," "psychotic" (including borderline cases), and "asocial." We regard the psychotic and asocial features as serious pathology and the corresponding "neurotic" descriptive items as signs of minor pathology, transitional disturbances, or within the normal range of developmental problems.

To find out which are the important ones of these 100 items, an item analysis was performed and four "prognostic" classes formed on the basis of the sum total of the best items describing psychosis and/or asociality. This procedure showed that our items differentiate our diagnostic categories as we define them in clinical practice. Table 7 gives correlations of descriptive items to their diagnostic category for most of the items describing children and fewer items describing families. Chi-square values refer to significances of differences between prognostic classes. As these classes are based on the number of items referring to serious pathology, prognostic Classes 1 and 2 include only children with clinical diagnosis of neurosis, with psychotic and asocial children clustering in Classes 3 and 4. So many significant differences between these prognostic classes gave us confidence to experiment with this classification as we proceed to follow-up information.

Qualities and Results of Treatment

Out of a total patient population of 323, 131 were treated in the ward only, 142 were outpatients for some part of their treatment, and 50 were treated only as outpatients.

Treatment motivation refers to that of the parents, and a three-level scale was formed: weak motivation (65 percent), distinct motivation but strong resistance (20 percent), and good motivation (15 percent).

The result-of-treatment-scale was condensed to four levels: (1) no change, (2) symptomatic change, (3) signs of deeper change,

Table 6   Phases of the Study

1. Systematization of data from the clinical records of all patients population (363), of which 40 had to be excluded because of deficient or too scanty informations.
2. Developing of a more comprehensive evaluation scheme (ca. 100 items) on characteristics of child and family. Coding of data from clinical records of long-term patients (87) applying this scheme.
3. Tracing of patients and inviting them to follow-up interview by personal phone call or, exceptionally, by letter. All those were invited who were under 11 when admitted for treatment of 6 months or more in 1956 to 1962 and were 18 or older in 1970.
4. Interviews by a psychiatrist (74) and testings by a psychologist (72).
5. Collecting of facts from registers of local mental hospitals and child welfare and national criminal register.
6. Determining of reliability of diagnostic categories.
7. Cross-tabulations (all patients population, 323) on a great number of variables: early and final stages of treatment as well as follow-up information.
8. Item analysis for a prognostic category breakdown of long-term patient population (87).
9. Working out an assessment scale, based on psychiatrist's follow-up interview (74 cases). Only variables "stress endurance" and "working ability" are used in this report.
10. Comparison between the prognosis categories, results of treatment, and follow-up variables of long-term patient population. Comparing cases showing the same (good or bad) or opposite trends in this comparison.

and (4) a new development trend and/or working through problems (child and/or parents).

Tables 8 to 10 give distribution of our population according to duration of treatment and the results of treatment by diagnostic categories. Table 11 gives the relationship between various qualities of treatment and the corresponding levels of significance. In this connection only our most significant findings can be reported.

The qualities listed in Table 11 are defined as follows: *parents' psychopathology*—immature personality, psychosis (actual or in history), severe neurosis, and no information of those mentioned earlier and *family problems*—disturbances in the interaction between the members and in adjustment to the community. These evaluation scales of several degrees were condensed to dichotomies in statistical computations.

Table 7   Significant Relationships of Treatment Qualities, All Patients

Treatment qualities, crosstabulated	Significance level, p >
Motivation/social class	0,001
Motivation/parental immaturity	0,01
Motivation/serious conflicts in family	0,001
Motivation/duration of treatment	0,001
Motivation/manner of terminating treatment	0,001
Duration of treatment/serious conflicts in family	0,001
Duration of treatment/diagnosis	0,01
Change during treatment/motivation	0,001
Change during treatment/duration of treatment	0,001
Change during treatment/diagnosis	0,001
Change during treatment/age at treatment	0,001
Change during treatment/intelligence level	0,1
Change during treatment/serious conflicts in family	0,01
Change during treatment/social maladjustment of family	0,05

Table 8   Total Duration of Treatment as In- and Outpatients
(1—Less Than 7 Years, 2—7 to 10 Years, 3—More Than 10 Years)

Duration of Treatment (Months)	Age			Total
	1	2	3	
Under 2	1	5	3	
2–5.5	11	8	14	
6–12	27	35	26	
12–24	6	19	11	
24–36	4	3	1	
Over 36	8	8	2	
Total	57	78	57	192
Under 2	2%	6%	5%	
2–5.5	19%	10%	25%	
6–12	47%	45%	46%	
Over 12	32%	39%	24%	
Total	100%	100%	100%	

Table 9   Duration of Treatment on Ward
(1—Less Than 7 Years, 2—7–10 Years, 3—More Than 10 Years)

Duration of Treatment (Months)	Age			Total
	1	2	3	
Under 2	19	34	24	
2–5.5	32	50	34	
6–12	28	31	12	
12–24	3	3	2	
24–36	0	0	0	
Over 36	1	0	0	
Total	83	118	72	273
Under 2	23%	30%	33%	
2–5.5	38%	42%	47%	
6–12	34%	26%	17%	
Over 12	5%	2%	3%	
Total	100%	100%	100%	

In the interaction disturbance scale, in one group conflicts did not have violent manifestations, although the relationships could be limited and scanty, whereas in the other group the relationship between the members was chaotic, and there was often excessive drinking and physical violence.

In the maladjustment scale one group was formed of families where there were parents' immature personalities, asocial tendencies in the family, and nonconsistent or impulsive way of life. The other group was comprised of families with no features similar to these. It could be mentioned that in these two evaluations one-third of the families was in the poorer evaluations. Serious disturbances in mother-child relationship refer to conspicuous inability of contact in mother, symbiotic mother-child relationship, and distinct rejection of the child.

Social Class I includes professionals, higher officials, managers, teachers, and so on. Social Class II consists of employers in small enterprises, own-account workers, technicians, foremen, higher clerical workers, nurses, and so on. Skilled workers, lower-grade clerical employees, shop assistants, drivers, and kindred workers have been classified under Social Class III. Social Class IV consists of different kinds of unskilled workers, maids, charwomen, janitors, and so forth.

Table 10   Results of Treatment (Duration over 2 Months)
by Diagnostic Category
(N—"Neurotic," P—"Psychotic," A—"Asocial")

Results	Diagnosis			Total	Percent
	N	P	A		
Marked change	39	7	7	53	21%
Signs of "deeper" change	78	10	18	106	42%
Symptomatic change	29	3	26	58	23%
No change	14	2	19	35	14%
Total	160	22	70	252	100%
Marked change	24%	32%	10%		
Signs of "deeper" change	49%	45%	26%		
Symptomatic change	18%	14%	37%		
No change	9%	9%	27%		
Total	100%	100%	100%		

Table 11 indicates that the lower the social class, the weaker is motivation for treatment. The improved motivation results in progress in treatment, better results, and terminating the treatment by a mutual agreement instead of interrupting it or letting it drop. Of the diagnostic groups, the psychotic children had the longest treatment. Various manifestations of serious disturbances in the family and its members have a negative influence on the treatment. Younger age at admission and higher intelligence improve the result of treatment. Of the diagnostic groups, the psychotic children had changed most and the asocial ones least. There is no significant difference in the results between the social classes but there are many more (40 to 59 percent) subjects unchanged or changed only as to their symptoms in Social Classes III and IV than in I and II (32 percent).

Psychotherapy was given as individual therapy for 69 percent of the children. Nearly all the mothers had case work and had their own therapy and so did 74 percent of the fathers, but often for a shorter period. Most of the therapies of children and mothers did not reach high figures, either (28 percent of children, 15 percent of mothers for more than 30 sessions). There are, however, some quite long therapies (more than 300 sessions). The longest therapy and most frequently was given to the psychotic children. Therapy groups were organized mostly for parents.

Table 11 Significant Relationship of Treatment Qualities

Treatment Qualities, Cross-tabulated	Significance Level, $p >$
Motivation/social class	.001
Motivation/parental immaturity	.01
Motivation/serious conflicts in family	.001
Motivation/duration of treatment	.001
Motivation/manner of terminating treatment	.001
Duration of treatment/serious conflicts in family	.001
Duration of treatment/diagnosis	.01
Results of treatment/motivation	.001
Results of treatment/duration of treatment	.001
Results of treatment/diagnosis	.001
Results of treatment/age at treatment	.001
Results of treatment/intelligence level	.1
Results of treatment/serious conflicts in family	.01
Results of treatment/social maladjustment of family	.05

Through the consecutive year groups 1956–1957, 1958–1959, and 1960–1962, a tendency to treat the patients more thoroughly can be observed. This became manifest as a significant increase in both the duration of treatment and the amount of psychotherapy.

After-care placement was recommended in 50 cases and carried out in 17. The majority of these belonged to the asocial category ($p > .001$). School arrangements after treatment have been most frequent in the psychotic group.

Follow-up Information

Facts from official records (323) were collected about all the patients in those years. This took place 10 to 15 years after the beginning of their treatment, so that the youngest were 16 and the oldest in their late 20s (by the end of 1972).

The child guidance centers in Helsinki have been contacted in 51 cases of former patients (16 percent) after the treatment at hospital. Child guidance center visits of these patients were 67. The asocial group has used these services most.

The child-welfare authorities have applied placement in 31 cases after treatment; 20 of these belong to the asocial group, and 15 were over 10 years of age when under treatment.

The records of two mental hospitals have been perused. These records consist of all the patients from the city and surrounding province. The migration trend in the country is toward Helsinki, and the migration in the opposite direction has been insignificant. Table 12 shows the distribution in mental hospitalization by diagnosis. Naturally, those in the psychotic group have been hospitalized most frequently, but those in the asocial group have also had later hospitalizations four times more frequently than neurotics. The differences are of the same significance regardless of the indication for treatment (psychosis or other reasons).

Most of those belonging to the neurotic or asocial group have been in mental hospitals only once or twice. On the other hand, in 70 percent of cases in the psychotic group, who were later hospitalized, the hospitalization took place three times or more, and only six of these because of psychosis. Three of these cases were sent immediately to a mental hospital for adults because of schizophrenia manifested in early puberty. Only one in the neurotic group had a psychosis later, and none in the asocial group. Out of those patients on our ward, who were under child psychiatric treatment in their early teens, significantly more have been in mental hospitals than have those who were younger when admitted to treatment. Those who had difficult family problems have had more mental hospital outpatient visits than did the others. They are 24 (7 percent) of the total patient population. The possibilities of private psychiatric treatment during the past decade have been fair, but it remains outside our study.

The national criminal records show only the more serious offenses leading to imprisonment. In the criminal records of the country there were 40 boys (19 percent) and 7 girls (6.5 percent)

Table 12   All Patients by Mental Hospital Inpatient Care
at Follow-up and Diagnosis

Hospitalizations	N	P	A	O	Total	Percent
None	193	15	71	11	290	91%
One or two	5	3	13	0	21	6%
Three or more	3	7	1	1	12	3%
Total	201	25	85	12	323	100%

of the total patient population (323). The percentage of those sentenced among the Finnish total population of the same age is 1.5 percent (men) and 0.05 percent (women). Four girls and four boys had a long and seemingly continuous series of offenses against property. In these cases it may be a way of life. Of the long-term population (87), 10 boys (19 percent of the boys) and no girls had a criminal record. Four of the boys had offenses against property, and four had traffic offenses. One had been sentenced for wounding and another for a narcotics offense. One may have taken to a criminal way of life. Six failed to attend our follow-up interviews, one of them being sentenced to hard labor and another one waiting for the beginning of a term of imprisonment. In addition, information on juvenile delinquency cases were received from the city child-welfare authorities. These records also included offenses that had not led to sentences. In the long-term population (87) this information is the more significant the worse the prognostic category.

Table 14 shows the age of the offenders by the offense from both the records and the distribution of the offenders by the diagnostic categories. Mostly this information concerns the asocial group. The psychotics have not committed crimes. Offenses committed at age 15 to 17 as seen from the information from the child-welfare or criminal records are more frequent the older the child when under treatment. Various gross family problems increase the criminal frequency to some extent. Those whose treatment result was poor also had more offenses than those whose treatment was better. Table 13 indicates the degree of statistic significance of relationship between certain treatment variables and follow-up variables concerning delinquency and mental-health services.

Follow-up Interview Facts

One of the 12 who did not attend the follow-up could not be contacted, and one did not answer the letter and turned out to be serving his hard labor sentence. Parents gave some information about the life of 10, and seven young people themselves were interviewed over the telephone. This talk was very limited with most of them because of their defensiveness. The majority of

Table 13   Relationship of Treatment Variables to Follow-up Variables, Significance Levels

Treatment Variables	Follow-up Variables	Significance Level, $p >$
Prognostic category	Working ability, assessment	.1
Prognostic category	Endurance under stress	.001
Prognostic category	Delinquency under 18	.05
Diagnosis: A	Delinquency from 15 to 17	.001
Diagnosis: P	Mental hospital: psychosis	.001
Diagnosis: P	Mental hospital: other	.001
Treatment age	Delinquency from 15 to 17	.1
Treatment age ±10	Mental hospital: psychosis	.01
Treatment age ±10	Mental hospital: other	.01
Social maladjustment of family	Delinquency from 15 to 17	.05

**Table 14   Offenders by Age of Offense and Diagnosis
(N—"Neurotic," P—"Psychotic," A—"Asocial," O—"Organic")**

Age of Offenders (Years)	N	P	A	O	Total	Age group at follow-up Percent	Total
15–17	7	1	17	1	26	8%	323
18–20	7	0	9	1	17	6%	294
21+	8	0	5	0	13	6%	217

those who refused to attend the follow-up belonged to the worst groups in prognostic evaluation. Of those interviewed, 26 (30 percent) had passed or were taking the Finnish matriculation examination. Approximately 20 percent of the age group pass the matriculation examination in Finland. The distribution into social classes of those who had passed this examination is I, 14; II, 7; III, 4; and IV, 1. On the basis of an intelligence test at the time of treatment, 11 were average and 15 above average in intelligence. Table 15 shows the level of schooling of those interviewed by prognostic categories.

The working ability of the 10 who were not interviewed was estimated on the basis of telephone information, but it seems to be overestimated rather than underestimated.

Table 15   Long-term Patients by Prognostic Category and
Education at Follow-up

Years Training Completed	I	II	III	IV	
12 (+ 1–2 at university)	8	8	7	1	
9–11 (or vocational training)	6	8	9	7	
8–9	4	5	6	9	
Drop-out	0	1	2	3	84

Follow-up Interviews: Assessments

From the beginning one of the basic principles was that mental
health is not unambiguous or one-dimensional. The study team
has been very well aware of its close connection with culture and
environment. When the children of this study were child
psychiatry cases we regarded as the risk groups psychotic/
borderline states and those deviating toward character disorders
who we called asocial. Within adult psychiatry, in the follow-up
assessments their mental health should be analyzed from a more
multidimensional point of view. One of the important dimensions
for these young adults is the potential of continuous personality
development that includes orientation toward future and identification with wider contexts. This we consider an age-adequate
developmental task in Erikson's sense.

Many other aspects have been assessed on the basis of the information from interviews and tests, but as this chapter is being
written only the extreme groups of narrow though important
estimates on working ability and stress endurance are available.
By "poor stress endurance" we mean not only the threat of
psychotic breakdown but also character disorders, character
neuroses, and psychoneuroses of a degree that threatens a person's capacity for bearing the strain of life. Under stress, people of
poor stress endurance lack strength or even attempt to pull themselves together and thus find themselves incapacitated for work
and psychiatric treatment becomes necessary. As a rule they act
below the level of their resources, and in the evaluation interview
most of them are estimated to have less than adequate working
ability or to be incapable of work.

The subjects estimated to belong to the "good endurance"

group are those who in the interview gave an impression of having strength to withstand conflict or failure as well as to pull themselves together even after straining experiences and to mature in relation to other people. The material from the interview did not give reliable bases for estimating the subjects' working ability better than adequate and hence the working ability evaluations do not differentiate the "good" group.

We want to emphasize that the classification given here is only one way of evaluating the mental health of these young adults and different starting points would give different results. We deal with them later as well as the evaluations and classifications made by a psychologist based on a projective test. Obviously, the psychiatrist who made the evaluation of adult mental health has not dealt with childhood information. Neither has she been aware of the prognostic categories of the subjects.

Table 16   Long-term Patients by Prognostic Category and Working Ability at Follow-up

	I	II	III	IV	
Ordinary	18	18	18	15	
Limited	0	3	4	2	
Precarious	0	1	1	5	85

Longitudinal Survey: From Prognostic Categories to Interview Information

Figure 1 draws a parallel between the information about the prognostic categories during treatment and follow-up. The four double columns show the subjects in the different prognostic categories so that the left column indicates the diagnostic characteristics of the child in the evaluation during treatment and the right column indicates those of parents. This indicates if the characteristics seen in the clinical records are dominatingly "neurotic," "psychotic," or "asocial." The letter on the right side of the column shows the clinical diagnosis. The symbol on the right side of the double column shows the result of the treatment (four grades), evaluation on the stress endurance (three grades), and working ability evaluation (two grades). In addition to this, an occasional letter can be seen in Figure 1 referring to use of psychiatric services after treatment or a criminal record. It shows that in the best prognostic category neurotic features are dominate both as to the child and the family. In the second prognostic category the same is true in almost all the cases, in the third in only a few cases, and in the fourth in none.

In this connection it could be recalled that the prognostic category was determined on the basis of the number of items describing psychotic and asocial features of the child and the family. Figure 1 also compares the relative similarity or dissimilarity of the prevailing item descriptions as for child and family. It also shows to what extent they correspond to the clinical diagnosis or differ from it. Table 7 contains some information about the diagram.

Both the Figure 1 and the Table 7 show that the result of treatment is distinctly best in the first and poorest in the fourth prognostic category, but mixed in the second and third. All the other information gets consistently worse when going toward the worse prognostic categories.

The children in the first prognostic group have almost always good or fair follow-up information, whereas about half of those having poor starting result in a quite poor present situation.

In the first prognostic category there is one subject with a good result in treatment whose stress endurance in the present estimation is quite poor and who has twice been sentenced for offenses against property. In the follow-up interview he proved to be a young man easily led by others and with poor self-confidence. He also described his relationship with his father as very disappointing. In the fourth prognostic category there is a boy coming from very difficult family circumstances and with a clinical diagnosis of "asocial." In the follow-up interview at the age of 24 he had reached the identity of an energetic free entrepreneur and gave quite an adult impression. He had kept in contact with his female therapist after the long successful treatment and regarded his relationship with a male occupational therapist in a school for delinquent boys as very significant for his development.

The other cases (10) in which the development has been from good starting point to poor result or vice versa belong to the prognostic middle categories, which is easy to understand. Their analysis is deferred until later.

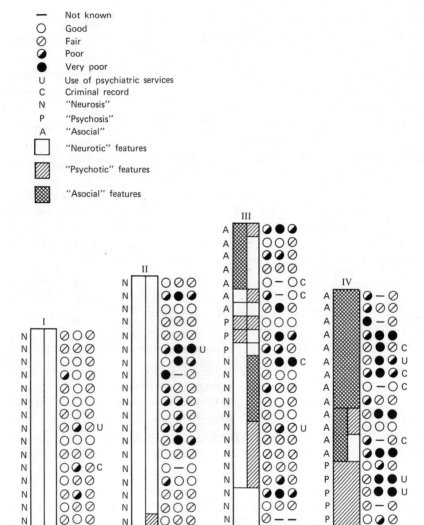

Figure 1   Prognostic categories during treatment and follow-up.

Table 17   Follow-up Information by Prognostic Categories

	I (N = 18)	II (N = 22)	III (N = 26)	IV (N = 21)
Treatment result good or fair (%)	94	68	73	62
Endurance under stress (%)	82	60	52	33
Ability to work (%)	100	82	79	67
Use of psychiatric services (N)	1	1	3	3
Criminal record (N)	1	—	4	5
Worst grade follow-up information (N)	—	5	6	8
Refusals (N)	1	2	3	6

The majority of even the long-term population belongs to the ▬▬stic category of neurotics. In the prognostic distribution, they fall mainly into the first to third categories, having the amounts 18, 22, 16, respectively. There were only two in the fourth category. One could suppose that the third prognostic category would show more severe pathology under a relatively milder clinical picture. The results of treatment and follow-up information should prove if this is true.

When comparing those with the diagnosis neurotic in the different prognostic categories, it can be seen that those in the first prognostic category do distinctly better on both results of the treatment and the follow-up. The same is not true with those in the second and third prognostic categories, where the evaluation of the results of the treatment is mixed. Good or moderate follow-up information has been obtained in 90 percent in the first prognostic category and in 70 percent in both the second and third as to stress endurance and/or working ability.

It may be concluded that the pathology criteria applied are significant when missing or when accumulating in a particular case but that their nature seems more important that the amount. The only subject who seems to have taken "a criminal career" belongs to the third prognostic category and the neurotic diagnostic category. His treatment at its time had petered out as unsuccessful.

Conclusions

We have reported the most central preliminary findings of our study. Some of our findings confirm previously reported insights and some, our clinical experience.

1. "Psychotic and borderline" children have more MBD signs and mothers with a history of psychotic breakdown than other groups.
2. "Asocial" childrens' background has plenty of immaturity in either or both parents, chaotic interaction in the family, and family's maladjustment in society. Most of them come from the lowest social classes.
3. Our diagnostic categories in childhood seem to have clear prognostic significance. Follow-up information on clinical psychiatric morbidity and social maladjustment is nificantly poorer for our "psychotic" and "asocial" group than for our "neurotic" group. Thus the childhood diagnosis implies different styles of disturbance in adulthood.
4. Our prognostic categories, based on certain characteristics of child and family, seem prognostic of working ability, stress endurance, and social adjustment in young adulthood.
5. Early treatment improves prognosis as it reduces juvenile delinquency and the need for psychiatric services.
6. Difficult family problems are the greatest threat to a good result of treatment and a favorable prognosis. Particularly parents' immaturity brings forth severe problems in the child and renders it more difficult for the family to seek treatment or build a therapeutic relationship. It is extremely difficult to communicate the aims of treatment to these families as well as to gain their confidence. The immaturity consists of such inconsistency and impulsivity that treatment, which is based on the clients' voluntary and spontaneous decisions, tends to fail.

Critique

As there are value judgments in all evaluations we make of human beings, those values have to be expressed and justified. We do not subscribe to a division of the healthy and the sick except for the presence or absence of clinical symptoms. We also consider it very problematic to decide which pathology is "sicker" than the other because of noncommensurability of different types of problems. Psychiatric illness in adulthood we regard as extensive nonuse of human innate potentials and marked limitations for self-satisfying work, to a point where the person is repeatedly or continuously in need of care or treatment. Mental disturbance is expressed also as inflicting much suffering on other people or being a cause of unreasonable social expenditure.

Classification is necessary, however, if points of prognostic value are to be shifted out of a multitude of observations. In our description of the children and their families we try to concentrate on features that either promote or hamper the development of stable warm relationships and strengthening of the child's ego and maturing of his conscience.

Some of our information is fairly reliable fact; however, most of our variables are estimates and evaluations. The possible sources of error are numerous—understanding the patient at the time of treatment, writing clinical records, and interpreting them into estimations. Although a carefully prepared coding system was devised, the coded items differ widely in importance. Author Malmivaara, who did the coding of clinical records (written 10 to 15 years earlier), has been the head of the unit from the early years under study. This can be considered both an advantage (personal acquaintance of patients) and a drawback (dependence on memories of patients).

The follow-up information was kept separate and handled by author Saarelma, who conducted the interviews. She had no knowledge of patients' prognostic category placement, although she had known a number of patients at their time of treatment. Author Keinänen, who did the psychological testing, worked blind.

Much thought and care has been put into developing various scales and estimates of both treatment and follow-up variables. It seems to bear fruit in the fact that findings are consistent with clinical experience and are never contradictory. This is true for both treatment and follow-up findings. Cross-validation by other people using our criteria on this or a similar population has not yet been done, but we are looking forward to it with expectation.

References

1. Anthony, E. J. A Clinical Evaluation of Children with Psychotic Parents. *Annu. Progr. Child Psychiat.*, 487–500, 1970. Chess, S. & Thomas, A., Eds. New York: Brunner/Mazel.
2. Anthony, E. J. and Benedek, T. *Parenthood: Its Pathology and Psychopathology.* Little, Brown, London, 1970.
3. Arajärvi, T. Psykoottisten ja rajatilapsykoottisten lasten hoitoja jälkitutkimus. *Duodecim,* 81 (1965), 1029–1039.
4. Aräjavi, T., Torma, S., and Mervaala, A. Lastenpsykiatrisen hoidon tuloksista koulunkäynnin ja yhteiskuntaan sopeutumisen kannalta. *Sos. lääket. aikak.*, 5, 1967.
5. Bell, R. Q., Waldrop, M. F., and Weller, G. M. A rating system for the assessment of hyperactive and withdrawn children in preschool age. *Amer. J. Orthopsychiat.*, 42, 1972.
6. Beller, E. K. *Clinical Process.* The Free Press, New York. 1968.
7. Bender, L. A Longitudinal Study of Schizophrenic Children with Autism. *Annu. Progr. Child Psychiat.*, 402–416, 1969.
8. Bratfor, O. Transition of neurosis and other minor mental disorders into psychosis. *Acta Psych. Scand.* 46 (1970), 35–49.
9. Caplan, Ed. G. *Prevention of Mental Disorders in Children.* Tavistock, London, 1961.
10. Chassan, J. B. Population and sample: A major problem in psychiatric research. *Amer. J. Orthopsychiat.*, 40 (1970), 456–462.
11. Cunningham, J. M., Westerman, H. H. and Fischhoff, J. A follow-up study of patients seen in a psychiatric clinic for children. *Amer. J. Orthopsych.*, 26:602, 1956.
12. Erikson, E. H., *Childhood and Society.* Imago, London, 1951.
13. Escalona, S. and Heider, G. M. *Prediction and Outcome.* Imago, London, 1959.
14. Fish, B. and Shapiro, T. A descriptive typolagn of children's psychiatric disorders. II: A behavioral classification. *Amer. Psych. Assoc.*, (1964), 75–86.
15. Fish, B., Shapiro, T., Cambell, M., and Wile, R. Classification of schizophrenic children under five years. *Amer. J. Psychiat.*, 124 (1968), 1415–1423.
16. Freud, A. *Normality and Pathology in Childhood.* International Universities Press, London, 1965.
17. Frijling-Schröder, E. C. M. Borderline state in children. *Psychoan. Study Child,* 24 (1969), 307.
18. Garmezy, N. and Nuechterlein, K. Invulnerable children: The fact and fiction of competence and disadvantage. *Amer. J. Orthopsychiat.*, 42 (1972), 328.
19. Goldfarb, W. Childhood psychosis. In *Manual of Child Psychology.* Wiley New York, 1970, Ed. G. Carmichael.
20. Goodman, C. and Putter, Z. Children of mentally ill parents: Whose responsibility? *Amer. J. Orthopsychiat.*, 42 (1972), 329.
21. Gosset, J. T., Lewis, S. B., Lewis, J. M., and Phillips, V. A. Follow-up of adolescents treated in a psychiatric hospital. *Amer. J. Orthopsychiat.*, 43 (1973), 602–610.
22. Graham, P. and Rutter, M. Organic brain dysfunction and child psychiatric disorder. *Annu. Progr. Child Psychiat.*, (1969), 521–539.
23. Graham, P., Rutter, M., and George, S. Tempermental characteristics as

predictors of behavioral disorders in children. *Amer. J. Orthopsychiat.*, 43, (1973), 328–339.

24. Hansen, N. Cerebro-organic pathogenesis in 110 children follow-up subsequent to admission to a child psychiatric department. *Acta Psych. Scand.*, 46 (1970), 399–412.
25. Havelkova, M. Follow-up study of 71 children diagnosed as psychotic in preschool age. *Amer. J. Orthopsychiat.*, 38 (1968), 846–857.
26. Herzog, E. and Sudia, C. E. Fatherless Homes: A Review of Research. *Annual Progr. Child Psychiat.* (1969), 341–451.
27. Holder, A. Theoretical and clinical notes on the interaction of some relevant variables in the production of neurotic disturbances. *Psychoan. Study Child*, 23 (1968), 63–85.
28. Holmström, R. *On the Picture of Mental Health. A Psychiatric Approach.* Munksgaard, Copenhagen, 1972.
29. Jonsson, G. *Delinquent Boys, Their Parents and Grandparents.* Munksgaard, Copenhagen, 1972.
30. Jonsson, G. and Kälvesten. *222 Stockholms pojkar.* En socialpsykiatrisk undersönkning av pojkar i skolåldern. Almqvist & Wicksell, Uppsala, 1964.
31. Kaffman, M. Characteristics of the emotional pathology of kibbutz children. *Amer. J. Orthopsychiat.*, 42 (1972), 692.
32. Kahana, B. and Anthony, E. J. Combining research and service: a multidisciplinary intervention program with children of psychotic parents. *Amer. J. Orthopsychiat.*, 42 (1972), 333.
33. Kogelschatz. J. L., Adams, P. L., and Tucker, D. Mc. K. Family styles of fatherless households. *J. Child Psychiat.*, 11 (1972).
34. v. Kraevelen, A. Prognosis of childhood neurosis and psychosis. *Acta Paedopsychiat.*, 1967. 34:104–111.
35. Kris, M. The use of prediction in a longitudinal study. *Psychoan. Study Child*, 12 (1957), 175–189.
36. Kütemeyer, W. *Die Krankheit in Ihrer Menschlichkeit.* Vandenhoeck & Ruprecht, Gottingen, 1963.
37. Laik, N. J. The classification problem in child and adolescent psychiatry. *Acta Psych. Scand.*, 49 (1973), 131–147.
38. Lempp, R. *Frühindliche Hirnschädingung und Neurose.* Verlag Hans Huber, Bern, 1970.
39. Lockyer, L. and Rutter, M. A five to fifteen year follow-up study of infantile psychosis. Psychological aspects. *Annu. Progr. Child Psychiat.*, 445 (1969).
40. Lukianowicz. N. Juvenile offenders III–IV. *Acta Psych. Scand.*, 48 (1972), 400–422.
41. Mahler, M. S. On human symbiosis and the vicissitudes of individuation. *Annu. Progr. Child Psychiat.*, (1968), 109–127.
42. Malmivaara, K. *Lasten psykoosit ja rajatilat seurantatutkimuksen valossa.* Psykoterapeuttinen Aikakauskirja II. Therapeia-Säätiö, Helsinki, 1972.
43. Malmivaara, K., et al. Granskning av vårdresultaten. *Nord. Psych. Tidskr.*, 4 (1962), 310–321.
44. McDermott, J. F., Harrison, S. I., Schrager, J., Lindy, J., and Killins, E. Social class and mental illness in children. The question of childhood psychosis. *Annu. Progr. Child Psych.*, 437–448 (1968).
45. Minde, K., Weiss, G., and Menderlson, N. A five year follow-up study of 91 hyperactive school children. *J. Child Psychiat.*, 11 (1972).

46. Mulligan, G., Douglas, J. W. B., Jammond, W. A., and Tizard, J. Delinquency and symptoms of maladjustment. The findings of a longitudinal study. *Proc. Roy. Soc. Med.*, 56 (1963), 1083.

47. Määttänen, M. Sosiaalisten sopeutumisvaikeuksien psykologisista ja sosiaalisista yhteyksistä. *Suomen virallinen tilasto. Sosiaalisia erikoistutk.*, 32 (1972), 28.

48. Nagera, H. *Early Childhood Disturbances. The Infantile Neurosis and the Adulthood Disturbances.* International Universities Press, New York, 1966.

49. Newman, M. B. and Martino, M. S. The child and the seriously disturbed parents. Treatment issues. *J. Child Psychiat.*, 12 (1973).

50. Otto, U. Spontant tillfrisknande hos barn och ungdom med psykiask störning. *Svenska Läkartidn.*, 65 (1968), 3935.

51. Rauhala, U. Koulokotipoikien ja nuorisovankien myöhemmät elämänvaiheet. *Suomen virall. tilasto. Sosiaalisia erikoistutkimuksia.*, 32 (1972), 30.

52. Robins, L. N. *Deviant Children Grown Up.* Williams & Wilkins, Baltimore, 1966.

53. Rosenthal, Ed. D. and Kety, S. S. *The Transmission of Schizophrenia.* Pergamon Press, London, 1969.

54. Rutter, M. *Children of Sick Parents: An Environmental and Psychiatric Study*, Oxford Press, London, 1966.

55. Rutter, M. L. Relationship between child and adult psychiatric disorders. *Acta Psych. Scand.*, 48 (1972), 3–21.

56. Rutter, M., Greenfeld, D., and Lockyer, L. A five to fifteen year follow-up study of infantile psychosis. *Annu. Progr. Child Psychiat.*, 449–496 (1968).

57. Rutter, M. Lebovici, S. Eisenberg, U. et al., A triaxial classification of mental disorders in childhood. *J. Child Psychol. Psychiat.*, 10 (1969), 41–61. 10 (1969), 41–61.

58. Siirala, M. *Medicine in Metamorphosis.* Tavistock, London,

59. Siirala, M. Schizophrenia—a human situation. *Sos. laaket. aikak.*, (1966),

60. Siirala, M. Our changing conception of illness. *J. Relig. Health*, 5 (1966), 105–118.

61. Siirala, M. *The Voice of Illness. A Study in Therapy and Prophecy.* Fortress Press, Philadelphia, 1964.

62. Speer, D. C., Fossum, M., Lippman, H. S., Schwartz, R., and Slocum, B. A comparison of middle- and lower-class families in treatment at a child guidance clinic. *Amer. J. Orthopsychiat.*, 38 (1968), 814–822.

63. Sundby, H. S. and Kreyberg, P. C. *Prognosis in Child Psychiatry.* Dreyer Aksjeselskap, Stavanger, 1968.

64. Thomas, A., Chess, S., and Birch, H. G. Behavioral problems revisited: Findings of an antrospective study. *Annu. Progr. Child Psychiat.* (1968a), 335–344.

65. Thomas, A., Chess, S., and Birch, H. G. *Temperament and Behavior Disorders in Children.* New York University Press, London, 1968b.

66. Thomas, A., Chess, S., Birch, H. G., Hertzig, M. E., and Korn, S. *Behavioral Individuality in Early Childhood.* University of London Press, London, 1964.

67. Uddenberg, N., Almgren, P.-E., and Nilsson, Å. Birth order and sex siblings: Influence on parental identification. *Acta Psych. Scand.*, 47 (1971). 324–333.

68. Weizsacker, V. *Pathosophie.* Vandenhoech & Ruprecht, Göttingen, 1967.

69. Werry, J. S., Minde, K., Grezman, A., Weiss, G., Dogan, K., and Hoy, E.

Studies on the hyperactive child. VII. Neurological status compared with neurotic and normal children. *Amer. J. Orthopsychiat.*, 42 (1972), 441.

70. Winnicott, D. W. *The Family and Individual Development.* Tavistock, London, 1965a.

71. Winnicott, D. W. *The Maturational Processes and the Facilitating Environment.* Hogarth Press, London, 1965b.

Outcome of Adolescent Psychiatric Disorders: A Long-term Follow-Up Study

Michael J. Shea, Ph.D., A. Jack Hafner, Ph.D., Wentworth Quast, Ph.D., and Joel H. Hetler, Ph.D. (U.S.A.)

The history of outcome research gives ample testament to the researchers' persistent quest to unravel the mesh of vulnerability, competence, and subsequent life events. Multiple subject groups, research strategies, and instruments have been employed in attempts to establish order and utility amid a myriad of variables and factors. To this end, some investigations have focused on "normal" populations [9, 36, 73], and others have chosen generally maladjusted children [82]. This latter approach has often yielded generalized results, limited in usefulness because of the heterogeneous populations.

Other wide-scope studies have addressed a range of specified symptoms and subject types, though usually not in sufficient depth, regarding the significant variables to satisfy the requirements of causal connection and specific etiological significance. Rather, they tend to provide leads for exploration through more intensive research programs, as in the high risk or target group approach [21, 31, 44]. This method holds great promise for intensive study of specific syndromes following a clearly delineated hypothesis. The unknowns in this method involve the actual yield from the group selected as high risk and the eventual usefulness of the instruments and variables chosen for the study.

Outcome studies have encompassed a variety of techniques from the case history method, an approach often educational but rarely of general validity, to the small- and large-scale follow-back and follow-up studies. The former has established limitations and generally has given way to follow-up studies. The latter has been conducted either prospectively as in the Mednick and McNeil [44] project or retrospectively using records to select subjects and determining their current as compared to their reconstructed past status. The best example of the latter kind of life history research is the Robins study [58] of referrals 30 years previously to a court-connected clinic. The usefulness of this study is limited only by the preponderance of antisocial and conduct problems in the sample and the lack of more sophisticated attempts to use the large amount of data gathered to maximize predictive ability across a range of outcome variables. Robins has investigated promising variables more extensively in subsequent research [59].

The subject age at which data collection begins has ranged from infancy [12] to elementary-school ages [72] to adolescence [40–42, 58] and beyond. The time spans covered have included periods of a few months or several years, as well as 20 or more years [55, 58]. Age at initial selection is an important issue as demonstrated by Roff's [62] finding that the preadolescent and adolescent socialization pictures of subsequent schizophrenics can be greatly disparate. Age at outcome measurement is equally critical; the case of male antisocial behavior has a fairly well-established pattern of gradual diminution through progressive age periods. Attrition of subjects and the related biases introduced, along with the lack or inadequacy of control or comparison groups, has been problematic in many studies.

Various methods of rating and classifying pathology have been used. Rutter has made the important point that any classification system should have predictive ability. There have been multiple criticisms of categorization as signifying "states" rather than "traits" and for being potentially damaging to the person being labeled. To defend that enterprise as more beneficial than harmful, adequate outcome research is essential. Multiple classification categories have been used by: (1) diagnosis [40, 56, 58, 75], (2) symptom types [1, 32, 70], (3) legal status [52, 57, 80], (4) temperament [12, 13, 69,], (5) psychological test results [2, 28], and (6) global ratings [71]. The relative strength of the various labels as measures of outcome is largely unclear. Outcome studies differ, furthermore, in the settings from which subjects are selected, and efforts to determine effects of treatment have been hindered by the differences both within and between groups in the type, intensity, and quality of treatment the subjects had received.

The outcome for groups having various symptom groupings and diagnoses has produced mixed findings. Those evidencing the greatest number and severity of antisocial symptoms carry the poorest prognosis [58]. Children who have internalizing or neurotic symptomatology seem to fare relatively better in adulthood [10], although many remain shy and retiring. The outcome for psychotic syndromes tends to be poor [17], but this heterogeneous group requires specifications of the type of disorder [60].

Numerous classification systems have been constructed [5, 25, 66, 67] in an attempt to specify the symptom patterns in a way that will foster better understanding of etiology as well as course than the existing diagnostic systems originally derived from the domain of adult psychopathology [76]. Most diagnostic systems are not studied to determine their predictive validity. Few have taken sufficient account of the age period specificity versus continuity of some disorders [5, 66]. Thus the enormously important but complex issue of the meaning of psychopathology and normality within the context of developmental phases has not been integrated successfully into our diagnostic systems.

Although outcome research has produced a multitude of findings, among which many have not been reconciled, several factors have repeatedly emerged as related to the outcome of some adolescent problems. The quality of peer relationships [61–65] is clearly an important precursor of later adjustment. School adjustment and performance [11, 58, 59] also stand out as important. Both of these are major problem areas for acting-out children and especially for seriously antisocial children [58]. Although many life-history studies have supplied pieces of the puzzle regarding interrelationships of types of variables, not enough is known about the relative contribution of each to outcome in specific child and adolescent groups.

The adolescent follow-up study described in this chapter investigates the relative contribution of a large number of variables and attempts to begin the complex process of specifying which factors are important and for whom. Earlier substudies in the project have investigated the relatively poor outcome for lower functioning adolescent subjects [51] and the importance of analyzing outcomes for males and females separately [35]. In the latter study the variables related to later adjustment differed by sex. A third study by Shea [70] has shown the symptom grouping of internalizing or turning against the self versus the externalizing or turning against others to be related to adult adjustment. An internalizer, externalizer, and control were individually matched at adolescent contact on the variables of sex, age, intelligence, intactness of family of origin, socioeconomic level of family of origin, and urban versus rural residence. The male and female externalizing subjects, consistent with the Robins [58] study, had more difficulty with school, poor relations with family, and significantly less successful marital and friendship relationships. In addition, unlike the internalizing and medical patient comparison group, they failed to improve their social class standing over that of their parents, had histories of poor job adjustment, many job changes, and surprisingly isolated lives despite their outgoing personality types.

The adolescent follow-up study was conceived for the purpose of investigating the long-term outcome of adolescent psychiatric patients. The primary study group had a sufficiently large number of psychiatrically disturbed adolescents to ensure a representative sample of the psychiatric problems occurring among adolescents. For comparative purposes, a group of adolescent pediatric patients without psychiatric problems was also studied. Adult outcome for both groups was evaluated through structured personal interviews with the subjects, psychological testing, and corroborating records.

Subjects

The sample was comprised of 1108 former adolescent patients seen at the University of Minnesota Hospitals at ages 13 through 17 during the years 1938 through 1950. The mean age of the subjects at the time of the follow-up contact (21 to 33 years later) was 38.7 years, indicating that sufficient time had elapsed from adolescence to adulthood to assure that the study was truly sampling adult outcome.

The psychiatric sample consisted of 866 consecutive inpatient and outpatient referrals to the University of Minnesota Child Psychiatry Unit. Nonwhite patients were not included in the study, as there were too few for proper investigation. The comparison group of 242 nonpsychiatrically disturbed patients was chosen from the Department of Pediatrics. Each of these patients was individually matched with a randomly selected psychiatric counterpart by age, sex, and date of referral. Patients were excluded from the nonpsychiatrically disturbed pediatric group who carried a diagnosis of brain syndrome or mental deficiency since such diagnoses are classified as mental disorders in the American Psychiatric Association Diagnostic Manual [4]. Pediatric patients were also excluded if the hospital record indicated significant law violations or serious acts of delinquency. Eight pediatric patients with minor law violations were retained in the study. The University Hospital draws referrals from throughout Minnesota; the subject population for the study was representative of the population of the state at that time with respect to such factors as socioeconomic status, geographic location, religion, and population density of the area of residence.

It was intended to interview each subject individually whenever possible. The first phase of this approach was the development of extensive location procedures, following a systematic checklist of sources that included the subjects' relatives, telephone books, telephone directory-assistance operators, state drivers' license bureaus, Polk city directories, credit-bureau yellow books, and district Internal Revenue Services. Additional information came from records supplied by public agencies and institutions, such as high schools, state hospitals, corrections institutions, state criminal apprehension bureaus, the Federal Bureau of Prisons, armed services personnel, and state departments of vital statistics. Although stringent safeguards were used to protect the individuals' privacy and confidentiality of records, it is doubtful that a study of this kind could be undertaken today in face of the current regulations on research.

Three sources provided location information for 83 percent of all the subjects located. Telephone or letter contact with a subjects' relatives provided the highest location yield (62 percent of all subjects located). The next best source was telephone books or directory-assistance operators, yielding 11 percent of the located subjects, followed by drivers' license bureaus with a subject location yield of 10 percent.

Positive location was made for 89.9 percent of the subjects (unlocated $N = 112$). Among the located subjects, 73 percent were in Minnesota and surrounding five-state area, whereas 27 percent resided outside that area. Of those positively located, 5.2 percent ($N = 58$) refused to cooperate in the study, and 9.8 percent ($N = 109$) were dead. Interviews were obtained with relatives of 88 of the 109 deceased subjects (80.7 percent). Data from those interviews are not included in this chapter.

Tests were carried out using the following adolescent variables to determine whether selection biases were introduced through the attrition of subjects: (1) group (psychiatric or medical), (2) sex, (3) age at adolescent University Hospital contact, (4) religion, (5) rural or urban residence, (6) social class of family, (7) adolescent mental health rating (MHR), (8) diagnosis, (9) intelligence, (10) intactness of family (living with both natural parents or with adopted parents since infancy), and (11) number of symptoms.

There were no differences between groups or sexes in the numbers of subjects unlocated or lost due to death. The number of uncooperatives from the psychiatric group was significantly greater than chance expectation (93.1 percent of the uncooperatives were adolescent psychiatric patients, whereas only 78.2 percent of the total study sample were psychiatric). The unlocated and uncooperative psychiatric females came from nonintact families significantly more often than the located and cooperative psychiatric females. In addition, a disproportionate number of psychiatric females diagnosed as antisocial personality were unlocated, and a disproportionate number from lower social classes were uncooperative. For psychiatric males the only significant finding was that the unlocated subjects were from lower social classes than the located ones. It was judged unethical to make MHRs on uncooperative subjects. It seemed likely that this group included a disproportionate number of severely disturbed adolescents; however, the small number of uncooperatives hopefully minimized this source of bias. Where it could be tested, rates of attrition were found to be unrelated to adolescent MHRs. Medical males who were not located were significantly more often of religious faiths other than Protestant or Catholic than were the located medical males. There were no variables on which the unlocated or uncooperative medical females differed from their located and cooperative counterparts. The deceased subjects in all groups did not differ from the living subjects on any of the adolescent variables evaluated.

Among those who died, the mean age at death for the medical group (21.4 years) was younger than that for the psychiatric group (27.4 years). The difference was due largely to the fact that a significant portion of the medical patients who died eventually died of the disorder for which they had originally been seen. This group difference is similar for both sexes but only statistically significant for the males. There was no significant difference between the sexes regarding age of death.

The subjects lost from the study group through several types of attrition did differ on several variables, notably family intactness for psychiatric females and social class for both psychiatric males and females. Differential attrition is an unavoidable phenomenon in studies of this type; however, it seemed to be small enough here to not have seriously biased the accuracy of other findings.

Analysis for this study eliminated all psychiatric subjects diagnosed as mentally retarded ($N = 35$), epileptic ($N = 34$), or having organic brain syndromes ($N = 18$). These groups are extremely important, but analyzing them together with the rest of the psychiatric subjects would contaminate the data and cloud the meaning of the results. Proper analysis of these groups is beyond the scope of this presentation.

The number of remaining subjects in these four categories of subjects retained for this analysis is as follows: (1) psychiatric males, 265; (2) medical males, 90; (3) psychiatric females, 282; (4) medical females, 105.

Data

Data collection began with the extraction of information from the University Hospital medical records, which included histories, physical examinations, laboratory studies, and consultation evaluations by specialists. The charts also contained information gathered at the time of adolescent referral from sources in the community such as schools, public-welfare departments, and social agencies, as well as information about previous hospital contacts. For the psychiatric group most records also contained social histories and comprehensive psychological and physical examination results. The records were generally quite complete, but the psychiatric records were more so.

The hospital records, supplemented with information from schools, contained one or more IQ scores for most of the subjects. If there were several tests, the highest score attained on a test of acceptable reliability and validity was used with individual tests taking precedence over group tests.

In spite of the problems with the reliability, validity, and utility (concurrent as well as predictive) of psychiatric diagnoses with children and the multiple number of poorly agreed-on diagnostic systems used with children [25], diagnoses, in some form, are widely used and will probably continue to be. One of the purposes of this study was then to investigate the usefulness of adolescent diagnosis. Psychiatric diagnoses were recorded as made at hospital contact and were transformed into the nomenclature of the current American Psychiatric Association (APA) system [3, 4] using APA suggested rules. Subjects lacking diagnoses were not given diagnoses by the investigators. Too few adults had known diagnoses to allow analysis.

Some of the adolescent psychiatric patients had been administered the MMPI, an objective personality inventory composed of 556 true-false questions, many of them similar to questions asked in a psychiatric interview [27]. Some MMPIs were also obtained from a large percentage ($N = 531$) of the subjects at follow-up. The MMPI is one of the most widely used objective personality inventories, having the advantages of low administration costs (in time and money) and a wealth of validity studies [14, 79].

Standard scores were available for adolescent MMPIs, but the item responses were not. K-Corrections were not available for many of these MMPIs since they were administered prior to the derivation of the K scale. The Marks, Seaman, et al. [39] norms were used to compute non-K-corrected T (standard) scores on the adolescent MMPI profiles. Three MMPI signs were computed on both adolescent and adult MMPIs: Gough's Character Disorder Sign [(Pd-(Pa + Sc/2)] [24]; The Welsh Internalization Ratio [(Hs + D + Pt)/(Hy + Pd + Ma)] [78]; and Goldberg's Psychotic-Neurotic Index [(L + Pa + Sc) − (Hy + Pt)] [22], on which a high score is a psychotic indication. The use of these signs on the adolescent MMPIs were unorthodox as they were applied to non-K-corrected adolescent scores, although they had been developed on K-corrected adult profiles. K-Corrected scores were used for computing these signs on the adult MMPIs, but non-K-corrected scores have been used in all other applications. In addition, average elevation of clinical scales, except 5 and 0, were computed for all adolescent and adult MMPIs. If the T score on F equaled or exceeded 80 or if L or K (when known) equaled or exceeded 70, MMPIs were deleted from the study as invalid. Additionally, for the adult MMPI, profiles were eliminated if 58 or more items were unanswered (T score 60).

Presenting symptoms were recorded on a 92-symptom checklist. Care was taken to avoid halo effects and other inferences in recording symptoms. All adolescent psychiatric subjects were rated on Achenbach's [1] factor analytically derived bipolar symptom grouping of "internalizing" (turning against self) versus "externalizing" (turning against others) or I-E, which accounted for the largest part of the variance in his study and had shown prognostic significance in a previous study [70]. Psychiatric subjects were also rated on Achenbach's second factor, "severe and diffuse psychopathology" (S-D), which contains a number of psychotic and generally more bizarre symptoms.

Achenbach and Shea each classified their subjects as I or E if 60 percent of their total symptoms were of that type (and the total number of symptoms was at least three). In this study three separate scores—the number of I, E, and S-D symptoms—were computed for each subject with three or more total symptoms. These scores were highly correlated with the total number of symptoms and were subsequently standardized by dividing each by that total. The final I, E, and S-D scores all had negligible correlations with the total number of symptoms. The I and E scores had a large negative intercorrelation but were both retained for the study. The S-D score had low or negligible correlations with the other two scores.

As a supplement to the psychiatric diagnoses and psychometric indices, a MHR similar to the rating used in the Midtown Manhattan Study [71] was assigned to each patient based on all appropriate information. The ratings were made by two of the principal investigators, who were experienced clinical psychologists. Ratings were made for the period of University Hospital contact in adolescence (1 year prior to Hospital contact to 1 year after) using only information about that period of time. Hence the ratings of adolescent mental health were done blind in that the raters had no access to any information about subsequent adjustment. Similarly, a blind rating was made for the period of time beginning 1 year after the University Hospital contact and ending five years before the date of the follow-up interview (interim period). A third MHR was made at outcome using information spanning the 5 years previous to the follow-up date (adult period). The ratings were then done on all 1108 study subjects for these three time periods and were uncontaminated, since a third researcher had separated the information by time periods. Although the same raters made all three ratings, the fact that all 1108 ratings for one period preceded those for the next period precluded remembering information about the same subject across periods. A study of the reliability of the mental health ratings found that there was a high degree of agreement between the two raters when rating a given subject independently. The ratings were then made jointly by the two raters.

The MHR consisted of five categories, ranging from symptom-free adjustment to extremely incapacitating symptomatology. The list that follows defines the five levels of the MHR:

0— No information; insufficient information to make an MHR.
1— Positive mental health; evidence of noteworthy positive mental health. Above average in total life adjustment.
2— Problem behavior not incapacitating; problem behavior not apparent or not interfering with life-adjustment factors to any significant degree.
3— Problem behavior mildly incapacitating; some evidence of problem behaviors interfering with life-adjustment factors.
4— Problem behavior moderately incapacitating; significant impairment of functioning in life-adjustment factors.

5— Problem behavior severely incapacitating; impairment in life-adjustment factors to degree that individual is essentially unable to function autonomously and requires institutionalization and/or primary support and protection by others.

The life-adjustment factors that were considered in determining the degree of incapacitation during adolescence and adulthood are as follows:

1. School adjustment: academic achievement (effective utilization of abilities), interpersonal relationships.
2. Social relationships: quality of relationship with parents; quality of relationship with siblings; number and closeness of friendships in and out of school; degree of social isolation; adequacy of heterosexual adjustment; dyssocial activity; quality of relationship with adults and authority; breadth of interests and social participation (clubs, organizations, activities).
3. Autonomous functioning: self-sufficiency; appropriately independent; financial responsibility; jobs.
4. Self-concept: positive attitudes regarding self.
5. Vocational competence (primarily in adulthood): job stability; effective utilization of abilities (achievement level); employability.

Weighing problem behaviors necessitated taking into account the frequency, intensity, and pervasiveness of the behavior, that is, the number of episodes of the problem behavior, the strength or magnitude of the problem in terms of its maladaptive nature, and the relative number of life-adjustment factors affected.

The subjects were interviewed at outcome using a 200-question structured interview form. A small proportion received a mailed questionnaire that had been found equivalent [8]. Interviews or questionnaires were completed by 73.5 percent of the subjects. In cases where a subject had died or was too disturbed or retarded to answer interview questions, interviews were completed by relatives (10.8 percent of the sample). In only 15.7 percent of the cases was no follow-up interview obtained. At the time of the interview, the MMPI was left with the subject to be completed and returned by mail.

Finally, collateral sources of information obtained through searches of school, military correctional, welfare, and psychiatric records provided validating data for the interview information. Data from the various subjective and objective sources was cross-referenced for reliability and validity.

Methods

In studies of this magnitude one runs the risk of finding many significant but unreplicable results due to the number of statistical tests involved, as well as the risk of detecting reliable but trivial differences or correlations because of the relatively large sample sizes. Several steps were taken to circumvent these problems. Conservative p-value cutoffs were used in determining significance. One-tailed tests were used when appropriate and $p = .005$ was taken as the cutoff. For two-tailed tests $p = .01$ was the cutoff. In addition, whenever possible, reports of significance were accompanied with statistical estimates of the strength of association or importance of the findings.

It should be noted that although strength of association measures are often correlation-like in form, they are not always subject to the same interpretation as correlation. When one or more of the variables involved was ordinal, Kendall's τ was used, which generally gives somewhat lower estimates of strength of relation than Spearman's ρ, which is the formal equivalent to the correlation for ordinal data. However, τ is considered to be more appropriate than ρ when the number of ordinal categories is small compared to the number of individuals measured.

The general plan of the analyses was to first analyze psychiatric versus medical patient and male versus female differences in adolescence and adulthood and then try to identify useful predictors of adult outcome. Analysis of variance was used to study group and sex differences on continuous variables. Whenever it was used the regression model (main effects corrected for other main effects and for interactions), rather than the classical-experimental model (main effects corrected for other main effects only), was applied. This is recommended by Overall, Spiegel, et al. [54] as the most appropriate approach in analyses of variance with unequal cell frequencies. It also gives a more conservative test for significance of main effects. In studying group and sex differences, we were sensitive to the possible presence of interactions between these factors, for example, larger sex differences within the psychiatric sample than within the medical comparison sample. It was often impossible to test directly for interactions; however, attempts were made to report them whenever they appeared to be present.

The relations between pairs of adolescent and adult variables were evaluated, and some beginning attempts were made to investigate the predictive power of groups of adolescent variables. To do this, multiple regression was used but not always in completely rigorous manner [e.g., ordinal variables—MHR and SES (socioeconomic status)—] were sometimes the dependents). These analyses were preliminary but potentially valuable heuristic aids in examining the complex relations between adolescent status and adult outcome.

Results

Of the large number of group comparisons made, there were relatively few significant differences in adolescence between the psychiatric and medical groups, as shown in Table 1. The groups did not significantly differ in terms of variables of sex distribution and mean age (two of the matching variables) or family social class or SES [34]. The mean IQ was higher in the medical group (ca. 6 points). Fewer of the psychiatric group came from intact families (a difference of 20 percent). The MHR was significantly lower for the psychiatric group, and more of the psychiatric group had been placed in foster homes or institutions during adolescence. Also more of the psychiatric group had committed minor or major law violations (nontraffic) in adolescence, an effect more marked among the males.

The lack of group differences on social class may have been partly artifactual, due to greater attrition among psychiatric subjects from lower social classes. Kohlberg, Lacrosse, et al. [37] found that IQ was a significant though weak predictor of adult adjustment, and hence differences on this might be important. The differences in family intactness, MHR, foster home or institutional placement, and law violations all seemed consistent with the

Table 1 Adolescent Variables: Group Values, Significance Tests, and Strength of Association

	Psych. Males	Psych. Females	Med. Males	Med. Females	Group Effect	Sex Effect	Interaction (Group × Sex)
Demographic							
Mean age at Univ. Hosp. contact (years)	14.7	14.9	14.5	14.8	NS	NS	NS
Distribution by sex (%)	48.5	51.5	46.2	53.8	NS	NS	NS
Intelligence (mean IQ)	98.9	100.6	104.2	106.1	$r = .128^c$	NS	NS
Socioeconomic status (SES) classes 1–5 (median)	4.57	4.71	4.57	4.66	NS	$T = .100**$	NS
Urban/rural residence	45.3/54.7	37.01/63.0	20.0/80.0	25.5/74.5	NS	NS	$r = .23^{c,e}$
Religion (%)							
Protestant	62.6	66.3	67.8	65.7			
Catholic	25.3	27.0	27.8	31.4	NS	NS	NS
Other	12.1	6.7	4.4	2.9			
Family							
Intactness (%)	50.6	54.1	71.6	72.6	NS	NS	NS
Father's job stability (% unstable)	23.1	26.7			—	NS	NS
Parents' marital problems							
Father (%)	29.7	24.3			—	NS	—
Mother (%)	31.8	26.1			—	NS	—
Father's psychiatric history (% with apparent problems)	38.4	41.0			—	NS	—
Mother's psychiatric history (% with apparent problems)	35.7	36.7			—	NS	—

Relationship with father (% poor)	62.6	60.7	—	—	—	NS	—
Relationship with mother (% poor)	57.3	63.1	—	—	—	NS	—
Relationships with siblings (% poor)	61.5	55.9	—	—	—	NS	—
Relationships with peers (% poor)	62.5	62.7	—	—	—	NS	—
Father's history of law violations (nontraffic)	4.9	6.1	—	—	—	NS	—
Mother's history of law violations (nontraffic)	2.0	1.9	—	—	—	NS	—
Patients' psychiatric and legal history							
Inpatient psych. at Univ. Hosp. (%)	42.2	50.0	—	—	—	NS	—
Adolescent placement in foster home or institution	43.8	40.6	7.9	6.7	$r = .327$[d]	NS	NS
Duration of complaints in months (median)	6.5	6.5	—	—	—	NS	—
Number of symptoms							
Mean	4.93	4.85	—	—	—	NS	—
SD	2.78	2.91					
Discharged to family (%)	60.3	69.5	—	—	—	NS	—
Law violations before age 18 (mean)	1.51	0.32	0.08	0.00	$r = .231$[c]	$r = .274$[c]	Sex difference greater within psych. group[c]

545

Table 1 Adolescent Variables: Group Values, Significance Tests, and Strength of Association (Continued)

	Psych. Males	Psych. Females	Med. Males	Med. Females	Group Effect	Sex Effect	Interaction (Group × Sex)
Diagnoses: 40.4% (107/247) of males and 49.7% (140/282) of females received diagnoses							
Psychotic	17.8	12.9	—	—	—	NS	—
Neurotic	16.8	51.4	—	—	—	$r = .356^d$	—
Antisocial	22.4	10.7	—	—	—	NS	—
Adjustment reaction	23.4	12.1	—	—	—	NS	—
Other	19.6	12.9	—	—	—	NS	—
Adolescent MHR (1-5) (mean)	4.03	3.90	2.32	2.21	$\tau = .644$	NS	NS
MMPI							
Adolescent (non-K) MMPI scales $L, F, K, 1, 2, 3, 4,$ 6, 7, 8, 9	—	—	—	—	—	NS	—
Mean elevation	55.19	55.17	—	—	—	NS	—
N-P Sign[f]	49.3	49.4	—	—	—	NS	—
CD Signs[g]	3.72	0.27	—	—	—	NS	—
I Ratio	0.99	1.07	—	—	—	$r = .299^{a,e}$	—

Strength of association: $t-\tau$; $r-$Pearson r; $R-$multiple R.

[a] $p < .01$.
[b] $p < .005$.
[c] $p < .001$.
[d] $p < .00005$.
[e] Two-tailed test.
[f] N = P—Goldberg's neurotic-psychotic sign.
[g] CD—

psychiatric versus nonpsychiatric distinction and were not considered to reflect mismatching of the two groups.

Data were not available for the medical patients on some adolescent variables. They had not been administered MMPIs at adolescence, and in general their adolescent records were not as complete as those of the psychiatric subjects. Thus group comparisons as well as male-female comparisons within the medical group were not possible on all variables of interest.

Adolescent data were also analyzed by sex. Comparisons were across both groups when possible and between psychiatric males and females otherwise. No sex differences across groups were found for age at contact, intelligence, family intactness, or percent ever placed in a foster home or institution. In addition, no differences were found between psychiatric males and females on parents' marital problems, inpatient versus outpatient status at adolescent contact, whether patients were discharged to their families, number of symptoms, parents' history of mental problems, and relationships with family members and peers. There were no sex differences on the adolescent MMPI scores and, in fact, the average MMPI elevations were almost identical (males 55.19, females 55.7). Therefore, the sexes were comparable on a number of important variables, except for a few variables, such as social class of the family. Also, whereas the MHRs did not differ by sex in the medical group, the ratings of the psychiatric males were significantly poorer than those of the psychiatric females. More psychiatric males came from urban and suburban areas than did control males.

Table 2 shows the variables examined at adult outcome (a period that included the 5 years preceding the follow-up interview). The mean age at follow-up was 38.7. There were no group differences on age at interview, age at first marriage, or self-reported health.

The groups did differ, however, on a number of other variables at outcome. The medical patients had completed significantly more schooling, 1 year for the medical males and 70 percent of a year for the females on the average. The psychiatric group had poor job stability, as measured by the length of time at their current job and the number of jobs held since finishing school. The medical patients' greater achievement was reflected in high in-

Table 2 Adult Variables: Group Values, Significance Tests, and Strength of Association

	Psych. Males	Psych. Females	Med. Males	Med. Females	Group Effect	Sex Effect	Interaction (Group × Sex)
Demographic							
Age at interview ($\bar{x}$ years)	38.5	38.7	38.5	39.2	NS	NS	NS
Highest grade completed ($\bar{x}$)	10.9	10.9	11.9	11.6	$r = .135^c$	NS	NS
Jobs since school ($\bar{x}$)	9.73	4.72	6.06	3.63	$r = .114^c$	$r = .239^c$	NS
Years on current job ($\bar{x}$)	5.97	2.60	8.25	2.82	$r = .082^b$	$r = .332^c$	NS
Annual income (median)	7600	7500	8200	7800	$t = .133^c$	NS	Group difference between males accounts for group effect ($\tau = .171^c$)
Adult SES (median level)	4.19	4.14	3.70	3.85	$t = .167^d$	NS	Group effect larger within males ($\tau = .204^d$)
Number of places lived ($\bar{x}$)	11.7	8.28	7.02	7.55	$r = .108^b$	NS	Group difference between females accounts for group effect $r = .139^b$
Never married	16.7	12.1	11.1	2.9	$r = .102^b$	NS	NS
Age at first marriage ($\bar{x}$)	23.5	20.3	22.7	20.7	NS	$r = .343^c$	NS
Married at interview (%)	71.6	75.2	85.6	90.5	$r = .155^d$	NS	NS

								Psychiatric males have significantly fewer children
Number of children if ever married ($\bar{x}$)	2.87	3.56	3.61	3.25	NS	NS	NS	
Mental health, health, and law violations:								
Health (self-report) (%)	14.7	29.4	10.0	16.2	NS	NS	NS	NS
Total times drunk in last 12 months ($\bar{x}$)	2.97	0.964	2.97	0.175	NS	r = .124[c]	NS	NS
Adult inpatient or outpatient psychiatric treatment episodes (% of occurrence in last 5 years)	8.9	14.0	0.0	4.6	r = .141[c]	NS	NS	NS
Adult outpatient *only* psychiatric treatment episodes (% of occurrence in last 5 years)	6.9	11.6	5.6	12.5	NS	NS	NS	NS
Adult inpatient *or* outpatient psychiatric treatment episodes in last 5 years (% occurrence either or both)	14.6	22.5	5.6	15.4	NS	r = .111[b]	NS	NS
Adult law violations (non-traffic) ($\bar{x}$) number with arrests in 5 years (%)	10.9	2.4	5.7	0	NS	r = .175[d]	NS	NS
Adult MHR (median)	3.08	2.96	2.42	2.59	T = .214[d]	NS	NS	NS

Table 2 Adult Variables: Group Values, Significance Tests, and Strength of Association (continued)

	Psych. Males	Psych. Females	Med. Males	Med. Females	Group Effect	Sex Effect	Interaction (Group × Sex)
Adult MMPI ($N = 531$)							
Overall difference	—	—	—	—	$R = .239^c$	$R = .433^d$	NS
L, K, F, 1, 2, 3, 6, 7, 8, A, R	—	—	—	—	NS	NS	NS
4 ($\bar{x}$)	59.5	58.4	54.0	54.1	$r = .177^d$	NS	NS
5 ($\bar{x}$)	55.8	50.4	55.8	46.9	—	—	Group effect within females ($r = .184^b$), NS within males
9 ($\bar{x}$)	54.7	50.3	53.1	47.9	NS	$r = .227^c$	NS
0 ($\bar{x}$)	51.8	58.8	52.9	57.6	NS	$r = .285^d$	NS
Es ($\bar{x}$)	56.0	51.8	55.2	53.8	NS	$r = .173^b$	NS
$\bar{x}$ Elevation	53.8	54.5	53.3	52.2	NS	NS	NS
N-P Sign, I Ratio	—	—	—	—	NS	NS	NS
CD Sign	7.27	3.39	2.49	2.06	$r = .133^d$	NS	NS

Strength of association: $t - \tau$; r — Pearson r; R — multiple R.

[a] $p < .01$.
[b] $p < .005$.
[c] $p < .001$.
[d] $p < .00005$.

come levels as well as a higher mean social class at outcome. Significantly more of the medical patients were married at the time of interview. A multivariate analysis of variance revealed an overall group difference on the MMPI profiles. This was probably due mainly to a difference on Scale 4, which was the only individual scale that showed a group difference. Scale 4 (psychopathy) includes a number of items about milder nonconformity, more serious antisocial behavior, and a history of poor relationships with family members and authority figures. The average elevation of the MMPI profiles did not differ between groups, however. In terms of psychiatric disturbance at outcome, significantly more of the psychiatric group had been inpatients, but the groups did not differ in the percent of each that had received outpatient therapy.

There were no sex differences in the outcome variables of social class, age at interview, highest grade completed in school, number of places lived, whether the subject was married at interview, or self-report of health. Significant sex differences, however, appeared in the subjects' age at first marriage (females married younger), the number of jobs held since school, and the length of time on the current job (if any). The females in this study were less likely to be employed outside the home than were the males. They differed, too, in median family income.

Significantly fewer medical than psychiatric females had never been married prior to follow-up. The differences between the medical and psychiatric males were not significant on this variable, and their rates of never marrying were comparable to those for the psychiatric males. Among those subjects who did ever marry, psychiatric males had fewer children than either psychiatric females or medical males and females.

Multivariate analysis of variance indicated an overall sex difference in the MMPI profiles in addition to the group difference. In terms of individual scales, the females had lower scores on Scale 9 (mania) and higher scores on Scale 0 (social introversion), indicating that the females had a lower energy level overall and were more introverted compared to the males. Further, the psychiatric females had higher scores on Scale 5 (masculinity-femininity) than did the medical females. The Scale 5 group difference did not hold within the males. The females had significantly lower scores on Barron's ego-strength scale [7].

There was a significant sex difference in adult law violations. These were confined almost entirely to the psychiatric males with no violations occurring among the medical females and very few in the other two groups. There were no significant sex differences in the percent receiving inpatient treatment, but there was a significant difference in adult outpatient treatment. More psychiatric group members received inpatient treatment as adults, whereas sex differentiated the outpatient treatment recipients from non-recipients and group membership did not. This is consistent with the treatment literature suggesting that females are more likely than males to receive outpatient psychiatric treatment, although not necessarily in reflection of the prevalence of disturbance in the population. Outpatient therapy in this study tended to be short-term treatment of anxiety and depression, often accompanied by psychotropic medications as either the primary treatment or an adjunct.

A more detailed analysis of psychiatric treatment after the University Hospital contact revealed a variety of courses and outcomes. In the male psychiatric group, 68.2 percent and in the female psychiatric group, 56.4 percent had no treatment after the adolescent contact. Another 17.2 percent of the males and 21.1 percent of the females had inpatient or outpatient treatment but by follow-up were not in treatment. During the 5 years prior to follow-up only 14.6 percent of the males and 22.5 percent of the females received any treatment. A small number of subjects seemed to require more intensive treatment at outcome than during the interim period (5.4 percent of the males, 9.5 percent of the females). Thus few adolescent psychiatric patients had any psychiatric treatment in adulthood and of the few who did, most were no longer in treatment by their middle to late 30s. The major exception to this good prognosis pertains to those who received interim inpatient treatment. Among the males, 39.2 percent and of the females, 46.3 percent, who received treatment then were still receiving treatment in the adult period, with 29.4 percent of the male and 31.3 percent of the female interim inpatients still receiving inpatient treatment.

Among the medical patients, 89.9 percent of the males and of the females, 76.9 percent never received any psychiatric treatment. Of those who did, only 2.2 percent of the males and 5.8

percent of the females had been inpatients at any time. During the 5 years prior to follow-up only 5.6 percent of the medical males and 15.5 percent of the medical females received treatment. There were 4.6 percent of the females and none of the males in inpatient treatment. These events are infrequent among the medical patients and thus likely to be difficult to predict. Although the rate of psychiatric treatment in the medical group may serve as a basis for comparison with the psychiatric group, mental illness incidence estimates vary greatly [15].

Law violations subsequent to age 18 were most common among psychiatric males. About one-third (32.3%) had convictions after adolescence, a decrease from the 50.2 percent who had law violations before 18. The frequently cited "burn-out" phenomenon reported for antisocial behavior can be observed in this group. Of the 32 percent still in trouble after age 18, only 20.9 percent had been convicted within the 5-year period preceding interview. Among the psychiatric females, 5.9 percent had convictions after age 18, with 2.4 percent having convictions during the 5 years preceding follow-up. Of the medical males, 12.6 percent had postadolescent convictions. In the 5 years prior to follow-up 5.7 percent had convictions. Only one medical female had any convictions, and this did not occur in the 5 years prior to follow-up.

Among the psychiatric females, however, the probability of an offense in adulthood if there had been one in adolescence was 29 percent, or nine times the probability for the nonoffense psychiatric females (3.2 percent). Thus the psychiatric females' course of trouble with the law should be much more predictable. The low rate of adult law violations among females, however, makes it extremely difficult to improve over a base rate prediction of no problem in adulthood.

Relationships between adolescent variables and a selected set of adult outcome measures were evaluated for the psychiatric males and females. Correlations reported gave a preliminary view of the relations between adolescent status and adult outcome. Statistically significant correlations should not, however, be overinterpreted as reflecting ability to predict outcome. This is particularly a problem when the outcome of interest is a rare phenomenon. Further analyses need to be carried out to determine the true extent of our ability to predict any given outcome.

The tables showing relationships between adolescent and adult variables include all relationships fulfilling one of these criteria: (1) the adolescent variable and adult outcome had a statistically significant association (r or τ); (2) a multiple regression equation was not significantly related to an outcome without the presence of that variable; or (3) the addition of a variable to an already significant multiple regression equation significantly increased the multiple R between the adolescent variables and the particular adult outcome. Table 3 shows that adolescent MHR was a good predictor of adult MHR in both female and male psychiatric groups. The two were also significantly related among medical males ($T = .312$; $p < .001$), but not medical females. This later finding seemed mainly to be due to the lack of any substantial numbers of 1, 4, or 5 ratings at either period for this group. In fact, it was probably more surprising to have found a significant relation among the medical males (where a similar restriction of range in MHR scores pertained) than to have not found it among the females.

Quality of peer relations at adolescence had the strongest association with adult MHR of any adolescent variable in both female and male groups. Additionally, amount of adolescent symptomatology as reflected by number of symptoms noted on the symptom checklist, anxiety level as reflected in MMPI Scale 7 and whether the subject had been in a foster home or institution during adolescence were significantly correlated with adult MHR in both sexes.

There were more significant relationships between adolescent variables and adult MHR in the females than in the males. This seems partly to be due to the greater association between diagnosis and adult MHR among the females. In general, the variables relating to adult MHR suggested that global severity of disturbance at adolescence was related to global severity of disturbance at outcome. Among women the specific presence of psychotic and/or delinquent indicators seemed also to be related to adult MHR. Adult SES appeared to have among the strongest relations to adolescent variables as judged by its large number of significant relationships. Adolescent IQ and SES related significantly to adult SES in both groups. It was noteworthy that these two variables did not have significant associations with any of the other adult out-

Table 3 Mental-health Rating: Significant Relationships with Adolescent Variables

Adolescent Variable	Psychiatric Male	Psychiatric Female
Adolescent MHR	$\tau = .252^d$	$\tau = .280^d$
Poor peer relations	$\tau = .335^b$	$\tau = .346^b$
Number of symptoms	$\tau = .230^c$	$\tau = .201^c$
Inpatient at Univ. Hosp.	$\tau = .199^b$	
Severe and diffuse symptoms		$\tau = .131^b$
Urban residence		$\tau = .176^b$
Psychotic diagnosis		$\tau = .292^c$
Neurotic diagnosis		$\tau = -.188^c$
Antisocial personality diagnosis		$\tau = .150^b$
Ever in foster home or institution		$\tau = .320^d$
Number of law violations		$\tau = .148^d$
MMPI K (Defensiveness)	$\tau = -.311^c$	
MMPI 7 (Anxiety)	$\tau = .210^b$	$\tau = .205^b$
MMPI 8 (Schizophrenia)	$\tau = .252^c$	

NB: Since an MHR of 5 is a low rating and 1 is high, positive correlation with MHR imply that high scores on the adolescent variable are associated with lower adult MHR ratings.

[a] $p < .01$.
[b] $p < .005$.
[c] $p < .001$.
[d] $p < .00005$.

comes studied. The results shown in Table 4 suggest that psychoticism or perhaps schizoidness as measured by the MMPI had a strong association to adult SES. In both the female and male psychiatric group, MMPI scales F (infrequent responses) 8 (schizophrenia), and Goldberg's Psychotic-Neurotic sign (more psychotic score associated with lower adult SES) were among the variables most highly related to SES at outcome. Additionally, a higher MMPI Scale 6 (paranoia) was significantly related to lower social class in males. Interestingly, though, non-MMPI indices of psychoticism, such as psychotic diagnosis and the severe and diffuse pathology scale of the symptom checklist, did not relate significantly to social class in either males or females.

Among males, but not females, quality of adolescent peer relationships had a very strong relationship with adult social class. Among females there was some suggestion that adolescent delinquency [as indicated by number of adolescent law violations and

Table 4   Adult Social Class: Significant Relationships with
Adolescent Variables

Adolescent Variable	Psychiatric Males	Psychiatric Females
Social class	$\tau = $ .237[d]	$\tau = $ .144[b]
IQ	$\tau = -.310$[d]	$\tau = -.229$[d]
MHR	$\tau = $ .130[b]	
Age when at Univ. Hosp.	$\tau = -.142$[b,e]	
Urban residence	$\tau = $ .255[c]	
Ever in foster home or institution	$\tau = $ .198[b]	
Poor peer relations	$\tau = $ .325[b]	
Number of law violations		$\tau = $ .118[b]
Number of symptoms	$\tau = $ .110[b]	
MMPI F (infrequent responses)	$\tau = $ .335[c]	$\tau = $ .349[c]
MMPI 6 (Paranoia)	$\tau = $ .222[b]	
MMPI 7 (Anxiety)		$\tau = $ .202[b]
MMPI 8 (Schizophrenia)	$\tau = $ .284[c]	$\tau = $ .271[c]
MMPI 9 (Hypomania)	$\tau = $ .267[c]	
MMPI P-N Sign	$\tau = $ .290[c]	$\tau = $ .305[c]

NB: Since Social Class VI is "lower" than Social Class I, positive correlations with social class imply that high scores on the adolescent variables are associated with lower adult social class.

[a] $p < .01$.
[b] $p < .005$.
[c] $p < .001$.
[d] $p < .00005$.
[e] Two-tailed test.

MMPI Scale 4 (psychopathy)] was related to lower social class at outcome. There was a possible, but much weaker, suggestion of this finding among males indicated by the relation of MMPI Scale 9 (high energy level and impulsiveness) to social class.

The variables measuring adult psychiatric treatment included whether a subject received any inpatient or outpatient treatment during the 5 years prior to follow-up (adult period). Additionally, the two variables were combined to give an index of incidence of any type of treatment in this period. The results shown in Table 5 suggest that general severity of disturbance in adolescence was related to incidence of both inpatient and outpatient treatment in the adult period. The number of symptoms from the symptom checklist was related to all three outcome measures among females and to incidence of inpatient treatment and total treat-

Table 5 Adult Psychiatric Treatment: Significant Relationships with Adolescent Variables

Adolescent Variable	Psychiatric Males	Psychiatric Females
Any Adult Treatment		
Number of symptoms	$r = .233^c$	$r = .263^c$
MHR		$\tau = -.197^c$
Maternal history of psychiatric problems		$\tau = .158^c$
Ever in foster home or institution		$r = .260^d$
Internalizing symptoms	$r = .224^e$	
MMPI K (Defensiveness)	$r = -.402^b$	
MMPI 5 (Masculinity-femininity)		$r = -.180^e$
MMPI 9 (Hypomania)	$r = .255^e$	
MMPI P-N Sign		$r = .251^e$
MMPI Internalization ratio	$r = .175^e$	
Inpatient treatment or both inpatient and outpatient treatment		
Number of symptoms	$r = .283^c$	$r = .201^c$
MHR		$\tau = .155^c$
Religion	$r = .210^c$	
Ever in foster home or institution		$r = .312^d$
Inpatient treatment at Univ. Hosp.		$r = .100^e$
MMPI L (Naive defensiveness)		$r = .232^e$
MMPI 3 (Hysteria)		$r = -.131^e$
MMPI 4 (Psychopathy)		$r = .149^e$
Outpatient treatment only		
Neurotic diagnosis		$r = -.254^b$
Number of symptoms		$r = .194^c$
MMPI Internalization ratio	$r = .311^e$	
MMPI P-N Sign	$r = .150^e$	

$^a p < .01.$
$^b p < .005.$
$^c p < .001.$
$^d p < .00005.$
^{e} Included because of regression analysis.

ment among males. In addition, adolescent MHR was related to these two outcomes among the females.

There was a possible interaction between severity of disturbance and internalization. One hypothesis might be that internalization was associated with outcome among more (but not less) severely disturbed subjects. This interaction seemed most clear for outpatient and total treatment incidences among males. The symptom checklist internalization score when added to the number of symptoms score produced a significant increase in the correlation with total treatment incidence among males. The MMPI internalization ratio in conjunction with the neurotic-psychotic sign gave a significant correlation with incidence of out-patient treatment among males, whereas neither MMPI sign alone had a significant relation to that outcome. There was a suggestion of the same effect among women. A combination of the MMPI neurotic-psychotic sign and Scale 5 (masculinity-feminity) was significantly related to total incidence of adult treatment, although again neither variable alone had such a relationship. Although masculinity-feminity is not an equivalent dimension to externalization-internalization, the adolescent psychiatric women in this study were significantly more internalizing then their male counterparts, and thus there may have been overlap between the two dimensions here.

Religion had a significant relationship with incidence of inpatient treatment among males. Of Catholic males, 17.7 percent received adult inpatient treatment, whereas only 4.8 percent of Protestant males did so.

Prior institutionalization (ever in a foster home or institution; inpatient at the University Hospital) was significantly related to incidence of adult inpatient treatment in women. Presence of a neurotic diagnosis was associated with low incidence of adult out-patient treatment among women. The combination of MMPI Scales L (naive defensiveness or lying), 4 (psychopathy), and 3 (hysteria) correlated significantly with incidence of inpatient treatment among females, whereas none of those scales had significant individual correlations with inpatient treatment. There was no obvious hypothesis to explain this finding.

Two adult variables reflecting antisocial outcome were studied: presence or absence of law violations (nontraffic) in the 5 years prior to follow-up and number of times drunk (as reported by the subject) in the year prior to follow-up. The incidence of inebriation and adult law violations were quite low among the female psychiatric sample (3.6 percent, more than four drunks and 2.4 percent, with any law violations). The lower rates for these phenomena make it quite difficult to improve on a prediction of no antisocial outcome among females. Nevertheless, correlations were found between adolescent variables and antisocial outcome in females. These relationships have been presented here (see Table 6) but should be interpreted cautiously.

Variables reflecting antisocial behavior at adolescence accounted for the majority of significant relationships with antisocial outcome. Number of adolescent law violations and diagnosis of antisocial personality accounted for all the significant relations with antisocial outcome among women. These variables also had important relations to antisocial outcome among males. It was noteworthy, though, that diagnosis of antisocial personality was not significantly related to presence of adult law violations among males. Several other variables (MHR, number of symptoms noted on the symptom checklist) that may perhaps reflect general severity of adolescent disturbance among males were also significantly related to adult law violations among males. Occurrence of foster-home placement or institutionalization also had a significant relation to adult law violations among males.

Average elevation of MMPI clinical scales [except 5 (masculinity/femininity) and 0 (social introversion/extroversion)] was used as an indication of general severity of disturbance. This index had the advantage of being a simple summary of a large

Table 6 Antisocial Outcome: Significant Relationships with Adolescent Variables

Adolescent Variable	Psychiatric Males	Psychiatric Females
Presence or absence of adult law violations (nontraffic)		
Number of law violations	$r = .301^c$	$r = .301^c$
Antisocial personality diagnosis		$r = .370^c$
MHR	$\tau = .141^c$	
Ever in foster home or institution	$r = .236^c$	
Number of symptoms	$r = .165^b$	
Number of times drunk in past 12 months		
Antisocial personality diagnosis	$r = .258^b$	$r = .465^b$
Number of law violations	$r = .324^c$	$r = .238^c$

[a] $p < .01$.
[b] $p < .005$.
[c] $p < .001$.
[d] $p < .00005$.

amount of information; however, it was not felt that it necessarily represented all the information contained in the MMPIs. Further investigations in this area are planned. There was a clear difference between the variables associated with MMPI elevation in the male and female psychiatric groups (see Table 7). As might have been anticipated, a number of adolescent MMPI scales and signs, including average adolescent MMPI elevation, correlated significantly with average adult MMPI elevation. It was notable that the only neurotic scale correlating with adult MMPI elevation was Scale 7 (anxiety), which, however, is also known to have a high correlation with Scale 8 (schizophrenia) [14].

This seemed to suggest that the severity of schizoid or possibly psychotic pathology as reflected in adolescent MMPIs was associated with general severity of disturbance at outcome. No non-MMPI variables had significant association with average adult MMPI elevation among the males.

No adolescent MMPI scales were significantly related to average MMPI adult elevation among females. Rather, several variables that were also frequently related to other outcome measures had significant associations with severity of adult disturbance as indicated by the MMPI. There was no clear explanation for the

Table 7   Average Adult MMPI Elevation: Significant Relationships with Adolescent Variables

Adolescent Variable	Psychiatric Males	Psychiatric Females
MMPI F (Infrequent responses)	$r = .448^c$	
MMPI K (Defensiveness)	$r = -.431^b$	
MMPI 6 (Paranoia)	$r = .577^c$	
MMPI 7 (Anxiety)	$r = .378^c$	
MMPI 8 (Schizophrenia)	$r = .467^c$	
MMPI $\bar{x}$ Elevation	$r = .451^c$	
MMPI P-N Sign	$r = .400^b$	
MHR		$\tau = .126^b$
Ever in foster home or institution		$r = .202^b$
Poor peer relations		$r = .428^c$

$^a p < .01.$
$^b p < .005.$
$^c p < .001.$
$^d p < .00005.$

difference between types of variables associated with adult MMPI elevation in the males and females.

Marital status at outcome was examined for two categories: those who had never married (long-term marital status) and those who were married at the time of follow-up. It was expected that the former would be more strongly related to adolescent characteristics than the later, since it is likely reflective of more enduring character traits than status would be at a given point in time. Marital stability among those ever married was not examined for the purposes of this work but is to be studied at a later time.

The results shown in Table 8 indicate that adolescent characteristics did in fact have fewer significant relationships with marital status at follow-up than with never having been married. Moreover, almost all variables with significant relations to follow-up status were also significantly related to long-term status. The one relatively minor exception was MMPI Scale F (unusual responses), which did not have significant individual associations with either marital status variable, but did add significant information to the relationship between MMPI Scale 7 and status at follow-up.

The data showed a significant relationship between adolescent psychoticism (psychotic diagnosis; severe and diffuse symptoms) and subsequent marital status among women. There was also an apparent negative relationship between impulsive, poorly controlled behavior at adolescence (MMPI character-disorder sign) and a tendency among women not to marry. It might be hypothesized that impulsivity was not correlated with status at outcome because impulsive individuals might have more unstable marriages and thus be evenly distributed among the married groups at any given time.

Quality of peer relations and severity of disturbance as measured by adolescent MHR and average MMPI elevation were significantly related to both long-term marital status and status at follow-up. In addition, there were significant relationships between never marrying and neurotic and/or internalizing symptomatology [MMPI Scales 1 (hypochondriasis); 7 (anxiety); internalization ratio; negative relation with externalizing symptomatology]. These relationships were not so clear in relation to marital status at follow-up. One hypothesis is that those

Table 8   Adult Marital Status: Significant Relationships with
Adolescent Variables

Adolescent Variable	Psychiatric Males	Psychiatric Females
Never Married		
MHR	$\tau = .149^b$	
Psychotic diagnosis		$r = .377^c$
Poor peer relations	$r = .301^b$	
Externalizing symptoms	$r = -.193^b$	
Severe and diffuse symptoms		$r = .187^b$
MMPI 1 (Hypochondriasis)	$r = .354^c$	
MMPI 7 (Anxiety)	$r = .433^c$	
MMPI 8 (Schizophrenia)	$r = .308^b$	
MMPI $\bar{x}$ Elevation	$r = .337^c$	
MMPI Character disorder sign		$r = -.343^c$
MMPI Internalization ratio	$r = .375^c$	
Married at follow-up		
MHR	$\tau = -.195^c$	
Psychotic diagnosis		$r = -.222^b$
Poor peer relations	$r = -.355^c$	
MMPI F (Unusual responses)	$r = -.020^e$	
MMPI 7 (Anxiety)	$r = -.333^b$	
MMPI $\bar{x}$ Elevation	$r = -.291^b$	

$^a p < .01.$
$^b p < .005.$
$^c p < .001.$
$^d p < .00005.$
^{e} Included because of regression analyses.

who were neurotic at adolescence but did marry were more likely to stay married and thus might be relatively more common in the married group at any given point in time.

Relations between adolescent variables and adult outcomes may be examined variable by variable as well as outcome by outcome; a number of adolescent variables had no significant relationship with adult outcomes. These included duration of complaints, discharge to other than family, intactness of adolescent family, quality of subjects' relationships to parents and siblings at time of hospitalization, parental histories of legal, marital, or occupational problems, father's history of psychiatric problems, diagnosis of adjustment reaction, and MMPI Scale 2 (depression). Adolescent social class, IQ, and age at University of Minnesota Hospital contact were significantly related to adult social class but not to any other outcome variables.

Another group of variables had only a few significant relations with outcomes. These included urban residence (associated with lower adult MHR in males), religion (greater incidence of adult inpatient treatment among Catholic males), maternal history of psychiatric problems (associated with incidence of any type of adult psychiatric treatment among females), MMPI Scales *L*, 3, and 4 (associated with incidence of adult inpatient treatment in females) and MMPI Scales 5 for females and 9 for males (associated with incidence of any type of adult treatment). These variables may have been important in relation to those specific outcomes but did not seem to be generally related to adult outcome, nor did they seem to fit into broader patterns of relationships between sets of adolescent variables and adult outcomes.

A third group of variables also related to only a few outcomes each but seemed to fit into general patterns of relationship when they did occur. These included inpatient versus outpatient hospitalization at University of Minnesota Hospital adolescent contact, scores on the internalizing, externalizing, and severe and diffuse symptomatology scales, MMPI Scales 1 (hypochondriasis) and 6 (paranoia), the MMPI character-disorder sign, internalization ratio, and average MMPI elevation (see specific outcome sections for these relationships).

A number of adolescent variables had significant relations to a variety of adult outcomes. Among psychiatric males, these included adolescent MHR, the number of symptoms on the symptom checklist, quality of peer relationships, foster-home or institutional placement, and MMPI Scales *F* (infrequent responses), *K* (defensiveness), 7 (anxiety), 8 (schizophrenia), and the P-N sign. Among females, these included adolescent MHR, number of symptoms on the symptom checklist, neurotic, psychotic, and antisocial personality diagnoses, adolescent law violations, quality of peer relations, and foster-home or institutional placement.

Discussion

The majority of adolescent psychiatric patients in this study did not continue to have serious problems as adults. By follow-up there was an approximately 50-percent drop in the number of both male and female subjects rated as having moderately or severely incapacitating problems and an approximate drop of 80 percent among both males and females in the number of those with law violations.

However, the former adolescent psychiatric patients did continue to have problems in adulthood at rates exceeding those found for the nonpsychiatric sample. There were differences at follow-up between the two groups on social class, MHR incidence of inpatient psychiatric treatment, and number of subjects never marrying. The MHR differences were less than they had been at the time of adolescent contact but were still significant. Although the group differences in social class had not been present at adolescent contact, there were significant differences between the groups at that time on variables that were correlated with adult social class. Intelligence quotient was correlated with adult social class in both psychiatric males and females and was lower in the psychiatric group than in the medical group at adolescence. Urban residence was correlated with lower social class for psychiatric males and was significantly more common among them at adolescence than among psychiatric females and medical males and females. The large number of other adolescent variables relating to adult social class in the psychiatric group suggests, however, that the adult group differences on this variable reflected the effects of continuing incapacitation among some of the psychiatrics as well as the effects of the mismatching on these nonpsychiatric variables. Interestingly, there were no differences between the psychiatric and comparison groups in the incidence of outpatient psychiatric treatment or overt antisocial behavior (law violations, inebriation) in adulthood. Sex-role expectations and other factors may play a more powerful part in determining these outcomes by the time of follow-up than do adolescent psychiatric problems. Women were found to have higher rates of outpatient treatment than men, whereas men had higher rates of antisocial problems than did women. There were differences between former psychiatric and nonpsychiatric subjects on subtler indications of antisocial orientation [MMPI Scale 4 (psychopathy)]. However, the ramifications of this were not evaluated in this chapter.

A subset of adolescent psychiatric patients, then, do not recover or do not recover completely from their early problems. A number of adolescent characteristics are related to the adult outcomes for this group and may ultimately lead to improved prognostic ability.

General, nonsymptom specific measures of adolescent adjustment—namely, the MHRs and a simple count of the number of symptoms present on Achenbach's symptom checklist—were found to be related to a wider variety of adult outcomes than were other measures. These general severity or extent of pathology indices were related to degree of general incapacitation in adulthood (adult MHR) in both male and female psychiatric groups. However, severity of adolescent problems correlated with a greater variety of outcomes in males than in females. Adolescent severity was correlated with incidence of inpatient treatment for both sexes (though only number of symptoms, not MHR, was correlated with this outcome for males). For males, however, it was also correlated with adult social class and never having married. It seems reasonable to hypothesize that social status and marriage are more dependent on general social competence among males than among females in our society. Then, if general severity of adolescent disturbance was in fact related to severity of adult disturbance, these results would make sense.

General severity of disturbance in adolescence was also related to incidence of law violations among males, but not females. This may in part have been due to the previously mentioned difficulties in predicting the rare event of adult antisocial behavior in females. However, the relationships between adolescent and adult antisocial behavior and severity of disturbance seemed to have been different among males and females.

Antisocial behavior at adolescence (antisocial personality diagnosis; number of law violations) was correlated with antisocial behavior at outcome (incidence of law violations; self-reported number of times drunk in the last year) in both sexes. Also, there was a suggestion that subtler acting-out tendencies (externalizing symptomatology in males; MMPI character-disorder sign in females) were related to likelihood of every marrying in both sexes. However, adolescent antisocial behavior was also correlated with general severity of disturbance in adulthood (adult MHR) and adult social class in females, but not males.

It thus appears that antisocial behavior at adolescence had more pervasive implications for females than for males. The data also seemed to suggest that adolescent antisocial behavior was a more necessary precursor for adult antisocial behavior in females than in males. However, this can be only conjectural in light of the small numbers of females showing adult antisocial behavior in this study.

There has been considerable controversy over the utility of diagnoses with adolescents. The data from this study show that diagnoses among adolescent males were not generally related to their adult outcomes. However, certain diagnoses among females were. In particular, adolescent diagnosis of psychosis was correlated with lower adult MHR and never having married among females. Diagnosis of antisocial personality was correlated with lower adult MHR and greater incidence of law violations and times drunk in the last year. Among females, neurotic diagnosis was associated with better-than-average outcomes, including better MHR and less outpatient treatment. The diagnosis of adjustment reaction of adolescence was not found to relate significantly to either good or poor adult outcome.

A subset of adolescent MMPI scores, generally including Scales 7 (anxiety) and 8 (schizophrenia), along with various combinations of Scales F (infrequent responses), low K (defensiveness), 6 (paranoia), and the P-N sign and average MMPI elevation, related significantly to several adult outcomes in males, including general severity of adult disturbance, adult social class, never having married, and average adult MMPI elevation. These results suggest that schizoidness or psychoticism as measured by the adolescent MMPI were related to those adult outcomes.

Surprisingly, adolescent MMPIs were related to adult social class but little else among the females. Moreover, whereas adolescent MMPI scores from this group were the only adolescent variables related to adult MMPI elevation among the males, none of these scores had significant correlations with adult elevation among the females. It is not clear why this might have been. Adolescent MMPIs were available for only about 25 percent of the psychiatric sample, and thus MMPI results may be less reliable than for other adolescent variables.

There were suggestions of interesting relations between internalization (MMPI internalization ratio; internalizing symptomatology on the symptom checklist) and the incidence of outpatient treatment, as well as never having married among males. This is consistent with Gardner's [19] finding that certain neurotic symptoms in males are related to a poor prognosis in males and that counter sex-role symptomatology interferes more with male social and interpersonal adjustment since a boy who is shy and timid is more likely to be rejected than is a girl with similar characteristics. Internalization correlated with long-term marital status, but not with marital status at the time of follow-up. The relationships with adult treatment were more complex. It seemed likely that internalization was related to incidence of outpatient treatment and total incidence of adult treatment, but only in conjunction with measures of schizoid or psychotic pathology. More work needs to be done to disentangle these relations. Internalization was not related to these outcomes among females.

Two other adolescent variables, quality of peer relationships and placement in foster home or institution, had important correlations with adult outcomes. Poor adolescent peer relations were associated with general severity of adult disturbance (MHR) in both males and females. In addition, it was related to adult social class and never having married among males and to adult average MMPI elevation in females. Placement in foster home or institution during adolescence was correlated with adult severity of disturbance, incidence of inpatient treatment, average MMPI elevation among females, adult social class, and incidence of law violations among males. There is no clear theoretical explanation why these variables should have been more strongly related to adult outcome than, for instance, relations with parents, duration of complaints, or any of the many other variables studied. However, these relationships are consonant with what other researchers have found. The peer-relationships result is consistent with the findings of Roff [61–65] that quality of peer relationships is a powerful predictor of later adjustment. The finding regarding the outcome for subjects placed in foster home and institutions is echoed by Murphy's [49] discussion of the apparent lasting impairment among children who have been in long-term foster care, as well as the finding that placement in inadequate institutions, though not necessarily in adequate ones, was related to significant later impairment [68]. This renders these high-risk children a primary target for ameliorative efforts.

Few of the remaining variables had any significant relations with adult outcome. Particularly surprising was the failure to find any relationships between characteristics of the adolescents' families, including parents' treatment, legal and marital histories, and adult outcomes (the sole exception was an association between mothers' history of psychiatric problems and total incidence of adult treatment among women). Adolescent social class and IQ were found to be associated with adult social class but not to any other outcome variables. As in any study of this sort, it is difficult to tell whether negative results such as these are due to problems of collecting accurate, nonretrospective data or to a true lack of relationship.

In summary, this study found, as had been expected, that the majority of adolescent psychiatric patients did not continue to be notably disturbed in adult life. It was also clear, however, that a number of former psychiatric patients did continue to have difficulty. A first step has been made toward identifying which adolescent factors are associated with subsequent poor outcome. The correlational analyses presented in this chapter have helped to indicate which adolescent characteristics might have potential as predictors of adult outcome. The next step is to directly assess the predictive value of these characteristics. To be considered useful, prediction from these variables will have to be shown to have significantly greater accuracy than prediction from known adult base rates for the various outcomes. Such analyses must also take into account the costs of various types of misprediction (e.g., the cost of misclassifying an individual likely to have a poor outcome when in fact he does not). In addition, it will be interesting to learn the characteristics of those who ought to have had a poor outcome but did not (the invulnerables). Finally, it will be important that the resulting instruments and decision rules be straightforward and generally applicable to the settings of other clinicians and researchers. Such analyses will make the difference between a project whose results are merely interesting and one whose results have practical application.

References

1. Achenbach, T. M. The classification of children's psychiatric symptoms: A factor analytic study. *Psychol. Monogr.*, 80: 7 (1966), whole issue No. 615.

2. Albee, G. W., Lane, E. A., and Reuter, J. M. Childhood intelligence of future schizophrenics and neighborhood peers. *J. Psychol.*, 58 (1964), 141–144.

3. American Psychiatric Association. *Diagnostic and Statistical Manual: Mental Disorders.* American Psychiatric Association, Washington, D.C., 1952.

4. American Psychiatric Association. *Diagnostic and Statistical Manual of Mental Disorders*, 2nd ed. Washington, American Psychiatric Association, D.C., 1968.

5. Anthony, E. J. *Classification of Psychiatric Disorders in Adolescence.* Unpublished WHO working paper, UNESCO, New York, 1967.

6. Anthony, E. J. The behavior disorders of childhood. In *Carmichael's Manual of Child Psychology*, Vol. 2, P. H. Mussen Ed. Wiley, New York, 1970, pp. 667–704.

7. Barron, F. An ego-strength scale which predicts response to psychotherapy. *J. Consult. Psychol.*, 17 (1953), 327–333.

8. Boulger, J. G. A comparison of two methods of obtaining factual and subjective life history data in follow-up studies: Structured interview vs. questionnaire. Unpublished doctoral dissertation, University of Minnesota, Minneapolis, 1969.

9. Bayley, N. Individual patterns of development. *Child Devel.*, 27 (1956), 45–74.

10. Bennett, I. *Delinquent and Neurotic Children.* Basic Books, New York, 1960.

11. Bower, E. M. and Shellhamer, T. A. School characteristics of male adolescents who later became schizophrenic. *Amer. J. Orthopsychiat.*, 30 (1960), 712–729.

12. Chess, S., Thomas, A., and Birch, H. G. Behavior problems revisited: Findings of an anterospective study. *J. Amer. Acad. Child Psychiat.*, 6 (1967), 321–331.

13. Chess, S. Thomas, A., Birch, H. G., and Hertzeg, M. Implications of a longitudinal study of child development for child psychiatry. *Amer. J. Psychiat.*, 117 (1970), 434–441.

14. Dahlstrom, W. G., Welsh, G. S., and Dahlstrom, L. E. *An MMPI Handbook.* Vol. 1. *Clinical Interpretation.* Univ. Minnesota Press, Minneapolis, 1972.

15. Dohrenwend, B. P. and Dohrenwend, B. S. Psychiatric epidemiology: An analysis of "true prevalence" studies. In *Handbook of Community Health*, S. E. Golann and C. Eisdorfer, Eds. New Appleton-Century-Crofts, New York, 1972.

16. Eisenberg, L. The autistic child in adolescence. *Amer. J. Psychiat.*, 112 (1956), 607–612.
17. Eisenberg, L. The course of childhood schizophrenia. *Arch. Neurol. Psychiat.*, 78 (1957), 69–83.
18. Frazee, H. Children who later became schizophrenic. *Smith College Studies in Social Work*, 23 (1953), 125–149.
19. Gardner, G. G. The relationship between childhood neurotic symptomatology and later schizophrenia. *J. Nerv. Ment. Dis.*, 144 (1967), 97–100.
20. Garmezy, N. Vulnerable children: Implications derived from studies of an internalizing-externalizing symptom dimension. In *The Psychopathology of Adolescence*, J. Zubin and A. M. Freedman, Eds. Grune & Stratton, New York, 1970.
21. Garmezy, N. The study of competence in children at risk for severe psychopathology. In *The Child in His Family: Children at Psychiatric Risk*, E. J. Anthony and C, Koupernik, Eds. Wiley, New York, 1974, pp. 77–98.
22. Goldberg, L. R. Diagnosticians vs. diagnostic signs: the diagnosis of psychosis vs. neurosis from the MMPI. *Psychol. Monogr.*, 79: 9 (1965), whole issue No. 602, 1–28.
23. Goldberg, L. R. The search for configural relationships in personality assessment: The diagnosis of psychosis vs. neurosis from the MMPI. *Multivariate Behav. Res.*, 4 (1969), 523–536.
24. Gough, H. G. Personal communication. Cited in Goldberg, L. R., Diagnosticians vs. diagnostic signs: The diagnosis of psychosis vs. neurosis from the MMPI. *Psychol. Monogr.*, 79: 9 (1965), whole issue No. 602, 1–28.
25. Group for the Advancement of Psychiatry, Committee on Child Psychiatry. Psychopathological disorders in childhood: Theoretical considerations and a proposed classification, 6 (1966), report No. 62.
26. Hafner, A. J., Quast, W., and Shea, M. J. The adult adjustment of one thousand psychiatric and pediatric patients: Initial findings from a twenty-five-year follow-up. In *Life History Research in Psychopathology*, Vol. 4, R. D. Wirt, G. Winokur, and M. Roff, Eds. Univ. Minnesota Press, Minneapolis, 1975, pp. 167–186.
27. Hathaway, S. R. and McKinley, J. C. *The Minnesota Multiphasic Personality Inventory*, rev. ed. Psychological Corporation, New York, 1951.
28. Hathaway, S. R. and Monachesi, E. D. *Adolescent Personality and Behavior: MMPI Profiles of Normal, Delinquent Dropout, and Other Outcomes*. Univ. Minnesota Press, Minneapolis, 1963.
29. Hathaway, S. R., Monachesi, E. D., and Salasin, S. A follow-up study of MMPI high 8, schizoid, children. In *Life History Research in Psychopathology*, Vol. 1, M. Roff and D. F. Ricks, Eds. Univ. Minnesota Press, Minneapolis, 1970.
30. Hays, W. L. *Statistics for Psychologists*. Holt, Rinehart and Winston, New York, 1963.
31. Heston, L. L. Psychiatric disorders in foster home reared children of schizophrenic mothers. *Brit. J. Psychiat.*, 112 (1966), 819–825.
32. Hewitt, L. E. and Jenkins, R. L. *Fundamental Patterns of Maladjustment: The Dynamics of Their Origin*. State of Illinois, Springfield, Ill., 1946.
33. Hobbs, N., Ed. *Issues in the Classification of Children*, Vols. 1 and 2. Jossey-Bass, San Francisco, 1975.

34. Hollingshead, A. B. *Two-factor Index of Social Position.* (Printed privately), New Haven, Conn., 1957.

35. Johnson, L. B. Psychiatric diagnosis, the MMPI psychiatric symptom cluster, and severity of disturbance in adolescence as predictors of adult adjustment. Unpublished doctoral dissertation, University of Minnesota, Minneapolis, 1972.

36. Kagan, J. and Moss, H. A. *Birth to Maturity.* Wiley, New York, 1963.

37. Kohlberg, L., LaCrosse, J., and Ricks, D. The predictability of adult mental health from childhood behavior. In *Childhood Psychopathology*, B. Wolman, Ed. McGraw-Hill, New York, 1972, pp. 1217–1284.

38. Lane, Ellen A. and Albee, G. W. On childhood intellectual decline of adult schizophrenics: A reassessment of an earlier study. *J. Abnorm. Psychol.*, 73 (1968), 174–177.

39. Marks, P. A., Seeman, W., and Haller, D. L. *The Actuarial Use of the MMPI with Adolescents and Adults.* Williams & Wilkins, Baltimore, 1974.

40. Masterson, J. F., Jr. Prognosis in adolescent disorders. *Amer. J. Psychiat.*, 114 (1958), 1097–1103.

41. Masterson, J. F., Jr. *The Psychiatric Dilemma of Adolescence.* Little, Brown, Boston, 1967a.

42. Masterson, J. F., Jr. The symptomatic adolescent five years later: He didn't grow out of it. *Amer. J. Psychiat.*, 123 (1967b), 1338–1345.

43. Mednick, S. A. A longitudinal study of children with a high risk for schizophrenia. *Ment. Hygiene*, 50 (1966), 522–535.

44. Mednick, S. A. and McNeil, T. F. Current methodology in research on the etiology of schizophrenia: Serious difficulties which suggest the use of high risk group method. *Psychol. Bull.*, 70 (1968), 681–693.

45. Meehl, P. E. *Nuisance Variables and the Ex-Post Facto Design.* Unpublished manuscript, University of Minnesota, Minneapolis, 1969.

46. Michael, C., Morris, D. P., and Soroker, E. Follow-up studies of shy, withdrawn children. II. Relative incidence of schizophrenia. *Amer. J. Orthopsychiat.*, 27 (1957), 331–337.

47. Morris, D. P., Soroker, E., and Burruss, G. Follow-up studies of shy, withdrawn children. I. Evaluation of later adjustment. *Amer. J. Orthopsychiat.*, 24 (1954), 742–754.

48. Muldoon, L. B. *Psychiatric Diagnosis, Psychiatric Symptom Types, and Severity of Disturbance in Adolescence as Predictors of Adult Adjustment.* Unpublished manuscript, University of Minnesota, Minneapolis, 1973.

49. Murphy, H. B. M. Long-term foster care and its influence on adjustment to adult life. In *The Child in His Family: Children at Psychiatric Risk*, E. J. Anthony and C. Koupernik Eds. Wiley, New York, 1974, pp. 425–446.

50. Nie, N. H., Hull, C. H., Jenkins, J. G., Steinbrenner, and Bent, D. H. *SPSS Statistical Package for the Social Sciences.* McGraw Hill, New York, 1975.

51. Olson, D. The severely disturbed adolescent: Prognostic implications and long-term adjustment. Unpublished doctoral dissertation, University of Minnesota, Minneapolis, 1972.

52. Otterstrom, E. Delinquency and children from bad homes. *Acta Paediatrica*, 33 (1946), Suppl. 5.

53. Overall, J. E. and Klett, C. J. *Applied Multivariate Analysis.* McGraw Hill, New York, 1972.

54. Overall, J. E., Spiegel, D. K., and Cohen, J. Equivalence of orthogonal and nonorthogonal analysis of variance. *Psychol. Bull.*, 82 (1975), 182–186.
55. Ricks, D. P. and Berry, J. C. Family and symptom patterns that precede schizophrenia. In. *Life History Research in Psychopathology*. M. Roff and D. Ricks, Eds. Univ. Minnesota Press, Minneapolis, 1970, pp. 31–50.
56. Robins, E. and O'Neal, P. Clinical features of hysteria in children with a note on prognosis. A two to seventeen year follow-up study of 41 patients. *Nerv. Child*, 10 (1953), 246–271.
57. Robins, L. N. and O'Neal, P. The adult prognosis for runaway children. *Amer. J. Orthopsychiat.*, 29 (1959), 752–761.
58. Robins, L. N. *Deviant Children Grown Up*. Williams & Wilkins, Baltimore, 1966.
59. Robins, L. N. An actuarial evaluation of the causes and consequences of deviant behavior in young black men. In *Life History Research in Psychopathology*, Vol. 2, M. Roff, L. N. Robins, and M. Pollack, Eds. Univ. Minnesota Press, Minneapolis, 1972, pp. 137–154.
60. Roff, J. Adolescent schizophrenia: Variables related to differences in long-term adult outcome. *J. Consult. Clin. Psychol.*, 42 (1974), 180–183.
61. Roff, M. Childhood social interactions and young adult bad conduct. *J. Abnorm. Soc. Psychol.*, 63 (1961), 333–337.
62. Roff, M. Childhood interactions and young adult psychosis. *J. Clin. Psychol.*, 19 (1963), 152–157.
63. Roff, M. *Some Developmental Aspects of Schizoid Personality*. U.S. Army Medical Research and Development Command, Contract No. DA-49-007-MD-2015, Report No. 65-4, March 1965.
64. Roff, M. A two-factor approach to juvenile delinquency and the later histories of juvenile delinquents. In *Life History Research in Psychopathology*, Vol. 2, M. Roff, L. N. Robins, and M. Pollack, Eds. Univ. Minnesota Press, Minneapolis, 1972, pp. 77–101.
65. Roff, M. & Sell, S. B. Juvenile delinquency in relation to peer acceptance-rejection and socioeconomic status. *Psychology in the Schools*, 5 (1968), 3–18.
66. Rutter, M. Classification and categorization in child psychiatry. *J. Child Psychol. Psychiat.*, 6 (1965), 71–83.
67. Rutter, M. Classification and categorization in child psychiatry. *Internat. J. Psychiat.*, 3 (1967), 161–187.
68. Rutter, M. *Maternal Deprivation Reassessed*. Penquin Books, Hamondsworth, Middlesex, England, 1972.
69. Rutter, M., Birch, H. G., Thomas, A., and Chess, S. Temperamental characteristics in infancy and the later development of behavioral disorders. *Brit. J. Psychiat.*, 110 (1964), 651–661.
70. Shea, M. J. A follow-up study into adulthood of adolescent psychiatric patients in relation to internalizing and externalizing symptoms, MMPI configurations, social competence, and life history variables. Unpublished doctoral dissertation, University of Minnesota, Minneapolis, 1972.
71. Srole, L., Langner, T. S., Michael, S. T., Opler, M. K., and Rennie, T. A. *Mental Health in the Metropolis: The Midtown Manhattan Study*, Vol. 1. McGraw Hill, New York, 1962.
72. Stennett, R. G. Emotional handicap in the elementary years: Phase or disease? *Amer. J. Orthopsychiat.*, 36 (1966), 444–449.

73. Terman, L. M. and Oden, M. H. *Genetic Studies of Genius, V: The Gifted Group at Mid-life.* Stanford University Press, Stanford, Calif., 1959.
74. Tuddenham, R. D. The constancy of personality ratings over two decades. *Genet. Psychol. Monogr.,* 60 (1959), 3–29.
75. Walker, C. F. Hysteria in childhood: A follow-up study. *Amer. J. Orthopsychiat.,* 17 (1947), 468–476.
76. Warren, W. Some relationships between the psychiatry of children and of adults. *J. Ment. Sci.,* 106 (1960), 815–826.
77. Weiner, I. B. *Psychological Disturbance in Adolescence.* Wiley-Interscience, New York, 1970.
78. Welsh, G. S. An anxiety index and an internalization ratio for the MMPI. *J. Consult. Psychol.,* 16 (1952), 65–72.
79. Welsh, G. S. and Dahlstrom, W. G. *Basic Readings on the MMPI in Psychology and Medicine.* Univ. Minnesota Press, Minneapolis, 1956.
80. Wirt, R. D. and Briggs, P. F. Personality and environment factors in the development of delinquency. *Psychol. Monogr.,* 73 (1959), whole issue No. 485.
81. Wirt, R. D., Hampton, A. C., and Seat, P. D. The psychometric prediction of delinquency. In Life History Research in Psychopathology, Vol. 2, M. Roff, L. N. Robins, and M. Pollack, Eds. Univ. Minnesota Press, Minneapolis, 1972, pp. 66–76.
82. Zax, M., Cowen, E. L., Rappaport, J., Beach, D. R., and Laird, J. D. Follow-up study of children identified early as emotionally disturbed. *J. Consult. Clin. Psychol.,* 32 (1968), 369–374.

The Vulnerable Child and Positive Outcomes: A Case History of Delinquent Behavior in Perspective

Waln K. Brown, Ph.D. (U.S.A.)

Introduction

The study of vulnerable children, and how many come to realize invulnerability, is a new and exciting area of research in the behavioral sciences. Although the bulk of such research has been directed toward psychiatric disorders, such as schizophrenia and other psychoses, other psychological—as well as sociological—forces that contribute to vulnerability need also be studied. The potential findings of such a research effort have tremendous ramifications for a number of fields of endeavor that study human behavior.

Nowhere is the research concerning vulnerability studies more needed than in the field of juvenile justice. The vulnerable children who "break down" under the burden of their stress-producing experiences often find themselves enmeshed in the juvenile justice system as a result of antisocial reactions to their particular dilemmas. A large percentage of these children remain enmeshed in the juvenile justice system throughout their adolescence, and many graduate into the adult justice system.[1]

Some vulnerable children, however, totally extricate themselves from the justice system and assimilate a more socially acceptable life-style. These children, and those who never "break down" despite the obvious existence of stress factors that render them vulnerable, hold valuable information in determining what factors produce invulnerability. Such information can help behavioral scientists and juvenile justice personnel isolate those acquired or innate factors that help promote resilience against delinquency. In turn, this information can be used to help vulnerable children guard against delinquent actions as well as help deter them from a life of crime.

The result of such applied findings constitutes the study of "positive outcomes," a new concept in the field of juvenile justice.[2] The thesis behind the study of positive outcomes is basically a two-part philosophical question that asks why, given all the risk factors of growing up, do most vulnerable children turn out relatively free from antisocial behavior and a juvenile or adult crime history, and, further, why do many vulnerable children who do experience deviant behavior leading to juvenile crime extricate themselves from the juvenile/adult justice system and realize a more positive life-style?[3]

The concept of studying positive outcomes has been long overdue in the field of juvenile justice. Researchers and other professionals in this field of study have had an enduring penchant to focus on the negative outcomes relative to juvenile delinquency and juvenile justice and have generally ignored both the potential for existence and reasons for occurrence of delinquents who have experienced positive outcomes.[4] Like the half-full/half-empty

---

[1] It is generally recognized that juvenile offenders have a high potential for becoming adult offenders. For one study of the relationship between juvenile institutionalization and subsequent adult institutionalization see the article by Rist and Reis [1].

[2] The concept of positive outcomes was originated by Hunter Hurst, Executive Director, National Center for Juvenile Justice.

[3] This philosophical question is an expansion of a theoretical comment proposed by my colleague and fellow researcher on positive outcomes, Richard Gable.

[4] A good example of this negative approach is the predictability literature, which focuses on failure rather than success rates. Sheldon and Eleanor Glueck have pioneered this

dichotomy in psychological testing, juvenile justice personnel seem to note only the empty aspect of the glass. The psychological implications of such a deleterious perspective need not be elucidated, and the stagnant state of the juvenile justice field should be sufficiently indicative.

Yet why has this negativistic approach persisted over such a prolonged period of time? Perhaps the answer rests somewhere in the fact that the juvenile justice field has, by definition and design, always been responsible for dealing with negatively defined behaviors. This predisposition for dealing with deviant behavior—coupled with the myriad of factors generally held to constitute the genesis of aberrant behavior (e.g., poverty, family instability, past family history of criminality or psychiatric disorder), as well as the high recidivism rates for juvenile offenders—has created something of a mind-set for studying delinquency. Thus the literature is couched in bleak undertones that emphasize failure rather than success. Nowhere is there light to provide relief, give perspective, or offer hope. Instead, we find analysts writing in negative terms about negative behavior. In the mathematics of the juvenile justice field, two minuses do not constitute a plus.

There is yet another major reason for couching studies of juvenile justice and delinquency in terminologies that emphasize negative outcomes. It is simplest to conjecture why delinquent children fail, because their repeated deviancies are easily traceable and constitute further information that can be analyzed and related to former failures. This is one major reason why recidivism studies that focus their attention primarily on failure rates run rampant through the juvenile justice literature. In the immense literature on recidivism, there are several noteworthy sources that focus specifically on juvenile recidivism [5–7]. It is most expedient to build a house where a foundation already exists. Success, on the other hand, is not so readily traceable. Those juvenile offenders who ultimately extricate themselves from the justice system become lost sources of information because of their lack of accessibility. Also, there is no theoretical foundation from which to assess

---

approach to the study of recidivism. See any of their works in general, or specifically see Glueck and Glueck [2]. There are other studies also worth noting [3, 4].

their success except to note that, statistically, they ceased to recidivate, and *why* they did not recidivate is left to conjecture. That conjecture usually derives its explanation from some sort of mystical, "logical" extrapolation that posits that the antithesis of the reasons for failure constitute the reasons for success. Not only is this theoretical approach scientifically naive, it is both untenable and unproductive. At least one other source [8] has noted that recidivism cannot be explained by greater degrees of negativism.

An alternative strategy to this area of inquiry is to examine directly those factors that appear to be related to an individual's passage into adult life, free from ongoing involvement with the law. Such a research paradigm can be invoked at two points in time and, consequently, with two separate populations of interest. Whereas it can be asked what differentiates those individuals who become, but later cease to be delinquent from those who persist in deviant acts throughout childhood and adolescence, it can also be asked what factors are associated with those children who never become involved in a delinquent career even though they possess many characteristics that would predict potential delinquency. It is in these two questions that the subtle differences between the terms "positive outcome" and "invulnerability" emerge. Contained within each question there are two broad categories of information required to gain an understanding of the process. The first category deals with the external influences that act on a child's life and are seen as helpful in deterring ongoing delinquent activity. Included in such data would be information about the effect of various societal systems such as the school, the juvenile court, and the residential institution—to name only a few. The second category focuses on the characteristics of the individual child that appear to protect him from a predicted delinquent life-style and that also seem to allow for or enhance the remedial effects of the juvenile justice system's intervention. The two categories of information are obviously related, with the former attempting to understand what works with whom, and the latter more concerned with the mechanisms involved in that process.

The study of positive outcomes is an attempt to provide a much needed perspective for the field of juvenile justice and delinquency. That perspective will emphasize success rather than failure. The research will draw its data from life-history interviews. It will identify a population of juvenile offenders who have succeeded in divorcing themselves from continued encounters with the justice system and developed a more acceptable life-style. With the information rendered by these "successful" ex-offenders, those important life forces that helped to promote their positive behavioral change might be identified. Through the continuous accumulation of these life histories, and careful factor analysis, this information will help determine specific factors intrinsic to producing positive outcomes. The following case history will serve to illustrate the proposed research.

CASE HISTORY[5]

The subject is a male caucasian. He was born on October 14, 1944 to middle-class parents. His birth was the result of a full-term pregnancy but was complicated by forceps delivery wherein a nerve was severed in an eye. The subject's mother reports that at birth he was a "bloody mess." He is far-sighted and has worn glasses since the age of 3 years. At age 4 he suffered a mild case of rheumatic fever. He continued to be enuretic until age 9.

In the first grade the subject was taken to a child guidance counselor on the advice of the first-grade teacher, who considered him "moody." Several visits were made to the counselor, and the parents were informed that the schoolwork was not sufficiently challenging for the subject, and that the subject felt rejected by his father. The father attempted to compensate for this but never developed a close affection for the child. The mother feels that this was due to the fact that the father was in military service until the subject was more than a year old.

At 8 years of age the subject and his younger brother (age 4) were involved in a bicycle accident. Both children were hospitalized for several weeks. The younger brother suffered a mild concussion. A local psycologist thought that the subject had deep feelings of guilt. He believed the subject to be insecure and felt responsible for his brother's suffering. The subject dramatically threatened suicide and took a large amount of medicine, requiring an emetic. He remained under psychological observation for several years.

During this period the subject became aware of parental household tensions. Arguments became increasingly persistent and more intense. The father began to absent himself from the home for prolonged periods of time, while the mother became progressively subject to depressions and developed a neurotic compulsion for cleanliness.

[5] Case-history information was assembled from official probation reports, court transcripts, hospital records, and school records. It is realized that these records are not always accurate, but in this particular case, inconsistencies were easily identifiable.

When the subject was 11 years of age a third child (girl) was born into the family. Immediately following the birth of this child the father abandoned the household. The mother and three children went to live with the maternal grandparents, both of whom were in their late 60s and suffered from failing health. Shortly after residence was established with the grandparents, the mother secured a job to financially maintain the household. She worked long, odd hours so that much of the responsibility for supervising the children was borne by the grandparents. This proved to be a trying experience for all concerned. The grandparents were too elderly and infirm to deal with the diverse exigencies of three children, and a tense atmosphere permeated the household. The mother suffered several psychoemotional breakdowns. The subject became withdrawn, hypersensitive, and emotionally unstable.

At age 13 the subject was placed in a Lutheran Home for orphaned, neglected, and dependent children. His placement resulted from an increasing difficulty in adapting to the family situation, which caused further dysfunctioning in extrafamilial activities. This problem was further complicated by the genesis of acute acne vulgaris. The subject began to miss school due to contrived illnesses.[6] These feigned illnesses (over 35 days of school absence) almost caused the subject to repeat the seventh grade. He also began to direct aggressive, antagonistic behavior toward his family. The family felt incapable of handling this negative behavior, so they placed the subject in an environment where they felt his behavior would gain the benefit of better control. After 2 weeks at the Lutheran Home the subject was returned to the natural home. The administration felt that the subject was not taking advantage of the opportunities available to him at the orphanage, as exhibited by his attempt to run away and his total dissociation from students and staff.

Following release from the Lutheran Home the subject underwent prolonged psychiatric observation at the County Mental Health Center. This was done at the recommendation of the County Probation Office, which had been made aware of the subject's difficulties by a local psychologist involved with the case. The Probation Office handled the matter in an unofficial capacity.

Despite psychiatric help the subject continued to have problems adapting to his situation. He persistently absented himself from school and also began to absent himself from home. He became involved in minor delinquent activities such as fighting and destruction of property. During his freshman year in high school he managed to fail three courses and had to repeat the grade.[7]

At age 15 the subject was suspended from school. A joint court complaint was filed against the subject by his mother, a psychiatrist at the County Mental Health Center, and by the high-school principal. The complaint pointed to the fact that the subject refused to obey the reasonable and lawful commands of his family, was emotionally disturbed, and had been suspended after engaging in a fight at

[6] There is an observable relationship between delinquency and school nonattendance. For one analysis of this relationship, see Tennent [9].

[7] Academic failure and delinquency have a definite relationship. For a review of research on the school-related etiology of juvenile delinquency, see Silberberg and Silberberg [10].

school. The subject was placed in the County Detention Facility until a juvenile court hearing could be held and remained in the detention facility until the day of the hearing. The presiding judge placed the subject on probation and released him to the custody of the family. The subject was required to meet with his probation officer at least once a month and was also allowed to return to school.

Two months following the hearing the subject was placed in the County Hospital for observation as a result of a suicide threat and accompanying erratic behavior. While in the hospital the subject assaulted various hospital staff and had to be heavily sedated. He was placed in a solitary confinement cell where he threatened self-destruction, attempted to assault others, and refused nourishment. After 3 days he collapsed from exhaustion and submitted to treatment.

Under the direction of the court, the subject was immediately removed from the County Hospital and committed to the State Hospital for psychiatric observation. He remained there for 2½ months. The staff psychiatrists diagnosed the subject as a schizoid personality with noticeable signs of autism. Their prognosis indicated a high potential for schizophrenia. They recommended release only if the subject was kept under close psychiatric observation by the County Mental Health Center and had frequent visits with the probation department. An outpatient program with the State Hospital was also recommended.

Several months after his release from the State Hospital the subject resumed his former pattern of school absenteeism. After outright refusal to attend, the school administration instituted proceedings against the subject and his mother. Shortly thereafter a juvenile court hearing was convened, and the subject was placed in the County Detention Facility and held there until suitable placement could be secured elsewhere.

Placement was secured at the Pennsylvania George Junior Republic School for Boys, a privately owned, mass-congregate institution for court-adjudicated delinquents. The subject remained at the institution for 18 months, during which time he successfully completed his sophomore and junior years of high school. He became involved with the school paper, was selected as the outstanding student of the tenth and eleventh grades, and began to exhibit some leadership characteristics. On completion of the eleventh grade, the subject was released to the custody of the court, which placed him back in the natural home and continued to monitor his activities through the probation office.

With only minor incidents (e.g., school-related problems, fighting, drinking), the subject managed to graduate from high school. In December of his senior year he was released from probation. There were no further recorded incidents of aberrant or delinquent behavior, nor did any recorded criminal incidents ensue.

Subsequent behavior. Although the subject finally extricated himself from the juvenile justice system and never officially penetrated the adult justice system, further developmental information provides enlightenment concerning the residual effects of the vulnerable state and the by-products of institutionalization.

Immediately following release from the Republic School the subject was involved in a number of aggressive encounters both at school and in the general community.[8] They continued to occur, in diminishing proportion, for a number of years, and in several cases bodily harm resulted for the subject's adversaries. These encounters were never officially recorded.

The subject also had trouble adapting to the social and academic life in public school.[9] Although he did manage to graduate, his grades were barely passing, and he did fail one course. This occurred even though his schedule was dominated by shop courses and study periods. Accompanying this poor academic showing was poor social interaction with fellow students. He seldom associated with his classmates and preferred to interact with underclassmen and students from other schools. The reasons for this failure to adapt to the social and academic life in the public school appear to be multifold. Since the school was small and many of the staff and students were aware of his previous institutional history, he conjectured that they perceived him as a failure. The subject also considered himself to be a social and academic failure and accepted this self-identity.[10] The one asset that the subject believed differentiated him from others was his physical aggressiveness. This perception gained reinforcement through a variety of interactions and verbal comments received from classmates and acquaintances. People seemed to tolerate him only because they were afraid to do otherwise. Thus the subject's major source of positive self-identity was proficiency in this deviant behavioral trait (i.e., aggressive behavior) and, as a result, other more positive aspects of his personality development suffered.

A deep-seated rejection anxiety further compounded the subject's development. He interpreted his past experiences with family and community as signs of rejection. His father had rejected him in his infancy, and this was later reinforced by his father's abandonment of the family. His mother and grandparents had rejected him by initiating or condoning his various institutionlizations. The school administration had rejected him by not ministering to his needs and by desiring to remove him from the student body because of his disruptive, antinormative behavior. His classmates had rejected him because of his acute acne condition, his unrefined social demeanor, and his poor academic proficiency. The feeling of rejection greatly retarded the development of a strong, positive personality.

For several years following high school graduation the subject floundered aimlessly from job to job while the majority of his peers pursued academic or vocational careers. His family relations remained strained, and after leaving the household he maintained only minimal contact with family members and former acquaintances. Due to a strong feeling of distrust he found it difficult to establish

[8] Aggression and its relationship to delinquency and the delinquent personality has been the subject of a number of studies [11, 12].

[9] Reintegration into the public high school by an institutionalized delinquent is a difficult task. For two studies that have keyed on this difficult transition, see Pfeil [13] and Novotny and Burnstein [14].

[10] Poor self-concept or a self-derogating attitude is often associated with deviant behavior. For a general approach to this theory, see Kaplan [15]; how this relates to schools is revealed in Fisher [16].

lasting friendships. Relationships tended to be ephemeral and manipulative on his part. He was unable to "risk" marriage. Remnants of the inferiority/rejection syndrome persisted.

Positive Outcomes

The information thus far presented concerning the subject would certainly seem to negate the potential for positive outcomes. Yet positive outcomes have been realized. Just the fact that the subject learned to adapt his behavior to conform more closely with the dictates of society, therefore managing to extricate himself from further negative involvement with the justice system, is enough to constitute a positive outcome. Add to this fact the consideration that the subject has suffered from no further psychological disorders and has maintained economic self-sufficiency, and one must concede that positive outcomes have been realized.

At this juncture it is important to determine the reasons intrinsic to the promotion of this metamorphosis. First of all, it must be noted that the subject possesses above-average intelligence. This fact in itself would be instrumental in allowing him to synthesize the information necessary to promote adaptation. But given the fact that the subject had the capacity to make his own choices, there would seem to be an equal chance that he could have adapted his behavior in a further deviant manner—rather than a positive one—if he desired to adapt it at all. Those factors that helped him to make the choice that led to the actualization of positive outcomes are of particular importance. Therefore, innate intelligence may be one of the reasons for a resultant positive outcome, but this should not be considered the total reason. However, various sources have noted a correlation between intellectual superiority and nonrecidivism [17–19].

During the critical period of vulnerability, the introduction of the court as a guidance agency was instrumental in providing stability for both the subject and his family. The improvement of family stability was necessary because the growing emotional instability in the household was instrumental in fostering the subject's aberrant emotional responses. More importantly, however, the court's role as an authority figure imposed otherwise nonexistant external behavioral guidelines on the subject. When the subject continually failed to make the appropriate behavioral changes in the home environment, the court sought further expert help.

Commitment to the Pennsylvania George Juvenile Republic School for Boys was a timely and necessary step in controlling the subject's accelerating delinquent behavior. He seemed bent on self-destruction. At the school his deviant/self-destructive behavior underwent controls that were formerly nonexistent; a strong disciplinary code checked his aberrant, acting-out behavior. His life was structured, he was given responsibilities, expected to attend school, and realized successes commensurate with the application of his abilities. Due to the length of his commitment, his behavioral changes had a chance to be internalized and gain substance. Had the court not interceded during this crisis period and secured appropriate placement, the subject would probably have either destroyed himself, totally disrupted his family, suffered further emotional problems, or followed a life of crime. Most certainly his chances of experiencing positive outcomes would have been diminished.

The successful completion of high school is of great importance because it allowed the subject to pursue a number of opportunities that otherwise would have been either closed or exceedingly more difficult to attain. The external pressure exerted by the court and the juvenile institution literally forced the subject to complete his high school education. Family pressure to do so was insufficient. If it had not been for external pressures, the subject would have dropped-out.

Separation from the peer group that had formerly supported and influenced the subject's delinquent behavior proved exceedingly beneficial. The group had functioned as a gang and was constantly involved in negative group activities. All had poor home lives, most were school failures, and none saw life as a positive experience. Their influence on each other was destructive. Removal from this deviant reference group was critical for developing a more positive outlook.[11] On release from the Republic School, the subject no longer associated with this group.

---

[11] How reference groups influence delinquent behavior has received much attention. For an analysis of reference group theories, see Clark [20].

Finally, the subject's desire to change his life role provided the internal impetus necessary to sustain a behavioral change. This desire grew gradually, but gained its initial incentive from the before mentioned experiences. The subject did not want to endure institutionalization again, nor did he want to continue to experience the destructive lifestyle that had for so long dominated his existence. He wanted to be accepted rather than rejected, and as he matured his desire to prosper increased. In fact, the maturation process has been cited as a significant factor in the reformation process [21–23].

Conclusion

The preceeding case history is just one of the many examples of "vulnerable" children who have endured a stressful youth, succumbed to emotional overload, penetrated the juvenile justice system, and yet experienced "positive outcomes." The literature seldom cites such cases; rather, the failures receive the bulk of attention. We have thus a plethora of information that analyzes failure and its causative factors, but almost no data that notes "positive outcomes" and the reasons for their occurrence. Before we can expect to help vulnerable children achieve invulnerability it is of paramount importance to understand what factors influence positive behavioral changes. This cannot be done effectively by accentuating the negative.

This, then, is the *raison d'être* for the study of positive outcomes. It is an attempt to understand those factors that promote invulnerability. Those factors may be many and diverse, but it is hypothesized that they have many characteristics in common. Those common characteristics will help determine how the juvenile justice system can more effectively meet the needs of the vulnerable children whom it attempts to serve. The case history outlined here presents the major factors that influenced one vulnerable child to experience subsequent positive outcomes. To those behavioral change agents, the author is greatly indebted. They prompted the subject of this chapter to become its author.

References

1. Rist, W. N. and Reis, E. Juvenile corrections: It starts here. *Personnel and Guidance J.*, 53: 2 (1974), 142–145.
2. Glueck, S. and Glueck, E. *Predicting Delinquency and Crime.* Harvard Univ. Press, Cambridge, Mass., 1959.
3. Hathaway, S. R. and Monachesi, E. D. *Analyzing and Predicting Juvenile Delinquency with the MMPI.* The Psychological Corporation, New York, 1954.
4. Simon, F. H. Statistical methods of making prediction Instruments. *J. Res. Crime Delinquency*, 9: 1(1972), 46–53.
5. Sakata, R. and Litwack, L. Recidivism among juvenile parolees. *Psychol. Rep.*, 29: 2 (1971), 351–355.
6. Ganzer, V. J. and Sarason, I. G. Variables associated with recidivism among juvenile delinquents. *J. Consult. Clin. Psychol.*, 40: 1 (1973), 1–5.
7. Roberts, A. H. Demographic variables base rates and personality characteristics associated with recidivism in male delinquents. *J. Consult. Clin. Psychol.*, 42: 6 (1974), 833–841.
8. Dettenborn, H. Relationships among psychologically relevant causes of juvenile delinquency. *Probleme und Ergebnisse der Psychologie*, 39 (1971), 27–79.
9. Tennent, T. G. School non-attendance and delinquency. *Educ. Res.*, 13: 3 (1971), 185–190.
10. Silberberg, N. E. and Silberberg, M. C. School achievement and delinquency. *Rev. Educ. Res.*, 41: 1 (1971), 17–33.
11. Redl, F. and Wineman, D. *The Aggressive Child.* The Free Press, New York, 1957.
12. Bandura, A. and Walters, R. H. *Adolescent Aggression.* Ronald Press, New York, 1959.
13. Pfeil, M. P. It's hard to come back. *Amer. Educ.*, 6: 5 (1970), 3–6.
14. Novotny, E. and Burstein, M. Public school adjustment of delinquent boys after release from a juvenile corrective institution. *J. Youth and Adolescence*, 3: 1 (1974), 49–60.
15. Kaplan, H. B. Sequelae of self-derogation: Predicting from a general theory of deviant behavior. *Youth and Society*, 7: 2 (1975), 171–197.
16. Fisher, S. Stigma and deviant careers in school. *Soc. Prob.*, 20: 1 (1972), 78–83.
17. Singh, V. P. Personality profiles of recidivists and nonrecidivists. *Ind. J. Soc. Work*, 35: 3 (1974), 227–232.
18. Cymbalisty, B. Y. Achievement level, institutional adjustment and recidivism among juvenile delinquents. *J. Community Psychol.*, 3: 3 (1975), 289–294.
19. Haskin, M. B. A comparison of graduate and recidivist WISC IQ scores in a delinquent treatment program for girls. *J. Clin. Psychol.*, 30: 3 (1974), 319–320.
20. Clark, R. E. *Reference Group Theory and Delinquency.* Behavioral Publications, New York, 1972.
21. Glueck, S. and Glueck, E. *Later Criminal Careers.* The Commonwealth Fund, New York, 1937, pp. 106, 124.
22. Glueck, S. and Glueck, E. *Juvenile Delinquents Grown Up.* The Commonwealth Fund, New York, 1940, pp. 94, 98.
23. Sealy, A. P. and Banks, C. Social maturity, training, experience and recidivism among British Borstal boys. *Brit. J. Criminol.*, 11: 3 (1971), 245–264.

ROLE OF PREVENTIVE MEASURES IN VULNERABILITY

Planning of Comprehensive Preventive Care for the Vulnerable Child Population

Joseph Marcus, M.D. (U.S.A.)

Infants at Risk (Stream 1)

A VULNERABILITY REGISTER

The first step in planning a preventive program has been the attempt to establish *at-risk registers* of vulnerable children, which have been used mainly for the planning of follow-up examinations by pediatricians. Such registers have been in use particularly in Britain [1, 2]. If the criteria of risk are too broad, too large a percentage of births is included, and the load may become too high for adequate follow-up of all children considered at risk. If the criteria are stricter (such as those of Oppe [2]), then many children who later manifest handicaps "slip through the net." Nonetheless, Forfar [3] stressed in a recent survey that the use of such registers is worthwhile. Further exploratory studies will no doubt evolve more accurate methods of pinpointing during infancy those children destined for deviant development.

A FULL ASSESSMENT OF THE VULNERABLE CHILD IN HIS FAMILY

These registers have most often been used as a check on the ultimate appearance of physical handicaps and in ensuring adequate general pediatric care of the children. However, insufficient attention has been given to closer investigation of the

589

earliest signs heralding functional disorder or disturbed infant-mother interaction, and of family relations (including the guidance of parents in individualized adaptation of, and to, the handicapped child). Any comprehensive plan of treatment and management for this group of children requires a full assessment of the family status and of the child within it, as well as pediatric, neurological, and other specialized evaluation of the child and his handicap. The capacity of the child to respond to treatment depends not only on the nature and severity of the physical handicap, but also on his ability to adapt to environmental demands and to comprehend and respond positively to training and teaching procedures. This ability will be influenced by his intellectual level, any distortions of perception that may exist, the psychiatric consequences of brain damage, and the psychological reactions to the physical handicaps. The child-parent relationship will also be affected by all these factors, as well as by the parents' reactions to the child's behavior and to the necessary restrictions dictated by the handicap. Furthermore, the possibility of formulating an optimal program for the parents with regard to the handling of their child's physical and behavioral difficulties requires an individualized, systematic assessment of the child's developmental level and psychological status, his vulnerability and his assets, and sometimes the parents' own capabilities.

Finally, the decision as to whether a child with a physical, emotional, or intellectual handicap will require day-care service outside the home or residential placement and treatment, as well as the type of care or placement required, will be influenced by his developmental psychiatric as well as pediatric evaluation. Many of these facets of examination and care have been well discussed in a recent book on early child care [4].

A PROGRAM OF INTERVENTION

Having identified and fully assessed those infants and families who are at risk, there remains a wide range of interventions that may be made to ameliorate, minimize, or treat deviant development. Such anticipatory guidance and care could be in the following areas:

1. Special protection in groups of mothers at high risk, including those suffering from eclampsia, preeclampsia, diabetes,

threatened abortion or previous abortions, antepartum, hemorrhage, low statural height (known to enhance perinatal mortality and morbidity, which may be averted by appropriately timed cesarian section).

2. Direct guidance during the lying-in period regarding handling of the infant, and support and help to the mother when immediate pathology or difficulties are identified.

3. Biochemical screening in depth for known inborn biochemical defect, with protection, or institution of elimination diets where indicated.

4. Special pediatric care (e.g., dietary control in malabsorption, diagnosis and management of mucoviscidosis, observation and care, anomalies of heart, hearing, vision).

5. Continued guidance by developmentally trained pediatricians, psychologists, and infant nurses professionally experienced in and geared to the needs of the multiply handicapped or deviant child. Planned programming of the care and education of these children.

6. Special nursery and kindergarten care to provide emotional, social, and cognitive enrichment, together with specialized therapy to foster motor and speech development or to alleviate hearing or sight deficiencies, and so on.

However, there must be *a warning* at this point. *There can be many pathogenic effects in preparing risk registers if proper care facilities are not developed concomitantly by the community.*

The foregoing descriptions have touched on some of the relatively clear parameters of development, but it must be stressed that perinatal and familial conditions and vicissitudes and deviations of infant and child development is an area replete with unknown and uninvestigated parameters. *True prevention and treatment of deviant development still requires a great deal of basic research into the etiology and evolution of handicapping conditions in the infant and young child*, as well as a deeper knowledge of the processes of normal neurological and behavioral development. The justification for the comprehensive clinical service that will be proposed later is reinforced by the proposed concurrent research program. This would be aimed principally at: clarification and definition of the potential etiological factors that may result in handicap, operating from the preconceptual phase through pregnancy, the perinatal period, and beyond; the refinement of clinical tools to enable more exact and fuller assessment (including the definition of developmental norms); and the investigations of different treatment modalities in the medical, psychological, social, and educational spheres.

Prompt Coordinated Developmental Care of Those Infants Born Handicapped (Stream 2)

As distinct from vulnerable infants potentially facing handicap, there are those born with either manifest anatomical malformation or physiological or functional handicap, evidence of which is elicitable neonatally or emerges gradually during infancy and early childhood.

HOSPITAL SCREENING

Hospital screening clinics, in collaboration with a malformation survey, could be utilized to identify the malformed, and to a gradually widening extent, the functionally handicapped.

The appropriate specialist for the primary defect, whether neurosurgical, plastic, orthopedic, genitourinary, or other, should be utilized. After consultation with and assessment by a developmental unit and a special rehabilitation advisor, a team of specialists appropriate to any particular handicap or child could be gradually coordinated for immediate action and for the graduated long-term management.

Early guidance and other assistance to the family of the handicapped would be a vital component of the management, and in this sphere a family social worker could be responsible for initiating and integrating social action in close collaboration with municipal social-welfare departments and with the social work units of community hospitals.

SERIAL DEVELOPMENT ASSESSMENT

Serial developmental observation of the handicapped child should continue in peripheral municipal clinics and central assessment units, according to the nature of the handicap and the specific observations to be made. (For example, growth recording by a specialized growth unit may only be required at 3- or 6-month intervals in some cases.)

The developmental assessment, in relation to the maturation of intellectual, psychoemotional, social, and adaptational aspects, should be especially geared to: (1) avoiding specific learning aberrations and (2) enhancing the development of relatively high adaptability or skills in any particular sphere of activity. The excellence of the interdisciplinary preoccupation with the primary malformation or handicap must not be allowed to obscure this aspect. Indeed an important basic conception of any program for the manifestly handicapped child should be the special interest in the "whole child," as well as principal interest in his optimal fulfillment through the detection and fostering of his potentiality, adaptability, or earliest stirrings of individual talent, irrespective of the nature of the known handicap. This must be supplemented by consideration of family dynamics.

Possible Model for a Community Program

The screening, assessment, and care of the vulnerable child as described in the preceding paragraph might be achieved by an infant and child development center. Such a center could be conceived of as a special, independent unit that at one and the same time has clearly defined and integrated clinical and research functions—in other words, it would be multifunctional. As it is aimed at providing a wide service to a whole community, it should be multiinstitutional, and as it is aimed at providing a complete assessment and care program to the "whole" child and his family, it should also be multidisciplinary.

THE DEVELOPMENT CENTER

Figure 1 schematically describes the structure of such a program. The development center itself would carry out the specialized assessment of infants and young children and their families who were referred through the screening clinics (see Figure 1). The multidisciplinary team would also outline a therapeutic program. Parts of the therapy or care could be done by the staff of the center, but much would be carried out by other facilities in the community (general medical center, maternal and child-care centers, social-welfare agencies, educational facilities) in collaboration with the development center. Connection of the center with university departments could provide the possibility of developing both teaching and research functions. Connection with other facilities would provide for full community participation in the overall program. (A program such as this was planned for the city of Jerusalem [5], and certain fragments of it are being carried out by various agencies.)

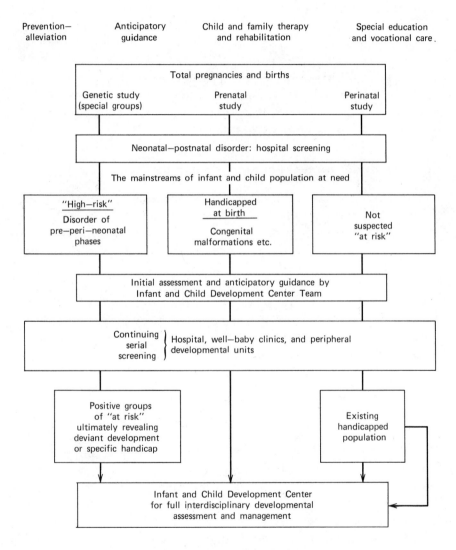

Figure 1   A community development project for vulnerable and handicapped children.

ASSESSMENT PROCEDURES

A variety of procedures from the biological, psychological, and social fields could be used. Briefly, these would include: (1) pediatric-biological assessment, (2) neurological and neurophysiological assessment, (3) behavioral and psychiatric assessment, (4) psychological assessment, and (5) parental and environmental assessment.

TREATMENT PROCEDURES

Following the thorough assessment of children found to have deviancies of development, programs of care would be outlined so as to provide the specific therapies and general enrichment necessary to ensure optimal programs. Such therapies could include specific dietary control, physical-rehabilitation techniques, establishment of orderly routines of care (at home, school, or elsewhere), parental guidance and therapy, family group work, and emotional, motor, cognitive, and speech stimulation through planned programs such as therapeutic day nursery and kindergarten.

RESEARCH PROGRAM

It is proposed that the research program be focused on basic scientific problems, but in close relationship to the functional and clinical problems of mentally, emotionally, and physically handicapped children. The research program could develop and provide extra tools for the early diagnosis and care of a wide range of handicaps and at the same time provide new dimensions for clinical work and education. When seen together, the behavioral and neurological data obtained would constitute a longitudinal study of behavioral, psychological, neurological, and physiological development. As such, they are of basic scientific importance but are also directly relevant to the more effective diagnosis and care of vulnerable children.

Following is an outline of some of the principal developmental studies that could be carried out:

1. A study of the comparative development of groups of children taken from the population of a perinatal study, divided into *perinatally damaged* and *normal* control groups.

2. A study of the development of infants born to schizophrenic parents.
3. Long-term behavioral and other developmental changes in children born: (a) following pregnancies complicated by hormonal treatment or other methods, (b) with delivery by vacuum-extraction method, (c) to mothers suffering from postpartum depression, and (d) with vision or hearing defects.
4. A study of comparative development of controlled groups of vulnerable infants and young children who do and do not receive planned treatment and enrichment programs.

References

Chandler, C. A., Lourie, R. S. and Peters, A. D. (1968) *Early Child Care.* New York: Atherton.

Forfar, J. O. (1968) "At-risk registers," *Developmental Medical and Child Neurology. 10*:384–395.

Marcus, J. and Russell, A. (1970) "The vulnerable and the handicapped," In *Children and Families in Israel–Some Mental Health Perspectives.* A. Jarus, J. Marcus, J. Oren, C. Rapaport, eds. New York: Gordon & Breach Science Publishers, pp. 385–426.

Oppe', T. E. (1967) "Risk registers for babies," *Developmental Medical and Child Neurology. 9*:13–21.

Sheridan, M. D., (1962) "Infants at risk of handicapping conditions," *Monthly Bulletin Ministry Health Labor Service. 21*:238.

Mental Health at Preschool Level: A Preventive Approach with a High-risk Population

Peggy L. Vaughan, M.S.S., A.C.S.W., Ellen Boorse, M.A., and Susanne S. Jakobi, M.S.W., A.C.S.W. (U.S.A.)

Introduction

The Irving Schwartz Institute for Children and Youth in Philadelphia, Pennsylvania, serving a catchment area as part of the Community Mental Health, Mental Retardation program, is an outpatient child guidance clinic offering a wide range of service for children and their families. This includes the services of a Pre-School Unit with a staff of three people. In weekly consultation to public elementary schools over a 3-year period, the Pre-School Unit staff became aware that a number of kindergarten children were showing emotional and behavioral problems within the classroom and that preventive measures were needed. In an effort to provide these measures at the preschool level, contact was made with the chief psychologist of Get Set Day Care for the purpose of sharing these observations and concerns. A program has been developed through this collaborative effort.

The first step was the presentation by the Irving Schwartz Institute Pre-School Unit staff of a 1-day workshop for Get Set Day Care personnel of that catchment area. This focused on the personnel's concerns with the emotional well-being of the children in their centers. As a result, the participants' desire for ongoing consultation service was expressed. Groundwork by the Pre-School Unit staff, along with Get Set Day Care psychological services' administrative personnel, culminated in the establishment of a consultation program to two Get Set Day Care centers. However, since the 18 centers in that catchment area, with 160 personnel serving approximately 850 children, began to request consultation services, the opportunity to reach them by expanding the program was met by the development of an in-service training seminar. It was determined that this could be accomplished initially by offering the seminar for lead teachers, social workers, and supervisory personnel. Their particular positions and administrative responsibilities brought them into contact with the greatest number of Get Set Day Care staff and enabled them to disseminate the content of the seminar. The purpose of the seminar was to promote the emotional well-being of the children and families in the program by: (1) enhancing the Get Set staff participants' appreciation of their own roles, (2) increasing positive interdisciplinary staff relationships and interaction so that the staff could more effectively carry out their roles and responsibilities, and (3) enhancing the skills of the staff participants as elaborated in the following paragraphs and throughout this chapter.

The families involved were mainly urban, poor, lower to lower-middle class, and Black, with a large first- and second-generation Italian group included. These and other features qualified them as a "high-risk" population. Emphasis was placed on the necessity and opportunity for creating a positive emotional experience for children who spend many waking hours with a surrogate parent, and whose own parents spend much of their time and energy struggling with severe financial difficulties and in pursuit of the satisfaction of their own emotional needs.

The Get Set Day Care program is the first school experience for the children and may be the first school contact their parents have had since their own school days. A good initial school experience helps promote positive handling of subsequent educational contacts. Preventive mental health was our main goal, along with prompt and appropriate intervention if needed. The very young age at which children attend Get Set Day Care rendered both of these goals of prime importance for this population.

The focus of the seminar was on the emotional aspects of the children's lives, particularly in relation to the Get Set Day Care program. It was not placed directly on the curriculum or the educating process, but it did include the emotional impact of the content and techniques of the educational procedures. Much of what happens to children at the ages in which they are involved in Get Set has important emotional undertones. Therefore, it is important for teachers to recognize the need for a good emotional climate and be able to create one. Participants were given the opportunity to learn ways of handling emotional stress that made traumatic situations less draining and less upsetting to both staff and children. A child who learns to "fail" or is unhappy or afraid in Get Set may respond in the same way to future school situations.

A primary goal was attitude change where necessary in both staff and parents. For example, stress was placed on the need for realistic structure for children, on not being punitive, on not "shaming" a child, and on seeing children as *having* problems, not as *being* problems.

The earlier experiences of the Irving Schwartz Institute Pre-School Unit staff in consulting with schools and with the Get Set Day Care centers revealed the reluctance of school personnel to refer children with emotional problems for professional help. On the other hand, it was found that there were times when the normal developmental stages and processes created difficulties for the staff. Portions of the seminar were, therefore, geared toward helping participants distinguish the child who needed special help from ones who did not, and to distinguish needs of children that could be met in school from those that could not. Ways of meeting appropriate emotional needs in school were discussed at length and referral sources and procedures noted.

For many reasons parents often feel alienated from schools. This is exacerbated by the fact that most of the Get Set Day Care parents work outside their homes and cannot attend meetings or other daytime activities at the centers. They cannot enhance their children's school experiences in this way, and both they and the center personnel lose opportunities for much needed positive communication. With children as young, dependent, and vulnerable as these, staff members become quite emotionally invested in their relationships with them and in their responsibilities for them. As a result, feelings of rivalry and jealousy sometimes exist between parents and staff. Therefore, emphasis was placed on involving parents in the life of the center to prevent alienation and isolation and to promote positive feedback for both groups. There are, of course, many occurrences and aspects of the school and home lives of very young children that are important for both staff and parents to consider. These include illness, birth of a sibling, parental separation, school accidents, school projects, and absence or replacement of a teacher. Positive methods for communicating with parents and for handling stressful situations with them were presented and modeled for the seminar participants.

The body of material presented in lecture, written form, and informal discussion in the seminar was based on the authors' own eclectic understanding of personality development and psychotherapeutic change, including aspects of psychoanalytic, interactional, and social-learning theories. Considerable emphasis was placed on the importance of family interactional patterns in personality development.

In keeping with recognized interdisciplinary mental health teaching methods, the participants received instruction in the theory and practice of promoting mental health through readings in the literature, mimeographed material written by the seminar leaders, didactic lectures, practicums, and through the preparation and presentation of assignments. As part of the practicum, they observed family diagnostic and family therapy interviews at Irving Schwartz Institute.

The seminar consisted of eight weekly sessions, each devoted to a different topic. Every session included a 1-hour lecture for the entire group, followed by 1½ hours of discussion in which participants were divided into three smaller groups, each led by a Pre-School Unit staff member to enable fuller participation by all in attendance.

These three small groups used their time primarily to probe into the issues considered in the presentations. Participants were encouraged to raise relevant theoretical or factual questions, bring up practical examples or problems from their own work, and air their views or feelings about the subjects being discussed. Although there were some differences in the roles the group leaders took, we generally worked to:

1. Help the group keep discussion focused in the direction of the particular day's presentation.
2. Answer factual questions when the group itself did not have the answers.
3. Offer ideas and suggestions.
4. Facilitate discussion by asking leading or provocative questions.
5. Involve as many group members as possible in verbal participation.
6. Keep issues alive until useful answers or solutions had been well considered.
7. Model principles of group leadership being taught.

In some cases, role play was used to demonstrate interactions. Every effort was made to stimulate the groups' interest in examining meanings or implications of issues raised and in working on solutions to problems. A secondary use of group time was to discuss expectations for individual assignments and go over the participants' reports of the completed assignments. Participants were encouraged to read or tell about their family interviews and child observations. This provided support and feedback for the reporting participant as well as beneficial discussion for the other group members.

Seminar Content and Presentation

SESSION ONE: THE WELL-ADJUSTED FAMILY

The nature and origins of relations between family members within a well-adjusted family was chosen as the first seminar presentation. Relationships in such families are more often positive than negative. This gives the child his or her best opportunity for healthy growth and development. The participants were thus introduced to mental health as a positive concept and to the use of interpersonal relationships to promote mental health. This major means of understanding and intervening in family functioning was labeled "the use of process." "Process" was defined as verbal and nonverbal interactions and activities occurring here and now and over a period of time. "Process" reveals patterns of individual and family dynamics. It is seen in the way people talk to one another, behave toward one another, show their feelings toward one another, and listen to one another.

The material handed out described in both diagram and outline form the characteristics and behavior of a well-functioning family and the factors enabling them to function well. Emphasis was placed on the identification and understanding of strengths within the family to serve as a desirable goal for the participants to keep in mind when dealing with children and their families.

The outline depicted the well-adjusted family as a unit moving through the following significant phases of family life (adapted from [9]), beginning with the parents meeting each other:

1. Courtship.
2. Marriage.
3. Pregnancy and childbirth.
4. Integration of child into the family.
5. Integration of outside influences on child into the family.
6. Integration of the adolescent into the world.

Each phase was described according to the following categories: (1) behavior, (2) reality problem-solving, (3) strengths, and (4) origin of strengths (in parents' family of origin).

To illustrate, the first phase, courtship, is presented in cross-section in Table 1.

Each section of the outline was discussed in detail with frequent reference to the constructive nature of "process" within the well-adjusted family.

The participants were encouraged to use the lecture and written material as a basis from which they could ascertain, increase, and appreciate their knowledge of healthy family functioning. Destructive "process," which exists to a greater degree in families who do not function well, was more readily isolated against this background and formed the basis for the second seminar session.

SESSION TWO: THE FAMILY IN TROUBLE

Both the well-functioning family and the family in trouble were defined in terms of how the members of the family feel, relate to

Table 1   Basis for the Well-adjusted Family

	What a Healthy Family Is and Does		What Enables Them to Do It	
Behavior	Reality Problem-Solving	Strengths	Origin of Strengths
Courtship: attraction of two mature individuals	Meeting members of the opposite sex	Communication and Interaction	Family of origin provides good modeling and acceptance of instinctual feelings
Physical Emotional Intellectual		Self-awareness Empathy	
Getting to know partner-to-be	Openly facing differences and	Adaptation	Acceptance of people outside of the
Likes	negative feelings	Rationalization	family
Dislikes	Learning to deal	Identification	Attainment of
Background (in-laws)	with them	Idealization	physical, emotional, and intellectual maturity
			Acceptance of normal aggressive feelings

others, and work. It was posited that in a disturbed family, certain important messages within the family system are not being correctly communicated, satisfactorily responded to, or acted on, and so parts of the family members' emotional functioning may be cut off. A case example was described, showing in detail how messages and feelings may be miscommunicated and misunderstood, leading to poor interaction. Often misunderstandings arise from preconceptions about reality based on prior experience, and members in a family can grow to perceive one another inaccurately. Appropriate and inappropriate family roles were discussed, as well as ways to explore strengths that may be used toward promoting better functioning in a disturbed family.

SESSION THREE: INTERVIEWING SKILLS WITH FAMILIES

Teaching interviewing skills to Get Set Day Care social workers is important to their specific roles. It is also important, though perhaps less obvious, as a needed skill for classroom personnel. We were aware of the frequency of informal contact between classroom personnel and parents, siblings, and other relatives as they accompanied the children to and from the centers. We were also aware of the frustrations experienced by staff and families as a result of these contacts, which are so often used to air problems and complaints and to give instructions. To turn these informal contacts into positive communications and to encourage further more formal contacts between classroom personnel and families, we introduced material on "interviewing skills with families" in our third session. At the same time an assignment was given to the participants to interview a family, for which this session provided a background.

The participants were given written material at the beginning of the session presenting:

1. Important concepts in interviewing.
2. Outline of the basic steps in an interview.
3. Sample case material illustrating the basic steps.

This material was to be used both to follow the lecture and for future reference. The lecture was brief, elaborating on the written material.

The important concepts in interviewing were: (1) use of "process" (as described previously) in combination with "content" (background information, the topic being discussed, etc.) as the major technique in family interviewing, (2) recognition and use of the family's and individual's strengths, (3) and respecting the rights of families and of the individual family members, including the right to suffer and the right to choose to change.

The outline included these five basic steps:

1. Review of background material prior to the interview.
2. Introductory period of the interview (including explanation of the reason for the interview and a careful assessment of the family's present emotional tone).
3. Recognizing and labeling the family system (including roles, rules, levels of communication, alliances, strengths, and weaknesses).
4. Dynamic formulation of family functioning (based on the interviewer's observations and the family's stated needs).
5. Presentation of goals to the family (stated in the language of the present family system).

The sample case material consisted of segments corresponding to each of the basic steps in the interview. Two seminar leaders read aloud and role-played each segment in sequence, followed by a short discussion relating the role-playing to the interviewing concepts and skills. The need to role-play two therapists and four family members in this specific case was accomplished by designating separate chairs for each family member and changing chairs according to role. The use of role-playing illustrated and brought to life "process" and "content" as expressed in verbalizations, feelings, and accompanying body movements as well as seating arrangements, use of furniture, and use of play materials by family members and therapists.

SESSION FOUR: STAGES OF CHILD DEVELOPMENT

The ages during which a child is likely to be enrolled in a Get Set Day Care center include the important early stages and formative years of life. Along with parents and relatives, the personnel in a day-care setting where a child may spend many of his or her waking hours are among the most influential people in the child's life.

For the sake of both the children and center personnel, we felt it was important that the personnel be familiar with the stages of development in childhood. We were aware that at times in the centers there was alarm about responses and behaviors of the children, which actually reflected appropriate, though perhaps difficult, developmental processes. At other times potential problems were overlooked. We were also aware that in situations where there was a dependence on popular or idiosyncratic attitudes and convention regarding child-raising and/or situations where there was a dependence on rigid formalized training in child development, the abilities of the Get Set personnel to deal appropriately with the children were hampered. We felt these abilities would be enhanced and that confusion between maladaptive behaviors and appropriate responses or attributes would be lessened by providing a systematic, but less rigid, understanding of what children at various ages and stages were experiencing and what the children needed to accomplish to enable them to grow and move on to a new stage.

At the beginning of this session the participants were given material outlining the stages of child development. For the sake of clarity, the stages were divided up to correspond to the ages 0 to 6 months, 6 months to 2 years, 2 to 4 years, 4 to 6 years, and 6 to 12 years.

Each stage was then described in the written material by using the categories: (1) tasks in process, (2) physical characteristics, (3) cognitive characteristics, and (4) emotional characteristics. The following example (Table 2) is one full section taken from the written material.

A large blackboard was used to list the ages and titles of each stage as described by both Sigmund Freud [7] and Erik Erikson [5]. This was not discussed as such, but was only called to the participants' attention as a reference point for those who had heard the titles and wanted clarification.

The participants were also given a bibliography relating to the topic of the stages of child development and a scale listing the approximate age in months at which a child would be able to perform certain tasks or reach specific levels of socialization.

The lecture accompanying the written material dealt with a few general concepts regarding ages and stages of development including the importance of the flexibility and overlapping of stages, the wide range of acceptable behaviors and adjustments for all children, the interdependence of the physical, emotional, and cognitive characteristics of each stage, the groundwork laid during each stage in preparation for the succeeding stage and for adulthood, and the mutual regulation necessary between the parent (or caretaker) and the child during each stage. However, the greatest portion of the lecture was devoted to further elaborate on the emotional aspects of each stage and stressed Erikson's theories with less specific emphasis on the theories of Freud. The concepts and theories were illustrated by use of many examples from the seminar leaders' experiences with children in general and specifically with children and personnel in Get Set Day Care settings.

SESSION FIVE: SYSTEMATIC OBSERVATION OF CHILDREN

Observation of children is necessary to the thorough understanding of the concepts presented in this seminar. Although the Get Set personnel spend much time with children, it is important that they are acquainted with a systematic method for observing them. Such a system is useful as a teaching tool to sensitize the

Table 2   Age 2 to 4 Years[a]

Tasks in process
　　To differentiate self as a person
　　To secure a sense of autonomy and free will
　　To tolerate separations from mother
　　To master instinctual, emotional impulses (e.g., those connected with shame and doubt)
　　To reach physical plateaus (motor action, toilet training)
Physical characteristics
　　Exercises autonomy with body: eating and toilet training (gains control of sphincter muscles — bowels and bladder)
　　Improves finger control (fine-motor ability): draws vertical and horizontal lines, copies a circle, drops and throws things
　　Develops sufficient speech to be understood
Cognitive characteristics
　　Thinks about things in concrete and "magical" manner, but not logical (e.g., if asked to explain the sun's setting, the child will say it "goes to sleep")
　　Often unable to follow the reason and logic behind an idea, a direction, or discipline
　　Engages in investigative play and the beginnings of imaginative (abstract) play; also engages in imitative play
　　Learns language and actively explores world
Emotional characteristics
　　Development of a sense of autonomy and a will; characterized by holding on and letting go
　　Concern about the concept of control (control of self, control *by* others, control *of* others, sphincter control)
　　Concern about loss of control and self-esteem (from a sense of muscular and anal impotence and parental overcontrol comes a lasting sense of shame and doubt)
　　Ambivalence toward dependence and independence
　　Feelings of dependence on mother and separation fears
　　Behavior identification with parents, siblings, peers
　　Plays by self, parallel to others; beginnings of cooperative play

[a] Portions of this outline were compiled with the assistance of Rita Schonberg and reference to the work by Senn and Solnit [22].

seminar participants to the needs, feelings, and fantasy life of the children. It increases awareness of the stages and levels of development and of the growth processes. It is also useful for changing the "set" of the observer so as to see children differently. For example, seeing Joey as being "at it again" often precludes watching what he is really doing and feeling, what he is reacting to, what his frustration tolerance is, what role he is playing out, and what he is actually accomplishing. Or seeing Linda as "withdrawn" may cause her immature speech, awkward way of holding crayons, and lethargic movements to be overlooked. When all areas of functioning are considered together, a fragmented picture of the child is avoided.

The written material that was handed out to the participants listed and described the following fourteen categories to keep in mind while observing children:

1. Separation in waiting room or on entering day-care center.
2. Initial reaction to day-care situation.
3. Speech.
4. Motor development.
5. Activity level.
6. Attention span and distractibility.
7. Frustration tolerance.
8. Fantasy.
9. Conceptual development.
10. Play.
11. Relationships.
12. General prevailing behavior and affect.
13. Defenses.
14. Group interaction.

These categories were discussed in detail, as was the value of doing several observations of the same child over a period of time. Included in the written material was an actual summary of several such observations of a particular child that covered these 14 categories.

To sharpen observational skills, the seminar participants were asked to spend approximately 30 minutes observing one child and taking notes. They were instructed to learn the 14 categories before actually observing the child and to keep them in mind if possible, but to take notes on everything the child did in order of occurrence instead of taking them according to the categories. In their note taking they were asked to simply describe what the child did, without inserting any of their own comments or feelings. They were to be an uninvolved observer and engage in no interaction with any of the children except to encourage a child to talk about any fantasy in which he or she might be engaged.

After the observation the participants were to go over their notes carefully and prepare them in final form by using the 14 categories. A description of the child's physical appearance, primary activities, and productions was to be included. The final writing is similar to putting pieces of a puzzle together and often results in a very different picture than that given by the impression or feelings the participant had while observing that child.

SESSION SIX

The sixth session lecture was divided into two short sections.

Childhood Disorders.   Throughout this seminar, emotional well-being and mental health were stressed instead of mental illness and pathology. Therefore, much thought was given to the value of a lecture on childhood disorders. We were not trying to train Get Set personnel to be diagnosticians, nor did we want to orient them to categorizing children or to thinking in terms of "symptoms." However, we knew that there were children in their classrooms who needed professional help beyond that available in the centers, and who often went unrecognized. We had observed that without help many of these children continued to have troubles, experience pain, and decline in their functioning. Often they were regarded as "shy," or as unintelligent, or were chastised for being "bad," and this we hoped to prevent. For these reasons, and because one of our goals was to encourage prompt and appropriate intervention if needed, we devoted the first part of the sixth session to a brief and concise presentation of childhood disorders.

The participants were given material listing the general characteristics of each of these categories:

1. Minimal brain dysfunction (MBD) in children (including learning disabilities).
2. Emotionally deprived children.
3. Retarded children.
4. Neurotic children.
5. Psychotic children (i.e., cases of childhood schizophrenia and infantile autism).

Under each category title, and just above the listing of the symptoms, was printed the warning: "May have some but not necessarily all of the following characteristics."

The lecture began by stressing that each disorder involves a configuration or pattern of characteristics that must be found together. One or two characteristics do not necessarily cause a child to be emotionally disturbed. Thus it was noted that the participants would probably find many of the characteristics in the children in their centers, but that these traits in isolated form do not necessarily constitute a disorder. The ability of Get Set personnel to be objective, recognize problems, and obtain help for the children in their centers was discussed, as well as the availability of outside referral sources.

The lecture continued by following the written material closely with elaboration of the symptoms, explanation of the possible causes of each disorder, and discussion of some of the methods used in helping children suffering from each disorder.

Behavior Modification. A brief presentation on behavior modification was included in the seminar to give an added dimension for observing and influencing the children's development. Some basic principles of stimulus-response theory and behavior modification were presented, along with examples of possible applications of behavior modification in the classroom. Prior experience with Get Set teachers had led us to believe that they tended to be distrustful of using systematic rewards because they sometimes consider it bribery. A common attitude was that children should not be rewarded for doing something that is expected of them anyway. Because of these attitudes, ethical issues surrounding behavior modification were stressed. For example, our position was that teachers reinforce and extinguish children's behaviors regardless of whether they believe they are doing so, and that systematic rewards are designed to make the teachers' control of child behavior more effective. A second attitude we attempted to challenge in discussing behavior modification is the idea that the only disciplinary method that really works is corporal punishment. We presented the findings of stimulus-response learning theory indicating that punishment tends to be inferior to other methods for modifying behavior.

The classroom use of behavior modification for controlling aggression, hyperactivity, tantrums, and withdrawal and for promoting learning was discussed. Some of the limitations of the method were discussed, such as the need for the behavior being modified to be isolable. No attempt was made to train the seminar participants to be formal behavior modifiers. Rather, our purpose was to define behavior-modification for them, help them overcome misconceptions in relation to it, and give them an opportunity to explore its potential use in their classes. We advised that anyone wishing to use behavior-modification techniques to modify a child's behavior should seek expert help at first so as to avoid undesired effects. Each participant was given written material including definitions relating to behavior modification, an example of its use, and a brief bibliography.

SESSION SEVEN: THE CHILD IN SCHOOL

The material presented during the first six sessions was specifically designed to increase the participants' knowledge, understanding, and skills needed in their work with preschool children and their families. In the seventh session the focus was placed on the role of the participants themselves as agents for enhancing the emotional development of preschool children. In the written material given to the participants, four aspects of this role within a sound day-care program were listed: (1) knowledge of child development within our culture, (2) adult ability to empathize with children, (3) understanding the meaning of play, and (4) self-awareness. These served as the content for the first portion of the lecture.

A brief review of the first six seminar sessions was presented with the stated purpose of providing an overview to the participants of the extent of their experience and knowledge related to child development. The concept of empathy as a necessary added dimension of their role was defined as a two-part process in which the adult must first comfortably feel again, as when he was a child, the child's emotion, and then become aware of himself as an adult relating to that child. Empathy requires the adult to temporarily give up his own sense of self, and then to recapture it in a back-and-forth process. The child's feelings thus become the primary interest of the adult who is empathizing with the child in an effort to help him develop normally. Empathy often requires the adult to see through the child's overt behavior, which may hide the child's real feelings. The ability to empathize is not dependent on liking or loving the child. The lecture included factors that can impede the process of empathy in adults, such as the revival of troublesome feelings from childhood.

Sometimes the increasing pressure of our society to provide "disadvantaged" young children with "learning experiences," along with the stress of continued daily responsibility for their care, tends to overshadow the importance of play in the developmental process. Therefore, the meaning of play was given careful attention in this session. Play was described as the "work" of children, which is a means of learning and can also be simply a means of enjoyment. The nature of play changes as the child grows and is put to increasingly more complex use by the child. Play was shown to be the child's way of using model situations of his or her own creation in order to practice dealing with pleasurable and stressful life experiences such as the birth of a sibling, death in the family, or move to another home. Some fantasies that might be revealed in play were illustrated by examples provided by the seminar leaders. The participants were encouraged to share examples from their classrooms. Their willingness and enthusiasm in so doing created a ready transition into a discussion of the concept of self-awareness, the fourth aspect of their role in enhancing the emotional development of preschool children.

The last section of the written material was an actual outline of a day-care program in which six areas of learning related to the child's emotional development were elaborated. The child needs to learn:

1. How adults feel, think, and behave.
2. That he or she is a worthwhile person.
3. Satisfaction in the results of good work habits.
4. To express fantasies freely.
5. To work out problems that originate in family life.
6. Social living.

Materials and methods for teaching were included only when they specifically related to these six areas. The bibliography attached to the outline was briefly noted.

SESSION EIGHT: PARENTAL INVOLVEMENT

A lack of parental involvement in the life of the school is often a problem in inner-city Get Set Day Care Centers. Although parents are not generally invited to take active part in the school day, they are encouraged to attend educational meetings, organize fund-raising activities, plan activities, suggest curriculum alterations, and occasionally help out at school and on school trips. When on-going group meetings or activities are organized, Get Set staff and some of the parents often complain about the fact that many of the parents do not participate. There is frustration over the degree of apparent apathy.

In the presentation on "parental involvement," reasons for lack of involvement were discussed. Parental feelings of inadequacy, anger at institutions, preoccupation with earning enough for survival, and a sense of not having enough for oneself, let alone enough to give to the child and his school, were explored as possible explanations for noninvolvement. We used a case example of a shy, self-deprecating 20-year old mother of two, with a husband who seldom works. This was discussed in terms of the young woman's considerable needs and fears that would make it difficult for her to perceive participation in Get Set as a priority.

A strong case was made for the inclusion of parents in the child's Get Set life, in ways that might answer needs of parents who do not at present participate in school activities. For example, a coffee corner in a room, available in many centers, might be set up so that parents could meet informally over coffee in the mornings. We emphasized the staff's taking a warm, empathic, consistent interest in parents as human beings in their own right and encouraging parents to take part in Get Set activities that would be fun and nurturing for them as well as for their children. In addition, it was suggested that social and educational parent groups be organized, that school staff reach out to families by visiting them in their homes, and that interreliance and help be encouraged among parents by Get Set.

Several important reasons for this emphasis on involving parents were spelled out, including:

1. Get Set may be the first institutional liaison that young parents of high-risk children have. If this liaison is nurturing

and positive, it can form a sound basis for the family's relationship with the child's continued schooling.

2. Parents' good relationship with school will help them to adopt more fulfilling parenting patterns while the child is young and to seek outside or additional help for the child if necessary.

3. Some parents are still immature. Positive involvement with Get Set or another helping agency may aid them in maturing so that they may seek more fulfilling lives individually, socially, and politically.

Each seminar participant received sheets with suggested behavioral attitudes and actions to employ toward encouraging parental involvement. Types of parent group meetings and topics to discuss were included.

Evaluation and Implications

Seminar participants filled out final questionnaires evaluating the in-service training seminar and were also asked for verbal evaluation by members of the Get Set Day Care Psychological Services staff. Following is a summary of the major results:

1. The participants unanimously recommended the in-service seminar for all Get Set staff, including supervisors, teachers, assistant teachers, aides, and other staff involved with the children.

2. The seminar was given an overall rating of 8 on a scale of 1–10. In general, it was described as "the best" or "one of the best in-services" the participants had attended.

3. The sessions pertaining particularly to the child were considered more helpful and relevant than sessions on the family and on interviewing techniques. Observations of a family interview at the Irving Schwartz Institute and leaders' role play were considered the most enjoyable portions of the in-service seminar.

4. Participants in general believed the seminar had positively influenced their work functioning in that they understood children better as a result and were more able to see children as "having," rather than "being," problems.

5. Participants suggested that more time in small group discussions would be helpful.

A multiple-choice test of some concepts and facts covered in the seminar was administered to participants at the beginning and end of the seminar. It was hypothesized that posttest scores would be higher than pretest scores. A t-test for two correlated samples using pre- and posttest scores showed a significant increase ($p <$ .02) in scores, confirming the hypothesis and indicating that participants learned as a result of the seminar.

Overall evaluation of the in-service seminar was highly favorable. This includes a consideration of the participants' evaluation, increase in knowledge, and enthusiasm, as well as the cooperation and evaluation of the Get Set Psychological Services staff. Our own judgment about the quality of involvement of the participants and what they learned was also positive. The few difficulties and drawbacks that became evident to us serve as the basis for some changes being planned for future seminars. Regular attendance at the sessions was lower than hoped for. Of an initial group of about 50, fewer than 35 attended the last sessions. Although most of the absences were deemed legitimate (illness, class trips), the drop-off rate was nonetheless disappointing. In addition, lateness was a problem. Assignments were only sporadically completed, despite many reminders. Time did not allow sufficient supervision of assignments and thus we felt that participants were getting useful information about skills, such as observing children critically, but little experience in practicing them.

In planning for a second in-service seminar, the core of this preliminary series will be maintained. In accordance with participant request, greater stress will be placed on the child and less on the family, parents, and interviewing skills. However, it is felt that, whereas participants may not see the extent of relevance of these areas of information, this is material that inner-city Get Set personnel working with high-risk children should become familiar with and utilize. We believe that the child's school and life adjustment, as well as the parents' personal and educational growth, will be enhanced by a more secure, multi-dimensional liaison between school and family. Hence, material on families, parents, and interviewing will not be dropped. The plan is to stress less formal aspects of involvement with the child's family rather than planned interviews. Methods of interacting with a child's parents when they bring the child to school or attend a meeting will be presented, stressing positive, warm, and supportive interactional techniques. In addition, means to gain useful information about the family will be discussed to better help the child.

In an effort to solve the problem of low attendance, participants not holding the bachelors' degree will be given credits toward certification leading to higher pay, with attendance and completion of assignments as criteria for credit. Ten weekly sessions will be held in small groups, with one leader for each 10 to 15 persons, so that closeness, continuity, and greater individual contact with the leader may be enhanced. The first five sessions will be a presentation of a condensation of the didatic materials discussed in this chapter and altered in the fashions described herein. Emphasis in the second five sessions will be placed on the participants' practice of skills in observing and evaluating children, discriminating the well-functioning from the problematic, responding sensitively to other people's emotional needs, and working with groups of parents. They will also receive close supervision from their seminar leader on the practice of these skills. Research dimensions are planned to more objectively evaluate changes in participants' attitudes and in observed child behavior as a result of the in-service.

Conclusions

We have described a promising, efficient consultation program for persons working with young children. A large number of teachers, social workers, and supervisory personnel, who have responsibility for the care of nearly 1000 inner-city, high-risk, preschool children, received training in the theory and practice of promoting mental health. This effort maximized the use of the consultants' skills and time to provide a preventive program. This was accomplished through a collaborative effort of a child guidance clinic and a public educational institution reaching out to the surrounding community. The program was very well received by the participants, and present evaluation indicates that it

is potentially an effective model for training and consultation.
Further use, evaluation, and refinement of this model is planned.

References

1. Ackerman, N. W. *Psychodynamics of Family Life*. Basic Books, New York, 1958.
2. Bennett, C. C. chairman. *Community Psychology: A Report of the Boston Conference on the Education of Psychologists for Community Mental Health*. Boston, Mass., 1966.
3. Blackman, G. and Silberman, A. *Modification in Child Behavior*. Wadsworth Publishing Co., Belmont, Calif., 1971.
4. Caplan, G. *An Approach to Community Mental Health*. Grune and Stratton, New York, 1961.
5. Erikson, E. H. *Childhood and Society*. Norton, New York, 1963.
6. Fraiberg, S. H. *The Magic Years*. Charles Scribner's Sons, New York, 1959.
7. Freud, A. *Normality and Pathology in Childhood*. International Universities Press, New York, 1965.
8. Goldfarb, W. *Childhood Schizophrenia*. The Commonwealth Fund, Cambridge, Mass., 1961.
9. Grinstein, A. and Sterba, E. *Understanding Your Family*. Random House, New York, 1957.
10. Isaacs, S. *The Nursery Years*. The Vanguard Press, New York, 1968.
11. Jackson, D. *Therapy, Communication and Change*. Science and Behavior Books, Palo Alto, Calif., 1968.
12. Josselyn, I. M. *Psychosocial Development of the Child*. Family Service Association of America, New York, 1948.
13. Maier, H. W. *Three Theories of Child Development*. Harper and Row, New York, 1965.
14. Millon, T. *Theories of Psychopathology*. Saunders, Philadelphia, 1967.
15. Minuchin, S. *Families of the Slums*. Basic Books, New York, 1967.
16. Moelis, I. Psychoanalytic concepts of children's play. Unpublished paper presented to the staff of Irving Schwartz Institute for Children and Youth, Philadelphia, Pa., March 25, 1968.
17. Parker, B. Analysis of in-service training sessions with nursery school personnel. In *Mental Health In-Service Training: Some Practical Guidelines for the Psychiatric Consultant,* International Universities Press, New York, 1968, Beulah Parker (Ed.)
18. Peller, L. E. Libidinal phases, ego development and play. *Psychoan. Study Child,* 9 (1954), 178–198.
19. Piaget, J. *Origins of Intelligence in Children*. International Universities Press, New York, 1952.
20. Rimland, B. *Infantile Autism*. Appleton-Century-Crofts, New York, 1964.
21. Satir, V. *Conjoint Family Therapy*. Science and Behavior Books, Palo Alto, Calif., 1967.
22. Senn, M., and Solnit, A. *Problems in Child Behavior and Development*. Lea and Febiger, Philadelphia, 1968.
23. Signell, K. Kindergarten entry: a preventive approach to community mental health. *Community Ment. Health J.,* 8 (1972), 60–70.

24. Slaughter, S. S. *The Mentally Retarded Child and His Parents.* Harper & Brothers, New York, 1960.
25. Tobiessen, J. and Shai, A. A comparison of individual and group mental health consultation with teachers. *Community Ment. Health J.,* 7 (1971), 218–226.

A Compensatory Community Environment for the Culturally Disadvantaged Child*

Eva Rosenfeld, Ph.D. (Israel), and Lea Baider, Ph.D. (U.S.A.)

The aim of this chapter is to describe a community-based compensatory social environment for culturally disadvantaged children. The program was designed to first provide the missing facilitating experiences needed to develop basic ego capacities necessary to negotiate successfully the first grades in school and then to explore ways for fostering continued intellectual growth. The first, preventive, aim has been achieved, and we describe here the changes that took place in the children and the particular features of the program that appear to be both necessary and sufficient to bring these changes about. The second aim is much more difficult, and we have had less time to explore ways and means; however, we have some basis for raising a number of questions, both theoretical and concerning a strategy of social intervention.

The Population

The population for whom the program has been designed are the numerically dominant but socioeconomically and culturally

*The program reported in this chapter is the Community Education Program in South Talpiot, Jerusalem, which is under the auspices of the Jerusalem Department of Education. Funding has been provided by the Municipality of Jerusalem, The Israeli Ministry of Education, and the Jerusalem Foundation.

disadvantaged Jews who immigrated to Israel in the 1950s and early 1960s from the Arab countries of North Africa (predominantly Morocco) and Asia (predominantly Iraq) and whose absorption into the dynamic, modern Israeli society, dominated by earlier immigrants from European countries, has been relatively slow, generating a "social gap" that is of great concern to all Israelis.

The Afro-Asian families are not only in transition from a stable, preindustrial society to a dynamic modern society, but also in transition from a system of beliefs, a world view and a concept of man strongly influenced by Moslem fatalism, a view of man as helpless and family loyalty overriding individual aspirations [6, 9]. In Israel, normal difficulties of absorption and acculturation have been exacerbated by protracted dependency on a very complex and often incomprehensible bureaucratic network of many new social agencies. This has served to delay orientation in and mastery of the new social environment; rather, it has encouraged dependence on an often poorly defined and unpredictable authority. Frustrated and disoriented people turn to manipulation, cajoling, and physical force or threats to obtain arbitrarily defined benefits. The men, used to be in authority and to dealing with a familiar world of small-town power structures, had to reorient themselves to the new environment and often found the difficulties overwhelming; many experienced a loss of self-confidence and loss of face in the family. The women, on the other hand, whose homemaking role remained relatively unchanged, suffered less of the shock of transition; they learned to cope quite effectively with the daily tasks in the new environment.

Conceptualization

SOURCES AND DATA

Our approach to social intervention with this population is conceptualized in two interrelated models, which list: (1) the behavioral manifestations of basic ego and cognitive structures or *capacities* necessary for "school readiness" and (2) the *facilitating conditions* posited by psychoanalytic ego psychology and Piaget's cognitive theory as necessary for the development of these capacities. This conceptualization has been initially derived from a review of literature on cognitive development and cognitive re-tardation in general and of the available literature on the families and children of Afro-Asian immigrants in Israel [11]. It has been sharpened, revised, and expanded as our direct contact and famil-iarity with this population increased. Observations of children have been made in nursery schools, kindergartens, and elemen-tary schools, and interviews have been conducted with dozens of nurses and teachers [12]. Since the establishment of our program in August 1974 we have become increasingly familiar with the children who attend our after-school club and with their families. Home visits and interviews have been made with 40 mothers [2]. The behavior of the children in the club has been recorded dur-ing weekly staff meetings and summarized in monthly progress reports during 1975 and 1976. Changes in the behavior of eight children with whom a home tutor worked individually have been systematically recorded and analyzed [13]. The present form of the two conceptual models makes no claim to completeness in theoretical terms. We have included, however, all items that ap-pear relevant in our population. (see Table 1).

These two models are an integral part of our work with the children, their families, and their community environment. The model for behavioral manifestations of the major intrapsychic capacities serves to describe the children's initial profile, to note significant changes, and to establish criteria of successful outcome. The model of the facilitating environment serves to assess what is actually missing in the child's experience, to define our program in terms of the particular compensatory experiences that we con-sidered most essential to provide, and to focus our attention on the strategy, methods, and conditions essential for providing these experiences effectively.

ASSESSMENT OF CHILD'S EXPERIENCE AT HOME AND IN SCHOOL

Using the model of facilitating conditions as a guide, we note that only two appear to be present: (1) most families do provide good and loving care in infancy and good physical care later on and (2) most families provide stability, both of residence and by the pre-sence of an extended family network. But all the remaining condi-tions are either inadequate or missing altogether. This must be seen in the perspective of the parents' recent history. As we have

Table 1 Conceptual Framework for Basic Ego Capacities

A Model of Behavioral Manifestations of Intrapsychic Capacities in Young School Children	Model of a Facilitating Environment	
	Minimal Conditions, Sufficient for a Traditional Society	Optimal Conditions for a Modern Society
Interpersonal relations		
Has trustful attitude toward adults	Tender, loving care in infancy	Stimulation of social reflex
Can form attachments	Role assignment and recognition for grow- ing children	Response to baby's social initiatives
Attachments are stable	Stability of immediate environment	Development of empathy and self- awareness
Can express his needs clearly		Verbalization of feelings
Makes reasonable demands		Responsiveness to child's changing needs
Can express range of feelings		
Can stand up for himself		
Internalized controls		
Control of sexual impulses	Respect for child's body integrity	Democratic discipline: explanation of limits and norms
Control of aggressive impulses	Tolerable discipline and punishments	Verbal mediation of conflicts
Can wait, delay gratification, and	Comprehensible limits	

tolerate reasonable frustration
Can accept reasonable limits and directives
Can discharge tension in constructive ways
Can express anger in constructive ways

Competence and industry
Concept of self as good, lovable, and capable
Intrinsic motivation to explore, innovate, comprehend, solve problems, and create
Can persist in task despite difficulties
Enjoys working and playing
Takes pride in job well done

Possibility of reconciliation after rupture
Consistent models of social behavior

Encouragement of independence
Opportunities for interaction with physical environment

Interpretation of the larger social order, its values and goals
Integrity and consistency of adult behavior with respect to democratic values, fairness, and equality

Responsiveness to child's exploratory excitement
"Going into the world together," sharing experiences
Respect for child's productions
Appreciation of child's ideas, originality, initiative
Absence of pressure to achieve
Availability of help when child requests it

623

noted, most of the women are coping quite effectively with the daily homemaking tasks. However, their capacity for creating and sustaining structure in their families is very limited. Many of the mothers in our community have married very early (at 15 or 16) and, having begun childbearing immediately, carried a heavy burden of responsibilities before having had a chance to experience themselves as separate individuals. Many of them remained relatively undifferentiated. They tend to relate to their children in primitive, physical, and material ways; they do not know how to encourage separation and independence, nor how to relate emotionally to a growing child's changing needs. Infants are cuddled and often held by mothers or older siblings. However, there is very little eye contact, very little stimulation of social reflex, and the mothers repel the baby's attempts to explore their face. Infants appear placid, passive, slow to respond to a smile; they observe the world but do not reach out. When the baby begins to locomote and explore, the mothers become irritable, helpless, constricting the baby's movements, slapping him for being "naughty" and wanting to "touch and get into everything." Older children are asked to give in to the youngest when he screams for some object, even if it is the older child's precious possession. Thus each child becomes "dethroned" when the youngest begins to locomote. With all their children, the little ones and the bigger ones, the mothers are obsessed by a need to control, but their capacity for discipline is limited; their demands are arbitrary and inconsistent, and they give in when they tire of the child's whining or tantrums. Very few of the women are capable of establishing and maintaining a structure in the family, such as setting fixed times for meals, assigning age-appropriate tasks for each child, and providing a minimal amount of private space for each child. Feeding on demand continues into adulthood, and the child is very seldom asked to wait. Socialization consists primarily of telling the child that this or that is forbidden. Punishments include severe beatings and threats of abandonment and bodily harm. Rewards are primarily in the form of sweets or money for sweets. Children learn codes of social behavior primarily by imitation of peers outside the home. Adults do not seem to have much interest in children; they do not respond to their excitement, their humor or cleverness and do not seem to wish to share experiences together—to "go into the world together."

To complete the children's home environment, one must include the street environment, with its opportunities for stimulation and exploration and for play with peers. The Israeli climate permits street play uninterruptedly from April to November and frequently during the rainy season when the days are warm and sunny. Toddlers, from the age of 2 or 3, spend many hours daily in front of their homes under the care of older sisters or brothers. The younger children are shy at first and mainly observe what is going on. But from the age of 3 or 4, the small children take an active part in all the excitements of peer-group life and try to imitate the older children in whatever they do. There is much peer contact, fights and tears, and excitement. Here are the compensations for maternal constriction of the small child at home. The cognitive elaborations may be lacking, but the child has plenty of opportunities to see, hear, manipulate objects with his hands, run, jump, climb trees, play with stray cats and dogs, and observe the social scene—the strong and the weak, the manipulators and the victims, the boy-girl encounters. Not much of this experience will be used in kindergarten as the basis for cognitive training, and hardly any will be used in grade school.

Nursery and kindergarten experience exacerbates in some ways the failures of the home environment. The heavy emphasis on "school readiness" forces the teacher to turn her attention away from the child's present needs and interests and to teach, mechanically and sometimes desperately, certain subsidiary cognitive skills and concepts that are not as yet a part of the child's daily living experience in his autonomous acting-on-the-environment. The insistence on teaching skills and concepts "because they will need it in school" violates the child's integrity and often leads to a sullen antagonism against all teacher-pupil encounters.

THE CHILDREN'S BEHAVIOR

The children's perception of adults reflects their experience. As one would expect, they see adults as basically uninterested in their feelings and ideas, basically ungiving, inconsistent and arbitrary, intrusive and coercive. This view was revealed indirectly by contrast with the thoughtful comments made spontaneously by some of the children in our program about their home tutor and what is "special" about her: "You let me think for myself . . . you want me to do what I want . . . you understand what I feel . . . you keep your promises." More direct indicators can be found in their behavior toward adults in unstructured situations. Most of the children observed in the highly structured classroom situations in kindergartens and schools were obedient, constricted, passive, trying hard to please the teacher. Most of the Afro-Asian children are seen by teachers as poor thinkers, poor students, dull, sluggish, and uncreative. They have difficulty in grasping abstract concepts and in expressing their thoughts in writing. Their learning difficulties increase with each grade, as do the behavior problems. Children with severe behavior problems are transferred to special schools. But even the "good" children are tense, restless, and inattentive during lessons. They have "stopped being involved in the learning process." On the positive side, many teachers see the children as "sweet," generous, quick to identify with the weak, very willing to please the teacher, and very grateful and responsive; they make the motherly teachers feel appreciated in their nurturing role.

When our club was opened, the children (then aged 6 to 11) seemed to be flooded by tension. They seemed unable to grasp what sort of people we were. The workers' interest and friendliness evoked primitive expressions of dependency cravings; they touched and pinched us, "glued" their bodies to ours, and talked incessantly without any apparent expectation of response. They did not really listen to what we were saying to them. Some of the children had a seemingly irrepressible urge to tease and provoke us, and they observed our reactions with anxious excitement. They tended to become easily offended and would then stalk off with tears of rage and threats, "I will destroy the club and everything in it." Their attendance was very irregular; they came and went and forgot the days and hours during which the club was open. They did not trust us, did not believe that we would really come back; for months, they asked every time if every worker would come. They were watchful of each other to make sure that they got exactly the same amount of supplies and attention. They also tried to obtain more supplies by a variety of surreptitious, manipulative devices.

Their capacity for impulse control, delay of gratification, frustration, and tolerance was severely limited; they trembled with the intensity of their desires. They were in an almost constant state of war with each other, cursing, destroying each other's work, and fighting savagely.

Their work and play were marred by intense motoric tension and avoidance of reflection in favor of trial-and-error. They did not want to be helped to figure things out and absolutely refused to think ahead, plan, or figure out the best strategy. They trusted their intuition, but not their head; they did things "from the heart" (as one 7-year-old told us). They did not want to know the principle involved in the solution of a problem; they did it, and that was enough. They had a strong "thought aversion." They had no specific curiosity; they enjoyed variety and novelty in a sensuous way, in the here and now. They did not ask questions about the things they saw and if asked to explain apparent incongruities, gave superficial, nonrational answers. The only questions they asked were personal ones, about the worker's family, her origin, and her clothes.

In the light of their home and preschool experience, the children's interpersonal behavior is fully comprehensible. The demandingness and manipulativeness, the rivalry with peers and outbursts of rage express the "dethroned" child's attempts to regain the position of the favored youngest child and to recapture the brief experience of omnipotence. The vigor of their attempts suggests that some encouragement must be given to their hopes. The lack of time schedules at home, the continued on-demand feeding, and the mothers' inability to set and sustain clear and consistent norms, limits, and discipline, can be seen as such encouragement to the child's hopes. The fluid interpersonal situation could be cognitively mastered, keeping the child in a state of constant tension, interfering with internalization of controls, and absorbing the child's emotional energy and intellectual curiosity. Tension is discharged into motoric activity; this interferes with reflection and thoughtful action, which require delay of discharge in the service of the ego.

The Program

AIMS AND METHODS

Our program has been designed to provide, in the community and on a continuous basis, a compensatory subenvironment in which children from an early age (ideally from age 3) might obtain those essential facilitating experiences that are missing in their home, street, and school environments. In the first preventive stage, the program aims at the development of basic ego capacities necessary for a successful absorption of the child in the school system. The compensatory environment is provided in an after-school club where small groups of about 10 children aged 5 to 8 meet with a group worker three times a week throughout the year. The second stage begins when our 9-year-old children "graduate" after 4 years in the club; they are given free use of one of the rooms in the club and are provided with a variety of experiences that are likely to foster continued intellectual growth.

The first stage of the program can be described in terms of three major concerns. First and foremost, we create conditions conducive to the formation of *trust and attachment* between the children and their worker, as well as among the children. The club consists of a row of five smallish rooms in a dingy air-raid shelter in the community. The dinginess is an asset. Each group of children of the same age has its own room, which belongs only to them and which they are free to mess up, clean, decorate, and paint. The room is the children's own territory. The group workers are carefully selected and trained on the job; most of them are students, but some have just completed army training and have not begun higher education. Weekly staff meetings provide ample time to discuss any problems that may arise and to clarify our aims and methods. The more experienced workers take active part in helping new members of the staff [1]. Most of the workers stay for about a year. Change of workers does not appear to upset the children any longer, although they were very upset when their first workers left. The children form attachments easily with new workers but remember the old ones who keep in touch and come to visit, telephone, and write.

The program's second concern is to compensate the children

for their mothers' lack of *interest in them as unique individuals* and for being used by teachers as receptacles for future goals. Our workers are liberated from the task of teaching. They are only interested in the child, his feelings and ideas, and, as far as possible, they follow the child's wishes and choices. The wide range of activities—handwork, games, play, walks, and so on—are used as means toward creating child-oriented situations in which the worker uses the activity to engage the children in conversation about what is being done and introduces into the conversation, informally and spontaneously, new concepts, new awareness and understanding—stimulating curiosity, encouraging imagination, and developing a capacity for reasoning—but all this without pressure of any sort. Like the "good" mother observed by White [14], the group worker informs, explains, and interprets in the context of normal daily activities by responding to the child's interests and needs and by entering into the child's experience in a relationship of mutuality. Whereas the workers are trained to recognize the special needs of each age group and the cognitive skills that can be expected at each age level and to keep in mind the "key experiences" of basic intellectual processes [3], this awareness remains in the back of their minds as they plan activities and carry on conversations; they do not "teach" specific concepts or skills in a fragmented or piecemeal way.

Our third concern is to help the children *internalize* basic norms of conduct, develop impulse control and capacity to abide by limits, become aware of needs, feelings, and motives (their own and others'), and thus to reduce the level of tension that is generated by the incomprehensibility of interpersonal relations. The structure we provide is interpersonal, not external. The children are free to come and go as they please, do what they want as long as they don't bother other children, initiate their own activities, and, in general, "do their own thing." But they also know exactly what the basic rules and limits are and what they can expect of their worker if they should break them. Since some of our children have a strong need to force the adult to give in—by threats, pleading, cajoling, or manipulation—it is very important that the worker combine explanation of the reasons for the limits with firmness, that she stay in contact with the transgressing child even when the child has to be temporarily removed from the club, and that the rupture of contact caused by the child's anger is followed by reconciliation-made-easy.

THE DELIVERY SYSTEM

The location of the program in the community, the gradual addition of ancillary services, and the establishment of a network of personal contacts between our staff and teachers, social workers, nurses, police, and probation officers serving our area—are all features of our delivery system intended to intensify the impact of the club on the community, to assure continuity of contact with the children, their families, and the peer society, and to increase the comprehensiveness of our preventive efforts.

The club is in full view of the families and within the "turf" of the peer society. The arrival of the workers and the way they are greeted by the children and respond to their excited accounts of events are carefully observed by mothers leaning out of the windows and older brothers and sisters. The workers' obvious interest in the children's conversation and the manner in which they handle the frequent outbreaks of aggressiveness in the open area provide a model of child-adult interactions. Toddlers wandering in the area become familiar with the club. When they join, they already have certain expectations; they know that they are free to come and go, can demand explanations, insist on their rights, express their anger, and expect to be listened to. The club has become a clearly defined environment in which the children are well oriented and comfortable. The staff know each child's home situation and visit homes when the child is sick. The location of the program in the community assures continuity of contact with the children throughout the ups and downs of conflict and rage, when the child takes offense and stalks off or is being asked to get out to cool off—all the usual forms of rupture of contact. Yet, whatever has happened, we will see the child the next time and can pave the way to reconciliation without loss of face and without giving in on basic values and norms. These breaks and reconciliations are known and visible to all; the children are interested in our fairness and watchful of our consistency and reasoning.

The community is also the strategic arena for the coordination of the various services. We are within short walking distance from the kindergarten and school. We have frequent meetings with teachers and the school psychologist, watching over the children's progress at entry into first grade and taking part in decisions to refer some children for diagnostic assessment or to provide remedial tutoring. Faced with special needs of some of the children, we have added two important services. One is a *home tutor* for those children in our club who have difficulty in establishing contact with their group worker and have problems that require individual attention. The other, soon to be implemented, is a pair of *workers for a predelinquent group* of older boys and girls (aged 10 to 13) who have not attended our club (or have been asked to leave after a brief experience). These workers will be supervised by a highly skilled clinician. We hope to establish contacts with agencies providing rehabilitation, work, probation, alternative training opportunities, and other resources, so as to build around these workers a comprehensive outreach model. Finally, we have made several attempts to establish a meaningful contact with the parents of our children. Our efforts have so far not been successful, but we intend to try again in the near future.

Results

We report first the changes in young school children, reflecting our first aim of fostering basic ego capacities. Following this, we describe our efforts to foster continued intellectual growth among our "graduates."

CHANGES REFLECTING EGO DEVELOPMENT

The baseline behavior profile of the 5-year-olds who have joined our club in the last 2 years differs from the initial behavior of children who joined the club when we first opened. These new members are already familiar with the club and its atmosphere, staff, activities, and rules, since almost all of them have older siblings in the club and have had occasion to visit and observe. Thus they do not experience the shock of novelty, only the excitement of finally being admitted, having a room of their own, a group worker, toys, and opportunities for all sorts of activities. Some are a bit shy and some are overdemanding, but there is little, if any, teasing and provoking, which so plagued us at the beginning. The children express their wishes clearly, their requests are reasonable, and they demand to know the reasons for our refusal. They delight in grasping the few routines of clean-up, borrowing books at the end of the day, and the like. All new children are tense, however; they often go out and come back, becoming "bored" and asking for another toy or activity, as they are too restless to persist in any activity and are very distractable. As a rule, a few children in a new group of 10 are extremely shy, passive, and uncommunicative; one or two are overdemanding, quarrelsome, aggressive, envious, and weepy, demanding whatever toy another child is using. The shy children are given time to become oriented and are left alone with their toy, with only an occasional glance or smile from the worker. Within 1 to 2 weeks, they relax and become more active. The aggressive-demanding children usually respond well to individual attention and friendliness. A sensitive group worker can be expected to establish contact and, within a couple of months, achieve periods of quiet, pleasurable group activity. Nearly all children are very responsive to warmth and individual attention; those who are not have severe problems at home and require individual work. The following report on changes focuses first on overall group behavior and then on changes in individuals, some of whom were given a home tutor.

Group Behavior   The children have a strong sense of proprietorship in the club. On two occasions, on a day when the club was closed, the door opened due to a faulty lock. Some children stood guard at the door to prevent looting by nonmembers while others phoned the director to "come quick." They take care of their equipment and enjoy cleaning up their rooms, although there are some who don't like to clean up and some who try to sneak out paper, crayons, or pretty pieces of a game; they are usually observed by other children who run to tell the worker.

The children's behavior toward the staff and the director is free and spontaneous. They ask for help or favors easily, but most of them prefer to work independently. They accept without fussing the worker's requests to wait. Their demands are reasonable; they know what can and cannot be allowed or given. They express anger freely and sometimes walk out in a pique, but are ready to listen to explanations and allow themselves to be coaxed back. They call on the worker to intervene when bothered by another child, although sometimes they prefer to settle the conflict on their own by fighting it out.

They are usually friendly with each other and enjoy playing and working together. But some children dislike each other, and a few have a tendency to tease and provoke peers. Occasional outbursts of rage and fights become less frequent as the children grow older. The "graduates" occasionally quarrel but do not hit out; they do, occasionally, hit smaller children.

They have learned to accept our basic rules, prohibitions, and discipline. They take their punishments without protest and return after brief banishment without resentment. They do not plead to be spared because they know that it will not help; they accept the consequences of their actions. This is in stark contrast to the behavior of older children who have not attended our club; when their requests to "just come in and watch" or to borrow equipment such as hammers and saws are sometimes refused for good reasons clearly explained, they do not pay attention to what is being said and respond by saying: "So what? Never mind! But I want to . . ."—thus repeating with us the common pattern of persistent pleading with their parents, which in view of the parents' inconsistency and arbitrariness is often successful. Our children have also learned to accept delay, such as postponement of a promised trip, with good grace as long as the reasons are clearly explained. They are usually asked to share in decisions, and their preferences are sensible. Some have learned how to express their occasional "nervousness" and tension in constructive ways. They ask the worker to set up a wrestling match, or they take to the punching bag or wander off to another room where the mood is quiet and the worker is friendly, and they join the group in their activity or ask for a game to play by themselves.

Changes in autonomous achievement striving are less unequivocal. All children are highly motivated to please the adult and to receive praise for their work. They enjoy working with their hands and can persist in a task for the time of the meeting (2 hours), often pleading to stay and go on with the unfinished task. They are creative in their work and love building things. They like having their work displayed (they used to take their drawings home even though they knew that the mother would immediately throw it out). The atmosphere during work is usually relaxed and pleasant. However, their interest is short-lived; they very seldom wish to continue the same activity and cannot be induced to carry out a series of activities that will lead to a completed project, such as making a model of a town or a doll's house. They have an intense investment in the here and now; next week does not seem real. Their aversion to intellectual effort remains unchanged. Although they talk a lot, easily and clearly, can tell imaginary stories and relate real events in a sensible sequence and with a comprehensible point to the story, they are not reflective and do not ask questions, except to inquire into personal background of the workers or to explain simple mechanics. They "tune out" the worker's attempt to convey a more general idea; it appears useless to them, and they have no patience. Only on a very few occasions did the children (in a group of 6- and 7-year-olds) listen attentively and "take in" the worker's effort to explain and interpret a situation in general terms—and that happened when the children experienced deeply conflicting emotions (e.g., death of the duck in Peter and the Wolf) and the worker, herself deeply involved in the children's reaction, tried to make the event comprehensible.

Changes in Individuals. Some of the children with serious behavior problems—either extreme constriction or destructive acting-out—have improved over the years slowly, with many ups and downs, oscillating from one extreme to the other. They are now in our group of graduates, fully in control of their impulses, active, responsible, attending regularly and utilizing every opportunity for new experience. The process of change in these children paralleled the growing trust and deepening attachment to their worker and to the director, which allowed for free expression of rage as well as dependency needs, open confrontation of wills, and rupture of contact with confidence in an impending reconciliation. The children did not verbalize what they felt and had little patience with our attempts to explain what we thought was going on between us. Only sometimes, a phrase seemed to "click," as, for example, saying to a boy after his rage had been successfully directed by the worker to building something, "You see, you do have a choice when you become 'nervous'; you can destroy or you can build." This idea pleased him, and he repeated it excitedly. But most of the dramatic encounters that marked the process of gradual change were experienced by the children, obviously deeply, but without conscious awareness and with an active shrinking from any verbal clarification.

Eight children, most of them in the second grade, were provided with a home tutor for periods ranging from 4 months to 1½ years. Changes in the behavior of these children were carefully recorded at the end of every session (once or twice a week) and analyzed according to the model of behavioral manifestations of basic ego capacities [13]. The tutor provided facilitating experiences similar to those available in the club but modified to suit the face-to-face situation; some of the children were helped with learning difficulties that they themselves were eager to overcome. Significant changes took place in three of the children. In two cases, work is still continuing. In three cases, the home tutor could not establish contact with the child nor with the family.

A comparison of the families who were responsive to the home tutor and changed significantly with those who were unresponsive suggests that the mothers in the "unresponsive" group had not been able to provide loving care even in infancy. The family system was severely pathological—unstable, broken, confused, or paranoid—generating malevolent coalitions that trapped the child into a pathologic adaptation that was constantly reinforced by dominant members of the family. The children were too young and vulnerable to ally themselves with the facilitating adult, and we, too, were extremely sensitive to the danger of disturbing whatever pathologic equilibrium existed in these families. These were hard-core cases that are beyond the scope of any community intervention and, unhappily, often beyond the scope of existing welfare and mental health services.

The families of "responsive" children were able to let the child form a relationship with the home tutor and to tolerate greater maturity and independence in the child. Four of the mothers were not interested in establishing contact with the tutor. Only one mother, a self-pitying widow, used the opportunity to establish contact for her own sake; in this family, the home tutor succeeded in changing previous coalitions that had trapped the child (a 7-year-old boy) in the role of scapegoat, to a positive alliance between mother and son, which benefited both and helped curb destructive interference by an older daughter.

In summary, these results confirm, we believe, our strategy of intervention. A compensatory subenvironment available in the community on a continuous basis to children from the age of 5 (ideally, from age 3) can modify the children's initial negative view of adults to that of benevolent, trustworthy adults who are interested in each child as an individual, respect his autonomy, delight in his creativity, and also have firm convictions about certain values and norms of social behavior. Changes in the children's interpersonal behavior are paralleled by increased self-control based on imitation, identification, and internalization of our values and a sense of self as important, valued, and capable—thus providing the necessary foundation for a successful negotiation of the first three grades in school. Most of our children are doing well in school, and some are very good students. Obviously, we cannot claim that the children's school performance is due to the changes in their ego development. (We have not yet succeeded in obtaining funds for an outcome-evaluation study.) But the *process* of change in their interpersonal relationships, impulse control, and autonomous work is clearly related to the compensatory experiences they have been provided with in the club.

CONTINUED INTELLECTUAL GROWTH

Ever since we have brought up our first group of "graduates"—9 to 11-year-old children now in fourth and fifth grades, who had been attending our club for 3 years—we have been concerned about their continued intellectual development. We did expect that as they grew older their interests would expand in range and depth. But, although they attend regularly and enjoy every opportunity for new activity or experience, their interests still remain short-lived; they'd rather start a new activity than pursue the previous one, and they continue to work quickly and sloppily, solving problems intuitively rather than deductively. Their aversion to thought continues; they are too impatient to stop and think and are not interested in learning the underlying principle of their intuitive solutions. They aim not at perfection, but at speed of completion. They are still relating primarily to the personal achievement aspect of the task and resist any pooling of efforts for a cooperative venture. (The only exception is preparation for festivities and parties, which evokes a spirit of sharing.)

Our aspirations for the children are focused not so much on scholastic achievements as on intrinsically motivated interest and pleasure in solving problems by reasoning and an eventual commitment to intellectual mastery of a subject matter. Since we are not sure what the reasons are for their continued reluctance to use their minds, we felt impelled to review all known variables that are likely to foster or impede those personality traits associated with intrinsic motivation to learn; we could then try to provide those experiences that we know are missing in the children's natural environment. The relevant personality traits and the facilitating conditions are listed in Table 2.

All the personality traits listed here are associated, in Piaget's theory, with the operational stage of cognitive development; more specifically, they are contingent on the attainment of decentration. But the connection between decentration and intrinsic motivation is by no means simple. The fact that an individual (child or adult) is capable of holding in mind two or more aspects of a situation, and carrying out mental operations that include them all, does not necessarily impel him to seek the connection or to reconcile incongruities by accommodating familiar schemas to newly perceived complexities. Students of intrinsic motivation have been investigating the complex process and noting the many shadows that may fall between perception and conception (cf. the series of papers in Day, Berlyne, et al. [5]). A person capable of recognizing incongruities may not be sufficiently observant to notice them. If he does notice them, he may not be disquieted sufficiently to need to reconcile them within an objectively valid system. Or he may have the need but, unsure of his intellectual skills, may be threatened by the difficulty and may prefer to deny or avoid unassimilable problems. There is some evidence that interest in complexity is not correlated with either IQ or school grades [4]. The need for closure—for perceiving order and meaning in life and in the world—may be satisfied by intuitive, emotional, artistic understanding, and not necessarily by objectively validated schemas. Some children who have not as yet attained

Table 2 Conceptual Framework for Fostering Intellectual Growth
on Operational Level

Personal Attributes Involved in Intrinsic Motivation to Learn on Operational Level[a]	Environmental Conditions that Foster Various Components of Intrinsic Motivation
Interest in the environment and capacity for observation	Adults or older peers acting as guides "going into the world together"
"Closure motivation": observed incongruities and dissonance generate disquiet and a need for a rational explanation	Educators who point out or "create" incongruities, raise questions, ignite curiosity, stimulate imagination, and generate intellectual excitement
Readiness to make the required intellectual effort; prerequisites:	
Proficiency in reasoning	Training in logical thinking: language, precision and clarity, rules of evidence
Feeling of competence in using one's mind	Experience in arguing with peers— consensual validation
Concept of self as a thinking actor	Social emphasis on individual autonomy and responsibility
Intrinsic pleasure in thinking	High value placed on thinking in the religious and/or secular value systems
Knowledge believed to have value as means to power, status, social advancement, satisfying occupations, and so on	Value of learning[b] as means towards desirable ends is demonstrable in society

[a] The capacity for decentration and capacity for delay of gratification are presupposed.
[b] The value of learning is conveyed to individuals via their social reference groups, models among adults, and older peers and visible rewards.

conservation have a reflective turn of mind and ask questions about incongruous facts (two of our 8-year-olds are such children).

The same investigators have been exploring environmental conditions that facilitate (arouse and sustain) specific curiosity and a commitment to learning. Quite a few of these deal with the "match" between the stimulus and the individual's interests, capacities, and values. The role of emotions in the learning process has been convincingly argued by Jones [8]. Social scientists note the relevance of value systems (religious and secular, intrinsic and utilitarian), the image of man in the culture, and the availability of models, opportunities, and rewards in the social system—to the level of interest in intellectual pursuits.

The two models presented in Table 2 are, as the ones in Table 1, incomplete and theoretically eclectic. Our main concern was to include all variables that appear relevant in our population.

The behavior of our graduates, described in the preceding paragraphs, reflects an absence of all the essential traits of an intrinsically motivated individual. We cannot say what are the precise reasons for the reluctance to use their intellectual capacities. But when we examine their environment, we note that none of the facilitating conditions listed in the chart are present. The *value of independent thought* is not stressed in the religious convictions of the Afro-Asian Jews; they approach the Bible with passionate love expressed in faithful recitation of memorized passages, akin to the Muslim's approach to the Koran [9]. This is in sharp contrast to the mainstream of Judaic (Ashkenazi and Sephardic) system of values, which commands Jews to arrive at an understanding of the Bible through questioning and study of various scholarly interpretations and to accept God only out of personal conviction. We have already noted in describing our population the prevalent image of man as totally dependent on fate, the deprecation of the power of reasoning and of the exercise of will, the un-self-consciousness, and externalization of wishes and ideas—which reflect the many centuries of life in close proximity to Muslim neighbors [10]. The parents of our children show little interest in the child's questions, reflective comments, and original ideas [2]. Neither are the kindergartens and schools geared to develop intrinsic motivation to learn; like in most schools everywhere, the emphasis is on acquisition of specific skills and facts. None of the schools attended by our children have introduced modern self-discovery methods, small-group study, and independent work. Neither do the people in our community perceive intellectual effort, study, and learning as a demonstrable *means* to social and economic advancement or to satisfaction in life. Although in the country as a whole, the proportion of Afro-Asians attending universities and higher technical schools is slowly but constantly increasing, there is not a single boy or girl in our community who attends the university or technical college or even a first-rate high school. Two local girls attend a good vocational high school, and they are the exception. The peer society in our neighborhood is provincial, culturally inbred. They are not familiar with the norms, procedures, and criteria that govern access to higher education.

What can we provide in our limited subenvironment in the community? For one thing, we can make it clear in our contacts with the graduates that we *expect* them to develop their talents and interests and that we are ready to help. Two talented boys have been enrolled at the prestigious youth wing of the Israel Art Museum; this gives them a great sense of status as well as pleasure. To create a situation that would help the children stick to a subject, develop competence, learn skills and be forced to think, we have brought in a biology student to organize a nature club. We are observing very carefully the children's response to this experience and are constantly modifying both the content and methods so as to lessen frustration and to allow each child to find a level that matches his readiness for independent work, acceptance of delay, and intellectual grasp. The children are fully aware of our interest in their intellectual progress. We invited the two high-school students to visit the club and tell our graduates about their studies, about choice of careers, and about what it takes to get into a good high school. Our children seem to appreciate our concern. They are responsible, reliable, and eager to help with the little ones when a worker is absent. They respect their teacher in the nature club and are trying to control their impatience and to slow down so as to have a chance to think. They are doing it for our sake now; we hope that they will eventually acquire the "taste" and the intrinsic pleasure in thinking. They are teaching us how to help them become thinking actors. In another year or so we should be able to report results.

References

1. Baider, L. and Rosenfeld, E. Some aspects of the selection and training of group workers for after-school programs in culturally disadvantaged neighborhoods. *J. Jewish Communal. Serv.*, 53: 4 (1977), 345–355.
2. Baider, L. and Rosenfeld, E. The role of adolescence in the process of differentiation. Unpublished manuscript.
3. Banet, B. Toward a developmentally valid preschool curriculum. *High/Scope Educational Research Foundation Report, 1975–76*. Yipsilanti, Michigan.

4. Day, H. I. The measurement of specific curiosity. In Day, Berlyne, et al. [5].
5. Day, H. T., Berlyne, D. E., and Hunt, D. E., Eds. *Intrinsic Motivation: A New Direction in Education.* Holt, Rinehart and Winston of Canada, Toronto, 1971.
6. Geertz, C. *Islam Observed.* Univ. Chicago Press, Chicago, 1968.
7. Hunt, J. McV. *The Challenge of Incompetence and Poverty: Papers on the Role of Early Education.* Univ. Illinois Press, Urbana, 1969.
8. Jones, R. M. *Fantasy and Feeling in Education.* Penguin Books, New York, 1972.
9. Patai, R. *Tents of Jacob: The Diaspora—Yesterday and Today.* Prentice Hall, Englewood Cliffs, N.J., 1971.
10. Patai, R. *The Arab Mind.* Scribner & Sons, New York, 1973.
11. Rosenfeld, E. *A Strategy for Prevention of Developmental Retardation Among Disadvantaged Israeli Preschoolers.* The Henrietta Szold Institute, Research Report No. 175, Jerusalem, 1973.
12. Rosenfeld, E. First Progress Report on Community Education Program in South Talpiot. Unpublished manuscript.
13. Rosenfeld, E. and Baider, L. Accessibility of disadvantaged Afro-Asian families to varieties of social intervention. Paper read at the First International Symposium on the Child and his Family, under the auspices of the Research Center for Human Sciences, the Hebrew University, Jerusalem, August 17–18, 1977.
14. White, B. L. An analysis of excellent early educational practices: A preliminary Report. *Interchange*, 2: 2 (1971), 71–88.

The Vulnerable Child–in Retrospect

Albert J. Solnit, M.D. (U.S.A.)

In summing up what has been accomplished in this comparatively young field of vulnerability, I would claim that we have come encouragingly near to accomplishing some of the original aims that we set ourselves in the International Study Group four years ago. These included: (1) providing an inventory of our knowledge and the state of our art in this area, (2) Improving communication among the disciplines and across the cultural, geographic, and socioeconomic boundaries that separate us, (3) consolidating and clarifying our knowledge and understanding, (4) viewing critically the trends of our research, training, and service, and (5) formulating, as Piaget put it, "fresh paths to be explored or expected" in the future.

In preparing this summation I realized that I would have to try to present a useful sample since it was hardly possible to cover all aspects of the related scientific work. The field of concern seemed so extensive and with so many facets to it that I felt somewhat like Buckminster Fuller when he said, "How often I saw where I should be going only by setting out for something else." What I have selected to present understandably reflects my own experiences, preferences, priorities, expectations, and fantasies. I can only justify this to some extent by quoting Albert Einstein, who said, "Imagination is more important than knowledge."

Some Basic Concepts

In our approach to the theme of vulnerability (with its corollaries on risk and mastery), we have attempted to shift progressively from a small field of focus with a correspondingly large magnification of the child as an individual to the larger field of focus with a smaller magnification of the child in his family, in his school, and in his community. This outline was useful as a planning guide but not adhered to rigidly, and so, rather than follow the logical development of the different themes requested in this volume, I begin by examining the basic concepts underpinning the general theoretical and practical superstructure, hopefully revealing some of the pitfalls lying in the way of our efforts to understand children better, serve them better, and help others to understand and serve them more empathetically and effectively.

Vulnerability refers to actual and latent susceptibilities and weaknesses, immediate and delayed. This concept implies that there is an opposite tendency, that of invulnerability. Invulnerability can be viewed as strength, resiliency, and a capacity for resistance to stress, pressure, and potentially traumatic situations.

Risk refers to uncertainty about outcome when the child is challenged by environmental or internal stress. When there is great risk there is a likelihood of a disadvantageous outcome; when there is little risk there is likelihood of an advantageous outcome.

Mastery refers to the capacity to overcome (to be active in overcoming) a challenge from internal demands, environmental stresses, and conflicts between internal and environmental pressures. Adaptation is more reactive, and defense is most reactive. Mastery implies self-starting and self-directing capacities and behavior patterns. These basic concepts imply two large categories of assumptions: (1) that change, including growth and development, is inevitable and (2) that we have standards or criteria for what constitutes mental health.

First, change is inevitable. If it is not progressive and constructive, if it does not advance psychological resiliency and strength, it is most likely to be regressive and weakening. As Freud said, "Nothing is complete—we either go forward or backward."

Second, change always implies risk—there can be no psychological advance or improvement without risks. The question is whether the child can avoid or minimize the disadvantages of psychological risk, and with resiliency, take advantage of the opportunities for advancing development and increasing the capacity for mastery when change takes place.

Third, psychological risk is an overdetermined or multiply-determined condition reflecting the complexity of man interacting with his environment. Man is a social-psychological-physiological-anatomical being. We focus on one aspect or interphase for the purpose of discussion, but this is artificial and fractional, and we must bear this constantly in mind.

Criteria for Mental Health

Throughout this volume there is the implication that psychological or mental health is a state of being characterized by continuing development in which:

1. The individual's potential is maximized in the context of his family and community. Ordinarily there is a trend toward a balance between individual expression and the individual's contribution to his family, community, and society. Positive growth is indicated by the extent to which the potential of the individual has continued to unfold, by his continued adaptation to his surroundings, contributions to his community, and last but not least, by the progressive changes that he has brought about to the benefit of the next and successive generations.
2. Regressive behavior, when not pathologically extreme, provides a sort of moratorium (psychological rest and preparation) for the further unfolding of development and for the mobilization of inner resources to strengthen defensive and coping skills and bring into play the capacity for mastery. In contrast, regressive behavior that provokes destructive tendencies in the individual or group must be viewed as unhealthy.
3. Continuity of affectionate relationships between family members and between generations under conditions of mental health is viable and visible. Similarly, the continuity between different cultures and different historical epochs

can also be looked on as indices of constructive cultural and historical forces. Cultures and epochs are at risk of survival if isolated and unrelated. Furthermore, a sense of individual and group identity, promoting realistic self-esteem and respect for others, is also fostered by the process of continuity.

4. A community or society is capable of providing for "the best interests of the young child" by generating a health-promoting environment. In conceptualizing vulnerability in childhood, in her Foreword to this volume, Anna Freud summarized the criteria for healthy development as follows:

> I arrived at the conviction that vulnerability cannot be explained in terms of the qualities characterizing any individual child but has to be understood in more general and impersonal terms. I assume now that any child's forward move on developmental lines towards maturity depends on a number of favorable external influences to interact with favorable innate given and favorable internal structural advance. This means that all children born with normal potentialities also need sufficient bodily care, membership in an intact and welcoming family, affection and support on a continuing basis, ongoing stimulation of their intellectual capacities and opportunity for identification with parents who are themselves healthy members of a community.

Thus there can be no advance or improvement without risk. Those who avoid risk may forgo progression in the service of safety and security. By failing to exercise their powers of resiliency, they will be courting arrest or deviation of development.

Many of the chapters and discussions presented in this volume imply that when there is a "good enough" human environment, the child's strengths and healthy capacities are evoked, but that when there is a deficient or unbalanced milieu there is a tendency for vulnerabilities and weaknesses to be exposed.

What becomes increasingly clear is our difficulty in maintaining an awareness, simultaneously and serially, of all the variables that influence vulnerability and that play a role in determining the outcome of desirable and undesirable risks. There invariably appears to be an irresistable tendency to ask—is it nature or nurture; is it the child's inner psychic resources or his human social environment that determines whether he masters the risk or is weakened and set back by it? This was also clearly the dilemma in Volume III in this series (*Children at Psychiatric Risk*), where we considered the psychiatric risks to children in terms of their genetic endowment, constitutional characteristics, and early life experiences. It must be said again, as it was said then, that nature and nurture are always significantly represented, uniquely interwoven and inscribed in each child.

In the present volume, the pitfall of "either-or" thinking is still around to haunt us, chiefly because we also need in the interests of scientific clarity to focus, intensify, and converge on certain variables. Otherwise, we run into the opposite pitfall of "tunnel vision," namely, the problem of diffuseness and the inability to make reliable, valid comparisons.

The presentations express a stimulating awareness of the complex interacting patterns that are the outcome of intertwined genetic, experiential and cultural forces influencing each child and each group of children. We have tried to bring together our epidemiological concepts, genetic knowledge, and increased understanding of the infinite complemental combinations of endowment and living experiences.

Vulnerability, Environment, and Expectation

There is another pitfall that to some extent can be defined by an elaboration of Anthony's analogy of the three dolls, that is, the nonfacilitating environments in which the dolls are trapped. An example of this is when the milieu is so refrigerated and lacking in warmth that the inherent qualities are altered, making it difficult for even the doll of steel to emit a beautiful tone, or in the extreme case to be equally shattered as the glass doll.

The climate of human expectations also has a vital influence on the child's development and behavior. Expectations are both a suggestion and a demand of the human environment. The power of these expectations can become considerable in shaping the child and the family if the expectations are either positively or negatively realistic. If the expectations are unrealistic and beyond the child's capacity, then they either have little influence or a very negative one. Other qualities of expectations by parents, teachers, physicians, and others who form the human environment include the intensity and clarity of the expectations, their duration, their consistency or inconsistency, and the relative degree of support for the expectations in the child's environment. Of course, some expectations concentrate on intellectual and others on physical or social performance.

The viable alternative routes for achieving particular expectations are often a critical factor in determining the outcome of parental and paraparental anticipations and aspirations, and related to this is the child's awareness (or lack of it) of the options open to him. Other questions in the same context include as yet unresearched areas; for example, what does society provide to support or discourage family expectations? How do our research and technology influence expectations? And in what way do these forces alter the ethical and social value of our expectations? Behind all such expectations, anticipations, hopes, fears, and preparations looms the specter of the future; what kind of world are we preparing our children to cope with—peace or war? Feast or famine? International collaboration or national isolation? Acceptance of differences or mindless prejudice? All these considerations have a powerful conflicting impact on developing children, whether in Europe, Asia, America, or the antipodes. Bringing up children well is not necessarily the same as preparing them for life. The two must be related to each other.

Body and Mind in Vulnerability

There are several papers in which the physical and psychological aspects of vulnerability are considered together and not separately: (1) infant nutrition and infant mental health, (2) physical injury or illness and emotional reaction, (3) the brain-damaged child and the psychological sequela—all within the context of development. Both aspects are treated not only as part of the whole child, but also part of the surrounding milieu. The physical and emotional aspects of violence and neglect in childhood are frequently set in an environment of disadvantage, and the same is true of starvation and malnutrition. One needs to treat the child both physically and psychologically and his immediate world that militates against his recovery. Once again it is necessary to emphasize that one is dealing with multidetermined causes of vulnerability. But it is not enough to make a complete diagnosis; one also needs to train sufficient personnel to serve the needs of vulnerable children everywhere more effectively.

Mental-health Services and Preventive Measures for Vulnerable Children

Three problems exist in developing optimal services for children in the category of vulnerability. The first concerns the downgraded role of children in our society, one in which their rights and priorities are often pushed aside in favor of the needs of the adults and where the children are actually in competition with adults for limited resources, especially in regard to mental health services.

The second category of problems is rooted in the developmental complexities of childhood that sometimes tend to be oversimplified in attempts to find a useful and scientifically satisfactory classification of the deviations that continue to generate vulnerability throughout development and afterward. A glaring deficiency stems from the paucity of good epidemiological instruments and studies that would allow us to estimate the scope of the problem. We have no knowledge as yet of the incidence and prevalence of vulnerability in the general population of children since we have still to define risk, vulnerability, and resilience more precisely. Nor are we sure of the "natural history" of the vulnerable child, the impact of various preventive modalities and the accuracy of predictions regarding outcome, allowing for intervening developmental crises and shift in environment.

Third, there is still a huge insufficiency of qualified personnel trained not only to treat but also to prevent. Because of the multidimensional nature of the child's vulnerability, a multidisciplinary approach is required to deal with it, thus increasing the need for funds at a time when both state and federal financial assistance is in short supply. We are recognizing the need for and requesting an expansion of preventive services when the sources of supply are having a difficult time dealing with the urgent demands for curative facilities.

To meet this new emergency in mental health servicing, we need to augment our training programs as follows:

1. Training in the understanding of normal development in children of all ages, including competence in observing normal children systematically.
2. Training in the recognition and screening of vulnerable children, as well as in the evaluation of defenses, coping

skills, competences, resiliencies, "invulnerabilities," problem solving, and mastery.

3. Training in the strategies of preventive, mitigating procedures, including ways to bolster and buttress the physically and psychologically abused and neglected child. An effective preventive program is a community-based program. Peer organizations can be very helpful ("Brother helped by brother is a fortress; Proverbs 18, 19).

4. As there are many treatment modalities effective in secondary and tertiary prevention (inpatient, outpatient, individual, group and family therapy, and chemotherapy), training should aim at a high degree of proficiency in *at least one* kind of treatment.

5. Family therapy as a curative and preventive measure has gained recognition throughout the world, but it should be reserved primarily for disturbances in family relationships. This emphasizes the need for the trainee to understand family dynamics and the significance of scapegoating for vulnerability.

6. Training in the development of competence in consultation with schools, general health facilities, courts, and other community agencies that often act as "first aid stations" where the vulnerable child begins to experience difficulties.

Present Gains and Promising Future Developments

Studies and clinical experiences have made it clear that the discrepancy between our best knowledge and its application becomes increasingly risky for the children we serve and for the future support of our clinical, educational, and research activities.

I elaborate on this concept as it is one of the major mosaics that has emerged during the 4 years of work with the International Study Group on Risk and Vulnerability. First, it is clear that the understanding and care of children is being improved by questions and insights drawn from the social sciences and from biological studies.

THE SOCIAL-SCIENCE INTERFACE

At the social-science interphase, improved sampling techniques and the capacity to combine in-depth interviewing, direct observations, historical archives, questionnaire data, and sophisticated statistical analyses enabled us to learn more from our history, of developing data banks, of utilizing computer techniques, and of comparing individual clinical observation with selective group studies in an increasingly productive manner. This clinical-social science interphase has put us in the position to study such risk phenomena as divorce, drug utilization, twinning, failure to thrive, psychotic parents, single-parent families, differential achievements, and failures in various school settings. In this interphase there were also reports on the impact on the child when there is a death in the family or when catastrophic events take place in a given community or region. These advances also enable us to relate the physical and cultural conditions of the community to alternative developmental patterns that are promoted in specific settings. One can also understand the form and organization of the human habitat in terms of man's behavior and needs, physical and psychological. In fact, one can observe two facets of the problems of urbanization at two different levels of magnification. In the first facet there is a movement within a developing nation to render human conditions more satisfying in villages and thus to stem the move of young people to the larger cities, and in the other there is a movement to plan for the large cities of the future partly on the assumption that the movement of people from rural areas to large cities is inevitable.

From the various studies reported in this volume there are good indications that we can gradually achieve a better balance of anterospective and retrospective studies because of the improved sophistication and versatility of our clinical and social-science methods of study. Or, to put it metaphorically, that we can become more effective in putting together microscopic and macroscopic views of problems and solutions. A promising sign is that clinicians are increasingly more comfortable with the collaborative efforts of their social-science colleagues.

There is an underlying assumption in this interpretation of trends, namely, that the social sciences may lose a crucial opportunity if they do not confront their problems of theory building with the issues of the real world in all of their complexity. The same impression is strongly conveyed in somewhat different terms in our clinical and epidemiological studies, namely, that we shall face the likelihood of a downward spiral if we do not find out how we can use our new or refined knowledge to influence social policy without becoming too involved in partisan politics.

For example, there appears to be a seriously threatening crisis in many countries around the proliferation of day-care services without the benefit of the knowledge we now have and without the personnel we know how to train. There is an urgent need for teachers, clinicians, administrators, and economists and other social scientists to collaborate effectively in this area.

On the other hand, in early child education, the deliberate study of the U.S. Head Start Program—a dynamic expression of social policy—will make more explicit its impact not only on children and their families and on education and health care for children, but also on how social scientists and practitioners must work together. Many such day-care programs in the United States, Britain, the Scandinavian countries, China, eastern Europe, and the *kibbutzim* in Israel have constituted both the application of our best understanding as well as a reflection of the need to refine our understanding about early childhood. Our evaluative methods and tools are good, but not yet good enough.

In fact, we should also realize from the currents of our own exchanges that we always face the risk of premature closure of our knowledge because of our tendency to develop "tunnel vision" when struggling to put our knowledge to work. This involves the implementation and evaluation of social policy at the same time as we continue to extend and refine our knowledge about early childhood. However, a certain amount of "tunnel vision" is necessary to spread our attention evenly over all aspects and magnifications of a particular phenomenon. Thus central and peripheral vision must be well balanced in dealing well with the needs of children served by our knowledge and social policies. As yet we are not capable of long-term predictions, but in our omnipotence we find it hard to accept such limitations and work toward this goal constructively. What we need is an international and cross-cultural set of studies to help us in this regard. There are several issues to keep in mind in bringing together best knowledge, practical needs, available resources, and the changing socio-politicoeconomic conditions:

1. The quality of life for children now and tomorrow may be

an adequate justification for a program or a change in conditions. Cost accounting must include quality of life as well as other values.

2. There is no one model that is satisfactory for providing for children's needs. They need daily care, affection, and nourishment (the nutritional model). They need to be "immunized" or strengthened periodically for developmental and environmental crises that are expectable or predictable—for example, for a world of automation, or, sadly, for a world in which violence and wars are a fact of life (the immunological model).

3. Cultural characteristics and preferences are crucial considerations in adapting concepts, programs, and evaluative efforts to a particular child or group of children.

4. Long-term planning, with regard to education, health services, and human resources may remain limited for some time to come (however expertly we plan long-term visits to the moon or the destruction of our planet!).

THE BIOLOGICAL INTERFACE

At the biological interface there has been a proliferation of concepts and techniques that enable us to use biochemical, genetic, endocrine, and radioactive tracer knowledge to the better understanding of affects, tensions, attentional characteristics, aphasia, and so on.

It would seem likely that there may be advances, perhaps breakthroughs in the next 5 to 10 years in connection with certain aspects of the biological basis of personality development. These advances will include studies of CNS dysfunctions that may underlie a broad spectrum of clinical disorders, including psychosis, hyperactivity, and other disorders. In these conditions we can expect that endowment vulnerability will be described and the combination of biological and psychological therapies in conjunction with special education will enable children to master the risks associated with their vulnerability. Other areas in which advances are anticipated include molecular genetics and neurophysiological models of learning and adaptation.

Conclusion

One lesson to be learned from this volume is that we need, very urgently, to move toward the mastery of the professional risks of isolation, parochialism, and shallowness in our humanitarian and scientific concern for children. Like our great pioneering predecessors, we must develop the heart and mind to serve children and their parents in a bold and imaginative fashion, bringing the gains of the past to the present and assuring continuity of the gains into the future.

I close with two quotations that might inspire us in our forward movement. The first is from Herman Melville, who said, "From without, no wonderful effect is wrought within ourselves, unless some interior responding wonder meets it."

And the second from Walt Whitman, who wrote:

There was a child went forth everyday,
And the first object he looked upon, that
    object he became,
And that object became part of him for
    that day or a certain part of the day,
Or for many years or stretching cycles
    of years.

Epilogue

Margaret Mahler, M.D., Sc.D. Med. (U.S.A.)

Our highly esteemed colleague, James Anthony, wrote me a thought-provoking letter that stimulated me to some soul-searching. The question he posed was the following: "If you had stayed in Europe, is it possible that you would have been as creative or produced as much?" To which he added the comment:

I recognize this as tantalizing because the answer could tell us so much about the potent forces released by the mastery of vulnerability and there are few states that engender as much vulnerability as immigration and cultural uprooting: yet at the same time, the question is unanswerable since we cannot go back in history to the crossroads that led toward and away from the United States, choosing, this time, a second course. If the universe had been constituted in terms of second chances, what a more interesting place it would be and how much more we would learn about better courses of action. There is, however, one thing that we can say, and as was said by Ernst Kris, that for many potentially creative people, stressfulness could act as a stimulus to creativity.

Let me say, in at least a partial reply, that whether or not the work I produced since my arrival in America deserves the epithet of "creative," I am quite certain that both in quality or in scope, I could not have produced it had I remained in Vienna. Now I want to discuss why I think this is so. Had I been totally unproductive in this country, a case might have been made for the assertion that the vulnerability stemming from emigration might have been responsible for my intellectual paralysis. Both viewpoints could be correct: the stresses of uprooting can at times (and this has been

655

manifested many times in history) unleash the forces that lead not only to physical and psychological survival but also to an enhancement of natural talents and epistemophilic drives. When one enters a new territory there is a drive in some to explore it and make it their own, whereas for others there is a regressive drive to become dependent, helpless, and needy. Still others distort their new environment to suit their ends so that paranoid psychoses intervene. I think that in the positive cases, a second individuation ensues with emigration, a new psychological birth, and perhaps a new perspective of the world.

In the novel environment that I found myself, the wish to master the stresses involved prompted me to put into form, integrate, and fully express and communicate to others the rich and varied basic experiences I had obtained during my formative years in Europe. What I am saying here is that I did not start my new life in America with a blank screen on which primary experiences engraved entirely fresh constructions. I came across from Europe with a mind already teeming with basic experiences. However, had I stayed in Europe, these basic experiences might have led to the development of professional skills. I might well have emerged as a clinician and teacher within a small setting of students and colleagues. It is my belief, but this, of course, could be wildly speculative, that the process of psychological rebirth in a new country may be related in some way to the cardinal theory of separation-individuation that has shaped so much of my recent work in the areas of both normal and abnormal development.

However, before dealing with the extrinsic factors that catalyzed my intrinsic need to become a clinician, teacher, and researcher, let me say a few words about those early formative years in Europe because it was there that my more-than-average curiosity and eagerness to find out and influence others to find out first showed itself. Psychoanalysis and self-analysis helped to uncover the sources of my strong exploratory interests. For example, I can well remember a memory (presumably a screen memory) that dated from about my fifth year. What I recall is that a neighbor's cat whelped and was housed with her litter in the attic. One day, I crept clandestinely up to the attic and was appalled to discover that the newborn kittens could not see because their eyes were tightly closed. I promptly attempted to pry the eyelids apart, quite unaware of the danger to my own eyes on the part of the mother cat, who might instinctively have attacked me in defense of her young. But I wanted the kittens to see the world into which they had been born, and I clearly wanted to experience their seeing and to observe how they set about seeing.

I think that in this little episode there lies the germs of two of my later articles, "Pseudo-imbecility: A magic cap of invisibility" [1] and "Les enfants terribles" [2]. It was necessary for me at this early age to see what was covered up, open what was closed, and discover what was hidden. It was also important for the baby kittens to see the world around them; it was wrong to keep anyone in the dark. Here one notes the origins of the epistemological urge. In the case of the *enfant terrible* and also of the pseudoimbecile child, the first, expressed openly, is the counterpart of the second, maintained covertly, but both stem from the same intense inquisitiveness overlying deeper anxieties. In its sublimated form, the impulse becomes the basis for later scientific investigation, but in the absence of resolution a chronic castration complex is established. The pseudoimbecile child hides his wishes under a magic hood of apparent stupidity while the *enfant terrible* displaces his need to know by throwing the superior adults off balance by means of provocative, pseudonaive, and embarrassing remarks or actions. The desire to know what the adult already knows generates a peculiar vulnerability in the child that he needs to master if he is to make anything of his talents.

Growing up in Hungary was like growing up in other parts of the world as far as tedium and stimulation was concerned. For the eager child, as for the excited toddler, the world can be full of fascination for those who are ready to conduct a love affair with it, to use Greenacre's analogy. Was it coincidental that my choice of friend at high school was Alice Balint, who later became a pioneering psychoanalyst specializing in the nursery child, and with whom I spent many exciting hours during periods when schoolwork was boring, reading Ferenczi's newly published essays on Freud's psychoanalytic theory? It was perhaps not the most conventional way for schoolgirls to relieve the monotony of dull class routines. Was it coincidental that while still at high school, I came briefly into contact with the magnetic personality of Ferenczi himself? Retrospectively, such occurrences often seem like lucky chances, but as I have since discovered, in prospective studies, there is a certain logic of development that leads one inevitably to particular destinies. My move into medicine, then into pediatrics, and finally into psychoanalysis had its own inevitability based on the early identification with my physician father and the influence exerted by Sandor Ferenczi.

Having completed my medical training, I returned to Vienna (about 40 miles from my home town of Sopron on the Hungarian border) and joined the residency program in pediatrics at the University Children's Hospital. At the same time, I attended the Department of Pediatric Psychiatry at the same hospital, which once again showed the course of my developing interests. It was, however, the pediatric psychiatry of 50 years ago that left much to be desired from a dynamic point of view. Yet it was this experience with both psychologically normal and emotionally disturbed children that further reinforced my growing determination to preoccupy myself with the psychological and developmental side of human health and illness. Even the negative aspects of this hospital experience—the aseptic, isolating arrangements for infants with severe nutritional disease and the consequently high mortality rate—confirmed my intention to do something for these psychologically abandoned children. Already in me there was this pressure to express and communicate by observations and experiences so that these few pediatric years brought forth seven pediatric papers, none of them memorable except one that was singled out for inclusion in Aschoff's *Textbook of Pathology* [3] which was obligatory reading for the medical student and pediatric resident at that time.

The two streams of my life, my pediatric work with children and my training in psychoanalysis, now began to run in parallel, the one influencing the other. My application for training to the Vienna Psychoanalytic Institute was triggered when I listened to one of Anna Freud's lectures to which members of the Pirguet Clinic staff had been invited. Soon after, I left the clinic and became a Health and Welfare physician to the public school system of the City of Vienna and later director of one of the well-baby clinics.

My employment by the city brought me into close contact with August Aichhorn, and I took every opportunity to accompany him on his roaming visits to various school districts where problem children, mostly with conduct disturbances, were brought to the educational counseling service centers for evaluation, short-term treatment, or disposition. My close apprenticeship with Aichhorn contributed more to my future career as therapist and teacher than any other influence during those formative years. His contact with children and their parents and his style of working could not be imitated or learned; they could only be assimilated. With his encouragement, I established the first psychoanalytically oriented child guidance clinic in Austria from which most of the original children undergoing child analysis were referred. Many of these have become classic cases in the literature, for example, the patient with night terror treated by Waelder-Hall.

By this time, my allegiance to psychoanalysis was almost complete. I became an eager participant in Anna Freud's child-analytic seminars from their inception, and I have since remained a student who was constantly in the throes of learning something new from the children that she saw. But here I have to record an unusual fact that is very close to the theme of this presentation. There was a long hiatus between my last pediatric and my first psychiatric-psychoanalytically oriented paper. I was to undergo a series of transitions, not only from one discipline to another, from one way of looking at children to another, but from one continent to another. This was my vulnerable phase, my critical period. In my long apprenticeship with Aichhorn, Anna Freud, and others, I was among the Titans of my profession. I lived in the shadow of their ideas and I learned from them. The experience was rich, unique, and considerable. But, and this was the crucial "but," my own ideas, own particular orientation, and own approach to development could not seem to gel until I was able (or rather, compelled) to separate myself from these primary sources and thus undergo my own particular individuation as a contributor. This, then, was what emigration did for me; it removed me and my slumbering ideas from the psychological capsule that was Vienna and exposed me to an alien environment, the newness of which aggravated the vulnerabilities of transition. But when I had mastered these early anxieties and insecurities, it led to a resumption of my productivity and to the emergence of my developmental theory. Vulnerability, like many other human conditions, is a two-sided process; it can lead to intellectual paralysis and emotional stagnation, or it can cause a blossoming of latent potentials.

References

1. Mahler, M., Pseudo-imbecility: a magic cap of invisibility, *Psychoanal. Quart.,* 11 (1942), 149–164.
2. Mahler, M., Les "Enfants Terribles", in K. R. Eissler, Ed., *Searchlights on Delinquency,* International Universities Press, New York, 1949.

Index